Contemporaries in Cultural Criticism

The "Cultural Criticism" series consists of three volumes:

Classics in Cultural Criticism I: Britain,
edited by Bernd-Peter Lange

Classics in Cultural Criticism II: USA,
edited by Hartmut Heuermann

Contemporaries in Cultural Criticism,
edited by H. Heuermann and B.-P. Lange

Hartmut Heuermann
Bernd-Peter Lange (eds.)

Contemporaries in Cultural Criticism

PETER LANG

Frankfurt am Main · Bern · New York · Paris

Die Deutsche Bibliothek - CIP-Einheitsaufnahme

Contemporaries in cultural criticism / Hartmut Heuermann ;
Bernd-Peter Lange (eds.). - Frankfurt am Main ; Bern ; New
York ; Paris : Lang, 1991
   ISBN 3-631-43052-3

NE: Heuermann, Hartmut [Hrsg.]

ISBN 3-631-43052-3

Table of Contents

Preface

This sequel to the two collections of essays published in 1990 as *Classics in Cultural Criticism* was part of the original design to round off the survey of traditions and patterns in British and American cultural criticism. Not only was the projected volume on contemporary critics devised to help transcend the barrier between national lines in cultural debate which in the twentieth century have become largely obsolete (and had even previously separated two interrelated cultures engaged in a continuous process of exchange), a supplement to the series also suggested itself because of an ongoing debate that unfolds in ever widening circles. It is safe to say that cultural criticism today is livelier and more controversial than ever before, which is just another way of saying that it is also felt to be more necessary than before. The most obvious reason for editing this concluding volume, however, follows from the authoritative voice and cultural weight of the critics highlighted in the essays, their active role in today's critical discourse and, especially, their frame of reference in the present day world. Since the line between undeniable relevance and impending obsolescence is always a fine one, there may admittedly be borderline cases where an inclusion can well be disputed. If so, this probably has something to do with the much accelerated turnover in critical thought conditioned by a rapidly changing environment, or else reflects a bias on our part in giving preference to particular figures to the exclusion of others.

There are additional reasons for a shifting of focus from a national onto an international scene in the English speaking world. Not only has there been, in recent decades, a striking diversification of cultural discourse, both geopolitically and thematically, but we also observe an increasing fragmentation due to intensified topical interests and a growing awareness of regional problems. Conditions and concerns of almost global import go along with, and are contrasted by, processes of quite specific relevance. The historical development of cultural criticism in the twentieth century has indeed been marked by a contradictory process of universalization and particularization. On the one hand, the mainstream of British and American criticism seems to have been diffused into divergent currents, the only common source being a growing discontent with present social conditions. While, in the past, a core of general interests could still be taken for granted at least in regard to certain dominant and pervasive themes (such as the classic tradition and the humanist heritage in philosophy and the arts), this core has dissolved into a plurality of paradigms and perspectives that reflect the heterogeneous interests of English speaking communities. On the other hand, there has been a trend toward the transcendence of national boundaries and a convergence upon global concerns. A geocultural expansion, notably in the direction of Third World problems, has been accompanied by an overriding commitment to international issues and a growth of cosmopolitan awareness. This gradual expansion has continued through all shifts in cultural debate and has made possible a link-up of minority cultures across the English speaking world.

A further expansion in the range of contemporary criticism concerns the cultural spheres that serve as the objects of debate. However *inclusive* some earlier definitions of culture purported to be, traditional criticism, on account of its equation of culture and aesthetic achievements (preferably literature), tended to be *exclusive* of non-aesthetic domains – more exclusive, at any rate, than would be possible at the end of the twentieth century. By and large, literature has been ousted as the dominant frame of reference and the acknowledged repository of cultural values, becoming replaced with (or joined by) other realms of cultural experience that increasingly involve the social sciences. This makes a debate such as the one about the "Two Cultures" conducted between C. P. Snow and F. R. Leavis in the fifties look dated and parochial today. Consequently, cultural criticism at present is a much more heterogeneous and variegated affair than the mainstreams of British and American discourse could ever be in the past.

Difficult though it is, in view of the centrifugal tendencies mentioned, to characterize the current situation, a few distinguishing traits can still tentatively be noted: There has been, to begin with, a general growth of theoretical awareness and a concomitant trend toward theorizing which often entails a recognizable de-emphasis on empirical facts, personal judgment and immediate experience. Where the majority of the nineteenth century critics tended to rely on their own observational power or personal taste when debating the issues of their times (such figures as Matthew Arnold and Alexis de Tocqueville come to mind), most contemporary critics have recourse to theories and concepts that abstract from and range far beyond personal experience, however seminal such experience may originally have been. This can be seen as a consequence of an increasing sophistication in dealing with present-day culture and its world-wide ramifications, while it may also be suggestive of a growing self-consciousness in the articulation of ideological or philosophical positions. Increasingly, theoretical discourse has produced a kind of metacriticism that is probably as much an indication of hightened sensitivity as it is a symptom of intellectual doubt and social crisis. Where it is felt to be difficult to come to satisfactory terms with cultural reality, the conditions and preconditions of these terms rather than the terms themselves become the focus of interest. The frames of reference that determine particular approaches such as Neo-Freudian, Feminist, or Poststructuralist criticism sometimes eclipse the personalities of those who advance them, creating camps and schools of thought that enter into what may be called depersonalized competition. In turn, these divisions have often been popularized in the media of mass communication and popular journalism.

Moreover, much criticism today is characterized by an overriding political interest – defined in a more inclusive way – and thus exhibits a strongly politicized consciousness, even where the positions taken may be relatively remote from either political science or practical politics. This holds true especially for feminist criticism as one of the dominant strands of criticism after 1970. Feminism provides a powerful impetus to Kate Millett's anti-sexist polemics, to Adrienne Rich's poetic visions and even to some extent to Susan Sontag's pro-modernist aesthetics. Similarly, Marxist critics share an important family likeness in spite of doctrinal or theoretical differences among them. A historian such as E. P. Thompson covers an impressively wide range of cultural interests and topics, but has never relinquished an essentially humanist kind of Marxism. Fredric Jameson and Stuart Hall between them exemplify, in their criticism of the media and other forms of mass culture, a Neo-Marxist attempt to cope with the challenges of structuralist and poststructuralist theory. Raymond Williams bridges the gap between these positions in his trajectory from older traditions to a Marxism responsive to new theoretical challenges. Hall, for biographically germane reasons, in his pronounced emphasis on the problems that spring from the highly charged confrontation of the First and the Third World in turn shows some affinity to Edward Said's campaign against ethnocentricity. In a more radical way this is also a major concern with black author C. L. R. James who, like James Baldwin but from an orthodox Marxist viewpoint, reflects on the ethnic barriers that have proved such a baneful legacy of Western imperialism.

The other critics included tend to center their works on various aspects of a cultural hegemony that they suspect of impoverishing society and manipulating the individual. It is observable that the cultural watershed of the protest movement in the sixties told heavily on their work, even if it is rooted in earlier periods. This applies to Daniel Bell's political sociology as a plea for moral and cultural regeneration as well as to Theodore Roszak's project of a counter-culture devised to rejuvenate what he took to be a decrepit and corrupt society. It holds equally true for Neil Postman's critique of American media culture and his diagnosis of the harmful effects on the mental life of the audience. A major concern in that profound crisis in Western culture, addressing itself to both the anger and the emancipatory hopes involved, is the individual's and society's psychic condition. It is here that Leslie Fiedler endeavors to evoke and exorcize the age-old demons that he believes keep haunting the collective mind of the American people. And it is here, too, that Christopher Lasch subjects his countrymen to a Neo-Freudian analysis that spells out their emotional life in terms of a dangerous cultural narcissism.

Compared with the two preceding volumes, *Contemporaries in Cultural Criticism* exhibits a changed emphasis in the relationship between individual critics and representative positions. The focus is on the latter. It seems no longer feasible to construct a pantheon of Grand Old Men whose selection is vouchsafed by their reputation alone, as was possible in the mainstream traditions of criticism in the past. But regardless of whether or not the Grand Old Men have vanished (as claimed by Russell Jacoby in *The Last Intellectuals*), the fact is that contemporary positions are often evolved and taken by more than one brilliant exponent. Hence more difficult choices had to be made when selecting the critics for this volume as against those in the *Classics*. But while the multiplicity of theories, methods, themes and concerns that cultural criticism reveals today rules out any attempt at comprehensiveness in the selection of critics, it is hoped that the spectrum presented is still wide enough to accommodate the most significant preoccupations and positions.

All essays in this collection are modelled on those published in the *Classics*: After a biographical sketch of each critic, his/her work is placed in context and then discussed at some depth and length, with emphasis on the intellectual profile of the critic and the specificity of his/her approach. After an assessment of the contribution to contemporary cultural debate, some final consideration is given to the critical reception among experts, colleagues, or cultural institutions. With some variation, the authors have tried to adhere to this pattern. In some cases, though, biographical information was either difficult to come by or was felt by the authors to be marginal to the critic's achievement. In other cases, the public and/or critical response proved, for inexplicable reasons, less pronounced than might be expected in view of the critic's stature. Sometimes, the ongoing debate has not settled into anything approaching a coherent picture as yet, so that judgments must needs be provisional and tentative.

Finally, for all the heterogeneity of approaches that constitutes the universe of discourse and for all the severity of critical arguments that instills more skepticism than faith, it is reassuring to know that none of the critics saw it expedient to withdraw into the cynicism or negativism that lies on the far side of hope. It is indeed noteworthy that all of them proffer some positive idea of a cultural change apt to transcend the present crisis and lead the way toward improvement. If the public fails to pay heed to and act upon what the latterday prophets proclaim it is surely, as in the days of old, not the prophets who are to blame. Their arguments, though often debatable, are urgent enough to warrant attention.

May 1991

Hartmut Heuermann
Bernd-Peter Lange

Jens-Ulrich Davids

C. L. R. James

(1901-1989)

> For my generation, James is the essence of political legend:
> organizing the Africa Bureau with George Padmore, beard-
> ing (!) with Trotsky in Coyoacan, organizing sharecroppers
> in Missouri, hailing Nkrumah as the Black Lenin in Accra,
> wandering into a Havana revolutionary congress with a vol-
> ume of Michelangelo plates.[1]
> ... the West Indian historian of the future has a crucial
> role to play in the education of the West Indian people in
> their own history and in the merciless exposure of the shams,
> the inconsistencies, the prejudices of metropolitan histori-
> ans.[2]
> In my private mind, however, I was increasingly aware of
> large areas of human existence that my history and my poli-
> tics did not seem to cover. What did men live by? What did
> they want? What did history show that they had wanted? ...
> What exactly was art and what exactly culture?[3]

To try and present C. L. R. James as a theorist of culture is a daunting task
for various reasons. The first is his tremendous output of essays, books, letters, talks and articles which cover subjects ranging from criticism of art, politics, Marxist dialectics to ancient Greek political organisation, slave rebellions, American popular culture, cricket and world revolution. The second is
the unfortunate fact that not all of this has been published so as to make it accessible. The third lies in the position James's life and work occupy at the
juncture of major political and cultural shifts and faultlines in the twentieth
century: only against this backcloth will their meaning and profile become
fully visible. Consequently, after a brief initial survey of his life, I felt it reasonable to delineate, in a movement not unlike perhaps that of growing circles, and not too briefly either, the historical forces that influenced him, the
crossroads at which he stood, the socio-political milieux he was a part of. As
far as his works are concerned, I have concentrated on those that are of relevance here (excluding, for instance, most of the considerable body of his
writings on Marxist theory).

Cyril Lionel Robert James was born in Trinidad in 1901.[4] His father was a
schoolmaster in the small town of Tunapuna. He grew up with literature, with

which his mother familiarized him, and cricket. "Our house was superbly situated, exactly behind the wicket", he wrote later. As a small boy of six, when standing on a chair, he could

> watch practice every afternoon and matches on Saturdays ... From the chair also [I] could mount onto the window-sill and so stretch a groping hand for the books on the top of the wardrobe. Thus early the pattern of my life was set.[5]

He learned to play the game to a rather good standard and became interested in its intellectual aspects early on. In 1910 he won a grant to Queen's Royal College, the leading educational establishment on the island. After eight years of schooling James became a school-master himself. He started earning his living as a teacher while playing a considerable amount of cricket at the same time. He also reported cricket for a number of Trinidadian newspapers.

Towards the end of the 1920s he increasingly turned his attention to writing fiction, publishing short stories and essays. The literary circle he moved in was part of a wider cultural and political upheaval which criticised colonial government and strove towards political and intellectual autonomy. Learie Constantine, the superb Trinidadian cricketer, asked James to join him in Nelson, Lancashire, England, where he had been playing professionally for some years, requesting James to take a hand in writing his autobiography. In 1932 James sailed from the colony to the metropolis.

In Nelson he was witness to a massive industrial dispute in the textile industry. According to his own account, here he learned a lot from the day-to-day struggles of the workers, and particularly from their disillusionment with the Labour Party. James himself joined the Independent Labour Party. He was active as a speaker mainly on the subject of the conditions in the West Indies. In 1932 he became a cricket reporter for the *Manchester Guardian*. The following year he moved to London, the heart of the Empire. Over the next five years, till he left England, he produced a tremendous amount of written work while at the same time reading up on Marxist political theory and getting intensively involved in the political life of the country. Within the ILP he entered the Trotskyist Marxist Group and became a leading spokesman on revolutionary politics, noted for his fierce denunciation of Stalinism.

The books he wrote in this period dealt in one way or another with the two overreaching themes of imperialism and world revolution. In 1933 his biography of Cipriani was published as *The Case for West Indian Government*; in the same year , Constantine's *Cricket and I*, which James had co-authored, was printed. *Minty Alley*, his novel about West Indian barrack-yard life, saw publication in 1936, as well as his one and only play, *Toussaint L'Ouverture*, in which he himself acted, while Paul Robeson[6] was seen in the title role on stage. The historical subject matter he used in the play, the revolution in Saint Domingue in 1791, which led to the first Black independent state in the New World, Haiti, in 1804, had been on his mind for some years. He had been to France to do research, and in 1938 his magisterial *The Black Jacobins* was published.

From 1938 till 1953 James lived in the USA. He became a member of the American SWP (Socialist Workers' Party), a Trotskyist organisation. He undertook speaking tours, spent some time with Trotsky in Coyoacan, Mexico, and wrote numerous articles for the SWP. He also tried to come to grips with American culture, which he considered a culture in its own right, quite distinct from that of the West Indies or Europe. A manuscript containing his observations here, *Notes on American Civilization*, has yet to be published. James did produce a book, though, which offers a vision of American society, encoded in an audacious reading of Herman Melville's works: *Mariners, Renegades and Castaways* (1953). James wrote a first draft while interned on Ellis Island. McCarthyism had reached him and he was expelled from the USA. James returned to England in 1953.

He took up reporting on cricket again and started preparing his classic *Beyond a Boundary*. The completion of this study was closely related to his return to the West Indies in 1958. During the run-up to independence, Dr. Eric Williams, noted anti-imperialist historian, who had been James's pupil at school in the twenties, preserving contact over the years, and was now the leader of the Trinidadian PNM (People's National Movement) and was later to become Trinidad's first Prime Minister, invited James to return and edit his party's paper. James accepted and reorganized the paper under the title *The Nation*. He also became secretary of the West Indian Federal Labour Party, an organisation committed to promoting a federation of the emerging West Indian nation states. His sojourn came to an end in 1962 when he fell out with the Prime Minister over his policies. James could not stomach Williams's decision to allow the USA to retain a naval base at Chaguaramas. His lectures on this issue were suppressed by Williams.

Another Third World country he became involved in was Ghana. In 1960 Kwame Nkrumah, whom he knew as an associate of George Padmore and a fighter for Pan-Africanism in the London of the 1930s, now the leader of the liberation movement and first head of state, invited him to participate in independence celebrations. From then on, he followed the development of the new state closely. As early as 1962 and again in 1963 he warned Nkrumah of the dangers to his government deriving from his autocratic style. His advice went unheeded. In 1977 James published *Nkrumah and the Ghana Revolution* in which he explained his break with the African leader.

Beyond a Boundary was published in England in 1963 to great critical acclaim. Soon afterwards James was commissioned to write up the England cricket tour of the West Indies by the *Times* and the *Observer*. On arriving in Trinidad he was placed under house arrest by Williams but freed after a public campaign. The next year he re-entered active politics in Trinidad founding the Workers' and Farmers' Party and its newspaper *We, the People*.

From the mid-1960s James travelled extensively through Africa, Europe and America. He gave lectures on politics, history, literature and, of course, cricket. He spoke to African villagers, Trinidadian oil-workers and Canadian intellectuals. He concerned himself with the colonial legacy in African and West Indian societies and cultures. He held a number of teaching posts in North America between 1968 and 1975 and initiated the Sixth Pan-African Congress in Tanzania in 1974. From 1981 till his death in 1989 he lived in Brixton, London, giving talks, publishing articles and corresponding widely as a major Black Marxist intellectual.

James's particular approach to cultural criticism can only be appreciated fully by a broad consideration of the social and historical context of which James was a part. The brief biography above enumerated steps he has taken in his lifetime; now we need a larger picture of the spheres he took these steps in.

The slave-trade followed a triangular route, with the merchant ships setting out from Europe, sailing to (mainly West) Africa to barter manufactured goods like knives and guns for Africans, who were transported on the Middle Passage to the slave markets in the Americas, and setting out again from there with slave plantation products like sugar, rum, tobacco or coffee in their holds for European consumption. James's life in body, soul and intellect moved in the area thus circumscribed. He grew up in the British Caribbean, where slavery was abolished in 1833, amongst the descendants of enslaved Africans (one of his own grandfathers had been a sugar-estate panboiler), he moved to the United States, whose cotton plantations in the South had used African unfree labour; he moved to Britain, whose Industrial Revolution had been partly financed with the copious proceeds from the slave-economy; and he paid visits to Africa, the continent depopulated by slavery variously estimated at between 20 and 50 million people. Africa, America and Europe are also the continents, whose people in different ways lived and still live under the necessity of having to come to terms with the horrendous heritage of slavery.

James was also born in the heyday of the British Empire, only two generations after it had abolished slavery, as a Black colonial lower middle-class subject of Queen Victoria. Admittedly he himself had taken no cognizance of it during the first twenty years or so of his life – "The race question did not have to be agitated. It was there. But in our little Eden it never troubled us."[7] "But [the Queen's Royal College] was in a colony ruled autocratically by Englishmen. What then about the National Question? It did not exist for me."[8] Trinidadian society observed a strict hierarchy of skin colour with the few Whites on top and the large numbers of Blacks at the bottom, it was divided by the relevance of shades, the status attached to them, the opportunities connected with them, the injustice imparted through them. In the British territories there were 128 shades of skin colour, each with its own name. There was, additionally, the hierarchy of colony and metropolis in all aspects of life: London controlled the government, which was largely white, and in its turn ruled autocratically. Along the lines of political decision, economic advantage and cultural dominance, England was the fount of profit and power. The third faultline ran between poor and rich, landowners and landless workers, capital and labour, as is usual in capitalist societies.

Trinidad as a lesser jewel in the Imperial crown partook of the blessings of British education. Those who could somehow rise from the illiterate majority were taught by England-trained masters or masters trained by these. Following British models and bound to the British external examination system which based its requirements entirely on matters British, the "secondary school curriculum in the British Caribbean ignored everything West Indian – West Indian history, geography, economics, community organisations and problems."[9] The children and young people were thoroughly anglicized. James tells us how his first books were passed on from his mother, a voracious reader. What where they? Shakespeare's plays. George Lamming, in his novel *In the Castle of my Skin* (1953), describes Black schoolchildren as not having the faintest idea what the slave-trade and slavery had been. The West Indian secondary schools, among them James's Queen's Royal College, were modelled on the British public schools. What did this imply as to school subjects, educational ethics and politics? Here again Trinidad can be seen as one example of the entire imperial educational set-up. Public schools in Britain were provided for the élite of the country. During the last quarter of the nineteenth century the moral accent in these schools moved from godliness to manliness[10] as part of a shift towards a set of morals designed for future rulers of the Empire. Obviously, its application to learners in colonial schools was liable to engender contradictory and perhaps undesired effects.

Literary criticism looked exclusively to England: *good* literature could only be *English*. There were effectively no publishing houses on the islands. If you wanted a novel published you had to go to the metropolis.[11] When James started writing during the late twenties, very few attempts had been made in the British Caribbean to write without condescension on West Indian subject matter, to place West Indian people centre-stage, to regard West Indian experience as worthwhile of literary endeavour. There had been quite a few travelogues and descriptions of social life by travelling English people, also novels and poems, but *not by Blacks*.[12] Now, during the twenties and thirties and forties, a powerful literary explosion took place, in which James provided his own fireworks. Its origins are essentially the same as those of the labour movement and the nationalist political parties; two major factors have been identified, the First World War, and the Russian Revolution. The emerging writers of the West Indies "were influenced by political events and contributed as exponents of cultural nationalism to the struggle for independence".[13] A considerable part of West Indian literature then was published in little reviews which emerged in almost every territory. James helped found two, *Trinidad* (1929-30) and *The Beacon* (1931-33); he also published some short stories, amongst them "Triumph" and "La Divina Pastora" (and in 1936 his novel, *Minty Alley*, published, however, in Britain), in which he presented the beliefs, attitudes and everyday lives of common people.

Thus, all was not quiet in this corner of the Empire. Side by side with the literary movement towards cultural autonomy, in the political and economical spheres, the ideas of self-rule, parliamentary democracy and equitable working conditions, of socialism and communism fired the upheavals which shook the Caribbean and the entire Empire between the wars. Captain Arthur Andrew Cipriani was active in Trinidad at the same time as Gandhi and Nehru in India. James saw in him "the greatest politician in the democratic tradition whom the West Indies have ever known"[14], and started collecting material for a biography. Cipriani was very much a man of the thirties, the decade in which political parties were founded in Jamaica and Trinidad, besides other colonies, which organised the struggle for independence. On the oil-fields of Trinidad and in the sugar-mills of Jamaica trade-unions started to be organised along British lines. When James left Trinidad in 1932 he took with him a well-informed consciousness of these struggles.

England was not peaceful either. Economic and social conditions were abominable. The decline of the British basic industries (ship-building, iron and steel, textiles and coal) had been exacerbated by the world-wide crash of 1929 and the ensuing depression. Widespread unemployment, poverty and an autocratic right-wing National Government contributed to an explosive situation. As in other European countries, a fascist party (the *British Union of Fascists*, under Sir Oswald Mosley) had been established, partly as an answer to the Russian Revolution and the existence of a *Communist Party* (founded in 1920). Industrial disputes – like the one James witnessed in Nelson, Lancashire – put political strategies and theories on the agenda. The thirties were also called "the red decade". Social democratic ideas like the "gradualism" advocated by the Fabians inside the Labour Party, the socialism as propagated by the Independent Labour Party, – the radical element in the Labour Party which had now been an independent organisation since 1932 – and Communism were the major notions of the Left. Communism, although the Communist Party itself had less then 10,000 members, was fairly popular with the working class. Two major orientations had developed, the one following Stalin and his idea of "one socialism in one country", the other following Trotsky and his idea of "permanent revolution". Both considered Marx, Engels and Lenin as their ideological ancestors. Imperialism was also a subject on the political Left; this took a new turn in 1935 when the Moscow-oriented Communists, following the new Popular Front guidelines started considering France and England as "democratic imperialisms" which could be neglected in order to concentrate all forces against the Fascists. This decision of the seventh Comintern inevitably alienated quite a number of anti-imperialists from the colonies who had seen themselves as Communists. One of them was George Padmore, James's boyhood-friend, a communist and a leading figure in the Pan-African Movement, – later "designated the Father of Pan-African Emancipation"[15] – who was resident in London at the time. It was he who convinced James of the centrality of Africa in the anti-imperialist struggle.

This brings us to a political dimension in the England of the Thirties which for James became as influential as Marxism: Pan-Africanism. (This term denotes the search for unity on the African continent, *and* the idea of a community of interests among African people all over the world, *and* the feeling that all of Africa should exclusively belong to Africans.) Both Marxism and Pan-Africanism together became interwoven into an intricate pattern of thought and action and formed the major current of what has come to be called Black radicalism in England before the Second World War.

When James arrived in Britain, there were already several Black organisations, of which Harold Moody's moderate League of Coloured Peoples commanded most attention and membership. Pan-Africanism had become an integral part of their thinking.[16] They looked back upon an appreciable tradition of struggle for Black emancipation: the long list of slave rebellions and nationalist uprisings in the colonies; the first Pan-African Conference held in London in 1900; ideas of Black nationalism emanating from the U.S.A. since the Civil War; the black sailors in Cardiff and Liverpool with their record of forceful and considered labour struggles. All these went into the weaving of an anti-imperialist, partly Marxist, radical Black consciousness in Britain.

These Pan-Africanists, mostly middle-class people, were in Britain because here they perceived the "centre of gravity"[17], the source of authority for the Empire, the site so persistently and idyllically envisioned in the literary and historical texts of their colonial schools. It was here, they felt, they could extend their intellectual and professional attainments, and where, in contrast to their home countries, they could speak up openly and criticize heavy-handed British rule throughout the world (even if they were observed and harrassed by "MI5, Scotland Yard and agents of the colonial office".[18]) Here, as a major figure in their midst, Ras Makonnen, was later to observe, they "were operating in the midst of radicalism unmatched in Europe", and, he adds, it was "a period of purposefulness. You had the feeling that the truth was being told once and for all."[19] The invasion of Ethiopia focussed the purpose further. James, together with George Padmore, Jomo Kenyatta, Ras Makonnen and others founded first the IAFE (International Friends of Ethiopia) and later the IASB (International African Service Bureau). He wrote numerous articles for *International African Opinion*, IASB's publication which he edited during 1937 and 1938, as well as for ILP's *New Leader*. In 1945 another important Pan-African Congress was held in Manchester (James came over from the USA to attend).

James left England in 1938 for the United States. Here, too, he got involved in the dual conflict zone of class and "race". Capitalism here had produced not only a vast and rich popular culture, but also a strong difference between rich and poor, economic distress, unemployment and social unrest. At the same time, the twenties had inaugurated an upsurge of Black nationalism. Black emancipation in its various forms was advocated by men like W. E. B. DuBois and Marcus Garvey, the Harlem Renaissance, that magnificent unfolding of Black arts like jazz and literature, – all this gave additional impetus to Black pride. The militant mood of Black people was directed against structural and personal racism (like for example the Ku Klux Klan) *and* economic deprivation. New Deal measures could only relieve the situation to a limited extent.[20] Thus James was confronted with what was then called the "Negro Question". (In 1942, for example, he became active in a Black sharecroppers' strike as an organiser and published a pamphlet called *Down With Starvation Wages in South East Missouri*).[21]

So far, Trotskyism had not addressed the "Negro question" adequately; within the SWP no particular policy had been formulated and sections were divided on whether Black people should be organised *alongside* the white working class members or in *separate* units. James, who later stated that he "constituted the Third World in the Trotskyite party",[22] advocated the idea of an autonomous Black mass movement. The other issues that still moved him profoundly were: Communism, the character of the Soviet Union, the concept of the vanguard party, the trajectory of world revolution. Was the Soviet Union a workers' state along the lines of Marx and in particular Lenin's ideas of the revolution brought about by the proletariat? Trotsky and the SWP majority defended the Soviet Union as a workers' state which was deformed by having fallen under the heavy hand of a powerful bureaucracy. After some time James discarded this view and proposed the theory that the Soviet Union represented an entirely new mode of production, i.e. state capitalism (of which the Stalinist party was an organic part). A series of articles and an account of American Marxism, *The Balance Sheet* (1947), a critical analysis of party rule in the Soviet Union, *The Invading Socialist Society* (1947), a general theoretical treatise, *Notes on Dialectics* (1948), and another detailed statement on the Soviet Union, *State Capitalism and World Revolution* (1950), prepared and documented his break with Trotskyist thinking. In the end, McCarthyism, anti-Communism run wild, was responsible for driving the Black Marxist James out of the country in 1952/53.

The England he came to had established a Welfare State. The Labour landslide victory after the war had inaugurated a nationwide consensus to fight all kinds of want by an all-encompassing net of social security. Successive postwar governments also presided over the dissolution of the Empire. The colonial peoples fought their white British masters, and Britain, weakened by general decline and the war effort, could not withhold independence. New states emerged in Asia, Africa and the Caribbean. James saw the approach of independence especially in the Caribbean as a unique historical moment.

During the same years economic shifts in Europe led to massive labour migrations: British firms invited hundreds of thousands of non-white workers from India, Pakistan, Jamaica and other countries to work in the factories, hospitals and transport systems of the former imperial centre. Over the years they and their families came to form a noticeable minority in Britain. They also provided a public for those writers, especially from the Caribbean, who transferred themselves to the metropolis in order to write and publish there, people like Edgar Mittelholzer, George Lamming, V. S. Naipaul or Wilson Harris, most of whom James knew personally. In the sixties the Black Power movement reached Britain from the United States, the deepening economic crisis sharpened the class conflict, and by and by the Black British developed ways and means to further their own emancipation. James played an important role in this. Finally, to round off this brief sketch of the contexts James moved in: further economic decline, the gradual collapse of the political consensus, and widespread dissatisfaction with political parties and Labour organisations encouraged the emergence of new social movements around issues of peace, equality and ecology, given ideas and form especially by young people, women and members of the ethnic minorities. These James supported, to these he looked for social change. He died in 1989 in Thatcherite Britain.

James has never, as far as I can see, developed a consistent "theory of culture" in abstract terms. Neither has he used the term 'culture' in quite the sense that has become usual in academic language. Nevertheless his concept is close to the understanding of culture as developed from Raymond Williams's dictum of culture "as a whole way of life". This paper also follows this tradition:

> The study of culture is primarily concerned with how the meanings are generated and circulated in modern societies, and especially how these meanings are put together by people so that they *interpret* (make sense of, or represent) social change in particular ways. Quite clearly, the myriad social groups that go to make up society will have different meaning systems (or cultures). These 'maps of meaning' ... may be relatively discrete, or they may overlap substantially.[23]

James's beginnings seem rooted in a kind of tropical idyll:

> It was only long years after that that I understood the limitation of the spirit, vision and self-respect which was imposed on us by the fact that our masters, our curriculum, our code of morals, *everything* began from the basis that Britain was the source of all light and leading, and our business was to admire, wonder, imitate, learn; our criterion of success was to have succeeded in approaching that distant ideal – to attain it was, of course, impossible. Both masters and boys (in the schools of Trinidad, D.) accepted it as in the very nature of things.[24]

Recording his formal education James describes himself as being entirely anglicized, but clearly British cultural hegemony did not penetrate totally. This became apparent when he wrote his political tract against the inequities of colonial rule (although then he did not question the parliamentary system itself), when he had a hand in publishing a nationalist literary journal and when he wrote narrative prose. The fiction he wrote was on the one hand indebted to the English literature he absorbed, on the other it introduced people of the lower strata of society as central characters, especially the plebeian populace in the barrack-yard on No. 2, Minty Alley, Port-of-Spain, Trinidad. He deviated from the received colonial literary practice up to then in that he made the real experiences of non-white lower class people the subject matter, without the condescension white writers had repeatedly brought to such an enterprise (notable exceptions such as de Lisser's *Jane's Career*, 1913, notwithstanding).[25] He defined his world anew, for all to read, and celebrated the West Indian experience. He was a fore-runner of the generation of West Indian writers (like V. S. Naipaul, Sam Selvon, George Lamming and Vic Reid) who, starting in the late 1940s, made the West Indian novel world famous. He helped not only to bring about the "awakening of a West Indian sensitivity"[26], but his "reinterpretation of history", which he continued later in his capacity as a historian, started here, thereby creating new ways of seeing, new maps of meaning, a critique of the dominant culture in the form of belles-lettres.

In the novel *Minty Alley* we find for the first time James's preoccupation with *the intellectual*. The narrator Haynes is a clerk in a bookshop, a cool observer, a maker of speeches. He comes to live in the yard when "in terms of real living, his life is a blank".[27] He sees and tells us about his neighbours, he registers their problems as well as their energy and liveliness, but he cannot share with them, he remains aloof, in distance, alienated. These people will return later in James's work as "the black masses", the cricket spectators, the social movements of the 1980s. James does not idealize them: they are as envious, racist, sexist, violent, stupid, greedy and jealous as the next man, but they have what the proto-intellectual Haynes is lacking: vigour, fighting spirit, highs and lows of emotion, a remarkable sex-life. This Haynes has to learn from Maisie. The personal is also the political:

> ... the novel implies that the Caribbean petit-bourgeoisie class had been rendered relatively impotent by its education and stood to benefit from more exposure to the passions of the lower class.[28]

In his book on Herman Melville, *Mariners, Renegades and Castaways*, written in 1952, James demonstrates an equally acrimonious, but more clearly political opinion of the petit-bourgeois intellectual. On the ships in his novels, which he sees as "symbolical of the real world"[29], he detects two of them, Ishmael and Pierre. They are so very distasteful to him (as are the authors of works like *The Waste Land, Journey to the End of Night, Darkness at Noon, A Farewell to Arms* or *The Counterfeiters*) because "they know nothing about work and workers, the living experience of the vast majority of living men". Their "self-examination and self-pity", are worthless compared to

> the warmth, humour, the sanity, the anonymous but unfailing humanity of the renegades and castaways and savages of the *Pequod* rooted in the whole historical past of man, doing what they have to do, facing what they have to face.[30]

The intellectuals are reduced to self-centred isolation and uselessness; they can only reflect their own misery, but they have nothing to give to wider society. Literature, values, social life and history are linked in this vision, in which Ahab's ship is "a microcosm of the newly emerging industrial society".[31]

In creating Ahab, the autocratic captain, whose dinner table is "the symbol of his social isolation"[32], who is the embodiment of a wholly new human type, the captain of industry "and ultimately the modern totalitarian dictator"[33], Melville took an important step towards embodying in his novel "what the future of capitalism was going to be".[34] But his

most intriguing step forward is the manner in which he now treats the crew. ... For him now the crew embodies some type of social order. Their association at work gives them interests, ideas and attitudes that separate them from the rest of society.[35]

They are the counterforce to the monomaniacal power of Ahab, in their heroism, spontaneity and collective anonymity they represent the ordinary people of the world[36], they demonstrate "the creative power of the popular mass".[37] They are, as James points out in much detail in his *Notes on American Civilization* (1950), the key to humanity's future: not the crew of the *Pequod* any more, but the general population of the United States of America:

Cultured they are not, in the old European sense, and that is one of their chief virtues ... In social culture, technical knowledge, sense of equality, the instinct for social co-operation and collective life, the need to live a full life in every sphere and a revulsion to submission, to accepting a social situation as insoluble, they are the most highly civilised people on the face of the globe. They combine an excessive individualism, a sense of the primary value of their individual personality, with an equally remarkable need, desire and capacity for social cooperative action. And, when you consider the immense millions of them, they constitute a social force such as the world has never seen before.[38]

"Culture" for James here is apparently "highbrow culture" or "élite culture", which he rejects; and "civilisation" is the value system he believes to be that of the ordinary Americans, is *their* culture. This he defends vehemently against any sort of denigration, especially by people who uphold European (élite) culture which, according to James, is "rotten". The main reproach he has in store for "the petty imitators of things European in literature and politics" is that they are "far removed from the lives of the people of the United States"[39], through whom real humanity can be found, as in No. 2, Minty Alley:

I am profoundly conscious of the deficiencies of American civilization. But they are as nothing to the fact that America is unburdened by the weight of the past which hangs so heavily on Europe, that as a result there is here not (the wrong type of élite, D.) culture but a need for human relations of a size and scope which will in the end triumph over all deficiencies.[40]

Melville's vision makes him the 'only' "representative writer of industrial civilization."[41] In his novels he "worked out an entirely new conception of society", which is not based on profits and private property, but on a new kind of relations "between man and man, between man and his technology and between man and Nature"[42]. Melville's future man will overcome the fragmentation which grows from the division of labour, he is "a total, complete being, participating in all aspects and phases of modern existence"[43]. In this future society, which begins with industrial civilization,

nature, technology, the community of men, science and knowledge, literature and ideas are fused into a new humanism, opening a vast expansion of human capacity and human achievement.[44]

Melville, therefore, in writing *Moby Dick*, has taught James "the inseparability of great literature and of social life",[45] being, like Aeschylos and Shakespeare, an author who is "aware that one great age is passing and another beginning".[46] He expresses this in his art, "primarily in terms of new types of human character, with new desires, new needs, new passions".[47]

James also saw this "new humanism", this integration of various dimensions of life, foreshadowed and partially achieved in the "arts of the masses" in the USA; they contained in essence the fundamental contradiction between the "development of the individual personality, the need for free individuality, and the reality of an oppressive, mechanised society".[48] For him the popular arts were part of the movement of the modern world towards a future in which "art and life were in an active, evolving relationship".[49] In this way an image appears, a futuristic vision of breaking down the divisions between artist and audience, culture and political life; he wrote:

It is not difficult to imagine a social situation in which, by means of fine artists and gifted performers, there will be an almost day-to-day correspondence between the ordinary experiences of many millions of human beings and their transmutation into artistic forms. There *enters into the field of art a closeness to life* unknown in past periods of human history which will not fail to have farreaching consequences on both.[50]

By paying serious attention to "the movies, the Hollywood star system, the detective novels, soap operas, jazz – in short, to the popular arts of the American people"[51] and on the basis of his "recognition of the creative capacities of ordinary men and women"[52], James saw in the USA a movement towards "the creation of man as an integral human being"[53], i.e. towards the reconstruction of "the human subject", integrating lives "fragmented by the division of labour"[54]. Thus, James had given to popular arts as supreme an importance as he ascribed to the artist in the shaping of humanity's destiny.

After having been thrown out of the United States, and living in Britain for some years again, and especially after having been invited to Trinidad by Eric Williams to give a hand in bringing about independence, James focussed on the West Indies and made it quite clear what he thought was required of

the West Indian artist in order to make him "great". Thus he identified the
first condition to be a kind of belonging, of rootedness:

> mastery in the medium is intimately related to the natural surroundings in which the
> artist has grown up, to the society in which he lives, and his national or even regional an-
> cestry.[55]

The artist is the product of "a long and deeply-rooted national tradition",
and he appears "at a moment of transition in national life with results which
are recognised" in the whole "civilised world". In this respect the West Indies
are no different from phases in the European past:

> The Greeks and the Florentines of the great period understood the direct, the immediate
> influence of the great artist upon the society in which he actually lived. But today in par-
> ticular he is a tremendous force while he lives, and particularly to people like us, with our
> needs.[56]

If he is really "great", he can "construct the personalities and relations of
the future, rooting them in the past and the present". Thus he "exercises an influence on the national consciousness which is incalculable. He is created by
it but he himself illuminates and amplifies it".[57]

All this the artist can do best if he can use a medium that has persisted in
his country, which, though "transported" (brought into the country from Europe), is "so well established that it has created a Caribbean tradition of its
own"[58]. And he explicitly names two art forms in which this is being
achieved: cricket and calypso, the popular music of Trinidad. At this juncture
it becomes quite clear that for James the artist, rooted as he has to be in his
society ("Local men playing for local people"[59]), comes into his own finally
and truly only within the *popular* culture. Then he makes his medium "a genuinely national expression and possession"[60]. Artistic capacity and popular
response must in the end be achieved together, "then the artists in the Caribbean will have arrived".[61] In Greece, once, that had already been the case.

Greece runs through much of James's writing. It supplies an inexhaustible
treasure-house of references, literary examples, philosophical notions, and it
is also a very superior example of what he thought humanity in general and
the West Indies in particular ought to aspire to. The Greece he thus makes
use of is Athens during the classical age of Pericles and Plato. James sees this
as a period of transition from the old aristocratic order to the beginnings of
democracy, built upon the recognition of individual personality and accompanied by a magnificent outburst of creativity and by the evolution of new artistic forms. In his essay "Every Cook Can Govern", first published in 1956,[62]
he systematically develops his particular vision of Greek democracy. His two

major concerns are the concept of direct democracy, combined with a high esteem for ordinary people, and his vision of the integration of the individual and society, of art and life, including the role of the artist.

In the Greek democracy described by James, both political leadership as well as administration were staffed by men from the ordinary people. (Women and slaves, he has to admit with regret, were not included at all.)

> The essence of the Greek method ... was the refusal to hand over these things to experts, but to trust to the intelligence and sense of justice of the population at large, which meant of course a majority of the common people.[63]

"Experts" were later to become his favourite bogeymen in Britain's welfare state, as were the bureaucrats in the Soviet Union under Stalin – both going back to his early enemy, the intellectual. The heroes, as always with James, are the common people:

> At every turn we see the extraordinary confidence that these people had in the ordinary person, the grocer, the candlestick-maker, the carpenter, the tailor, the sailor. Whatever the trade of the individual, whatever his education, he was chosen by lot to do the work the state required.[64]

Every citizen was believed to possess the "capacity, judgment and ability to represent the whole body of citizens"[65], and thus "every citizen could and did govern equally with every other citizen", so that "equality was carried to its extreme".[66] And it was precisely this radical democracy that created "world-historical achievements".[67] This total equality presupposes, of course, that a permanent division of labour has not yet divided the populace; the "creative power of freedom and the capacity of the ordinary man to govern"[68] are the result, and product of, what Karl Marx called the "fully developed individual"[69], the integral human being we have already encountered in connection with American popular culture. James found this "capacity of the ordinary man to govern" also in other historical periods and geographical regions, for example in the black masses, especially in the person of Toussaint L'Ouverture, who achieved Haiti's freedom from slavery and France during the French Revolution; the integral human being in pre-Victorian Britain, in the men fighting for Ghana's independence. It had, however, to be fought for: "The common people won [their democracy] only after generations of struggle"[70].

This seems a good point of departure to look at his concept of history, closely interwoven as it is with his notion of culture.

Two overriding aspects of James's view of history relevant here are the search for the subject of the historical process, and the use made of the concepts of "race" and "class".

For James as a Marxist who understands history in the light of the theories developed by Hegel, Marx, Lenin and others, history has a goal, a telos, a movement towards a society without the contradictions of class. In his effort to reach this goal, man is constantly seeking "to negate what impedes his movement towards freedom and happiness."[71] The eventual instrument in bringing about the necessary changes is the industrial proletariat emerging in the capitalist social formation. To this orthodox Marxist view of the coming world revolution James brings his contention of the special role of *Black* workers.

> ... the development of capitalism ... has created Negro proletarians and has placed them as proletarians in what were once the most oppressed and exploited masses. But in auto, steel, and coal, for example, these proletarians have now become the vanguard of the workers' struggle and have brought a substantial number of Negroes to a position of primacy in the struggle against capitalism. The backwardness and humiliation of the Negroes that shoved them into these industries is the very thing which today is bringing them forward, and they are in the very vanguard of the proletarian movement from the very nature of the proletarian struggle itself.[72]

His Marxist outlook merges with his stance as a Black West Indian nationalist and as adherent of Pan-Africanism; "race" or ethnicity becomes for him a pivotal category concerning the past, the present and the future of Black people like himself. He never claims superiority of Africans over white people, but he does insist on a place of pride for them in world history. On one hand, this is fused with his Trotskyist principles which during his American years are central to him (rejection of Lenin's theory of the vanguard party, support for the control of industry by workers, amongst others), on the other hand it informs his fight against what he discerned as the main current of British historiography.

"I began to study the history of the islands"[73], and what he finds is a white Whig interpretation of history which does not correspond with the experience of "the black masses"[74]. Combatting the white interpretation of history leads him, for example, to write an enthusiastic essay introducing a reprint of J. J. Thomas's *Froudacity*, a Trinidadian rejection of a devastatingly high-handed, arrogant and downright racist 'analysis' of the West Indies by the English academic historian James Anthony Froude. *Froudacity* had first appeared in London in 1889 and was published a second time in 1969. James here marks the West Indians as a "particular social product" and goes on to say:

We of the Caribbean are a people more than any other people constructed by history, and therefore any attempt not only to analyse but to carry out political or social activity, in connection with ourselves and in relation to other peoples, any such attempt has got to begin and constantly bear in mind how we came into being, where we have reached, who we are and what we are.[75]

The answers to these questions awaken a sense of pride:

We were brought from Africa and thrown into a highly developed industry (sugar industry, D.) and a highly developed language. We had to master them or die. We lived.[76]

James countered the "historical racialism"[77] most successfully in his widely acclaimed magnum opus, *The Black Jacobins*, of 1938. The subtitle runs "Toussaint L'Ouverture and the San Domingo revolution". It was, as a history, a scholarly intervention in the social, political and cultural upheavals taking place at that time not only in Europe, but also prominently in many parts of the British Empire, including the West Indian colonies. It also addressed the issue of West Indian identity which even today commands attention and causes heartburn; the question of identity still is

of the greatest interest to our insular societies because, born from colonial slavery, they are marked by the experience of the loss of identity which is traumatic.[78]

I shall not even attempt to give a summary of James's book here. Suffice it to say that he described the Haitian revolution, which started in 1791 and led to an independent state under Black leadership in 1804, as a product of European economic interests, the ideas of the French Revolution, the tradition of "Negro Revolt",[79] the military power of the African fighters, the overwhelming statesmanship of their leader Toussaint and the fortunate coincidence of men, ideas and events. He stressed the Africans' ability not only to rebel and to fight, but also to learn, to organize and plan farsightedly and show themselves in many respects equal to their European enemies. It was not for nothing that Toussaint was called the "Black Napoleon".
The Haitian revolution had a tremendous impact on world history. The fighting spirit spread to Louisiana, Virginia and Brazil[80], its success set an example for the Latin American colonies[81] and was one of the factors that forced the British to abolish the slave trade. James's book showed, in his own words, "the role the Blacks played in the creation of modern Europe"[82]. In the United States, the runaway slaves fired the public imagination and helped create abolitionism, in fact, "the slave community itself was at the heart of the abolitionist movement"[83]. Abolitionisms then got involved in the most significant struggles for human emancipation that were going on in the Unit-

ed States and went on to bring about "improved methods of eduation" and "set in motion the liberation of women"[84].

To return to "race" and "class", *The Black Jacobins* offered a demonstration of their complex relationship. The historical example was seen as also highlighting contemporary on-going struggles in this respect; as James was to comment later, it

constantly implied that the African revolution would be similarly contingent upon the socialist revolution in Europe.[85]

The dialectical relationship between "race" and "class" is thus interwoven with the dialectic of Europe and Africa as the intellectual and physical 'homes' of the revolutionary subject. Here, too, we find an intricate pattern:

... unless we have a profound historical conception of where the African people are going and where they have come from ... That is the ocean of thought and feeling from which emerge historical manifestations as Marcus Garvey, Aimé Césaire, George Padmore, Frantz Fanon ...[86]

And then there is the European line of experience and analysis:

The future of Africa will be rooted in the African experience of African life. Yet nobody, European or African, can make anything clear and consistent of the developing pattern in Africa unless upon the basis of the substantially documented and widely debated historical experiences of Western civilisation.[87]

Europe and Africa, they both come together in a history of domination and maltreatment to which James belongs:

I am a Black man in the sense that Blacks are maltreated in the world up to this day, as no section of society is maltreated. And part of the maltreatment is the discrediting of the great achievements made in the building of civilization, the very formation of Culture in Africa.[88]

This statement was made in an interview in 1981. In an earlier essay, published in 1948 in the United States of America, James delineated more precisely in which way culture was important as a factor in the revolutionary struggle of which the Blacks (James: "the Negro people") were the subject.

Let us not forget that in the Negro people, there sleep and are now awakening passions of a violence exceeding, perhaps, as far as these things can be compared, anything among the tremendous forces that capitalism has created. Anyone who knows them, who knows their history, is able to talk to them intimately, watches them at their own theatres, watches them at their dances, watches them in their churches, reads their press with a discerning eye, must recognise that although their social force may not be able to compare with the social force of a corresponding number of organised workers, the hatred of bourgeois society and the readiness to destroy it when the opportunity should present itself, rests among them to a degree greater than in any other section of the population in the United States.[89]

Thus Blacks, as a force in the class struggle, are distinguished through their culture (as manifested in theatre, dances, press, hatred) which becomes "a basis for the revolutionary transition"[90]. The Black workers' contribution is not only economic, social and political, but also cultural.

James in his search for the subject of history finally arrived at a broad vision of neither the working class nor the Blacks nor the West Indians shouldering the responsibility for the ideal society, but, again, the ordinary people *outside* self-appointed vanguard organisations, in other words, the new social movements which James saw as "the fundamental movement".[91]

And as to culture: James's prime example is the game of cricket and the role it came to play in history.

Cricket, like football, has an ancient history and strong popular roots; games between villages are recorded in the seventeenth century. From the Restoration onwards, it was patronized by the aristocracy and royalty.[92] From the earliest stages it had a "democratic character": the best batsmen and bowlers were employed to strengthen a team, "from whatever station in life they came".[92] Its development during the nineteenth century is inextricably linked with the public schools, where cricket thrived and was perfected and given binding rules. It took off during the 1840s when the first All-England Eleven toured the country. Signs of the growing enthusiasm were the publication of Wisden's *Cricketer's Almanack* in 1864 and the first county championship in 1873. Cricket was played at an international level as early as 1860; the Imperial Cricket Conference was formed in 1909.[93]

Towards the end of the nineteenth century the game came to be closely associated with the virtues males were supposed to need in order to rule the Empire, and together with the administrators of the vast colonies it was carried there. It was one of the colonisers' favourite games and belongs to the things British which the colonised people "assimilated whole", perhaps, as Bernard Porter suggests in a slightly malicious aside, "because colonial rulers, who were gentlemen and therefore usually batsmen, needed to teach natives to bowl to them"[94]. As imbued with, and transporting, the public school ethic, cricket shared the ambiguity inherent in this code. On the one hand there were the virtues of "manliness and honour"[95], "courage, self-discipline, honesty, a sense of service and loyalty to the group"[96]. Even today the English language uses the phrase "it isn't cricket" in the sense of "it is morally unacceptable". On the other hand, cricket and the manly virtues it was supposed to teach became linked to Empire, domination of colonised peoples, and war. This orientation put

a new premium on discipline, authority, and team spirit ... a discipline which would create responsible, honorable boys, willing to give their lives unquestionable to the preservation and expansion of Empire.[97]

One of the most famous expressions of this linkage is found in Sir Henry Newbolt's poem *Vitai Lampada*, first published in 1897, which connects the schoolboys' cricket pitch with a battlefield in some outpost of Empire. The schoolboy has become a young officer:

The sand of the desert is sodden red, – / Red with the wreck of the square that broke; – / The Gatling's jammed and the Colonel dead / And the regiment blind with dust and smoke. / The river of death has brimmed his banks / And England's far, and Honour a name, / But the voice of a schoolboy rallies the ranks: / "Play up! Play up! And play the game!".[98]

In order to appreciate this poem's full significance we have to see it in the context of the social-Darwinistic ideas of racial superiority and the firm belief in the English people's God-given right to govern their vast colonial possessions, – inhabited by people Rudyard Kipling had characterized as "half devil and half child". Such ideas were part of the public school curricula at the time and constituted an ideology well suited to a 'master-race'. The fact that the game of cricket, and the public school ethic that went along with it, was widely accepted by the colonised peoples seems rather baffling. As contradictory as the ethic itself, however, were the significations that came to be attached to it. It was indeed used to create a loyalist culture, but at the same time

Cricket was a far more complex social force than imperial propagandists realized. Playing Anglo-Saxon games did not make all sportsmen reassuringly pro-British.[90]

In a host of journalistic articles, in a large number of letters, and, most importantly, in his book *Beyond a Boundary*, published in 1963, James has written on cricket at length. The book's title already transcends the understanding of cricket as a sporting activity alone. The *boundary* is the outer circumference of the cricket field: if the batsman hits the ball beyond the boundary he gets the highest number of points (6) for one stroke. The boundary is the thin line between the microcosm of the game and the outer world. Looking from the centre of the game's dramatic activity – the pitch with the wickets – the eye settles on the world beyond the boundary where forces are at work which this side of the line have significantly less power. At the same time the microcosm echoes the macrocosm of wider society. Thus, the game does, and does not, equal society. James introduces cricket to us as a ground where men meet, this side of social hierarchies where they compete as athletes and not as class-bound or ethnically divided members of society. Thus the title prepares us for James's multiple reading of cricket not only as a game in colonial and post-colonial contexts, but also as a ritual, a metaphor, a symbol.

Cricket has been part of every period in the history of England and the colonial territories, says James, and "an integral part of British civilization": "I believe that whatever road that civilization takes, it will take cricket with it."[100] And: cricket and football

were the greatest cultural influences in nineteenth-century Britain, leaving far behind Tennyson's poems, Beardsley's drawings and concerts of the philharmonic society."[101]

We can discern the outlines of a wide, non-elitist concept of culture, in which cricket figures hugely. The history of which cricket is a part, is one of decline, starting from the times of the Industrial Revolution and Romanticism, which formed a high plateau of attitudes and morals:

In all essentials the modern game was formed and shaped between 1778, when Hazlitt was born, and 1830, when he died. It was created by the yeoman farmer, the gamekeeper, the potter, the tinker, the Nottingham coal-miner, the Yorkshire factory-hand. These artisans made it, men of hand and eye.[102]

Thus cricket from the beginning incorporated "native artistic instincts" of "rural and artisan Englishmen"[103]. It has an essentially preindustrial (James also uses "pre-Victorian") character. From then on society declined, but cricket did not. It remained "a genuine national art form ... founded on elements long present in the nation, profoundly popular in origin".[104] At the time when Wordsworth, in his *Lyrical Ballads*, published in 1798, urged the preservation of the "inherent and indestructible qualities of the human mind" from the devastations of the coming industrial age, cricket was born, and cricket "in its own way did what Wordsworth was trying to do."[105] We must bear this profoundly humanistic task which James ascribes to cricket in mind to understand the scope and reach of his multi-faceted concept of the game.

The next great era is the Victorian age. At this time, the British "wanted a culture, a way of life of their own." They found it

symbolized for them in the work of three men, first in Thomas Arnold, the famous headmaster of Rugby, secondly in Thomas Hughes, the author of *Tom Brown's Schooldays*, and lastly in W. G. Grace."[106]

Arnold, who stood for character, religion, high morals, and "the role of the intellect", was accepted as to his aims and his methods. But the English ruling classes devised "one of the most fantastic transformations in the history of education and culture" in separating from the public school curriculum "the cultivation of the intellect" and substituting for it "organized games, with cricket at the head of the curriculum" (159/60). Thus through cricket moral excellence could be inculcated, "but intellectual passion was left out". (163) The "moral excellence" was found in the values of

loyalty and self-sacrifice, unselfishness, co-operation and *esprit de corps*, a sense of honour, the capacity to be 'a good loser' or 'to take it'. (162)

All this the Victorians made into "what can only be called a national culture", (163) which was embodied in a person of outstanding personality, a cricketer, the third man in what James deems the guiding triad of nineteenth-century England: the cricketer W. G. Grace. In him we have a kind of apotheosis of everything that was best in English culture, especially pre-industrial culture. A few phrases illustrate this: "all his physical and spiritual force was at his disposal" (175), he used all available techniques, he was the maker of modern batting, "science was his servant, not his master" (178), he lifted cricket into a "national institution" (178). Into an age, which was one of "iron and steel" (180), he carried over and incorporated into national life as an art form "cricket, the most complete expression of popular life in pre-industrial England" (169), he was a "pre-Victorian (!) militant" (176). He preserved what had been good before in the *way* he played cricket. He was close to his spectators, so close that he embodied *their* "passions and forces". He could ignite what James has pointed to many times as "the most potent force in our universe": "the spontaneous, unqualified, disinterested enthusiasm and goodwill of a whole community. "(182)

Through W. G. Grace, cricket could be a "guardian of morals" (182), but afterwards the game declined together with the whole, which is characterized by James as

the whole crumbling edifice of obeisance before Mammon, contempt for Demos and categorizing intellectualism. (183)

Expressed in terms of a less poetic nature, what James here sees at the centre of decline is the pivotal role of money under capitalism, the lack of democratic spirit and organization and the dissociating and separating properties of an intellecutal, bureaucratic and isolating approach to viewing the world.

The story of decline, of the "crumbling" of the edifice after W. G. Grace also includes the development of cricket. It, too, goes downhill. I shall quote the two major instances James uses to describe this process. The first is "bodyline", a technique of bowling in which the bowler aims at the batsman instead of at the wicket. It was introduced in 1932, and it "was the violence and ferocity of our age expressing itself in cricket" (186). The two players accused of "ruthlessness" in this connection are Jardine and Bradman. With them decline accelerates: "chivalry" begins to fade (189), "Captains encourage their bowlers to waste time", wickets "are shamelessly doctored", there are other "immoral practices" (189). What little remains of the old cricket-code

is being finally stifled by the envy, the hatred, the malice and the uncharitableness, the shamelessness of the memoirs written by some of the cricketers themselves. (190)

The chapter in which James exposes these features of "crumbling" is entitled "Decline of the West"; although he never mentions the name (and hardly ever gives the sources of quotations), the shadow of Oswald Spengler's concept of the occident's decline seems to be quite visible behind James's moving cricketers.

The next ominous step in the same direction is characterized by James's phrase of "The Welfare State of Mind". Again he finds the movement and forces of wider society expressed through cricket, as for instance in the (apparently insidious) "routine leg-side slip field for fast bowlers" (207). The new attitude displayed by cricketers now, in the 1950s, is summed up in one word, "security". This is wrong because it separates the players from the public. The public, "those who support the Welfare State idea in politics and social life do not want it on the cricket field". The other negative aspect of Welfare State cricket is that the cricketers play "the cricket of a specialized stratum, that of functionaries in the Welfare State" (211), by playing a highly professionalised style. The grievance is again about the separation of what should be connected:

The cricketer needs to be returned to the community (as so many of our professional experts in so many different spheres of life need to be returned). He must do a job of work with his fellows so that cricket, an artistic expression of life, becomes an artistic expression of his own individual life." (212)

The unspoken keyword here seems to be 'wholeness', the wholeness of the human being in human society. Cricket has a role in bringing it about; to do so, it must be integrated into the historical and cultural process if it is not to fall victim to that categorization and specialization, that division of the human personality, which is the greatest curse of our time. (191)

It should be remembered that cricket can and will save "the inherent and indestructible qualities of the human mind"[107]. It is in a position to do this because it is an art form, and the artists who fulfil the task are the outstanding West Indian cricketers.

As in Britain, cricket in the West Indies is expressive of, and formed by, history, as James exemplifies in the cricketer Garfield Sobers, whom he does not see as

a fortuitous combination of atoms which by chance have coalesced into a superb public performer. He brings what he is (and I bring what I am), for me his command of the rising ball in the drive, his close fielding and his hurling himself unto his fast bowling, are *a living embodiment of a tortured history*.[108]

In spite of the slavery past, the gloomy prospects of British culture are emphatically *not* in evidence in the West Indies, at least as far as cricket is concerned. There, grounded in the British tradition, cricketers are involved in their societies in a constructive way. There, cricket is part of an utopian vision, feeding mysteriously on ancient Greek democracy and the capacities of ordinary people. There, cricket is the centrepiece of a different 'map of meaning', whose richness and complexities James unfolds in considerable detail. There, it has, from the beginning to this day, "expressed with astonishing fidelity the social relations of the islands".[109]

James relates how in his youth the cricket clubs of Trinidad formed a hierarchy along the lines of class and skin colour. Top of the list was *Queen's Park* whose members were "for the most part white and often wealthy", followed by *Shamrock*, "almost exclusively white", *Constabulary*, whose team was all black, but "captained by a white inspector". *Maple* was "the club of the brown-skinned middle class", *Shannon* was the club of "the black lower middle-class", and at the bottom was *Stingo*: "They were plebeians: the butcher, the tailor, the candle-stick maker, the casual labourer, with a sprinkling of unemployed. Totally black and no status whatsoever."[110] The social stratification was additionally displayed during matches, when the enthusiastic support of the crowds for their side "showed the social passions which were using cricket as a medium of expression."[111]

But there is more to it: cricket has been "a permanent source of serious matters, social growth and differentiation, national unity, and social awareness"[112], and has transported what James has called the "subterranean aspirations"[113] of the West Indian populace. To understand this, we have to cast a glance back to Britain whence the game came, along with the public school:

These Oxford and Cambridge men taught us Latin and Greek, mathematics and English literature, but they also taught, rather diffused, what I can only call the British public-school code. ... Very rapidly we learned to 'play with the team', which meant subordinating your personal inclinations and even interests to the good of the whole. We kept a 'stiff upper lip' in that we did not complain about ill fortune. We did not denounce failure but 'well tried' and 'hard luck' came easily to our lips. ... We absorbed the same discipline through innumerable boys' books: books by G. A. Henty ... The masses of the people paid little attention to this code but they knew it ...[114]

Leaving aside the racist, imperialistic and violent side of the public school ethic, James sees it perpetuated by West Indian cricketers. What has been destroyed in Britain by industrial capitalism, can be preserved here in the *form and style* of a game. The new world saves the old. The periphery takes over where the metropolis gives up. The erstwhile marginals and outsiders are the builders of a better future. The first step is that they create their own positive image, their own frame of reference:

The West Indian's very consciousness is the product of his cricket in a very definite sense. In Britain, Drake and mighty Nelson ... Shakespeare, the Charge of the Light Brigade, the success of parliamentary democracy, the few who did so much for so many, these constitute a continuous national tradition. Underdeveloped, newly independent countries have to go back many decades, sometimes centuries, to find one. The West Indian people have none, at least none that they know anything about. To such people, Ramadhin and Valentine wrecking English batting ... fill gnawing gaps in their consciousness and in their needs.[115]

They create by playing cricket successfully on an international level their own positive, heroic tradition, in the same vein that for instance Jamaica, on becoming independent, created a new tradition by installing a group of "national heroes" (including black freedom fighters like Cudjoe and Paul Bogle from the days of slavery). In this way the West Indian discourse about national identity is given a positive twist.

However cricket transports more than the old British values. In its very enactment in the Caribbean, flows a hidden stream of values and capacities and constructive meanings which are not of European origin. This makes West Indian cricket something unique. James traces the West Indian specificity in a number of outstanding cricketers. For us, a few examples will suffice.

The first is Mathew Bondman. Socially, Bondman, whose family were neighbours to the Jameses in Tunapuna, was not acceptable to the respectable lower middle class James comes from: "My grandmother and my aunts detested him." But, this man could play cricket.

For ne'er-do-well, in fact, vicious character, as he was, Mathew had one saving grace
– Mathew could bat. More than that, Mathew, so crude and vulgar in every aspect of his
life, *with a bat in his hand was all grace and style.*[116]

In the context of James's book, "grace and style" gain the significance of a
submerged quality in a man outside the influence and reach of metropolitan
bourgeois culture. Bondman can be seen, in his abominable existence,

as the end result of a historical process which had built a world that had no place in it
where Bondman could realize his powers. Establish his identity. Enact his radical historicity.[117]

Bondman's humanity can only find expression in his batting (the same way
as W. G. Grace's pre-Victorian humanity was expressed in how he played the
game). Bondman is, according to Sylvia Wynter, "immersed in the imperatives of the popular underground counterculture of Trinidad, a culture derived
from Africa, yet toughened"[118], and "African norms were frustrating to capi-
talists".[119]

Leary Constantine also "belongs to that distinguished company of men
who, through cricket, influenced the history of their time"[120]. He was an "independent spirit" (106), he taught James to see their worth as Black men by
saying "They are no better than we" (116), and that was "a slogan and a ban-
ner. It was politics, the politics of nationalism" (117). Constantine's book, co-
authored by James in the thirties, was "a protest against racial discrimination"
(128). He played professionally in England, as the only Black cricketer in his
team, and he used "his reputation and his financial competence ... as a means
of advancing the cause of the West Indian people". (122)

Lastly, I should like to mention Frank Worrell, in whom the Black nationalist aspirations of West Indian cricket fans, including James, reached their
height. He was a Black man, and James himself, as a cricket journalist,
fought long and hard for Worrell to be made the captain of the West Indian
team (a position so far occupied exclusively by white men). Worrell's ap-
pointment was for James a victory for the drive towards self-government and
the original cricket code. Worrell apparently was of a stature to carry this
twofold symbolism. He was

a most finished personality, who knows his business, theory and practice, and knows modern men. (249)

His batting in one famous innings of the 1961 test match against Australia
"was simply a return to the batting of the Golden Age". (250) This means that
Worrell took up where W. G. Grace left off, defending "the beauty and digni-

ty of the human mind" of the pre-Victorian mould. At the same time, Black pride and West Indian pride had a field day:

> ... when over a quarter of a million people in an Australian city came into the streets to tell Worrell's team goodbye, a spontaneous gesture of affection and respect, *the West Indies, clearing their way with bat and ball, had made a public entry into the comity of nations.*[121]

James's reading of cricket as a multidimensional cultural energy which blossoms especially in the West Indies is difficult to grasp. Central to his concept is the combination in the game of the aesthetic and the social: the interrelation between its form (its "style") and its social function (its roles as a ritual, a receptacle of norms and values and a cathartic event). Cricket is many things, it is a game "and we have to compare it to other games", it is an art "and we have to compare it to other arts", and first and foremost it is "a dramatic spectacle"[122].

In three steps James develops in which way cricket *is* drama. Firstly: all games are dramatic, but cricket has a unique quality as drama:

> It is so organized that at all times it is compelled to reproduce the central action which characterizes all good drama from the days of the Greeks to our own: two individuals are pitted against each other in a conflict that is strictly personal but no less strictly representative of a social group. (192)

Whereas the dramatist, novelist or choreographer must *strive* to make their characters symbolic of a larger whole, cricketers have this relation built into the structure of their game:

> This fundamental relation of the One and the Many, Individual and Social, Individual and Universal, leader and followers, representative and ranks, the part and the whole, is structurally imposed on the players of cricket ... Thus the game is founded upon a dramatic, a human relation ... (193)

Secondly, in its composition of event and design, episode and continuity, diversity and unity, the battle and the campaign, cricket is "structurally perfect" in a way soccer or baseball are not. Using Aristotle's aesthetics, James attributes to it the basic dramatic requirements:

> It has a beginning, the ball bowled; its middle, the stroke played; its end, runs, no runs, dismissal. (193)

Thirdly, although cricket cannot allow "that representation or suggestion of specific relations as can be done by a play", it does offer

elemental human activities, qualities and emotions – attack, defence, courage, gallant-
ry, steadfastness, grandeur, ruse ... They are the very stuff of human life. It is of this stuff
that the drama of cricket is composed.(194)

The combination of "measured ritualism" and "varied and intensive physical activity" allow "human personality" to shine through.

What we glimpse here is the outlines of a holistic concept of the world of
humans, in which polarities have ceased to exist, between art and popular
games, artist and public, specialist and common man or woman. Like Aes-
chylus or Shakespeare or Michelangelo or Picasso (on all of whom James has
written analytically), the eminent cricketer brings into the lives of his contemporaries the idea, the notion, the foreshadowing (and I believe Ernst
Bloch's term is appropriate her) of "the beauty and dignity of the human
mind"[123]. Culture is seen as an active energy in the evolution of humanity:
cricket can do what Wordsworth was trying to do: "preserve the "inherent
and indestructible qualities of the human mind"[124] because cricket, too, is
art.[125] As classical Greece's newly fledged democrat found his need for a
"fuller existence fulfilled in the tragic drama", so the Victorian found his
need for a "further expansion of his aesthetic sense" fulfilled in cricket.
Cricket might have its limits of expression, as it cannot express the emotions
of an age: it must repeat.

But what it repeats is the original stuff out of which everything visually or otherwise
artistic is quarried. The popular democracy of Greece, sitting for days in the sun watching
The Oresteia; the popular democracy of our day, sitting similarly, watching Miller and
Lindwall bowl to Hutton and Compton – each in its own way *grasps at a more complete
human existence.*[126]

There seem to be enormous contradictions in James's intellectual make-up:
the Black man from Trinidad who went to Britain as a "British intellectual"
(114); the Marxist who insisted that "Thackeray, not Marx, bears the heaviest
responsibility for me" (47); the *aficionado* of British cricket who was a Pan-
Africanist, the Trotskyist who harked back to ancient Greece for a model of a
popular democracy; the socialist, who saw in US-American popular culture,
and in cricket, the fibres of a consciousness which might one day change the
world. It is a very strange quirk of history, indeed, that at the same time that
George Orwell came to hate the British Empire and the role which the public
school code played in it (as expressed in his novel *Burmese Days*, published
in 1934), a colonial gentleman extracted positive values from that very same
hegemonic culture and proposed their application as behavioral guidelines:
"the British reticence, the British self-discipline, the stiff lips, upper and low-

er" (48). He put his dialectical approach to West Indian identity in a nutshell when he said about his *Beyond a Boundary*:

> The book is West Indian through and through ... But the book is very British. Not only the language, but on page after page the (often unconscious) literary references, the turn of phrase, the mental and moral outlook. That is what we are, and we shall never know ourselves until we recognize that fully and without strain.[127]

This did not prevent him from claiming uniqueness for the West Indian people, especially in cricket and literature. Accepting the British cultural heritage, he was also a Black nationalist. He used Marxism to give a theoretical foundation to Black radical history[128], and ancient Athens to give a vision to the Black masses. In this way, he fused in himself different strands of world history, of the experiences and ideas of different peoples, feeding them into his notion of culture. He created a new 'map of meaning' for the underprivileged, black and white. He dismantled "European discourses" and put them to his own use at the same time. Coming from a colonial past, he energized in himself the "dialectical relationship" which the following paragraph ascribes to post-colonial culture:

> The contemporary art, philosophy, and literature produced by post colonial societies are in no sense continuations or simple adaptations of European models ... a much more profound interaction and appropriation has taken place. Indeed, the process of literary decolonization has involved a radical dismantling of the European discourses ... Post-colonial culture is inevitably a hybridized phenomenon involving a dialectical relationship between the 'grafted' European cultural systems and an indigenous ontology, with its impulse to create or recreate an independent local identity.[129]

It is clear from this that, although James's life and work were partially anchored in British culture, he could not be incorporated easily into some sort of metropolitan all-encompassing embrace: he charted a 'map of meaning' subversively different. From early on in his life he set about to explode the colonial myth that anything worthwhile could only come from the metropolis (England, Europe); to the end he combatted systems of dominance, from the colonial to the post-colonial capitalist system; wherever colonised peoples strove for independence and cultural self-determination, he was there to support their struggles. And finally he transcended the limitations of ethnicity and upbringing and suggested a concept of a future world, in which "a more complete human existence"[130] of undivided personalities, "pre-Victorian" values and the reintegration of fragmented lives will be made possible by "the people" and their popular arts, including cricket.

In order to arrive at this point James had to rewrite history. Perhaps this is his most enduring achievement.[131] Following the twin perspectives of Marxism and Black nationalism, he gave back to the kidnapped, transplanted and oppressed people from Africa the eminent place in world history which colonial historical discourse had denied them. He challenged the European ideological construction of the West Indies and other parts of the African Diaspora in a similar vein as Edward Said who challenged the construction of the "Orient"[132]. Opposing those writers, politicians and historians who wrote about Africans within a framework of hegemony, which included the idea of "European identity as a superior one in comparison with all the non-European peoples and cultures" (7), James was part of the "counter-articulation" (11). A short passage from a British school-book published in 1911 demonstrates what he was up against. It quotes from a description of the life of the freed slaves in the West Indies; here, the Black man of the Caribbean is depicted as

lazy, vicious and incapable of serious improvement or of work except under compulsion. In such a climate a few bananas will sustain the life of a negro quite sufficiently; why should he work to get more than this. He is quite happy and quite useless and spends any extra wages which he may earn upon finery.[133]

In his later years James stopped seeing exclusively the West Indian people (or generally people of African descent) as the future subject of history and assumed a broader view. Till the end, though, he stuck to the occidental, Hegelian-Marxist confidence that an ideal society lies at the end of human evolution. The historical subject which would attain this goal continued to be, according to his "80th Birthday Lectures", the working class:

the working class has not only to emancipate itself but it has to emancipate the society as a whole.[134]

But beyond this somewhat orthodox term "working class" we glimpse something else. Referring to E. P. Thompson, whom he saw as a kindred spirit, James stressed that the impetus towards revolutionary change cannot come from the old parties or the traditional unions, but from "the *fundamental movement*" (43): "from these committees, the black committees, the shop stewards' committees, the women's groups, and the rest of them" (33). Especially the Blacks

must prepare for a situation ... where [they] will be in the vanguard of the revolutionary elements in this society. (33)

This "fundamental movement" is inspired by culture. Culture, for James, is a major energizing force in the flow of history, informing and directing human action. Unlike what has been termed "lazy Marxism" (Stuart Hall),

James did not see a rigid determinist relationship between base and super-structure; he was not an economistic Marxist. His reading of cricket, for example, places him rather in the neighbourhood of "culturalism", and his work in this field has found wide acclaim.[135] Although he might not have used these terms: for him cricket became a cultural form with a content, an assemblage of signs, a cluster of significations, a social ritual with a bearing on the lives of people and expressive of their aspirations, a complex symbol to be decoded within its historical contexts. This holistic treatment of a cultural phenomenon seems to bring him methodologically close to *symbolic anthropology*.[136]

We can see he never stopped sharing the optimism of modernist thinking. He believed in the inherent goodness of the human species and the perfectability of human society. In popular culture and in the arts he detected a counter-hegemonic energy unspoilt by industrial capitalism. He believed in a universal set of values – including the British public school code and socialism – and the universality of the objectives mankind should fight for. In all this, as I mentioned before, he belonged strictly to the 'project of Modernity', following the

'grand narratives' (Lyotard) of progress, development, Enlightenment, Rationality and Truth.[137]

I should like to end with these lines by the poet Aimé Césaire from Martinique which James liked to quote:

... and no race possesses the monopoly of beauty,
of intelligence, of force, and there is
a place for all at the rendezvous of victory.[138]

Notes

1   David Widgery, "A Meeting With Comrade James", in: *Urgent Tasks* 12 (1981): 115-117; p. 115.
2   Eric Williams: *British Historians and the West Indies*. 1966:234.
3   C. L. R. James: *Beyond a Boundary* 1963: 149-150.
4   In this short biography I follow largely Anna Grimshaw's "Notes on the Life and Work of C. L. R. James", in: Paul Buhle (ed.): *C. L. R. James: His Life and Work*. 1986:9-21.
5   C. L. R. James: *Beyond a Boundary*. 1963:13. (from now on: *Boundary*)
6   Cf. James's "Paul Robeson: Black Star" in his *Spheres of Existence*, 256-264.

7   *Boundary*, 39.
8   *Boundary*, 38.
9   Eric Williams: *From Columbus to Castro: The History of the Caribbean 1492-1969*. 1970:461.
10 John Lawson/ Harold Silver: *A Social History of Education in England*. 1973:355.
11 Cf. Kenneth Ramchand: *The Background of the West Indian Novel*. 1978.
12 Cf. Bruce King (ed.): *West Indian Literature*. 1979.
13 Reinhard Sander, "The Thirties and Forties", in: loc.cit. 45-62, here: 46.
14 C. L. R. James: *The Black Jacobins*. 1980 (1938). With an appendix, "From Toussaint L'Ouverture to Fidel Castro", 391-418. Here: 402.
15 loc.cit., 399.
16 Cf. Ron Ramdin: *The Making of the Black Working Class in Britain*. 1987.
17 Ras Makonnen: *Pan Africanism from Within*. 1973:152.
18 Cedric J. Robinson: *Black Marxism*. 1983:374.
19 Ras Makonnen, loc.cit., 147.
20 Cf. Howard Zinn: *A People's History of the United States*. 1980.
21 Published in his *The Future in the Present*: 89-94 (from now on: *Future*).
22 Paul Buhle: *C. L. R. James: The Artist as Revolutionary*. 1988:69.
23 Nigel Thrift, "Images of Social Change", in: Chris Hamnet et al. (eds.): *The Changing Social Structure*. (Restructuring Britain). 1989:14.
24 *Boundary*, 38-39.
25 Cf. Bruce King: *West Indian Literature*. 1979: chapters 2 and 3.
26 Cf. Hena Maes-Jelinek, "The Awakening of a West Indian Sensitivity", in: Reinhard Sander (ed.): *Der karibische Raum zwischen Selbst- und Fremdbestimmung*. 1984:189-203.
27 E. Elliot Parris, "Minty Alley", in: Paul Buhle (ed.): *C. L. R. James: His Life and Work*. 1986:200-202, here 201.
28 loc.cit. 202.
29 C. L. R. James: *Mariners, Renegades and Castaways*. 1985 (1953):89. (= *Mariners*).
30 *Mariners* 121.
31 Anna Grimshaw, "Popular Democracy and Creative Imagination: The Writings of C. L. R. James, 1950-1963." In: *Third Text* 10 (1990):11-24. Here: 16.
32 *Mariners* 87.
33 Grimshaw 1990:16.
34 C. L. R. James, "Afterword" to *Mariners*, written in 1978. *Mariners* 174.
35 *Mariners* 88.
36 Grimshaw 1990:16.
37 *Mariners*, "Afterword", 174.
38 C. L. R. James: *Notes on American Civilization*, manuscript written in 1950, not yet published. Quoted from Grimshaw 1990:15-16.
39 *Mariners* 167.
40 *Mariners* 168.
41 *Mariners* 96.
42 *Mariners* 96.
43 *Mariners* 95.
44 *Mariners* 124.
45 *Mariners* 132.

46 *Mariners* 124.
47 *Mariners* 124.
48 Grimshaw 1990:15.
49 loc.cit. 15.
50 James, *Notes on American Civilization*, quoted in Grimshaw 1990:15. My emphasis.
51 Grimshaw 1990:11.
52 James, *Notes on American Civilization*, quoted in Grimshaw 1990:12.
53 Grimshaw 1990:12.
54 Grimshaw 1990:12.
55 C. L. R. James, "The Artist in the Caribbean", in his *Future*: 183-190. Here: 183.
56 loc.cit. 186.
57 loc.cit. 185.
58 loc.cit. 187.
59 loc.cit. 188.
60 loc.cit. 190.
61 loc.cit. 188.
62 C. L. R. James, "Every Cook Can Govern", in his *Future*: 160-174.
63 loc.cit. 162.
64 loc.cit. 163.
65 loc.cit. 163.
66 loc.cit. 166.
67 loc.cit. 166.
68 loc.cit. 169.
69 loc.cit. 167.
70 loc.cit. 171.
71 C. L. R. James, "Dialectical Materialism and the Fate of Humanity", 1947, reprinted in his *Spheres of Existence* (from now on : *Spheres*), 1980:70-105; here: 85.
72 C. L. R. James, "The Revolutionary Answer to the Negro Problem", first published in 1948, reprinted in his *Future*, 119-127; here: 126.
73 *Boundary* 188.
74 *Boundary* 188.
75 C. L. R. James, "Introduction" to J. J. Thomas: *Froudacity*. West Indian Fables by James Anthony Froude, Explained by J. J. Thomas. 1969 (1889):23-48; here: 27.
76 loc.cit. 46.
77 loc.cit. 47.
78 Roger Toumson, "The Question of Identity in Caribbean Literature", in: *Journal of Caribbean Studies* 3 (1986): 131-143; here: 131.
79 James published another monograph, *A History of Negro Revolt*, in the same year.
80 Cedric J. Robinson: *Black Marxism*. 1983:203.
81 C. L. R. James, "Presence of Blacks in the Caribbean and its Impact on Culture", first published 1975, reprinted in his *At the Rendezvous of Victory* (hence *Rendezvous*): 218-235; here: 218.
82 From an interview with C. L. R. James, printed in: Henry Abelove et al. (eds.): *Visions of History*. Interviews. 1983: 263-277; here: 275.
83 C. L. R. James, "The Atlantic Slave Trade", published 1970, reprinted in his *Future*: 235-264; here: 253.
84 loc.cit.

85 C. L. R. James: *Nkrumah and the Ghana Revolution*. 1977:68.

86 Introduction to *Froudacity*: 45.

87 *Nkrumah and the Ghana Revolution*: 12.

88 From an interview with C. L. R. James, in: Paul Buhle (ed.) 1986:164-167; here: 167.

89 C. L. R. James, "The Revolutionary Answer to the Negro Problem", in his *Future*: 126-127.

90 Paul Buhle, "Marxism in the USA", in: Paul Buhle (ed.): *C. L. R. James: His Life and Work*. 1986:81-104; here: 96.

91 Margaret Busby and Darcus Howe (eds.): *CLR James's 80th Birthday Lectures*. (Lectures delivered in 1981 in London) 1984:33.

92 Robin Simon and Alastair Smart: *The Art of Cricket*. 1983:2.

93 James Walvin: *Leisure and Society 1830-1950*. 1978:92-93.

94 Bernard Porter: *The Lion's Share*. 1975: 346-347.

95 R. Simon, A. Smart: *The Art of Cricket*. 1983:49.

96 C. C. Eldridge, "Sinews of Empire: Changing Perspectives", in: C. C. Eldridge: *British Imperialism in the Nineteenth Century*. 1987 (1983): 168-189; here: 186.

97 Edward Mack: *Public Schools Since 1860*, p. 130, quoted in: John Lawson and Harold Silver: A Social History of Education in England. 1973:345.

98 Quoted in Patrick Howarth: *Play up and Play the Game*. 1973:i.

99 Richard Holt: *Sport and the British*. 1990:221.

100 C. L. R. James: *Cricket*. Ed. by Anna Grimshaw. 1989:276 (= *Cricket*).

101 *Boundary* 70.

102 *Boundary* 158.

103 *Boundary* 164.

104 *Boundary* 158.

105 CLR James, "Garfield Sobers" (1969); *Cricket* 227.

106 *Boundary* 159-160.

107 CLR James, "Garfield Sobers" (1969); *Cricket* 227.

108 loc.cit. 232, my emphasis.

109 CLR James, "Cricket in the West Indian Culture" (1963); *Cricket* 119.

110 *Boundary* 55-56.

111 *Boundary* 60.

112 *Cricket* 119.

113 *Boundary* 77.

114 C.L.R. James, "Cricket in the West Indian Culture" (1963): *Cricket* 121.

115 loc.cit. 123-124.

116 *Boundary* 14, my emphasis.

117 Sylvia Wynter, "In Quest of Matthew Bondman: Some Cultural Notes on the Jamesian Journey", in: Paul Buhle (ed.): *C. L. R. James: His Life and Work*. 1986: 131-145; here: 138.

118 loc.cit. 139.

119 loc.cit. 144.

120 *Boundary* 109.

121 CLR James, "Cricket in the West Indian Culture" (1963); *Cricket* 124. My emphasis.

122 *Boundary* 191-192.

123 *Cricket* 227.

124 loc.cit.

125 Cricket, according to James, is also a visual art. He deals with this aspect of the game
    at some length in *Boundary*, especially pp. 195-205.
126 *Boundary* 206, my emphasis.
127 Letter to V. S. Naipaul, (1963); *Cricket* 116-117.
128 Cf. Cedric J. Robinson: *Black Marxism*. 1983: 386.
129 Bill Ashcroft et al.: *The Empire Writes Back*. 1989:195.
130 *Boundary* 206.
131 Especially his *The Black Jacobins* is treated as a classic.
132 Edward W. Said: *Orientalism*. 1978.
133 C.R.L. Fletcher and R. Kipling: *A School History of England*. 1911:240. Quoted in
    Valerie E. Chancellor: *History for Their Masters*. Opinion in English History Text-
    book: 1800-1914. 1970:124.
134 *C.L.R. James's 80th Birthday Lectures*, 23.
135 Cf. for example Chris Searle, "Race before wicket: cricket, Empire and the White
    Rose. For C.L.R. James (1901-1989)". In: *Race & Class* 3 (1990):31-48.
136 Cf. Michi Knecht, "Höflichkeitsverhalten als öffentliches Ritual. Ansätze ethnolo-
    gischer Symboltheorie." In: *Tübinger Korrespondenzblatt* Dec 1990: 7-18.- Knecht's
    use of *symbolic anthropology* (amongst others he refers to Clifford Geertz's work)
    seems to suggest James's proximity to this approach to culture.
137 Stuart Hall, "The Meaning of New Times", in: Stuart Hall and Martin Jacques (eds.):
    New Times. 1989: 116-133; here: 122.
138 These lines from Césaires *Return to My Native Country* are quoted in CLR James:
    Kwame Nkrumah and the Ghana Revolution, 1977:22.

The Works of C. L. R. James

Listed below are James's major writings, with emphasis on those available today. An extensive bibliography, including articles, essays, reviews and lectures by him can be found
in his collection *At the Rendezvous of Victory*. Articles of his which have been reprinted in
one of his three anthologies have not been listed separately. As to the vast amount of material which has been published in little magazines, in the form of pamphlets or leaflets, as
well as far as his *Notes on American Civilization* and other unpublished manuscripts are
concerned: bibliographies attached to the anthologies list the various archives, universities
and private institutions and collections where they can be found.

The Life of Captain Cipriani: An Account of British Government in the West Indies (Nel-
    son, Lancs., England 1932).
Minty Alley (London 1936).
World Revolution 1917-1936: The Rise and Fall of the Communist International (1937,
    repr. London 1970).
The Black Jacobins: Toussaint L'Ouverture and the San Domingo revolution (London
    1938).
A History of Negro Revolt (London 1938).

The Invading Socialist Society (New York 1947, repr. with new preface by James, Detroit 1972).

Notes on Dialectics: Hegel, Marx, Lenin (1948, repr. London 1980).

State Capitalism and World Revolution (Detroit 1950, repr. Detroit 1969).

Mariners, Renegades and Castaways: The story of Herman Melville and the world we live in (New York 1953, repr. London 1985).

Modern Politics (Port of Spain 1960, repr. Detroit 1973).

Party Politics in the West Indies (Port of Spain, Trinidad 1962).

Beyond a Boundary (London 1963. repr. London 1980, New York 1984).

The Future in the Present, Selected Writings vol. 1, (London 1977).

Spheres of Existence, Selected Writings vol. 2, (London 1980).

Walter Rodney and the Question of Power (London 1983).

80th Birthday Lectures (London 1983).

At the Rendezvous of History, Selected Writings vol. 3, (London 1984).

Cricket, Selected Writings, ed. Anna Grimshaw (London/New York 1986).

Walter Kühnel

Leslie A. Fiedler

(1917-)

In 1948 *Partisan Review* published a short essay entitled "Come Back to the Raft Ag'in, Huck Honey!" The title was innocuous enough to fool even the most recent reincarnation of Anthony Comstock. Its contents, though, would launch its author into the contemporary orbit of cultural criticism as few other short essays had done in the past or would in the next future. And its message sent some of the established authorities of American literary and cultural criticism reeling. Actually, Philip Rahv, the editor responsible for its publication, later claimed that he was sure that the author "did not really mean it," that it was an aspiring young novelist's *jeu d'esprit* which had produced "Come Back ...".[1] Few saw it as the first of the many gauntlets which its author would throw in a long career. Today, we can safely say that no anthology or history of American literary or cultural criticism in the 20th century is complete without accounting for both the impact of "Come Back ..." and the irritating, or stimulating – which may be the more concise word – but, in any case, the undeniably long-lived presence of its author. In 1948 he first exhibited his unique talent, i.e. a beast of prey's instinctive knowledge of its victim's jugular. He was not meant to become just another choir boy. Nor was he prepared to kneel at the feet of the champions of established cultural criticism. "Come Back ..." was not incensed, it was incendiary.

The author was one Leslie A. Fiedler, a young assistant professor of English from the University of Montana. Only a few years before, Fiedler had roamed the stacks of the Widener Library, had gone through the Harvard routine, e.g. "the class in Modern American Poetry, to which we came faithfully three times a week." Strangely – or understandably – enough, he failed to ingratiate himself with the Harvard crowd. At Cambridge, Fiedler merely felt Harvard's "whole exhilarating-melancholy weight." But he came to see himself – with the rest of the 1946-1947 class of Rockefeller Foundation grantees – as destined for a career as either novelist, poet, or critic. In a more or less fictional recall of his days at Cambridge, Fiedler would come to view his "prolonged recess in a surreal playground" as a waste of time – shades of young Fitzgerald at Princeton, no doubt. And rather than attending another boring academic committee meeting, he set about to "slowly, slowly ... become a writer."[2]

He tried poetry and he began to write short stories, some of which would later be collected and published in *Pull Down Vanity*, or *Nude Croquet*. With *The Second Stone, Back to China*, and *The Last Jew in America*, Fiedler was to win modest fame and recognition as a promising young American novelist. There is actually one secondary source which regards him as a peer of, if not an equal to, the likes of Nathanael West, Bernard Malamud, Norman Mailer, and Saul Bellow.[3]

But it was only with "Come Back ..." that Fiedler found his true vocation and his voice – as a cultural critic. He had tried his best – and would try again – to become a *bona fide* novelist. But his best was not good enough. Trying as hard as he might, Fiedler never managed to transcend the awkwardness of an Ernest Hemingway in his declining years, to rise above the embarrassing "was-it-good-for-you-too?"-syndrome which so effectively marred *For Whom the Bell Tolls*. He just adds positional precision when he has one of his female characters straddle her lover in her preferred manner while the suggestive picture and stills from *Hiroshima, Mon Amour* slowly fade "from consciousness in the final explosion of love."[4]

Though he would keep the novelist's shop open for some time to come, Fiedler must have known that not even "Nude Croquet" would get him anywhere near the wicket. The responses to "Come Back ...," though, could easily teach him that, rather than breaking into the well established canon of poetry and fiction, its irreverent reexamination or explosion was worth his while.

It is tempting to retrace the steps which, slowly but surely, led Fiedler to see himself as neither poet nor novelist – led him to accept his true calling and undisguised self: that he was an extremely gifted essayist, that the scholarly and the not-so-scholarly essay was the one and only genre "in which my street-corner voice learned to criticize my street-corner self."[5]

The publication of "Come Back ..." surely changed an academic career which had progressed smoothly enough. Born in Newark, N.J., in 1917, Fiedler had earned his B.A. at New York University in 1938 and then transferred to the University of Wisconsin, at that time one of the first addresses of American liberalism. He graduated with the class of '39, and completed the Ph.D. program with a thesis on "The Medieval Background of John Donne's 'Songs and Sonnets'" – a dyed-in-the-wool new critic, most unwary readers assumed, with some justification. They were in for a surprise: for the publication of "Come Back ...", a first treat to the stunning argument, the even more stunning methodological about-face, and the verbal felicity which Fiedler would, later on, develop into his distinguished trademark.

His first professional teaching assignment exiled Fiedler to the University of Montana. He was obviously ill prepared for Missoula, Mont. A contemporary commentator gleefully evokes the picture of "the burly Fiedler ... bundled by implacable fate into the train that would haul him off kicking and fuming to the academic Gulag in Montana."[6] Here, as in many other instances, it is much more satisfying to listen to the original voice than to that of his hagiographers or detractors. According to Fiedler, he approached Montana with little more than shabby remnants of a romanticistic myth of the West gleaned from popular culture. But he was also grimly determined (shades of popular culture, no doubt) to prove himself an eastern academician, i.e. "to face down any student who came to argue about his grades armed with a six-shooter."[7]

The Montana residence taught Fiedler a lot; certainly more than most of his critics imagine. Allison Lurie actually held "places like Buffalo and Montana" (a beautiful juxtaposition of a city and a whole state!) accountable for subsequent Fiedlerisms, by making a case "for the ill effects of this kind of enforced isolation on the American writer, who typically finds himself cut off from most of his natural peers on some cold far-flung campus."[8] Upon closer reading, though, we learn that the Montana experience taught Fiedler, first of all, to resist the "enervating effect of the mountains," to retain his "desire to revile my fellow-men for their weaknesses." It certainly helped him "to leap to my feet and drive, past the rusty beer cans and the white roads back to town."[9] And there can be no doubt that it encouraged Fiedler in more than one way to pass the rusty beer cans and white roadsigns of traditional cultural or literary criticism and proceed in a different direction – a road that would lead, strange as it may sound, to Nigger Jim's plaintive "Come Back ...".

The evidence is overwhelming: the Montana experience did influence, or better yet: it shaped or at least shaded, the cultural critic's view of things and persons, yet in a way inconceivable by his "natural peers." After all, Fiedler encountered, no, not the student who wanted to argue about his grades with a six-shooter, but that "Montana Face" which would, simultaneously, awe and appall the Jewish Eastern Liberal. That face seemed, at first glance, just "reticent, sullen, weary – full of self-sufficient stupidity." After a while, though, Fiedler would resign himself to the conclusion that this face was developed for neither sociability nor feeling, its one and only redeeming function was "facing into the weather."[10] The observable reality, the ubiquity of that face taught Fiedler not only that there is a considerable discrepancy between fact and fiction. Its undeniable presence in Missoula and within a 500 mile-wide perimeter, must have suggested the idea of a pattern, of an essence beneath the individual phenomena. Was there a sort of genetic mould which churned out this endless sequence of but superficially individualized faces? Could it be that there was something like an ...? Oh, well, prototype? Were social conditions potent enough to reduce individuality to ... well what? Archetypes?

But, then, we might as well assume that, in order to avoid yet another encounter with just one more of those faces, Fiedler simply returned to his den. And, rather than oiling his six-shooter or uncorking the magnum Moet-Chandon which he could not yet afford, he simply returned to that slender, yet well-thumbed book which must have fascinated him from the first: D. H. Lawrence's *Studies in Classic American Literature*. If so, it does not require an overly speculative mind to imagine that the somber notes of Lawrence's introductory chapters struck a sympathetic chord in someone who had just learned that Rousseau's dream "reaches a cul-de-sac at the Lions Club in Two Dot, Montana."[11]

What was the deeper meaning of this Montana face? One is tempted to visualize Fiedler in his den, pondering the lines of that face over a can of *Coors*. It is even more tempting to imagine that this was the moment when he decided to take a closer and harder look at cherished American myths and realities, to redefine their tenuous relationship. Had not Lawrence asked the pertinent questions? Called attention to the conflict which marked not only the boundaries between fact and fiction but also between rhetoric and reality? Had he not suggested that substance is veiled by appearance – in the New as much as in the Old World? And that it is the cultural critic's true vocation to look behind the masks and reveal the true identity of the characters as well as the original nature of the play? "Never trust the artist. Trust the tale," Lawrence had admonished both readers and critics.

It may thus be not entirely amiss to trace Fiedler's relentless search for the mythical character underneath all fiction – a term which would soon juxtapose literature and politics – and to reach one's destination in those few lines wherein Lawrence as grandly as beautifully imagined the inception of America and the images which would forever haunt and distinguish American literature:

> What did the Pilgrim Fathers come for, then, when they came so gruesomely over the black sea? Oh, it was in a black spirit. A black revulsion from Europe ... You have got to pull the democratic and idealistic clothes off American utterance. And see what you can of the dusky body of IT underneath.
> 'Henceforth be masterless.'
> Henceforth be mastered.[12]

It was, may be, at this moment that Fiedler decided to really pull the democratic and idealistic clothes off American utterances and to expose the dusky body underneath. Because that is exactly what Fiedler did – and with that vengeance which surprised not only the then reigning Miss Watsons of academia. Was *Huck Finn* no more than but another novel in that canon which he had been hired to uphold and transmit? The newly gained insight into the true nature of the "Montana Face," its archetypal rather than individual significance gave a new ring to Lawrence's words. To "pull the democratic and idealistic clothes off American utterance," ... and to reveal the dusky body underneath! Here was the New World – of cultural criticism. It was *that* kind of cultural criticism which would transcend both New Criticism and the by now discredited Marxist cant of Mike Gold. Fiedler was free now to proceed from "Ethics and Aesthetics to Ecstatics," as he would later entitle one of his essays.[13] Or were the ecstatics of cultural criticism still reserved for the eventual publication of *Love and Death in the American Novel* in 1960?

On the other hand, Cambridge, Mass., rather than Missoula, Mont., may deserve the blame for or may claim the honor of having given rise to the eventual emergence of Leslie A. Fiedler, myth critic, whom few would love, many despise, and most remember as "the guy who wrote that stuff about Huck Finn." Harvard's claim to Fiedler-fame or -infamy rests on the fact that in 1946 Fiedler was made Rockefeller Fellow of the Humanities and for about a year became a presence on the lawns of the venerable institution. It is a safe assumption that the Widener Library holdings include C. G. Jung's collected works, probably even a few of Jung's early manuscripts. It certainly did not need the *Gesammelte Werke* to introduce or reintroduce Fiedler to Jungian concepts. Whether it was in the Widener Library or somewhere else that Fiedler was introduced or reintroduced to Jungian ideas must remain a moot point. Yet, as in the case of Lawrence and Fiedler, there can be no doubt as to Jung's and Fiedler's conceptual contiguity. From time to time, Fiedler will call the reader's attention to this Jungian connection, e.g. by calling himself an "anti-Jungian Jungian."[14] Fiedler's words suggest a tenuous kinship. But whatever trust the reader is willing to place in Fiedler's claims or disclaimers: he is well advised to enjoy not only Fiedler's conceits, similes and metaphors, in short, Fiedler's smoothly flowing rhetoric. He should also remember how Gerhart Hauptmann defined the essence of all fictional production. "Dichten heißt," Hauptmann alleged in a memorable a priori, "hinter Worten das Urwort erklingen lassen." Translated into what Jung calls "psychologische Sprache," the critic must be guided by one question only: "To which primordial image of the collective unconscious can we trace the image developed in the work of art?" Defining in no uncertain terms "the primordial image" as "archetype" or that figure which, "whether demon, man or event, ... repeats itself in the course of history wherever the creative imagination is freely exercized," Jung laid the foundations of cultural criticism which today is known as myth-criticism and whose most prominent and provocative practitioner is one Leslie A. Fiedler – because Fiedler, better and more convincingly than his peers, put into criticial practice what were but logical implications of such Jungian concepts as divesting *daimon*, man, or conditions of their historical robes and props, i.e. transcending "the course of history." He would pull off the democratic and idealistic clothes more radically, and much more imaginatively, than Northrop Frye, Maud Bodkin, Richard Chase or R.W.B. Lewis.

A closer look at contemporary phenomena, Jung maintains, will reveal their ephemeral nature, will reveal that what poses as historical drama is but the reenactment of mythology. History is but a costume-change on a stage that exists since time immemorial, the historical actors are but contemporary variations of the limited number of archetypes. Or as Jung puts it:

> If we take a closer look at these images, we will discover that they are so to speak the formulated resultant of countless typical experiences in our ancestral line. They are as it were the psychic residue of innumerable events of the same type. They depict myriad individual experiences in terms of a human average and thus give us a picture of man's psychic life split and projected into the various figures from the mythological pandemonium.[15]

What finally generated the proposals and projections which made "Come Back ..." such a memorable event in recent cultural criticism is thus not beyond all conjecture. Jung's idea of a mythological pandemonium is quite obviously one of its most inspiring sources. And so is Lawrence's definition of the critic's proper function as that of "saving the American tale from the American artist."[16] In his later work Fiedler gave ample credit to Jung, but has always short-shrifted Lawrence's impact by nonchalantly relegating *Studies in Classic American Literature* to a few footnotes. Montana finally earned not only a place in the cultural topography of the nation by Fiedler's hard looks into the "Montana Face." It helped him to extend his mythopoetic readings to the interpretation of life as well as literature. Compared to this experience Harvard only serves to grace the cultural critic's biography.

But all conjectures must remain moot points compared to the impact this little essay had on the career of its author and the development of an unmistakable voice in American cultural criticism. "Come Back ..." *made* Fiedler. Before its publication he was just a face among many others at the annual MLA meetings. Now he was the guy who "dared suggest that Huck and Jim were queer as three-dollar bills"[17] – not the least achievement in the otherwise mousy groves of academe. Even if, at that time, not even Fiedler fully realized the implications of that "irreverent first-person meditation," as he would call it some thirty-odd years later, "Come Back ...," like few other cultural analyses, entered the public domain, as Fiedler claims with his usual modesty – adding with that equally characteristic spite for the academic establishment that the essay is fast "becoming in effect itself popular literature." In modern cultural criticism the impact of "Come Back ..." is unrivaled. That it entered the public domain, i.e. that it gave uncommon status to an academician, can be learned from the responses Fiedler received. In "Who Was Leslie Fiedler?" the sage from Buffalo gleefully recalls that there was this middle-aged commentator who, in the pages of the hallowed *New York Times*, complained that his son had gone off "on a raft with Nigger Jim or Leslie Fiedler."[18] And when Fiedler met Ernest Hemingway, "Papa" asked: "Fiedler? Leslie Fiedler. Do you still believe that st- st- stuff about Huck Finn?"[19]

There is ample evidence to conclude that it was this "st- st- stuff about Huck Finn" which made Leslie A. Fiedler one of America's most talked about, cherished as well as reviled cultural critics. That "stuff" resurrected Twain's novel from an untimely death on the dusty shelves of lending libraries or, worse yet, from an even less deserved death in the lecture halls of yet another English Department. It is only fair to let the author summarize his original intention. Some thirty-odd years later Fiedler said:

> What I actually contended, referring not just to *Huckleberry Finn* but other American classics like *Leatherstocking Tales* and *Moby Dick*, was that, in a society characterized in the conscious level by fear and distrust of what I called then "homoerotic love" ("male bonding" has since become the fashionable euphemism) and by mutual violence between white and nonwhite Americans, there has appeared over and over in books written by white American authors the same myth of an idyllic anti-marriage: a lifelong love, passionate though chaste, and consummated in the wilderness, on a whaling ship or a raft, anywhere but "home," between a white refugee from "civilization" and a dark-skinned "savage," both of them male.[20]

It goes without saying that such a reading of some of America's most revered literary classics would not only ruffle feathers but rattle cages in God's own country on the eve of the Eisenhower era and the concomitant renaissance of the Daughters of the American Revolution. Was this inspired re-reading of Cooper, Dana, Melville, and Twain, this reinterpretation of what had long been shelved as harmless books for children, for good and God-fearing American adolescents, Fiedler's way past all of Montana's rusting beer cans, "back to the city?"

The discovery of "the Montana Face" added insult to injury. Wasn't it enough to have one's favorite literary heroes reduced to a bunch of socially irresponsible queers? Did that same Eastern dude have to revile the backbone of American society by calling the good people of Montana "a kind of parody of the Noble Savage, the Healthy Savage – stupidity as mental health?"[21] Was Fiedler pillorying Middle America in order to make his way past the boringly white roadcrossings "back to the city?"

If Fiedler was seriously considering a move from Missoula back to the East Coast and its ivy-covered halls, he certainly missed the road to the big cities and the East's major colleges by seriously antagonizing what was left of the leftist establishment. Outraging the poor hicks in Montana was one thing, incurring the wrath of the hidebound hordes on the little magazines' editorial boards was quite another. Yet with the same zeal that had inspired his Montana campaign, Fiedler, in the early Fifties, threw himself into the hot battle raging over the Cold War and the American cultural critics' role in this historical Jihad.

While a rainbow-coalition of former cardholders, fellow-travellers, *bona fide* liberals, and other newspaper readers yelled either bloody murder or demanded a retrial of the Rosenbergs, Fiedler cooly – or hotly? – set out to transcend the historical actors of that drama in much the same way he had transformed Nigger Jim and Huck Finn from individual literary characters into American cultural archetypes and exactly in that manner which helped him reify the "Montana Face".

Why should not Whittaker Chambers, Alger Hiss, the Rosenbergs, or, for that matter, even Joe McCarthy, be just players in a much broader scenario, characters in a primordial drama?

As ham actors going through the script written by out-of-court agencies they were merely pitiable, Fiedler suggested. As contemporary reincarnations of a perennial struggle they gained a stature which no editorial in the *New Masses* could provide. Even McCarthy is dehistorisized, becomes a "symptom" of the eternal struggle between two forms of totalitarianism – the totalitarianism of populist Red-baiting as well as the fetish of an hysterical Liberalism. The arsenals of both liberal and populist mythology are depleted "until what began as a genuine bill of particulars ends at paranoid speculation, paranoia answering paranoia."[22] Although clearly no follower of McCarthy, Fiedler gained few friends in the academic community by his contention that, in their own way, a sizeable segment of the intellectuals were as paranoid as the most rabid Commie-baiters. Could this guy be serious? Why would he insist on viewing and evaluating Hiss, Chambers, even the Rosenbergs as archetypes? Why didn't he discuss the specifics of their cases or the irregularities of the trials? The antagonism was deeply felt. It certainly was not just Fiedler's "affinity for the wrong journals" which impeded or slowed his return to the East.[23] Until today Fiedler has to answer "his rattlebrained image of McCarthy as the *victim* of the masses."[24] It certainly did not help to smooth the way back into the city. But in no way did Fiedler intend to break "his previous allegiance with progressive liberals," as several contemporary readings of his essays "Hiss, Chambers, and the Age of Innocence," or, more pertinently, "Afterthoughts on the Rosenbergs," and "McCarthy and the Intellectuals" would have us believe.[25] Once again, it is tempting to speculate, to ask what motivated Fiedler to write those essays which, as he must have well known, would catch as much flak from the liberal establishment in the East – as he knew only too well, didn't he? – his "Montana"-essay had to cause tornado-like disruptions in and around Missoula. Could it be that he was not planning his return to the big cities? That, instead, he was still desirous "to revile my fellow-men for their stupidity?" Or that he saw himself in the position of that literary angel who had been promised a return ticket but which, somehow and somewhere, and without the owner's knowledge, had been invalidated? If so, what would be the web, and what could be the rock in the near future?

Or Fiedler simply enjoyed kicking at rusty old beer cans. After all, in the early Fifties literary as well as cultural criticism had more empty than full bottles to offer plus a good number of rusting cans. There was still a sizeable number of containers marketed by the successors of the Michael Gold-company. Yet they would only go through a few more Hickups, a malaise which no Aptheker could cure. Nor was Mr. Warren's trade still energetic enough to sustain the promises made by either Spingarn or Eliot, Richards or Winters. The *Partisan Review* symposium on 'Our Country and Our Culture' amply demonstrates this quandary in American literary, cultural and social Criticism. Daniel Bell was ringing in the end of all ideologies. And more and more formerly dedicated class-strugglers became stranglers in the managerial revolution. Quite a number of them must have relocated their cherished Joe Hill records to the attic in order to discover the man in the gray flannel suit. Which, in turn, would lead them to worry about the plight of the newly discovered lonely crowd and the impact of industrial capitalism on the psyche rather than the poor worker's mangled body, sometimes even creating a new concern for the individual rather than "the masses," which had by that time somewhat miraculously been rechristened as "the people." In the Fifties, the number of rusty beer cans littering the country from New York to Los Angeles, and especially from Boston to Baltimore must have been a tempting sight for a punter.

Whatever his motives, Fiedler chose to expand his ideas yet further by applying in what was to become a heated debate of the political scene. Jung's concept of the archetype had served him well in the rereading of classical American literature and in the examination of local features. Why should it fail him in the assessment of contemporary politics? In the three essays which were to become part I of *End to Innocence*, Fiedler redeemed the cultural bane of the Fifties by mythicizing the detail and by elevating the unsavory strife. Earlier on he had made the historical Daniel Boone over into, no, not the Natty Bumppo of the *Leatherstocking Tales* but one of the grand-dads of

America's infatuation with miscegenous dreams. Later on he had comprised whatever unpleasant encounters with Montanans he actually had into the un-flattering archetype of the face which is made not for human sociability but only good to face the weather. In the "Rosenberg et al."-essays Fiedler mere-ly turned from literature and social psychology to politics. But he had not changed his approach: once again he gave status to a decade by turning histo-ry into mythology. And we should not forget that it was the decade when the word greatness was reserved, even in the school readers, for the golfing pro-pensities of the president of the United States.

In spite of all his extreme judgments Fiedler tried desperately to convince himself and others that he was merely balancing a precarious middle against the inroads of radical ends in both literary and cultural criticism.[26] But he was clearly propelled towards the Scylla and Charybdis of mythopoetic criti-cism, towards the extremes rather than the middle: The question where arche-type ends and where signature begins, or *vice versa*, how the poet can assert himself against the poem. It is, of course, that question which Lawrence had answered in such unequivocal manner in 1922.

Here Fiedler comes as close to a definition of his key concepts as never be-fore and never again. Any work of art, he says, is both: archetype *and* signa-ture:

> The word Archetype ... I use ... to mean any of the immemorial patterns of response to the human situation in its most permanent aspects: death, love, the biological family, the relationship with the Unknown etc., whether those patterns be considered to reside in the Jungian Collective Unconscious or the Platonic world of Ideas. The archetypal belongs to the infra- or meta-personal, to what Freudians call the Id or the Unconscious; that is, it be-longs to the Community at its deepest, pre-conscious level of acceptance. I use signature to mean the sum-total of individuating factors in a work, the sign of a Persona or Personal-ity, through which an archetype is rendered ...
>
> Literature, properly speaking, can be said to come into existence at the moment Signa-ture is imposed upon the Archetype. The purely archetypal, without signature-elements, is the Myth.[27]

Fiedler later claimed that at that time he was a "pontifical fellow with a pretentious middle initial who wrote articles with even more pretentious ti-tles."[28] Even a friendly critic will hesitate a moment before he contradicts the pontifical fellow. But the contours of the critical program are discernible. Ac-cepting Jung's definition of the archetype as the recurrent and immutable pat-terns of human existence beyond all historical variables, Fiedler had nonethe-less transcended the rigid Jungian system by adding the individual artist's sig-nature and defined cultural expression as the dynamic interaction of ontogeny and phylogeny: Literature is a palimpsest, the original texts can never be fully erased, new signs – or signatures – may be superimposed in the language of the day, yet the hieroglyphics of the old message will always shine through.

But Fiedler also disagrees with Jung on another important topic: he wants to balance psychological and sociological factors. Or, as he said in the preface to the second edition of *Love and Death in the American Novel*, all revisions of the original text aimed at the further clarification of "the balance between psychological and sociological insights essential to my approach."[29] He further widened the gap between himself and Jung in an unpublished letter to the author of this article, explaining that, to him, "all literature ... is not [just] words on a page but images in the head and the head in society." For that part of literature which reveals or reflects the impact of society on those images, neither Jung nor Freud have provided satisfying answers. And thus, Fiedler adds, "What I reject completely ... is the autonomous status of the archetypal: Jung's notion that they are eternal, given, as it were."[30] He thus correctly called himself an "anti-Jungian Jungian" when, in *What Was Literature*, he said: "In any case, I have never used my criticism as a way of denying history," and adding, for explication's sake, "For me the archetypes are not eternal but socially determined, changing as our relationship to the environment and each other change."[31] Thus Fiedler claims for himself what much earlier Lawrence had demarcated as the province of his type of cultural criticism. Both critics maintain – in full accordance with C. G. Jung – that the cultural archetype cannot be denied. But both critics also assert – in opposition to Jung – that under the new robes, in a new socio-political environment, the cultural archetypes can, and most likely will be so significantly modified as to warrant the idea of national cultures or literatures.

For Lawrence the archetypal American conflict is one of blood-consciousness versus abstract cognitions. Relying on the Enlightenment's promise of making man the subject rather than the object of history, the American is forever oscillating between cognitively defined plans for social improvement and "what IT wishes done." And Lawrence poetically paraphrases the American archetype as a mixture of Caliban and Pilgrim Father. As a nation, the U.S., to Lawrence, is politically dedicated to Jefferson's and Lincoln's dedications: "THOU SHALT NOT PRESUME TO BE A MASTER. Hence democracy. 'We are the masterless.' That is what the American Eagle shrieks." But the Enlightenment only broke the chains and fetters of feudalism. No cognition could liberate the Americans, "the runaway slaves," from blood-consciousness: "We cannot see what invisible winds carry us.... We are not the marvellous choosers and deciders we think we are. IT chooses for us, and decides for us.... IT drives us and decides us."[32] Subsequently, all American art-speech will betray a duplicity which exists between the official surface

and the submerged meaning of the text. And it is this duplicity which gives
classic American literature its unmistakably indigenous ring: "The old American art-speech contains an alien quality, which belongs to the American continent and to nowhere else."[33]

Here, once again, hypothesis darkly yet temptingly beckons. Can we safely
assume that the combination of traditions, conditions, methodologies mentioned before actually suffice to explain the Leslie Fiedler who, in 1960,
would startle the academic community, and this time for good, with the publication of *Love and Death*? Where and when did Fiedler learn to evade the
pitfalls of "pure" mythopoetic criticism? To evade the nemesis of all myth
critics, i.e. to view not only American, but world literature and history as "the
tireless history of the Same?"[34] In other words, how can the critic reconcile
the conflicting ideas of archetype and "the spirit of place"?

The early encounter with "secular liberalism" or Marxism – if not in New
York, then quite certainly at Madison – prevented an unconditional surrender
to orthodox Freudianism as well as what only seemed to be revisionist Jung-
anism. But the growth of Fiedler's belief in the necessity of juxtaposing
archetypes and history might also be traceable to his European experiences in
the early Fifties. The years he spent as Fulbright Fellow and visiting professor in Italy honed his sense of cultural differences. Thus, the wonderful little
essays collected in part II of *End of Innocence* may also help to explain how
Fiedler learned to transcend the merely archetypal, the psychologist's rather
sterile history of the same and progressed from Jungian a prioris to a stimulating discussion of *the archetype in time and place*.

In "Italian Pilgrimage" Fiedler describes how changed historical conditions
recast what to him are a community's deepest phantasies. Surveying past and
present Italian images of America from Checci to Pavese and Pintor, he reaffirms the existence of an archetype and simultaneously rehistoricizes it,
claiming, e.g. that America is to contemporary Italy "what Italy itself had
been to England in the Renaissance, what Germany to Europe when Romanticism was beginning."[35] To the historian, even the literary historian, this
sweeping statement is and ought to be an annoying irritation, raising questions rather than answering them. But to the cultural critic it clearly suggests,
in methodological terms, the author's grown awareness of conditioning factors beyond the psychologist's conceptual grasp. The latter's ahistorical and
apolitical stance has been significantly expanded. Cultural utterance is no
longer the timeless peddling of either well- or ill-wrought urns containing the
ashes of mere archetypes. The Italian years may thus have contributed more
to the theses informing *Love and Death* than even its author realized. The
"Italian Pilgrimage," as the essay's subtitle suggests, was another step towards the "Discovery of America," or, as Fiedler says in "Looking Back-

ward": "The end of the American artist's pilgrimage to Europe is the rediscovery of America."[36]

The rediscovery of America in *Love and Death*, though, entailed much more than "Ah, Genoese! Thy dream ... ." And, no doubt, it was a genuine intellectual effort rather than a merely syncretical yoking together of old and new approaches in cultural criticism, or just the cavalierly transformation of his borrowings, as Fiedler maintains in what is a gifted raconteur's ingenious *captatio benevolentiae* rather than the academician's usual preface to the first edition of his *magnum opus* (*LaD*, p. 14). By now, Fiedler's views were commodious enough to accommodate Marx and Jung, C. S. Lewis and D. H. Lawrence, an explosive congeries of sources and inspirations.

During the Christian Gauss Seminars at Princeton in 1957, Fiedler may have worked out almost all of part three of *Love and Death*, as he claims, (*LaD*, p. 15). Yet the ground had been well prepared by "Montana," "Looking Backward," by "McCarthy and the Intellectuals" or "Adolescence and Maturity in the American Novel."[37] But there can also be no doubt that, more than any other, "Come Back ..." had charted the course which *Love and Death* would take. The key concepts and the unifying approach had been explored and tested in the field of literature, social psychology and politics. Fiedler was ready and more than willing to "redeem our great books from the commentaries on them" (*LaD*, p. 11) – words reminiscent of the Lawrentian "saving the American tale from the American artist."[38]

But in *Love and Death* Fiedler not only takes up or merely expands Lawrence's argument: He actually explodes it. The point of departure is the assertion of a categorical difference between European and American fiction. To write about the American novel is "to write about the fate of certain European genres in a world of alien experience" (*LaD*, p. 31). American literature is, for Fiedler, the sum total of socio-politically conditioned variations of European prototypes which, themselves, are but expressions of an archetype. American fiction acquires its uniqueness in the specific way it modifies a generic model of the novel, or "Ur-roman":

A continuing tradition of prose fiction did not begin until the love affair of Lovelace and Clarissa ... had been imagined. The subject par excellence of the novel is love or, more precisely ... seduction and marriage; and in France, Italy, Germany, and Russia, even in England ... love in one form or another has remained the novel's central theme ...
But our great Romantic *Unroman*, our typical anti-novel, is the womanless *Moby Dick*.

Consequently, Fiedler sees in Irving's Rip Van Winkle the patron saint of the American novel, the prototype memorializing the "male protagonist of our fiction ... a man on the run ... to avoid 'civilization' ... which is to say, the confrontation of a man and a woman which leads to the fall to sex, marriage, and responsibility." Spurning social responsibility is no liberation, though. Rip's world is one of loneliness and fear. With the male protagonist shirking society for an "endlessly retreating vision of innocence," the American novel becomes "pre-eminently a novel of terror."[39] Its true domain is the frontier. In a brilliant paraphrase of Turner's famous hypothesis, that region is defined as "the margin where the theory of original goodness and the fact of original sin come face to face" (*LaD*, pp. 26-27, *passim*). The archetypal configuration in American literature, Fiedler argues, replaces Eros by Thanatos – in a not too covert translation of some of Freud's central concepts which explain the book's title. The flight from society leads to a latently homosexual relationship with nature's creature, the dark-skinned male companion, pagan yet pure: Chingachgook in Cooper's *Leatherstocking Tales*, Hope in Dana's *Two Years Before the Mast*, Queequeg in Melville's *Moby Dick*, Nigger Jim in Twain's *Huckleberry Finn*, King Dahfu in Bellow's *Henderson*. (In the retrospective "Who Was Leslie Fiedler?" he cites as additional evidence of the myth's persistence movies such as *The Defiant Ones, The Fortune Cookie,* or *One Flew Over the Cuckoo's Nest* as well as TV series such as *I Spy, Tenspeed and Brown Shoe, Chips, Hill Street Blues* or *Star Trek*.[40]) In accordance with his idea that the American novel is preeminently a novel of terror, Fiedler also evokes the Janus-face of the archetype: Chingachgook is also Injun Joe, "the killer in the graveyard," Nigger Jim is also the Babo of "Benito Cereno," and finally "the dark-skinned companion becomes the 'Black Man,' which is a traditional American name for the devil himself" (*LaD*, p. 26). So far Fiedler's explanation for the ubiquity of this archetypal pattern in the American novel is heavily if not exclusively indebted to psychological concepts. To redress the imbalance in terms of the reasons given in the preface to the second edition ("the balance between psychological and sociological insights") he now proceeds to a sweeping survey of American history. Terror is "essential to our literature," he says:

> But it is not merely a matter of terror filling the vacuum left by the suppression of sex in our novels, of Thanatos standing in for Eros. Through these gothic images are projected certain obsessive concerns of our national life: the ambiguity of our relationship with Indian and Negro, the ambiguity of our encounter with nature, the guilt of the revolutionist who feels himself a parricide (*LaD*, p. 27).

Any conceptualization of a society in terms of its "obsessive concerns," must, of necessity, remain unspecific and finally ahistoric – in spite of all claims to a balance of psychological and sociological concerns. Unwilling to pay heed to social actualities or essential changes of major issues on the historical agenda, it must remain sociological in name only. Reising correctly pointed out the unbridgeable discrepancy which exists between Fiedler's claims and his practice in *LaD* by calling attention to its very methodology as "a framework antithetical to social and historical specificity."[41] Fiedler claims that *LaD* relates cultural products to historical changes, promises to elucidate the complex interactions of social conditioning and fictional representations. The promised historicity, though, never acquires a new quality beyond the succession of archetypes, e.g., "the substitution of the Indian for the Inquisitor, the symbol of untamed nature for that of corrupt civilization" (*LaD*, p. 14). The emphasis on the archetype and its variations prevent a truly convincing connection of life and literature. And we should agree: the archetype is just that, why should it accommodate transitory reality?

Love and Death is an extremely amusing book. In academic discourse, references to entertainment are normally used as a soft guillotine, dispatching its victim without openly singing the executioner's song. As a cultural critic, Leslie Fiedler has displayed a refreshing sense of what ought to inspire criticism. It is thus not too far amiss to enjoy *Love and Death* as fiction in its own right. The reader should pay Fiedler the well deserved compliment, i.e. calling him an irreverent, an arrogant, an intriguing reviewer and interpretator of carefully selected American classics. *Love and Death* should thus remain – whatever the edition, revised or unrevised, – "to new readers and old ... as lively and in the best sense of the word, as vulgar as ever" (*LaD*, p. 8).

In terms of the history of American cultural criticism it is both a rejection of the progressivists' untenable mimetic obsession and the New Critics' equally reprehensible separation of fact and fiction. Most memorable will remain the sharp and pertinent assessments transcending rather than merely anticipating literary fashions, e.g.: "In the work of William Faulkner, the fear of the castrating woman and the dis-ease with sexuality ... attain their fullest expression" (*LaD*, p. 320) – a sentence which should make the ears of some feminists ring who would, much later, revile the likes of Mailer et al. for their misogynist leanings – ignoring Faulkner.

Or it ought to be remembered for the sleight-of-hand conceptualizations combining a new critic's reverence for the text with a detached cultural critic's concern for overlapping patterns. Few Hemingway critics have as pointedly and feelingly defined Hemingway's use of geography as cultural chiffre as Fiedler did in his discussion of *The Sun also Rises*. One short paragraph in *LaD* lights a funeral pyre for an inordinate number of approximations to Hemingway's novel, past and present. No sensitive reader can ignore the conjoint powers of the new critic as myth critic in passages such as the following:

One must not be confused by the exotics of expatriation: bullfights, French whores, and *thés dansants*. Like the American East, Paris in Hemingway's book stands for the world of women and work, for 'civilization' with all its moral complexity, and it is presided over quite properly by the bitch-goddess Brett Ashley. The mountains of Spain, on the other hand, represent the West: a world of male companions and sport, an anti-civilization, simple and joyous, whose presiding genius is that scarcely articulate arch-buddy, 'good, old Bill' (*LaD*, p. 355).

The enjoyment of *Love and Death* should be balanced by a sober sense of its bias, its methodological problems, and its omissions. Irving Howe was understandably displeased by what, to him, was yet another form of Fiedler's treason. Consequently, he ignored Fiedler's plea in the preface and magisterially reprimanded him for inexcusable omissions. "What Fiedler disregards," Howe accusingly howled, "is awesome."[42] Howe consciously chooses to ignore Fiedler's concession that he never pretended "to deal with all the remembered novelists" and his argument is invalidated by Fiedler's anticipation of "certain partisan readers [who] will doubtless resent the passing mention or the total silence accorded such novelists as William Dean Howells, Sinclair Lewis, John Dos Passos, or Thomas Wolfe" (*LaD*, p. 11). Rather than writing another literary history of the United States, Fiedler was trying to reveal hitherto neglected patterns in American fiction – covert codings of guilt and longings, repressed but nonetheless real themes of a uniquely American experience, sufficiently frequent – though not ubiquitous – to suggest and affirm the existence of a "covert culture"[43] in the pages of even those books which the custodians of tradition had commissioned to the children's section of public libraries and classroom anthologies. Fiedler never claimed to have written a comprehensive study of American literature. In his inimitable modesty he merely lays claim to the much more explosive discovery that "American literature is distinguished by the number of dangerous and disturbing books in its canon – and American scholarship by its ability to conceal this fact" (*LaD*, p. 11).

Rather than deploring Fiedler's disregard for mimetic poetics and social concerns, the reader and the critic ought to be concerned with the insouciant confession that the author has liberally sacked "certain fictionists ... who do not share what I believe to be the major concerns of our tradition" (*LaD*, ibid.). Instead of criticizing Fiedler for lacunae admitted well in advance, Howe might have asked Fiedler to reveal the criteria of his "beliefs," might have wondered on what principles Fiedler's cocksure knowledge of "the major concerns" in American literature actually rest. Comprehensiveness may be a problem. A selection of the available body of texts in terms of subjectively held beliefs is a much more grievous violation of scholarly standards. However acrimonious the reviews of *LaD*, and whatever invectives were hurled at Fiedler: nobody can accuse him of ever having tried to *falsify* rather than verify his provocative views by testing them against the obstinate presence of the very writers who do not share his "beliefs," his exquisite definition of "the major concerns."

Sir Karl Popper and his concept of falsification as the true parameter of scholarship, no doubt, takes second seat to C. G. Jung in all of Fiedler's writings. And an almost visceral self-assurance nips all tender off-shoots of a methodological self-reflection in the bud. It is only fair, though, to add that the most stimulating pages in Fiedler's work owe their thrust to what Lawrence would have called "blood-consciousness," those pages when the native hue of resolution is never sicklied o'er with the pale cast of methodological qualms. Or, in those pages which only too clearly substantiate "my not-so-secret motto ... 'Often wrong, but never in doubt.'"[44]

Even more problematical is the ease Fiedler displays in joining psychoanalytical concepts with those gleaned from what, *expressis verbis*, claims to be historical materialism. It poses a number of truly staggering problems to reconcile the concept of an archetype, or Jung's "Urbild," and Marxist ideas of the mind's social conditioning by time and place. Marxists have justifiably criticized the mythopoetical approach for its endemic ahistoricism, if not idealism. Myth critics have, with like methodological sneers, marveled at the Marxists' ease in translating imaginative worlds into indictments of a society's deficiencies. Fiedler unraveled the Gordian knot with Alexandrian determination and ruthlessness: for the "anti-Jungian Jungian" the archetypes are not eternal but socially determined. This is, of course, a conveniently bilingual rosetta stone, a too-beautiful-to-be-true Golden Gate Bridge across the straits separating two mutually exclusive approaches to cultural criticism. And more: The New Criticism's allegedly pure textual horizon is, by mere affirmation, broadened to encompass the psychologist's archetype which then becomes – a *non sequitur* in its own right – the expression of an historically and socially constituted political universe: a breathtaking methodological *tour de force*, indeed!

Howe might also have, with reason, pointed out that Fiedler is "maddeningly vague,"[45] on historical particulars. The text and the contentions of *LaD* actually strain Fiedler's own *captatio benevolentiae* in the preface, i.e. that this is not "an academic or scholarly book," a book "which depends not on faithfulness to 'fact' but on sensitivity to insight and nuance" (*LaD*, p. 9). And the contemporary reader may also consider what Kenneth S. Lynn alleged with his usual vitriol: that Fiedler "in defining the sexual vision of ... 19th-century authors ... merely imposed upon them a 20th-century view of male sexuality," or, more precisely, that Fiedler "distorted the masculine relationship in the *Leatherstocking Tales, Moby Dick,* and *Huckleberry Finn* in order to bring them into line with the sensational assertion in *Sexual Behavior in the Human Male,* by Alfred C. Kinsey and associates."[46]

However deserved or undeserved, vitriolic or enthusiastic the criticism of *LaD*, Fiedler expanded his original thesis and used an identical methodological approach in *Waiting for the End* and *The Return of the Vanishing American*. In conjunction with *LaD*, the later books are, according to the author himself, "an effort to define the myths which give a special character to art and life in America," even more succinctly, they constitute "a single book, the first of whose parts concerns itself with *eros* and *thanatos*; the second with the hope of apocalypse and its failure; the third with the Indian."[47]

Waiting for the End is, and, in all probability, will remain Fiedler's most 'literary' book – a collection of essays unusually subdued in tone, though reiterating his favorite themes. *Waiting*, I think, should be best remembered for its elegiac mourning of the "Death of the Old Men," the sensitive and sympathetic obituaries for Hemingway and Faulkner. It also contains the germs of those two books Fiedler had been promising himself for so long and never wrote. "War, Exile, and the Death of Honor," "The Beginning of the Thirties: Depression, Return, and Rebirth," "The End of the Thirties: Artificial Paradises and Real Hell,"[48] were obviously meant to provide the conceptual framework for earlier essays on John Peale Bishop and Henry Roth, and are, taken together, preludes to the full-length study of the thirties which would remain a writer's dream, i.e., which never reached publication. And "Academic Irresponsibility" in conjunction with "The New Mutants" were but bits and pieces of another abortive dream, hardly enough to console the by now growing number of Fiedler fans waiting for – not the end, but the "inclusive and conclusive book on the university."[49]

To be fair, though, no examination of Fiedler's work should neglect his earlier or later walks in the groves of academe, in essays such as "The War Against the Academy,"[50] or "On Remembering Freshman Comp."[51] In the late seventies Fiedler made a tentative foray into the history of the institutionalized study of literature.[52] The views expressed there were repeated and intensified in the first part of *What Was Literature?* The enemy territory is demarcated as those "English departments of the American mass university ... [where] there are not likely to be many teachers passionately engaged with literature and capable of responding in kind to its special use of language and evocation of image."[53] But, more importantly, in this book Fiedler comes close to a definition of his idea of literary – or cultural – studies by taking them from ethics (the New Humanism) and aesthetics (the New Criticism) to ecstatics (Fiedler). Accordingly, he rejects what he refers to as pro- and prescriptive critics and their obsolete notions of what constitutes literary excellence. And, of course, he also condemns the "autotelic" criticism from the New Critics to the postmodernists. Literary criticism is the search for "the *mythoi* which lie at the heart of all works which please many and which please long."[54] With his emphases on *all* works and the pleasure of the *many*, Fiedler had, of course, opened up the canon long before challenges to established canonicity became the *de rigeur* of modern criticism. And opening the canon in search of the archetype's affective potential, its power to move the recipient to a "privileged insanity," Fiedler legitimized popular culture studies certainly more elegantly and probably also more convincingly than most members of the Popular Culture Association.

Defining "classic" literature as the many-faceted expressions of the living archetype, and the modernist classics such as Joyce's *Ulysses*, Eliot's *The Waste Land*, or Pound's *Cantos* as "secondary mythology," Fiedler redeems popular culture as "not mythology once removed but primary myth."[55] And all manifestations of primary myths deserve and require academic attention and discussion. So, the expansion of Fiedler's canon, the tender embrace of "the many mothers of *Uncle Tom's Cabin*," the inclusion of *Gone With the Wind* as "the feminization of the anti-Tom Novel," or Alex Haley's *Roots* as an Uncle Tom's rewriting of *Uncle Tom's Cabin*, in the second part of *What Was Literature?*[56], cannot surprise the reader. Nor does it come as a surprise that *What Was Literature?* caught as much as or even more flak than *LaD*, "Montana" or "The new Mutants." For Vernon Young *What Was Literature?* is "virtually unreadable," because of Fiedler's "undying spite." It is, in addition, "the most offensive, ill-informed, and incoherent study of any aspect of literature that I have read in years." Alfred Kazin accused Fiedler of having "embraced the cultural values of his students, and that is what *What Was Literature?* is really about." Similarly, Kenneth Lynn indicted Fiedler for courting "the most immature members of his audience." Worse yet, Lynn targeted Fiedler as that professor who worked harder than any of his despicable peers "to prepare the way for the anarchic hedonism that overtook our colleges and universities in the 1960's ... . Fiedler ... has done his best to impoverish the study of literature by breaking down standards and transforming academic study into a theater of the self." Finally, Lennard J. Davis disparaged the book as the "old academic claptrap in street clothes," in which the author "is playing fast and furiously with this hidden image of himself as demagogue."[57]

Now, there can be no doubt that Fiedler is an attentive observer of contemporary trends. But that does not make him an uncritical patron of students' values. And in spite of Prof. Lynn's amply demonstrated acumen and perspicuity, it is hard to believe that Mr. Fiedler ever meant to impoverish the study of literature. What the critics fail to realize is that *What Was Literature?* becomes a companion piece to *LaD* in Fiedler's insistence on the existence of a "counter-myth" to the one "I had been exploring with almost monomaniacal exclusivity for all of my critical career." There is, Fiedler explains, "a second myth of equal importance, to which I regret having paid so little attention for so long." To the myth of "Home as Hell" investigated in *LaD*, he now adds what he calls "the myth of Home as Heaven," classically formulated in Beecher-Stowe's *Uncle Tom's Cabin*. In this counter-myth "home is portrayed as the earthly paradise, and marriage and integration into the family not as a fate to be fled for the sake of freedom, but as one to be sought in quest of maturity, responsibility and Christian salvation."[58]

Thus, Fiedler is only marginally interested in opening up the canon. He should by no means be bracketed with or mistaken for one of the numerous canon critics yelling bloody murder in the name of politics, race or gender. One might justifiably argue that, in fact, he is not even opening the canon at all but simply buttressing his old arguments with new materials. We might also argue that he covertly yet effectively defends them against any type of criticism questioning and challenging the highly selective filters of *LaD*. Any well-read literary critic could have charged the Fiedler of "Come Back ..." or *LaD* with a highly reductionist selection of American literary history, might have cited not only Howells, James, Dreiser, or Dos Passos, but the likes of Susanna Rowson, E.D.E.N. Southworth, Beecher-Stowe, William V. Moody, D. G. Phillips, Ellen Glasgow, Elizabeth M. Roberts etc., etc. He might also have asked Fiedler to account for contemporaries such as J. C. Oates or Joan Didion. And he might have added the charge that someone who claims to be well aware of the historical conditioning of cultural production and reception had actually wielded dehistoricizing a prioris with the recklessness characteristic of the proverbial hoodlum's use of a blunt instrument in an aggravated assault on an unsuspecting genre. He might actually have reminding Fiedler and the reader of the heinous "The subject par excellence of the novel is love, or, more precisely, ... seduction and marriage" (*LaD*, p. 25), and might have asked, "Who spread the linen, Prof. Procrustes?" But only a German critic would actually challenge Fiedler to answer Goethe's proverbial expansion of the theory of the novel, magisterially introducing and legitimizing the genre as that "Tier mit dem breiten Rücken," which defies formal definitions as well as all restrictions with regard to its contents.

With the addition of the counter-myth, though, Fiedler transforms quite a number of potential witnesses for the prosecution into circumstantial evidence for the defense. *What Was Literature?* is thus less a landmark in the debate over canonicity but crucial to a belated reaffirmation of the interracial male bonding thesis informing *LaD*. All critics unwilling to accept the reduction of females in American fiction to either fair maiden or sultry temptress, or the reduction of male protagonists to Good Bad Boys escaping from female control and symbolically mating with a colored boon companion, are now stripped of some of their most cherished and convincing contrapuntal evidence, i.e. the myriads of literary characters who contradict rather than substantiate Fiedler's original contention. Ricks may be right in surmising that "Fiedler in his prime would not have allowed himself so many of the *somehows* that are exactly what a critic has to convert into a true *how*."[59] But he is dead wrong in the allegation that the word "canon" is essential to Fiedler's argument. On the contrary, *What Was Literature*? is but a concerted effort to validate *LaD*, a point missed by even the most hostile critics. Fiedler did not cave in under the pressures of canon revisionists, nor did he, in a fit of impending senility, become pop critic. And he certainly did not propose that "the academic distinction between high and low culture be completely obliterated."[60] With admittedly too many *somehows*, Fiedler merely stretched and "somehow" strained the gratifyingly elegant argument sustaining *LaD*. But neither the "uncanny instinct for cultural fashion" nor the "gift for racy language"[61] explain Fiedler's interest in canon reformation. Instead, canonicity becomes the handmaid of methodology.

But absolving Fiedler from the sin of embracing the students' values should not be misrepresented as a general amnesty. The assertion that popular culture products reflect – however obliquely – primary myths, can lay claim to a venerable tradition. It does not, however, automatically lay to rest the disquieting idea that popular culture is but the product of what Adorno and others used to call *Kulturindustrie*, a serialized commodity rather than the autochthonous expression of a culture's *Urbilder*. Fiedler persistently ignores conditioning forces in both the productive as well as the receptive areas. And this is and remains an irritating "archetypal bias" in a critic who is wont to emphasize the balance between psychological and sociological factors. He means to bridge the gap, no doubt, but rests his argument, much as he did in his earlier work, on ahistorical, on anthropological *données* rather than historical variables. The furor which *What Was Literature*? generated is thus a crying over the milk spilled many years before. Fiedler simply resorted to his well established methods of publishing, swearing another oath of allegiance to the well-tried methodology of his publications: He cannibalized his *Inadvertent Epic*[62], and retained and expanded the ideas informing *LaD*.

This, in itself, is a pattern governing Fiedler's entire work. "The Jew in the American Novel," first published in 1959, would later come to serve as the backbone of *To the Gentiles* (1971)[63], only to have parts of it resurfacing in *The Stranger* in *Shakespeare* (1972)[64]. Fiedler himself calls his method "a continuation of certain speculations begun in a time that now seems relatively peaceful and innocent," and freely admits to cannibalizations à la Chandler.[65] It is thus not too surprising to learn that his "impossible book" on Shakespeare ends with the same paragraph as his original lecture (presented in 1948) on the four essential myths, i.e., the woman, the jew, the moor, and the New

World savage as strangers in Shakespeare's work, "only a little changed to suit its new context."[66] Once again, Fiedler sets out to "penetrate beneath the surface of what men say or do," in short, to reveal the "hidden meanings"[67] – with predictable results. De-individualizing Shakespeare's characters, Fiedler turns them into variations of a limited number of proto- or archetypes. A perfect example is Fiedler's reading of *Henry VI*. There are three female characters: Joan of Arc, the Countess of Auvergne, and Margaret, the later Queen of England. But, "mythologically speaking, they *are* one, being all 'black,' all French, and all bent on betraying the male champion of the English."[68] And, once again, the archetype is much more important than the differences between the historical characters: The archetype eclipses history in a, by now, only too well-known manner. History is but a change of props in a primordial conflict defined in terms of human antagonisms. "Both of these particular strangers," Fiedler claims, "the woman and the Jew, embody stereotypes and myths, impulses and attitudes, images and metaphors." The alleged preponderance of archetypal patterns is further reinforced, or, more precisely, becomes the DNS in the creation of symbolic meaning. After all, "whatever superficial changes have been made in the stereotypes and myths ... they still persist in the dark corners of our hearts, the dim periphery of our dreams."[69]

Accidence and essence are thus clearly defined, history can but superficially change "hearts," i.e. the Enlightenment can do but little to illuminate those dark corners to the right or the left of our cardiac valves. Visceral depths will always be much too profound to yield their secrets to mere cerebration. Dupin's ratiocination surely taught him "what song the sirens sang" and thus helped him to unravel a few negligible murders committed without spite and malice in a fictional Rue Morgue. But mere ratiocination can never successfully explore the dark regions, i.e., the forbidden territory covered by an officially prescribed chastity belt or jockstrap. The "stranger," though, reveals his true qualities to the mythopoetic critic. Fiedler is thus making, once again, liberal use of his "anti-Jungian Jungian" arsenal which provides him with all the conceptual weaponry he needs. And Fiedler does not disappoint his readers: all the "Strangers" in Shakespeare are familiar characters – not necessarily for the Shakespeare fan but for the devoted Fiedlerite.

After all, Fiedler read *Henry VI, The Merchant of Venice*, and *The Tempest* in much the same manner he read Irving, Dana, Cooper, Twain, et al. In more than one way, his Shakespeare does come – to paraphrase and correct a claim Fiedler makes in the preface – "out of my own head and the text before me."[70] This explosive interaction makes *The Stranger* another extension of the thesis expounded in *LaD*; the method developed for the investigation of American novels is now projected onto the Elisabethan stage. Once again,

Fiedler combines inspired close reading with provocative a prioris and thus "saves the tale from the artist," with predictable results. Except that *The Stranger*, more than any other of Fiedler's books, thus becomes a fascinating meditation on life rather than a new critical investigation of textual structures, becomes itself literature rather than literary exegesis as the beautifully elegiac final passage clearly shows:

> Only the failure, the castaway, the irredeemable stranger succeeds in dreams – dream-magic being granted in exile and loneliness – a means to drive out the usurper or to create a 'brave new world' in which love is ceremonial innocence. But the perfection of the dream is the dream's ending, and the dreamer must finally let fall his cloak and wand, bid the powers of air depart, stand outside the last illusion. Only then, knowing himself naked as all men are naked, estranged as all men are estranged, a slave as all men are slaves, can he learn to ask the prayers of others as he had once sought their applause.[71]

But despite the power of the archetype to generate an emphatic response in the reader, he is well advised to consider the fact that, once again, Fiedler reduces his textual sample by strapping it to the Procrustes bed of his *Urbilder*. And that in this relentless search for the *Urbild*, Fiedler simultaneously stymies and explodes the characters under review. Asserting the virtual identity of Joan of Arc, Margaret, and the Countess of Auvergne in *Henry VI*, he resorts to that method of telescoping literary characters which helped him, in *LaD*, to fuse or even amalgamate such opposites as Chingachgook and Injun Joe, or Babo and Nigger Jim. The same method was employed in *What Was Literature?* when Fiedler asserted that the reader must realize "the degree to which, metaphorically, mythically, Tom is female and white."[72] This search for the *Urbild* in both type and antitype has, naturally, provided more ammunition for hostile critics than all other Fiedlerisms. It is, one might argue, an almost unassailable bastion, a singularly clever form of self-immunization. This, in itself, explains the size of the clubs used in yet another Fiedler-bashing, explains the bitter indictment that only "Mythic criticism allows you to do things like this – people turn into other people, people become myths, myths become other myths."[73] Kenneth S. Lynn, in a savage panning of *What Was Literature?*, would diagnose Fiedler as a self-parodist beyond hope or cure.[74]

Harsh as it may sound, this criticism has a point. Fiedler never deviates from his well-travelled roads. It is thus understandable that some hostile – and some merely angry – critics vilified Fiedler for having recycled rather than effectively disposed of all the rusty beer cans along the winding roads which seem to connect Missoula, MO, and Buffalo, N.Y. Such criticism might also be applied to *The Return of the Vanishing American* or Fiedler's essay collection *To the Gentiles* in which he specifically and correctly summarizes the train of his thoughts as "a continuation of certain speculations."[75]

Nor does *Freaks* (1978) alter the established pattern. Again, Fiedler is not content with a factual history of recorded physiological irregularities or aberrations. The historical freaks are viewed, as the subtitle indicates, as "Myths and Images of the Secret Self." In other words, it is an investigation into the cultural patterns evolved in the historical responses to such creatures who, on "the more archaic levels of our own minds are ... omens and portents." His true interest, linking the book to the rest of his work, is Fiedler's pursuit of "certain long-lived fantasy creatures with no prototypes among actual Freaks ...," the monsters "men have needed to believe in" and will create for themselves even if there is *no* empirical evidence for their existence.[76]

The freak suits the pursuit of archetypes in an appealing manner; Fiedler confesses that:

Confronting them, I could feel the final horror ... a kind of vertigo like that experienced by Narcissus when he beheld his image in the reflecting waters.... . In joined twins the confusion of self and other, substance and shadow, ego and other, is more terrifyingly confounded ... standing before Siamese Twins, the beholder sees them looking not only at each other, but – both at once – at him.

Freaks becomes another *tour de force*, with Fiedler roving the etymology of "freaks" as well as the images of the freak in contemporary popular culture, until he settles for another probing of the metaphors elucidating the *condition humaine*. It is also another self-reflexive book, an excursion into what he calls the dark places of his own psyche. Its final conclusion shows Fiedler at his best, or worst, depending on the reader's faith in or doubts about the power of cognitions in human affairs. In spite of all observable physical differences he rejects the idea of a categorical distinction between "... we and them, normal and Freak," because, he claims, in the final analysis any such distinction "is revealed as an illusion, desperately, perhaps even necessarily, defended, but untenable in the end."[77]

Fiedler actually alleges that all distinctions between two- and three-legged creatures are but artificial categorizations of man as logician, desperately trying to rationalize "primordial fears ... about scale, sexuality, our status as more than beasts, and our tenuous individuality."[78] Here, more than elsewhere, Fiedler stretches myth criticism's admirable aversion against logical positivism and technical monosignation, takes it to the point where even the sympathetic reader must pause and seriously ponder the question whether there are any limits to connotative plurisignation. There is no doubt that the suggestive language of myth is much more appealing than the declarative, unequivocal terms used by logic and science, and we should be grateful for all reasonable attempts at establishing and affirming the former's legitimacy or, even more so, its psychological necessity.[79] But the resentment of steno-language does not automatically immunize all flights of an imaginative fancy. And the one-two-three count is not necessarily a representational fallacy, nor does it deny the affective power of art.

Here – as well as elsewhere – Fiedler pushes "his best observations to the edge of [self-]parody."[80] And here and elsewhere, the reader is well advised to remember what Fiedler himself said about his method in a different though related context, cautioning himself and calling the reader's attention to all the hazards and temptations pertaining to an approach which invites the critic to write "literature about literature, fiction about fictions, myth about myth." Denying any differences between "we and them" is a bold but questionable stroke of methodological unconcern, virtually disregarding all, even the most relativistic considerations concerning object-subject relationships. It thus qualifies as mythopoetic fiction rather than scholarly tenet – it may actually be "untenable in the end." And viewing all cognitive distinctions as mere rationalizations of "primordial fears" is to credit the unconscious with limitless and irresistible power and could well be but another fiction from that strange land of Id where Fiedler reigns as Grand Wizard. All such assumptions might themselves qualify as handy "mega-myths," which Fiedler once aptly described as those unassailable attempts "not to prove or disprove, construct or deconstruct anything, but to compel an assent scarcely distinguishable from wonder." To elicit this very rapport is Fiedler's greatest talent, the quality which distinguishes and inspires both his writing and his lectures. He can sway the reader and the listener, like few of his peers, into a temporary suspension of disbelief, thus making his criticism almost indistinguishable from the fiction it is meant to elucidate.

Yet, as a cultural critic, he is most admirable in those preciously few moments when he reminds the reader that even mega-myths might or should be read as inspired flights of fancy, "written not with the methodological rigor of the sciences, soft or hard, but with the openness, the ambiguity, and the contempt for logic or mere 'truth' of the myths they subsume."[81]

Fiedler's work never generated a "school", nor can he be easily classified as a disciple of any preceding school of cultural criticism. There is a heavy indebtedness to the ideas of C. G. Jung, quantitatively as well as qualitatively eclipsing the debit to Karl Marx. For sure, D. H. Lawrence stimulated his thinking and writing more than Fiedler cared to admit. His work is a unified whole, so unified that sometimes it skirts the hazy borders of self-plagiarism. There is a fair number of key-concepts which link his books and articles to the work of Maud Bodkin, Northrop Frye, Philip Wheelwright, or R.W.B. Lewis, Richard Chase, Kenneth Burke, and – to a degree – Stanley Hyman.

But it must be obvious that this is not the company he cherishes most. Fiedler was and is a maverick, in spite of all the affinities to and affiliations with other "myth critics". Thus, in all the churches of contemporary American cultural and literary criticism which he tried to secularize by insisting that the Gutenberg galaxy has been most recently refurbished with the furniture that stares back at you, there ought to be a separate pew – marked L.A.F. or, at least, *LaD* – reserved for someone who will, at best, remain a corresponding member only. What he shares with that motley fraternity is his unshakable belief that American literature is but a palimpsest of the secret cultural history of the USA, from puritanism to narcissism. With his distant confrères, Fiedler is convinced that Freud's demand for the functional reorganization of the id was a plea rather than an inventory of reality. Ego *should be*, Fiedler is willing to grant, yet, a capitalized Id *is* and lurks behind all the happy and moral endings designed to satisfy the demands of any middlebrow reader or viewer, constituting the "profound duplicity" of American *Art-Speech* as well as the vernacular of American popular culture. Even in the highly mimetic the myth cannot be denied, mythos always precedes logos.

And there can be no doubt that Fiedler is perfectly well aware of the painfully real dichotomy separating the *explication* of literature from its *experience*. The "Anti-Jungian" Fiedler is Jungian enough to bemoan the fact that "We must interpret, we must find meaning in things ... well knowing that in doing so we are getting further away from the living mystery."[82] Fiedler is wont to say that he loathes being called "provocative" or "controversial." But he has done little do countermand such an image. After all, he must know that the blurb in most of his books introduces or reintroduces the man who loves to read fairy tales to his grandchildren as the most voluble, diverse, uneven, divisive, rambunctious of modern cultural critics, or, quite modestly, a bombshell. And most accounts of his academic career will, consciously or unconsciously, deemphasize his gracious and inspired defense of literature's affective potential by their very emphasis on the "provocative" nature of his approach. Fiedler had encouraged rather than discounted such views by advertising himself as the only professor of English who was ever busted and, on Thursday, April 9, 1970 was found guilty of "maintaining a premise" where marijuana had allegedly been smoked.[83] Some of his critics have ventilated the blurb only rather than read the works themselves and disdainfully dismissed Fiedler as a publicity hound.

Any such view is patently unfair and often merely reflects the critic's indebtedness to Irving Babbitt rather than analyzing Fiedler's work or providing a critical perspective which would help the reader to determine Fiedler's actual methodological position. It should suffice to say that in some instances Fiedler has done too little to keep his own "Urbild" from being used for promotional magnification. And that he has displayed an almost gleeful pride in having his work reviled as either "subversive," or, yes, even "freakish."

And neither sympathetic nor hostile readers will deny that Fiedler knows how to functionalize a *captatio benevolentiae.* Or that he will use its power knowingly, – or "consciously?" – or simply "too consciously" for an experienced explorer of the collective unconscious? Consider, for example, the charming and disarming honesty displayed in *What Was Literature?*:

I have written and talked all my life under the sponsorship of anyone willing to let me publish what I believed at the moment (my-not-so-secret motto being 'Often wrong but never in doubt') and to pay me for my effort. Such sponsors have ranged from a magazine later revealed as subsidized by the CIA to the magazine which revealed that fact to institutions funded with money left by America's robber barons and the Writer's Union of Rumania.[84]

Who, in the pantheon of American cultural criticism has ever so candidly acknowledged past errors of judgment? Who, in cultural criticism's hall of fame (wherever it may be), has so freely admitted that there is a "lucre connection?" Will a bust and a subsequent conviction make or break a cultural critic, prove or disprove the validity of his or her argument? Considerations such as these will only help to obliquely enhance Fiedler's status as cultural critic. The candid confessions of this sort merely serve to direct the reader's attention to the subtle similarities existing between a contemporary critic and his lionized and anthologized predecessors.

What Fiedler is actually saying, with a smirk indicating that he enjoys Fielding as much as Shakespeare, is: My dear reader, before you cast the first – or, in my case, a second – stone, you might as well remember a few pertinent facts. You may want to recollect that a certified American cultural critic, named R. W. Emerson, made most of his money on the Lyceum racket and never had the decency to thank George Redpath or the Boston Lyceum Bureau. (And who, by the way, settled Edmund Wilson's expense account on his deservedly famous trip *To the Finland Station*?)

Another illustrious American cultural critic, dear reader, the famous Henry Adams, quite clearly misread the second law of thermodynamics, yet used it unsparingly as a kind of rosetta stone in his analysis of modernity. What could he do, poor guy, always right and never in doubt, but terminate his education with an inconclusive incomplete? But, does that make his apprehensions less significant? Will that little misunderstanding totally invalidate his melancholy conclusions?

And what constitutes H. D. Thoreau's claim to fame, my dearest reader? A night in Concord's communitarian center or the resultant reinvestigation of the relationship between individual and society? The famous "majority of one"-dictum might thus be no more and no less convincing than the conclusions which a certain Leslie A. Fiedler read aloud "late one night to a quite noncommittal audience of two cats and a dog,"[85] upon learning that the Appellate Court had ruled against him.

As I have said before: Once we meet Fiedler on his own terms, neither the origins nor the ramifications of his cultural criticism can be easily or precisely stated. In order to understand and adequately represent Fiedler, the reader himself must be "twice removed," and certainly unhampered by a representational fallacy. There can be no doubt, though, that Fiedler's work, much as that of his fellow myth critics, is a plea for the reintroduction of the mythical and the mysterious into the actual, a defense of literature's potential to move, to assuage, to cheer and to delight. In an age which has reduced literature to the incestuous discourse of discourses, it is heartening to listen to a voice defiantly clamoring that literature is more than "just words on the page."

To do the Lacan-Can on a luxury liner captained by Derrida or Stanley Fish may be tempting enough for the contemporary cultural critic. But, on the other hand, few can be heedless enough to ignore Mark Twain's "there warn't no home like a raft, after all."[86] Or unfeeling enough to miss the appeal of sentences like the following:

There *is* a place in men's lives where pictures bleed, ghosts gibber and shriek, maidens run forever through mysterious landscapes from nameless foes; that place is, of course, the world of dreams and of the repressed guilts and fears that motivate them. This world the dogmatic optimism and shallow psychology of the Age of Reason had denied (*LaD*, p. 140).

In his long career, Fiedler has ceaselessly wandered the world of dreams and found quite a number of repressed guilts and fears which, according to his views, motivate men and women. In that process his critical allegiances have been both far-ranging and conspicuous. There have been, as the last quote indicates, quite a number of cheap shots at the Age of Reason, or the critics who "simplify" literary studies by their close examination of the textual surface rather than its latent meaning. But it requires neither Freudian nor Jungian exegetics to explain why Fiedler knew no other way to end *LaD* the way he did. Once again, we should honor and appreciate Fiedler's fine sense of textual perspicuity. And we might end on yet another conjecture. Better yet, we ought to ask if he was merely enticed by Melville's famous Hawthorne-review because he knew that it actually captured and encapsulated – better and more succinctly than any other evaluation – the essence of Hawthorne's writings. Or was he, deep in his heart, delighted to learn that a great American writer had, long ago, anticipated what Leslie A. Fiedler would want to say? To write one – or many more – "wicked" books, to yell "No! in thunder," and yet to feel, simultaneously, spotless "as the lamb?" (see *LaD*, pp. 504f.) Fiedler thus eludes easy categorizations. He can be – and has been – indexed under "the sociological mode of myth criticism."[87] Yet no discussion of Fiedler's work will come close to the subject under review if it fails to heed what, long ago, another maverick in the field of cultural studies tried to hammer into the boneheads pursuing principles. They fade and quiver, he said, almost as soon as they are stated. But other things live.

And why? Because there is in them the flavor of salient, novel and attractive personality, because the quality that shines from them is not that of correct demeanor but that of creative passion, because they pulse and breathe, and speak ... So with criticism. Let us forget all the heavy effort to make a science of it.; it is a fine art, or nothing. If the critic, retiring to his cell to concoct his treatise upon a book or play or whatnot, produces a piece of writing that shows sound structure, and brilliant colour, and the flash of new and persuasive ideas, and civilized manners, and the charm of an uncommon personality in free function, then he has given something to the world that is worth having.[88]

Who would dare contradict Mencken on questions of the critical process? And, if it is true what Mencken says, then Fiedler gains stature beyond contemporary pertinence – or impertinence. Because no reader of his work will remain unaffected by, or indifferent to, what is, quite clearly, a highly interesting and stimulating cultural critic. Because whatever has been said – or may be added to what has been said – about his work: there can be no doubt that he has generated a *reaction*, reaching far beyond the incestuous groves of academe. So, in that definition, at least, Fiedler matches Mencken's definition of the critic who is "alive." (Any writer who manages to galvanize both Kenneth S. Lynn and Irving Howe into retributive action must be very much alive.)

Thus, whether one feels a sympathetic concurrence with his views or entertains an unmitigated disdain for Fiedler's methods and conclusions, must remain a moot point in all questions concerning his critical stature. And reading Fiedler one cannot help reassessing and reconsidering Mencken's dictum that it requires a lot of intellectual ability and enterprise to make the leap from the work of art to the vast and mysterious complex of all the phenomena behind it. To claim competence in matters of cultural criticism should, then, not be mistaken for a contemporary Boswell's untenable pretense to know all the strangers in Leslie A. Fiedler.

Notes

1 Leslie Fiedler, *What Was Literature? Class Culture and Mass Culture* (New York: Simon and Schuster, 1982), p. 15.

2 Leslie Fiedler, *Being Busted* (New York: Stein and Day, 1969), pp. 44-48, passim.

3 Max Schulz, *Radical Sophistication: Studies in Contemporary Jewish-American Novelists* (Athens, OH.: Ohio University Press), pp. 154-72.

4 Leslie Fiedler, *The Second Stone: A Love Story* (New York: Stein and Day, 1963), see ch. 2 passim.

5 Fiedler, *Being Busted*, p. 48.

6 Hugh Kenner, "Who Was Leslie Fiedler?" *Harper's*, Nov. 1982, p. 69.

7 Fiedler, "Montana: Or the End of Jean-Jacques Rousseau," *An End to Innocence* (New York: Stein and Day, 1972), p. 134.

8 Allison Lurie, "To the Sideshow," *The New York Review of Books*, March 23, 1978, p. 23.

9 Fiedler, "Montana: P. S." *Unfinished Business* (New York: Stein and Day, 1972), p. 143.

10 Fiedler, *End to Innocence*, p. 135.

11 Ibid., p. 137.

12 D. H. Lawrence, *Studies in Classic American Literature* (Harmondsworth: Penguin, 1971), pp. 9 and 14.

13 Fiedler, *What Was Literature?*, pp. 126-42.

14 Ibid., p. 17.

15 C. G. Jung, "Über die Beziehungen der Analytischen Psychologie zum Dichterischen Kunstwerk," *Gesammelte Werke* 15 (Olten and Freiburg: Walter, 1971), p. 92. See also and especially p. 94f. for Fiedler's indebtedness to Jung's definition of the work of art and its impact, or Fiedler's and Jung's understanding of the nature of the creative process: "Wer mit Urbildern spricht, spricht wie mit tausend Stimmen, er ergreift und überwältigt, zugleich erhebt er das, was er bezeichnet, aus dem Einmaligen und Vergänglichen in die Sphäre des immer Seienden, er erhöht das persönliche Schicksal der Menschheit ... . Der schöpferische Prozeß, soweit wir ihn überhaupt zu verfolgen vermögen, besteht in einer *unbewußten Belebung des Archetypus* ... . Die Gestaltung des urtümlichen Bildes ist gewissermaßen eine Übersetzung in die Sprache der Gegenwart." (My italics).

16 Lawrence, *Studies*, p. 9.

17 Fiedler, *What Was Literature?*, p. 15.

18 Ibid., p. 15.

19 Fiedler, "An Almost Imaginary Interview: Hemingway in Ketchum." *Unfinished Business*, p. 157.

20 Fiedler, *What Was Literature?*, p. 15.

21 Fiedler, *End to Innocence*, p. 135.

22 Fiedler, "McCarthy and the Intellectuals," *End to Innocence*, p. 75.

23 Kenner, "Who Was Leslie Fiedler?", p. 20.

24 Andrew Ross, "Intellectuals and Ordinary People," *Cultural Critique*, 9 (1988), p. 82.

25 Donald A. Pease, "Leslie Fiedler, the Rosenberg Trial, and the Formulation of an American Canon," *Boundary* 2, 17 (1990), pp. 155-198; see also Ross, pp. 74-82.

26 Fiedler, "The Middle Against Both Ends," *Mass Culture: The Popular Arts in America*, ed. Bernard Rosenberg and David Manning White, pp. 537-48.

27 Fiedler, "Archetype and Signature: A Study of the Relationship Between Biography and Poetry," *Kenyon Review*, 60 (1952), p. 261f.

28 Fiedler, *What Was Literature?*, p. 15.

29 Fiedler, *Love and Death in the American Novel*, rev. ed. (New York, 1966), p. 8. (This and all further quotes from *Love and Death* refer to the Delta Book edition issued by Dell Publishing Co., 1967, and will be bracketed in the text).

30 Leslie Fiedler, "Letter to W. Kühnel," Oct. 16, 1989, p. 2.

31 Fiedler, *What Was Literature?*, p. 17.

32 Lawrence, *Studies*, p. 11ff.

33 Ibid., p. 7.

34 Russell Reising, *The Unusable Past: Theory and the Study of American Literature* (New York and London: Methuen, 1986), p. 137.

35 Fiedler, *End to Innocence*, p. 101.

36 Ibid., p. 124.

37 Ibid., pp. 191-210.

38 Lawrence, *Studies*, p. 9.

39 It is a truly remarkable fact that two critics who have virtually nothing in common were equally intrigued by the gothic element in American literature. Paul Elmer More in his discussion of Poe's and Hawthorne's "unearthly visions" stated that they were "in no wise the result of literary whim or unbridled individualism, but are deep-rooted in American history." Daniel Aaron, ed., *Paul Elmer More's Shelburne Essays on American Literature* (New York: Harcourt, Brace & World, Inc., 1963), p. 87.

40 Fiedler, *What Was Literature?*, p. 16.

41 Reising, p. 132.

42 Irving Howe, "Literature on the Couch," *New Republic*, Dec. 5, 1960, p. 17.

43 For the concept of 'covert culture' see: Bernard Bowron, Leo Marx, and Arnold Rose, "Literature and Covert Culture," *Dominant Ideas and Images*, ed. Joseph J. Kwiat (London 1971), pp. 84-94.

44 Fiedler, *What Was Literature?*, p. 22.

45 Vernon Young, "Waiting for the Barbarians: Fiedler on the Roof," *American Scholar*, 52 (Aut. 1983), p. 564.

46 Kenneth S. Lynn, "Back to the Raft," *Commentary*, Jan. 1983, p. 66.

47 Fiedler, *The Return of the Vanishing American* (New York, 1967). (Quoted from Granada's Paladin edition, London, 1972, p. 7). In his introduction to the second edition of *End to Innocence* Fiedler affirms: "I myself, for instance, have expanded the central insights first developed in the few pages of "Come Back to the Raft Ag'in Huck Honey!" into the thousandpage trilogy which begins with *Love and Death in the American Novel*, goes on to *Waiting for the End*, and concludes with *The Return of the Vanishing American*" (Fiedler, *End to Innocence*, p. ix).

48 Fiedler, *Waiting*, pp. 20-64.

49 Fiedler, *Unfinished*, p. 3.

50 Fiedler, *Waiting*, pp. 138-54.

51 Fiedler, *Unfinished*, pp. 163-68.

52 Fiedler, "Literature as an Institution: A View from 1980," *English Literature: Opening Up the Canon,* ed. Leslie A. Fiedler and Houston A. Baker (Baltimore and London, 1981), pp. 73-91.

53 Fiedler, *What Was Literature?*, p. 109.

54 Ibid., p. 37.

55 Ibid., p. 130f.

56 Ibid., pp. 168-231.

57 Vernon Young, "Waiting for the Barbarians." p. 563; Alfred Kazin, "Honoring the Dark Impulse," *Atlantic,* Jan. 1983, p. 93; Kenneth S. Lynn, "Back to the Raft", p. 68; Lennard J. Davis, "Myth America," *The Nation,* Dec. 11, 1982.

58 Fiedler, *What Was Literature?*, pp. 153-55.

59 Christopher Ricks, "I Contain Mobs," *The New Republic,* Dec. 20, 1982, p. 31f.

60 Lynn, "Back to the Raft," p. 68.

61 Christopher Lasch, *The Agony of the American Left* (New York: Random House, 1969), p. 71.

62 Fiedler, *The Inadvertent Epic: From Uncle Tom's Cabin to Roots* (New York: Simon & Schuster), 1979. (The second part of *What Was Literature?* is a virtual transcript of *The Inadvertent Epic* which is a transcript of the 1978 Massay Lectures aired by CBC in its IDEAS program).

63 Fiedler, *To the Gentiles* (New York: Stein and Day, 1971), ch. 6.

64 Fiedler, *The Stranger in Shakespeare* (New York: Stein and Day, 1972). See especially ch. II.

65 Fiedler, *To the Gentiles,* p. 4.

66 Fiedler, *The Stranger,* p. 9. (Quoted from Granada's Paladin edition, London, 1974.)

67 See Ronald S. Crane, *The Languages of Criticism and the Structure of Poetry* (Toronto, 1953), p. 193.

68 Fiedler, *Stranger ...,* p. 40f.

69 Ibid., p. 82f.

70 Here Fiedler claims that "... my sense of the dialectical relationship between poet and living audience comes *not* (emphasis added) just out of my own head and the text before me" (Ibid., p. 10).

71 Fiedler, *The Stranger ...,* p. 212.

72 Fiedler, *What Was Literature?*, p. 173.

73 Davis, "Myth America," p. 630.

74 Lynn, "Back to the Raft", p. 68.

75 See footnote 59.

76 Fiedler, *Freaks: Myths and Images of the Secret Self* (New York: Simon and Schuster, 1978), pp. 20 and 27.

77 Ibid., p. 35f.

78 Ibid., p. 34.

79 See e.g. Philip Wheelwright, *The Burning Fountain: A Study in the Language of Symbolism* (Bloomington: Indiana University Press, 1954), especially ch. 4.

80 Allison Lurie, "To the Sideshow," p. 23.

81 Fiedler, *What Was Literature?*, p. 131.

82 See, among others, Vincent B. Leitch, *American Literary Criticism from the Thirties to the Eighties* (New York: Columbia University Press, 1988), pp. 120-144; or Reising, *The Unusable Past,* pp. 129-140.

83 Fiedler, *Being Busted*, p. 1.

84 Fiedler, *What Was Literature?*, p. 22.

85 Fiedler, *Being Busted*, p. 245.

86 Mark Twain, *The Adventures of Huckleberry Finn* (Cambridge: Riverside Editions, 1958), p. 99.

87 See Leitch, *American Literary Criticism*, p. 131.

88 H. L. Mencken, "Footnote on Criticism," *Prejudices: Third Series* (New York: Alfred A. Knopf, 1922), p. 94f.

The Major Works of Leslie A. Fiedler

Criticism:

An End to Innocence: Essays on Culture and Politics. Boston: Beacon Press, 1955 (including "Hiss, Chambers, and the Age of Innocence," "Afterthoughts on the Rosenbergs," and "McCarthy and the Intellectuals;" "Italian Pilgrimage: The Discovery of Europe," and "Looking Backward: America from Europe;" "Montana and the End of Jean-Jacques Rousseau," "Come back to the Raft Ag'in, Huck Honey!" and "Dead-End Werther: the Bum as American Culture Hero").

The Art of the Essay. New York: Crowell, 1958.

The Jew in the American Novel. New York: Herzl Press, 1959.

Love and Death in the American Novel. New York: Criterion Books, 1960; rev. ed. New York: Dell Pub., 1966.

No! In Thunder: Essays on Myth and Literature. Boston: Beacon Press, 1960 (with the important early essays "In the Beginning Was the Word," "Archetype and Signature," or "Negro and Jew: Encounter in America").

Waiting for the End: A Portrait of Twentieth-Century American Literature and Its Writers. New York: Stein and Day, 1964 (containing "The Death of the Old Men," "The War Against the Academy," and "Towards the Suburbs: The Fear of Madness, and the Death of the 'I'").

The Last Jew in America. New York: Stein and Day, 1966.

The Return of the Vanishing American. New York: Stein and Day, 1968.

Being Busted. New York: Stein and Day, 1969.

The Collected Essays of Leslie Fiedler. New York: Stein and Day, 1971.

Cross the Border – Close the Gap. New York: Stein and Day, 1972.

To the Gentiles. New York: Stein and Day, 1972 (resurrecting "The Jew in the American Novel" and adding "Master of Dreams: The Jew in a Gentile World").

The Stranger in Shakespeare. New York: Stein and Day, 1972.

A Fiedler Reader. New York: Stein and Day, 1977.

Freaks: Myths and Images of the Secret Self. New York: Simon and Schuster, 1978.

The Inadvertent Epic: From Uncle Tom's Cabin to Roots. New York: Simon and Schuster, 1980.

What Was Literature? Class Culture and Mass Society. New York: Simon and Schuster, 1982.

Olaf Stapledon: A Man Divided. New York: Oxford U. Pr., 1983.
Fiedler on the Roof: Epistle to the Apostles. Boston, 1991.

Fiction:

Pull Down Vanity and Other Stories. Philadelphia: Lippincott, 1962.
The Second Stone: A Love Story. New York: Stein and Day, 1963.
Back to China. New York: Stein and Day, 1965.
The Last Jew in America. New York: Stein and Day, 1966.
Nude Croquet: The Stories of Leslie A. Fiedler. New York: Stein and Day, 1969.
The Messengers Will Come No More. New York: Stein and Day, 1974.

Heinz Tschachler

Daniel Bell

(1919-)

In 1938-39, Daniel Bell, then a graduate student in sociology at Columbia University, enrolled in a course on "Social Evolution." Summoned to discuss the topic of his term paper, Bell was asked, "What do you specialize in?" Without self-consciousness or irony, he replied, "I specialize in generalizations."[1] Almost forty years later, Bell, then a professor of sociology at Harvard University, opened his book *The Cultural Contradictions of Capitalism* with a quotation from Nietzsche's *The Will to Power*. In the passage quoted, Nietzsche predicts the end of the project of modernity. But while for Nietzsche the "advent of nihilism" was a matter of "the history of the next two centuries" (p. 3), for Bell this conclusion to history is a matter of fact: "Today modernism is exhausted. The creative impulses have gone slack. It has become an empty vessel. The impulse to rebellion has been institutionalized by the 'cultural mass' and its experimental forms have become the syntax and semiotics of advertising and haute couture. As a cultural style, it exists as radical chic, which allows the cultural mass the luxury of 'freer' life-styles while holding comfortable jobs within an economic system that has itself been transformed in its motivations" (p. 20).

Yet while *Cultural Contradictions* is shot through with references to Nietzeschean "nihilism," it is the Joseph Conrad of *The Secret Agent*, the Freud of "Civilization and Its Discontents," and Henry David Thoreau, rather than Nietzsche, who serve as Bell's culture heroes. Words and phrases like "taming," "constraint," "held in check," "transcendental ethic," "normative rules," "belief," and "the return of some conception of religion" (pp. 19-29) define Bell's self-image, that of a tragic protagonist in a cultural battle. While Bell does not see the decline of the West as inevitable as Spengler, references to "tension," "contradictions," "conflicts," "adversary relations," "the disjunction of realms" within bourgeois society (which is what Bell, following Werner Sombart, means by "capitalism") suggest that his main concern also is an impending disaster of apocalyptic dimensions. As he writes in another chapter of the book, society lacks a "center," that is, "any sure moral or cultural guides as to what worthwhile experiences may be" (pp. 102, 145). Thus it is not amiss to say that Bell's concern proper is "the great instauration" (p. 146) that would reverse the dominant trend of bourgeois society, that is, the passing of the "legitimations of social behavior [...] from religion to modernist culture" (p. xxiv).

If Bell is acutely aware of a sociocultural crisis, he contends that this crisis originates from cultural modernization, which spreads nihilism, egotism, and hedonism at the same time as it undermines cultural excellence. In effect, this is a questioning of the Enlightenment belief that reason can contribute to the construction of a rational and good society. In view of the failure of secular reason to fashion symbolic structures that can provide compelling universal values and orientation that would give coherence and meaning to our lives, Bell looks to a religious revival to initiate sociocultural renewal: "If science is the search for the unity of nature," he writes in the 1978 foreword to *Cultural Contradictions*, "religion has been the quest for the unity of culture in the different historical periods of civilizations. To close that circle, religion has woven tradition as the fabric of meaning and guarded the portals of culture by rejecting those works of art which threatened the moral norms of religion" (p. xxi).

But then, Bell's work apparently contains its own antithesis. Next to the apocalyptic theme we have sketched, there is also belief in what Steven Seidman has called the "millennial importance of modernity."[2] This is a belief that seems to have come down to Bell's posthistoric myths in a direct line from Condorcet's *Sketch for a Historical Picture of the Progress of the Human Mind*, Herbert Spencer's *Evolution of Society*, and Talcott Parsons's *The Evolution of Modern Societies*. The common thread in this line is a story of human events from the beginning of history to the present that is framed in terms of a meta-narrative of progress. Thus underlying Bell's end-of-ideology thesis is the idea that since the great systemic social conflicts have come to an end, we are about to enter an age of consensus: "Few 'classic' liberals insist that the state should play no part in the economy, and few serious conservatives, at least in England and on the Continent, believe that the Welfare State is 'the road to serfdom.' In the western world, therefore, there is today a rough consensus among intellectuals on political issues: the acceptance of a Welfare State; the desirability of decentralized power; a system of mixed economy and of political pluralism" (*EI*, p. 373).

Not only does the system described in the concluding chapter to *The End of Ideology* allow for a diversity of views and behavior which Bell finds to be missing in the "closed systems" of Marxism and other classic ideologies; also, it seemingly leaves only particular, local problems. This means that essentially in a postindustrial society, the coming of which Bell came to envisage in a book of that title, published in 1973, ideologists will give way to administrative-technocratic experts whose task is merely to fine-tune an already well-functioning social machine. But in spite of what has been said to the contrary,[3] Bell is far from complacent about this. His time, the late 1950s, marks "a disconcerting caesura" not despite but because "the old passions are spent. The new generation, with no meaningful memory of these old debates, and no secure tradition to build upon, finds itself seeking new purposes within a framework of political society that has rejected, intellectually speaking, the old apocalyptic and chiliastic visions" (*EI*, p. 374). Although there was considerable yearning for change, reform, and critique, what Bell believes to be missing is a discourse which would define the content of the "cause." In other words, the real problem is not the legitimacy of radical criticism but, "that the old politico-economic radicalism (preoccupied with such matters as the socialization of industry) has lost its meaning, while the stultifying aspects of contemporary culture (e.g., television) cannot be redressed in political terms" (*EI*, p. 374).

Thus we might tentatively say that what characterizes Bell's work is a mix of millennial and apocalyptic themes. Not unlike Peter Berger, Daniel Bell appears "to endorse both notions that modernity marks an epoch of unprecedented social progress and that the secularization produces an ongoing cultural crisis."[4] That Bell actually holds such a view is evident from a passage in the foreword to *Cultural Contradictions*, in which he characterizes his position in terms of being "a socialist in economics, a liberal in politics, and a conservative in culture" (p. xi). As we shall see, this is but shorthand for a set of visions based upon two related theses, that each social realm follows its own characteristic rhythm of change while social differentiation ("disjunction" is the word used by Bell) is itself an essentially modern phenomenon. At the same time, Bell's conviction that if one is a conservative in one realm one does not necessarily have to be conservative in the others as well is a denial that his intellectual development falls easily into the familiar pattern of a journey from radicalism to conservatism. Bell would agree, on the contrary, that his position is itself the product, at least in part, of the ex-radical intellectual, the remnant of the Old Left of the 1930s who reconciled himself with the order of power in America. But for Bell such reconciliation was not an easy one. If many of the leading American intellectuals of the immediate post-war years were former socialists who had retreated from the authoritarian Stalinism of leftist politics, what Bell believes to have inherited from them and their experiences was largely "pessimism, evil, tragedy, and despair" (*EI*, p. 287).

The image emerging of Bell – that of a moralist trying to establish a political and moral basis for modern liberalism as a philosophy of political pluralism and limited social planning – is a context that can serve as a starting point for analyzing his position as a cultural critic of post-industrial society. But Bell got there only after a long intellectual journey, which in the preface to a collection of essays written between 1960 and 1980 and published as *The Winding Passage*, he describes in Dantean terms as "a movement out of the netherworld to the fires of redemption" (p. xxii). Let us begin, then, with the early years. Daniel Bell was born in New York City on May 10, 1919 into a family of Polish-Jewish immigrants earning a modest living as garment workers on the Lower East Side. Until the age of six, when he began to learn English, Daniel Bolotsky, as he was then called, spoke only Yiddish. We do not know when he changed his name to Bell, but by the time he was thirteen, his voracious reading had taken him beyond the usual fare of boys' books to Karl Marx and John Stuart Mill, whose theories he tried to expound as a young orator for Norman Thomas, leader of the Socialist Party. In a personal memoir Bell recalls having come "to political awareness in the Depression and [having] joined the Young People's Socialist League in 1932, at the precocious age of thirteen."[5]

In 1935, at the age of sixteen, Bell graduated from Stuyvesant High School and entered City College of New York, where he received his B.S. in sociology in 1938. By that time, his political views had already taken shape. The Depression years, together with his immigrant background, inevitably made politics a crucial element in his own education as much as that of his classmates at City College, which included several students who were to achieve professional renown – the literary critic Irving Howe, the sociologists Nathan Glazer and Seymour M. Lipset, and the writer and editor Irving Kristol. Like them, Bell became part of the anti-Communist left, a group consisting of radicals of various persuasions, some of them anti-Stalinist or anti-Soviet and others like the Young People's Socialist League, which was more concerned with positive programs for social reform. Bell joined the latter group, although he never felt at ease when aspects of ideological dogma were concerned. This led him to align himself, following the 1936 split in the Socialist Party, with the Old Left in its formation of the Social Democratic Federation.

Following his graduation from City College Bell moved on to graduate work in sociology at Columbia University. There he studied the work of Wilhelm Dilthey, L. T. Hobhouse, and Max Weber, and he frequented the evening seminars conducted by the Frankfurt School exiles – Max Horkheimer, Theodor W. Adorno, Herbert Marcuse, Leo Löwenthal, and others. Also while a graduate student at Columbia, Bell began to work as a staff writer for the socialist journal *The New Leader*. He became a managing editor of *The New Leader* in 1941 and of *Common Sense* in 1945. Both in these functions and as a labor editor for *Fortune* (1948-1958), he wrote voluminously on labor as well as on a wider variety of social subjects, such as economics, changes in the occupational and class structure, and the expanding role of big business and government. He even started on a book, a project he later abandoned, entitled *The Monopoly State*, which apparently anticipated some of the theories of corporate capitalism proposed by New Left writers of the sixties. It was in those years that Bell acquired a thorough knowledge of Marxism, which became fully embodied in his first book, *Marxian Socialism in the United States*, published in 1952. (The book was reissued in 1967, with a new introduction, as a paperback by Princeton University Press.) The fifties also saw the publication of *Work and Its Discontents* (the result of his long concern with labor questions), and, growing out of a seminar Bell conducted, with Richard Hofstadter and Seymour M. Lipset, at Columbia University, two collections of essays dealing with McCarthyism and the radical right, entitled *The New American Right* (1955) and *The Radical Right* (1963), respectively.

In 1951 Bell, in a move that even to his closest friends must have come quite unexpectedly, left *The New Leader* to become labor editor for *Fortune* magazine, apparently the voice of American big business. The move clearly reflects his loss of faith in political radicalism. Convinced that dogma obscured critical vision, Bell rejected the "military-industrial complex" idea as a mere shibboleth. Instead, in a review of Irwin Ross's book on the *Politics of the Mixed Economy* published in *Commentary* in December, 1949, Bell, in what clearly anticipated *The Coming of Post-Industrial Society*, proposed that American society could for analytical purposes be divided into three institutional realms, the economy, the polity, and the culture. At the same time, he began to shift to a politics of moderation, particularly as embodied in the Welfare State liberalism of the 1940s. In an article on "America's Un-Marxist Revolution," published in *Commentary* in 1949, there is, supplementing the discussion of the changing structure of American society, a first call for a new public philosophy, a philosophy of the "public household." By this concept is meant a system of reciprocal relations between the federal government and the major interest groups dependent on it and competing with each other, through legitimate political means, for greater rewards from the government.

In his book on the history of *Marxian Socialism in the United States*, Bell struck a similar note. For all its historical analysis, the book also expresses Bell's disillusionment with the socialist movement in terms of the Party's (or any Leftist movement's) inability to determine whether it was to function as a political party or an ethical movement. Convinced that "it is only on the field of politics that [the struggle for power] can take place," Bell in an article published in *Modern Review* in January 1949 criticized the Socialist Party for being "in but not of the real world" (p. 347). If for all his criticism, Bell in 1973 found much praise for the socialist paper *The New Leader's* "moral vision," with the messianic and utopian elements in Marxism he was merciless. Drawing on the Weberian distinction between the ethics of responsibility and the ethics of conscience, Bell insisted that a political group must recognize that success in politics means the acceptance of relevant alternatives. Thus his rejection of Marxism would be "on moral grounds," as he wrote in a symposium on "Liberal Anti-Communism Revisited" sponsored by *Commentary* in September 1967. There, Bell denounced Communism as "a social philosophy which, in the name of rationality and humanism, imposes a repressive regime on people, on the principle that only a vanguard or a conscious elite knows the 'truth' or what is best for everyone. [...] Such a regime, whatever its claims, leads to a denial of those liberties and protections without which free inquiry cannot function" (p. 36).

It was no coincidence that the symposium on "Liberal Anti-Communism" was sponsored by *Commentary*. Under the editorship of Elliott Cohen, the magazine had been expressing the impatience of many intellectuals with Marxist panaceas. Also, well into the fifties the magazine, founded in 1938 as *Contemporary Jewish Record* (the name was changed to *Commentary* only in 1945), continued to mirror the fears and aspirations not only of Bell but of an entire generation of New York Jewish intellectuals gathered under the umbrella of the American Jewish Committee.[6] The discussions spawned by the Committee not only sparked a deep-seated sense of camaraderie; also, their effects registered in Bell's writings and in his political activities, that is, for instance, in his participation in the 1955 Milan Congress for Cultural Freedom meetings, where he presented two papers: "The Ambiguities of the Mass Society and the Complexities of American Life," and "The Breakup of Family Capitalism." But Bell's involvement with the Congress for Cultural Freedom extends back to the early 1950s when with Sidney Hook, Irving Kristol, J. K. Galbraith, David Riesman, Nathan Glazer, and J. Robert Oppenheimer, he helped organize meetings for the Committee for Cultural Freedom, the Congress's American affiliate.

The Congress for Cultural Freedom itself was an international organization of intellectuals from the United States and Western Europe who, at the Berlin Congress for Freedom meetings in June of 1950 (participants included Ignazio Silone, André Malraux, Arthur Koestler, John Dos Passos, Arthur Schlesinger, Sidney Hook, and James T. Farrell), had pledged themselves to encourage Eastern European intellectuals to resist communist tyranny as well as to prevent Western European intellectuals from making compromises with Stalinism. With such goals, from its very beginnings suspicions were voiced about the Congress's claim to independence. These suspicions were reinforced when in 1966, an article in *The New York Times* reported the CIA support of the Congress and its magazines, in particular the London-based *Encounter*. The rumors were silenced by vigorous denials from Kristol and others, though, until a year later a former CIA official, confronted with other

CIA manipulations, told reporters of the *Saturday Evening Post* that not only had CIA money supported *Encounter* but also that the CIA had planted agents both in the editorial office of the magazine and in the Congress. The agent in the Congress, executive director Michael Josselson, offered his resignation, which, however, was not accepted. As a result Bell, who had voted with the majority, and who had served, in the years 1956-57, as director of the seminar program of the Congress in Paris, was accused of rightwing sympathies.[7]

While it is true that the CIA did not dictate the policy of either the Committee or the Congress or the journals sponsored by it, there is no question about the political line. The mission was not only to be anti-communist but to be anti-anti-American, that is, to fight whatever might provoke thoroughgoing opposition to America. This is not to say that anti-communism originated with the CIA, much as the CIA could not take credit for the rapid and widespread acceptance of the Congress's Berlin program; even so, the elective affinities were such that even the CIA recognized that the credibility of a front had to be maintained "by not requiring it to support every aspect of official American policy."[8] But Bell, at that time, was hardly one to offer a fundamental criticism of America or American foreign policy. Not only was he convinced that "one can be a critic of one's country without being an enemy of its promise." In 1965 Bell and Irving Kristol, then a registered Republican, had launched *The Public Interest*. This fact was taken as evidence that Bell had risen to a position within a privileged class, with institutional affiliations and commitments that made him more dependent on and more grateful to the existing social order.

Also by that time, Bell's career had shifted focus from journalism to academe, a move not uncharacteristic of 1950s intellectuals. But Bell's development has its own idiosyncracies. While still mainly a journalist, he taught, at various times between 1940 and 1960, at Columbia University and at the University of Chicago, where he worked with a group of thinkers that included Riesman, Edward Shils, and Philip Rieff. In 1959 Bell was appointed associate professor of sociology at Columbia University. He had left *Fortune* magazine, and was ready, in order to receive his Ph.D. from Columbia, to revise those sixteen essays that were eventually to be published as *The End of Ideology*. Publication of this book led to his reputation as one of America's foremost academic sociologists, who taught at the Salzburg Seminar of American Studies, and was Visiting Fellow at the London School of Economics in 1976-77. From 1969 to 1980 Bell was professor of sociology at Harvard University, before becoming Henry Ford II Professor of Social Sciences at that institution, a post from which he was recently emerited. In 1987 he was appointed Pitt Professor of American Studies at King's College in

Cambridge, England. However, Bell is not only a foremost academic sociologist but also one of the leading intellectuals in the United States, whose work covers a wide range of topics – apart from the ones mentioned, these comprise technology and culture, religion and personal identity, the intellectual and society, the special role of the Jewish intellectual, the validity of the concept of class, social forecasting, the universities, ideology, the race issue, and ethnicity.

While some of Bell's works are so highly specialized that they are hardly for the general reader and, moreover, truly beyond the scope of this essay – works like *Capitalism Today, The Crisis in Economic Theory, The Social Sciences Since the Second World War, The Deficits: How Big? How Long? How Dangerous?*, even several of the essays collected in *End of Ideology* and *Post-Industrial Society* – the tenor in all his works clearly is from an older, humanistic sociological tradition. In fact, none of Bell's works has reached the pitch of abstraction and formalism of a Talcott Parsons or a Jürgen Habermas. This is the result, at least in part, of the fact that Bell was never solely an academic. Characteristically, he derides the "lockstep" career from student to graduate student to instructor to tenured professor (*WP*, xii). And while he was probably aware of the Ph.D. as a ticket for a professorship, he was not going to have it over nerve-consuming years of planning and executing. Not only did a Ph.D. project on trade-union oligarchy, begun in Chicago in the late 1940s, remain uncompleted; when the question of a Ph.D. came up at the time he was about to be granted tenure at Columbia, Bell answered that he did not have a Ph.D. because he never submitted a thesis. This situation was happily resolved by rewarding him a Ph.D. for past work, the collection of essays originally written for several magazines and published as *The End of Ideology*.[9] Once Bell was part of academe, he would not succumb to the dictum of publish or perish. Cherishing direct and elegant writing, he was never one to substitute substance for form, never allowing his work to deteriorate into unreadable communiques, summaries of arguments or findings.

Clearly, then, Bell's style is different from the style of those "high-tech intellectuals, consultants and professors" who according to Russell Jacoby "direct themselves to professional colleagues but are inaccessible and unknown to others" and thus have ceased "to enrich public life."[10] But if Bell belongs to the group of "transitional" intellectuals who continue to elicit interest and discussion, this position has never been an easy one. For instance, in the concluding chapter to *The End of Ideology*, Bell describes the differences between the intellectual and the scholar. The intellectual, Bell explains, "begins with *his* experience, *his* individual perceptions of the world, *his* privileges and deprivations, and judges the world by these sensibilities;" conversely, the scholar "is less involved with his 'self' [since] he has a bounded field of knowledge, a tradition, and seeks to find his place in it, adding to the accumulated, tested knowledge of the past as to a mosaic" (*EI*, p. 372). In this sense, Bell's work is proof of the tug of war between the morality of intellectual journalism and the skepticism of academic scholarship, between interests and ideals, subjective purposes and objective structures; yet underlying these dualisms is Bell's concern, of many years' standing, with cultural crisis.

In *Post-Industrial Society* Bell writes of the "moral unity" of the scientific community, of which one becomes a member not by subscription but by election; moreover, in order to belong one needs to both realize a "calling" and make a "commitment" – to an ethos that combines faith, passion, and mystery in the search for certified knowledge, and that bases its hierarchies and prestige rankings on achievement and confirmation by peers (pp. 379-83). But while following Tönnies, Max Weber, and Polanyi, Bell characterizes academe as a *Gemeinschaft*, "a primary group bound by intimate ties regulating itself through the force of tradition and opinion," he is too shrewd and troubled a thinker not to have noticed the disjunction, repeating the disjunction of capitalist ethos and the cultural style of modernism, between scientific ethos and the organization of science, and the reality of the structure and role of science as a *Gesellschaft*, "the large, impersonal society of secondary associations regulated by bureaucratic rules and tied together by the sanctions of dismissal" (p. 383). Even so, sense of calling and commitment as well as a deeply felt belief that for those who "devote themselves to the temple of science" there is still a "transcendent ethic" (p. 480) motivate Bell's trust, a trust vigorously denied by Irving Howe, that the university could actually be the natural home of intellect.[11]

While Bell's defense of academic life can be explained as the result of intellectual and spiritual homelessness, this was a condition which clearly parallels his Jewish experience. To be sure, by 1960 very few would find, as T.S. Eliot did before the war, the moving of "a large number of free-thinking Jews" into the universities "undesirable;"[12] even so, Lionel Trilling was still the first Jew to be appointed to the English faculty at Columbia. Thus in a lecture on "The 'Intelligentsia' in American Society," delivered in 1967 and later collected in *The Winding Passage*, Bell, with a mixture of admiration and bewilderment, speaks of the fact that the New York Jewish intellectuals "inherited the cultural establishment of America in ways that they, and certainly their fathers, would never have dreamed of" (p. 129). Behind the jubilant note of the lecture, however, there lurks the spectre of anxiety that can be traced back to Bell's early years. In an article called "A Parable of Alienation" published in *The Jewish Frontier* in 1946, Bell had written that both the modern temper and Jewishness condemned the intellectual to an experience of homelessness and consequently to a sense of tragedy by not being able to know the limits of possibilities in a world that their restlessness – their need to know – compels them to explore. These conundrums could be resolved, Bell was hoping then, through an understanding of both the creative potentialities and the limits that enrich and constrain the intellectual's activities.

There is a different perspective, though. In the general retreat from radicalism which set in after the war, non-Jewish intellectuals (like C. Wright Mills, Michael Harrington, Edmund Wilson, J. K. Galbraith, and others) were apparently more inclined to remain devoted to a radical vision than their Jewish fellow-travelers. As Russell Jacoby suggests, while a "solid American background" allowed a distancing that "sustained radicalism for the long haul," for the Jewish intellectuals, "the angst that expresses the pain of separation also craves union – or its substitute, recognition and acceptance. The social critique founded solely on alienation also founders on it."[13] As if aware of this thesis, for Bell, the rise of the Jewish intellectuals, animated by a "hunger for culture" (*WP*, p. 131) that is in itself the result of an acute sense of separation, entails a sense of social responsibility that cannot be explained except in terms of a craving for union. Convinced that limits are as necessary to intellectual endeavors as creative potentialities, Bell attacks, in an essay first published in *Encounter* in 1960 and later reprinted in *The Winding Passage*, C. Wright Mills's supposed "vulgar sociology."

Mills, in a "Letter to the New Left," had asserted that in view of the dearth of revolutionary potential among the working classes or the peasantry the intellectuals must become the new "historic agencies for change."[14] But the function Bell envisages for the intellectuals, as removed from Mills's "rock-throwing from the podium" as Jack London's views apparently were from socialism (*WP*, p. 142), draws upon the example of the high moral purpose of the English intellectual aristocracy of the nineteenth century (Arnold, Macaulay, Trevelyan, Darwin). Like them Bell demands that the intellectual rather be a force of social stability (*WP*, pp. 147, 158). In effect, after the demise of extremist political ideologies and with the emergence of post-industrial values (reflecting a dislike of materialism and an emphasis on the quality of life), for Bell the moral vacuum was calling for the stabilizing function of the intellectual. This is the subject also of an address entitled "The Intellectual and the University" and delivered in 1966, at the 119th Charter Day Convocation marking the founding of the City College of New York, in which intellectuals (at least those whose institutional affiliations are with the university) are celebrated as the ones entrusted with "the maintenance of right or true belief." If Bell calls upon intellectuals to confront the modern with tradition and the rational intellect, this is also the general goal of a liberal arts education. Thus in a book on *The Reforming of General Education*, significantly dedicated to Lionel Trilling, Bell undertakes a defense of the liberal arts college on the basis of the "civilizing role" of the humanities (pp. 54-58, 180-83).

Such discourse, shot through with references to limits and the maintenance, through the workings of a living tradition, of right and true belief, has little to do with the "explosive" style of Mills and the New Left, whose purpose in Bell's eyes, is merely to create a "tumult" (*WP*, p. 138). Rather it is the group of thinkers and intellectuals that has become known as anti-communist liberals and, more recently, as neo-conservatives that defines Bell's place in American culture and society.[15] What characterizes this group is, as Bell wrote in 1957, an intellectual journey that began in the 1930s when many of the writers and intellectuals who dominated the period – Lionel Trilling, Sidney Hook, Edmund Wilson, Dwight Macdonald, Reinhold Niebuhr, John Dos Passos – were "intense, hortatory, naive, simplistic and passionate but, after the Moscow trials and the Soviet-Nazi pact, disenchanted and reflective" (*EI*, p. 287). The question whether the success of a revolution always depended on the ability of a single party to control the pace and define the goals of social change had been a theoretical one until the Cold War. But with Stalin in power and the Cold War in full swing, it became one of extreme urgency. For a few years after World War II, the cold war was not only a political and military conflict but also a cultural combat, an intellectual battle in which the image of the Soviet Union was reshaped from that of a wartime ally against fascism to that of an empire of evil, while on the home-front the agenda was the celebration of America.

What many former radical intellectuals found praiseworthy about America can be summarized in the formula of the benefits of liberalism in promoting social improvements without inhibiting personal freedom and self-development. Other concepts in the political discourse of the time were the tactics of bargaining and compromise, the virtues of pluralism and interest-group competition, the superiority of Keynesian economics and the limited welfare state. All this was part of a consensus, among many intellectuals of the 1950s, that the problems of modern America were no longer ideological but technical and administrative, and that these problems could be solved by knowledge experts rather than by mass movements. But such a consensus was not the product of a home-spun ideology of liberalism. What had drawn so many divergent views together was apprehension about the appeal of communism, not so much to American as to Western European intellectuals who, as Sidney Hook complained, were unable to see that in spite of all its flaws America was still preferable to the Soviet Union. Even so, what had started as counterpropaganda eventually became the ideology of those whose stature in the intellectual community had risen steadily, "not only because of the quality of their minds and the excellence of their work, but also because they seemed to flourish equally well in a variety of environments: in elite universities and research institutes, on the lecture circuit, in the world of specialized as well as mass circulation magazines, even in political campaigns."[16]

But the conclusions reached by intellectuals like Bell, Schlesinger, Boorstin, Lipset, Trilling, and Niebuhr, were not only the result of their retreat from socialism. Much of it came from a questioning of liberalism itself, in particular its tendencies toward self-aggrandizement and uncritical belief in progress. For instance, in Trilling's position of "moral realism," defined as the willingness to work for change combined with an awareness of the "dangers" that lie "in our most generous wishes," there is a more tragic view of human nature – in Reinhold Niebuhr's words, "both strong and weak, both free and bound, both blind and far seeing." From such a view follows a strong conviction of the folly of efforts to completely remodel the world. The sentiment is repeated in Bell's assertion that the "radical intellectual who had articulated the revolutionary impulses of the past century and a half" had forgone all "chiliastic hopes," messianic dogmas, or "apocalyptic thinking." Indeed in the 1950s, the standards of public behavior were informed by the implicit agreement not to convert "concrete issues" into "ideologically tinged conflicts" that would polarize the nation but rather to follow a "democratic politics" that was defined as "bargaining between legitimate groups and the search for consensus."[17]

But if the retreat from socialism, the (often qualified) praise for capitalism and the welfare state, and the emphasis on the political restraint of the broker state, spawned an intellectual environment that permitted writers to deal with America as they thought it was rather than as they might have once wished it to be, such an attitude did not go unnoticed. For instance, in books like *The American Political Tradition* (1948) or *The Age of Reform* (1953), Richard Hofstadter criticized all forms of national self-congratulation, be it hero-worship or rosy depictions of America's past. More intense was the critical examination of a "liberal consensus" among Americans, undertaken by Louis Hartz in a book, published in 1955, on *The Liberal Tradition in America*. Hartz complained that the untrammeled success of capitalism in America had virtually eliminated any need or desire for alternatives. Thus liberalism, "a doctrine which everywhere in the West has been a glorious symbol of individual liberty," exerted in America a "tyrannical compulsion" which "posed a threat to liberty itself." In particular, when faced with "military or ideological pressure" from abroad, the dogmatic belief in liberalism, always prepared to convert "eccentricity into sin," could easily generate mass hysteria in the form of red scares and witch hunts.[18]

Neither Hofstadter nor Hartz were revolutionaries. They mainly wanted to strengthen liberalism as a political philosophy at a time when they felt it was under pressure. As it happened, during the cold war years this was hardly a purely theoretical position. But the narrowing of academic freedom and civil liberties during the McCarthy years did not just happen. As Richard Pells notes, to most intellectuals the security measures imposed by the Truman administration may have been unfortunate but were still considered necessary. To them, communists were beyond the pale of civil liberties – they were thought to function as virtual "agents of a foreign power" (Sidney Hook), using Marxist ideas solely as "stratagems" to further the "national interests of the Soviet Union" (Irving Kristol); consequently, they could be identified as participants in a "conspiracy to end forever the whole conception of a society based on free discussion" (Arthur Schlesinger), while Daniel Bell was convinced that communist intrigues constituted "a clear and present danger" to democracy. The anti-communism of these intellectuals had its limits, though. For instance, at an executive meeting of the American Congress for Cultural Freedom in April 1952, Bell and Kristol submitted a resolution condemning both communism and MacCarthyite types of anti-communism. Similarly, at a panel discussion held at the New York Tamiment Institute in 1952, Bell sharply attacked what he called the "breakdown in rational discourse in this country."[19]

However, when in the mid-1950s a group of writers that included Bell tried to assess the larger significance of McCarthyism for American history and society, they were less concerned with formulating strategies to resist its pressures than with understanding its origins and contemporary manifestations. These efforts led to the publication, in 1955, of a book edited by Bell entitled *The New American Right*, which explains McCarthyites as preoccupied not with wealth or property or power but with their slippery status in the American race for success. In view of the somber diagnosis – xenophobia and racism, anti-Semitism, anti-intellectualism, hatred of parliamentary and constitutional democracy – one of the lessons the contributors drew was that "Wall Street was closer to the liberal intellectual on civil rights and liberties" than "pseudo-conservative" McCarthyites. In effect, each of the contributors to *The New American Right*, with varying degree of enthusiasm, was advising his fellow intellectuals to "greatly strengthen" the "elite" and to become authentically conservative.[20]

If the book on the New American Right did little to effectively dispel the red scare or rightist extremism because the contributors were not yet ready or able to disavow their own ideological premises, it is still of interest insofar as it shows that characteristically social predicaments could not be analysed other than in cultural terms. This shift in the conceptual framework was recognized by a contributor to *Commentary*, who in 1957 remarked that "almost all the problems that were once called 'political,' now belong to a different context, psychological, sociological, and cultural." Even so, with Bell's *Work and Its Discontent* there is evidence that an apparent advocate of pragmatism and compromise would worry about the effects of psychological manipulation, the suppression of conflict, and the demise of job satisfaction to employees. Thus despite its shortcomings – Bell obviously does little to explain how the changes he recommends be brought about and neither does he seem to suggest that the individual psyche could hardly be remodeled without restructuring society itself – *Work and Its Discontent* still stands as "a model of criticism" in an age that "allegedly wanted only statements of affirmation."[21]

If the attacks on conformity, by Bell much as by other intellectuals of the 1950s, contained radical implications, at the same time they articulated "many of the issues that would galvanize the young in the following decade."[22] The emphasis on personal integrity and existential honesty led, in the 1960s, to a yearning for moral confrontations over concrete issues, and to a reliance on civil disobedience and public demonstrations as a means of expressing authentic commitment to a particular cause. Clearly, this was not fundamentally different from what the older generation of intellectuals had wanted. Thus when Bell refused to believe in alienation as a positive force in reshaping American life, what was different was not the issue itself, the sense of a cultural crisis, but the key words of the discourse. For instance, George Levine felt that "a high moral sense of vocation" had become untenable in the context of the dissolution of the individual, of alienation, fragmentation, uncertainty, and the crisis of liberalism, in fact had given way to a struggle for coherence, connection, and the reshaping of consciousness.[23] Bell, on the basis of an older, more humanistic ideal of community, would not surrender hope in social change so easily, although in view of the "lack of a rooted moral belief system" (*CPS*, p. 480), his hope was qualified.

The extent to which Bell's hope was qualified is evident from his conviction that social change is a matter of culture, not politics. "Ideas and cultural styles do not change history – at least, not overnight. But they are the necessary preludes to change, since a change in consciousness is what moves men to change their social arrangements and institutions" (*CPS*, p. 479). The notion that history progresses through human consciousness is not an original one. It was first propagated by Marx's great predecessor, G.F.W. Hegel. In both the *Philosophy of History* and *The Phenomenology of the Spirit* Hegel conceived of the historical drive as existing first of all in the realm of human consciousness. What Hegel had in mind, though, were ideas in the sense of large unifying world views, that is, value systems or ideologies shared by a great many members of a society. Bell's concern, however, is rather more with the individual. This can be inferred both from his proclamation of the "end of ideology" and the importance he ascribes to the intellectual. In effect, for Bell, concern with the individual is a matter of moral belief.

As Lionel Trilling remembers, among the questions the editors of *Partisan Review* posed to themselves and other leading intellectuals in 1952 were the following: "Must the American intellectual and writer adapt himself to mass culture ... which will overrun intellectual and aesthetic values traditional to Western civilization?" Or, if a re-affirmation and rediscovery of America is under way, "can the tradition of criticial nonconformism ... be maintained as strongly as ever?"[24] The argument apparently depended on a political definition of the individual and his or her own rights. For instance, in Trilling's collection of essays entitled *The Opposing Self*, the master theme of the literature of the last century and a half is described as the "idea of the self." But while classic liberal political theory concerns itself with the protection and affirmation of the self vis-à-vis society and its political institutions, Trilling in his 1965 collection of essays, *Beyond Culture*, refines this argument to the point that the self, when allied to the arts, could perform a transcendent function, that is, "to liberate the individual from the tyranny of his culture in the environmental sense and to permit him to stand beyond it in an autonomy of perception and judgment."[25]

I have made reference to Trilling here mainly for two reasons: on one hand because of Trilling's close relationship with Bell and, on the other hand, in order to show how the two men may have had common intellectual ancestors but have come to differ widely in their opinions. Both writers had come up from a cultural "Stalinism" that involved the rejection of experimental modernism and bourgeois high culture on the grounds that often they were negative, elitist, and too complex for the masses. Similarly, both writers responded with a generalised culture of humanism that, by marrying Marx to Matthew Arnold, seemingly overrode ideological contradictions and divisions. However, Bell was not prepared to follow Trilling into a rehabilitation of a Romanticism that celebrated the concept of individual transcendence as a basic source of energy and a governing methodology. For Bell, the passionate individualism of Trilling and other anti-communist liberals clearly had its limitations.[26] While he admits that the achievements of Romantic individualism have been considerable, he is at the same time convinced that the original heroic energies of the individual have degenerated into a narcissistic idolatry of the self and a value system in which "the impact on the self, not the moral consequence to society" has become "the source of ethical and aesthetic judgments" (*CCC*, p. 19). In other words, the overvaluation of the rights of the individual has helped build an economic system in which "the cultural, if not moral justification of capitalism has become hedonism, the idea of pleasure as a way of life" (*CCC*, pp. 21-22).

Given this view, for Bell, social values, taboos and restraints that crowd in on the individual are no longer the tyrannical system they were for Trilling. Rather, culture and society need to be protected from the individual which is no longer "held in check by Puritan restraint and the Protestant ethic" (*CCC*, p. 21). Yet as Bell explains in the preface to *The Winding Passage* (p. xii), his major interest has been, not moralizing but the recasting of sociological theory, in particular the methodological repudiation of "holistic" interpretations of society. Rather than describing society as some kind of historical period or closed system, integrated through the mode of production or a dominant value system and consequently following the belief that all other realms (superstructural or peripheral) are determined by or predominantly influenced by a principle of "totality" or "integration," Bell argues for a view of society as being composed of separate realms, each following a different "axial" principle which becomes the regulative or normative standard, the legitimating principle of action.

"Analytically," Bell explains in *Post-Industrial Society*, "society can be divided into three parts: the social structure, the polity, and the culture" (p. 12). With regard to his premise, that each part of society "is ruled by a different axial principle," Bell expounds his argument as follows:

In modern Western society the axial principle of the social structure is *economizing* – a way of allocating resources according to principles of least cost, substitutability, optimization, maximization, and the like. The axial principle of the modern polity is *participation*, sometimes mobilized or controlled, sometimes demanded from below. The axial principle of the culture is the desire for the *fulfillment and enhancement of the self* (*CPS*, p. 12).

In the past, Bell continues, these realms "were linked by a common value system," while in the present, "there has been an increasing disjunction of the three" (*CPS*, pp. 12-13).

In *Post-Industrial Society*, concern is with the consequences of the disjunction of realms for both the social structure and the polity.[27] Thus it is to the later book on *The Cultural Contradictions of Capitalism* that we need to turn for Bell's thoughts on the relation of the disjunction of realms to modern culture. "The fundamental assumption of modernity," he writes, "the thread that has run through Western civilization since the sixteenth century, is that the social unit of society is not the group, the guild, the tribe, or the city, but the person" (*CCC*, p. 16). On one hand, this phenomenon is manifested in the bourgeois entrepreneur, who may be following the principles of laissez-faire while remaining subject to individual conscience as established by the protestant ethic. On the other hand, there emerged the figure of the individual artist, freed from patrons and institutions, while, like his or her entrepreneurial counterpart, operating in a market economy. From these sociocultural premises Bell derives his main thesis. While he admits that the energies and principles of modernity released individuals from the restraints of feudalism and the church, he now sees them as "exhausted," redundant, and inhibiting progress, particularly in the realm of culture. According to Bell, this process began in the nineteenth century when, "radical in economics, the bourgeoisie became conservative in morals and cultural taste" (*CCC*, p. 17). With the controls of censorship and morality tightening, an adversary relationship between the artist and society developed. Artists like Baudelaire began to subvert bourgeois values, attempting to disrupt and challenge the rationality, the well-tempered narrative sequences and the ideological optimism of the bourgeoisie by creating a culture of experiment, abstraction, and the whole range of 'isms' from impressionism to surrealism and cubism that challenged the basic aesthetic premises of bourgeois art, in particular that of mimetic realism.

The development of an adversary aesthetic would not have been possible, Bell continues, without an increasing ability of artists to justify what they were doing not to the general public, the bourgeois world, as it were, but to coteries of fellow artists, critics, and supporters who constituted what has come to be known as an avant-garde culture and audience. This process culminated in the period from 1890 to 1930, "the great period of modernism, in its brilliant explorations of style and its dazzling experiments of form" (*CCC*, p. 115). Since, Bell claims, there has been a "break-up of aesthetic distance," the consequences of which he interprets in the sense that "for human beings, and for the organization of thought, there are no boundaries, no ordering principles of experience and judgment" (*CCC*, pp. 117, 199). Armed with catchwords such as "nihilism," "hedonism," and "narcissism," Bell launches his attack on a whole range of avant-garde phenomena in contemporary American culture. Having dismissed, in *The End of Ideology*, the beat generation of the 1950s as a "hopped-up, jazzed-up, self-proclaimed group of outcasts" (p. 35), he goes on, in *Cultural Contradictions*, to denounce the 1960s counter-culture as nothing more than "the fantasies and sexual demands of childhood acted out during adolescence on a mass scale unprecedented in cultural history" (p. 144).

But in spite of his self-image of a protagonist in the battle against an impending apocalypse, Bell is far from complacent about the autonomy of realms he posits for analytical purposes. As we have seen, his strategy for remedying the disjunction of realms is an identification with "secular humanism," the traditional moral and ethical continuities that have accompanied Western civilization since Aristotle and the Renaissance. Recalling arguments by cultural critics from Arnold to Trilling, Bell believes this tradition of "secular humanism" capable of guarding society "against religious fanaticism, ideological extremism, or mindless activism, political or cultural" (*WP*, p. 229). In Bell's formulation, taken from an article on "Liberalism in the Postindustrial Society" collected in *The Winding Passage*, secular humanism comprises classic liberalism, which, he argues, was as much a system of restraints as of permissions. The new forms of individualism have transformed an historically acceptable idea of individual liberty into the idea of liberation that he defines as a "psychological impulse," that is, the desire "to be free of all restraints, to achieve extasis, freedom from the body itself" (p. 231).

This is not the place to concern ourselves with the political implications of Bell's call to the first principles of liberalism. At this point, what concerns us are his proposals for checking the cult of liberation in the cultural sphere. In effect, his main concern is, first, to disengage culture from economics and politics and then to recover the historic connections between culture and religion. This is based on the theoretical assumption that culture is not inextricably linked to a particular mode of economic production or to a particular political ideology. As he writes in *Cultural Contradictions*, "A machine or a process that is more efficient or more productive replaces one that is less efficient. This is one meaning of progress. But in culture, there is always a ricorso, a return to the concerns and questions that are the existential agonies of human beings" (p. 13). These concerns and questions find expression in "those efforts in painting, poetry, and fiction, or within the religious forms of litany, liturgy and ritual, which seek to explore and express the meanings of human existence in some imaginative form" (p. 12). Deriving its themes "from the existential situations which confront all human beings, through all times, in the nature of consciousness" (p. 12), ultimately for Bell culture transcends time and place.

Historically, Bell argues, this kind of transcendental metaphysical culture has "been fused with religion" (*CCC*, p. 12). Thus, as he wrote elsewhere, the major themes in this culture as religion are "cultural universals, to be found in all societies where men have become conscious of the finiteness of existence." The list of cultural universals recalls Aristotle's elevation of tragedy over comedy, pain over pleasure, "how one meets death, the meaning of tragedy, the nature of obligation, the character of love" (*WP*, p. 333). But the high moral and spiritual tone of Bell's critique of modernist culture was anathema to critics of a succeeding generation. For instance Susan Sontag, in an essay entitled "Against Interpretation" called out polemically that, "in place of a hermeneutics, we need an erotics of art."[28] For critics like Sontag, the fusion of restraining religions and culture Bell advocates – favoring the tragic and Dionysian over the comic and erotic, the mind over body, pain over pleasure, and moral content over formal innovation – apparently creates a value system that denies a whole range of human experience. In turn Bell, in his essay on "The Sensibility of the Sixties," written in 1969-70 and first published in *Commentary* in 1971, dismisses both Sontag's views and practices and those of the counter-culture as "the pathetic celebration of the self — a self that had been emptied of content and which masqueraded as being vital through the playacting of Revolution" (*CCC*, p. 144).

Why had Bell singled out Sontag as a promotor of cultural hedonism? After all, they have much in common, if not in rhetoric at least in the fact that the radicalism of the 1960s, like that of the preceding decade, was primarily cultural rather than political or economic. Also, the 1960s radicals were informed by the values of individual dissent, authenticity, existential honesty and personal commitment coupled with a distrust of ideology and chiliastic hopes, much as their reliance on strategies of civil disobedience and public demonstrations was in the manner of a cultural avant-garde. To the extent that the counter-culture was an adversary culture, it was as antagonistic to middle-brow standards as Bell himself. Indeed, Bell, during the time of student riots, instead of going along with the provost's decision of bringing the police in, strongly pressed for a student-faculty senate at Columbia. Moreover, both his book on *The Reforming of General Education* and his article on "Columbia and the New Left" (in a collection of essays entitled *Confrontations* and edited by Bell and Irving Kristol in 1969) show that he had wanted students to be provocative, to take risks and to raise important questions, challenging the policies of the corporations and the government.

Possibly, therefore, it was the fact that Sontag, like other critics of the sixties, belonged to a different generation (that is, a generation which, as Bell writes in his genealogical tree of New York intellectuals, had come "of age" in the late 1940s and early 1950s) which made Bell's sense of threat into more than a mere "playacting of revolution." This younger generation of critics were attacking the older liberal intellectuals as having grown administrative and managerial, as having confused intelligence with expertise, as having exchanged trust in social criticism for a dependence on technology and specialization. Consequently, they began to reject recruitment through the customary channels, that is, through a combination of journals, circles, and political parties, controlled by the older intellectuals; indeed, they began to reject the very idea of a life built mainly on the foundation of intellect as opposed to action and feeling. Hence the mounting hostility of older intellectuals toward the young radicals, to the extent that what we have been witnessing is very nearly a ritual killing of the fathers, who in turn strike back by dismembering their children.[29] This thesis also explains Bell's attacks on Norman Mailer, Mark Rothko, or the abstract expressionism of Jackson Pollock (clearly a descendant of Cubism), at the same time that he was paying little attention to mainstream literature, let alone to the utopian aspirations expressed from such diverse perspectives as the feminist movement, the environmental movement, or the civil rights movement. In sum, what the essays Bell wrote during the sixties and later collected as *Cultural Contradictions* convey, is, in a very literal sense, a "fear of the demonic, of human nature unchecked" (p. 19). So strong was this fear that on one hand Bell publicly supported McGovern in 1972, while on the other hand he sought refuge, not in "the multiplicity of exotic consciousness-raising movements – the Zen, yoga, tantra, I Ching, and Swami movements – which have spread so quickly among the *culturati*" (*WP*, p. 348), but in "the great historical religions" (p. 19).

Bell's concern with the function of religion goes back to *The End of Ideology*. In the epilogue to that book he asserts that "frenzies and mass emotions" – such as "fanaticism, violence, and cruelty" – "could be displaced, symbolized, drained away, and dispersed through religious devotion and practice" (p. 371). The experience of the 1960s gave Bell's hope in religion a more fervent character. Convinced that "new religions" will arise, he trusts, in an essay on "The Return of the Sacred," that they will "return to the past, to seek for tradition and to search for those threads which can give a person a set of ties that place him in the continuity of the dead and the living and those still to be born. Unlike romanticism, it will not be a turn to nature, and unlike modernity it will not be the involuted self; it will be the resurrection of Memory" (*WP*, p. 349). This resurrection, Bell continues, may take many forms – fundamentalist religion, moral redemptiveness on the part of the intellectual and professional classes, the strengthening of mediating institutions such as family, church, neighborhood and voluntary associations, and, finally, the return to and simultaneous transformation of mythic and mystical modes of thought.

If for Bell all these forms of resurrection are essentially "religions," he also knows that religions "cannot be manufactured" (*CCC*, p. xxviii). This fact raises an important metamethodological problem, a problem that, once it is resolved, would be the anwer to the question raised by Bell himself, "Can we set a limit to *hubris*?" (*CCC*, p. xxix). On one hand, the problem of the "*cultural* contradictions of capitalism and its deceptive double, *semblable et frère*, the culture of modernity" (*ibid.*), can be resolved through finding an answer to the question, what is culture? Is it a coercive order that is determined, objectively or mechanistically, by its environment, or is it rather an ideational order that is itself the product of actions motivated by something inside the person.[30] If this is a matter of choosing between Marx and Hegel, Bell, as we have seen, is rather following Hegel. I shall come back to this presently. What concerns us here is the problem sketched above, which apart from being a problem of the definition of culture is as much a theological problem, a problem of faith.

In a "Symposium on Morality," sponsored by *American Scholar* in 1965, Bell found himself in the dilemma of having to say either that morality is "what I feel it to be," or that there is "a common morality" derived from Mosaic law, from the word of God or from some other transcendent element (p. 352). But there as ever, Bell is unable or unwilling to decide the issue, asking instead if there is, perhaps, "some procedural method [...] of testing values" (p. 356). Such caution, insofar as it is grounded on belief in the sacredness of the individual, has been taken as evidence that Bell's critique remains essentially "within the immanent horizon of modernity." If, as Bernard Zylstra contends, Bell is "a victim of modernity," he, Bell, "does not have faith."[31] This means that Bell must necessarily remain content with a defense of culture, if by culture is meant those symbolic activities – like language, ideas, beliefs, customs, codes, institutions, tools, techniques, works of art, rituals, ceremonies – the function of which is "to make life secure and enduring for the society of human beings living within the cultural system."[32] Unable to provide a theology, Bell offers a "kind of social compact" based on the *a priori* condition of "some transcendent tie to bind individuals sufficiently for them to make, when necessary, the necessary sacrifices of self-interest" (*CCC*, p. 281).

Insofar as the social compact envisaged by Bell is the framework for the remaking of self and society, Bell remains essentially in the tradition of those "grand theories" which since the beginning of the process of modernization have served as substitutes for Christian and Aristotelian cosmologies. According to Steven Seidman, the function of these theories is to provide, often in the guise of scientific discourse, an integrated picture of humanity, or, as grand narratives, to explain who we are, where we come from, what our place is in history, and our likely future.[33] As we have seen, Bell defines a likely future in terms of the binding force of some transcendent tie. This puts him, on one hand, squarely in line with the sociological romanticism of the nineteenth century, which (mainly in the theories of Tönnies, Simmel, Durkheim, and Max Weber) had been idealizing the traditional community of *Gemeinschaft* while lamenting the alienation of the individual, thrust into the contemporary "mass society," from traditional society. Yet regardless of their respective ideological analyses, Bell, like Lipset, Shils, or Talcott Parsons, has never welcomed theories of mass culture.[34] Thus on the other hand, Bell's thesis laces into a debate among the Founding Fathers of the republic over equality and liberty, and the prospect of democratization. With regard to the values Bell cherishes most – harmony, order, stability, virtue, reverence, loyalty, self-discipline, restraint, and moderation – we can indeed say, as John P. Diggins has done, that the "philosophical conservatism" of Madison, Hamilton, and John Adams is more similar to Bell's position than Lockian liberalism.[35]

Does this mean, then, that we have once and for all positioned Bell in the political spectrum from right to left? Perhaps it is well to remember, at this point, that today conservatism is no longer a reaction against bourgeois emancipation but rather defends the legitimacy of bourgeois society. If this is true, we can say, as Louis Hartz has said, that liberal theory itself has nurtured deeply conservative instincts. With no perspective outside of Lockianism from which to critically examine Lockian orthodoxy, liberalism has virtually preempted conservatism as the bearer of traditional American values. As a result, the word 'liberal' is used not so much to describe Americans as liberals (if by that term is meant a deep commitment to the Bill of Rights and the ideals of the Declaration of Independence), as rather to describe a mentality that, following Tocqueville, desires change as much as it resists it, that stands in awe of economic transformations as much as it recoils in fear of political radicalization.[36] Thus when in 1967, at the time of the Detroit and Newark riots, the *New York Review of Books* featured a diagram showing a Molotov cocktail on its cover while its lead article apparently called for revolution, Bell was truly alarmed. To him, the incident was a symptom of a larger historical development, that is, of the renewed commitment to radical ideologies (declared prematurely dead in *The End of Ideology*).

To which Bell would have added that there is a difference between the post-1960s radicalism and that of earlier times: while for the latter, ideologies were frameworks in the struggle for political power, post-1960 radicalism is rather more that of marginal social groups whose ideologies but legitimize their particular social conventions and cultural productions.[37] This does not mean, though, that Bell is more sympathetic to these than he had been to more traditional forms of ideology such as socialism and fascism. On the contrary, in a retrospective essay called "The Revolt Against Modernity" and published in *Public Interest* in 1985, he argues that since the 1960s radicalism has been merely a form of anti-modern traditionalism, a leftist populism whose high moral tone is but a symptom of the inability to formulate a coherent political philosophy (pp. 53-57). If the revolt against modernity is seen as a threat to the "utopia of enlightenment" (p. 54), by the same token Bell has consistently rejected the demands and special pleadings of underprivileged or minority groups who claim preferential treatment or quotas on the basis of historial injustice and inequity. Asserting that ascriptive criteria such as "birth, or race, or color, or religion, or social class are irrelevant to judging the individual," Bell concludes that rather "achievement is to be judged on the basis of merit, talent and work" (*WP*, p. 230). If classical liberalism has always been hostile to rights movements that demand redress on the basis of gender, color, or other ascriptive criteria, so has the neo-conservatism of Irving Kristol and Daniel P. Moynihan. There is yet another aspect that apparently links Bell to the revival of conservatism in the United States since the 1970s. Unable to accommodate himself to rights movements, Bell has consistently favored the role of voluntary associations as important mediating structures between the individual and the state. Rejecting the notion, defended by David Riesman and others, that American society had become a "lonely crowd" of atomised, alienated individuals, Bell claims, instead, that "in no other country in the world, probably, is there such a high degree of voluntary communal activity, expressed sometimes in absurd rituals, yet often providing real satisfaction for real needs" (EI, p. 32).

Yet while Bell has repeatedly declared himself to be a conservative, at least in matters of culture, we should also remember that he has consistently rejected the label "neo-conservative."[38] Perhaps he has done so for good reason. For once, the term itself implies a far greater degree of cohesion than one finds evidence for in Bell's work. Secondly, the term is not so much an analytic category (that is, a category used to identify a particular function) as it is a defining one, signifying a set of features. This means that it is not irrelevant by whom Bell is termed a neoconservative – by those who argue that Bell's critique, insofar as it is cultural rather than political, has no room for farreaching changes, or by those who charge that Bell lacks a normative basis to define the bond he invokes. Let me explain. The reception of *The End of Ideology*, in particular the exchange between Bell and Dennis Wrong, an editor of *Dissent* magazine, is a good example of leftist objections to the book and to Bell's consistently cautious approach to social change. While conceding that ideological fanaticism prompted humans to entertain unreasonable hopes about the future, Wrong argued that "the reality and indestructibility" of their hopes were not negated.[39] In reply, Bell, who had readily accepted the designation, given to him by Wrong, of a "centrist," agreed that the end of ideology ought not to mean the end of utopian thinking, a point he would make again and again in his later works; at the same time Bell emphasized the 'nonideological' quality of his utopia insofar as it was based, not on a "faith ladder" but an empirical one, that is, on a "procedural method of testing values": "A utopia has to specify *where* one wants to go, *how* to get there, the costs of the enterprise, and some realization of, and justification for the determination of *who* is to pay" (*EI*, p. 405).

If the reception of *The End of Ideology* keynoted the debate over Bell's approach to social change, Jürgen Habermas in an essay called "Modernity versus Postmodernity" and first published in *New German Critique* in 1981, sees Bell as a veritable avatar of the neoconservative intellectual scene of the 1970s. Repeating what Peter Steinfels felt to be the essence of neoconservatism, Habermas reasons on the shifting "onto cultural modernism [of] the uncomfortable burdens of a more or less successful capitalist modernization of the economy and society."[40] By doing so, the charge runs, neoconservative doctrine fails to uncover the economic and social causes for the altered attitudes toward traditional values and life styles. Instead, it draws uncomfortable connections between an adversary mentality and various forms of extremism: hence modernism becomes nihilism, government regulations become totalitarian, criticism of the 'defense' budget becomes subservience to communism, women's liberation becomes the destruction of the family, etc. But is putting a limit to libertinism so that the ethic of discipline and work be established really Bell's sole concern? What makes Habermas assume that the expectations Bell harbors toward new norms "will put a break on the leveling caused by the social welfare state, so that the virtues of individual competition for achievement can again dominate"? If it is true that Bell's discontents with modernity is rooted "in deep-seated reactions against the process of societal modernization," in what sense is Bell's concept of a "public household," the product of an essentially modern administrative and technocratic rationality, conservative?[41] And was it not the very issue whether social science knowledge or common sense was to be the basis of public policy that led to Bell's resignation, in 1973, from the editorship of *The Public Interest*? (Bell also stepped down from the honorific post of chairman of the publication committee in 1982.) Finally, to make Bell the ideological culprit for Reaganomics and the idea of non-interference of the state is to ignore the fact that in a study devoted to the problem of the national deficit, Bell and co-author Lester Thurow came to the chilling conclusion that none of the proposals they envisaged (in particular, tax increases to alleviate the plight of the have-nots) are "*politically* feasible."[42]

If under the label of 'neoconservatism,' Bell has been accused of hostility to modernization and government interference, under yet another label the picture is reversed. The remarks Bell made in *Life* magazine in 1967 toward the necessity of a welfare state based on a strong centralized government were taken, by the author of the *Biographical Dictionary of the Left*, as a typical example of "left-liberal pessimism concerning people's ability to regulate their economic, political and social lives." But right-wing populism, it is perhaps worth mentioning, has traditionally been anti-intellectual, invoking common sense rather than experience. Thus what is under attack here is hardly someone's "pessimism" but rather emphasis on social science knowledge as the basis of public policy. Not surprisingly, therefore, also in this publication the scholars and intellectuals who in 1955 had contributed to the symposium on *The Radical Right* (essentially, these were Glazer, Lipset, Parsons, Riesman, and Viereck) are treated to the honorific title of "leftists ... who could be relied upon to vilify Joseph R. McCarthy and all other influential anti-Communists."[43] Presumably such tripe discredits itself. If it does not, we might add that a considerable number of "other influential anti-Communists," far from feeling "vilified" apparently had no objections to coming under Bell's influence.

Prominent among those reached by Bell are members of a social group that according to Kadushin is comprised of "politically appointed administrators."[44] It is hard to imagine this group of policy makers as "leftists," but it might be well to remember, just in case, that assessment of Bell's impact is based on the trajectory of *The Public Interest*, a magazine Bell launched, along with Irving Kristol, in 1965. With Daniel P. Moynihan, Robert A. Nisbet, and Nathan Glazer among the magazine's most prestigious contributors, its circulation rose from the 5,000 originally anticipated to about 11,000 in 1973; this is the result, at least in part, of consistently professing what the editors, following Walter Lippmann's definition, meant by the "public interest," that is, "what men would choose if they saw clearly, thought rationally, acted disinterestedly and benevolently." If this is a description of the magazine's policy, it is clearly not that of "leftwingers." Yet neither was the report on undergraduate education that Bell submitted, in 1965, to the faculty of Columbia College. In this report, Bell stood up for the traditional values of general education, in particular for a renewed emphasis on the liberal arts, which he felt to be endangered by the prevalence of specialized training in a particular discipline. At the time, Bell's proposals for educational reform did not produce *any tangible* results; if they were neglected, they were so not because of a supposed leftist bias but because they were considered too conservative.

It is when Bell uses sociology for social forecasting that his impact has been more widely felt. In books such as *The Year 2000*, published by Herman Kahn and Anthony J. Wiener in 1967 and which Bell helped prepare and to which he wrote the introduction, and *Toward the Year 2000*, edited by Bell in 1968, the predictions he and his associates on the Commission on the Year 2000 made are drawn from four sources: technology; the diffusion of existing goods and privileges in society toward greater equality; structural developments toward a post-industrial society; and the relation of the United States to the rest of the world. While some of what the contributors predicted seemingly points to quite a rosy future if not the technological paradise critics have noted, there is also concern about the psychological damage caused by the current trajectory, such as a decline in privacy, a greater confusion about educational goals, and a pervasive sense of alienation and depersonalization as people become more mobile and traditions less viable. It was in the hope of averting such possibilities that Bell and his colleagues continued their efforts in forecasting. Thus at the core of Bell's book on *Post-Industrial Society* is the wish "to let people choose if they can ... to change to a different path" (p. xi).

This, as we have seen, has been the goal also of *The Public Interest*; presumably it likewise informed Bell's affiliation with various government agencies, such as the President's Commission on Technology, Automation and Economic Progress, on which he served from 1964 to 1966, or the Government Panel on Social Indicators, on which he was, first with William Gorham and then with Alice Rivlin, from 1966 to 1968. Both Bell and Kristol contributed articles to a special issue of *The Public Interest*, published in the fall of 1970, on aspects of capitalism and modern life. The issue appeared as a book, *Capitalism Today*, in 1971. From 1976 to 1979 Bell was the United States representative on the O.E.C.D. project, *Interfutures*, which examined the common problems of the advanced industrial societies within a ten-year period. In 1980, he was named by Jimmy Carter to the President's Commission for a National Agenda for the 1980s. At the time, he was a trustee of the Institute of Advanced Study at Princeton and a director of Abt Associates Inc., another high-powered think tank. Other memberships and fellowships include the Council on Foreign Relations, the Century Association, the American Academy of Arts and Sciences. From 1957 to 1961 Bell was a member of the board of directors of the American Civil Liberties Union. He is the recipient of honorary degrees from Grinnell College and Case Western Reserve University and of the Borden Medal of the American Council on Education, awarded in 1966 for his book on *The Reforming of General Education*. Bell's work in editing includes membership on the editorial boards of the *American Scholar* and *Daedalus*.

The enormous range of activities, together with the excellence achieved, have catapulted Bell into the intellectual elite, ranking, in the study completed by Charles Kadushin in 1970, among the ten most prestigious contemporary American intellectuals.[45] Curiously enough, however, Bell does not appear on a list of "influentials," if by that are meant those intellectuals (like Milton Friedman, J. K. Galbraith, or Daniel Patrick Moynihan) who are sufficiently recognized as influential by both other intellectuals and by the leadership. How do we account for this phenomenon, which obviously contradicts Steinfels's view of Bell as one of "the men who are changing American politics"? Presumably, this is a result, at least in part, of personal style. As Kadushin explains with regard to a disastrous lunch Norman Podhoretz once had with John F. Kennedy, "Policymakers need specific advice on technical matters, not general theory ... . If one is a general critic one simply has not much to say of interest to men of action." But then Bell, as we have seen, is as much an expert on issues of foreign policy and domestic reform as he is concerned with the social, political, and economic system as a whole. Moreover, through such activities as consulting and policy advising he became more involved in high-level channels than the classic "literary" intellectuals who have rarely reached a position "intermediary" between the circles of elite intellectuals and the men of power. On the other hand, as an intellectual concerned about culture – in his self-styled role as a "specialist in generalizations" – Bell apparently comes close to being ineffective, were it not, as Kadushin asserts, for "creating an atmosphere that may permeate the centers of power."

The extent to which Bell has succeeded in creating an atmosphere permeating the centers of power may be inferred from a more recent invitation, extended to him by the Munich-based Carl Friedrich von Siemens-Stiftung, to participate in a series of lectures. These lectures were later collected and published, under the editorship of Heinrich Meier, as *Zur Diagnose der Moderne*.[46] As Meier explains in the introduction, the title of the collection refers to a large intellectual debate that has come to agree that, with the triumph of modernity over its adversaries (the feudal social order, the church, absolute monarchy, classical philosophy), the very concept 'modern' has lost its critical acumen. From the Enlightenment the term 'modern' was taken to mean the development of the sciences, morality and law as well as the arts, both in terms of their functional autonomy and with a view of a reasonable (that is, emancipatory) organization of society. However, 'modern' has become a problematic term insofar as the connection of functional autonomy and practical-emancipatory reason has been lost. Consequently, Meier contends, late modernist or post-modernist culture has become exhausted, the unsavory product of nihilism and cultural laissez-faire (p. 10).

Bell, it will be remembered, has come to similar conclusions. But is it really true, as he claims, that "modernism has been the seducer" (*CCC*, p. 19), enticing contemporary men and women to forego their moral, political, and economic sanities? To say that the tawdriness of much of modern America is the result of a crisis both of values and of mediating institutions like church and family is, essentially, to deny the existence of larger socio-economic processes, or of decisions being made outside the scope of church and family, which determine their fate or alter their structure. If such a view is part of Bell's intellectual universe, we cannot say, as Joseph Featherstone does, that Bell's thought is obscured by a portrait of capitalist innocence – of a capitalist economy happily persevering in its activities along its governing principle of functional rationality at the same time that the nihilism of modern advertising and high-pressure salesmanship is the result not of the imperatives of capitalism but of a modernist "life-style."[47] "The breakup of the traditional bourgeois value system," Bell writes in *Cultural Contradictions*, "was brought about by the bourgeois economic system," and he goes on to characterize this system in terms of "the free market ... mass production and mass consumption [and] the creation of new wants and new means of gratifying those" (pp. 20, 21).

For all its differences, this bears a striking similarity to Herbert Marcuse's thesis, developed in *One-Dimensional Man* (1964), of the commodification of culture. This thesis has been rephrased more recently by Marshall Berman, who in a book on *The Experience of Modernity* writes that, "under the pressures of the modern world *economy*, the process of development must itself go through perpetual development. Where it does, all things, institutions and environments that are innovative and avant-garde at one historical moment will become backward and obsolescent in the next." This means that under late capitalism, all individuals, groups and communities are under constant, relentless pressure to reconstruct themselves; if they stop to say to the moment, "Verweile doch, du bist so schön," they will be swept away in the rat race for survival in an economic system that is denying an ever-increasing number of people the necessities of health and life.[48] If Bell were to agree to this, he would nonetheless object that Berman's picture of historical necessity was too narrow or, to use Bell's own terminology, too holistic insofar as it conceives of society as integrated through the mode of production or a dominant value system that determines or influences all other realms. Conversely, what scandalizes Bell's critics is hardly an alleged primacy of culture ("what ultimately provides direction for the economy ... is not the price system but the value system of the culture in which the economy is embedded" [*CPS*, p. 279]); after all Bell, while denying that change in the social structure actually determines corresponding changes in the polity or the culture, quite readily concedes that these changes "pose questions" for the rest of society (*CPS*, p. 13). What really scandalizes the holists is what Bell in "The End of Ideology Revisited" describes as an "unwillingness [...] to put forth a formulation of *the* single problem, or of a single answer to complex questions" (p. 140).

While this, as we have seen, is the premise of Bell's thesis of the disjunction of realms, at the same time it bears a deeper significance, revealing a profoundly modern temper. Talking to Ron Chernow, Bell, remembering a series of seminars he gave at Columbia with Lionel Trilling and Steven Marcus, admits that he owes the very notion of disjunctive modes to the literary sensibilities these critics made him aware of. "A nineteenth-century novel of Trollope or Jane Austen looks at society as if it's an ordered world with an ominiscient narrator who is telling you what is going on. And this is, in one sense, what functional sociology and Marxist sociology try to do. But if you look at the modern novel, you get the introduction of a narrator who tells you from his point of view. For example, in Faulkner's *The Sound and the Fury*, you're getting a multiple set of visions."[49] This, I have been trying to show, is also what we are getting from the work of Daniel Bell: a multiple set of visions that not only discerns different rhythms of change in the different realms of society but that regards the very disjunction of realms, as well as the fragmentation, into autonomous or monadic entities, of all aspects of life, as essentially modern ("Resolving the Contradictions of Modernity and Modernism," pp. 45-46). At the same time, the attempt to establish a classicist order, symmetry, proportion, or the correspondence theory of truth must lead, if not into an aporia but to a discourse whose "key terms," as Bell remarked long ago, are "irony, paradox, ambiguity, and complexity" (*EI*, p. 287).

If these terms are the key terms of modernism, modernism itself, while providing a framework for the discontents of radical intellectuals denies the possibility of resolving them. When Bell, in *the End of Ideology*, points out the futility of grounding political radicalism in the cultural stance of modernism (p. 251), he is commenting on this very depoliticizing effect. And neither was he sure if the national consensus apparently resulting from the end of ideology would not itself prove to be "illusory" (p. 287). Modernism, Bell laments also in *Cultural Contradictions*, "leave[s] us without a resolution." It offers "no positive viewpoint" (pp. 118, 42). What Bell defines as the problem to solve is, ultimately, the substitution of "cultural radicalism [which is] largely rebellious only," for "political radicalism [which is] revolutionary, and seeks to install a new social order in place of the previous one" (p. 120). If this is true, cultural modernism has come to stand in as a substitute for a program of action aiming to overcome it.[50] This means, in effect, that if the antinomian culture which Bell denounces is the banality of a largely rebellious modernity, the very distinction he makes between culture and society reflects a dualism that structures his thought at its deepest level and that falls in line with the poles of skepticism and morality, interests and ideals, objective structures and subjective purpose.

In sum, then, Bell's diagnosis of the modern is at one and the same time a coming to terms with his own self. Indeed, in what resembles the disenchanted radicalism of the Frankfurt School, Bell long ago resolved for himself that the intellectual "can live only in permanent tension and as a permanent critic" ("Parable of Alienation," p. 190). From what we have seen, it is fruitless to read Bell's work in terms of its relative position to either the cultural or the social principles of the modern (the one antinomian, the other instrumental); but if we cannot say that Bell has come to conservatively reject the cultural principles of modernism while embracing the social principles of modernization, that is, scientific rationality and rational efficiency, it is perhaps well to be looking for a "missing third term, a rational collective, a reason of common ends." This is what Howard Brick, in what is perhaps the most perceptive study of Bell's thought to date has suggested, and which is a view I accept: that the voice speaking to us in Bell's works is "the unhappy consciousness of social democracy at an impasse, trapped by its commitment to seek reform under the umbrella of capitalism." Thus when all is told, Bell's theory emerges as "a theory of an unconquered contradiction, an unfinished dialectic."[51]

Notes

* This article is part of a larger work begun during free time made available to me by two summer grants from the Research Committe of the University of Klagenfurt, for which I am most grateful. My debt to Glen and Rhoda Love of Eugene, Oregon, U.S.A., exceeds anything I could acknowledge here.

1 Quoted in Peter Steinfels, *The Neoconservatives: The Men Who Are Changing America's Politics* (New York: Simon & Schuster, 1979), p. 161.

2 Steven Seidman, "Moral Order and Social Crisis," in *Culture and Society: Contemporary Debates*, ed. Jeffrey C. Alexander and Steven Seidman (Cambridge: Cambridge UP, 1990), p. 220.

3 See the articles by Henry David Aiken, Joseph La Palombara, Robert A. Haber, and Dennis Wrong, all in *The End of Ideology Debate*, ed. Chaim I. Waxman (New York: Funk and Wagnalls, 1968).

4 Seidman, "Moral Order and Social Crisis," p. 222.

5 EI, p. 286; for the biographical section to follow, I am particularly indebted to Nathan Liebowitz, *Daniel Bell and the Agony of Modern Liberalism* (Westport, CT: Greenwood P, 1985), and Howard Brick, *Daniel Bell and the Decline of Intellectual Radicalism* (Madison: U of Wisconsin P, 1986).

6 See Daniel Bell, "The 'Intelligentsia' in American Society" (1976), in *The Winding Passage*, pp. 119-37, Irving Howe, "The New York Intellectuals," *Commentary* 46 (Oct. 1968), pp. 29-51, Alexander Bloom, *Prodigal Sons: The New York Intellectuals* (New York: Oxford UP, 1986), Howard Simons, *Jewish Times: Voices of the Jewish Experience* (Boston: Houghton Mifflin, 1988).

7 Cf. Christopher Lasch, *The Agony of the American Left* (New York: A. Knopf, 1969), pp. 78-98, and Steinfels, *The Neoconservatives*, pp. 83-90.

8 Cited in Steinfels, *The Neoconservatives*, p. 85.

9 Cf. Brick, *Decline of Intellectual Radicalism*, p. 105.

10 Russell Jacoby, *The Last Intellectuals: American Culture in the Age of Academe* (New York: Basic Books, 1987), p.x.

11 Cf. Irving Howe, "This Age of Conformity," *Partisan Review*, 21 (1954), pp. 10-14.

12 T. S. Eliot, *After Strange Gods: A Primer of Modern History* (London: Faber & Faber, 1934), p. 20.

13 Jacoby, *The Last Intellectuals*, pp. 88-90.

14 *New Left Review*, 5 (Sept./Oct., 1960), pp. 18-23.

15 Cf. Steinfels, *The Neoconservatives*, pp. 25-48, 49-69; for the section to follow I am indebted to Christopher Brookeman, *American Culture and Society Since the 1930s* (London: Macmillan, 1984), chs. 1 and 2, John P. Diggins, *Up from Communism: Conservative Odysseys in American Intellectual History* (New York: Harper & Row, 1975), and Richard H. Pells, *The Liberal Mind in a Conservative Age: American Intellectuals in the 1940s and 1950s* (New York: Harper & Row, 1985).

16 Pells, *Liberal Mind in a Conservative Age*, pp. 130-31.

17 References in this paragraph are to Lionel Trilling, *The Liberal Imagination* (New York: Viking, 1950), pp. 212, 215, Liebowitz, *The Agony of Modern Liberalism*, p. 89, and Bell, *The End of Ideology*, pp. 301f., 393, 402, 404, 104, 112, 121.

18 References in this paragraph to Hofstadter are in Pells, *Liberal Mind in a Conservative Age*, pp. 150-55; references to Louis Hartz are to his *The Liberal Tradition in America* (New York: Harcourt, Brace, 1955), pp. 10-12, 17-18, 175-76, 285-86.

19 References in this paragraph are to Pells, *The Liberal Mind in a Conservative Age*, p. 268, and Diggins, *Up from Communism*, pp. 327, 281f.

20 References to *The New American Right* are to the 1964 edition and to contributions by Bell, Talcott Parsons, Hofstadter, and Peter Viereck.

21 Pells, *Liberal Mind in a Conservative Age*, p. 195 and p. 185 for reference to *Commentary*.

22 Pells, *Liberal Mind in a Conservative Age*, p. 248.

23 George Levine, "Our Culture and Our Convictions," *Partisan Review*, 39 (1972), pp. 63-79.

24 Trilling, *A Gathering of Fugitives* (Oxford: Oxford UP, 1980), p. 68.

25 Trilling, *Beyond Culture* (1965; repr. Oxford: Oxford UP, 1980), pp. 4-5.

26 Cf. a. Brookeman, *American Culture and Society*, pp. 112-23; I am also following, in subsequent paragraphs, ch. 2 of this valuable book.

27 For critical examinations of Bell's model of the postindustial society, cf. Krishan Kumar, "Industrialism and Post-Industrialism: Reflections on a Putative Transition," *Sociological Review*, 24 (1976), pp. 439-78, Laurence Veysey, "A Postmortem on Daniel Bell's Postindustrialism," *American Quarterly*, 34 (Spring 1982), pp. 49-69, and Walter L. Bühl, "Die 'postindustrielle Gesellschaft': Eine verfrühte Utopie?," *Kölner Zeitschrift für Soziologie und Sozialpsychologie*, 35 (1983), pp. 271-80.

28 *Against Interpretation and Other Essays* (New York: Dell, 1966), p. 14.

29 Cf. Pells, *Liberal Mind in a Conservative Age*, pp. 404-9. A symposium sponsored by *Commentary* in September 1990 and called "The American '80's: Disaster or Triumph" is a good example of the continuing exorcism of the 1960s (see esp. the contributions by Jeane J. Kirkpatrick, John B. Judis, Charles Horner, James Nuechterlein, and Hilton Kramer).

30 Cf. Jeffey C. Alexander, "Understanding the Relative Autonomy of Culture," in *Culture and Society: Contemporary Debates*, ed. Jeffrey C. Alexander and Steven Seidman (Cambridge: Cambridge UP, 1990), pp. 1-2.

31 Bernard Zylstra, "Daniel Bell's Neoconservative Critique of Modernity," in *Hearing and Doing: Philosophical Essays Dedicated to H. Evan Runner*, ed. John Kraay, Anthony Tol (Toronto: Wedge, 1979), p. 30.

32 "Culture," in *The New Encyclopaedia Britannica*, 15th edn., vol. 16, Macropaedia (Chicago: Encyclopaedia Britannica, 1983), p. 926.

33 Cf. "Moral Order and Social Crisis," p. 218.

34 For instance, in an essay entitled "America as a Mass Society," published in 1956 and later included in *End of Ideology*, Bell dismisses the mass society thesis as "a *presumed* scientific statement" concerning the disorganization of society created by industrialization and the demand of the masses for equality, a thesis that in his eyes little reflects or relates to "the complex, richly striated social relations of the real world" (EI, pp. 21-25, my italics). Cf. a. Brookeman, *American Culture and Society*, chs. 5 and 8, for a general discussion of mass society theses. For Bell's relation to sociological romanticism, cf. John O'Neill, "Religion and Postmodernism: The Durkheimian Bond in Bell and Jameson," *Theory, Culture & Society*, 5 (1988), pp. 493-508.

35 Diggins, *Up from Communism*, pp. 390-92.

36 Cf. Diggins, *Up from Communism*, pp. 387-89.

37 Cf. Seidman, "Moral Order and Social Crisis," p. 234.

38 Cf. *New Sociology*, 54 (13 Nov. 1980), p. 340, *American Quarterly*, 34 (Spring 1982), p. 85. Cf. a. Liebowitz, *The Agony of Modern Liberalism*, pp. 251-59.

39 Dennis Wrong, *Commentary*, June 1960, *Dissent*, Summer 1960 and Winter 1961, later collected, as "Reflections on the End of Ideology," in *The End of Ideology Debate*, ed. Chaim I. Waxman, pp. 116-25. More sympathetic to Bell's thesis were the contributors, mostly from Europe and Japan, to M. Rejai, ed., *Decline of Ideology?* (Chicago: U of Chicago P, 1971). Bell has responded to his critics in the new Princeton edition of the book (1988) and in "The End of Ideology Revisited," *Government and Opposition*, 23 (1988), pp. 131-50, 321-31.

40 Habermas, "Modernity versus Postmodernity," in *Culture and Society: Contemporary Debates*, ed. Jeffrey C. Alexander and Steven Seidman (Cambridge: Cambridge UP, 1990), p. 346. Reference to Steinfels is to *The Neoconservatives*, p. 65; in fairness to Steinfels it needs to be said that his exposition of Bell's neoconservatism is much more cautious (cf. pp. 165-74) – to the point that if Bell had not been put in the context of other neoconservatives like Moynihan, Glazer, and Kristol, one would probably term him a conventional New Deal liberal; or, seen from a different perspective, would Steinfels (or anyone else) habe labeled Bell a neoconservative if it had not been for personal ties to other neoconservatives?

41 References in this paragraph to Habermas are to *Culture and Society*, ed. Jeffrey C. Alexander and Steven Seidman, pp. 345, 347.

42 Cf. *The Deficits*, pp. 62-67, 110-20, my italics! Political feasibility (that is, essentially, the voting habit of Americans) may, therefore, jeopardize Mr. Bush's recent calls for tax increases: cf. *DIE ZEIT*, #30 (July 20, 1990), p. 21, and #31 (July 27, 1990), p. 39.

43 Francis X. Gannon, *Biographical Dictionary of the Left* vol. 2 (Boston-Los Angeles: Western Islands, 1971), pp. 224, 223.

44 Kadushin, *The American Intellectual Elite*, p. 325.

45 Charles Kadushin, *The American Intellectual Elite* (Boston: Little, Brown, 1974), p. 30; also on this list were Noam Chomsky, J. K. Galbraith, Irving Howe, Dwight Macdonald, Mary McCarthy, Norman Mailer, Robert Silvers, Susan Sontag, Lionel Trilling, and Edmund Wilson. Other references in this paragraph to Kadushin are to pp. 311, 323.

46 Heinrich Meier, ed., *Zur Diagnose der Moderne* (Munich-Zurich: Piper, 1990).

47 Cf. Joseph Featherstone, "A Failure of Political Imagination," *The New Republic*, 15 Sept. 1973, pp. 26-27.

48 Marshall Berman, *All That Is Solid Melts Into Air: The Experience of Modernity* (London: Verso, 1983), p. 78.

49 Ron Chernow, "The Cultural Contradictions of Daniel Bell," *Change*, 11 (Mar. 1979), p. 14. Cf. a. Steinfels's view that "the modern 'disjunction of realms' is not for Bell simply a fact, it is a *problem*" (*The Neoconservatives*, p. 169).

50 Cf. a. Günter H. Lenz and Kurt Shell, Introduction to *Crisis of Modernity* (Frankfurt am Main: Campus-Boulder, CO: Westview, 1986), p. vii: the very absence of ideology that would inform "the perspective of a utopia of enlightened rationality" suggests that the crisis of the project of the modern is, at one and the same time, "a crisis of critical theories of society and culture that have radically questioned bourgeois culture and capitalist society and economy."

51 Brick, *The Decline of Intellectual Radicalism*, p. 209.

Works of Daniel Bell

With Douglas G. Webb's project presumably abandoned (WP, p. xii), there is as yet no complete bibliography of Bell's works. Both Nathan Liebowitz (*Agony of Modern Liberalism*) and Howard Brick (*Decline of Intellectual Radicalism*) have good bibliographies, though.

"A Parable of Alienation," *The Jewish Frontier*, 14 (Nov. 1946), pp. 12-19.

"American Socialist: What Now?," *Modern Review*, Jan. 1949, pp. 345-53.

"America's Un-Marxist Revolution," *Commentary*, Mar. 1949, pp. 207-15.

Marxian Socialism in the United States (Princeton, N.J.: Princeton UP, 1952).

Ed., *The New American Right* (1955); *The Radical Right. The New American Right*, expanded and updated (Garden City, N.Y.: Doubleday, 1964).

Work and Its Discontents (Boston: Beacon, 1956).

The End of Ideology: On the Exhaustion of Political Ideas in the Fifties (Glencoe, Ill.: Free P, 1960); abbr. as 'EI'.

"Symposium on Morality," *American Scholar*, 34 (Summer 1965), pp. 347-69.

The Intellectual and the University (New York: City College, 1966).

The Reforming of General Education (New York: Columbia UP, 1966).

"Liberal Anti-Communism Revisited," *Commentary* 44 (Sept. 1967), pp. 31-39.

"Introduction," in Herman Kahn, Anthony J. Wiener, *The Year 2000: A Framework for Speculation on the Next Thirty-Three Years* (New York-London: Macmillan, 1967).

Ed., *Toward the Year 2000: Work in Progress* (Boston: Houghton Mifflin, 1968).

and Irving Kristol, eds., *Confrontation: The Student Rebellion and the Universities* (New York: Basic Books, 1969).

and Irving Kristol, eds., *Capitalism Today* (New York: Basic Books, 1970).

The Coming of Post-Industrial Society: A Venture in Social Forecasting (New York: Basic Books, 1973; London: Heinemann, 1974), abbr. as 'CPS'.

"The Moral Vision of *The New Leader*," *The New Leader* LVI (24 Dec. 1973), pp. 9-12.

The Cultural Contradictions of Capitalism (New York: Basic Books, 1976), abbr. as 'CCC'.

The Winding Passage: Essays and Sociological Journeys, 1960-1980 (Cambrigde, Mass.: Abt Books, 1980), abbr. as 'WP'; British edition, *Sociological Journeys: Essays 1960-1980* (London: Heinemann, 1980).

and Irving Kristol, eds., *The Crisis in Economic Theory* (New York: Basic Books, 1981).

The Social Sciences Since the Second World War (New Brunswick, N.J.: Transaction Books, 1982).

"Mr. Veysey's Strabismus," *American Quarterly*, 34 (Spring 1982), pp. 82-87.

"Our Country – 1984," *Partisan Review*, 51 (1984), pp. 620-37.

"The Revolt Against Modernity," *Public Interest*, 81 (Fall 1985), pp. 42-63.

and Lester Thurow, *The Deficits: How Big? How Long? How Dangerous?* (New York: New York UP, 1985).

"The End of Ideology Revisited," *Government and Opposition*, 23 (1988), pp. 131-50, 321-31.

The End of Ideology, rev. edn., with an afterword (Cambridge, Mass., Harvard UP, 1988).

"Resolving the Contradictions of Modernity and Modernism," *Society*, 27 (1990), 3, pp. 43-50, and 4, pp. 66-75.

Tony Pinkney

Raymond Williams

(1921-88)

Raymond Williams is, we might say, a 'thinker of the copula,' or so at least we might be tempted to conclude from the sheer number of his books which feature that grammatical item in their titles: *Reading and Criticism, Culture and Society, The Country and the City, Television: Technology and Cultural Form, Marxism and Literature, Politics and Letters, Problems in Materialism and Culture*. Williams clearly, on this showing, is one of our most profoundly anti-dualistic theorists of art and culture, seeking in study after study to break open the rigid binary pigeon-holes in which contemporary society conceptualises its experience. Long before 'deconstruction' became a fashionable slogan, Raymond Williams was, in his critical practice, deconstructing many of the most fundamental dichotomies of our cultural thinking. It once happened that, through accidents of teaching, the present author found himself reading Williams's *The Country and the City* and Jacques Derrida's *Of Grammatology* simultaneously. There was little sense of strain in moving across the two volumes, each of which seemed engaged on a common project. Both are powerful, seminal attempts to defeat our entrenched habits of thinking our social experience and history through binary oppositions and a theological myth of the Fall: from innocence through unthinkable cataclysm to fallen experience. Indeed, Williams's country/city couplet may be seen as a special case of Derrida's more general critique of the speech/writing opposition. In both cases, the former term is conventionally seen as the site of pristine authenticity and value, and the latter taken to be the realm of corruption and chaos. And for both Derrida and Williams, this binary conceptual apparatus – 'metaphysical' for the former, 'ideological' for the latter – masks a more fundamental continuum: 'proto-writing' or the integrated experience of a whole society, respectively.

To read Williams as a deconstructive thinker is to see how richly, some twenty or thirty years beforehand, he anticipated that central feminist slogan: 'the personal is the political'. If Jacques Derrida has done much to dismantle received conceptual boundaries between literature and philosophy, so too has Raymond Williams done much the same for literature and cultural theory. There are strong autobiographical elements in many of his more theoretical writings, with the first chapter of *The Country and the City* forming perhaps the most impressive example. But, on the other side of the binary fence as it were, Williams is also an important novelist, whose novels in their turn often have far-reaching political and theoretical implications. His first novel, *Border Country*, provides in its very title yet another version of the characteristic Williams 'and', that tense but productive no man's land liminally situated between the major binary categories of a culture; and it was, Williams often maintained, the very experience of writing and rewriting the drafts of this novel which enabled him to formulate the concept of 'structure of feeling' which later became so distinctive a mark of his cultural theory. His second novel, *Second Generation*, broaches in the noun of its title an issue – the transmission and transformation of culture through time, through the different times of the 'residual', 'dominant' and 'emergent' – which would exercise him as much conceptually as it does in his literary practice throughout the novels. His fourth novel, *The Fight for Manod*, bears the closest relation to Williams's concerns in *The Country and the City*, and in my view pushes his thinking on the city several stages further than it is developed in the latter text. A similar account could be given of his third novel, *The Volunteers*, in relation to *Television: Technology and Cultural Form*; and if we take *The Volunteers* and *The Fight for Manod* together, with their linked preoccupations with television, terrorism, the simulacrum, multinational capital and a new utopian kind of city, we would have virtually a flown-blown theory of postmodernism which is everywhere present but nowhere fully articulated in Williams's later non-fictional writings.[1]

Williams's preferred term for himself was 'writer', thereby undercutting received binary contrasts between 'literary' and 'non-literary', 'experience' and 'theory'. This last dichotomy, and its practical undoing in his lifetime's oeuvre, is a particular important one. Deconstruction can be, and has been, extracted as a handy method from the voluminous writings of Jacques Derrida, becoming in the process a portable tool-box whose spanners and screwdrivers ('supplement', *'pharmakon'*, 'invagination') can be applied to a whole host of non-philosophical writings; thus there was, in the early 1980s, a generation of American Derrideans in the field of literary criticism. There are not, however, despite the man's remarkable influence on several generations of radical critics and cultural theorists, 'Williamsites' in the way that there are Derrideans or once were Leavisites. Deconstructionist to his very roots Williams may be, but this impulse to undo binary categories is not extractable from his work like the kernel of a nut; it is, rather, grounded in a formative biographical and social experience whose contours we must now seek to trace. Its grounding there gives it an impressive concreteness and authority, but also means that Williams's cultural theory, as he himself often enough insisted, will have to be made and remade by new intellectuals in new situations rather than being graven on tablets of stone as a transhistorical truth which disciples could simply evoke. In Williams's final novel, *People of the Black Mountains*, the young student Glyn Elis sets out across the dangerous terrain of these Welsh mountains to find his lost grandfather, the fount (as it seems to Glyn) of all local lore and wisdom. But he never does find him, just as we, now, shall never receive a final, authoritative word from Raymond Williams. What Glyn has in effect to learn is that his own active process of search *is* his grandfather's legacy to him, just as for radical critics today 'Williams-ism' is a whole series of active reappropriations and developments of his work, not a codified body of truths that we could imbibe with our daily milk at junior school.

Williams was born in 1921 in the Welsh border village of Pandy, a 'liminal' geographical location which from the start displaced him from the certainties of both official English (or 'British') and official Welsh culture – though a return to a Welsh identity is a notable feature of his later work. His father was a railway signalman, though more than half the population of the village were small farmers. If from the former he derived an attachment to socialist class politics that remained unswerving throughout his life, from the latter, from a profound feel and respect for physical work on the land, came both that intense hostility to upperclass 'pastoralisation' of the countryside which is memorably expressed in *The Country and the City* and a rich potential connection to the emergent ecological politics of the late 1970s and 1980s. He went to Abergavenny Grammar School in 1932, followed by Cambridge University in 1939, thus following that trajectory of a 'voyage out' from the local community into the alienating routines of a class-bound education system which he was later to see as the essential vision of so many of the novelists he wrote about in *The English Novel from Dickens to Lawrence*. At Cambridge Williams joined the Communist Party, though when his membership lapsed during his wartime service he never renewed it, and it was as a student that he first came into contact with the modernism (James Joyce in literature, Sergej Eisenstein and Fritz Lang in film) which would so deeply shape many of his later cultural judgements.

Williams returned to Cambridge in late 1945 to complete his degree, and there encountered the increasingly influential views of F. R. Leavis; these were to have a deep impact on his early work, which has been dubbed by many commentators as 'left-Leavisism'. Leavis may have been anti-Marxist, but then, so crude had been the British Marxism of the 1930s against which he tilted, that Williams could share his main polemical emphases: the refusal of merely derivative or 'superstructural' status for literature and culture, the development of techniques of close reading – 'practical criticism' – far subtler than any literary analysis British Marxist critics of the thirties had ever pro-

duced. Moreover, Leavis's endorsement of T. S. Eliot's theory of some catal-
clysmic 'dissociation of sensibility' in the mid-seventeenth century led him
towards a powerful critique of the whole period of capitalist modernity.
Where Williams dissented from Leavis in his early work was, first, in a more
nuanced view of the modern period which had, in good dialectical fashion,
brought forth real gains in democracy, technology, communications and living standards as well as appalling economic exploitation and destruction of
the natural environment, and, second, in his resolute refusal of Leavis's cultural pessimism and elitism. For Leavis and his followers, once the capitalist
'dissociation of sensibility' had set in, history was a long downhill slide into
the mass-cultural vulgarity and the opposed political extremisms of the early
twentieth century. All one could pit against civilisation's lemming-like race to
the abyss was the 'minority culture' of the university English Faculty, bravely
upholding 'standards' and the literary tradition as a desperate break on accelerating cultural decline. Williams, as a socialist, inevitably rejected the social
positions that accompanied the valuable analytical reading methods of Lea-
visism. For him, Leavis's 'organic community' was to be actively built rather
than passively mourned; it pertained more to the struggles of twentieth-century working men and women than to a (thoroughly mythic) history of the
sixteenth-century English peasantry.

In 1946 Williams took a job in adult education, the field in which he
would continue to work until he returned to Cambridge in 1961 as Lecturer in
English; and it was in this educational framework, outside the reified academic protocols of the university and with a profound commitment to a
democratic education, that his earliest distinctive work – *Culture and Society*
(1958), *The Long Revolution* (1961) and *Communications* (1962) – took
shape. Adult education was also the terrain on which projects very close to
Williams's own took shape in these same years: Richard Hoggart's *The Uses
of Literacy* (1957) and E. P. Thompson's *The Making of the English Working-Class* (1963). This body of texts constitutes the founding moment of
what we have since come to call 'cultural studies', but Williams insisted often
in his later writings (true in this to the principles of his own 'cultural materialism') that the history of that discipline should not be written in idealist terms
as a body of texts but rather in terms of a 'formation', of men and women
working within these marginal educational institutions which, through their
very marginality, allowed important new forms of teaching and intellectual
breakthrough. It was a phase he often contrasted favourably with that later
moment, in the mid-sixties and seventies, when cultural studies decisively
entered the universities, with real gains in conceptual sophistication but crucial losses in terms of audience and political direction.

But if adult education was the immediate institutional matrix of cultural studies, the political events of 1956 organised it into an actual political generation and movement, the 'New Left' (or perhaps better, to differentiate this moment from the student revolts of 1968, the 'first' New Left). Williams's simultaneous sense of the loss of impetus of the 1945 Labour Government and of the impossibility of rejoining the Communist Party meant that he had, objectively, been situated in a 'New Left' position for some years; but now the Anglo-French invation of Egypt in the Suez crisis and the Russian invasion of Hungary meant that a whole generation, to the Left of Labour but bitterly opposed to the Stalinism of the international Communist movement, joined him there. It was a generation which found its intellectual voice and organisational focus with the founding of *New Left Review* in 1959, a journal whose editorial board Raymond Williams himself joined. Williams was a seminal presence, both politically and intellectually for this 'first' New Left, but while such fellow-thinkers as Hoggart and Thompson have tended to remain fixed within this early formative political moment, often responding hostilely to later intellectual developments on the Left, Williams throughout his life showed a remarkable capacity to 'go on thinking' (to borrow a phrase Stuart Hall has several times used in relation to him), proving as inspirational to the 'second' New Left of 1968 as he has to a 'third generation' or postmodern New Left of the 1980s.[2]

The first formulation of cultural studies in the cluster of founding texts by Williams, Hoggart and Thompson has often been termed (usually by its critics) 'culturalism'; and certainly 'culture', in several senses, was at the very core of what it stood for. Its most immediate derivation was from the very tradition of English literary studies that Williams had surveyed in *Culture and Society*: Matthew Arnold's *Culture and Anarchy*, F. R. Leavis's and Denys Thompson's *Culture and Environment* and T. S. Eliot's *Notes Towards A Definition of Culture* form some of the landmarks of this particular lineage. 'Culture', taken over from these sources, was then a politically resourceful concept. The stress on the particular and the empirical in this British intellectual tradition could be counterposed to the crude abstractions of Marxism-Leninism: it licensed the study of actual rather than 'imputed' working-class consciousness and experience (Hoggart's *Uses of Literacy* is precisely a detailed study of contemporary working-class reading habits), and an emphasis on the particularities of local or national experience as against the abstract internationalism of the Communist movement. And if the idealism of this intellectual tradition was in one sense an object of attack for a socialist like Williams, it too had its strategic value in polemic with the crude reductions of culture to mere 'echo', 'reflection' or 'precipitate' in any rigidly applied 'base-superstructure' model. At the same time, however, the tradition provided a powerful set of emphasis for attacking the emergent consumer capitalism of the late 1950s and early 1960s. As memories of 1930s mass unemployment and real material deprivation were displaced by the new 'affluence', with its social rhetoric of new council estates, working-class car and television ownership and access to education and holidays, so an older Labour or Communist critique of capitalism – that the anarchy of the market would necessarily 'fail to deliver the goods' – had less and less purchase on contemporary social reality – a fact made evident enough by the Labour Party's defeat in the General Elections of 1951, 1955 and 1959. However, since the Arnold-Eliot-Leavis mode of social critique had never paid much attention to questions of material prosperity in the first place, its emphasis on a *qualitative* rather than quantitative critique of capitalism, on the cultural impact of television or the motor car on social and family relations rather than on the mere statistics of ownership, provided real intellectual resources for a Left faced by the baffling new social experiences of working-class 'apathy' and the sheer undeniable success (in its own terms) of capitalism.

Culture and Society and (in more theoretical mode) *The Long Revolution* set out to effect a junction between two currently dominant definitions of culture: the literary and the anthropological. In this sense, the two books constitute the first of Raymond Williams's many exercises in deconstruction, though this time of dualistically opposed meanings within a single term rather than of a binary opposition proper (Arnold's culture/anarchy, say). For the literary tradition, culture is a body of privileged texts or activities (art, ballet, painting, the writing of poetry) which constitute a storehouse of values in the name of which a degraded social present can be measured and condemned. In its weakest forms this constitutes mere social snobbery; in its strongest forms, as with Eliot and Leavis, for whom literature is the last memory-trace of the lost 'organic community', it can be the basis of a powerful 'romantic anti-capitalism' (with all the political ambivalence that that term implies). This stress on values, on the 'qualitative', remains important to Williams even as he seeks to democratise the built-in elitism of this version of culture, which he precisely does by invoking the anthropological use of the term as a neutral, blanket description of *all* the habits and practices of a community: 'Welsh culture', 'working-class culture'. Concerning itself with the production of values, the literary version of culture is impressively active but too socially restrictive; surveying the whole range of social practices, the anthropological use is generously capacious but also rather inertly descriptive. Weld these two uses together, however (and transmute the whole debate into characteristic Williams terminology), and culture becomes the 'making and taking of meanings' in a 'whole way of life'. Literature is, *pace* Leavis and Eliot, a particularly intense form of this common social process, but it is, precisely, only one form among many others; it is not to be counterposed, as an utterly unique practice, to a banal social reality beyond it: Arnold's 'anarchy' or Leavis and Thompson's 'environment'. On the other hand, if culture is now the 'whole way of life' and not just literature and the arts, then we cannot, *pace* Marxism, mark out a certain area of social reality which we could dub the 'base' or the 'truly real' and then contrast to a ghostly or mirroring 'superstructure' which would be less than utterly real. And on the basis of his new definition of culture Williams proposes that 'working-class culture' should be understood not as a handful of already highly dated 'proletarian novels' from the 1930s, nor even (as Richard Hoggart was wont to do) in terms of the traditional working-class terraced neighbourhood (many of which were being bulldozed as slums while their inhabitants were relocated on the new estates or new towns), but:

> rather, the basic collective idea, and the institutions, manners and habits of thought, and intentions which proceed from this ... The culture which it [the working class] has produced, and which it is important to recognise, is the collective democratic institution, whether in the trade unions, the cooperative moment, or a political party. Working-class culture, in the stage through which it has been passing, is primarily social (in that it has created institutions) rather than individual (in particular intellectual or imaginative work).[3]

Williams's account of culture as the giving and taking of meanings, the slow process of movement towards *common* meanings, in a whole way of life, necessarily makes of culture an intensely active, creative process; indeed the first chapter of *The Long Revolution* is an extended historical and theoretical meditation on the idea of the 'creative mind'. This is an emphasis at one with the whole New Left stress on 'experience', 'consciousness', the lived, 'agency', the active making of history by men and women, in sharp contrast to the rigid economism and determinism of the official Communist tradition. Thus the 'making' of Thompson's *The Making of the English Working Class* is not a matter of a mode of production calling into being the men and women who are to be its supports, transforming rural labourers into industrial proletarians, but rather of the ways in which those new proletarians actively organised *themselves* into new identities, new institutions, a movement and a culture. New Left cultural studies, that is to say, is 'humanist' through and through, concerned more with the ways working people consciously experience and shape their history rather than with the determinate, given conditions in which this 'making' necessarily takes place. In terms of theory, therefore, the stage was set for some fierce and intensely polarised polemics when French structuralism in general, and Louis Althusser's structuralist-inspired Marxism in particular, crossed the Channel and deeply influenced a younger generation of British cultural critics from, say, 1968 on. E. P. Thompson, above all in his book *The Poverty of Theory* (1978), set himself up as the scourge of Althusserianism, savagely denouncing its reduction of working-class men and women to the mere unconsious 'bearers' or structural supports of a mode of production. Williams's own position, in these sometimes brutal battles between agency and determination, conscious and unconscious, experience and structure, was always a more nuanced one, subtly deconstructive rather than binarily assertive. And if we look back to his early works, we can now see why this should have been so; for we can trace a second definition of culture at work in these texts, above all in *The Long Revolution*, and one which points more towards the *un*conscious that structuralism would later one-sidedly valorise than the conscious creativity of the 'giving and taking of meanings' in a whole way of life.

The question of whether culture was conscious or unconscious had already been a vexed issue in the very 'culture and society' tradition from which cultural studies itself emerged. For liberal humanists like Matthew Arnold, culture was necessarily conscious, the possession of the lucid, self-assured, 'Hellenic' individual subject. But for conservative organicists like Eliot, Leavis and Lawrence, it was largely *un*conscious, an inarticulate collective force which consciousness could at its best serve and further but was more likely than not to betray, plunging us into dire 'dissociations of sensibility'. Williams's second early version of culture, expounded in the chapter on 'The Analysis of Culture' in *The Long Revolution*, itself veers towards the inarticulate and unconscious. He here aims to 'define the theory of culture as the study of relationships between elements in a whole way of life':

> A key-word, in such analysis, is pattern: it is with the discovery of patterns of a characteristic kind that any useful cultural analysis begins, and it is with the relationships between these patterns, which sometimes reveal unexpected identities and correspondences in hitherto separate activities, sometimes again reveal discontinuities of an unexpected kind, that general cultural analysis is concerned.[4]

The most interesting of such patterns are not the relatively formalised belief or value systems of a group or period, what Williams terms the official 'social character', but rather reside (in a clearly Leavisite turn of phrase) in the 'felt sense of the quality of life at a particular time and place'; and Williams's term for these deep, emergent patterns is 'structure of feeling': 'it is as firm and definite as "structure" suggests, yet it operates in the most delicate and least tangible parts of our activity'.

This emphasis on culture as pattern or structure of feeling has several immediate theoretical advantages for Williams. As with the stress on a 'whole way of life', it too is radically opposed to Marxist formulations of base and superstructure. For if deep, underlying structures can be traced across various social domains which had initially seemed separate, then no single such domain can be dubbed 'infrastructural' with the others reduced to its mere 'epiphenomena'. The Marxist concept of 'determination' gives way to a thoroughly interactionist model of the social formation, in which no level or instance is inherently assigned priority over any other. 'Structure of feeling' also gives him a suggestive way of thinking about problems of cultural *emergence*, a theoretical preoccupation which is at the root of his ability to remain so remarkably open in his responses to the new political and intellectual developments after the initial moment of the New Left in the late 1950s. Defined in contrast to a more or less preformed 'social character', structures of feeling are, almost by definition, at the very edges of semantic availability in any period; they are the very sites on which the forms and conventions through which a new cultural generation will recognise itself come tentatively and falteringly into being. A privileged example in Williams's work, which he first notes in *The Long Revolution* but returned to in more detail several times thereafter, was the new generation of British novelists – Dickens, Thackeray, Gaskell, the three Brontë sisters, Disraeli – which suddenly emerged in the late 1840s. Scribbling alone at their desks up and down the country, such writers can none the less, in analysis, be shown to be articulating a new shared structure of feeling – of exposure, isolation, victimisation, full recognition of which is often evaded by 'magical' fictional devices – as a major cultural response to a newly dominant industrial capitalism. Williams's work on late nineteenth and early twentieth-century drama, which begins with *Drama from Ibsen to Eliot* in 1952 and receives full institutional recognition when he became Professor of Drama at Cambridge in 1974, is itself largely concerned with tracing the characteristic structures of feeling of Naturalist and the many varieties of modernist play-writing.

But perhaps the long-term advantage of the notion of 'structure of feeling' for Williams's cultural theory was its determinedly oxymoronic character. Structures and feelings, after all, are usually taken to be deeply antagonistic terms, opposed to each other as the abstract to the 'felt', the anonymous to the immediately personal, the unconscious to the conscious. There has, accordingly, been much debate as to what exactly the force of this notion is in Williams's work and as to how viable it might be to us, as a general contribution to cultural theory. We need not here enter the full detail of those arguments, but should note how the presence of the term 'structure' in Williams's earliest, most 'humanist' writings, prepared him in advance for a fertile encounter with the fullblooded structuralism which was waiting in the intellectual wings just across the Channel. Williams himself first marked his rapprochement with this whole new field of work in an essay on the 'genetic structuralism' of Lucien Goldmann in 1971: 'I found in my own work that I had to develop the idea of a structure of feeling ... But then I found Goldmann beginning ... from a concept of structure which contained, in itself, a relation between social and literary facts. This relation, he insisted, was not a matter of content, but of mental structures ... The stress there on the interactivity of practices and on the underlying totalities, and the homologies between them, is characteristic and significant'.[5] But this moment, when Williams begins to resituate his own early 'left-Leavisism' with its dogged native strengths *and* intense parochialism in a wider context of European Marxist cultural debate, is also the moment of the 'second' New Left, of the 'generation of 1968', which constitutes the second formative shaping context of Raymond Williams's intellectual work.

Williams's growing disillusionment with the Labour Governments of the 1960s (he resigned from the Labour Party in July 1966) had already propelled him in the political direction of the 'new' New Left which emerged around the key events of 1968: the May events in Paris, the Prague Spring in Czechoslovakia, the Tet offensive in Vietnam and the international student rebellion. This second New Left, which took intellectual shape around *New Left Review* under the editorship of Perry Anderson, far from seeking a midway position between Social-Democracy and official Communism, tended to reject both in the name of Maoism or Trotskyism. Far from rejecting Stalinist internationalism in the name of the specificities of the British experience, as had the first New Left, it affirmed a new, more rigorous internationalism with a strong emphasis upon the Third World – an affirmation which took practical shape in its work for the Vietnam Solidarity Campaign, in which Raymond Williams too was much involved. Internationalism in the realm of theory meant a systematic importation, through the pages of *New Left Review*, of a whole series of 'Western Marxisms' – Lukács, Korsch, Gramsci, Benjamin, Adorno, Marcuse, Goldmann and, above all, Louis Althusser – who were, so it was assumed, to be a decisive Marxist antidote to the intellectual torpor and empiricism of British culture in general and the British Labour Party in particular. As the boom years of postwar affluence drew to a close and a new period of sharper class-struggle began, so the old cultural or 'qualitative' critique of the first New Left began to lose ground to a new, harder and more 'classical' Marxism – a move represented above all by the works of Louis Althusser, with their rejection of the early humanist Marx in favour of a more rigorous, 'scientific' and anti-humanist one, and their sustained invocation of Lenin's political practice as a model for all subsequent Marxisms.

We can gain a sense of the transformation in Williams's work during these years by considering the odd symbiotic relationships between two pairs of books: first, *Drama from Ibsen to Eliot* (1952), which is rewritten as *Drama form Ibsen to Brecht* in 1968, and second *The English Novel from Dickens to Lawrence* (1970), many of whose analyses reappear in a new context in *The Country and the City* in 1973. But a prior issue should be mentioned here, since it is acutely posed by these texts and we shall have to return to it later in the context of postmodernism: the issue of Raymond Williams's relation to modernism. Williams's enthusiasm for the experimentalisms of the early twentieth-century avantgarde in his drama books sits oddly both with the exclusively English focus – 'from Dickens to Lawrence' – of his study of the novel and with the focus on a narrowly English tradition of social criticism in *Culture and Society*. Moreover, his own early novels also belong to this English-realist tradition: *Border Country* is an impressive treatment of the theme of the 'return of the native' at the core of Thomas Hardy's fictional vision, while Williams's second novel *Second Generation* ambitiously seeks to recreate the totalising forms of an earlier Victorian realism, to be, as it were, the *Middlemarch* of the early 1960s. And these predilections for realism at the levels of literary criticism and practice have their equivalent in cultural theory in Williams's sustained admiration for the work of Georg Lukács. A chapter on 'Realism and the Contemporary Novel' in *The Long Revolution* offers a critique of modernist culture in precisely Lukácsian terms, seeing it as collapsing out into an abstract objectivism (Wells, Bennett, Galsworthy) and an abstract subjectivism (Woolf, later Lawrence), and calls for a revival of realism defined in terms of Williams's own formulation of 'culture': 'When I think of the realist tradition in fiction, I think of the kind of novel which creates and judges the qualities of a whole way of life in terms of the qualities of persons ... Neither element, neither the society nor the individual, is there as a priority'.[6] Williams's younger readers in the late 1960s and early 1970s – above all Terry Eagleton in *Criticism and Ideology* in 1976 – tended to dismiss his work as hopelessly parochial in its attachment to a realist aesthetics. His work on European modernist drama, which would have decisively challenged such critiques, tended to be marginalised in these polemics. We need not adjudicate the issue here, but we should beware of one-sided formulations of Williams's own positions: he is, simultaneously, both deeply for *and* against modernism. As a realist, he is deeply suspicious of its tendencies towards solipsism, myth, ontology rather than history, but he is also – paradoxically – aware of it as an epochal cultural breakthrough that there is no going back behind, and from *The Fight for Manod* on his own fiction effectively abandons realist forms (even as early as *The Long Revolution* he was arguing that 'the old, naive realism is in any case dead'). To be both pro- and anti-modernist in this way is, as I shall suggest later, an ambivalence characteristic of what we have since come to term *post*modernism.

Drama from Ibsen to Eliot concludes by praising the experimental drama of W. B. Yeats and T. S. Eliot as flawed but worthwhile attempts to break beyond the claustrophobia of Naturalism – strange judgements indeed for a socialist, given the profoundly reactionary values built into the very forms of such works. *Drama from Ibsen to Brecht*, sixteen years later, has many critical things to say of the works of Bertolt Brecht, and is far removed from the Brechtian euphoria of much radical theatre and theory of its time; yet it recognises that this *Marxist* modernism is now the fundamental dramatic breakthrough of the century. Indeed, in Williams's view, Brecht must be rescued from his admirers, who have fetishised a few key slogans and methods – *Verfremdungseffekt* above all – and ignored the full material complexity and power of the plays. So too does *Modern Tragedy* (1966), which is a sustained polemic against George Steiner's elitist defence of 'tragedy' as an index of cultural seriousness threatened by the mass-democratic societies of the twentieth century, end with a chapter on 'A Rejection of Tragedy: Brecht'. *The English Novel from Dickens to Lawrence* is a similarly sustained reworking of F. R. Leavis's *The Great Tradition*, which it thoroughly democratises. Charles Dickens and Thomas Hardy, both of whom Leavis had denigrated, emerge as central to Williams's account: the former because of his ability to draw on the rich forms and traditions of urban popular culture, the latter as the key continuity between George Eliot and early D. H. Lawrence, and as vital in his exploration of the social 'border country' between education and the local, customary community. Yet though much of the material of *The English Novel* reappears word for word in *The Country and the City*, the political and intellectual context of the discussion is remarkably transformed, producing what is by general consent Williams's finest single volume. All readers of the book will have noted how the occasionally circumlocutory, oddly formal tone of Williams's earlier writings is replaced here by a new, harder and colder political anger – over both the actual exploitation and destruction of the natural environment under capitalism, and the wilful ideological mystifications of rural social relations in pastoral poetry. Some of Williams's polemical ire is reserved for F. R. Leavis, and the myth of the 'organic community' has rarely been more effectively demolished than in the first chapter of this book; but the fundamental intellectual framework of *The Country and the City* is not English criticism, but rather European Marxism. The book concludes with a searching examination of Marxist attitudes to the polarity of city and country, rounding upon the glib preference for urban modernity implicit in Marx's notorious phrase about the 'idiocy of rural life', but approving Engels's vision of socialism as 'abolishing the contrast between town and country, which has been brought to its extreme point by present-day capitalist society' – an abolition which Williams sees as practically under way in the Chinese Revolution (a political preference which has led one commentator to characterise *The Country and the City* neatly but too simply as a work of 'Leavisite Maoism'). And these rapprochements with Marxism in *Drama from Ibsen to Brecht* and *The Country and the City* culminate in *Marxism and Literature* in 1977, where Williams formally situates his work within the Marxist tradition: 'it is a position which can be briefly described as cultural materialism: a theory of the specificities of material cultural and literary production within historical materialism ... it is, in my view, a Marxist theory ... part of what I at least see as the central thinking of Marxism'.[7]

I have suggested that Raymond Williams is a 'thinker of the copula', and any copula – Williams and Marxism in this instance – both connects *and* divides; for the question of whether cultural materialism is indeed a Marxist theory is one which has exercised many commentators since Williams's death. This debate will no doubt rage on for many years to come, but let us first sketch the contours of the theory, of cultural materialism as formulated in Williams's later works, before returning to it. In *Marxism and Literature* Williams aligns himself with the work of V. N. Volosinov in seeking to think through the nature of language without capitulating to the abstract polarities of two powerful, opposed traditions in linguistics: idealistic subjectivism, on the one hand, for which individual speakers freely create meanings of which *langue*, or the system of language, is the reflection or product, and abstract objectivism, on the other, for which individual *parole* is pre-programmed in advance by the rules of *langue*. As a theory of culture, cultural materialism similarly threads its way between Scylla and Charybdis. On the one hand, it refuses all idealist models of culture as an autonomous realm of values or unconstrained creativity, insisting instead that cultural production is an integral part of the general material social process; but on the other hand, it also refuses the cultural reductionism of vulgar Marxism, which also dematerialises art and ideology as mere 'forms of social consciousness' wholly determined by more fundamental processes which take place elsewhere. As H. Gustav Klaus insists, in an excellent 'summary of principles' of cultural materialism, Williams typically speaks of 'cultural practices' rather than of 'text', 'artefact' or 'object';[8] indeed, one of his fiercest critiques of the Marxist-structuralist and deconstructive criticisms of the late 1970s was precisely that they took the reified, academicist object 'text', rather than an active 'practice', as their object of analysis. But the stress on social agency and intention built into the notion of 'practice' is at once constrained by a firm emphasis on the technical, physical, material conditions of any communicative or aesthetic mode – a stress exactly captured in the subtitle of *Television: Technology and Cultural Form*. If the mass media of the late twentieth century are particularly evident instances of the principle, it none the less applies all the way down even to language itself, which Williams describes in *Marxism and Literature* as material 'practical consciousness'. This insistence on the material dimension of cultural and communicative practices – both acquired bodily skills and socially available materials and technologies – does not lead to 'technological determinism', to which Williams devotes some finely polemical pages in his *Television* book. New technologies are not just 'bumped into' by scientists pursuing their own autonomous goals; they are, rather, discovered by intensive research programmes which are shaped to their roots by existing social values and priorities. But even so, at the moment of scientific breakthrough, the social uses of the new technology remain an open question, a site of struggle: nothing in the physical technology of, say, radio or television pre-programmed them for the essentially passive, privatised mode of reception which is our dominant experience of them under late capitalism. But, none the less, Williams's emphasis on the materiality of cultural practices does, in his view, ward off another – and unacceptable – materialism, that would reduce them to the mere echo, precipitate or ghostly reflection of the economic base. As he puts it in *Politics and Letters*: 'my aim was to emphasize that cultural practices are forms of material production, and that until this is understood it is impossible to think about them in their real social relations – there can only ever be a second order of correlation'.[9]

Cultural practices, then, are not an autonomous or a derivative but rather a *constitutive* social process; but the precise status of this claim is not always easy to decipher in Williams's work. Is it a historical point, such that cultural production perhaps once was secondary in the Marxist sense but now *isn't*? It wouldn't be difficult to argue that late capitalism has witnessed not just a quantitative but a qualitative expansion of culture, so that with its commodification in the culture industries and the attendant general 'aestheticisation of everyday life', culture is now socially central in a way it has never previously been in human history – to the point, indeed, where all those supposedly 'hard' activities that we could once distinguish from it – economics, politics, even war – are now saturated with it through and through. Williams often does cast the case for cultural materialism in these historical terms, including in those pages from *Politics and Letters* from which I have just quoted. And when he does so he seems (without ever naming them) to align himself with theories of postmodernism for which, after 1956 or 1968 or whenever, we do indeed enter an unprecedented new epoch in which a 'society of the spectacle' can no longer tell image and referent apart, or more radically, as Jean Baudrillard would have it, we suffer the 'precession of simulacra' and so-called 'referents' are only the echoes of their own echoes. In his inaugural lecture as Professor of Drama at Cambridge, on 'Drama in a Dramatized Society', Williams moves very close to such accounts. Noting that a human being today can watch more drama in a week than any of his or her ancestors could in a lifetime, Williams speculates that this marks a qualitative transition in human consciousness, a radical dismantling of the boundaries of fact and fiction, base and superstructure: 'dramatised society' is his equivalent of Baudrillard's 'simulacrum' or Fredric Jameson's 'image culture'. Yet on many other occasions cultural materialism's insistence on the constitutive nature of culture is argued through as theoretical principle rather than as historical description, as holding good since the moment when some shaggy human ancestor picked up the first flint rather than coming into force only with the invention of the video recorder. And Williams's premature death means that this particular ambivalence in his work is not now going to be settled either way.

But if culture is constitutive rather than reflective, what becomes of the Marxist concept of 'determination'? This, it seems, has become the key issue in theoretical wrangles over whether cultural materialism is or is not a Marxist theory. Williams and his *New Left Review* interviewers debate the problem at some length in *Politics and Letters*, and it has dogged every subsequent account of Williams's work. Determination had, indeed, been an issue in Williams's earlier work, since the definition of culture as the 'study of the inter-relations between elements in a whole way of life' seemed to imply a circular notion of the social totality in which – such were the intricate complexities of its lived relationships – no area of practice could inherently be assigned priority over any other. In those early studies, Williams rejects the Marxist model of base and superstructure on Leavisite or phenomenological terms. No social actor *feels* or experiences some activities as infrastructural and others as 'merely' superstructural: all are intensely real to the individual agent in the indissociable complexity of his or her total social existence. But, as Williams's Marxist critics were quick to point out, the base/superstructure doctrine operates on an analytical, not experiential, plane; it does not offer to describe the actual feel of different bits of social reality, but rather offers an abstract, conceptual apparatus for thinking through the relationships between them. At this point, then, still strongly in the grip of a Leavisite premium on the 'lived', Williams comes down too heavily on the 'feeling' side of his splendidly oxymoronic or schizophrenic concept of 'structure of feeling'.

In his later writings, this lop-sided phenomenology is succeeded by the emphasis on the materiality of cultural practices; and in this sense Williams is now *more* Marxist than Marx, who was too often inclined to define culture as mere disembodied 'forms of social consciousness': 'instead of making cultural history material, which was the next radical move, it was made dependent, secondary, "superstructural"'.[10] But once it *is* made material, do we not again, *though* in startlingly altered form, face problems of circularity? The 'base' of course is material; classical Marxism had always asserted this, and Williams agrees. But now the superstructures are material as well, so how do we tell the two apart? What is the force of the description of practices as 'material' if the adjective now has no opposite? If everything is material, from robot-operated car factories through making a film to literary devices such as enjambement or the use of a naive narrator, does the term any longer mean anything? Have we not rather expanded its meaning so far that any explanatory or polemical force it might once have had has now haemorrhaged away? In an excellent account of Williams's later cultural theory, Terry Eagleton has argued that Williams takes the base/superstructure metaphor as a description of social reality, and rejects it as such. Without denying that it has indeed been this in some incautious Marxist formulations, Eagleton maintains that it is, at its best, an *explanatory* schema. Far from describing some social regions as grittily material and others (art, culture) as aethereally spiritual, the base/superstructure schema happily concedes the material reality of all social practices but insists none the less that some are more *determining* than others. Williams has thus taken the weakest, rather than strongest, versions of classical Marxism as a way of distinguishing his own position from it, just as he regularly erects a weakly external concept of 'ideology' (as a relatively formal set of conscious ideas) before knocking it off its pedestal with his own appropriation of Gramsci's concept of 'hegemony'; there are, however, much richer models of ideology in the Marxist tradition than this 'vulgar' one. Thus, as Eagleton wryly notes, 'the effect of Williams's increasing *rapprochement* with Marxism during the 1970s was not, paradoxically, to lead him closer to the base/superstructure model, but to lead him further away : In extending Marxist logic, Williams partly undoes ist'.[11]

We might well generalise this remark across the various Williams texts I have been surveying. Brecht may have replaced Eliot as the highpoint of avantgarde theatrical achievement in *Drama from Ibsen to Brecht*, but this was a distinctively 'Williams-ised' Brecht, and not the Brecht we are familiar with from the writings of, say, early Roland Barthes or Colin MacCabe or Terry Eagleton himself. Similarly, though *The Country and the City* finds resources for thinking productively about urban and rural inter-relations within the Marxist tradition (Engels, William Morris, Mao), we can also see the book as contributing powerfully to an emergent ecological politics which through the 1980s would be a major challenger to Marxism for radical hearts and minds. And the self-declared Marxism of *Marxism and Literature* has, as we have seen, proved unpalatable to more classically minded Marxists such as Eagleton. The notion of a 'rapprochement with Marxism' through the 1970s, then, though it captures an important element of Williams's development, is far from exhausting it, and will not account adequately for his writings of the 1980s. I have spoken so far of two formative political moments in Williams's career: 1956, which finds political expression with the first New Left and intellectually sees the emergence of cultural studies; and 1968, whose political form is the second New Left and whose intellectual framework is European Marxism. We must now move on to a third crucial moment, which in Britain is signalled by Margaret Thatcher's first election victory in 1979: the moment – a very long moment, which is perhaps only now coming towards its end – of the emergence of the New Right and of the Left's responses to it.

An internal signal of the impact of this new political moment in Williams's work is the transformations his fiction undergoes during these years. The early novels, including the conveniently titled *Second Generation*, are preoccupied with a clash of political values between two generations. It may be crude, in reading *The Fight for Manod*, to draw up the equation: Matthew Price = 1956 or first New Left, Peter Owen = 1968 or second New Left; but it is not wrong to do so. But an important shift sets in with *Loyalties* in 1985. Though the body of the novel enacts yet another version of the clash between the first two political generations, this action is framed by a new force in Williams's work – the young television researcher Jon Merritt, representing an untried, as yet largely undefined *third* generation which might be able to break beyond the impasses in which the first two are now hopelessly locked. This narrative framing device is massively developed in Williams's last novel, *People of the Black Mountains* in 1988, where the second generation has disappeared from the text altogether (killed off in an air crash on page nine!). The crucial issue here is whether the young student Glyn can find his lost grandfather, whether – to put it a little too crudely – meaningful political relations can now be established between the first and third generations. That they could be is suggested not so much by *People of the Black Mountains*, which remains unfinished after its author's death, but by his earlier book, *Towards 2000*, published in 1983.

In his extended obituary of Williams, Andrew Milner has spoken of 'a third generation, a "postmodern" New Left, which has endured that prolonged extension of "the winter of 1979" which has been the 1980s'; and he has characterised this 'postmodern Left' as, first, opening out socialist politics towards ecology, feminism, the peace movement, resistance to racial oppression, and nationalism (Welsh, Scottish and Irish in the British context) and, second, as abandoning Leninist notions to the vanguard party in favour of renewed relationships with the Labour Party or the new-model, post-Leninist Communist Party. Williams's *Towards 2000*, on this showing, emerges as a virtual manual of postmodern politics, seeking to integrate economics and ecology, traditional class politics and the new social movements, and striving to think through the relations between the most rootedly local and breathtakingly international dimensions of the new, late-capitalist world order and of possible resistance to it. The old nation-state, as Williams notes, has precious little purchase on the new world of multinational corporations, and he now strives determinedly to think both 'before' and 'after' its boundaries – a paradoxical project which is memorably signalled in a phrase from *Marxism and Literature*, where the Leavisite 'Englishness' of some of Williams's early work gives way to a new identity as a self-declared 'Welsh European', yet another suggestive 'border country' to inhabit. In terms of practical politics, the last decade of Williams's life was taken up in a full involvement in many of the projects of this new, postmodern Left: he played an important role in Welsh nationalist politics, moved closer to the new forces in the Labour Party while still insisting on the need to create a socialist opposition beyond it, helped found the Socialist Society to advance socialist education, research and culture in 1982, and played a role from the late 1970s in the Socialist Environmental Resources Association (SERA). As Milner puts it, 'Williams surely succeeds in recuperating the positive, though not the negative, moment within postmodern leftism'.[12]

I have alluded to the question of postmodernism on and off throughout this essay, and now wish to address it directly as a way of moving towards a conclusion and of trying to summarise Williams's importance for us today. His was an intellectual career of some forty years, beginning with the appearance of *Reading and Criticism* in 1950 and ending with the posthumous publication of *People of the Black Mountains* and *The Politics of Modernism* in 1989. Some of its earlier moments, in particular, now seem very arcane and distant from us: who, after all, apart from academic specialists, now remembers who F. R. Leavis is, and thus still cares much about Williams's fraught struggles to break away from his influence? Yet much in that early work can still be close and suggestive for us, and it seems to me to be the framework of the postmodernism debate that best reveals that to be the case. As I remarked at the beginning of this essay, Raymond Williams never did develop his thoughts on postmodernism explicitly or at length (he planned to conclude *The Politics of Modernism* with a chapter on postmodernism, but died before he could do so); but then more interesting than Raymond Williams *on* postmodernism, I suspect, is an attempt to see Williams *as* postmodernist. My broad framework for construing Williams in this way is provided by Fredric Jameson's powerful essay of 1984 on 'Postmodernism, or the Cultural Logic of Late Capitalism'.[13]

Postmodernism, above all in architecture, is an 'aesthetic populism', a return to local, vernacular, even commercial traditions after the stringent, high-tech impersonality of the modernist buildings of Le Corbusier, Walter Gropius, Mies van der Rohe. But Raymond Williams's early work is also an eloquent assault upon the cultural elitism of both traditionalist conservatives and the modernist avantgarde: his early slogan, 'Culture is Ordinary' (the title of an essay of 1958) bears comparison with the postmodern populism catchily expressed in the titles of Robert Venturi's *Learning from Las Vegas* and Tom Wolfe's *From Bauhaus to Our House*. Or if – to express the same point in a different way – postmodernism is characterized by a collapse of the barriers between high culture and mass culture, then the discipline of 'cultural studies', in the emergence of which Williams's early work played so crucial a role, might be seen as an archetypally postmodern phenomenon. Moreover, that dismantling of the high/low binary opposition in the field of culture is enacted in Williams's own fiction which, after its early realism, moves with *The Fight for Manod* and *The Volunteers* decisively into the popular terrain of detective fiction and political thriller. And the charge of 'populism', both cultural and political, as a belief that ordinary men and women creatively shape their own meanings and projects, was repeatedly hurled against Williams during the Althusserian onslaught of the early 1970s. In this sense, Althusserianism, in its view of men and women as mere *Träger* of social structures of which they remain unaware, reverts to the contemptuous dismissal of the 'cretinised' (Leavis's term) masses characteristic of high modernism itself.

Architecture is a key instance in the postmodern debate because in its modernist form, the International Style, aesthetics and philosophy dovetail neatly. If Le Corbusian architecture is in one sense a distinct set of stylistic features – flat roofs, white facades, rectilinear construction, *pilotis*, and so on – in another it can be seen as a particular embodiment of a much grander project – the project of modernity itself. In its refusal of popular taste and historical traditions as mere 'prejudice', in its devotion to austere functionalism, to an internal logic of construction and the most scientifically advanced technologies and materials, International Style buildings can be seen as an expression of Enlightenment rationality, spurning the merely local or subjective in the name of the axioms of Universal Reason. Postmodernist architecture, then, in its relaxed populism and historicism, reaffirms these despised marginal forces, the actual life-world, against the totalitarianism of pure reason. One way of returning to Williams's *Culture and Society* in the context of today's preoccupations is to read its retrieval of a conservative social critique from Edmund Burke onwards precisely as an attack upon the project of Enlightenment modernity and its brutal 'top-down' reshaping of the life world (whether in the form of capitalist or Stalinist 'planning'). His later study of *The English Novel from Dickens to Lawrence* is also a sustained meditation on these issues, using a body of literary texts to ponder the general relations between the 'lived', local community, in which wisdom is a matter of accumulated custom and tradition, and the Enlightenment rationality implicit in modern educational systems (even if often deformed there by the operation of class interests). In insisting, true to the deconstructive impulse that runs throughout his work, that we can come down on neither side of this binary division, but must rather inhabit a tense, difficult 'border country' that somehow encompasses both, Williams emerges as a truly postmodernist thinker, giving both the prefix and the adjective itself equal weight, critiquing but never simply regressing behind the project of modernity. And it is striking how often formulations of the aesthetic and philosophical principles of postmodern architecture are phrased in terms extremely close to Williams's metaphor of a 'border country' between the popular and the élite; Charles Jencks's seminal study of *The Language of Post-Modern Architecture* is a mine of such parallelisms.

Once the elitist enclosure of the high-modernist building is broken open, so that it now enters into relations with its local context and the latter's assorted styles and traditions, postmodern architectural thinking moves swiftly from the question of the single artefact to that of the city as a whole. The rationalised, sanitised space of Le Corbusier's *ville radieuse* gives way to what Colin Rowe famously terms 'collage city', a detotalised city space of randomness, pluralism, discontinuity, aleatory encounters. This postmodern 'turn to the city' seems to me as productive a context for thinking about Williams's *The Country and the City* and his novel *The Fight for Manod* as the notion of a 'rapprochement with Marxism'. The utopian city of the latter, 'Manod' itself, has clearly broken with the relentless logic of Le Corbusian urban space; its high-tech communications networks function in the name of decentralisation, multiplicity, a new integration of the urban with its natural environment. And if *The Country and the City* moves closer to Marxism, we must also stress that Marxism, during these very years and precisely under the impact of postmodernist culture, is pondering the question of the city, of 'the specificity of the urban', and the role of space in social relations, as never before. Key works of this moment would include Henry Lefebvre's *La Revolution Urbaine* (1970) and *La Pensée Marxiste et la Ville* (1972), Manuel Castells's *La Question Urbaine*(1972) and David Harvey's *Social Justice and the City* (1974). And as Edward Soja has insisted in his *Postmodern Geographies*, the city is not simply yet another object to which one can apply a Marxist method that already exists in advance.[14] It rather transforms the method *as* it is applied, giving rise to a new, 'postmodern Marxism', which is summed up in Soja's own slogan of a 'topian Marxism' or in David Harvey's call for a 'historico-geographical', rather than plain old-style 'historical', materialism. Raymond Williams's cultural materialism may not, in conventional terms, be a Marxism, but then, after its encounter with the postmodern city, Marxism was no longer its old self; and the relations between a 'postmodern geography' and cultural materialism remain to be thought through in depth.

Populism, historicism and the decentred city by no means, naturally, exhaust the field of the postmodern. A second series of postmodernist preoccupations circulate around such terms as pastiche, depthlessness, one-dimensionality, spectacle, image, media, communications, technologies of reproduction; and Guy Debord and Jean Baudrillard are more relevant theoretical names here than Robert Venturi and Charles Jencks. Of the centrality of these themes to Raymond Williams's work, from *Preface to Film* in 1954 through *Communications* (1962) to *Television: Technology and Cultural Form* in 1974, there can be no doubt; the latter work, indeed, was begun while Williams was visiting professor at Stanford University, in the heart of the most image-ridden of all cultures, and its central concept of 'total flow' has been repeatedly invoked by later theorists of the postmodern. I have argued above that Williams's 'dramatised society' serves in his work the function of Debord's 'spectacle' or Baudrillard's 'simulacrum'; but his fullest development of such issues is his novel *The Volunteers*. Already in *The Fight for Manod*, through the figure of Juliet Dance, the distinction between organic and inorganic, human original and its mechanical simulacrum, is breaking down bewilderingly. But this process is radicalised in the multinational, postmodern terrorist world of *The Volunteers*, whose hero Lewis Redfern works for an international satellite television agency, and where 'lived' experience is entirely a matter of the production of signs, styles, images and pastiche. Fredric Jameson has argued that contemporary communication technologies serve, in many recent novels and films, as figures for the barely imaginable totality of the multinational capitalist world order itself; he terms such moments, at which in oblique but awesome ways, one seems fleetingly to come into contact with the very limits of the system itself as the 'hysterical' or 'technological sublime'. It should then come as no surprise, though I have no space to demonstrate the point in detail here, that this postmodern sublime is the fundamental aesthetic experience of Raymond Williams's most interesting fiction, emerging with impressive force at the end of both *The Fight for Manod* and *The Volunteers*.

In terms of both its stress on the local rather than the universal, and of the depthless nature of its ubiquitous images and simulacra, postmodernism has often been described as a *spatial* culture, an unprecendented culture in which, experientially and theoretically, space is visible as never before; hence the subtitle of Edward Soja's seminal study, *Postmodern Geographies: The Reassertion of Space in Critical Social Theory*. Space and geography, however, are central to Williams's work from beginning to end. One has only to consider the spatial signals emitted by his first and last novels, *Border Country* and *People of the Black Mountains*; and we could certainly read all his novels in such a way as to reveal a fully developed 'socio-spatial dialectic'

(Soja's term) operative in them. From these fictional concretions, there arises eventually an articulated postmodern political position; 'a new theory of socialism', Williams argued in 1984, 'must now centrally involve *place*'.[15] 'Place' in such formulations, naturally, is not an appeal to a pre-given positivity, but rather indicates the baffling postmodern space of being a 'Welsh European', an extraordinary intersection of the local and the global within the forcefield of the postmodern. Raymond Williams's lifetime work as a literary critic, socialist and cultural theorist is a strange intersection of a related kind. Earlier, 'local' images of him, as Leavisite English-realist in the early 1960s or even as a more Europe-orientated Marxist in the 1970s, still obscure his immediate relevance to today's fully international debate on postmodernism. Yet it seems no accident that Williams's last (and uncompleted) critical study was devoted to *The Politics of Modernism*, and that it is as deeply ambivalent about that early twentieth-century cultural moment as only a full postmodernism (and no mere anti-modernism) could be. Marxist in any simple sense, no; but 'postmodern cultural materialist'? We have still to take the full measure of that description of Raymond Williams's cultural theory.

Williams's work, as I have tried to suggest in this essay, is still in many ways so close to us that it seems premature to attempt an account of the history of its reception or even of a 'critical heritage' in relation to it. None the less, some important landmarks from amidst the mass of commentary on it can be pointed out. Significant early responses include Victor Kiernan's 'Culture and Society' in *The New Reasoner* 9 (Summer 1959) and E. P. Thompson's 'The Long Revolution' in *New Left Review* 9 and 10 (May/June and July/August 1961); the latter deplored the academicist tone of Williams's early writing and famously proposed 'whole way of life'. Michael Green's 'Raymond Williams and Cultural Studies' in *Cultural Studies* 6 (Spring 1975) is a useful survey of Williams's contributions to this emerging field of study. In 1976 Terry Eagleton's article on 'Criticism and Politics: the Work of Raymond Williams' in *New Left Review* 95 (January/February 1976) initiated a new phase of commentary on Williams; it also appeared as the first chapter of his *Criticism and Ideology* later in the same year. A former student of Williams's, Eagleton launched a fierce broadside against his mentor, damning his work as 'empiricist', 'realist', 'English'; in this way, an Althusser-inspired younger generation of socialist theorists, in the grip of something akin to Harold Bloom's 'anxiety of influence', sought to settle accounts with their commanding precursor. Williams still had his defenders, as in Anthony Barnett's 'Raymond Williams and Marxism: A Rejoinder to Terry Eagleton' in *New Left Review* 99 (September/October 1976), but Eagleton's attack set the terms of debate on and with Williams for several years. This remains true in the interviews between Williams and the editors of *New Left Review* which are collected in *Politics and Letters* (1979), though what is noteworthy here is how far Williams himself has taken on board the Eagletonian critique of his early work.

Empiricist, realist, English: these charges are still occasionally levelled against Williams's work, but what they now essentially denote is that the critic stopped reading it sometime in the mid-1960s; for the later Raymond Williams is none of these things. One attempt to redefine his significance is my essay on 'Raymond Williams and "the Two Faces of Modernism"' in *Raymond Williams: Critical Perspectives*, edited by Terry Eagleton (1989) and the Editor's Introduction on 'Modernism and Cultural Theory' to Williams's posthumously published *The Politics of Modernism* (1989), both of which seek to establish the formative presence of European modernism in Williams's life and thought. This effort of redefinition, by a generation of Left critics who now tended to be the students *of* Williams's students, is continued in a Special Issue of the journal *News from Nowhere* devoted to 'Raymond Williams', points to an issue that is becoming increasingly important in assessments of Williams's thought. The latest stage of redefinition seeks to forge relations between Williams and the postmodern rather than modernism: Andrew Milner's fine obituary, 'A Young Man's Death', in *Thesis Eleven* 20 (1988) and my study of *Raymond Williams: Postmodern Novelist* (Cardiff, 1991) are straws in this particular wind.

Realist, modernist or postmodernist? These debates will no doubt continue, as they should; but Williams's death has also led to another impulse – not so much to wrangle over his legacy as to attempt some broad overall survey of it, to take the full measure of it across the many years and genres of its writing. Eagleton's introduction to his *Raymond Williams: Critical Perspectives* volume is a moving attempt to do just this, as are several of its contributions; and Alan O'Connor's *Raymond Williams: Writing, Culture, Politics* is a broad, meticulously researched introduction for the general reader. If such studies lack the fire of the old polemics, they also perform the essential service of making Williams available for today's students, young readers who have no personal acquaintance with the man and have not eagerly bought his books as they have appeared, one by one, across the years. What shape *their* Raymond Williams – a 'fourth-generational' Raymond Williams – will take remains to be seen.

Notes

1 For a detailed reading of this kind, see my *Raymond Williams: Postmodern Novelist* (Seren Books, 1991).

2 For an excellent brief account of these 'phases' in Williams's work, see Andrew Milner, 'A Young Man's Death: Raymond Williams 1921-1988', *Thesis Eleven*, no 20 (1988), pp. 106-117. My 'Editorial: Third Generation' in *News from Nowhere* no 6 (February 1989), pp. 3-11, also develops this notion.

3 Raymond Williams, *Culture and Society 1780-1950* (London, 1958), p. 327.

4 Raymond Williams, *The Long Revolution* (Harmondsworth, 1965), p. 63.

5 Raymond Williams, 'Literature and Sociology', in *Problems in Materialism and Culture* (London, 1980), p. 23.

6 Williams, *The Long Revolution*, p. 304.

7 Raymond Williams, *Marxism and Literature* (Oxford, 1977), pp. 5-6.

8 Gustav Klaus, 'Cultural Materialism: A Summary of Principles', in *Anglistentag 1989, Würzburg* (Tübingen, 1990), edited by Rüdiger Ahrens, pp. 66-78. As Klaus notes, the American anthropologist Marvin Harris also lays claim to the term 'cultural materialism', but in a sense far removed from Williams's own.

9 Raymond Williams, *Politics and Letters: Interviews with New Left Review* (London, 1979), p. 353. The half-dozen pages which surround this remark are of the utmost importance for Williams's definition of his own position.

10 Williams, *Marxism and Literature*, p. 19.

11 Terry Eagleton, 'Base and Superstructure in Raymond Williams', in *Raymond Williams: Critical Perspectives*, edited by Terry Eagleton (Oxford, 1989), pp. 171-2.

12 Milner, 'A Young Man's Death', pp. 107, 112-15.

13 Fredric Jameson, 'Postmodernism, or the Cultural Logic of Late Capitalism', *New Left Review* 146 (July/August 1984), pp. 52-92.

14 See Edward Soja, *Postmodern Geographies: The Reassertion of Space in Critical Social Theory* (London, 1989), chapter four. See also my 'Space: the Final Frontier', *News from Nowhere* no 8 (November 1990), pp. 10-27.

15 Raymond Williams, *Resources of Hope: Culture, Democracy, Socialism*, edited by Robin Gable (London, 1989), p. 242.

The Works of Raymond Williams

Reading and Criticism (London, 1950)
Drama from Ibsen to Eliot (London, 1952)
Preface to Film (with Michael Orrom), (London, 1954)
Drama in Performance (London, 1954)
Culture and Society 1780-1950 (London, 1958)
Border Country (London, 1960)
The Long Revolution (London, 1961)
Britain in the Sixties: Communications (Harmondsworth, 1962)
Second Generation (London, 1964)

Modern Tragedy (1966)

Drama from Ibsen to Brecht (London, 1968)

The English Novel from Dickens to Lawrence (London, 1970)

Orwell (London, 1971)

The Country and the City (London, 1973)

Television: Technology and Cultural Form (London, 1974)

Keywords: A Vocabulary of Culture and Society (London, 1976)

Marxism and Literature (Oxford, 1977)

The Volunteers (London, 1978)

The Fight for Manod (London, 1979)

Politics and Letters: Interviews with New Left Review (London, 1979)

Problems in Materialism and Culture: Selected Essays (London, 1980)

Culture (London, 1981)

Towards 2000 (London, 1983)

Writing in Society (London, 1984)

Loyalties (London, 1985)

People of the Black Mountains (London, 1989)

Raymond Williams on Television: Selected Writings, edited by Alan O'Connor (London, 1989)

Resources of Hope: Culture, Democracy, Socialism, edited by Robin Gable (London, 1989)

The Politics of Modernism: Against the New Conformists, edited by Tony Pinkney (London, 1989)

What I Came To Say, edited by Neil Belton, Francis Mulhern and Jenny Taylor (London, 1989)

Klaus Ensslen

James Baldwin

(1924-1987)

Baldwin's production spans a period from the rise of McCarthyism in the late 1940s, through the so-called Second Black Renaissance and the rise of militant political currents including black nationalism in the 1960s and early 70s, to the upsurge of conservative stances and the concomitant discrediting of radical social vision in the Reagan phase of the 1980s. Too young to have been affected by World War II or by the leftist radicalism of the pre-war decade, Baldwin profited from Richard Wright's pioneering literary works as stepping stones for launching his own confrontation with the social norms and concepts, first of his more circumscribed specific world (the ghetto of Harlem and its storefront churches), but very soon also with the state of the nation and its mainstream culture, and eventually with the Western world as one ideological complex. Wright's example was particularly effective in showing Baldwin the value of autobiographical self-analysis: Wright's flight away from the suffocating forces of a murderously race-ridden South (*Black Boy*, 1945) became a model for Baldwin's analogous emancipation from the stifling constraints of poverty and its social anodyne, the black church. But Baldwin's reenactment of Wright's life-saving flight from the outset contained the creative germ of a determined criticism of Wright's rejection of most forms of black community – a critically informed emulation of the liberating exodus pattern which was to provide the main creative tension to Baldwin's quickly emerging role as public spokesman of black America, drawing on both the unbroken participatory empathy for his ghetto origins and the painfully sought for distancing power of the prophet in exile.

James Baldwin was born on August 2, 1924 in New York City as the oldest of nine children of a typically ghetto-bound family. His stepfather tenaciously maintained subsistence level family coherence by holding a steady job in a factory (no small feat in depression years) while also preaching in a storefront church. Treating his children with more severity than sympathy, he remained a polarizing factor for his adolescent stepson (as the recurrent attempts of James the writer to fathom his character, or to come to terms with him as a father in retrospect, serve to document). James early showed interest in reading and writing (for the school newspaper which he edited), but his formal education ended with his graduation from De Witt Clinton High

School. He became a boy preacher in his father's church at the age of fourteen, but dropped this role with seventeen to drift from one occasional job to the next in and around New York. In these formative years Baldwin intermittently lived in Greenwich Village and met a number of writers and artists, among them the black painter Beauford Delaney, a life-long friend, and Richard Wright, who encouraged him in his writing and helped him to get the Eugene F. Saxton Award for the completion of his first novel. The accumulated pressure of racial discrimination, poverty and an unresolved professional perspective, the dilemmas of his sexual coming of age and the personal responsibility for his family after his stepfather's sudden illness and death in 1943 – all these factors made Baldwin's state of mind in the post-war years so explosive (i.e. beset by violence as a symptom of and a reaction to his society) that he decided in 1948 to leave America for Paris.

Paris brought Baldwin the space he needed to breathe more freely and the vantage point to look at his society and the black man's situation in it with some critical detachment. Although it was another five years before he published his first novel, Baldwin broadened his contributions to various magazines (like *The Nation, Partisan Review*, and *Commentary*), after his initial apprentice work in reviewing books for *The New Leader* and trying his hand at reporting in New York. He broadened his scope to include reflexions on Americans in exile, observations on intercultural and interracial tensions in France and a systematical probing of his debt to and detachment from Richard Wright. Exile gave Baldwin more existential elbow room (especially after his reputation was assured with his first two books), and a distance conducive to clarifying his critical position towards his own culture.

But exile in France also implied the price of not taking part in the dramatic changes of the political climate back home during the accelerating civil rights struggle. Intensive discussion in Paris of the literary craft of Henry James, André Gide, Marcel Proust and others were one thing – the surge of hope for a healing of American society through racial integration and legal reform after the Montgomery bus boycott was an appeal to black solidarity that went well beyond the role of public witness Baldwin had chosen in his expository pronouncements. Neither personal friendships (like the one with Lucien Happersberger, the Swiss painter in whose chalet in the mountains Baldwin had finished his first novel) nor professional contacts with writers like Chester Himes or Norman Podhoretz in Paris could eventually replace direct participation in the new spirit of black civic protest. What Baldwin had repudiated in the Wright school of fiction, now caught up with him in political reality.

Except for one short visit to New York in 1952 and a longer stay (backed by a Guggenheim grant) from 1954 to 1955 (both related to the publication of his first books and to finding his place in the American literary scene), Baldwin had not planned on leaving Paris. In 1957 he decided to return to America and demonstratively began his lasting commitment to the civil rights struggle with his first visit to the American South, establishing active contacts to Martin Luther King, Bayard Rustin, Kenneth Clark and other public figures (among them also Harry Belafonte and Marlon Brando). Back in New York he assisted Elia Kazan in two theater productions and met the dramatists Tennessee Williams and Lorraine Hansberry, as well as novelists James Jones, John A. Williams and Norman Mailer, the black actor Sidney Poitier, and a little later (after a trip to Ingmar Bergman's film studio in Sweden in 1959) also William Styron, the white Southern novelist in whose guest house in Connecticut Baldwin would work on *Another Country* – a novel he was to finish in 1961 in Istanbul.

Istanbul in the next ten years became a repeatedly sought refuge from the hazards of literary fame, political advocacy and personal entanglements. Baldwin's role as a witness and spokesman for the situation of black Americans gathered momentum with discussions at Howard University, a Nobel Prize dinner at the White House and a black ministers' conference with King in 1962, followed by contacts with Malcolm X and the Black Muslims, a new trip South to support James Meredith at "Ole Miss" (the University of Mississippi at Oxford), and finally reached its peak in the consultation meeting with Attorney General Robert Kennedy and a group of black and white civil rights leaders and public spokespersons on May 24, 1963. Baldwin's presence at the Washington march (August 1963) and at James Forman's SNCC voter-registration drive in Selma, Alabama, that same fall mark other steps of his political commitment, with its literary collateral in the writing and staging of his play *Blues for Mister Charlie* in 1964. The controversial public response to this play, on the eve of the birth of a new black theater in the spirit of LeRoi Jones, drove Baldwin back to Paris and Europe, although he maintained a New York apartment. Geographic distance, however, made neither Malcolm's assassination in 1965, nor the growing American involvement in Vietnam, nor the sharpening of the domestic racial climate (culminating in King's assassination in 1968) any less painful. Baldwin's identification with more militant black stances shaped both his expository and fictional work in the late 1960s and early 1970s and took him to Hollywood on Kazan's and Alex Haley's invitation to consider a play and later a screenplay (for Columbia Pictures) based on *The Autobiography of Malcolm X*. The abortion of this film project added to Baldwin's disenchantment with the political climate and the media and public opinion pressure of his country on his own person. In 1971 he chose a more permanent exile, after the irregular flights to Istanbul and Paris, with his new residence at St. Paul-de-Vence on the Côte d'Azur. With the option of voluntary returns to New York and trips to other places more available because of his secured financial status, he was to live and work in Southern France until his death on December 1, 1987.

Baldwin brought two immutable conditioning factors to the assessment of his own culture: his socially ostracized status as a black American, and his precarious sexual self-image as a homosexual. The former contained the advantage of the painfully earned "birthright" of all black Americans: the outsider's sharpened perception of social and cultural norms, tested by both personal and collective experience. Baldwin's sexual marginality, on the other hand, constitutes more of a liability than a strength. In his fictional texts Baldwin appealed to a broader audience by counterbalancing homosexuality with the postulate of bisexuality where he did not eliminate or suppress it altogether (as he did in *Go Tell It On the Mountain, Going to Meet the Man* and *If Beale Street Could Talk*). But neither this tactical camouflage nor the more adamant dramatic treatment of homosexuality in some novels (especially *Giovanni's Room, Another Country* and *Just Above My Head*) seem to have released in the writer the interest for questioning culturally transmitted traditional gender roles. As Baldwin's conversation with Nikki Giovanni (*A Dialogue*, 1973) proves, his insecure sexual status reinforced the unconscionable privileging of the male position and the mechanisms for its defense, making him blind to new female self-concepts. As a more recent monograph shows, Baldwin's fictional portrayal of women almost unswervingly adheres to the ascription of serving, suffering, and supporting functions.[1]

Sexuality for Baldwin is a privileged arena for self-knowledge, or for showing the diseased condition of American society: The exclusion of blacks in America results from the entrenched evasion in the white American psyche of the black other as part of the composite nature of America. To understand the position of racial groups within American society in such terms rather than as the result of power and politics enhances the possibilities of moral suasion, of individual self-reform, and of both the warning and the healing power of the written word. The passion of Baldwin's jeremiad in this sense derives largely from his closely linking personal experience with structural analysis. His stance is that of eyewitness and exhorter, rather than of the social scientist. The object of his analysis is not systematic inclusiveness or a social theory, but an emotionally charged dynamics of deductions from tangible experience over time.

Baldwin gained a broad national audience and reputation primarily through the brilliance, rhetorical energy and argumentative incisiveness of his first essays. A survey of his writings would suggest that Baldwin's novels, stories and plays are dramatized extensions of the author's explicit public debate over ingrained concepts and precepts of his society. Baldwin's essays continue to gather analytical force and persuasive power all the way into *No*

Name in the Street (1972) and *The Devil Finds Work* (1976), while his fiction shows diminishing expressive force after *Tell Me How Long the Train's Been Gone* of 1968.

Baldwin always meant to address a broad national (i.e. a predominantly white) audience. He therefore toned down the repetitious, emotionalizing, and highly metaphorical techniques of black preaching by joining them to a basically rational tenor of argumentation. More important even, he offered the general reader in his earliest essay from *Notes of a Native Son* of 1955 ("The Harlem Ghetto", February 1948, *Commentary*)[2] a strategic device bridging the antagonism of black and white by shifting from the specific "I" of the black reporting voice to the "We (Americans in general, that is)" – thus identifying himself rhetorically with the white reader while at the same time claiming his full place in American society and anticipating the proclaimed community of interests for all Americans. Baldwin was to perfect this technique in later essays as a double-edged linguistic vehicle for rhetorically aligning himself with the white reader without lifting the didactic pressure from that reader's consciousness, with its burden of unacknowledged (or suppressed) facts.

Baldwin's first essay touches upon a great number of concrete details and arguments in a seemingly unsystematic way, but with the firm objective of indicating the plethora of conscious and unconscious emotional currents in the Negro community of Harlem and its ties to "this democracy" (59) or to "American reality" (70). The note of protest is as yet camouflaged beneath a stance of controlled reporting which only momentarily points to "the cancer" of racism which "attacks the mind and warps it" (71), which produces frustration and contradiction for Negro leaders and forms the groundswell of "bitterness", "innate desperation" and "rage" among ghetto people (65). Even the black church here functions as an "exquisite fantasy revenge" of "the long overdue punishment ... of the white American" (66) who has diverted black hatred to the Jew as the most visible instrument of white exploitation (70). To avoid being "irreparably scarred" and "growing into stunted maturity" (as so many "Negro boys and girls" "all over Harlem" were doing, 71) – a danger Baldwin also dramatized in his first story "Previous Condition"[3] – the author chose to leave America.

In Paris he began to exorcize Wright's literary shadow and the meaning of violence in his native country with the essays "Everybody's Protest Novel" and "Many Thousands Gone" (first published by *Partisan Review* in 1949 and 1951). In the first essay Baldwin argues an analogy between Beecher Stowe's *Uncle Tom's Cabin* and Wright's *Native Son* because Uncle Tom and Bigger Thomas remain defined by the ideology of their oppressors. "Bigger's tragedy is ... that he has accepted a theology that denies him life, that he admits the possibility of his being subhuman and feels constrained, therefore, to battle for his humanity according to those brutal criteria bequeathed him at his birth" (22-23). In Baldwin's view the main failure of the protest novel of this type is in accepting social categorization as more real than the capacity of the individual to transcend stereotypes and thereby create his own freedom. Baldwin here subscribes to theorems with existentialist overtones about the protean and ambivalent nature of man which also inform Ellison's *Invisible Man* (1952) and his apologetic essays of the late 40s and early 50s in *Shadow and Act* (1964).

The essay "Many Thousands Gone" shifts the argument away from the dichotomy between sociology and literature to the more tangible opposition of black and white Americans: The exclusion of the story and voice of the Negro American from American culture is seen as a post factum justification for the enslavement of Africans, and for the denigrating "myths we perpetuate about him" (27) which imply a "dehumanization of ourselves" (25). Baldwin's criticism of Bigger Thomas here gains sharper contours: Wright's limitation is seen in denying Bigger "the shared experience" of Negroes "which creates a way of life", and in suggesting "that in Negro life there exists no tradition, no field of manners, no possibility of ritual or intercourse" (35-36). Wright's "failure to convey any sense of Negro life as a continuing and complex group reality" (39), his elision of "the ironic ... in Negro life" (43) is thus embedded in the pressure exerted by the whole culture, with explosive black hate as the only possible reaction. Baldwin counters this by the reminder that black-white relations also represent a "*blood* relationship": "Negroes are Americans and their destiny is the country's destiny." (42)

Baldwin clearly stands in abhorrence of the criminal potential dramatized in Wright's Bigger Thomas, and in the title essay "Notes of a Native Son" he locates the autobiographical origin of this horror in an incident back in New Jersey where his accumulated rage and hate threatened to sweep away all other impulses and to make him a potential murderer (95-98). Baldwin's life can be understood as the continuing effort to escape this inherent threat of the black ghetto: to succumb to the self-hatred and fear suggested by the opressive stereotypes of the dominant culture and to counteract the denial of self-value purely by uncontrolled violence.

The experience of exile for Baldwin is addressed in three essays ("Encounter on the Seine", 1950; "A Question of Identity", 1954; "Equal in Paris", 1955) and initially helped to counteract "the alienation of the American from himself" (137) – before allowing a broader comparative perspective. After the comic treatment (in "Equal in Paris") of how Baldwin experienced threatening white power of the French brand, the concluding essay of

Notes of a Native Son, "Stranger in the Village" of 1953, proceeds to a more far-reaching confrontation of West European culture.

Finding himself in an isolated Swiss mountain village (where Baldwin was finishing his first novel) the naive curiosity of the natives leads the writer to reflect on his status as the exotic other. Perceived more as a symbol of Africa than as a person, Baldwin contrasts the villagers' sense of belonging to a culture and its inherited symbols (Bach, Chartres etc.) with his own awareness of being disinherited, "trapped in history" (163), heir to the "loss of power" and "loss of past" resulting from slavery, "[finding] myself among a people whose culture controls me, has even, in a sense, created me, people who have cost me more anguish and rage than they will ever know, who yet do not even know of my existence" (164). Whereas for Europeans the black man "remained comfortingly abstract" as part of the distant colonies, "in America, even as a slave, he was inescapably part of the general social fabric and no American could escape having an attitude toward him. Americans attempt until today to make an abstraction of the Negro, but the very nature of these abstractions reveals the tremendous effects the presence of the Negro has had on the American character" (170/71). The adoption of white supremacy (i.e. "that white men are the creators of civilization", 172) has made the American vision of the world "a dangerously inaccurate vision", promoting a national "moral high-mindedness at the terrible expense of weakening our grasp of reality" (174-75).

Baldwin locates the central problem of American culture in the battle between the white man trying to protect his false and overbearing sense of reality and the black man trying to establish an identity: "And despite the terrorization which the Negro in America endured and endures sporadically until today, despite the cruel and totally inescapable ambivalence of his status in his country, the battle for his identity has long ago been won. He is not a visitor to the West, but a citizen there, an American; as American as the Americans who despise him, the Americans who fear him, the Americans who love him" (173). Therefore, American culture can heal its own psychopathic traits only by coming to terms with the most comprehensive argument of the essay (and book) in its conclusive sentence: "This world is white no longer, and it will never be white again" (175). In domestic terms, Baldwin deduces from this the following psychogram of the white American and suggests a possible therapy (172-73):

At the root of the American Negro problem is the necessity of the American white man to find a way of living with the Negro in order to be able to live with himself. And the history of this problem can be reduced to the means used by Americans – lynch law and law, segregation and legal acceptance, terrorization and concession – either to come to terms with this necessity, or to find a way around it, or (most usually) to find a way of doing

both these things at once. The resulting spectacle, at once foolish and dreadful, led someone to make the quite accurate observation that "the Negro-in-America is a form of insanity which overtakes white men."

One has to add to the arguments discussed so far the hesitant but highly
sensitive and differentiated observations contained in "Princes and Powers"
(January 1951), an essay incorporated in Baldwin's second volume *Nobody
Knows My Name*, to get the full breadth of his critical concerns. In his report
on the Conference of African Writers and Artists 1950 in Paris, Baldwin first
pursues the question of what all the black delegates (from Africans like Sen-
ghor and Césaire to West Indians like George Lamming and the American
Richard Wright) might have in common, and against all the claims scattered
through various addresses for typically African elements in art, Baldwin tentatively offers his own conclusion: "What [all black people] held in common
was their precarious, their utterly painful relation to the white world. What
they had in common was the necessity to remake the world in their own
image, to impose this image on the world, and no longer be controlled by the
vision of the world, and of themselves, held by other people" (35). Such a
reversal of image control would presuppose a clear-headed analysis of the
experience of black people in Western culture, and it is here where Baldwin
locates the key role of black Americans, "for the American Negro is possibly
the only man of color who can speak of the West with real authority, whose
experience, painful as it is, also proves the vitality of the so transgressed
Western ideals" (28). "We could ... in a way, be considered the connecting
link between Africa and the West, the most real and certainly the most shocking of all African contributions to Western cultural life" (30). Measured
against this hypothesis of the African American as a connecting link between
black and white culture with a privileged potential for the revitalization of
black cultural values, neither Du Bois' nor Richard Wright's contribution to
the conference could convince Baldwin: Du Bois (who had been denied a
passport by the US government) had sent a statement advising black artists
and countries to look for guidance in the socialist doctrines of Eastern Europe
rather than to fall victims to the colonizing influence of America. Wright, on
the other hand, in Baldwin's opinion took a very high-handed attitude towards
black cultures by calling the enlightenment a gift of Europe to the "irrational"
past of Africa, and by conceding a leading role to Western cultures in the
reshaping of Africa and other colored parts of the world. Baldwin's initial
respect for Wright perceptibly makes room for a growing irritation on what
appeared to be provocative but confused and inconsistent arguments. The
right to view Wright critically stands in telling contrast to Baldwin's hesitation to evaluate the African speakers who remain somewhat opaque and

impenetrable to him – an attitude towards Africa that Baldwin throughout his life was never quite prepared to replace by a more substantial immersion.[4]

Baldwin's expository prose shows that by 1955 he had focused his critical confrontation with America around some basic psychological and conceptual observations on that culture; he had widened his scope, through the new vantage point of the exiled, to include considerations on European or Western culture; and he had substantiated his conclusions on the tangible level of autobiographical experience. Compared to this, the thematic focus of his first fictional texts is narrower and more particularized. Baldwin's first novel *Go Tell It On the Mountain* (1953) focuses on the relatively closed world of the black storefront church as part of the black ghetto and inscribes in this setting the central autobiographical experience of the writer's relation to his father. The one new element in this text is the portrayal of the Southern experience of black city dwellers, recapturing the origin of people in the black ghetto before their migration to the urban centers of the North. Except for one subplot (the story of Elizabeth and her lover who commits suicide after he has been brutalized in jail by white police) the novel stays within the narrowly circumscribed black community. Gabriel Grimes is the central figure of the novel, but the dramatized perspective of his son John opens and closes the novel, framing the flashback chapters, or "Prayers of the Saints," allotted to Gabriel, his sister Florence and his wife Elizabeth. Gabriel, the dominating father and husband of the book, is totally defined by his character, including his sexual drive and religious obsession, without any indication that the outside pressure of the white world has contributed anything towards conditioning this character. (This would enter into the repeated and increasingly sympathetic portrayals of his father in Baldwin's essays, and it also informs the later dramatization of his father in *Tell Me How Long the Train's Been Gone*.)

Similarly, the world of the storefront church community is presented as part of a self-contained black ghetto world largely isolated from the surrounding context. When Gabriel's rebellious favorite son Roy returns with a bloodied face, we are told that he has deliberately gone to the West side to fight a gang of white boys. To acknowledge the presence of the dominant white world is thus given as an explicit act of transgression in a black world whose norms postulate the denial of the larger white world.

This places the whole burden of deficits of the black ghetto world squarely on the black characters themselves. *Go Tell It on the Mountain* shows a family torn by strife and dissent between father and sons, husband and wife, brother and sister; of all the major characters, only Elizabeth has shown in an earlier phase of her life that she is capable of love, but through no fault of hers she now finds herself passively serving both husband and sons. Others (like Florence, Roy, and to a degree even John) are animated more by hatred than by sympathy: the chorus-like church members show formalized rather than socially vital interrelations. Church and familiy community are both presented as rather bleak and loveless worlds, and the initiation into the former for John is more like the closing of a trap than the opening of new horizons. The subliminal homoerotic attraction exerted by Elisha, a young church member of good standing, contains the promise not of community but of seduction, as a surrogate for Elisha's ostracized relation to a young woman. In sum, the symbolic action of the novel and the ascription of character traits result in a relatively negative portrayal of black family and church life, seen as stifling and incapacitating rather than as enabling forms of community.

A critical portrayal so exclusively addressed to inner conditions of the black community must raise certain questions about its place within Baldwin's perspective on his culture. On the autobiographical level, one could say that by equating the father figure with the church Baldwin exorcized his dependence on both and used writing as an act of emancipation, or escape. The tight, symmetrical structuring of the novel, the deliberate use of biblical imagery and rhetoric, the equilibrium between extended flashbacks and the dramatizing of action through individual characters as centers of consciousness all indicate that Baldwin modeled his novel more strongly on mainstream literature from Henry James to William Faulkner than on any specifically African-American tradition. Only the writer's ear for the spoken idiom in dialogue point to that heritage. Whether Baldwin had in mind a double-edged (and thereby blues-related) critique of pentecostalism and religious ecstasy as both escapist and resisting gestures of a pauperized ghetto group vis-à-vis the oppressive dominant culture[5] would seem more than doubtful given the extremely individualistic perspective of the characters or their life histories.

With his second novel Baldwin abandoned both the black setting and black speech. *Giovanni's Room* (1956) takes up the search for sexual identity and for a viable cultural space of a white American in France. The novel's frank focus on homosexuality broke new literary ground for post-war American fiction; it deals with this topic very directly, but refracted through the consciousness of a man who still takes the view of the majority to be the morally desirable one. David has not only deserted his first boy friend Joey and, running away from his inclinations, gone to Paris where he falls in love with Giovanni, an Italian barman; he also, despite his deep emotional involvement, abandons Giovanni after a few months of close partnership because he continues to see homosexuality as an aberration from which he flees once more. This time he rushes into the arms of his presumable fiancée Hella whom he had sent to Spain to wait for his own final word. While Giovanni, who had put his whole trust on David, after losing him in desperation kills an older substitute lover and is waiting to be executed, David discovers that he cannot love or marry Hella and decides to return to America by himself.

The culturally relevant implications of this dramatic action point towards a critique of the emotional or passional sense of identity of David as symptomatic of white American culture. Evasion of his sexual nature can be read as an analogy to the inability (or unwillingness) of the white American to face his own true nature. "Qualities repressed in our own self-images" correspond to "myths we have burdened the Negro with in this country" to justify his exclusion (*Nobody Knows My Name*, 112). *Giovanni's Room* thus probes the restrictive and stifling self-image (the white lie) of American culture by analogy, using homosexuality as a detector for what Baldwin elsewhere has called the American desire for innocence, or moral simplification.

This rather frightening view of the collective psyche of white America (which *Giovanni's Room* presents in a terse, récit-like form with ironical echoes from Henry James' *The American*) was taken up again by Baldwin in a more complex form in his third novel, *Another Country* (1962). Transposed to American ground (the civilized Babylon of Manhattan), the action here includes white and black Americans in the throes of their as yet unclarified social and sexual roles. A loose group of friends with artistic ambitions are shown in frantically driven interaction, sharing a sense of being threatened by destructive forces within and around themselves. These forces already have engulfed Rufus Scott, a black musician who commits suicide at the beginning of the novel by jumping from the George Washington Bridge because he is unable to stand the pressure of his own hatred and self-hatred which reflect his image and treatment in American society. Bisexuality and art mark him and most of his friends as outsiders; unstable love relations characterize the society in which they all suffer from self-alienation. Literary or artistic success are shown as forms of cooptation by an exploitative system which turns Rufus' sister Ida into a callous go-getter on her way to success as a singer. Only love seems to offer temporary stability and protection from the surrounding vortex of mutual distrust and destruction. Except for the actor Eric, a white Southerner who has returned from France and expects his lover Yves to join him, all other persons in the novel are on the point of foundering in one way or another, and since Eric's self-possession is not explained, but simply ascribed, it takes on the status of a utopian island in a treacherous sea.

Another Country presents a doomed society in which constructive impulses in the individual become thwarted, paralyzed, or deflected into greed for success and power. The main arena is the individual and its relation to other individuals, while art remains a more or less marketable and corruptible commodity. The resulting rejection of American society and its enacted values is wholesale and visceral rather than detailed and analytical, and the fictional space of New York is articulated by imagery connected with night-time, labyrinthine disorder and jungle-like feeding of individual characters on others (Ida on Vivaldo, the unpublished writer; the impresario Ellis on Ida; the successful writer Richard Silensky on his wife Cass; Rufus on his white girl friend Leona). In several regards the novel bears the marks of a highly ambivalent apprehension of urban American culture and correlates with Baldwin's intermittent returns to and absences from his country. *Another Country* can be understood as a violent gut reaction against America, and while his essayistic work would directly reflect his political involvement in the States from *Nobody Knows My Name* (1961) to *The Fire Next Time* (1963), it took Baldwin the fiction writer more time to articulate similar public themes in daylight settings, starting with a sensationalist play, *Blues for Mister Charlie* in 1964, through a subtly composite collection of stories in *Going to Meet the Man* (1965), to his most explicitly political novel *Tell Me How Long the Train's Been Gone* in 1968.

Baldwin's observations and first deductions from the civil rights struggle had been formulated in various articles right from or immediately after leaving the battle lines, and most of them were collected in *Nobody Knows My Name*. With "Notes for a Hypothetical Novel" (October 1960) this volume also contains what is probably the best anticipated conceptual frame of reference for *Another Country*: the germinal "image of a drunken man stumbling through his street" (119), "a handful of incoherent people in a violent world" (118), the shaky sense of identity of all Americans. "The bottomless confusion which is both public and private of the American republic" (122-23) for Baldwin is an expression of the moral evasion he diagnoses in all Americans, "revealed in those dreadful speeches by Eisenhower, those incredible speeches by Nixon" (125). The writer's task for Baldwin is to oppose this America of illusion and to "make it over" (126) by thoroughly reforming its values on the level of public and political morality.

For Baldwin the goal of the student civil rights movement was no less than this "liberation of the entire country from its most crippling attitudes and habits" (69). This statement from "East River Downton: Postscript to a Letter from Harlem" connects a reiteration of the systemic function of the black ghetto in "Fifth Avenue, Uptown: A Letter from Harlem" with a general assessment of the civil rights movement in its national context, before other essays (including the title essay) enter directly into Baldwin's personal experience with the South and the civil rights struggle there and elsewhere. The public housing of Harlem, "as cheerless as a prison", and the policeman "who moves through Harlem like an occupying soldier in a bitterly hostile country", reveal "how thoroughly the white world despises black Americans" (60-

61). The ghetto is living proof for "what we, this nation, have become"; "one cannot deny the humanity of another without diminishing one's own" (66). Two recent movements for Baldwin prove the fact "that the American Negro can no longer, nor will he ever again, be controlled by white America's image of him" (72): the Negro student movement, "the very last attempt made by American Negroes ... to force the country to honor its own ideals"; and the Black Muslim movement which, disbelieving any "American professions of democracy or equality," "insists on the total separation of the races" (69). Both movements have to do with the rise of Africa in world affairs and the reevaluation of her image.

Baldwin's own immersion in the American South at the moment of its being shaken by the accelerating civil rights struggle became a vivid object lesson. In many points it confirmed his views of American society as a whole; but it also gave him new insight into the strength of black people. Against the backdrop of the white Southerners' "defiance of change," of their "dishonest and insane arguments" against desegregation, or of the Southern mystique which even Faulkner actively prefers to defend ("Faulkner and Desegregation", Winter 1956), Baldwin provides some of the most sensitive and subtly shaded on-the-spot reporting one could wish for from an outsider to the actual political movement. The patient interviewing of the first black student, his parents and school principal in an unlocalized Southern high school ("A Fly in Buttermilk", October 1958); probing talks with black students in Tallahassee, Florida ("They Can't Turn Back", August 1960); and the programmatic "Nobody Knows My Name: A Letter from the South" (Winter 1959) – all these essays show the depth of Baldwin's concern as an engaged and increasingly uncompromising witness. He maintains that the South and the North differ not so much in the "spirit" of segregation as only in "the etiquette" (93); the entire nation has spent "a hundred years avoiding the question of the place of the black man in it" (98). In historical perspective, the South continues to use the Negro to assert its old identity in spite of the lost Civil War: "The North, by freeing the slaves of their masters, robbed the masters of any possibility of freeing themselves of the slaves" (105). Black men ("far stronger than the terrified white populace") and black women with their "as yet unwritten history" (99) are now witnessing their children, the student generation, "trying to save whatever good remains in those white people" (106).

Americans keep wondering what has "got into" the students. What has "got into" them is their history in this country. They are not the first Negroes to frighten the mob more than the mob frightens them ... But these young people are determined to make it [freedom] happen and make it happen now. They cannot be diverted. It seems to me that they are the only people in this country now who really believe in freedom. Insofar as they can make it real for themselves, they will make it real for all of us. The question with which they present the nation is whether or not we really want to be free. It is because these students remain so closely related to their past that they are able to face with such authority a population ignorant of its history and enslaved by a myth. And by this population I do not mean merely the unhappy people who make up the southern mobs. I have in mind nearly all Americans.[6]

The note of optimism one can still hear in this passage – and in "In Search of a Majority" of the same year – will not be so pronounced any more in Baldwin's assessment of his culture after the publication of *Nobody Knows My Name*. With *The Fire Next Time* the apocalyptic groundswell which is detectable in most of Baldwin's earlier writings becomes more pronounced, the appeal to the self-reforming potential of American society recedes before a more radical judgment, and a new militancy can be seen seeping into familiar key arguments, with bitterness as an explicit leitmotif (particularly in the first part, "My Dungeon Shook"). Once again, the black ghetto is seen as the primary symbol of American society, as well as the hotbed of a new awareness and the need for change.

The first part of the extended essay, subtitled "Letter to My Nephew on the One-Hundredth Anniversary of the Emancipation," launches its caustic argument "that the country is celebrating one hundred years of freedom one hundred years too soon" (22) with the unambiguous definition of the ghetto as a place intended to destroy its inhabitants, physically and mentally.

The historical proof for this rests in "the destruction of hundreds of thousands of lives" by an America which does "not want to know it" (15). The lesson from this for the black American, as the writer advises his nephew, is "to go behind the white man's definitions" (20), to shake off his conceptual control and subjugation as concretized in the ghetto and the term 'nigger.' The second part of the essay ("Down at the Cross: Letter from a Region in My Mind") undertakes this very act of liberation by delineating Baldwin's own road from his origins in the ghetto to a questioning of some of the conceptual main props of the American (or Western) nightmare and finally to a radical critique of Western history and religion. Since "the Negro's experience of the white world cannot possibly create in him any respect for the standards by which the white world claims to live" (35), the power of white people is generally considered "a criminal power, to be feared, but not respected and to be outwitted in any way whatever" (36-37). Since Negroes feel that the religious and ethical norms of the dominant society are instruments of subjection, they often will rebel against them and become criminalized. Baldwin himself chose the church to escape the pressure of the ghetto streets, but came to see the religious community as "a more subtle hypocricy", "a mask for hatred and self-hatred and despair" (57-58) and as lacking true love, yet at the same time as a realm of extraordinary "zest and joy" (59) creating an incomparable communal power for surviving and even forgetting oppression – all of which becomes manifest in the "tart and ironic, authoritative and double-edged" stance "that one hears in some gospel songs – and in all jazz" (60).

It took Baldwin a long time personally to disengage himself from the black church (whose blinding effect on dealing with the real world he was to dramatize most sharply in the figure of Leo Proudhammer's brother in *Tell Me How Long the Train's Been Gone*). A radical consequence in *The Fire Next Time* for Baldwin was a process of conceptual liberation: "To become a truly moral human being [one] must first divorce himself from all the prohibitions, crimes, and hypocricies of the Christian church" (67). For the white Christian "the spreading of the gospel ... was an absolutely indispensable justification for the planting of the flag" (65-66). To Baldwin "the fact of the Third Reich alone makes obsolete forever any question of Christian superiority, except in technological terms" (74). The Black Muslims in this perspective are doing conceptually (by opposing the myth of white supremacy with the message of black superiority) what the world in general will have to do in one way or another: "America and all the Western nations will be forced to reexamine themselves and release themselves from many things that are now taken to be sacred, and to discard nearly all the assumptions that have been used to justify their lives and their anguish and their crimes so long" (64). Encouraged by the rise of Africa (not by any change of heart of white Americans), the American Negro is now on the point of demanding "the most radical and far-reaching changes in the American political and social structure" (115), and by his demands to reform and save American society as a model for the world. As a last resort, if he cannot initiate these changes, he has the potential to cause the conflagration (if not the destruction) of this society.

Never before had Baldwin's thinking reached a similar point: Moral suasion and appeal to the self-interest of the dominant culture have given way to a radical critique of norms, values and self-concepts and to an explicit gesture of menace – still couched in biblical imagery but actualized by the respectful references to the Black Muslims. What made it impossible for Baldwin to fully agree with Elijah Muhammad and the Nation of Islam was his scepticism towards a black separatism resting on an "invented past" (111); and his insistence on the individual's worth and weight. "I am a writer. I like doing things alone" (97) was Baldwin's direct reply to Elijah, but behind it was his basic hesitation to view the problem of black Americans mainly on the level of power – "a principle that has nothing to do with love, a principle that releases them from personal responsibility" (110). And part of the inalienable personal responsibility of love for his people for Baldwin is his concern "for their dignity, for the health of their souls"; therefore he must "oppose any attempt that Negroes may make to do to others what has been done to them" – "Whoever debases others is debasing himself. That is not a mystical statement but a most realistic one, which is proved by the eyes of any Alabama sheriff – and I would not like to see Negroes ever arrive at so wretched a condition" (113).

The refusal to hate the white devil (in Black Muslim terminology) for Baldwin also implies the recognition of the kinship and mutual dependence of black and white Americans. "We, the black and white, deeply need each other here if we are really to become a nation" (131). With his better knowledge of the white man – a kind of parental understanding – the Negro has been led to feel comparatively little hatred, but instead "to dismiss white people as the slightly mad victims of their own brainwashing" (137). In such a view, the arena for a racial rapprochement is again mainly psychological, therapeutical, and dependent on individual consciousness (which Baldwin increasingly will subsume under the term "love") rather than on institutions and power control. Yet even on the level of individual awareness and psychological interrelatedness, Baldwin's writings after *The Fire Next Time* assumed a more uncompromising and radical note, implying a deepening psychological and moral antagonism between white and black and an increase on the writer's part of critical distance towards white history and enacted culture that was to culminate in *No Name in the Street* (1972).

The shift towards politically sharper contours can most clearly be seen in *Blues for Mister Charlie* (1964). Baldwin's second dramatic work instinctively goes for the more public didacticism of the stage at a time when LeRoi Jones was developing a self-consciously militant black theater addressed to an exclusively black audience. Baldwin was not interested in cultural black nationalism and therefore continued to have a mixed national audience in mind, but one can feel this audience split up along racial lines under the very impact of the play's stark and polemically charged oppositional images. Whereas Ida and Vivaldo at the conclusion of *Another Country* still kept open the chance for bridging their culturally conditioned antithetical origins and ambitions in an incremental act of mutual empathy, and while the oppositions of Baldwin's first play (*The Amen Corner*, written in 1954, but published only in 1968) still probed the options of a largely self-contained black world between secular and religious forms of moral or cultural identity (gospel vs. jazz, church vs. street, carnal vs. spiritual community, ending on a note of sentimental reconciliation of these diversionary forces), *Blues for Mister Charlie* sets Blacktown against Whitetown, the black church against white business and white law, and the reckless black rebel Richard Henry against the unrestrained white racist Lyle Britten. The play is allegorically located in "Plaguetown, U.S.A." as the stereotypical embodiment of a small

Southern town. And while Baldwin chooses the actual incident of Emmett Till's murder as germ of his plot, and strongly suggests the civil rights struggle through the figure of Richard Henry (son of the local minister Meridian Henry) who returns home after being made militant by his experience in the North, the play presents the conflict not as a political struggle but as an individual clash of stereotypical representatives whose sexual poses are the vehicles for expressing their political stances. The free use of cinematic techniques (simultaneous juxtaposition of different scenes and blending of time and sound levels) underline the collective implications of the action, while both the white liberal newspaper editor Parnell James and the black student Juanita (one of a whole group of demonstrating students who hopes she is pregnant by Richard) prove to be very ineffectual mediators for the murderous antagonisms between black and white. Even Juanita's and Meridian's love for Richard are powerless in the face of the public prejudice of Plaguetown, just as Lyle's and Parnell's earlier sex-affairs with black women have not changed their racial solidarity.

The drastic polemical simplifications of the cancer of white racism and the fever of black rage and resistance in *Blues for Mister Charlie* are replaced by more subtle dramatizations of these and related impulses in the black and white psyche in the collected stories of *Going to Meet the Man* (1965). The concluding title story is one of the most frightening and bitter enactments of Baldwin's persistent hypothesis of the diseased white mind: In the communal ritual of a lynching it tries to reveal the psychodynamics of white supremacy as sexual frustration merges with the lust for power. This syndrome is acted out by a white sheriff in the gruesome blending of the torturously empty sex act with his wife, the punishing of black protest marchers in prison on the preceding day, and the memory of his initiation when as a small boy he witnessed a lynching with his parents. "The Man Child" focuses on the interlinking of material greed and sadism in the lifelong 'friendship' of two white men unmasked in the final act of child murder. The aggressive tenor of these dramatizations of the white psyche is in stark contrast to the rest of the stories registering black states of mind. The early study of the effects of urban housing discrimination in "Previous Condition" is complemented by the sensitive portrait of a black professional woman in New York who begins to develop a new sense of her own worth as she overcomes her dependence on whites in "Come Out the Wilderness" (the jungle imagery referring unmistakably to white cultural norms). "The Rockpile" and "The Outing" take up the fictional world of John Grimes from Baldwin's first novel, but with a sharper sense of critical distance to the church and family community to whose restricting rules the sensuality of the young members forms a rebellious counternorm. "Sonny's Blues," usually considered the central text of the volume, uses music as a specifically black venue for reconstructing cultural and communal identity, as a self-directed creative impulse capable of counteracting the cooptation into bourgeois white values. The realigning of two alienated brothers by the communal force of black music anticipates some of the central concerns of Baldwin's last novel (*Just Above My Head*). "This Morning, This Evening, So Soon" goes one step further in showing a black protagonist and actor (who has found a positive identity through self-exile, work and marriage in Paris) on the eve of returning to America to confront the diseased norms of the dominant culture for which he has found an analogy in the relations between the French and the Algerians[7]. The majority of the texts in *Going to Meet the Man* articulate symbolic gestures of a more aggressive or combative spirit than were to be found in Baldwin's fictional work before, a tendency that was to gather momentum in his fourth novel.

Self-assertion without exile, but from the very heart of American society is the thematic focus of Baldwin's most openly political novel, *Tell Me How Long the Train's Been Gone* (1968). After a serious heart attack, the successful black actor Leo Proudhammer has occasion to reexamine in a series of flashbacks his whole life, which began under the constraints of the black ghetto, his father's social frustration and desperate black pride, his mother's capacity for enduring and his brother Caleb's late surrender (under the murderous repression of the prison system) to the opium of religion. The protagonist unswervingly seeks the public confrontation of the stage as a high status cultural institution, passing through the limbo of his actor's training under conditions of discrimination which he might not have survived without the alliance and love of his white co-student Barbara King, an heiress from Kentucky. Proudhammer eventually reaches a level of professional success where he becomes unassailable to social repression, at the price, however, of being cut off from his own group and of foregoing marriage with Barbara. This working arrangement between social status and symbolic representation of his group in his acting is seriously questioned when he meets and falls in love with Christopher, an example of the new black breed who believes in militant action. Proudhammer has to acknowledge the logic of armed resistance. Attending a rock concert with Christopher he cannot help but feel that the times have overtaken his conciliatory attitude. His admiration for the vital self-assurance of Christopher, a product of the ghetto streets like himself, is accompanied by consternation about his own tacit assumptions. The novel leaves us with the innuendo that Proudhammer might be at the beginning of a learning process with unforeseeable results.

The repercussions of the need for new forms of political action in the sense of organized militancy are most directly traceable in Baldwin's extended essay *No Name in the Street* of 1972. The title (a quote from a biblical prophecy of doom) explicitly locates the book in the streets of the ghetto, while the two parts of the essay (more evenly weighted than in *The Fire Next Time*) in their headings take up the religious imagery of baptizing, thus positing a semantic opposition between the lack of name and identity and the willed initiation of the author into a new community and sense of position. Once again the essay starts with an autobiographical self-examination: an analysis of the helplessness abutting in religious fanaticism of his father; the importance of Martin Luther King's assassination for Baldwin's political awareness; other moments of past and present experience that reveal the structure of American society. The concentrated probing of past moments in the light of a unifying political perspective bears the mark of kinship with *The Autobiography of Malcolm X* – Baldwin was concurrently working on a screen version of that book.

The nagging memory of his father's case is reinforced by Baldwin's awareness of his mental and material distance to a former classmate whom he revisits in order to let him have the new suit he wore only once, at King's funeral. This friend's narrow horizon of daily survival for Baldwin sets off a reconsideration of the ground he himself has covered since his flight from Harlem and America. Baldwin now realizes what he owes to the history of others, e.g. of the Algerians in France, in developing a sense of his own history. The Arab repression in a period of declining French colonial power becomes an object lesson for the fact that Algerians and American Negroes "were both, alike, victims of [European] history"; "their battle was not theirs alone but was my battle also" (41). The attitude of the French on the eve of Algerian independence recalls for Baldwin "the contemptible era" of the McCarthy years. What he witnessed on his first return to the States in 1952 opened his eyes "about the irresponsibility and cowardice of the liberal community" (30) – condoning the political climate and trying to coopt him as well. The role of Albert Camus in the France of the *plastique* bombs to Baldwin appears analogous to that of Faulkner in the initial phase of the civil rights struggle, with a partial exoneration for Faulkner who was "seeking to exorcize a history which was also a curse" (46). "For the subjugated, life itself depends on the speediest possible demolition of this history" (42).

Baldwin here takes a position close to that of Frantz Fanon when cultural concepts appear "as nothing less than a mask for power" (48). On joining the civil rights struggle in the South in 1957 (set off by a photo of 15-year-old Dorothy Counts in Charlotte, N.C., being reviled and spat upon by the mob), Baldwin had to face some of the most terrible people in the world ("as social and moral and political and sexual entities, white Americans are probably the sickest and certainly the most dangerous people, of any color, to be found in the world today", 55). However, "their wickedness was but the spirit and the history of America" (55). This uncompromising judgment on the dominant culture is hardly softened by Baldwin's also mentioning "the unbelievable dimension of their sorrow" or by his expressing a preference for Southerners over Northerners who have cold-bloodedly profited from the white folkways of the South (55-56). Inspite of Baldwin's having been torn between fear and rage while in the South, he clearly records a growing sense of identification with black people, a feeling of coming home, and explicitly stresses the daily heroism of black men (exemplified by the Reverend Shuttlesworth and his awareness "that the danger in which he stood was as nothing compared to the spiritual horror which drove those who were trying to destroy him", 66), and the secret strength of black women, "the most fearfully mistreated creatures of this region" (69) who appear to be imprisoned in their world. The first part of the essay ("Take Me to the Water") end on the radical statement that "slavery in America has not yet come to an end" and that "black men working for white men" is but a "democratic circumlocution for black men being owned by white men" (80).

The second part ("To Be Baptized") starts from the premise that "the West has no moral authority," and that its "immoral power has become a global problem, menacing the lives of millions" (85). "The failure of the moral energy of their oppressors," however, should encourage the oppressed "to forge a new morality" (90). The rest of the essay serves to point out and argumentatively support this new moral energy, first in memories of Baldwin's direct impressions of Malcolm X, a "true revolutionary" embodying "a virile impulse long since fled from the American way of life" (97-98), a man who "considered himself to be the spiritual property of the people who produced him" and who stood out not by his hatred for whites but his love for blacks, which made him "work on their hearts and minds to enable them to see their condition and change it themselves" (96-97). It is Baldwin's sense of obligation towards Malcolm's legacy, felt to be a continually growing force, that has taken him to Hollywood to work on the screenplay, and it is in the Beverly Hills Hotel that Baldwin experiences with renewed sharpness the conflict between his life as a writer and as a "public witness to the situation of black people". A broken black man (living out his mad fantasy as 'Prince of Abyssinia' in the Beverly Hills setting) and the unsolved fate of Baldwin's personal friend Tony Maynard (whom he has helped out of a Hamburg prison and continues to support against trumped up charges) serve to illustrate the situation of blacks in America: Not one black prisoner "has ever had a fair trial" (112), and the accumulated evidence of recent years and of history points toward something close to unconscionable genocide (129-31):

The truth is that this country does not know what to do with its black population now that the blacks are no longer a source of wealth, are no longer to be bought and sold and bred, like cattle; and they especially do not know what to do with young black men, who pose as devastating a threat to the economy as they do to the morals of young white cheerleaders. It is not at all accidental that the jails and the army and the needle claim so many, but there are still too many prancing about for the public comfort ... Some pale, compelling nightmare – an overwhelming collection of private nightmares – is responsible for the irresponsible ferocity of the Omnibus Crime Control and Safe Streets Act ... Black men have been burned alive in this country more than once – many men now living have seen it with their own eyes; black men and boys are being murdered here today, in cold blood, and with impunity; and it is a very serious matter when the government which is sworn to protect the interests of all American citizens publicly and unabashedly allies itself with the enemies of black men (129-31).

Baldwin sees the black ghetto "beleaguered, betrayed by the total lack of vision of the men in Washington," and using the example of the Black Panther Party for Self-Defense, introduces with growing vehemence the imagery of domestic colonialism to explain the relation between public policies and the existence of the ghetto. Ever since the March on Washington and King's "I have a dream" speech, the power structure and the interests behind it have struck back with increasing repression, culminating in the search-and-destroy operations against the Black Panthers (167). "I do claim that the law, as it operates, is guilty" (148); "the administration of justice in this country is a wicked farce" (149), and the "belief in due process" is a "self-delusion" (160), exacerbated by "the abject cowardice" of the "emancipated North" when faced with the suppression of the Black Panthers (164). Given this general assessment, Baldwin can only view the Black Panthers as "a great force for peace and stability in the ghetto," trying to ward off the "demoralization of the ghetto" by "restoring to the ghetto its honor" and by the necessary "creation and protection of a nucleus which will bring into existence a new people" (165). Apart from outspoken allies like Marlon Brando, whose participation in the Black Panther struggle Baldwin minutely reports, the only change in the dominant culture seems to occur among young people on whom the nature of their own culture is beginning to dawn (185). With Africa still only a potential cradle for a new black self-concept (191), Baldwin continues to view African Americans as pioneers in the struggle for "shaking off the control of the white man's fantasies": "To be liberated from the stigma of blackness by embracing it is to cease, forever, one's interior agreement and collaboration with the authors of one's degradation" (190). In this global historical sense, "Black is a tremendous spiritual condition, one of the greatest challenges anyone alive can face" (189-90). Baldwin ends the essay on this positive prospect for a new breed of blacks (which has caused him to replace the image of Dorothy Counts by that of the still endangered

Angela Davis), while he reiterates the threat of destruction for white culture from *The Fire Next Time*, but this time in the form of self-destruction through its own blindness, intransigence and 'innocence' (i.e., moral evasion).

Never before has Baldwin taken such a clearly partisan position for black militancy and its foundation in black history and collective black interests. And even though the ideologically charged concept of the individual and its indispensable value comes through in the portraits of Shuttlesworth, Malcolm, Brando and Huey Newton (and on a more personal level of polemics is admirably maintained in Baldwin's balanced and constructive judgment of Eldridge Cleaver who had so pitilessly calumniated him in 1968 in *Soul On Ice*)[8], Baldwin explicitly rejects any "separate peace" (126) for himself as an artist, writer and privileged spokesman of his group and claims his place as a moral witness and image maker if not as part of the heroically exposed front-line combat troops.

The spirit of opposition to persistent attitudes and values of the dominant power structure, and the concomitant public policies in the years after the black ghetto revolts culminating in the persecution of the Black Panthers, was to inform Baldwin's writing between 1971 and 1974. "An Open Letter to My Sister, Miss Angela Davis" (dated November 19, 1970) can be taken as a prelude to *No Name in the Street*, with the *New York Review of Books* (where it was published in January 1971) as a high caliber sounding board. Hailing "the enormous revolution in black consciousness" in the generation of Angela Davis, Huey Newton, George and Jonathan Jackson as the chance for "the beginning, or the end of America" (16), Baldwin contrasts their achievement ("that a whole new generation of people have assessed and absorbed their history and have freed themselves of it and will never be victims again") with the continuing "ignorance not merely phenomenal, but sacred, and sacredly cultivated" of white Americans unwilling "to become responsible for themselves, their leaders, their country, their children, or their fate" (15). The quality of America's leaders (Nixon, Agnew, Mitchell, Hoover, Reagan) spells the state of the nation's health, with numberless black prisoners "in our concentration camps" – all part of "a system ... whose only god is profit," "to be used by a carnivorous economy which democratically slaughters and victimizes whites and blacks alike" (15). The Marxist undertones of this assessment are not accidental and may contain echoes of some statements by Angela Davis herself. The war between the races is called "a civil war" between brothers, with the metaphor of the gas chamber as a reminder of genocidal tendencies in the culture. The willingness to fight for Angela Davis as for a common cause is unconditional: "For if they take you in the morning, they will be coming for us that night" (16). Baldwin's identification with a militant black liberation struggle (his letter was prompted by a *News-*

week cover photo showing Angela Davis in chains!) was never more explicit than here and in *No Name in the Street.*

The screenplay *One Day, When I Was Lost* (1972) was also a clear gesture of identification with Malcolm X, especially when taken in the context of Baldwin's refusal to give up control over his text and the envisioned cinematographic realization – a resistance to the suspected watering down and recharging of central images by the Hollywood establishment that eventually made Baldwin drop the film project and settle for the book publication. This act of solidarization with the antagonistic nature of Malcolm's vision should be respected even though Baldwin is guilty of eliminating key figures in Malcolm's social and political experience, of sentimentalizing personal and of simplifying power relations (especially those allegedly leading to Malcolm's assassination). But if the script falls short of capturing some of Malcolm's exemplary qualities, this seems due more to a failure of the shaping power within the required dramatic format and to attempts at popularizing Malcolm as a political hero, than to any basic disagreement with Malcolm's political message.[9]

Baldwin's two extended published dialogues (*A Rap on Race*, 1971, with the white anthropologist Margaret Mead; and *A Dialogue*, 1973, with the black poet and writer Nikki Giovanni) both testify to the writer's growing interest in voicing his views as a public witness of collective concerns. In the talk with Margaret Mead Baldwin reiterates many of his basic views on his own society and culture within the framework of Western culture, being well aware of the fact that he is addressing a white audience through a liberal mediator who agrees with most of his structural criticism but is not ready to accept his concept of collective guilt, nor of white being a state of mind from which all whites profit in some way. The dialogue becomes controversial when Baldwin places the burden for racial discrimination and its conceptual undertrimmings squarely on white culture ("The fact is I am an exile because I can't live in America under terms on which Americans offer me my life. And that says something about my country and nothing at all about me", 224).

Facing Nikki Giovanni (in London in November 1971, for the TV program "Soul!") was an act of willed identification with the young generation ("I have written off my generation", 91). Clearly admiring the new breed of writers like Giovanni because of their pride in being black and in providing their own definitions, Baldwin yet is wary of a new form of "romanticism" in setting up black as an absolute value, divorced from history, church and other collective experiences. Applying an earlier statement about Malcolm X from *No Name in the Street* to himself ("I am not responsible to anyone but the people who produced me", 73), Baldwin maintains that a black writer comes out of black traditions like the church, the music or the group history in his "responsibility to excavate the experience of the people who produced him" (80), in the sense of testifying and teaching a "buried history" (72), a black sense of life and a civilization which Europe attempted to destroy, but only managed to disperse (71). Just as Angela Davis was put in prison for teaching this new sense of black identity with its implicit rejection of white moral and aesthetic standards (75), so Baldwin feels called upon to give voice to the restorative and antinomian energy in the collective black experience ("You've got to liberate the energy in that word [black] – so it has a positive effect on the lives of people. There is such a thing as the living word", 89). His self-concept as a writer has moved away from the individualistic image of Leo Proudhammer towards the more collective orientation of testifying to the indestructible moral energy and vision in the black experience which American or Western culture – with its discredited morality, waning authority and threatened sense of identity – is in dire need of.

The position articulated in *A Dialogue* was to passionately inform and give unifying critical thrust to Baldwin's last convincing performance in the format of the extended essay, *The Devil Finds Work* (1976). This study of Baldwin's experience with American film again combines, as all his mature expository prose does, the incessant reexamination of the writer's own life and origins with the unremitting critical probing of cultural and psychological mechanisms of American society, especially in their unconscionably internalized forms. Film, for Baldwin, is an ideal medium for his testifying responsibility, because "the language of the camera is the language of our dreams" (34), and moviegoers as well as performers are exposed to the danger of surrendering to the projection of collective fantasies as they are thrown back from the screen (29). The cinema, as the most directly accessible cultural institution, for Baldwin very early became a testing ground not only for his interest in the fictional impulse, but also for his sense of life and identity and his growing awareness of 'otherness' within American culture. The book records in a freely associative and meandering (though basically chronological) progression Baldwin's odyssey through the bewildering Sargasso sea of the self-projections of a Hollywood-dominated commodity industry. Under the passionately anti-racist guidance of a rare white woman teacher, Baldwin gathers his first impressions of a black presence in theater and film; his return to these media initiates his liberation from a stifling church environment and becomes the vehicle for his increasingly sharp assessment of how blacks are inscribed in American films and of what this says about the tacit assumptions of American culture in putting them in their place. From desperate early attempts to discover even traces of his own existence or perception of reality in popular films of the 1930s and 40s (where only Bette Davis and Henry

Fonda seemed to possess traits which blacks could identify with), Baldwin comes of age via the life-giving discovery of the physical presence of black actors like Paul Robeson and Canada Lee and graduates to the analytical assessment of the ideological implications of a film like *The Birth of a Nation*, which through a "labyrinthine and preposterous plot" pretends to present history while it propagates "an elaborate justification of mass murder" with "the Niagara force of an obsession" (43-45). From the crucial parts of two mulattoes as symbols of evil in Griffith's film Baldwin deduces a general thesis on the inadvertent destruction (and denial) by America of its own children ("infanticide being just a step away from genocide"), this being "one of the keys to American history, present and past" (50). With growing subtlety and incisiveness, Baldwin then proceeds to demonstrate the convoluted motives and unconscionable implications of a culture struggling for nostalgic images about the relations of black and white while reiterating its old caricatures and murderous wishes in films like *In the Heat of the Night, The Defiant Ones* and *Guess Who's Coming to Dinner* – three films in which Sidney Poitier can insert a black subtext into the white-controlled plot-structure and discourse only in rare moments of sheer visual presence which capture a black sense of life through hidden reservoirs of feeling. Quoting a wealth of other films (Baldwin obviously was a ravenous moviegoer), Baldwin unremittingly pursues his hypothesis that American films could admit black characters and situations only on condition of siphoning out (97), sealing off (100) or distancing (109) and decontextualizing black experience and perception of reality, by ignoring the functional context of black life, and by underhandedly changing the testimony of the victim (110) in such a way as to make him instrumental to the "continued sanctification" (118) and/or justification of white history and its sense of life and morality (112-13). Films as different as *Lawrence of Arabia* and *Lady Sings the Blues* thus can be shown to grow out of a common deep structure intended to justify white history and empire (which "pivots on the infantile, and, in action, criminal delusions of possession, and of property", 115) and thus to also legitimize "the essential validity of the black condition" (112). But black actors, musicians and writers will continue to introduce another moral energy, even with the little space given them in white cultural institutions, rather than to "exist only in the brutally limited lexicon of those who think of themselves as white, and imagine, therefore, that they control reality and rule the world" (75). Poitier in *The Defiant Ones* uses that minimal space, when the film shows him thinking of his wife at one moment, and the real Billie Holiday in her autobiography (not the film on her) describes such a moment when she returns a stolen wallet to an unknown man ("Billie's morality, at that moment, indeed, threatens the very foundations of the Stock Exchange," 113). Baldwin, of course, knows from his own experience with the screenplay for Malcolm's autobiography how strong the mechanisms for removing any black ethos from products of the film industry are (he describes them tersely in practical terms, 95-99), and in his concluding film analysis (of *The Exorcist*) he shows how banal the self-propagated dramatization of the devil by white image makers is when compared with black people's testimony of evil in white society and culture. America and Hollywood have hardly yet begun to accept in their imagination the existence of black people and their experience.

Given the quality and range of Baldwin's critical perceptions in *The Devil Finds Work* it seems regrettable that he did not focus more often on film as a vehicle of culturally determinant images. Except for the early pieces on *Carmen Jones* and on *Porgy and Bess* (both published in *Commentary*, January 1955 and September 1956)[10], of which only the first unfolds a comparably sharp focus on image control in the interplay of physical presence with role ascription, Baldwin did not feel called upon at other times to write on film as reflecting cultural stereotypes and image manipulation. His exile from the States probably minimized the occasions for direct response to thematically pertinent American films. It is particularly to be regretted that we have no criticism from his hand on some black-directed films, or on films with a sharper emphasis on black self-assertion, as they set in at the end of the 1960s.

Whether prompted by his studies in film as a popular narrative form, or by the growing demand for self-references within black culture in the sense of community control and emphasis on the black oral tradition, Baldwin in his novel *If Beale Street Could Talk* of 1974 proffered in his own turn a sample of fictional didacticism geared towards boosting the image of black ghetto dwellers, and their capacity for self-reconstruction. Told in the untutored idiom of a young woman from the ghetto (the wife of a young black sculptor who is in prison on the false charges of having raped a West Indian woman), the novel shows the need for close family support and black solidarity in order to fight a social system and a legal machinery hostile to blacks on the one hand, and the false pretensions and religious addiction of a coopted black middle-class on the other. Black solidarity is seen as family-centered rather than political: his woman's unconditional loyalty, her expecting a child plus the full support of her parents will guarantee the prisoner's self-esteem and his release as an unbroken man – attitudes which are in sharp contrast to the lack of cohesion and self-respect in the young artist's own family (the despairing father commits suicide, the mother is a religious fool and hypocrite, and the sisters are caricatures of propriety). Unfortunately, the ascription of both constructive and disparaging traits is so glaringly exaggerated and schematized, the oral idiom so reductive and programmatic that the whole book reads more like the blueprint for a novel, than a fully imagined and dramatized situation. Baldwin in this book seems to write for a totally different audience, black rather than white or mixed, to be incited and driven into righteous rage rather than to be enlightened and mobilized on the cognitive level. The price the writer pays for this gut-level didactic appeal is a glaring reductionism on the psychological and linguistic level – the oral idiom, for example, seems rigid and gender-neutral, erasing the female narrator Tish to the point of making her a mere sounding-board for the dominant male characters, and therefore cannot come anywhere near the expressive force of the highly stylized, but mimetically true and gender-charged vernacular of Alice Walker's *The Color Purple* (1982).

Baldwin did not again seek the reductive didacticism of this social *roman à thèse* (to which he even sacrificed his unconventionally polymorphous concept of sexuality – in *If Beale Street Could Talk* all characters are either sexually very straight, or slanderously straight-laced). In his last fictional work, the novel *Just Above My Head* (1978), he returned to a clearly more individualized contextualization of family, art and sexuality in a social space which tries to bridge gospel music and individual pursuit of happiness, by testing the church through mundane forms of community like kinship, friendship and partnership. The recovery of life experience by memory and flashback again dominate the text, and through a feverishly obsessed concern with body sensations and a somewhat hysterical note of being threatened by decay (or dispersal on the social level), the rhetorical stance of the text in itself engenders a proliferating discourse of reported situations which makes this novel the longest in the Baldwin canon. The geographic mobility of its characters (between the South, New York and Europe) dissipates any feeling of rootedness, and the emphasis on sexuality as the main vehicle of self-definition somewhat narrows down the cultural and political implications of the book. Even music (the singing of gospel) becomes strangely subsumed, or absorbed, by the search for sexual fulfilment, like an iridescent disguise of the passionate longing for self-expression through physical union. It is probably far from accidental that the central female character, Julia, is shown as emancipating herself from sexual coercion to find self-realization in other areas, but at the price of largely fading out of the action, or the attention of the narrator (the bisexual brother of the homosexual protagonist). While the artist-protagonist dies a rather gruesomely lonely death in a toilet (symbolizing the wasteland of his unresolved social and sexual status), the narrator has himself escaped into the ostentatious security of marriage which is belied by his emotional identification with his brother.

Baldwin's last two novels in different ways bear the marks of the creative impasse of a writer no longer able to translate his vision of black culture within the context of American society into fictional terms. If we add to this the limitations of the narrative elaboration of Malcolm's career in *One Day, When I Was Lost*, Baldwin's failing skill for handling narrative discourse might prompt a reconsideration of the relative status of fictional and non-fictional works in his writing. Baldwin's expository prose up to *The Devil Finds Work* shows a continuing broadening of the writer's critical perspective on American and Western culture in their historical contexts, as well as a consistent radicalization of central concerns in his cultural critique. These can be traced all the way into his latest essayistic work, most clearly so to the introduction for *The Price of the Ticket*, Baldwin's collected (though regrettably not complete) nonfiction published in 1985, and with certain reservations also to *The Evidence of Things Not Seen* (1985). The latter text – a study of the so-called Atlanta murders (a series of unresolved assassinations of black children from 1979 into the 1980s) – was in several regards an unsuccessful attempt to analyze the social and administrative urban context in which a series of crimes was and continues to be couched, including structural conditions of the judicial and the publicity systems involved. With his last book Baldwin ventured into a field of investigation which proved far too charged with implications for the structure of American society as a power system for a writer inexperienced in the scrutiny of institutional networks, so that it was hardly to be expected that Baldwin would achieve more than a series of more or less inspired educated guesses about the forces involved. Although Baldwin pursues questions addressed to overall structural conditions of the society, thus remaining true to the broadened critical horizon of the late phase of his cultural critique, the book suffers from too many changes in focus and from a general inconclusiveness in the tracks pursued. Neither the destruction of black neighborhoods (like Auburn in Atlanta) through the imposition of one-way integration (22-25), nor the function of black administrators and mayors as masking the unbroken continuity of white power (26, 94-96), nor the desperate need for black solidarity as demonstrated by Ms. Camille Bell's founding the Stop the Murders Mothers Committee (54ff.) are treated in the book more than cursorily, and Baldwin is highly aware of his role in this investigation as "an interloper, a stranger" who "sometimes cursed the editor whose brainstorm this had been" (55). To write under contract did not improve the coherence of his long essay, and the most impressive statements are to be found not in the concretely detailed investigation of local and case-related conditions but on the level of reiterated general assessments of American culture – on its "ruthless dynamics of profit" ("The situation of Black Americans has been created, and is dictated by this motive, and there is no other single detail of American life more revelatory of Americans and, absolutely, no level of American life it does not corrupt", 31), on the moral vacuum "resulting in the betrayal of the social contract", with the doctrine of Manifest Destiny "nothing less than calculated and deliberate genocide" (42), and on "the real and unanswerable disaster" of white history based on "the cowardly delusion of White Supremacy" which has "transformed Africa" into a "horror" and the American dream into an "intolerable nightmare" (80, 82), with the ever receding, but not yet abandoned utopia of America as "the only nation under heaven that contains the universe," "that can hope to liberate – to begin to liberate – mankind from the strangling idea of the national identity and the tyranny of the territorial dispute" (124-125).

Baldwin has always remained true to his own critical vision of the black man as a touchstone for the moral and ideological fibre of the dominant culture surrounding him. The black ghetto of American cities as the exemplary symbol of his society for Baldwin expanded to all of Western culture and to its global context. Born into a Southern community displaced by migration to one of the urban centers of the North, Baldwin knew that he was kept intact by the communal protection of family members, teachers and neighborhood solidarity until as the oldest of nine children he could assume responsibility for the younger children and the survival of the family as a whole by consistently refusing to accept the conditions of a segregated and pauperized ghetto.[11] It was his ability with the living word that provided his main route of escape from the ghetto streets which were threatened not only by the habitual rage and hopelessness but also by the invasion of drugs after the end of the war. Self-tutored through reading, preaching, school journal and review writing Baldwin joined the public critical dialogue on American society and culture stimulated by liberal and leftist magazines (like *Commentary* and *Partisan Review*), using Richard Wright as a distancing amplifier for his own views on the uses of literature and race in America.

Claiming no school in support of his cultural assessments, Baldwin also left no school or disciples in his wake. Privileged by early success which earned him mass audience appeal after his first two book titles, Baldwin, who always preferred to think of himself as a witness responsible to all black Americans, soon found himself pushed into the role of spokesman for his black countrymen. Granting Baldwin this status reflected the opinion of a white national (and later also international) audience more consistently than the changing (and often revisionary) climate for black self-concepts. Baldwin remained the most lucid and persistent advocate for black Americans to white readers adding exhortatory edge to his pronouncements by his passionate belief in a common destiny (or "conundrum") of all Americans.

His self-exile never changed Baldwin's intense identification with America, but definitely added to his critical horizon and to an independence of judgment at a clear remove from interest groups and short-lived movements.

But Baldwin tried to assimilate specific radicalizations of black perceptions in a critical vision that tended to be comprehensive and categorical rather than practical and partisan. He gave vocal support to political leaders and movements without risking direct recruitment by them, and he always felt free to syncretize ideas from various quarters in his own broadside attacks on entrenched collective white attitudes and their socio-psychological subsoil. The personal and conceptual criticism he drew from black radical groups and positions (culminating in Cleaver's venomous attack) did little harm to either his audience appeal or the gradual broadening and growing incisiveness of his cultural critique.

The academic reception of his writing was most appreciative at the beginning of his career and began to fade with *Tell Me How Long the Train's Been Gone*. Despite the recognized brilliance of his essays, the discussion tended to privilege his fictional work, but even here the sum total of substantial critical comment is relatively slender considering the durable positive reader response to Baldwin's work. The accumulated critical writing on Baldwin's more than twenty booktitles clearly falls below the analytical attention accorded a contemporary black writer like Ralph Ellison (with only two books to his name until recently), both in quantity and in quality.

The main strength of Baldwin's critique rests in his eloquently and passionately reasoned indictment of culturally engrained disabilities in the historical, social and moral perception of American society, especially in its ubiquitous racism as a self-destructive cultural and psychological mechanism. This indictment is grounded in incontrovertible personal experience reflecting the symptomatic collective experience (and judgment) of black Americans vis-à-vis the moral and aesthetic norms of the dominant culture. The main weakness of Baldwin's critical vision may be located in his restricted focus on the arena of the individual social and moral sensibility as sharply illuminated and minutely analyzed fountainhead for social action, but stopping short of including institutional and economic factors in the analysis of the social and ideological structure of his society. This self-limiting focus (which in fictional discourse sometimes generates an excess of sentimentalism) in his political rhetoric enhances the therapeutic function of language in the sense of moral suasion, and thus salvages the utopia of a society based on the free consent of its individual members – a utopia which Baldwin expands from the founding promise of America into a multiracial society ready to replace domination and conquest by other, more brotherly values. Baldwin's voice was and remains a solitary one, with little support in social or political theory but with a powerful appeal to the social and moral imagination of readers in a post-nationalist world of increasingly global concerns which would include both the facing of new liabilities and the pursuing of age-old dreams.

Notes

1 Trudier Harris. *Black Women in the Fiction of James Baldwin*. Knoxville: University of Tennessee Press, 1985.

2 For all essays quoted here, the original date and place of publication can be found in *The Price of the Ticket* (see the listing of Baldwin's major works below). For reasons of accessibility, the page numbers for all quotes from Baldwin's works refer to paperback editions (as given in the title listing after the first edition in parentheses, usually under the date of the first printing of the softcover edition).

3 "Lockridge. 'The American Myth'" (originally in *The New Leader*, April 10, 1948), in *The Price of the Ticket*, 13-18.

4 Baldwin made two trips to Africa which both left no echo in his writing – a two month trip (with his sister) in 1962, and a shorter trip in December 1963 (with Sidney Poitier, Harry Belafonte and Thurgood Marshall). V. W. J. Weatherby, *James Baldwin. Artist On Fire*. N.Y.: Dell, 1989, 230-233, 267-268.

5 Hans-Christoph Ramm, *Modell für eine literarische Amerikakunde*. Bern: Peter Lang, 1989, 129-254.

6 "They Can't Turn Back" (originally in *Mademoiselle*, August 1960), in *The Price of the Ticket*, 228.

7 The same topic (and geographical consequence) was treated more extensively in the novel *The Stone Face* (N.Y., 1963) by William Gardner Smith, a black novelist from Philadelphia.

8 In "Notes On a Native Son" (*Soul On Ice*, N.Y. 1968, 97-111), Cleaver declares Baldwin to be an "intellectual sycophant", "a white man in a black body", and equates his tenuous masculinity with his lacking rapport to black people.

9 Cf. also Patsy B. Perry, "*One Day When I Was Lost*: Baldwin's Unfulfilled Obligation," in T. B. O'Daniel, ed. *James Baldwin: A Critical Evaluation*. Washington, D.C., 1977, 213-227.

10 "Carmen Jones: The Dark Is Light Enough" and "On Catfish Row" in *The Price of the Ticket*, 107-112, 177-181.

11 V. "Why I Left America. Conversation: Ida Lewis and James Baldwin" in A. Chapman, ed. *New Black Voices*, N.Y., 1972, 409-419.

Major Works by James Baldwin

Go Tell It On the Mountain. N.Y.: Alfred A. Knopf, 1953 (Dell, 1955), (novel)
Notes of a Native Son. Boston: Beacon Press, 1955 (Beacon, 1957) (essays)
Giovanni's Room. N.Y.: Dial Press, 1956 (Dell, 1958) (novel)

Nobody Knows My Name: More Notes of a Native Son. N.Y.: Dial Press, 1961 (Dell, 1963) (essays)
Another Country. N.Y.: Dial Press, 1962 (Dell, 1963) (novel)
The Fire Next Time. N.Y.: Dial Press, 1963 (Dell, 1970) (essay)
Blues for Mister Charlie. N.Y.: Dial Press, 1964 (Dell, 1965) (play)
Going to Meet the Man. N.Y.: Dial Press, 1965 (Dell, 1976) (stories)
The Amen Corner. N.Y.: Dial Press, 1968 (play)
Tell Me How Long the Train's Been Gone. N.Y.: Dial Press, 1968 (Dell, 1969) (novel)
A Rap On Race (with Margaret Mead). Philadelphia: J. B. Lippincott Co., 1971 (Dell, 1974) (dialogue)
No Name in the Street. N.Y.: Dial Press, 1972 (Dell, 1973) (essay)
A Dialogue (with Nikki Giovanni). Philadelphia: J. B. Lippincott Co., 1973 (dialogue)
One Day, When I Was Lost. N.Y.: Dial Press, 1973 (scenario)
If Beale Street Could Talk. N.Y.: Dial Press, 1974 (Signet, 1975) (novel)
The Devil Finds Work: An Essay. N.Y.: Dial Press, 1976 (Dell, 1990) (essay)
Just Above My Head. N.Y.: Dial Press, 1978 (Dell, 1980) (novel)
The Evidence of Things Not Seen. N.Y.: Holt, Rinehart and Winston, 1985 (Holt & Co., 1986) (essay)
The Price of the Ticket: Collected Nonfiction 1948-1985. N.Y.: St. Martin's/Marek, 1985 (essays)

For further bibliographical information consult:

O'Daniel, Therman B., ed. "A Classified Bibliography" in *James Baldwin: A Critical Evaluation.* Washington, D.C.: Howard University Press, 1977.
Standley, Fred L. and Nancy V. *James Baldwin: A Reference Guide.* Boston: G. K. Hall, 1980.
Porter, Horace A., "James Baldwin: A Selected Bibliography" in *Stealing the Fire: The Art and Protest of James Baldwin.* Middletown, Conn.: Wesleyan University Press, 1989.

Richard Stinshoff

Edward P. Thompson

(1924-)

In January 1990 the peoples of Eastern Europe had finally blown away their oppressors. The petrified structures of Stalinism had eventually come tumbling down; their shatters littering the streets of Budapest, Leipzig, Prague, and after a terrible bloodbath, Bucharest. For most politicians and intellectuals in the capitalist democracies of the West "the end of history", as a political advisor to the State Department in Washington, D.C. had called it in the summer of 1989, seemed to have come into its own. "The universalisation of western liberal democracy as the final form of human government" seemed to be near[1].

At this juncture Edward P(almer) Thompson, "historian, polemicist and prominent peace and human rights activist" as a recently published biographical dictionary introduces him[2], who had for the past ten years committed his energies to building a European Movement for Nuclear Disarmement (END), raised his voice issuing a prophetic warning. He appealed to the western peace movement

to enforce some major concessions from the west to match those made by the east. ... Let me give examples. The Brezhnev Doctrine has been explicitly renounced. But there has as yet been no sign whatsoever of the renunciation of the Truman Doctrine (1947) by which the US not only asserted a "right" to intervene in Greece and Turkey but also to intervene when *any* nation was threatened by communist "subversion". Nor is there any repudiation of the Eisenhower Doctrine (1957) which extended the US sphere of direct intervention to the middle east (further extended by Carter to the Persian Gulf). The Truman Docrine was nothing less than the direct passing-on of ugly British imperialist and royalist strategies to the United States during Attlee's bankrupt second Labour post-war administration. These doctrines license the perpetual presence in the Mediterranean and Persian Gulf of the US 7th Fleet. ... The cold war with the Soviet Union is not the true occasion for the deployment of the fleet, but the pretext – the plausible excuse for a wider exercise in imperialist control, an excuse made less plausible every day.[3]

Who is this man, who – from a marxist position critical both of Soviet 'nomenklatura' and of capitalist imperialism – dared to question claims that recent developments in Eastern Europe were "the victory of justice, of freedom over tyranny, the rallying of all good and reasonable men and women"?[4]

He also dared to remind us that it is movements like Charter 77 in Czechoslovakia or the Hungarian opposition groups to whom more credit might be due for challenging the petrified and repressive system of communist orthodoxy than to western style liberty and equality of opportunity. What strange tribe of intellectuals does this man belong to, who never went for more than a B.A. degree, but who eventually held a very prestigious university position from which he resigned, some years later proudly explaining that "socialist intellectuals must occupy some territory which is, without qualification, their own ... places where no one works for grades or for tenure but for the transformation of society"[5]?

How do we approach this distinguished historian enjoying international reputation for his pioneering study of the origins of the working class in England and at the same time marking for over 30 years one of the most original and unorthodox positions in European marxist thinking?

What are we to make of this unusual scholar who in his characteristic vein of self-confident doggedness for more than the last decade has committed most of his energies to the peace movement, thus almost totally interrupting his activities as a researcher and writer, yet publishing a utopian novel entitled *The Sykaos Papers* in 1988?

In this didactic piece of fiction the poet Oi Paz from the alien planet Oitar (= ratio, a place of supreme reason) endangered by the cosmic exhaustion of its solar system visits our planet exploring it for the purpose of intended colonization. He calls our earth Sykaos since to him the terrestrial environment for all its seductive beauty (threatened by nuclear holocaust and environmental collapse as the result of human behavior organized around the principle of individual free choice) appears both *psychotic* and *chaotic*. Under the impact of his home planet's doom to gradual extinction, Oi Paz, like the other Oitarians, has been programmed by the Gracious Goodnesses, a powerful super-computer masked as a cabinet of governing sages, to fulfil his assigned role. But Oi Paz very gradually comes to understand the principles of earthly behaviour because his programming allows for a certain degree of imagination. For all their individual free choices terrestrials to Oi Paz collectively seem just as programmed as he is. After escaping a paranoid web of international intriguing and Cold War politics Oi Paz is able to return to Oitar taking along Helena, en earthly anthropologist he has fallen in love with. In the end their son Adam defying Oitar's Gracious Goodnesses leaves the dying planet in a spacecraft together with a young Oitarian Eve called Vev looking for some distant habitable planet. Although in parts somewhat laboured and overblown with detail this contemporary fable tells us a lot about E. P. Thompson's frame of mind, more than about his perhaps less than ideally suited aspirations to writing fiction. It shows him as a thinker with a fundamentally optimistic vision of human future.

Amazingly, Thompson has been able to sustain this almost youthful optimism throughout the intellectual and political frustrations in his life, which were far from peripheral as we shall see. For this prominent trait in his character he may be just as indebted to a fairly exclusively English tradition as he is – according to his self-assessment – for his intellectual habits:

Take Marx and Vico and a few European novelist away, and my most intimate pantheon would be a provincial tea-party: a gathering of the English and the Anglo-Irish. Talk of freewill and determinism, and I think first of Milton. Talk of man's inhumanity, I think of Swift. Talk of morality and revolution, and my mind is off with Wordsworth's Solitary. Talk of the problems of self-activity and creative labour in socialist society, and I am in an instant back with William Morris – a great bustard like myself, who has never been allowed into the company of such antiquated (but "reputable") eagles as Kautsky or Plekhanov, Bernstein or Labriola – although he could, if given the chance, have given them a peck or two about their gizzards.[6]

Such an intellectual attitude has made him self-confident enough, as a committed Marxist and socialist, to put Marx into perspective:

I think there is, indeed, much energy and ability inside those barrels of enclosed Marxisms which stand, row upon row, in the corridors of Polytechnics and universities. By striking a sharp and bitter blow at the Althusserian bungs, I hope I may let a little of that energy get out. If it should do so, then the problems of creating in this country an independent Left engaged in a continual and fraternal dialogue of practice with the larger Labour movement, might not prove insuperable after all. Those massive and impassive "structures" of our time might prove to be more vulnerable to human agencies than the Marxisms suppose. And if any minds should get out, I hope they will bring Marx with them. I hope they will not bring *only* Marx; and they must certainly rid themselves of the truly scholastic notion that the problems of our time (and the experiences of our century) will become understood by the rigorous scrutiny of a text published one hundred and twenty years ago. To return, in every motion of analysis, to propositions of Marx is like going on a cross-country run in leaden boots. William Morris expressed the matter with unerring sanity. "Tough as the job is you ought to read Marx", he advised a correspondent: "up to date he is the only completely scientific Economist on our side." As the assembled ranks of Marxists express their sense of scandal, or dissolve into laughter, I will continue my argument. It is not on the question of whether or not it is adequate to describe Marx as an "Economist". This was the Marx available to Morris; and, one might add, it is the Marx to which the man is reduced, in effect, by "mode of production" manipulators and by *Capital* navel-scrutinising groups. The point is, that *Marx is on our side; we are not on the side of Marx.* His is a voice whose power will never be silenced, but it has never been the only voice, and its discourse does not have limitless range.[7]

This is the political approach which has, from the very first, influenced Thompson's work as a teacher, scholar and writer and which is at the core of his "socialist-humanist" understanding of Marx and Marxism, informing all of his scholarly and political or polemical writing. This is the stance that has made him such a well-known intellectual and political figure in Britain and beyond. Yet for all his achievements as a historian and political activist, Thompson originally wanted to become a poet like his father and brother. This is perceptible in his fluent, readable style, at its best in his long historical narratives like *The Making of the English Working Class*[8]. It may also be felt in his paramount inclination towards using the social and historical evidence extant in English literature, e.g. Blake, Wordsworth or Morris, as sources equal to any other when it came to demonstrating the impact the Industrial Revolution or Victorian Britain had not only on material and social change but also on changes in the minds of the people.

The range of E. P. Thompson's political and intellectual interests and activities has been so broad, the sheer amount of his writing so massive and diverse – including scholarly books, articles and reviews, philosophical and political polemics and essays, journalism and even fiction[9] – that it would be both difficult and bold to attempt a complete survey in an introductory essay like this. Fortunately there has been a fairly good amount of critical analyses of E. P. Thompson's works published in recent years[10]. This enables me to concentrate on highlighting, discussing, and putting into perspective the basic concepts for understanding history that Thompson has become so well known for. The recent war in the Persian Gulf with its terrible toll in human lives and ecological devastation was not only militarily but also ideologically used by the leading power in the alliance against Saddam Hussein, the USA, to launch an offensive towards a new "world order" after the breakdown of the USSR as a superpower.

Writing in the aftermath of this pivotal event it is worth while remembering some basic insights E. P. Thompson expressed on occasion of another of those hundreds of military conflicts since the end of World War II, most of them so called "low-level, low-intensity" warfare. The war waged by Britain in 1982 to recover the Falklands from Argentine for comparable reasons happened to get similarly spectacular media attention as the war in the Persian Gulf has now enjoyed. The Falklands – as we will remember – were invaded by Argentine, at that time a military dictatorship, which clearly was an act of unwarranted aggression on their side. Eventually the islands were recovered by a British task force, involving the loss of some 1,700 lives on both sides, not to speak of the 4 billion pounds spent by Britain alone on dispatching a major armada into the southern Atlantic. To the majority of her western allies Britain's claims to this tiny archipelago seemed historically somewhat questionable, and British enthusiasm for recovering them by military force hardly understandable. Yet the war proved immensely popular in Britain and crucially beneficial to Mrs Thatcher's popularity which happened to be at a low point due to the adverse effects of her policy of massive deindustrialisation between 1979 and 1982. E. P. Thompson's comment on the effects of this act of organized violence stands out among the few Britons who publicly raised their voices in condemnation of this madness:

The response to the Falklands crisis has been one of imperial atavism ... [and has] shown us at least this – how close to the surface of our even-tenored life the atavistic moods of violence lie. We shall pay for it for a long time, in rapes and muggings in our cities, in international ill-will, and in the stirring up of ugly nationalist sediment which will cloud our political and cultured life.[11]

This brief quote illustrates one of the most typical traits in the sphere in which he was brought up: In spite of his pugnacious mind and behaviour when it comes to taking on political or intellectual opponents he has always been convinced that non-violence is the only viable means of solving conflicts in human interaction. E. P. Thompson was born in 1924 into a family of liberal-radical dissenters[12]. His father, the writer Edward John Thompson (usually referred to as Edward Thompson), and his mother, an American by birth, were both known to be highly critical of British imperialism, which they had been able to experience during Edward Thompson's time as an educational missionary in India, where he had supported Indian nationalism and become a personal friend of Nehru. Growing up near Oxford E. P. Thompson was educated at Kingswood, a Methodist public school, entering Cambridge University in 1941, where he first read literature, later switching to history. E. P. Thompson's interest in Marxism was roused at the early age of sixteen. Only two years later, in 1942, he joined the Communist Party of Great Britain (CPGB) during his time at Cambridge, working on its Yorkshire district committee from 1948 onwards. After spending military service as an officer fighting in France and Italy Thompson went back to Cambridge receiving his BA degree in history in 1946 – the only formal academic qualification he ever cared to get. Inspired by the example of his older brother Frank, a war-hero and communist[13], E. P. Thompson also spent some time in Yugoslavia and Bulgaria as a volunteer working on basic reconstruction projects and building railways in Bosnia immediately after the war. This seminal period in his life seems to have formed Thompson's notion of communists as people committed to building mass movements close to the real needs of the people and capable of revolutionary initiative and of forging broad anti-fascist, anti-imperialist popular front alliances[14].

After the war at Cambridge E. P. Thompson met his future wife Dorothy, today a professor of history at the University of Birmingham, who was at that time very active in the *Communist Party Historians' Group* (CPHG), which had developed in 1946 as a consequence "from the need to discuss a new edition of A. L. Morton's *A People's History of England*, first published in 1938 by the Left Book Club."[15] Among those belonging to this group were Maurice Dobb and Dona Torr plus a number of younger historians such as Rodney Hilton, Christopher Hill, Eric J. Hobsbawm, E. P. Thompson and Dorothy Thompson, George Rudé, John Saville, Victor Kiernan and others, who had gotten their degrees either in the mid-thirties, like Hill and Kiernan, or just after the war. The influence of this group on Thompson was both enormous and lasting, even after it dissolved when most of its members left the party in the wake of the brutal suppression of the Hungarian uprising in 1956. Eric Hobsbawm recalls that for most of its members it was a circle about which "physical austerity, intellectual excitement, political passion and friendship are probably what the survivors remember best – but also a sense of equality."[16] This atmosphere also involved, as E. P. Thompson remembers, the ability of mutually providing and accepting rigorous intellectual criticism which he has since then considered an essential feature of the marxist method.

In 1948 the Thompsons moved to Halifax in Yorkshire, where E. P. had been able to get a position as lecturer in the Department of Extramural Studies at the University of Leeds, which he held until 1965. His teaching experience and research results in these years provided the foundation of his *The Making of the English Working Class*, a more than 900-page seminal study of the formation of the working class in England between the 1790s and the 1830s, first published in 1963 and eventually establishing the basis for Thompson's lasting reputation as a non-orthodox marxist historian. His specific concern for the history of the people and their movements, however, had transpired already in his first book, a voluminous political biography *William Morris – Romantic to Revolutionary* (1955), also developing from his teaching in adult education at Leeds University. The book on Morris essentially showed in which way Thompson would make use of history: To highlight what he considered basic issues of the present – such as the lack of social and political dynamism in the period of the Cold War – by carefully analyzing historically comparable situations without trivializing them into convenient blueprints for present-day problems. Using his characteristically epic narrative style to confront his readers with different and often seemingly incompatible layers of reality Thompson presented Morris as someone who was motivated by the beginning economic, cultural and intellectual crisis of Victorian Britain in the 1870s to cross – fairly late in his life, yet very deliberately – the "river of fire" between bourgeois and socalist thinking and acting. To have recovered Morris for those trying to think creative ways out of today's seemingly total cultural hegemony of advanced capitalism was not the least of E. P. Thompson's merits, yet one which today tends to be among the least remembered. He demonstrated how Morris combined aesthetic sensibility with an acute awareness of the "innate moral baseness" of Victorian society. As Thompson has argued in a more recent re-assessment:

In Morris's critique of capitalist society, there is no sense in which morality is seen as secondary, power and productive relations as primary. The ugliness of Victorian social relations and 'the vulgarities of civilization' were 'but the outward expression of the innate moral baseness into which we are forced by our present form of society ...'. This moral baseness was 'innate', within the societal form: 'economics' and 'morality' were enmeshed in the same nexus of systematized social relationships, and from this nexus an economic *and* a moral logic must ensue.[17]

Thompson here has apparently abandoned the beaten tracks of orthodox Marxist thinking which conceives of the economic mode of production as heuristicly prior to its cultural ramifications.

When Morris looked forward to the society of the future, he proposed that a quarrel between desire and utilitarian determinations would continue, and that desire must and could assert its own priorities. For to suppose that our desires must be determined by our material needs may be to assume a notion of 'need' itself already determined by the expectations of existing society. But desire can also impose itself as 'need'. In class society it may be felt in the form of alienation, desire unsatisfied; in the society of the future in the form of more open choices between needs.[18]

In 1956, still actively engaged in adult education in the West Riding of Yorkshire, Thompson came to experience the most important watershed in his intellectual and political career: In February of that year Chruchev gave his famous speech at the 20th congress of the Communist Party of the USSR, severely criticizing Stalin's dictatorship. When his speech was published in June, it immediately provoked fierce debates in most communist parties in the East and in the West about the terror and the atrocities of the Stalin era and about the crisis of international communism. The tenor of this speech, however, eerily resonated with the crushing of the uprisings in Poznan (in June) and in Budapest (in October/November) by Soviet troops. In July, E. P. Thompson and John Saville had begun to edit a journal called *The Reasoner – A Journal of Discussion*. Its motto was "to leave error unrefuted is to encourage intellectual immorality – Karl Marx", its objective was to focus the discussion of Stalinism within the CPGB. The third issue proved to be the last. After the tanks had ruthlessly put down the uprising in Budapest, Dorothy and E. P. Thompson together with most of their friends left the party, which lost almost 10,000 of its members between early 1956 and early 1958, because its leadership was unable or unwilling to initiate and permit a critical discussion of the ills of Stalinism. For the Thompsons as for many of their friends this step was a final consequence after many years of doubt and futile attempts to reconcile intellectually irreconcilable theoretical and political contradictions; most notably questions about the range and function of human agency in a societal setup determined by economically defined modes of production; or the leadership claim of the party and its cadres versus the role of ordinary people in revolutionary class struggle.

The once dissident faction within the CPGB – the Thompsons, Ken Alexander, Doris Lessing, Raymond Williams, Ralph Miliband and others – who had gathered around *The Reasoner*, now renewed this journal as a non-partisan programmatic voice of Marxist dissent *The New Reasoner – A Quarterly Journal of Socialist Humanism* (NR). In its ten issues published between 1957 and 1959 the journal successfully attempted to combine theoretical debate and current political analysis including cultural aspects of advanced capitalism. Its contents were a creative mixture of articles, reports reviews, fiction and poetry, at times trying to direct the attention of its readers towards the situation of dissidents in communist countries or towards third world issues. Foremost on its agenda was the rethinking of Marxism in terms of a non-bureaucratic Socialism and the developing of visions for changing and renewing society in a way that puts everyday people's needs first.

This impulse is mirrored in the very titles of some programmatic essays E. P. Thompson contributed – *Socialist Humanism* (NR 1, 1957); *Agency and Choice* (NR 5, 1958); *The New Left* (NR 9, 1959). The latter essay, for example, examined how grass-roots democratic socialist movements in the capitalist democracies of the West had grown out of what was initially a cultural opposition (Rock, Beat) to the decade of political apathy after World War II, characterized by the Cold War, the growing threat of nuclear war and the continuing colonial and imperialist repression both on the side of the USA and the USSR. For Britain, Thompson identified three strongholds of these tendencies: Dissident communists (ex-CPGB members), frustrated socialists on the left wing of the Labour Party, and independent young intellectuals such as those around the journal *Universities and Left Review* (ULR) edited by Stuart Hall in Oxford since 1956 as an authentical voice of the critical post-war generation. This strand of the New Left did not only define itself as opposed to the political and cultural establishment of the day, but also as opposed to the 'Old' Left in the labour movement, who failed to realize the potential of the New Left relying on people's growing awareness of new needs and interests and their increasing willingness to fight for self-realization instead of drowning in the sea of capitalist consumerism.

At the end of 1959 *The New Reasoner* and the *Universities and Left Review* merged into the *New Left Review* (NLR), edited by Stuart Hall, who was supported by an editorial board of 26 members. The editorial of the first issue expressed the policy of the journal which was also meant to be an organizational focus for the New Left movement sponsoring New Left clubs for political discussion and mutual education.

We are convinced that politics too narrowly conceived has been a main cause for the decline of socialism in this country, and one of the reasons for the disaffection from socialist ideas of young people in particular. The humanist strengths of socialism – which are the foundation for a genuinely popular socialist movement – must be developed in cultural and social terms, as well, as in economic and political.[19]

What the NLR subsequently offered were elements of a comprehensive economic, political and cultural examination of post-World War II capitalism. The range of issues included the analysis of specific features ensuring the remarkable resurgence and strength of advanced capitalism (like the consumerist manipulation of needs, the Fordist modernization of economic organization, and the lack of / necessity for workers' control), and last not least, a critique of mainstream western philosophy and social theory. Among Thompson's important contributions to these debates were essays like *Outside the Whale* [20], centering on Auden's *Spain* and Orwell's *Inside the Whale* and *Nineteeneighty-four* as documents of long pent-up frustration with communism voiced by intellectuals of the 1930s and 1940s, who like others of their generation (Koestler, Hemingway, Dos Passos) once had shown such fervent revolutionary zest.

In *Revolution*[21] Thompson presented a critique of the single-mindedness of both revolutionary and reformist strategies of the Old Left, advocating a more realistic model based on dialectically integrating revolutionary and reformist political practice. The essay prompted a vidid discussion causing Thompson to put forward a more elaborate version of his approach in a reply entitled *Revolution again! Or shut Your Ears and Run*[22] which, moreover, contained important insights into newly developing forms of proletarian consciousness. Another important contribution to NLR in this early period was Thompson's long review[23] of Raymond Williams's book *The Long Revolution* (containing a first elaboration of his concept of working class culture as "a whole way of life"), which Thompson used as the starting point for a highly original discussion of the history of class culture.

All this has to be seen against the backdrop of the developing New Left in Britain: In late 1960 there were as many as 45 New Left Clubs with a paying membership of 3,000 and NLR had a circulation of 10,000[24]. This potential, most unfortunately in Thompson's view, could not yet be harnessed to the traditional trade union and labour movement, although its mobilising strength and radicalism was already making itself felt in the Easter marches of the Campaign for Nuclear Disarmament (CND; founded in 1958 by Bertrand Russell) attracting tens of thousands of demonstrators every year. Despite his strategic and tactical criticism Thompson would some ten years later align himself again actively with CND, because it was "precisely the popular, extra-parliamentary, quasi-libertarian and democratic mass movement that has best represented ... [my] vision of a socialist future"[25].

Meanwhile in 1962/63, Thompson suffered from what he personally perceived as the most painful rupture in his career as a political activist: He, his wife and their political friends chose to withdraw from the editorial board of NLR, or, as other versions will have it, they were, for all practical purposes, ousted by a new editor, Perry Anderson and a group of younger New Left academics[26]. Thompson retreated choosing not to fight over the journal, although he was clearly outraged by what he described ten years laster as

a fracture in the passage from one tradition to another, which was never exposed to principled discussion. It was a very English transition: that is (according to one's viewpoint) gentlemanly and tolerant, or otiose and manipulative. It was not until 1965 that I raised ... objections to certain interpretations in the (mutated) *New Left Review*: these pointed to ulterior questions of some significance, although I was inhibited ... by my own sense of the shared fellowship of the Left ..., from pressing every objection home. In due course ... Anderson replied. His reply, in my view, neither answered my objections nor opened up new problems of significance.[27]

Without looking any closer at the details of the disagreements and arguments involved in this editorial reshuffle, it has to be borne in mind that they eventually triggered a long and bitter theoretical debate between Thompson and Anderson. It began as early as 1965 with a biting indictment issued by Thompson on a series of articles by Perry Anderson and Tom Nairn which "attempted to develop a coherent account of British society."[28] *The Peculiarities of the English* first appeared in a new journal *Socialist Register*, which was founded and edited by John Saville and Ralph Miliband, Thompson's old friends from the day of the CPHG and later the 'old' New Left, who had also withdrawn from the board of NLR. After the row at NLR Thompson considered the *Socialist Register* as "the last survivor in the direct line of continuity from the old New Left, and its editors and publisher have done much to keep alive a tradition of undoctrinaire, oecumenical, substantive Marxist analysis"[29]. *The Peculiarities of the English* was the first of Thompson's three great polemical essays, each of them very much in the English tradition of empirically based reasoning, yet at times rather flamboyant in rhetoric. In his argument Thompson undertook to show how unwarranted the essence of Anderson's and Nairn's claims was that

in the ... compromises of 1688 and 1832, the industrial bourgeoisie failed to attain to an undisputed hegemony, and to remake the ruling institutions of society in its own image. ... A premature bourgeois revolution gave rise to a premature working-class movement, whose heroic struggles during the Industrial Revolution were nullified by the absence of any commensurate theoretical growth ...[30].

Thompson then argued this case against Anderson's/Nairn's allegations of provincialism, backwardness, complacency and traditionalism in the social, political and cultural development of the English in considerable detail: He showed that in spite of the all-pervading "old corruption" of eighteenth century Whigs the bourgeoisie once again demonstrated its flexibility and capacity for modernisation in their first step towards widening the franchise in 1832. He went on by illustrating the historical effectiveness of the democratic and dissenting traditions from the seventeenth century onwards, and the equally progressive contributions of English (and Scottish) political economy and natural science. When these strands in the social and cultural development of the English converged in the nineteenth century, this eventually resulted in making Britain the most advanced and successful bourgeois nation. Thompson then challenged Anderson's and Nairn's verdict on the reformist character of the British labour movement after the defeat of Chartism, contending that they could only arrive at such a conclusion by misunderstanding Gramsci's notion of cultural hegemony merely as a quality of the ruling class, while failing to grasp its range as a comprehensive feature of societal relations. Finally Thompson criticized some major weaknesses in traditional Marxist class theory: This culminated in a coherent critique of economistic reductions of the relation between social being and social consciousness as expressed in the questionable image of base and superstructure. To this he added a refutation of reified notions of class as a living entity (individual people being just theoretical derivatives of such), instead pleading for an understanding of individual men and women as basic constituents of the notion of social class lest we should give up human agency as the central driving force in history.

Of course, there was a reply from Perry Anderson[31], whose basic proposition in *Origins of the Present Crisis* later on was taken up and developed into a study of *English Culture and the Decline of the Industrial Spirit 1850-1980* by the American historian Martin J. Wiener[32]. More recently Anderson himself has presented an updated version of his original argument, like Wiener contending that the English bourgeoisie was lacking in industrial spirit and capitalist ethos and prone to taking over aristocratic values and behaviour patterns, thus being responsible for Britain's economic and political decline from the 1870s to the present day[33]. Yet Wiener and Anderson so far have experienced much qualified and detailed criticism from both Marxist and non-Marxist historians drawing on a host of case studies[34]. This, in turn, has been borne out, amongst others, by comprehensive interpretations of Britain's social and political development from the eighteenth to the twentieth centuries like the one elaborated in Harold Perkin's two substantial studies[35], so that there remains hardly any doubt about subsequent historical evidence having basically vindicated Thompson's polemic dissent.

At the time this polemical essay was published Thompson seemed to have somewhat withdrawn from New Left politics: Gathering considerable reputation as a scholar and historian after *The Making of the English Working Class* was published in 1963, he left his teaching in adult education at Leeds University in 1965, when he was appointed director of the Centre for the Study of Social History at the University of Warwick. But he did not keep this position for very long; in 1970 he decided to give up academia altogether considering it an environment he was unfit to work in productively. Since then he has lived as a full-time writer and scholar, from the late 70s being increasingly involved as an activist in the international peace movement. The reasons for his resignation from Warwick are complex and may best be gleaned from his accounts of various conflicts in which he had passionately engaged. These conflicts arose from students' political agitation in the late 60s in an atmosphere that Thompson bitterly referred to as that of a "business university"[36]. His ironic comments on these events make good reading, specifically at a time when universities are again trying to streamline themselves for the advent of full-fledged European transnational capitalism (commonly referred to as "1992"), giving up much of their critical stance towards the framework in which such developments are occuring.

In the late 60s Thompson embarked on another of his political interventions: After Harold Wilson's Labour government had failed to live up to people's expectations of a promised modernization of Britain's economy and society, some of the 'old' New Left once again regathered their spirit and their trust in the resilience and better heritage of the British labour movement as Thompson had characterized it in *The Peculiarities of the English*. E. P. Thompson, Stuart Hall and Raymond Williams co-operated in producing a "May Day Manifesto"[37] trying to make a democratic-socialist impact on national politics by setting out an agenda for the trade union and labour movement. Alas, to no avail, as one might say with the benefit of hindsight.

The decade after leaving Warwick saw the core of Thompson's scholarly historical writing emerging, most of which is highlighted below[38]: In the

1970s more than ten substantial essays on eighteenth century English social history and his book *Whigs and Hunters* on the origin of the Black Act in 1723 were published, theoretically sophisticating and substantially expanding in scope what had been inaugurated by *The Making of the English Working Class* as the 'Thompsonian view' of English social history.

At the same time the second of his polemical essays *An Open Letter to Leszek Kolakowski*[39] appeared as an attempt at reflecting his political biography and vindicating his own position within what he identified as four major varieties of western Marxism:

– the doctrinaire variety of Marxism rampant as a party-political creed,

– the New Left intellectual fashion of Marxism as the quintessential method of true believers,

– the non-committal way of regarding Marxism as one more or less colourful item in the intellectual gallery of immortal ideas,

– Marxism as a living tradition for democratic movements that helps to endure the tensions between historical necessity and moral choice, between individual spontaneity and organizational constraints.

Putting himself among the ranks of those sticking to the latter variety Thompson maintained against Kolakowski, who had just crossed Morris's "river of fire" in the opposite direction, the Marxist notion of capitalism. He pinpointed it as an extremely flexible form of comprehensive social organization which for all its historical changes so far had effectively prevented any attempts at non-capitalist transformation. But he also defended the possibility of developing viable scenarios for a socialist future as alternatives to the contemporary reality of capitalism.

It is in his last, longest and most polemical of the three essays appearing in 1978 that Thompson took on what he considered as the most serious challenge to his concept of socialist humanism: The reading of Marx offered by the French structuralist Louis Althusser (among the foremost thinkers of the French communist party PCF) and his followers. *The Poverty of Theory* [40], ironically alluding to Marx's diatribe against Proudhon *The Poverty of Philosophy*, once again revealed the fundamental difference between the closed abstract character of contemporary Marxist theory in continental Western Europe and Thompson's 'experiential' method which he had demonstrated in such meticulous detail in *The Making of the English Working Class* and in *Whigs and Hunters*. His method, which subsequently has often been referred to as the "anglomarxist" approach to history, is derived from the Jacobin traditions of radical artisans in organizations like the *London Corresponding Society* or the *London Working Men's Association* and from the imaginative visions articulated by William Blake or William Morris. In E. P. Thompson's (as in Christopher Hill's or Eric J. Hobsbawm's) understanding historical and cultural materialism concentrates on the cultural experience of class struggle rather than on what he considered barren scholastic exercises in shifting categories within a hierarchically structured theoretical universe barely deserving the name of Marxism. The ferocity of Thompson's attacks and the bitterness of his scorn – yet compelling in their all-embracing sweep against ideological models of reified epistemology from Popper and Smelser to Althusser, whose thinking he could not refrain from indicting as "Stalinism reduced to the paradigm of Theory ... at last, theorised as ideology"[41] – can only be understood against the backdrop of his political biography. In his youth Thompson had experienced the exhilarating force of mass movement solidarity united by a common cause and a powerful ideology: The liberation of common people from fascist dictatorship and the attempts to improve their everyday lives in a communist society. Yet from 1956 onwards he could no longer evade facing his earlier delusions by Stalinist deceit and doublespeak. And he also had to come to terms with the fact that, in spite of the exposure of Stalinist betrayal and a growing awareness of the full extent of Stalinist terror, Stalinism as a frame of mind seemed to survive and proliferate into infinite varieties, both in the USSR and in Eastern and Western Europe. Probably Thompson had felt for a long time that the evil heritage of Stalin could only be overcome by the complete downfall of state socialism. Yet for all his efforts as a political activist he had to look on helplessly as the post-World War II world order unfolded before his eyes. He saw the two superpowers with their threats of mutual nuclear overkill driving the peoples of the world to the brink of global extermination. And at the same time he saw Marxist intellectuals refusing to take notice, instead carrying on with their business of producing ever more sophisticated, yet futile theoretical models, thus truly emulating the legitimation of capitalist status quo practised by mainstream western social theory and philosophy. Thompson furiously realized how easily impressionable the New Left in Britain as well as elsewhere was by such sophisticated forms of theorizing as for example Althusser's *Lire le Capital*:

... today's Western Leftist intelligentsia is distinguished by its lack of political experience and judgment. But this is not offered in any sense as an accusation of sin. It is a necessary consequence of the determinations of our time. We cannot remedy it by wishing it was otherwise. But it provides, nevertheless, the necessary ground within which the ideological deformations of our time are nurtured. Isolated within intellectual enclaves, the drama of "theoretical practice" may become a *substitute* for more difficult practical engagements. Moreover, this drama can assume increasingly theatrical forms, ... Since no political *relations* are involved, and no steady, enduring struggle to communicate with and learn from a public which judges, cautiously, by actions rather than professions, the presses may reek with ideological terror and blood. Moreover, this is precisely the ground which can nurture an *elitism* for which intellectuals, by a multitude of precedents, are only too well prepared. ... Once again, the intellecutals – a chosen band of these – have been given the task of enlightening the people. ... No doubt this ideological predisposition was itself nurtured within the terrible experiences of Fascism, of mass indoctrination by the media, and of Stalinism itself. But it is a sad premise from which socialist theory should start (all men and women, except for us, are originally stupid) and one which is bound to lead on to pessimistic or authoritarian conclusions. Moreover, it is likely to reinforce the intellectual's disinclination to extend himself in practical political activity. ... In this way, a "revolutionary" and "Marxist" critique which despairs of communication and which has only a fictional political correlative, and which, moreover, reveals that all social evils are insoluble within capitalism, ... becomes a licence for intellectual withdrawal.[42]

From this we may gather the motivational source that have always informed his political critique and practice: It is the unrelenting strength of his socialist-humanist imperatives to educate, agitate and organize people, so that they will eventually be capable to articulate their own desires and ideas for a better society.

Consequently Thompson did not hesitate, towards the end of the 70s, then in his mid-fifties, to once again throw himself into the arduous task of grass-roots political organizing when he realized the imminent danger of a new generation of nuclear overkill technology. The immediate cause for his concern were American Pershing and cruise missiles to be deployed in selected West European bases as a response to the threat posed by new SS 20 missiles which the USSR had stationed in various forward locations in Warsaw Pact countries. Thompson's pamphlet *Protest and Survive*[43] form 1980 onwards became the rallying point for a rejuvenated peace movement that he has so successfully been able to use for his initiative to create the world-wide organization for European Nuclear Disarmament (END). For the last decade he has, up to the point of physical exhaustion, devoted all his energies to the cause of the international peace movement. Therefore it should not be considered overly pathetic when he now finds it

...profoundly moving to see the forms of the old cold war dissolving before one's eyes, but dissolving most of all on the other side. The cold war has not been an heroic episode, an occasion for triumphs, but the most futile, wasteful, humanly destructive, no-through road in history. It has led to inconceivable investments in weapons with inconceivable destructive powers, which have – and which still do – threatened the very survival of the human species, and of other species perhaps more worthy of survival. It has nourished and reproduced reciprocal paranoias. It has enlarged authoritarian powers and the licence of overnight security services. It has deadened imagination with a language of worst-case analysis, and a definition of half the human race as an enemy Other. Its refraction into internal ideological and political life, and on both sides, has been malign. I need not document the offences against human rights on the other side. On this side we have had absurd spy games, MacCarthyism and red-baiting, the purging of trade unions and academies, the inhibition or closure of many intellectual areas ... If the cold war is coming to an end then perhaps my, and Dorothy's, years of political activity may be allowed to be coming to an end also. It is a long and thankless struggle to try and influence the course of history by little movements "from below", but maybe after four decades we have seen a little movement.[44]

Men make their own history, but they do not make it just as they please; they do not make it under circumstances chosen by themselves, but under circumstances directly encountered, given and transmitted from the past. The tradition of all the dead generations weighs like a nightmare on the brain of the living. Karl Marx, The Eighteenth Brumaire of Louis Bonaparte[45]

It could be argued that all of E. P. Thompson's historical writing so far has been a sustained attempt to demonstrate the validity of this statement. In fact, it characterizes, as I will show, Thompson's notion of history very conclusively because it emphasizes the active role of concrete historical people, meaning ordinary men and women, as the subjects of history. And it is this aspect of human agency that is so central to Thompson's concept of social and historical change and development focussing on "the crucial ambivalence of our human presence in our own history, part-subjects, part-objects, the voluntary agents of our own involuntary determinations."[46] In trying to outline this concept it seems helpful to start with some of its basic propositions:

In the wake of his traumatic experience of the events in Hungary in late 1956 Thompson had come round to accepting Stalinism not just as the perversion of an individual human mind and will but as a systematic *frame of mind or an ideology*: Ever since it has been one of Thompson's central theoretical and practical concerns to overcome a mechanistic and deterministic understanding of history as a process conceivable in terms of the dualistic 'base / superstructure' metaphor. Both his historical analyses of eighteenth and early nineteenth century England and his more theoretical and polemical essays have elaborated the central idea that

> Production, distribution and consumption are not only digging, carrying and eating, but are also planning, organizing and enjoying. Imaginative and intellectual faculties are not confined to a 'superstructure' and erected on a 'base' of things (including men-things}; they are implicit in the creative act of labour which makes man man.[47]

In other words, Thompson has consistently refused to conceive of social totality in terms of a material base narrowly defined as the economic process and the relations of production which, in turn, either mechanistically determine or somehow, in the last instance, are reflected in a (relatively autonomous) political, cultural, ideological superstructure.

In this ongoing theoretical debate among Marxists of very different political persuasions Thompson has tried to present an alternative that allows for a richer, fuller version of the world than that cultivated by orthodox communist parties or by structuralist Marxist philosophers like Althusser.

When we speak of the capitalist mode of production for profit we are indicating at the same time a 'kernel' of characteristic human relationships – of exploitation, domination, and acquisitiveness – which are inseparable from this mode, ... there is an economic logic *and* a moral logic and it is futile to argue as to which we give priority since they are different expressions of the same 'kernel of human relationship'.[48]

In this passage from his review of Raymond Williams's *The Long Revolution* Thompson indicated his characteristic understanding of historical materialism which has no room for any artificial division between a 'primary' economic, and 'secondary' social and cultural spheres. Any notion of capitalism to be used meaningfully in analysing its historical development would have to comprise both "'economic' institutions and practices and ... certain attendant norms and values that sustain the processes and relations of production and the system of power and domination around which they are organized"[49]. The idea of the mode of production operating both in its economic *and* cultural features is based on Thompson's reading of Marx, notably a passage from Marx' *Grundrisse*:

In all forms of society there is a specific kind of production which predominates over the rest, whose relations thus assign rank and influence to the others. It is a general illumination which bathes all the other colours and modifies their particularity. It is a particular ether which determines the specific gravity of every being which has materialized within it.[50]

Thompson discusses this passage in his essay *Folklore, Anthropology and Social History*:

What this emphasizes is the simultaneity of expression of characteristic productive relations in *all* systems and areas of social life rather than any notion of primary (more 'real') of the 'economic', with the norms and culture seen as some secondary 'reflection' of the primary. What I am calling in question is not the centrality of the mode of production (and attendant relations of power and ownership) to any materialist understanding of history. I am calling in question ... the notion that it is possible to describe a mode of production in 'economic' terms, leaving aside as secondary (less 'real') the norms, the culture, the critical concepts around which this mode of production is organized.[51]

Statements like this appear to lack clarity about the precise content of the term 'mode of production' which seems "to expand into an indeterminate totality of human relations"[52], yet this may turn out to be not so much a problem of Thompson's theoretical consistency rather than a methodological difficulty of mediating between social structure and human agency, which I will discuss below. What it does bring back to our minds, however, is that the material basis of history designated by the term 'mode of production' extends beyond the sphere of economy and technology and includes conscious human activity; and this is contained in Thompson's understanding of the term *social being*, when he tried "to find a model for the social process which allows an autonomy to social consciousness within a context which, in the final analysis, has always been determined by social being."[53]

Such a conceptual framework does, in fact, not discard the idea that both economic and non-economic spheres are affected by the determinative power of the mode of production. It also does not venture to describe or even predict the course of history in terms of more or less abstract 'laws' that would envisage a definite sequence of modes of production to evolve over time eventually leading to some last stage of social perfection. It rather concentrates on the dynamics of historical change and tries to discover the specific logic behind such processes. It is on such premises allowing for *human agency* as the decisive factor in history that Thompson may demand "the historian has got to be listening all the time"[54], rather than locking historical people and their actions into abstract structural categories. And yet he retains a materialist frame of reference when it comes to the problem of interpretation since "the meaning isn't there in the process; the meaning is in what we make of the process".[55] In this, however, he has always remained aware that historical "evidence is witness to a real historical process and that this process (or some approximate understanding of it) is the object of historical knowledge."[56]

E. P. Thompson has probably become most well and widely known for his contributions to historiography. And here it is specifically his momentous and monumental *The Making of the English Working Class*[57], a book that may have been more influential in British historical writing after World War II than any of its kind, which comes to mind when we think about his achievements as a historian. As Harvey Kaye has shown, MEWC was intended as a historical, theoretical and, at the same time, political work: It took issue with a number of mainstream traditions in history and sociology and also with a particular intellectual elitism among the 'old' and 'new' Left, whose manufacture of 'grand' theory suggested the course of history as a derivative of certain universal materialist laws[58]. The basic contention of this book – whose more than 900 pages, of course, cannot be summed up here – was that in Britain "the emergence of the working class was a product of the complex and contradictory *experience of workers* in the turbulent years from 1790 to 1832, and that it could not be understood apart from that experience."[59] The preface – one of the most frequently quoted and criticised pieces of scholarly writing in contemporary Britain – elaborates Thompson's idea of class and class formation:

> By class I understand a historical phenomenon, unifying a number of disparate and seemingly unconnected events, both in the raw material of experience and in consciousness. I emphasize that it is a *historical* phenomenon. I do not see class as a 'structure', nor even as a 'category', but as something which in fact happens (and can be shown to have happened) in human relationships. More than this, the notion of class entails the notion of historical relationship. ... it is a fluency which evades analysis if we attempt to stop it dead at any given moment and anatomize its structure. ... And class happens when some men, as a result of common experiences (inherited or shared), feel and articulate the identity of their interests as between themselves, and as against other men whose interests are different from (and usually opposed to) theirs. The class experience is largely determined by the productive relations into which men are born – or enter involuntarily. Class-consciousness is the way in which these experiences are handled in cultural terms: embodied in traditions, value-systems, ideas and institutional forms. If the experience appears as determined, class-consciousness does not. We can see a *logic* in the responses of similar occupational groups undergoing similar experiences, but we cannot predicate any *law*. Consciousness of class arises in the same way in different times and places, but never in just the same way.[60]

I have quoted Thompson at some length here to make sure that his basic points are not missed: Class, in his view, is a *relationship and a historical process*, based on *experience*, involves *human activity and consciousness*; I should perhaps add that he insists on *working class* rather than the descriptive term *working classes* "which evades as much as it defines"[61]. It hardly needs emphasizing that this now somewhat 'classical' definition – despite its seeming inconsistencies – posed a challenge to both marxist and structural-functionalist concepts of class. And it was definitely meant to be challenging these orthodoxies on both sides of the fence as Thompson made very clear throughout the rest of his preface. He notably turned against any reified definition of class which would either have class-consciousness deduced from Leninist theorists' or party activists' concepts or which would rather denounce class-consciousness as a thing sprung from the tiny minds of communist intellectuals trying to upset the benign efforts of Western social technology in persuading people to accept their assigned social roles for the benefit of capitalist democracy.

As I have already indicated, both among Marxist and mainstream academic historians there has been much censure and fault-finding with this innovative and original approach towards the problem of re-conceptualising 'class' as the focus and agent of social change for its lack of a clear theoretical mould. At the same time Thompson has also been commended over and again for his effectively freeing "labour history from the bonds of a rigid economic determinism"[62]. In trying to provide a more systematic insight into the basic propositions of Thompson's concept of history it may be helpful to examine two more fundamental objections concerning the clarity and consistency of his notion of class that have persistently been raised over the years and that, in my opinion, cannot be dismissed altogether:

First, defining 'class' as a relationship and a historical process inevitably raises the question, how it can be of any heuristic value in analysing structural features of a society. Thompson has, to a certain degree, sidestepped this issue by introducing a twofold meaning of the term as a descriptive and an analytical category: When used descriptively it will refer to empirically observable historical evidence whereas in its analytical meaning it may be used to organize such evidence[63]. Moreover, in his essays on eighteenth-century English society Thompson has made clear that

class, in its heuristic usage, is inseparable from the notion of 'class struggle'. In my view, far too much theoretical attention (much of it plainly ahistorical) has been paid to 'class', and far too little to 'class struggle'. Indeed, class struggle is the prior, as well as the more universal concept. To put it bluntly: classes do not exist as separate entities, look around, find an enemy class, and then start to struggle. On the contrary, people find themselves in a society structured in determined ways (crucially, but not exclusively, in productive relations), they experience exploitation (or the need to maintain power over those whom they exploit), they identify points of antagonistic interest, they commence to struggle around these issues and in the process of struggling they discover themselves as classes, they come to know this discovery as class-consciousness. Class and class-consciousness are always the last, not the first stage in the real historical process.[64]

This, for his critics, has by no means settled the issue. Yet I think by linking 'class' with 'class struggle' it clarifies the direction of Thompson's analytical interest beyond doubt: Rather than re-inventing categories for theorizing the structure of society he tries to improve concepts and terms for understanding human history and development. In this pursuit, he considers 'social structure' as the reified result of past collective human activity designating, at every given point in history, the periphery circumscribing the material opportunities for present human agency, both as constraining and – as Anthony Giddens in his theoretical approach to the analysis of social change has shown[65] – enabling factor. Thompson does, however, not consider structure and structural change worth analysing as such without centering on real historical people since it is they who by their conscious activities create and change these structures. Leaving them out would turn such analysis into a barren contemplative exercise in theoretical practice which Thompson did so ardently condemn throughout his polemic against Althusser and structuralist Marxism in *The Poverty of Theory*.

Second, another central feature in Thompson's notion of class that even today still attracts the arguable charge of being utterly muddled and unexplained and on which he himself – curiously enough – allegedly has remained fairly reluctant to provide clarifying explanations is *experience*. Thompson seems to suggest in the passage from the preface of MEWC quoted above, that experience mediates between productive relations and class-consciousness or "between 'social being' and 'social consciousness'. The problem with such a formulation is that experience appears to encompass both the terms between which it is supposed to mediate."[66] I do not wish to enter into a discussion of the inconsistencies that Sewell has meticulously identified (or so he thinks) in Thompson's use of the term which essentially center on the issue if 'experience' is supposed to designate a mode of perception or a structural device. At first the latter seems to be Sewell's misreading which he then discards to "deflate the concept" and restore the term to its meaning in everyday language as 'actually living through an event or events' which generate 'an effect on judgement and feeling'[67]. Incidentally Thompson never seems to have understood experience differently:

Experience arises spontaneously within social being, but it does not arise without thought; it arises because men and women (and not only philosophers) are rational, and they think about what is happening to themselves and their world. If we are to employ the (difficult) notion that social being determines social consciousness, how are we to suppose that this is so? It will surely not be supposed that "being" is here, as gross materiality from which all ideality has been abstracted, and that "consciousness" (as abstract ideality) is there? For we cannot conceive of any form of social being independently of its organising concepts and expectations, nor could social being reproduce itself for a day without thought. What we mean is that changes take place within social being, which give rise to changed *experience*: and this experience is *determining*, in the sense that it exerts pressures upon existent social consciousness, proposes new questions, and affords much of the material which the more elaborated intellectual exercises are about.[68]

This should sufficiently settle the issue about the status of experience in his concept: Experience is a structured and at the same time determining way in which men and women perceive their material and social environment; it is structured by past and present human action (social being). At the same time it again shapes human action by acting upon social consciousness. Thompson sees men and women "as persons experiencing their determinate productive situations and relationships, as needs and interests and antagonisms, and then 'handling' this experience within their *consciousness* and their *culture* ... in the most complex ... ways, and then acting upon their determinate situation in their turn".[69] Here he refers to the impact of experience on consciousness as a reflexive process of mental assimilation and conscious integration into patterns of everyday individual and collective behaviour (culture). It is this way of conceptualising social change over time (i.e. the movement of history) that has – particularly among Marxist philosophers, historians and sociologists in Britain and the USA – widely attracted (and still does) the charge of "culturalism" or "experientalism". Nevertheless I would contend that Thompson is at his most materialist when he portrays history through the eyes of those who experienced it, presenting such experience as "*structured* – by productive relations, political institutions, habits, traditions, values."[70] This makes history understandable as the result of human actions which, in turn, become explicable in a socially meaningful way.

The logic of such analysis is persuasively demonstrated in the organization of MEWC: Part I "The Liberty Tree" unravels the major strands of popular traditions in political culture. Part II "The Curse of Adam" looks at the economic and political transformations of the Industrial Revolution and how they were experienced and evaluated by different occupational groups of working people. Part III "The Working-Class Presence" shows how, during the heroic years of plebeian radicalism (1816-1820), from these heterogeneous groups as a response to their experience of industrialization an organized working-class gradually began to emerge – throughout this process drawing creatively on their inherited political culture. This is what Thompson meant when he claimed in his preface that the working class "was present at its own making".[71]

It was mentioned before that the theoretical propositions of this analysis have not deemed to meet the sophisticated standards of theoretical rigour academic Marxism or functionalist sociology would demand: yet the meaning Thompson assigns to 'experience' as one of his central terms enables him to bridge the gap between an 'objective' social structure and the 'subjective' vagaries of individual behaviour. Interestingly enough this fresh approach to the dialectical problem of human desire and volition vs necessities and constraints of circumstances corresponds with some recent developments in social theory:

In his outline of the theory of structuration Anthony Giddens represents all human beings as "knowledgeable agents" meaning that they "have, as an inherent aspect of what they do, the capacity to understand what they do while they do it."[72] "Knowledgeability" is a characteristic of their "practical consciousness" which "consists of all the things which actors know tacitly about how to 'go on' in the context of social life".[73] It underlies all of their actions and is based on what Giddens calls "reflexive monitoring of activity" which "is a chronic feature of everyday action and involves the conduct not just of the individual but also of others".[74] Although reasons or "rationalizations" for social interactions may be offered by the "discursive consciousness" of social agents, these tend to be rather inconclusive since "knowledgeability ... exhibits an extraordinary complexity ... often ... completely unexplored in orthodox sociological approaches, especially those associated with objectivism."[75] Yet knowledgeability, as that part of consciousness which continuously and purposefully assimilates *experience*, forms the crucial connecting link between 'inside' and 'outside', between agency and structure.

In the debate on how to conceive of the development of history and culture in theoretical terms, it is certainly one of Thompson's lasting merits to have defused, by introducing 'experience' as a basic category into the analysis of historical and cultural change, the epistemological tension between 'objective' and 'subjective' into a methodological aspect of analytical procedure. "Abstraction becomes only a moment in the analysis: a necessary strategic move in any complex historical argument."[76]

On this I agree with Sewell whose criticism of Thompson's lack of theoretical clarity in defining 'experience' I do not share. I rather think that despite some occasional murkiness[77] Thompson, just as well as Giddens, though perhaps in theoretically less sophisticated terms, sees 'agency' as the flipside of 'structure' "not as antagonistic but as indissolubly linked."[78] All you have to do is read for 'structure' 'historical situations and processes', which have continuously been the subject matter of Thompson's analytical efforts. Then it should be clear that understanding these as medium *and* result of human action, as constraining *and* enabling men and women who have always tried to make their own history not without purpose.

Thompson's central contention in MEWC that the working class was 'made' – or had largely made itself for that matter – by 1832 includes an important suggestion: The social formation that emerged was a *single unified* working class. Recently Geoff Eley, an American historian, has again challenged this view that there was a *single* working class by the beginning of the 1830s referring to the evidence of considerable disunity and sectionalism particularly between (a) skilled craft workers and artisans and (b) unskilled or casual workers and other sections of the labouring poor. Eley's main argument is that Thompson identifies "the 'making' of the working class with a transitional radicalism of the artisanate which bore a somewhat uncertain relationship to the working class as a whole" and he further argues that "although Thompson shows the existence of a rich and developing radical culture, the unifying power of that radical culture (its impact on the consciousness of the class as a whole) awaits proper demonstration".[79] Beyond this demand for further empirical analysis – "systematic and carefully specified studies of regional class formation"[80] – Eley's critique involves some basic questions on Thompson's understanding of history, notably that of the British state and society. These are questions about the connection between politics and culture, and questions about the nature of political and cultural hegemony. Addressing them will hopefully help to clarify another problem that I have already touched upon before: The formation of class through the process of class struggle or in other words, how the forces of historical change affected *The Origins of Modern English Society* as the title of Harold Perkin's well-known historiographical synthesis of that crucial period of English history runs.[81]

In fact, we have to turn to Thompson's eighteenth century studies for answers to these questions: Whereas MEWC focusses on the 'inside' perspective of those very diverse groups of artisans and labourers who, within a very short period of cataclysmic social change (commonly called *Industrial Revolution*) were forged into what Thompson sees as *the* working class, his essays and studies on the social history of eighteenth-century Britain look at the issue of class formation from a broader perspective of social totality. In several case studies, most extensively in his book *Whigs and Hunters*[82], Thompson has shown in remarkable detail, how the unstable balance of eighteenth-century British society was upset so that what he calls "the reciprocity of relations between rulers and ruled", that is between gentry and crowd, in what Peter Laslett once labelled a "one class society"[83], were restructured along class lines. It was in the last decade of the eighteenth century when

the relationship of reciprocity snapped. As it snapped, so, in the same moment, the gentry lost their self-assured cultural hegemony. It suddenly appeared that the world was not, after all, bounded at every point by their rules and overwatched by their power. A man was a man, 'for a' that'.[84]

What is referred to as 'cultural hegemony' here, needs some more detailed backgrounding: Among contemporary British historians and historically minded political scientists there seems little disagreement about the nature of the eighteenth-century British state[85]: According to the 'conventional wisdom' of liberal historians, it was seen as a strong and stable realm of consensus governed by the 'rule of law' within the perimeters of paternalism and deference: Today, in fact, the widely accepted view (incidentally shared by Thompson) is somewhat different emphasizing the origins of this state as a result of the seventeenth-century revolutions and the political compromise of 1688/89: This included a limited monarchy no longer encroaching on the property rights of the gentry and aristocracy and a parliament dominated by the propertied sections of society, who did not, however, form a socially or culturally cohesive ruling class. These origins translated into a structural frailty of the state which was (a) institutionally minimal in size, given the small number of central government agencies as an infrastructure for the exercise of central power and (b) weak because it lacked a strong military or police force or other means of coercion for actually asserting its virtual power monopoly.

In the absence of these features – markedly different from continental absolutist kingdoms like France – the problems of exercising political domination and control had to be solved differently:

The hegemony of the eighteenth century gentry and aristocracy was expressed, above all, not in military force, not in the mystifications of a priesthood or of the press, not even in economic coercion, but in the rituals of the study of the Justice of the Peace, in the quarter-sessions, in the pomp of Assizes and in the theatre of Tyburn.[86]

In his sweeping history of the so-called 'Black Act' passed in 1723 which responded to a number of disturbances around the forests of Windsor and in South East Hampshire (poaching, cutting down young trees, threatening forest officials with anonymous letters and the like) with drastically repressive measures ("legislative overkill") Thompson gets to the very core of Antonio Gramsci's notion of 'hegemony':

He "explores the passage of the Act in terms of both the *socio*-historical development of capitalism and the immediate needs of the political elite, especially Walpole and his fellow Whigs."[87] Thus the character of eighteenth-century British state and society is exemplified to have been in a precarious balance which in the transformations ahead would be teetering on the brink of collapse more than once:

At the turn of the seventeenth century still a largely direct paternalist social control was exercised by *parson* and *squire* over what was, at that point, a still largely half-free labour force bound to the landed property owners by countless forms of dependency (labour services, living-in etc.). As the eighteenth century progressed this control was gradually eroded because the ruling gentry increasingly disengaged from their direct involvement in the sphere of production (which at the same time was the sphere of exploitation and direct social control). They retreated to live parasitically within the confines of their landscaped estates continuing "to appropriate surplus value produced by the labouring poor but they did so through their tenants and by commerce or taxation".[88] It should be added that at the same time more fully blown forms of capitalist production and exploitation became more widespread and sizeable such as the manufacture of textiles, potteries, iron and other metal implements and articles etc., which had been in existence along with the pre-industrial agrarian and commercial economy since the late fifteenth century yet on a relatively small scale. Towards the end of the eighteenth century all these developments converged in the relentless "advance of free mobile wage labour".[89] In this context of weakening social cohesion and a decreasing political pattern of paternalism and deference Thompson argues that the Whig oligarchy came to employ the law as a chief instrument for defending and legitimizing its property and status, which they had been able to secure in their decisive victories both over the absolutist pretensions of the Crown and over the far-reaching participatory demands from "below" (for example from the Levellers). But he insists that this does by no means vindicate a view of the law as merely a feature of the superstructure: Although the law "may also be seen as ideology, or as particular rules and sanctions which stand in a definite and active relationship (often a field of conflict) to social norms; ..."[90], it was just as well

a definition of actual agrarian *practice*, as it had been pursued 'time out of mind'. How can we distinguish between the activity of farming or of quarrying and the rights to this strip of land or to that quarry? ... Hence 'law' was deeply imbricated within the very basis of productive relations which would have been inoperable without this law. And ... this law, as definition or as rules (imperfectly enforceable through institutional legal forms), was endorsed by norms, tenaciously transmitted through the community. There were alternative norms; that is a matter of course; this was a place, not of consensus, but of conflict.[91]

This is why we cannot simply write off 'law' as an ideological implement of the state apparatus of the ruling class! It should rather be clear that the 'rule of law' provides an excellent example of *hegemony* in a more sophisticated understanding, in that it was cultural and material at the same time, in that it was a necessary element of the social order and an area of contest between rulers and ruled, the outcome of which may have been grossly biassed in general, yet was anything but a foregone conclusion in particular cases. Thompson's notion of hegemony is not simply synonymous with social consensus along the lines of a hegemonial view of the world or hegemonial public discourse.

Rather it refers to an *order* of *struggle* that is constantly being disputed and negotiated, but does not become revolutionary conflict, nor entail the continuous use of physical force or coercion by the state (or similar authority) to maintain the social order.[92]

Eugene Genovese, who in his book *Roll, Jordan, Roll: The World the Slaves Made*[93] used the concept in this very way, in replying to his critics has stated very succinctly

Hegemony implies class struggles and has no meaning apart from them. ... It has nothing in common with consensus history and represents its antithesis – a way of defining the historical content of class struggle during times of apparent social quiescence.[94]

So much about the 'rule of law' and its hegemonial quality. There were, of course, other levels at which social control was challenged in the "banana republic" (Thompson) of eighteenth-century Britain. The food riots that he investigates in his essay on *The Moral Economy of the English Crowd in the*

Eighteenth Century[95] he interpreted as attempts at re-establishing the traditional moral economy of direct dependence and paternalist responsibility against the advancing impersonal economy of the market. They were "a highly complex form of direct popular action, disciplined and with clear objectives" and therefore have to be seen as well designed forms of political struggle that "the word 'riot' is too small to encompass".[96]

After elaborating the social and political content of hegemony in eighteenth-century Britain I would now wish to examine the remaining issues:

How did this process of struggle eventually result in the formation of class, namely the working class? And how does *culture* fit into this (and what is Thompson's version among the many available concepts of 'culture' anyway)?

In his essay *Patrician Society, Plebeian Culture*[97] Thompson has argued that hegemony as a social relationship and a political process was acted out on the side of the gentry in what he describeds by the metaphor of "public theatre" staged in "occasional dramatic interventions: the roasted ox, the prizes offered for some race or sport, the liberal donation to charity in times of dearth"[98]. As we can now imagine the administering of the law may be seen as the most regularized form of this public theatre. Public theatre, however, must not be confused with what Jürgen Habermas has conceptualised as the "public sphere" of the emerging middle class which developed throughout the eighteenth century as a specific form of mutual self-articulation, communication and assertion of a new set of norms and values culminating in demands for democratic rights and responsibilities made by a maturing segment of society who claimed their places as equal members of the body politic. Public sphere in this understanding "mediates between society and state, in which the public organizes itself as the bearer of public opinion."[99]

In one way, Habermas's concept, has been enormously useful in distinguishing between such different cultural modes of communication and interaction: 'Public theatre' designates the all-embracing traditional way in which pre-industrial political domination was publicly expressed and performed. 'Public sphere' circumscribes the origin of a new social 'locus' for an economically more and more successful, yet politically still relatively powerless segment of society to develop self-consciousness, identity and articulate common interests as a distinct social group.

In another way, employing 'the public sphere' perspective in detailed historical research has over the years led to a more sophisticated understanding of its nature: It was segmented into the more rationally arguing bourgeois radicalism of a nascent middle class (informed by the philosophical and political principles of Enlightenment thinking) and into a more plebeian insurrectionism of a socially heterogeneous crowd inspired by an emotionally based rebellious spirit. The latter was locally based on communal traditions and practices of protest and revenge incorporating many elements of older customs and symbols such as "the anonymous tradition" (sending or publishing anonymous letters), "the counter-theatre of threat and sedition" using such symbolic language as effigy burning etc and "the crowd's capacity for swift direct action" (destroying machinery, intimidating employers)[100]. Thompson considers such practices to be ultimately situated in what he pinpoints as "culture's material abode: the people's way of life, and above all, their productive and familial relationships"[101], thus clearly aligning himself with what has become known, through the works of Raymond Williams, as a materialist, "broad" notion of culture.

Not only did the bourgeois and the popular section of the 'public sphere' evolve on a different time-scale and develop different patterns of communication and interaction. There was also, as MEWC has demonstrated convincingly, considerable mutual influence between bourgeois radicalism and plebeian insurrectionism which eventually came to fruition in generating the radical and class-conscious cultural environment of the 1810s and 1820s in which people like William Cobbett, Richard Carlile, John Gast or John Wade were rooted. This environment, in turn, proved to be the fertile ground from which further working class experience of struggling and learning in the 1830s and 1840s would grow. The progress along this long and winding road towards improving working class institutions, spreading working class consciousness and culture and developing working class concepts for a new social order is littered with success and failure alike. This is what Michael Vester has shown in his pioneering *Die Entstehung des Proletariats als Lernprozeß*[102] which undertakes to re-interpret Thompson's MEWC, extending it to the time of Chartism and using the concept of a distinctly 'proletarian' public sphere put forward by Oskar Negt and Alexander Kluge in further elaborating Habermas[103]. Chartism can thus be seen as a first triumphant victory demonstrating that the working class had achieved an unprecedented strength and cohesion despite its many sectional divisions and was able "to raise an overt challenge to the emergent hegemony of the bourgeoisie, by elaborating an independent public sphere of its own"[104]. Yet Chartism must also be seen as its hitherto most serious defeat showing the impressive strength of the new hegemony in effectively neutralizing the potential antagonistic working class visions of an alternative social order into socially acceptable reforms and interventions[105].

This ambivalent significance of Chartism may vitiate any objections against Thompson's claim that the working class was 'made' by 1832. They would be tenable only on the premise that 'made' means 'completed'. This, I contend, has never been his claim. On the contrary, I would rather argue that Thompson takes a more long-term perspective on the formation and development of a social class: His essay *Eighteenth-century English Society: Class Struggle Without Class?*[106] re-examines the issue of class formation 15 years after MEWC had first appeared in print. More or less taking up many of the arguments that had been made against the theoretical assumptions implicit in his grand narrative about the origins of the working class he acknowledges and clarifies his position: Using his careful explorations of hegemony and class struggle in the eighteenth century as a backdrop he refers to the gradually emerging restructuring of social forces in terms of an aptly chosen image: He describes this process as a

societal "field of force" ... with, for many purposes, the crowd at one pole, the aristocracy and gentry at the other, and until late in the century, the professional and merchant groups bound down by lines of magnetic dependency to the rulers, or on occasion hiding their faces in common action with the crowd.[107]

The weakening of paternalist fetters in this 'field of force' was experienced by the labourers as a growth in self-determination and decrease of economic dependency at every level in their working lives. The ruling gentry, in turn, perceived these changes as growing "indiscipline of working people, their irregularity of employment ... and their social insubordination."[108] But they thought "the insubordination of the poor was an inconvenience; it was not a menace."[109] What Thompson has epitomised as "class struggle without class" presented itself as countless smaller and larger instances of local popular protest and rebellion which effectively combined to the redrawing of the political power lines. The exact role of the nascent middle class in this unstable "field of force" remains yet to be established in detail.

On balance such insurgent actions worked important changes in the modes of plebeian self-perception and their expression of common interests: Together with the experience of industrializing production these changes combined to fragment a rebellious, but traditional plebeian culture which was neither revolutionary nor deferential. Although divided by a wide gulf from patrician culture and its concomitant notions of social order – it had been lived within the confines circumscribed by this patrician culture. The fragments of the traditional plebeian culture eventually helped to recompose the social experience arising from changes and conflicts in the objective relations of the workers to the means of production in "class ways".[110]

Of course, E. P. Thompson's historical writing has to be seen in the context of a long-standing and distinctly non-orthodox Marxist tradition of historians of British culture and society, who have written and continue to write from a materialist point of view:

Marxist historiography was never, in Britain, deformed beyond recovery, even when failing to make a clear intellectual disengagement from Stalinism. We had, after all, the living line of Marx's analysis of British history – in *Capital*, in Marx and Engels' correspondence – continually present to us. To work as a Marxist historian in Britain means to work within a tradition founded by Marx, enriched by independent and complementary insights by William Morris, enlarged in recent times in specialist ways by such men and women as V. Gordon Childe, Maurice Dobb, Dona Torr and George Thompson, and to have as colleagues such scholars as Christopher Hill, Rodney Hilton, Eric Hobsbawm, V. G. Kiernan and (with others whom one might mention) the editors of this *Register*. [Th. is referring to John Saville and Ralph Miliband, editors of *The Socialist Register*, R.S.] I could find no possible cause for dishonour in claiming a place in this tradition.[111]

In considering this statement it might be useful to remember some things about Thompson's scholarly and political activities for the past 35 years. They may be seen as a sustained attempt to defend Marx's materialist critique of European history and his vision of an alternative social order against the terrible debasements it has suffered from Stalinism and from its successor regimes of state socialism in the USSR and most of Eastern Europe, with all the drabness of their physical environment and the barrenness and infertility of their intellectual traditions. Therefore Thompson may have held Marxist thought and political practice in the capitalist democracies of the western hemisphere (and in those parts of the third world that have been under their neo-imperialist control) by far the more promising branch of that tradition when it comes to developing scenarios of how we might survive into the next millenium. One should not be confused about his fundamental belief to that effect by his frequent railings against what he considers Stalinist aberrations within western Marxism (as in his attacks on Althusser in *The Poverty of Theory*) or by his sarcasm about British Marxist heritage in general:

We lie upon our heritage like a Dunlopillo mattress and hope that, in our slumbers, those good dead men of history will move us forward. We are dosed with eclecticism (or with opportunism given the brave name of empiricism) as regularly as we are dosed with librium; the public health service pays for one and the University Grants Committee pays for the other; it scarcely matters which pays for which, since the Government pays for all. Someone will make huge profits one day from the public dispensation of Marxism as Heritage.[112]

This was written in the good old days of 'labourism'; Mrs Thatcher had not yet left her marks on British post World War II history, and there is definitely a good degree of self-complacency about it, a sin that Thompson in his rhetorically more inflated moments certainly likes to indulge in. Yet all this certainly does not militate against his proudly counting himself in the ranks of this very tradition.

Which brings me to another reminder, a brief and cursory characterization of this tradition: It goes back to the days of Marx and Engels and of William Morris. One can hardly overestimate the impact of the latter on the strong moral undercurrent in Thompson's Marxist beliefs, for which he himself not entirely by chance has accepted the label of "socialist humanism", thus clearly distinguishing himself from other contemporary Marxist traditions. Moreover, it has to be considered a tributary to that broader stream of independent radical, liberal, Fabian and other socialist thinking which in Britain from the days of theorists like J. A. Hobson and L. T. Hobhouse or writers with more leanings towards history and politics like Barbara and John Hammond, G. D. H. Cole, or Beatrice and Sidney Webb to this very day has never been allowed to run dry. In 1991 it may not go unmentioned that this stream from its very beginning, of course, has also included feminist historians like for example Maud Pember Reeves and other members of the Fabian women's group, who were pioneers in early women's history in Britain[113].

It is this context fostered by a general "modernisation and liberalization of the English intelligentsia at the time of the First World War and the 1920s"[114], which has helped to create a more liberal intellectual climate in twentieth century Britain. Even distinctly Marxist approaches like for example A. L. Morton's classic *A People's History of England* – originally published by the Left Book Club in 1938 and marking "the closing of a tradition of popular, political and non-academic history writing" within the Communist Party[115] – have always found attention and recognition even in mainstream academia. Professional historiography at British universities, notably in Oxford and Cambridge, despite never being over-sympathetic towards scholarly positions informed by Marxist thinking, has also never totally ignored or even exiled them from history departments to such degree as has been the case in post-World War II West Germany or the USA.

As a consequence Britain has so far seen a critical, yet fruitful debate of the practical results and theoretical premises of Marxist historiography, most notably that flowing from the pens of members of the Communist Party Historians' Group between 1946 and 1956, who after dissolving in 1956, because most of them had left the party, turned out thousands of pages of historical writing determinedly unorthodox in its Marxist propositions[116]. This debate, although not always led in an overly fair or well-balanced manner, has certainly been the livelier for having lacked most of the florid rituals of academic politeness and all sides have enormously benefited from it. This does not mean that the academic career path for Marxist thinkers has ever been anything like a high road to success and recognition in Britain, but their well-established presence in teaching, research and publishing gives evidence that a century of independent radical, socialist and marxist thinking can make a difference. Even beyond academic debating circles this tradition today is certainly not less felt than it was in the middle of the Cold War climate of the early fifties, when the first issue of what eventually became a very distinguished scholarly journal, *Past and Present*, was published. *Past and Present* over the years has been very successful in building bridges between Marxist and non-Marxist historians sharing common research interests. Moreover people like Christopher Hill, Eric J. Hobsbawm and Edward P. Thompson have been enjoying national and international reputation for their scholarly achievements or as politically minded and historically qualified commentators on current events or both.

Over the last ten to fifteen years or so a younger generation of socialist and feminist historians has emerged, committed to carrying on the efforts revived after World War II by the CP Historians' Group. These include Raphael Samuel – at one point the youngest member of the CPHG – who has been a leading figure of the *History Workshop* movement started at Ruskin College, Oxford, in 1966. Sheila Rowbotham, Catherine Hall, Dorothy Thompson, Richard Johnson, Royden Harrison, Gareth Stedman Jones, to name just a few more, may be found like others of their generation connected to journals like *History Workshop Journal* or as members of the *Society for the Study of Labour History*. Quite a few are more or less established at universities and polytechnics in history departments or in the recently burgeoning "cultural studies" programmes. They are all politically committed and actively involved in the more recent developments in workers' and women's history stimulated by the contemporary socialist and labour movement in Britain.

I have emphasized all this because – interestingly enough – outside Britain the tradition of British Marxist historians has never been widely received in mainstream academia beyond a small number of interested scholars, mostly liberal or left leaning historians, sociologists and political scientists, who in the seventies and early eighties eagerly read and discussed what today occasionally goes by the collective name of 'Anglomarxism'[117]. This has made E. P. Thompson into an intellectual figure often known only from hearsay outside English-speaking countries. Although *Poverty of Theory* and his major essays on the eighteenth century were, for example, translated into German back in 1980, *The Making of the English Working Class* was not translated until 1987[118], *Whigs and Hunters* yet awaits translation to this day. This means that MEWC did not become known to a wider German reading public until 25 years after it was first published and also more than twenty years after social history as a new fashion had begun to make major inroads into the bulwarks of conventional academic history wisdom. At that point publishers had already been cashing in on the general public's newly aroused craze for "everyday history", "oral history", and the like: These new tastes were, however, catered for by translations of major highlights from the French school of "history from below", which had developed as part of the *Annales* tradition[119] and is also informed by the materialist (but certainly non-marxist) concept of history originated from the works of Fernand Braudel, whose three-volumed *magnum opus* 'Civilisation matérielle, économie et capitalisme' appeared in a German translation only six years after it was published in French:[120]. In (West) Germany, the "anglomarxist" school of thought in historiography has on the whole remained in the shadow of these more widely received French examples, even if there are a few notable exceptions like E. J. Hobsbawm's *The Age of Revolution* and *The Age of Capital*, both available in cheap German paperback editions for many years.

Without belabouring this point any further this should make us aware that an interested public in this country so far has not been given an opportunity to engage in the critical discussion of E. P. Thompson's and others' distinctly non-orthodox Marxist approach in writing history which has proved so fertile in Britain. Reviews of the German translation of MEWC even by well-meaning scholars like Günther Lottes, who happens to be an expert on the period, have so far helped very little to change this deplorable situation[121].

Over the last ten years or so quite a few easily accessible comprehensive surveys have been published on the women and men who helped to build this tradition over the past century, on their social and cultural backgrounds, and on their specific interests shaped by various intellectual and political movements, socialist and non-socialist alike.[122] Therefore I will be able to confine myself to a brief concluding appraisal of E. P. Thompson's specific achievements within this tradition not needing to outline it in greater detail.

What Thompson, like most British Marxist historians, has in common with other critical strands of historiography is his overall endeavour to bring the common people, the masses, the crowd (back) into the scope of history writing. For this Raphael Samuel, Thompson's younger colleague from their days in the CPHG, has coined the unpretentious term "people's history".[123] Usually such orientations have become more well known by the name of "history from below", a term which goes back to Georges Lefebvre, one of the great historians of the French Revolution. "History from below" in this broader understanding draws on diverse traditions going back to the French *Annales* school: There is, for example, the history of material and cultural circumstances or of collective mentalities (as opposed to the more elitist history of ideas), both in the perspective of *longue durée*, meaning the impact of long term geographical or environmental changes on the everyday lives of common people or their self-images and thought. Moreover, there are ethnohistorical or modernization history approaches to common people's culture and experience.

From such concepts the British Marxist historians may be distinguished by their common approach towards history as Kaye[124] has recently pointed out: They insist on putting the study of common people's experiences into the frame of historically and politically specific class relations and conflicts involving the examination of the general interplay between power and subordination in society. This accounts for their frequently concentrating on resistance and rebellion as forms of conflict which try to break the mould of enforced consensus 'from above' or plainly coercive domination. Kaye[125] and others have termed this characteristic perspective as "history from the bottom up" (arguably not a very catchy designation). Both Thompson and other fellow Marxist historians are well aware that this kind of historiography needs to be supplemented by "history from above" in the sense of "studying the intricate machinery of class domination" as demanded by Perry Anderson[126].

This is another reason why the objections of 'culturalism' or 'experientalism' raised, above all, against Thompson in the extended debate on the theoretical premises of MEWC in *History Workshop Journal* in 1978-79[127] today seem – with the benefit of hindsight – somewhat ill-directed: Thompson's emphasis on the role of experience and practices, norms, values and ideas (the latter summarily referred to as *culture* in the broad sense of the term) of the common people in struggling to make their own history were denounced as lacking in theoretical rigour: These notions allegedly are anything but "definite and precise categories, necessary for a really systematic analysis, ..." in the sense of "genuine abstractions [which] are simplified formal representations of really-existing relations".[128] Such charges do not duly recognize that Thompson has always tried (like fellow historians as Hobsbawm or Hill) to reconstruct these struggles in the context of historical and societal totality without sacrificing Marx's central category of 'mode of production' relating it, however, to the level of real historical events in a meaningful way.

In fact, it is in his uniquely narrative, yet by no means untheoretical, presentation of these struggles through the eyes of those actively involved that we find one of Thompson's lasting achievements which has to be considered of pervasive influence on Marxist and non-marxist historians alike in Britain and the USA: His redrawing the theoretical and methodological lines of class analysis. By conceptualising class as historical relationship and process he did not only provide for class experience to become a central area of analysis in a host of subsequent studies. He has also been successful in helping to discard the determinism of both Leninist and structuralist class analysis in favor of human agency thus creating a more sophisticated marxist vision of history as an "active, though structured process"[129].

As I have pointed out above this has resulted in bringing Marxist attempts at theorizing history again somewhat closer in touch with more recent, creative non-marxist developments in social theory trying to solve the problem of "the mutual dependence of structure and agency" (A. Giddens) in history and culture. Thompson's contribution to this kind of theory-building has been qualified as an example of what the American sociologist of culture Clifford Geertz would consider an "interpretive theory" of history[130]. This is a type of theory different from those (as, for example in natural sciences or in some branches of empirical social sciences) formulating predictive hypotheses. It rather helps to make

thick description possible, not to generalize across cases but to generalize within them. ... Rather than beginning with a set of observations and attempting to subsume them under a governing law, such inference begins with a set of (presumptive) signifiers and attempts to place them within an intelligible frame.[131]

As Trimberger reminds us, Jürgen Habermas suggested many years ago that such theories are "*not* aimed at helping social scientists in their attempts at greater social control. Rather, it seeks to foster self-consciousness that will make humans into more conscious subjects who can actively affect the future."[132] While effectively distancing himself from any deterministic marxist model of social totality as comprised in the base / superstructure image, Thompson, in his attempts at recomposing and historicizing what Kaye aptly called "the traditional master category of mode of production", has always insisted on the "total character of the social relations of production"[133], yet without conflating them with class relations[134]. Therefore he would not reject the proposition that – theoretically – the nature of class conflict and class struggle as a political and cultural phenomenon is always circumscribed by the relations of production. He would however argue, that – in concrete historical situations – relations of production and class relations are mutually interactive through the process of human experience and agency. The latter as a reflexive instrument of mediation between productive base and social formation is the bone of contention at the bottom of the debates with structuralist critics like Perry Anderson[135]. Yet there are other voices – even in the factories of 'grand' theory around *New Left Review* which usually have been fairly unsympathetic to Thompson's approach – and these voices lately have been less reluctant to recognize the merits of his way of thinking: In a fairly original outline for a "political" Marxism Ellen Meiksins Wood has, for example, practically vindicated Thompson's position: She has tried to reconsider 'base' and 'superstructure' tying them together in the notion of an ultimately "social constitution of the economy" that emphasizes the *political* aspect of relations of production, "that aspect in which they are actually *contested*: as relations of domination, as rights of property, as the power to organize and govern production and appropriation." This stance she explicitly adopts in order to "illuminate the terrain of struggle by viewing modes of production not as abstract structures but as they actually confront people who must *act* in relation to them."[136]

On balance the conclusion seems justified that Thompson has greatly contributed to relieving Marxist historiography from forever being stuck in the dead alley of a dualistic materialism perceiving class in dichotomous terms of 'subjective' vs 'objective' or 'class in itself' vs 'class for itself'. He has tenaciously explored the many forms in which people were experiencing one of the crucial watersheds in modern history, the transition towards full-blown industrial capitalism in Britain. He has examined the many ways in which they articulated their interests and struggled for their realization. Thus he has taught us to make *the process* of class formation the central focus of attention in people's history. He has also taught us that this process has always been tainted with the contradictory behaviour of real historical people and therefore has never been easily domesticated by clear-cut theoretically derived structural tools.

Why history? It it over this fundamental question that Thompson the historian and theorist and Thompson the political writer and activist become eventually reunited. For him there can be no doubt that there is a moral purpose in history and in developing historical consciousness, after all. Not only do we need to understand the past in order to be able to actively and responsibly shape our present lives, "historical consciousness [also] ought to assist one to understand *the possibilities of transformation and the possibilities within people*."[137] This is how history can be useful in what William Morris, Thompson's great example, has called "the education of desire". Morris's prophetic warning

> If the present state of society merely breaks up without a conscious effort at transformation, the end, the fall of Europe, may be long in coming, but when it does, it will be far more terrible, far more confused and full of suffering than the period of the fall of Rome.[138]

seems to be more urgent than ever, now that the proudly celebrated "end of history" has come into its own – in the Gulf war. Developing the desire to create an alternative social order – this is what Morris had in mind and this is on the agenda now. In educating this desire history may serve to show how the present calamities of an utterly unbalanced world order may be overcome and in what ways human agents – we, the people – can be motivated to achieve this aim.

Notes

Reference to E. P. Thompson's writings is made by title or shortened title only, unless the item is not included in my selected bibliography below.

1 Francis Fukuyama, *The End of History*, The National Interest, Summer 1989; quoted after E. P. Thompson, *Decline of the West*, New Statesman and Society, January 12, 1990, p. 10.
2 Richard Taylor, *Article on E. P. Thompson*, The Blackwell Biographical Dictionary of British Political Life in the Twentieth Century, ed. Keith Robbins (Oxford: Blackwell, 1990), p. 398.
3 E. P. Thompson, *The Decline of the West*, New Statesman and Society, 12 Januar, 1990, p. 12.
4 Allan Bloom, quoted after E. P. Thompson, loc. cit., p. 10.
5 Michael Merrill, *Interview with E. P. Thompson*. Radical History Review 3, 1976, p. 25.
6 E. P. Thompson, *An Open Letter to Leszek Kolakowski*, p. 109-110, hereafter quoted as OpLet.
7 E. P. Thompson, *The Poverty of Theory*, p. 383-384.
8 Originally published by Victor Gollancz, London, in 1963; quotes in this essay are from the second edition, Harmondsworth: Penguin: 1968.
9 The most comprehensive bibliography on E. P. Thompson's works (including practically all his articles and major reviews in periodicals) may be found in Harvey J. Kaye and Keith McClelland (eds.), *E. P. Thompson, Critical Perspectives* (London: Polity Press, 1990), p. 276-280.
10 The most recent is the book by Kaye and McClelland; others include Harvey J. Kaye, *The British Marxist Historians* (London: Polity Press, 1984), p. 167-220; Bryan Palmer, *The Making of E. P. Thompson* (Toronto: New Hogtown Press 1981); and Ellen Kay Trimberger, *E. P. Thompson: Understanding the Process of History*, in Theda Skocpol (ed., *Vision and Method in Historical Sociology* (Cambridge: Cambridge University Press, 1984), p. 210-243.
11 E. P. Thompson, *Why Neither Side Is Worth Backing*, The Times, April 29, 1982.
12 For this biographical survey I have used the titles quoted in notes 5 and 10 and the following material: Dieter Groh, Einleitung zu Edward P. Thompson, *Plebeische Kultur und moralische Ökonomie, Aufsätze zur englischen Sozialgeschichte des 18. und 19. Jahrhunderts* (Frankfurt/M., Berlin, Wien: Ullstein, 180), p. 5-31; Michael Vester, *Edward Thompson als Theoretiker der "New Left" und als historischer Forscher – Notizen zu einer Bio-Bibliografie*, Ästhetik und Kommunikation 33, September 1978, p. 33-45; this issue also gives a shortened German translation of Michael Merrill's Interview with E. P. Thompson (cf. note 5) on p. 21-32; Michael Vester, *Edward Thompson und die 'Krise des Marxismus'* in E. P. Thompson, *Das Elend der Theorie, Zur Produktion geschichtlicher Erfahrung* (Frankfurt/M., New York: Campus, 1980), p. 13-38, (this is the German translation of *The Poverty of Theory* and also contains an interesting introduction by the "Institut für sozialhistorische Forschung").

13 The strong influence of his brother is felt in the biography that E. P. Thompson wrote together with his mother, cf. E. P. and T. J. Thompson, *There is a Spirit in Europe: A Memoir of Frank Thompson* (London: Victor Gollancz, 1947).

14 Cf. Michael Merrill, *Interview with E. P. Thompson*, loc. cit., p. 10-12.

15 Bill Schwarz, *'The People' in history: the Communist Party Historians' Group, 1946-56*, in Richard Johnson, Gregor McLennan, Bill Schwarz, David Sutton (eds.), *Making Histories, Studies in History-writing and Politics* (London: Hutchinson, 1982), p. 44.

16 E. J. Hobsbawm, *'The Historians' Group of the Communist Party* in M. Cornforth (ed.), *Rebels and Their Causes* (London: Lawrence and Wishart, 1978), p. 25.

17 E. P. Thompson, *Romanticism, Moralism and Utopianism: the Case of William Morris*, p. 105.

18 op. cit., p. 106.

19 New Left Review 1, 1960, editorial.

20 In E. P. Thompson (ed.), *Out of Apathy*, (London, 1960), p. 141-194.

21 In NLR 3, 1960, p. 3-9.

22 In NLR 6, 1960, p. 18-31.

23 In NLR 9-11, 1961.

24 Cf. Trimberger, op. cit. (see note 10), p. 217.

25 Richard Taylor, op. cit. (see note 2), p. 399.

26 For details see Trimberger, op. cit., p. 217; see also H. Gustav Klaus, *Politisch-kulturelle Periodika der englischen Linken (1945-1973)*, in Gulliver 1 (Berlin, 1976), p. 184 seq.

27 OpLet, p. 102. For Perry Anderson's version of these events cf. his book *Arguments Within English Marxism* (London: New Left Books and Verso, 1980), Chapter 5 "Internationalism".

28 E. P. Thompson, *The Peculiarities of the English*, p. 35; the most important of these essays were Perry Anderson, *Origins of the Present Crisis*, NLR 23, 1964, p. 26-53, and Tom Nairn, *The English Working Class*, NLR 24, 1964, p. 43-57.

29 OpLet, p. 102.

30 E. P. Thompson, *The Peculiarities of the English*, p. 37 seq.

31 Perry Anderson, *The Myths of Edward Thompson*, NLR 35, 1966.

32 First published by Cambridge University Press, 1981.

33 Perry Anderson, *The Figures of Descent*, NLR 161, 1987.

34 Cf. the discussion of Martin J. Wiener's book in Alan Sked, *Britain's Decline, Problems and Perspectives* (Oxford: Blackwell, 1987), or on Anderson's recent essay Michael Barratt Brown, *Away With All the Great Arches: Anderson's History of British Capitalism*, NLR 1967, 1988, p. 22-52.

35 Cf. Harold Perkin, *Origins of Modern English Society 1780-1880* (London: Routledge and Kegan Paul, 1969) and Harold Perkin, *The Rise of Professional Society, England since 1880* (London: Routledge, 1989).

36 Cf. his edited work *Warwick University Ltd*, and the section on Warwick University in his collection of essays from the 1970s *Writing by Candlelight*.

37 Raymond Williams edited a revised version (Harmondsworth: Penguin , 1968).

38 listed in detail in my select bibliography.

39 first published in 'The Socialist Register', London: Merlin Press, 1973, p. 1-100.

40 Published simultaneously in London and New York in a volume of collected essays *The Poverty of Theory and Other Essays*. I quote from the 3rd impression of the London edition, quoted hereafter as PoT.

41 PoT, p. 374.

42 PoT, p. 375, 377, 378.

43 Published by "Campaign for Nuclear Disarmament" in 1980 and running through several editions.

44 E. P. Thompson, *When the War Is Over*, New Statesman and Society, 26 January, 1990, p. 30 and 31.

45 Karl Marx and Frederick Engels, *Selected Works in two volumes* (Moscow: Foreign Languages Publishing House, 1958), vol. 1, p. 247.

46 PoT, p. 280.

47 E. P. Thompson, *Socialist Humanism*, New Reasoner 1, 1957, p. 130-131.

48 NLR 10, 1961, p. 28-29.

49 Ellen Meiksins Wood, *Falling Through the Cracks: E. P. Thompson and the Debate on Base and Superstructure*, in Kaye, McClelland (eds.), op. cit. (see note 9), p. 137.

50 E. P. Thompson, *Eighteenth-Century English Society: Class Struggle Without Class?*, p. 151, cf. Karl Marx, *Grundrisse*, (Harmondsworth: Penguin 1973), p. 106-107 for the translation quoted here.

51 p. 17-18 (quoted from the reprint of this essay, Brighton 1979).

52 Ellen Meiksins Wood, op. cit., p. 139.

53 E. P. Thompson, *The Peculiarities of the English*, p. 81.

54 Michael Merrill, op. cit. (cf. note 5), p. 15.

55 Michael Merrill, op. cit., p. 7.

56 PoT, p. 220.

57 Quoted hereafter as MEWC.

58 Cf. Harvey J. Kaye, op. cit., p. 176.

59 William H. Sewell jr., *How Classes Are Made,: Critical Reflections on E. P. Thompson's Theory of Working-class Formation*, in Kaye, McClelland (eds.), op. cit., p. 51.

60 MEWC, p. 9-10.

61 MEWC, p. 9.

62 Sewell jr., op. cit., p. 55.

63 Cf. E. P. Thompson, *Eighteenth-century English Society: Class Struggle Without Class?* p. 147 seq.

64 loc. cit., p. 149.

65 As for example in Anthony Giddens, *The Constitution of Society, Outline of the Theory of Structuration* (Berkeley and Los Angeles: University of California Press, 1984).

66 Sewell jr., op. cit., 59.

67 Cf. loc. cit., p. 60.

68 PoT, p. 200.

69 PoT, p. 356.

70 Sewell jr, op. cit., p. 65.

71 MEWC, p. 9.

72 Giddens, op. cit., p. 281 and XXII. My understanding of Giddens owes much to discussions with the sociologist Ilse Dröge-Modelmog (Oldenburg).

73 loc. cit., p. XXIII.

74 loc. cit., p. 5.

75 loc. cit., p. 281.

76 Sewell jr, op. cit., p. 66.

77 As in the passage quoted by Sewell jr, op. cit., p. 61 seq.

78 loc. cit., p. 66.

79 Geoff Eley, *Edward Thompson, Social History and Political Culture: The Making of a Working-class Public, 1780-1850*, in Kaye, McClelland (eds.), op. cit., p. 36.

80 loc. cit., p. 20.

81 see note 35.

82 First published by Allan Lane in London, 1975; my quotes are from the 1977 edition by Penguin Books, Harmondsworth; quoted as W & H.

83 Cf. Peter Laslett, *The World We Have Lost* (3rd ed., New York: Charles Scribner's Sons, 1984), chapter 2.

84 E. P. Thompson, *Eighteenth-century English Society: Class Struggle without class?* p. 165.

85 Cf. Andrew Gamble, *Britain in Decline* (3rd ed., London: Macmillan, 1990), p. 64-74.

86 W & H, p. 262.

87 Kaye, op. cit., p. 196.

88 Kaye, op. cit., p. 198.

89 ibid., Kaye here summarizes arguments from Thompson's essay *Patrician Society, Plebeian Culture*.

90 W & H, p. 260.

91 W & H, p. 261.

92 Kaye, op. cit., p. 197.

93 Published by Pantheon in New York 1974.

94 Eugene Genovese, *A Reply to Criticism*, Radical History Review 3, 1977, p. 98.

95 In 'Past and Present' 50, February 1971, p. 76-131.

96 Ibid., p. 78 and 79.

97 In 'Journal of Social History', 7, 1974, p. 382-405.

98 ibid., p. 389, 390.

99 Jürgen Habermas, *The Public Sphere*, New German Critique 3, Fall 1974, p. 49. This essay, of course, is a comprehensive rendering of his argument in *Strukturwandel der Öffentlichkeit* (Neuwied: Luchterhand, 1962).

100 Cf. E. P. Thompson, *Patrician Society and Plebeian Culture*, p. 399-401.

101 PoT, p. 368.

102 Published by Europäische Verlagsanstalt, Frankfurt 1970.

103 Oskar Negt and Alexander Kluge, *Öffentlichkeit und Erfahrung: Zur Organisationsanalyse von bürgerlicher und proletarischer Öffentlichkeit* (Frankfurt: Suhrkamp, 1972).

104 Eley, op. cit., p. 39.

105 cf. ibid.

106 in 'Social History' 3, 1978, p. 133-166.

107 ibid., p. 151.

108 *Patrician Society, Plebeian Culture*, p. 383.

109 ibid., p. 387.

110 Cf. Ellen Meiksins Wood, *The Politics of Theory and the Concept of Class: E. P. Thompson and His Critics*, Studies in Political Economy 9, Fall 1982, p. 50.

111 OpLet, p. 123.

112 OpLet, p. 116.

113 For a short rundown on this tradition see David Sutton, *Radical Liberalism, Fabianism and Social History*, in Johnson, McLennan, Schwarz, Sutton (eds.), loc. cit. (see note 15), p. 15-42.

114 Bill Schwarz, loc. cit. (see note 15), p. 45.

115 ibid., p. 44-45.

116 A short survey on the group is provided by Schwarz, loc. cit. For an insider's view cf. Eric J. Hobsbawm, loc. cit. (see note 16).

117 Some of the few West German scholars to have incorporated Thompson into their own approaches are Michael Vester, Hannover; Hans Medick, Göttingen; or Dieter Groh, Frankfurt.

118 Edward Thompson, *Die Entstehung der englischen Arbeiterklasse* 2 vols (Frankfurt: Suhrkamp, 1987).

119 Well-known examples of such translations include Jacques LeGoff, *Kultur des europäischen Mittelalters* (München, Zürich, 1970), or Emmanuel Le Roy Ladurie, *Montaillou* (Frankfurt, Berlin, Wien, 1983).

120 Fernand Braudel, *Sozialgeschichte des 15.-18. Jahrhunderts*, vol. 1 *Der Alltag*, vol. 2 *Der Handel*, vol 3 *Aufbruch zur Weltwirtschaft*, (München: Kindler, 1985 and 1986).

121 Cf. Günther Lottes, *Die Empörung aller Gerechten über die Verhältnisse*, in 'Frankfurter Rundschau', 3 October, 1987, p. ZB 4.

122 Cf. Harvey J. Kaye, *The British Marxist Historians*, (London: Polity, 1984); Raphael Samuel, *The British Marxist Historians I*, in NLR 120, 1980, p. 21-96; for the more recent developments and controversies in the wider context of Perry Anderson's *Arguments Within English Marxism* (London: New Left Books / Verso, 1980); and for the debate on the analysis of "culture" originating around Stuart Hall and the "Center for Contemporary Cultural Studies" (CCCS) at Birmingham University in the 1970s see Richard Johnson, *Culture and the Historians*, in John Clarke, Chas Critcher, Richard Johnson (eds.), *Working Class Culture, Studies in History and Theory* (London: Hutchinson, 1979), p. 41-74. On the *History Workshop Movement* Raphael Samuel has given a short overview in his afterword to Raphael Samuel (ed.), *People's History and Socialist Theory* (London: Routledge & Kegan Paul, 1981), p. 410-417.

123 Cf. Raphael Samuel, *People's History*, in Raphael Samuel (ed.), loc. cit. (see note 122), p. XV-XXXIX.

124 Kaye, op. cit., p. 221-249.

125 ibid., p. 228 and Harvey J. Kaye, *E. P. Thompson, the British Marxist Historical Tradition and the Contemporary Crisis*, in Kaye, McClelland (eds.), op. cit. (see note 9), p. 255.

126 Cf. Harvey J. Kaye, *The British Marxist Historians*, loc. cit., p. 229.

127 This debate was triggered by Richard Johnson's essay *Edward Thompson, Eugene Genovese, and Socialist-Humanist History*, in History Workshop Journal 6, Autumn 1978, p. 79-100. It went on for more than a year, mainly in the columns of that journal: its repercussions could still be felt in the section on *Culturalism* in Raphael

Samuel (ed.), *People's History and Socialist Theory* (London: Routledge & Kegan Paul, 1981), p. 375-408.
128 ibid., p. 96 and 97.
129 Kaye, op. cit. (see note 126), p. 235.
130 I owe this thought to Ellen Kay Trimberger, op. cit., p. 226 and 227.
131 Clifford Geertz, *The Interpretation of Cultures* (New York, 1973), p. 26.
132 Trimberger, op. cit., p. 227.
133 Kaye (1984), op. cit., p. 236.
134 Cf. Kaye (1984), op. cit., p. 237.
135 Cf. Perry Anderson, *Arguments within English Marxism* (London: New Left Books / Verso, 1980), specifically his second chapter on "agency", p. 16-58.
136 Ellen Meiksins Wood, *The Separation of the Economic and the Political in Capitalism*, in NLR 127, 1981, p. 77.
137 Michael Merrill, *Interview with E. P. Thompson*, loc. cit., p. 17 (my italics).
138 quoted in E. P. Thompson, *William Morris: Romantic to Revolutionary* (rev. ed., New York: Pantheon, 1977), p. 723 from May Morris, *William Morris, Artist, Writer, Socialist* (Oxford: Blackwell, 1936).

E. P. Thompson: A Selected Bibliography

This introductory bibliography focusses on books and longer political and historical essays and excludes all reviews. More comprehensive bibliographies may be found in Perry Anderson, *Arguments Within English Marxism* (London: New Left Books / Verso, 1980), p. 209-213; and in Harvey J. Kaye, Keith McClelland (eds.), *E. P. Thompson, Critical Perspectives* (London: Polity Press, 1990), p. 276-280.

Books and collected essays

William Morris: Romantic to Revolutionary, London: Lawrence and Wishart, 1955; rev. ed., New York: Pantheon, 1977.
The Making of the English Working Class, London: Victor Gollancz, 1963; 2nd ed. with a new postscript, Harmondsworth: Penguin 1968; 3rd ed.with a new preface, 1980.
Whigs and Hunters: The Origins of the Black Act, London: Allen Lane, 1975; repr. with a new postscript, Harmondsworth: Penguin, 1977.
The Poverty of Theory and Other Essays, London: Merlin, 1978 and NewYork: Monthly Review Press, 1978.
Writing By Candlelight, London: Merlin 1980 (collected essays).
Zero Option, London: Merlin 1982; published in the USA as *Beyond the Cold War*, New York: Pantheon, 1982 (collected essays).
Double Exposure, London: Merlin 1985 (collected essays).
The Heavy Dancers, London: Merlin 1985 (collected essays); in the USA under the same title published in New York by Pantheon, 1985; this edition includes the essays collected in *Double Exposure*, yet excludes some essays of the British edition.
The Sykaos Papers, London: Bloomsbury, 1988; New York: Pantheon, 1988.

Books edited

There is a Spirit in Europe: A Memoir of Frank Thompson, with T. J. Thompson, London: Victor Gollancz, 1947.
Out of Apathy, London: Stevens & Sons / New Left Books 1960.
The May Day Manifesto, with Raymond Williams and Stuart Hall, 1967; rev. ed. by Raymond Williams, Harmondsworth: Penguin, 1968.
Warwick University Ltd, Harmondsworth: Penguin, 1970.
The Unknown Mayhew: Selections form the Morning Chronicle 1849-1850, with Eileen Yeo, London: Merlin, 1971.
Albion's Fatal Tree: Crime and Society in Eighteenth-century England, with Douglas Hay et al., London: Allen Lane, 1975 and Harmondsworth: Penguin, 1977; New York: Pantheon, 1975.
Family and Inheritance: Rural Society in Western Europe, 1200-1800, with Jack Goody and Joan Thirsk, Cambridge: Cambridge University Press, 1976.
Protest and Survive, with Dan Smith, Harmondsworth: Penguin, 1980; rev. ed. in the USA, New York: Monthly Review Press, 1981.
Star Wars. Harmondsworth: Penguin, 1985.
Prospectus for a Habitable Planet, with Dan Smith, Harmondsworth: Penguin, 1987.

Pamphlets

The Communism of William Morris, a lecture given on 4 May, 1959, in the Hall of the Art Workers Guild, London; London: The William Morris Society, 1965.
Protest and Survive, CND / Bertrand Russell Peace Foundation, 1980.
Star Wars: Self-Destruct Incorporated, with Ben Thompson, London: Merlin, 1985.

Political Essays

Socialism and the Intellectuals, Universities and Left Review 1, Spring 1957.
Socialism and the Intellectuals: A Reply, Universities and Left Review 2, Summer 1957.
Socialist Humanism: An Epistle to the Philistines, The New Reasoner 1, Summer 1957.
Agency and Choice, The New Reasoner 5, Summer 1958.
The New Left, The New Reasoner 9, 1959.
Revolution, New Left Review 3, 1960.
Revolution Again! Or Shut Your Ears and Run, New Left Review 6, 1960.
A Letter to America, The Nation, 24 January, 1981.
Why is Star Wars? and *Folly's Comet*, in *Star Wars*, ed. E. P. Thompson (Harmondsworth: Penguin, 1985).
The Rituals of Enmity, in *Prospectus for a Habitable Planet*, eds. E. P. Thompson and Dan Smith (Harmondsworth: Penguin, 1987).

Historical Essays

Homage to Tom Maguire, in *Essays in Labour History*, eds. Asa Briggs and John Saville (London: Macmillan, 1960).
Time, Work-discipline and Industrial Capitalism, Past & Present 38, 1967.

The Political Education of Henry Mayhew, Victorian Studies 11, 1967.

Mayhew and the 'Morning Chronicle', in *The Unknown Mayhew*, eds. E. P. Thompson and Eileen Yeo (London: Merlin, 1971).

The Moral Economcy of the English Crowd in the Eighteenth Century, Past & Present 50, 1971.

Rough Music:Le Charivari Anglais', Annales ESC 27, 1972.

Patrician Society, Plebeian Culture, Journal of Social History, 7, 1974.

The Grid of Inheritance: A Comment, in *Family and Inheritance: Rural Society in Western Europe, 1200-1800*, eds. Jack Goody, Joan Thirsk and E. P. Thompson. (Cambridge: Cambridge University Press, 1976).

Romanticism, Utopianism and Moralism: The Case of William Morris, New Left Review 99, 1976.

Folklore, Anthropology, and Social History, Indian Historical Review, III (2), 1977; repr. in Britain as 'A Studies in Labour History Pamphlet' (Brighton: John L. Noyce, 1979).

Eighteenth-century English Society: Class Struggle Without Class? Social History, 3, 1978.

Agendas for Radical History, with E. J. Hobsbawm, Christopher Hill and Perry Anderson, in Radical History Review 36, 1986.

Eighteenth-century Ranters: Did They Exist? in *Reviving the English Revolution*, eds. Geoff Eley and William Hunt (London: Verso, 1988).

Elizabeth Meese

Adrienne Rich

(1929-)

Adrienne Rich, the philosopher-poet, is an astute critic of culture and one of the foremost feminist theorists of our time. Her work, spanning a period of more than thirty years, serves as both a touchstone against which we test ideas and feeling today, and a beacon that casts its light into the uncertainty that surrounds us. Whether she contributes most significantly as a poet, a critic, a friend or a citizen is not of concern here, and reflects the way in which generic conventions entrap as much as they enable. To speak of the poet Adrienne Rich as a feminist critical theorist requires certain differentiating moves, on her part as poet and ours as readers. We could consider here only her prose work – her three books and numerous other essays – allowing us the illusion of separating the critical theorist from the poet. But Rich helps us to reject this easy move through the way she resists the stasis and security of such delimiting categorical boundaries. The value of her writing, in any form, is that it represents a thoughtful response to these decades of momentous change for women (especially for feminists and lesbians), intellectuals, and literary critics. In particular, Rich's works to date explore the figuration of woman in various familiar positions along a continuum of possibilities: heterosexual lover, wife, mother, daughter, daughter-in-law, lesbian lover. The splendor of her writing results from a kaleidoscopic positioning and re-positioning as thinking, feeling and writing subject, looking for the breaks in the stitching, the flaws and the cracks in the apparently smooth surface of our literary and sociopolitical texts. By studying the sequential emergence of her work, we can chart the development of major philosophical and cultural positions in the late twentieth century. The trajectory of Rich's theorizing deserves exploration, in particular, as a useful record of the development of feminist critical theory in our time – the paths we have and have not taken, how and where we stand, and with whom.

Rich's work might be described in terms of her movement from an uncritical heterosexuality to a lesbian feminism with a global commitment, with an ever keener articulation of her position in relation to the production of literary work. We can see this convergence in Rich's writings through her simultaneous critique of language (the writer's means of production and point of relation to the mode of production) as both *form* (demanding a certain kind of

verbal structure) and *socio-political ethos* (demanding a certain kind of relation between the woman writer and the world).

Furthermore, her expression of this critique takes the form of a radical re-
positioning of the subject in relation to her audience as well as to the
demands of the artist in society – a positioning which we might call a "lesbian feminist method."

Rich's first book of poetry, *A Change of World* (1951), published the year
she graduated from Radcliffe, marks a point of departure for her lifelong artistic and analytic quest. Despite its title, very little of the concern for social
transformation which characterizes her later work is apparent in this volume
of youthful, highly formalistic "school poetry." Rich, the good student and
dutiful daughter, positions herself carefully in the place of the writer in a literary tradition that constructs the poet as a masculine speaker. She earns the
Yale Younger Poets Prize and Auden's praise for her mastery of form and
voice, for a notable "self"-restraint that obscures "Rich-as-woman" so successfully that she can present herself as the "poet" in (harmony with) tradition. Citing Yeats and Frost as progenitors, Auden, in his forward introducing
her volume to the world of letters, places her in that tradition: "In a young
poet, as T. S. Eliot has observed, the most promising sign is craftsmanship
for it is evidence of a capacity for detachment from the self and its emotions
without which no art is possible." Through craft and self-positioning, the
fashioning of an apparently objective, detached, and gender-neutral voice
which speaks to the "fathers" (a figure for the powerful arbiters of tradition),
these early poems win their place, just as they mark a point of departure for a
life's work.

Rich's next volumes, *A Change of World* and *The Diamond Cutter and
Other Poems* (1955), are principally those of the woman writing without
feminism, the speaker who, in pretending to be neither male nor female, or in
filtering her experience through male personae, adopts the (discursively
assigned) position typically reserved for the subject as generic masculine
speaker. Her next book, *Snapshots of a Daughter-in-Law: Poems, 1954-1962*
(1963), begins Rich's self-conscious examination of her socially and linguisti-
cally assigned position as woman through a process of feminist consciousness-raising designed to explore the dimensions of the female self in culture
(e.g. "The Loser" and "A Marriage in the Sixties"). This volume, as indicated
in the title poem, presents the poet's effort to (re)figure a sense of the
"woman" in culture. Even here, Rich notes later, "I hadn't found the courage
yet to do without authorities, or even to use the pronoun 'I' – the woman in
the poem is always 'she'" (*On Lies*, 45). Still, some suggestive shifts are
beginning to take place. In "The Roofwalker," for example, Rich blurs the

distinction between subject and object, female and male, difference and indifference, as the speaker realizes:

A life I didn't choose
chose me: even my
tools are the wrong ones
for what I have to do (63).

In this collection, Rich enacts a strategic re-positioning that asks us to construct the personal in a new way; that is, to read and to write woman's personal experience as the political text of a woman socially constructed in/by culture. Her shift in position places the reader in a different relation as well. Neither language ("neither words nor music are her own," *Snapshots*, 3) nor history ("Time is male," *Snapshots* 24) can be counted upon to articulate this new relationship. A measure of Rich's political radicality can be seen in the fact that her critical reception now becomes highly problematic. Rich's resistance, her stubborn pursuit of something "beyond," her desire to expose the social construction of "woman," encompasses at the time a consideration of the aesthetic and thematic shifts inherent in both personal and poetic re-positioning.

Her struggle with the social construction of woman is even more pronounced in *Necessities of Life: Poems, 1962-1965* (1966) where Rich undertakes the long process of re-interpreting women's lives, her own and others, that characterizes much of her later work. To re-interpret is to re-figure woman, beginning with her domestic relationships (her place in the production and reproduction of culture), as wife ("Like This Together"), daughter ("After Dark"), and mother ("In the Woods"). Rich reaches back, extending her consideration of women's relation to men to her foremothers like Emily Dickinson in "'I Am in Danger − Sir −'," intertexts for reading the woman poet's relationship to those who determine her interface with the public world of literary production.

The political ramifications of Rich's feminist re-positioning in and through language becomes increasingly evident in *Leaflets: Poems 1965-1968* (1969) and *The Will to Change* (1971). Just as she re-figures woman's place, Rich re-defines the poet's position in the world as requiring a "masculine ... singlemindedness." Through her reading of Dickinson, of Bradstreet in "The Tensions of Anne Bradstreet" (1966) and of Eleanor Ross Taylor in "Woman Observing, Preserving, Conspiring, Surviving" (1972), essays later collected in *On Lies, Secrets and Silence*, Rich studies herself as a poet. She plumbs her feelings, preparing to uncover (ex-pose) their political dimensions. She examines the personal implications of the public world as it presents itself in the death of a revolutionary ("To Frantz Fanon"), and the artistic implications of changing position – a resistance to conformity that desires to make words change us ("Implosions" 42), noting that "Every existence speaks a language of its own" (*Leaflets* 68). If this is so, then there are many more languages waiting to be heard, hoping to find form. Now the smooth lines of the poem break open, admitting uncertainty and violation, as in "Nightbreak" where the figurations of the poet's body and the bombed villages of Vietnam simultaneously coalesce as they are devastated. This vision requires a new language and an altered form to mark its way through the ruptured landscape and the female body at odds with their situations. Breaking with tradition to signal the breaks in tradition, to suggest the ways in which tradition has broken with us, Rich employs a more experimental style. The function of the poet, the woman, the feminist fuse in the imaginative and pragmatic quest to determine "how we can use what we have/to invent what we need" ("Leaflets" 56) as she tries "to drive a tradition up against the wall" ("Ghazals," ii, 62).

In *The Will to Change*, Rich deepens and particularizes her understanding of the relationship between the aesthetic, personal and political dimensions of experience. She materializes through language that maxim of the feminist movement, the cornerstone of consciousness raising practices, the ethic of an entire generation, "The personal is the political." In lines that characterizes this volume in their refusal to marginalize the political, she writes: "*The moment when a feeling enters the body*/is political" ("The Blue Ghazals" 24). It grows politically and artistically necessary to determine what it means to "speak as a woman." In "Planetarium," for example, she writes, "I am an instrument in the shape/ of a woman," and aligns herself with Caroline Herschel, the astronomer – "A woman in the shape of a monster/ a monster in the shape of a woman" (13-14). Critical re-vision gains a more radical function in the scene of writing: "I tear up answers/ I once gave ..." ("Letters: March 1969," 31). Like her subject, the poet persona transgresses boundaries, forbidden separations of outer and inner space, of the artistic and the political, the political and the personal. Through these crossings, interruptions and transgressions, which of course one is always risking, Rich demonstrates precisely what is at stake in her revolutionary texts.

The radical and monstrous violations that she commits in the interest of poetry and feminism are articulated as transgressions in her poetic language and structure, as in "The Burning of Paper Instead of Children," where sections of prose frame and interrupt passages of poetry. Except for lineation, one genre is indistinguishable from the other. Rich gives us a study of oppression and language in which the speaker observes: "'to hear a mother say she do not have money to buy food for her children and to see a child without cloth it will make tears in your eyes'" (16). The poem itself calls attention to this passage which it describes as

(the fracture of order
the repair of speech
to overcome this suffering) (16).

Rendering a material (ortho/graphic) representation of one of her final comments, "A language is a map of our failures" (18), the poem (re)presents the tension of Rich's most frequently cited lines:

this is the oppressor's language
yet I need it to talk to you (*Will* 16).

She engages the irresolvable dilemma of positioning, the paradox within language and culture of the speaker in the margins who realizes how language, necessarily in/of "the center" and "tradition," both liberates and entraps. The terrain grows more treacherous. Rich expresses her aim as "the relief of the body/and the reconstruction of the mind" (*Will* 14) – a subject which receives deliberate consideration in her landmark essay "When We Dead Awaken: Writing as Re-Vision" (1971). Her often cited definition of "re-vision" guided a decade of feminist intellectual work in the United States and elsewhere, and still articulates a pronounced desire of feminist criticism: "Re-vision – the art of looking back, of seeing with fresh eyes, of entering an old text from a new critical direction – is for women more than a chapter in cultural history: it is an act of survival" (*On Lies* 35).

Of the books most thoroughly expressive of Rich's and the country's emergent interest in feminism, *Diving into the Wreck* (1973) is her first. It concentrates on and extends Rich's consideration of categorical violation through transgressions of gender. In "The Phenomenology of Anger," she writes:

Every act of becoming conscious
(it says here in this book)
is an unnatural act (31).

Men are figured as adulterers, destroyers, murderers of babies, rapists, and women are their (unwitting) accomplices. Similarly, in the essay "Caryatid: Two Columns" (1973), Rich connects the violence in Southeast Asia with sexual violence at home: "Rape has always been a part of war" (*On Lies* 114). Women make only the most tentative gestures of solidarity and support, fashioning garments, deconstructing and reconstructing their materiality as a metaphor for the fabric of women's lives. The exercise of male power creates a world no better than "scarred volcanic rock" (*Diving* 12), and woman's psyche is imaged as somehow inaccessible, a huge lock without a key (6). Women are "outside the frame of his dream" (12), looking for ways to articu-

late their need and their anger, to intersect with the discursive structure that
writes them and the world they inhabit. To (re)write both of them demands
that the poet (re)frame the "American dream."

Playing with the law of gender, Rich frequently presents herself as the
androgyne (19), the mermaid and merman of "Diving into the Wreck": "I am
she: I am he" (19). This figure, commonly used to represent the artist,
assumes new significance in the polarized context of sexual opposition, anger
and devastation. The androgyne suggests, on the one hand, Rich's complicity,
and on the other her difference from the tradition of male poets and social
prescriptions for women. Rich's androgyne signifies the effects of exclusion
and repression – being "outside" the frame – needed for the "dead language"
to do its work:

> if they ask me my identity
> what can I say but
> I am the androgyne
> I am the living mind you fail to describe
> in your dead language
> the lost noun, the verb surviving
> only in the infinitive (19).

She articulates the rift between the language of things and the meaning of
things in their essence through an attempt to rewrite the antithetical, the contradictory – subject/object, masculine/feminine, self/other, inside/outside (see
Martin 191).

But a language of the rift is a language about the woman poet's struggle
with her culture's positioning of woman and the signifying capacity of language – what its lexicon, syntax and grammar permit and refuse, in what
relations it places us.

The political and artistic aim of her scorching anger is purification, to burn
away the enemy's masks, words, lies

> leaving him in a new
> world; a changed
> man (29).

Again, the enemy is figured as masculine, suggesting the power of the
oppositional logic. At the same time, Rich represents her utopic desire, not by
means of separatism or the destruction of men, but in terms of harmonious
life in a lush, green world of women and men, in a state of peaceful
human/ecological integration: "each with its own pattern –/a conspiracy to
coexist" (*Diving* 30). Critics interested in Rich as a theorist have paid considerable attention to this poem, noting how she links male and female princi-

ples in the androgyne figure, moving toward the development of a collective (feminist) women's voice (32). But what remains unremarked is how Rich negotiates the tension between the exclusion of the masculine which the collectivity of women requires for the construction of its singular identity and the more pragmatic need for a nonetheless u-topic negotiated coexistence.

The poems of this period signal an important shift with respect to Rich's project, a move that she makes clearer in her work beginning with *The Dream of a Common Language*. The development of Rich's feminist and lesbian/feminist aesthetic in the 1970s opens new possibilities for feminist criticism at the same time that it alienates some of her earlier critics and supporters who now take objection to her treatment of feminist principles in her poetry. In their view, her radicality exceeds art's capacity to contain or suppress it; she has stepped over the line that separates "art" from "politics." In a sense their objections parallel the point I just made concerning Rich's inability or unwillingness at this time to move beyond an oppositional logic of the sex/power/knowledge nexus of language.

The important difference between my observation and the complaints of these non- or anti-feminist critics is that they refuse to perceive the political importance of the reversal Rich enacts. Reinscribing the dominant hierarchy of sexual politics in the form of textual politics, Rich's opponents prefer a tidy, judicious art that resists the political implications of the quotidian detail. The poet's refusal to engage in a proper disciplining of the heart in the form(s) of tradition which offers to recuperate woman, to give the good girl her "place," sets her at odds with the part of her readership that finds its commitment ultimately with the artistic establishment. Their judgments and persistent, almost mechanical defense of the fathers, underscore the very purpose of Rich's feminist critique and her desire to forge an/other discourse for feminist writing.

Rich's book *Of Woman Born* provoked similarly hostile responses from non-feminist critics and readers. The volume's considerations, begun in a review essay, "The Anti-Feminist Woman" (1972), clarify Rich's views on women's "place" in patriarchal culture, what it is that she wishes to renounce. As the subtitle suggests, she attempts a tricky differentiation between "Motherhood as Experience and Institution." Her audience is not always able or willing to engage this subtle difference, when read in the context of her strong indictment of patriarchy, which she defines as "the power of the fathers: a familial-social, ideological, political system in which men – by force, direct pressure, or through ritual, tradition, law, and language, customs, etiquette, education, and the division of labor, determine what part women shall or shall not play, and in which the female is everywhere subsumed under the male" (57). Positioned in this way, women's bodies and their (re)productive capacities can be read, in the Foucauldian sense, as the locus of socially constructed regulative technologies.

The distinctions between experience and institutional effects pose problems for feminist criticism because the understanding of one cannot be neatly separated from the other. In its public form, motherhood, woman's socially pre-eminent role, exists under the control of men and is superimposed upon "the *potential relationship* of any woman to her power of reproduction and to children" (13). Experienced in this form, it is difficult to separate the alienating effect of woman's "place" in social institutions from the "actual fact" (experience) of woman as mother. Earning a place with works like Woolf's *A Room of One's Own* and *Three Guineas*, Rich provides one of the century's most astute explorations of how woman's identity is figured, that is, produced and socially represented, in Western culture. When she talks about her own transformation at twenty-five, she imagined that "new self" as male – "independent, astutely willing, original" (193). Through feminist analysis, she struggles to separate these and other desirable properties from their (en)gendered (em)bodiment in language so that one's (biological) "identity" as a woman and one's (social/discursive) potential for positive (re)presentation are no longer antithetical captives of gender opposition. Rich nonetheless resists biologistic essentialism, anti-intellectualism and separatism – all of which she has been accused of advocating. Here and elsewhere she focuses on a particular form of social transformation which she claims for radical feminism; citing Mary Daly, Rich maintains that radical feminism "alone opens up human consciousness adequately to the desire for non-hierarchical, non-oppressive society" (80). Still caught up in an exclusionary logic, Rich confronts the challenge of constructing a displacement, side-stepping the objection of some critics that she wants to make for radical feminism a singular access to the social truth.

Continuing to refine her notion of a feminist poetics, Rich characterizes "the true nature of poetry" as "The drive/to connect. The dream of a common language" (7) so that the personal, the political and the aesthetic share a common purpose in language. As she frees herself "*of the hunter, the trapper/the wardens of the mind* –" (8), she expands her image of the poet to include the mother "dumb/with loneliness" (15) in whose beginnings Rich recognizes her own trajectory of escape. Probing the limits, the "Cartographies of Silence," knowing that "Language cannot do everything –" (19), she imagines a poetics of silence, struggling at the perimeter, marking its opposite – sound, but returning always

> ... to the concrete and everlasting world
> what in fact I keep choosing

are these words, these whispers, conversations
from which time after time the truth breaks moist
    and green (20).

Rich's writings which explore the force of woman's anger and alienation, culminating in *Diving into the Wreck* and *Of Woman Born*, are supplanted more and more with explicitly lesbian works concerned with issues of possibility and connectedness between women, with the emergence of a positive community identification for women. The recognition of this move and the apprehension it generates determine to a degree the kind of accounting Rich's critics give of her work in this period.

Her desire to materialize the collective power of women in feminist/lesbian terms leads Rich to look for sources of reconstructive power in women like Marie Curie ("Power"), and in relationships between women in "Paula Becker to Clara Westhoff," with her own sister in "Sibling Mysteries," and with the women mountain climbers united by "*A cable of blue fire*," refusing "*to settle for less*" than the realization of their dream (6) in "Phantasia for Elvira Shatayev." Survival depends literally upon connectedness: "Until we find each other, we are alone" (14). However as a theorist Rich invokes no simple, romantic notion of woman as biological monolithic entity; the ideology of sameness or likeness receives as rigorous a critique as that of difference. Thus, Rich also refigures relationships with men in poems like "Natural Resources." It is as though the poet returns to set the record straight. What woman wants is "The phantom of the man-who-would-understand,/the lost brother, the twin —" (62), not the rapist, but "the comrade/twin": "Merely a fellow-creature/with natural resources equal to our own" (62). She (re)signs other possibilities expressed as "humanism" and "androgyny," words too shallow to express woman's difference in relationship to men, to other women, and to herself. Withholding these comfortable props, she forces the reader to engage her work as feminist, just as she enlists the reader's participation in refiguring women and sociopolitical relations. She rewrites the unwritten of tradition and continuity, casting her lot with "the raging stoic grandmothers," the nurturers and conservators of value

who age after age, perversely,

with no extraordinary power,
reconstitute the world (67).

As she reconstitutes the world as word, Rich wants to write an intelligent love which refuses what she sees as the heterosexist division of love and action, itself marked by an essential arbitrariness as the ostensibly "natural," but actually unbalanced figure for human relationship which few of her critics want to engage.

During this period, the sphere of Rich's political involvement broadens and her analysis sharpens, as demonstrated in the poem "Hunger," dedicated to Audre Lorde. She exposes the horizontal hostility articulated in the hierarchicization of suffering that patriarchal society promotes as a deterrent to the solidarity of oppressed peoples:

> The politics of hunger:
> The decision to feed the world
> is the real decision. No revolution
> has chosen it. For that choice requires
> that women shall be free (13).

Perhaps the suggestion that the freedom of women as a group will tip the balance of world decision in a life-preserving direction reflects a naive, partisan, even essentializing view, but the same logic (the logic of the same) also dictates that intervention in the balance of power (as a no-power/all-power im/balance) will demand a rewriting of relation, distribution, and production. Writing at the edge, where none of our rehearsed performances can be trusted, Rich questions the familiar discursive forms, the "oratory, formulas, choruses, laments" (75). She searches for what does not lie, like something she feels in the eyes of the lioness. Using the "oppressor's language," because she needs to talk to us, because it is her language as well, Rich harbors no illusions about the lesbian feminist's or anyone else's ability to escape the patriarchal province of language: "Poetry never stood a chance/ of standing outside history" (*Fact* 325). This "new" language of the disinherited, the undisciplined cry of the heart, is not really new in human and socio-political terms: "in fact we were always like this,/rootless, dismembered: knowing it makes the difference" (75). What *is* new is the process of trying to articulate the cry in a form which politicizes rather than recuperates or represses the disinherited. The knowledge that makes a difference is a knowledge of difference earned, in Rich's case, through her lesbian/feminist repositioning. As "Transcendental Etude" demonstrates most brilliantly, she returns repeatedly to material things – milkweed skeins, petunia petals, the feather of a finch – and to concrete gestures – composing valued objects on the scrub board – to reorient herself, to test out what matters, as a material antidote to "the arguments and jargon" that quickly fill a room and that we mistake for signification and signs of our connectedness. The representation of the material realities of women's lives, as they are textually remembered, preserved, examined and addressed, asks the writer and reader to reorient themselves personally and, thus, politically as well.

The concerns of her collection of essays, *On Lies, Secrets, and Silence: Selected Prose 1966-1978* (1979), overlap and reinforce those expressed in the poetry written during the same period. The introduction to the volume reveals a writer conscious of her position as a white lesbian/feminist living in the United States. The purpose of her work at this time is "to define a female consciousness which is political, aesthetic, and erotic, and which refuses to be included or contained in the culture of passivity" (18). While she continues the task of reclamation or repossession of her sources and foremothers, as in "Vesuvius at Home: The Poetry of Emily Dickinson (1975)," she sharpens her articulation of the goal of a feminist critique: to achieve "an end to male privilege and a changed relationship between the sexes" (153). This goal emerges as her response to the need for a new ethics to supplant the scandalous lies of the socio-political contract, and the common lies of both speech and silence. The notion of replacing the old with a new ethics implies that there is a singular "truth" that can be spoken; Rich, however, resists this presumptive move, maintaining in her essay "Women and Honor: Some Notes on Lying (1975)" that "There is not 'the truth,' 'a truth' – truth is not one thing, or even a system. It is an increasing complexity" (187). Throughout these essays she passes over the doctrinaire solution, "for certainty even at the cost of honesty, for an analysis which, once given, need not be reexamined" (193). She speaks in favor of an expanded rather than a reduced complexity, a point that is exemplified in "Power and Danger: Works of a Common Woman (1977)," where Rich pursues the questions of the political poem, the politics of poetics and the poetics of politics, through a discussion of Judy Grahn's work. Uniting two strains in her own writing – the poems of lesbian love and of politics – Rich claims "powerlessness and power" as textuality's common ground: "No true political poetry can be written with propaganda as an aim, to persuade others 'out there' of some atrocity or injustice ..." (251). The power of the love poem, like the political poem, resides in the turn it effects. How the poet creates a relationship to experience, or how the artistic and the political come together through the poet-in-the-poem (the woman as speaking subject) and her relation to the poem in tradition (the lesbian artist). Rich's rejection of the political tendency as determinative of value, like her earlier refusal to rest securely in her aesthetic accomplishment, or the artistic tendency, points toward the more complex view of indissolubly linked features requiring that the reader, no longer "out there," discover her or his own reconceived and revised means of producing the poems' meanings.

Seeking "a profound transformation of world society and of human relationships," Rich focuses ever more insistently on the refiguration of the socio-political context. The positive construction of relationships between women reaches its fullest elaboration in *Twenty-One Love Poems*, which was first published separately in 1976, not by Norton, her usual publisher, but by a women's press – a gesture which can perhaps be read as a statement about Rich's own relation to literary production. Two years later, these poems are included in *The Drama of a Common Language: Poems 1974-1977* (1978), a return to Norton, not in a countermanding gesture but as an insertion of the revolutionary within the space of the traditional. Testing feminism's radical potential and stretching the limits of discourse, Rich increases her commitment to writing lesbianism as the unspeakable, the unwritten text of women's lives, because "what has been kept unspoken, therefore *unspeakable*, in us is what is most threatening to the patriarchal order in which men control, first women, then all who can be defined and exploited as 'other.'" (308). The lesbian (black and white) and the black (woman and man) as the repressed "Other," are the "beyond" of sex and race with whom women must form solidarity. As such, they provide the inevitable subjects (as material and, in the case primarily of the white lesbian, as speaker) of Rich's revolutionary poetry and politics.

As Rich's work becomes more explicitly radical, the issues of masculine exclusion and culpability, feminist separatism and identity, constitute a battleground for contemporary feminist critical responses. In "Notes for a Magazine: What Does Separatism Mean?," she reverses the negative judgments of exclusion to construe separation as a positive gesture of "claiming one's identity and community as an act of resistance" (86), but for Rich separatism finally is as much an escape from the engagement with difference as it is a liberating move. In a note to the "Foreword" in *Blood, Bread, and Poetry: Selected Prose 1979-1985* (1986), she offers her most direct position statement: "At no time have I ever defined myself as, or considered myself, a lesbian separatist. I have worked with self-defined separatists and have recognized the importance of separatism as grounding and strategy. I have opposed it as a pressure to conformity and where it seemed to derive from biological determinism. The necessity for autonomous women's groups still seems obvious to me" (viii, fn 1). The essays collected in this volume reflect these views, and in fact gain their radical potential through the writer's commitment to forging larger coalitions. By writing alliances, Rich attempts to con/script others, to impose on us the task of co-authoring a new socio-political discourse. The most explosive of these gestures occurs in "Compulsory Heterosexuality and Lesbian Existence" (1980).

In this essay, Rich creates the mechanism for a startling effect in which the reader is asked to become a producer of refunctioned socio-political institutions. She accomplishes this through the unsettling move of plotting all women's lives on a "lesbian continuum," thereby stripping those sub/scribing to a socially "compulsory heterosexuality" of their unexamined position as exemplars of "*the* natural emotional and sensual inclination for women" (58). The subversive effects of this re-writing are several. In a disturbing reversal, the lesbian is publically, unabashedly figured as the "bottom line," the initial feature or common thread in women's lives. Just as Rich, who eventually publishes her lesbian love poems with Norton, places lesbian texts in the place of tradition, the lesbian of the continuum is inserted, takes a place, in tradition. And the heterosexual woman is shaken from her position of privilege and conscripted into the proscribed, socially reprehensible place of the lesbian as "deviant," "abhorrent" or simply "invisible" (26). Heterosexual women who want to preserve an identity of privilege and lesbian women, interested, according to the same logic, in maintaining "pure" identity, the power to determine membership in the lesbian community, are displaced through Rich's daring repositioning with respect to the way in which the dominant ideology constructs heterosexuality, as a socio-political institution. In effect, the text replicates the alienated conditions within which we live, and we are asked to reconsider what we hold to as identity, community and relationship, having been placed, at least discursively, in a new set of relationships.

Though frequently read as such, this essay is not about "compulsory lesbianism," for, indeed, who might compel women to adopt a "lesbian position"? How might lesbianism, in its own right, be written as a political institution? Indeed, the figure would not have such force had Rich presented it as a "heterosexual continuum" or an "androgyny scale." Through the figure of the "lesbian continuum," Rich suggests a range of experiences that any woman may have, regardless of how she identifies herself, whether or not she claims the name "lesbian." Through the "lesbian continuum," doubtless a problematic figure as all figures of a problematic are, Rich's revolutionary performance eludes assimilation and foregrounds critical examination as it positions women and their past experiences in relation to one another rather than, or at least in addition, to their relationships with men. Trying to move "beyond" the conventional binary oppositions, rather than simply negating them, Rich refigures lesbianism and heterosexuality along the continuum's subversive relational structure which connects women in their difference, asks each woman to identify the differences within herself, and relates one to another.

Any writer who has given us so much writing is a likely target or at least offers a ready supply of words that can be enlisted in the service of critical disputes. Rich's work has served as an arena for conflicting feminist critical arguments.

A writer like Rich whose thematic concerns alone have focused so unrelentingly on complexities and ambiguities of human language and experience puts us on notice. Contra/dictions characterize her life and work; they preoccupy her still, as the title of the third section of *Your Native Land, Your Life* suggests: "Contradictions: Tracking Poems." Rich summarizes her perplexity in the essay "Split at the Root," where she represents herself as "The middle-class white girl taught to trade obedience for privilege. The Jewish lesbian raised to be a heterosexual gentile. The woman who first heard oppression named and analyzed in the Black Civil Rights struggle. The woman with three sons, the feminist who hates male violence. The arthritic woman limping with a cane, the woman who has stopped bleeding are also accountable. The poet who knows that beautiful language can lie, that the oppressor's language sometimes sounds beautiful. The woman trying, as part of her resistance, to clean up her act" (*Blood* 123). These tensions are not easily reduced to a monolithic or single(simple)-minded vision, and efforts to do so tend to suggest more about her readers' anxieties and interests than hers.

Also deserving of mention is another related failure to read the lessons of Rich's texts. It would seem, in the abstract, that her long-standing, often expressed desire for a non-oppressive, non-hierarchical society of negotiated co-existence could not be easily overlooked by "liberal" and radical readers. Yet her work is frequently dismissed in critical and academic circles, or she is represented as a poet whose work stopped with the somewhat less threatening *Diving into the Wreck*. On charges of essentialism and separatism respectively, post-structuralist critics and creative writers in academic institutions have forged a curious coalition in their resistance to reading Rich. What these readers reject, if we can even for a moment take Rich at her word, is her u-topic desire for women and men to relate as understanding "comrade/twins" in a radically transformed structure of equals – a writing some refuse to read.

To figure the "beyond" of socio-political organization and relationship requires a "quantum leap," "a leap of the imagination" (271), "beyond" the oppositions the phallogocentric analytical method uses to produce heterosexism, racial dominance, and class oppression masquerading as knowledge. By looking "beneath what is apparent for what has been simultaneously true, though unseen" (299), a method she claims for radical feminism, Rich wants to displace the opposition of the One and the Other, white/black, rich/poor, of man's privilege and woman's "place," in favor of a something "otherwise" and "elsewhere." The separation from the other is a separation within the self, requiring us to undertake multiple, unending negotiations with the logic of identity. As early as "When We Dead Awaken," Rich described the transformative capacity of the imagination in terms of its power to undo conventional oppositions: "You have to be free to play around with the notion that day might be night, love might be hate; nothing can be too sacred for the imagination to turn into its opposite or to call experimentally by another name" (43). Despite the fears of the powerful, she is not talking about a reversal where women dominate men, blacks victimize whites, the homeless dispossess the possessed, or lesbians take over the world. Nor is she urging appropriation where the differences between black and white women are eliminated through "colorblindness," which she insists is not the opposite of racism (although perhaps it is, in terms of the constricting oppositional mechanics of racist grammar), but is instead "a form of naiveté and moral stupidity" (380) through which whites solipsistically deny the particularity of black experience.

The poems collected in her last three volumes – *A Wild Patience Has Taken Me This Far, Your Native Land, Your Life* and *Time's Power* – demonstrate how increasingly difficult it is to write beyond this point, that is, to manipulate language in order to negotiate the constraints of the metalogic. Perhaps no one has tried so hard for so long as Rich has. "The Images," for example, explicitly undertakes the problem of refiguring "woman," given the realization that "no-man's-land does not exist" (4), that separatism will neither reform nor displace the system of opposition. Only in the private world of intimate physical love is the speaker re-membered, fulfilling her need for assembling an alternative view of herself within the context of "the war of the images" (*Wild* 5). She reconsiders the split self again in "Integrity," where, like the spider, who brings to mind the powerful, mythic spider-grandmother, she spins and weaves simultaneously. Through her struggle with the word, the poet tests the limits of a singular meaning and a unicentered identity for woman and culture.

Rich writes her own account of "Culture and Anarchy," conspicuously stealing her title from Arnold and positioning herself at once in the culture of nineteenth-century women writers and in the anarchy of nature in August. She juxtaposes natural wildness with the oppressively orderly, unnatural constructions of culture (the tradition of continuity without rupture), by permitting the intertexts of feminism – Susan B. Anthony, Jane Addams, Elizabeth Barrett, Ida Husted Harper, Elizabeth Cady Stanton – to break open her text. The letters blur as *The History of Woman Suffrage* is transmuted into *The History of Human Suffering*. Exposing the price of order, Rich presents a litany of the omissions cultural tradition needs to construct itself. "For Julia in Nebraska" continues the accumulation of intertexts with the lesbian writer Willa Cather, "whose letters were burnt in shame" (*Wild* 17), analogous to the mute historical marker whose silence lies, concealing the "broken treaties, Indian blood/women wiped out in childbirths, massacres" (17) in the "American" desire to construct a narrative celebration of the frontiersman's "heroic conquest." This history is a pictograph, "neither your script nor mine," that asks for (re)interpretation.

Rich's search for a method that will take her out of the metalogical trap is well illustrated in "What Is Possible." The speaker exposes the path she chooses over and over in her poetry as a means of questioning oppositional thinking and of displaying analytical method with a truth as "true" as planetary motion. She sidesteps the "abstract and pure" (*Wild* 24), "knowing better than the poem she reads," but also "knowing through the poem" (25). She confunds the interior and the exterior, private and public. Figuring the interior as the "beyond" of an intimacy withheld from public discourse, she positions her speaker inside a house, surrounded by the killing wind of winter. At the same time, the speaker claims she could know what is "beyond" if only the mind were ever as simple as "a swept interior" and deciphering were as clear as "a comb passing through hair beside a window" (24). The poem creates the sense that these places and gestures have a "truthfulness" that writing or analysis never does or can have, and yet such concrete manifestations of life are not really interpretable either, irresolutely stubborn as they are in the silent immanental materiality of event and the elusive significance of affect until they enter the inescapably limiting and unnaturally orderly scene of language. In the most troublesome way, they are always already written. Such is the paradox of immanence: that properties appear to reside in the thing itself while they are effects of mind, one's subjectivity acting in and constructed by language. In "The Spirit of Place," Rich continues her struggle with the wor(l)d "as it is," as it has been represented, as it might be. She unsettles identity, just as knowledge itself. There is always a part of us "out beyond ourselves/ knowing knowing knowing" (45) – but what that is – the identity, the knowledge – is never fully articulated, ever returning to inform or motivate our struggles with language and action. She locates the text of the wor(l)d "as it is" with the repressed and victimized of history, the unspeakable and silent "Other" whose text "on a pure night" remains to be read. A perspective on the construction of knowledge, other than the view of it as a conclusive accumulation of knowledge, other than the view of it as a conclusive accumulation of logical and analytical detail, is at work in these poems. Instead, we are asked to engage the other woman, to look life in the face, in the eyes – to see and feel it: "look at her closely if you dare" (57), hoping somehow that the way we rewrite the wor(l)d will allow us to see her and it to write us with a difference.

Aware of the problematic nature of her project, Rich shares the preoccupation and strategies of other intellectuals pursuing philosophical and cultural problems; she explicitly takes up the question of framing, what is seen under what circumstances, how self-positioning entails a frame, a vision. In "Frame" the speaker regards another woman's victimization as she constructs her. Rich reiterates the refrain of her own self-positioning: "*I am standing all this time/just beyond the frame, trying to see*" (46). Similarly, *Sources*, published as a chapbook in 1983 and reprinted as the first section of *Your Native Land, Your Life*, explores the question of the subject position in terms of who one is and where one stands, the conundrum, she claims, of all her poems: "There is a *whom*, a *where*/that is not chosen that is given and sometimes falsely given" (*Your* 6). In this beautiful and very personal poem, Rich attempts to review as she reconstructs her history. The reflective anger of the poem belongs to one who grieves for what is lost; in fact the volume reverberates with echoes of the lesbian poet Elizabeth Bishop, particularly her "Art of Losing," which provides the occasion for the poem, "It's true these last few years I've lived" (98). Rich cannot take comfort in the knowledge of the common things she can name: "there is no finite knowing, no such rest" (27). She ends the poem, but not the quest, with a reflection on a line from Gordimer's *Burger's Daughter*: "When I speak of an end to suffering I don't mean anesthesia. I mean knowing the world, and my place in it, not in order to stare with bitterness or detachment, but as a powerful and womanly series of choices" (27; see note, 113). The poems seem to respond to the question, "What can I see from here?" This is not a new question, as evidenced by the title poem and epigraph from the collection *The Fact of a Doorframe: Poems Selected and New 1950-1984*. The self-reflexive poem from 1974 presents poetry as support, method, and view – "violent, arcane, common,/hewn of the commonest living substance." The frame, as a structure of figuration, is both inside and outside, the condition for seeing and part of what is seen.

Rich defuses polarization, particularly the "we"/"they" opposition that marks some feminist criticism, by accepting her own position with respect to her country's history: "What if I told you home/is this continent of the homeless" (*Fact* 323), a country which suppresses diasporas, refugees, taboo languages, the "trails of tears." In "North American Time," the title poem of the middle section of *Your Native Land, Your Life*, the poet suggests that there is no escaping our position, where we stand literally and metaphorically:

> Everything we write
> will be used against us
> or against those we love (33).

There is no hope of escaping history through language, because even if we were to move, change position, "our words stand." The poem signals a renewed commitment to global accountability, an idea which gains importance in the essays of *Blood, Bread, and Poetry: Selected Prose, 1979-1985*. In the title essay, "Blood, Bread and Poetry: The Location of the Poet" (1983), Rich pursues a line of inquiry which she extends further in "Notes toward a Politics of Location." Beginning with a need to understand how she is affected by "*location*" as a lesbian feminist poet and writer in the United States, Rich acknowledges in the later essay the ways in which her position in this country entails a particular perspectival politics. We might say that what bothers Rich most about location and the frame's effect are the assumptions of centrism and forgetfulness, a view she shares with many poststructuralist and cultural critics today. Wanting "to understand the politics of location," she begins with her body, which determines by sex and color "the places it has taken me, the places it has not let me go" (*Blood* 216). Rich is disarmingly self-critical, of her ideas and of the process of writing: "I wrote a sentence just now and x'd it out. In it I said that women have always understood the struggle against free-floating abstraction ... I don't want to write that kind of sentence now, the sentence that begins, 'Women have always ...' ... If we have learned anything, in these years of late twentieth century feminism, it's that that 'always' blots out what we really need to know: when, where and under what conditions has the statement been true?" (214). The application of such self-scrutinizing questions produces a challenge to the construction of feminist theory today. Rich's texts do more than present lesbian/feminist polemics; in their unrelenting insistence on the inextricable relation between form and content, one person and another, they perform their revisionary revolutions in the letter.

Struggling with feminism's definition of theory, Rich asks if it is "something made only by white women, and only by women acknowledged as writers?" (*Blood* 219). From her position in Nicaragua, the site of the earlier essay on location, Rich recognizes the inescapable importance of her position in North America to her perspective on identity and value. She opposes the oppositions, "the climate of an enormous either/or" (221), which masquerade in a politics of absolute choice. In several decentering moves, Rich unsettles Feminst Identity, questioning the pronoun of individual identity, "I," as well as the comfortable "we" of collective presumption. She no longer believes "that the white eye sees from the center" (226). In her summary of what white North American feminists in the United States have been told about the "other woman," Rich poses for herself and her readers some of feminist criticism's most pressing questions as it tries to escape the tyranny of Feminism, the proper name. Citing the resistance of women in South Africa, Lebanon, and Peru, Rich questions the view of White Feminism that this other woman's ideas "are not real ideas" and "that only when a white mind formulates is the formulation to be taken seriously" (230). She concludes with a difficult challenge to the perils of abstract theorizing: "Once again: who is we?" Similarly, she ends the series of contradiction poems (if we can say that there is an end to such poems for Rich) with the caution: "O you who love clear edges/more than anything watch the edges that blur" (*Your* 111).

The terms of a writing practice, though not the answer, are evident by now, although even those may blur before our eyes. In "Blood, Bread, and Poetry" Rich considers what is at stake in any effort at decentered, non-authoritarian feminist refiguration. She reflects on a comment from James Baldwin: "'Any real change implies the breakup of the world as one has always known it, the loss of all that gave one an identity, the end of safety'" (*Blood* 176). The threat of the coalescence of the political and the aesthetic rests in the power of language to destroy as it creates; the work of any (re)writing. Although we can understand in addition why the institution of literature, like any sociopolitical body with a stake in its perpetuation and preservation, writes so unceasingly against this powerful union of the political and the artistic, we can also recognize how an institution's life issues from the vitality associated with change and the "new."

In "Virginia 1906," Rich asks of her persona, "How does she keep from dreaming the old dreams?" (*Your* 43) By reiterating this question, which she and others have written and rewritten, Rich focuses our attention on what matters most in feminist cultural, artistic and philosophical work. The answer, her reader feels certain, will not result from abstraction floating free from the material reality of women's particular relationships within culture. As Rich explains in "Notes Toward a Politics of Location," "Theory – the seeing of patterns, showing the forest as well as the trees – theory can be a dew that rises from the earth and collects in the raincloud and returns to earth, over and over. But if it doesn't smell of the earth, it isn't good for the earth" (*Blood* 213-14). But I do not take this as a writing which favors experience over theory; rather, I read it as the writer's challenge to those of us, including herself, who are theorizing feminism. Through some metaphorical sidestep or quantum leap, feminist theory, like rain when it comes back down, must smell of the earth.

Rich's most recent work, reflected in *Time's Power*, suggests that the struggle has not ended. She continues to examine, expand, reconsider the contents of the perspectival frame, as it exists for her as a feminist, a poet, and a citizen of the United States. If anything, the vision has been extended here – stretching to encompass an understanding of life's relation to death: "death we talk to her/ daily, as to a neighbor" (8). She is intimate with her: "she has the keys/ to this house" (8). *Time's Power* is in some ways a somber volume, written, as it were, under the death sentence. The poet, like the lover of "Love Poem," carries on her critical work: "testing, testing the world/the word" (7), resisting the "pretty sonnet" as somehow aesthetically, culturally and political inappropriate to the lover, the act, the moment. In a world of power, where "guns are the language of the strong to the weak" (40), Rich observes that "Time's/power [is] the only just power" (50).

This is not to say, however, that wrongs right themselves in time, that all things shall pass, that things will gradually improve. Rather, it is to reinforce the need for memory, for analysis, for story. In poem after poem, "In Memoriam: D.K.," "Harpers Ferry," "Letters in the Family," "Sleepwalking Next to Death," "The Desert as Garden of Paradise," Rich recounts the lives of the struggling and the dead. If anything, these poems suggest the terms of the struggle, the cost to the poet in her unrelenting effort, as suggested in "Dreamwood," to decipher the rebus that presents itself as life, her own and others. These are the stories that explain the need for revolution, the poem as the report of the union of the material and the dream. A melancholy book, *Time's Power* is marked by the cultural revolutionary's weary awareness that one finally leaves the struggle through death, but the struggle continues, to be waged elsewhere, by others – the legacy of the next generation. It is, as she writes in the volume's final poem "Turning": "no task you expect to see finished, but/you can't hold back from the task" (53).

Rich's global phase, a looking "beyond" what she calls "North American Tunnel Vision," represents an agenda of magnitude and urgency for Rich, feminist critical theorists, and readers in the decades ahead. The revolutionary political and artistic force of Rich's work is that she tracks the contradictions and, doing so, holds us to these fundamental questions concerning one's position in relation to the world of production which the text of feminism must engage if it is to write itself. She reminds us, in book after book, of the need for revolution. Through her resistance to the easy course, she gives us an improved apparatus – texts which specify a method, though not the answer, and an improved politics which requires our involvement as critical producers if we are ever to speak of global feminism and to write (it) in other ways.

The Works of Adrienne Rich

Blood, Bread and Poetry: Selected Prose, 1979-1985. New York and London: Norton, 1986.

A Change of World. New Haven: Yale University Press, 1951; London: Oxford University Press, 1952.

The Diamond Cutters and Other Poems. New York: Harper, 1955.

Diving into the Wreck: Poems, 1971-1972. New York: Norton, 1973.

The Dream of a Common Language: Poems, 1974-1977. New York: Norton, 1978.

The Fact of a Doorframe: Poems Selected and New, 1950-1984. New York: Norton, 1984.

Leaflets: Poems, 1965-1968. New York: Norton, 1969; London: Chatto & Windus/Hogarth Press, 1972.

Necessities of Life: Poems, 1962-1965. New York: Norton, 1966.

"Notes for a Magazine: What Does Separatism Mean?" *Sinister Wisdom* 18 (1981): 83-91.

Of Woman Born. New York: Norton, 1976; London: Virago, 1977.

On Lies, Secrets, and Silence: Selected Prose 1966-1978. New York: Norton, 1979.

Poems: Selected and New, 1950-1974. New York: Norton, 1975.

Selected Poems. London: Chatto & Windus/Hogarth Press, 1967.

Snapshots of a Daughter-in-Law: Poems, 1954-1962. New York & Evanston: Harper & Row, 1963; London: Chatto & Windus/Hogarth Press, 1970.

Sources. Woodside, CA: Heyeck Press, 1983.

Time's Power: Poems, 1985-1988. New York and London: Norton, 1989.

Twenty-One Love Poems. California: Effie's Press, 1976.

A Wild Patience Has Taken Me This Far: Poems, 1978-1981. New York: Norton, 1981.

The Will to Change. New York: Norton, 1971; London: Chatto & Windus, 1972.

Your Native Land, Your Life. New York and London: Norton, 1986.

[Other versions of this text have appeared in the *Dictionary of Literary Biography: Modern Criticism since 1955*, ed. Gregory S. Jay (Detroit: Gale Research Co., 1988) and in my latest book, *(Ex)Tensions: Re-Figuring Feminist Criticism* (Chicago and Urbana: Univ. of Illinois Press, 1989]

Peter Ludes

Neil Postman

(1931-)[1]

During the sixties of the twentieth century, radical criticism of all realms of America's social life gained in impact on public opinion about "the Establishment." The erection of the Berlin wall in August 1961 literally petrified the borderline between the Eastern Bloc and Western European countries. The Cuban crisis in October 1962 made the world realize that nuclear war was not just a vision of sick brains. The increasing involvement of American troops in Vietnam and other parts of Indochina took the toll of hundreds of thousands of lives; news on this war, spread by journals and increasingly by television, shaped the public discourse on international affairs. The completion of a high-school education no longer automatically meant the beginning of vocational training or college education but could mean leaving one's home town and becoming "airborne" in a region of the earth that most American soldiers knew nothing about. No wonder that the American nation began to question education itself. No wonder that people began to have doubts about its importance for life.

Neil Postman, teacher at elementary and high schools, later professor of English at New York University, along with his colleague, Charles Weingartner, another former high school teacher and a professor of Education at Queens College, in 1969 published and propagated *Teaching as a Subversive Activity*. The book opens with the quote from a "subversive hit", popular in those days: "What did you learn in school today ... I learned that Washington never told a lie, I learned that soldiers seldom die ... that's what I learned in school." As in a nutshell, this song highlights Neil Postman's first major concern: "the deteriorating semantic environment"[2]. Since human life is impossible without the internalization and expression of thoughts conveyed by socially constructed, reconstructed, and transmitted language, the "inhalation" of misinformation – such was Postman's argument – endangered human achievements. "Never before, thanks to the techniques of mass communication, have so many listeners been so completely at the mercy of so few speakers."[3]

Neil Milton Postman was born in New York City in 1931. He studied at the State University of New York and earned his Ph.D. at Columbia University. In 1959 he was appointed professor of Communication Arts and Sciences at New York University. From 1976 to 1986, he was editor-in-chief of *ETC: the Journal of General Semantics*. He holds the Christian Lindback Award for Excellence in Teaching, and in 1987 he was given the George Orwell Award for Clarity in Language by the National Council of Teachers of English. Together with his colleague Charles Weingartner he delivered a major address at the 1963 meeting of the National Council of Teachers of English. Postman gave further major talks in Frankfurt, West Germany, in September and October 1984, and in March 1987 at the annual meeting of the Association of Supervision and Curriculum Development in New Orleans. He is married, has three children, and lives in Flushing, New York. According to his own perception, as stated in the preface to *Conscientious Objections*, his most recent collection of essays, he focused on three principal issues throughout his scholarly career: (1) on the triumph of "one-eyed technology" – a term he uses repeatedly; (2) on the decline or eclipse of the word; and (3) on education.

As early as 1969, Postman combined insights into the development of the established school system with observations about the development of the new electronic media in an attempt to assess the increasing dangers of "semantic pollution." On the basis of a critical diagnosis of major deficiencies in the American school system at a time of radical political and cultural changes, he advanced strategies for survival and what he called a "Soft Revolution"[4].

The revolutionary sixties were over when, in 1973, Postman and Weingartner raised the question of "what all the hollering was about." In 1976, Postman continued his publications without his former co-author and released *Crazy Talk, Stupid Talk*. At the end of the seventies he interestingly reached the conclusion that – given the historical changes plus the changes in his own thinking, feeling, and judgment – it might be better to propagate *Teaching as a Conservative Activity*.

During the eighties, Neil Postman was to emerge as the most famous successor to Marshall McLuhan, the controversial media theorist and critic who had died in 1980. Pushing his radical doubt about the possibility of education to its limits, Postman advanced a two-fold hypothesis, viz. that established educational institutions and activities would increasingly be replaced by television and that this process would be accompanied by what he called "the disappearance of childhood."[5] In contrast to what one reviewer called Postman's "grandiose misconceptions" of an all-pervading television impact on social behavior (during the past two or three decades)[6], Postman thought in terms of long-range developments, spanning several generations, which is to say, in the case of the "invention" and "disappearance" of childhood, from the invention of the printing press with movable letters in the fifteenth century to the invention of electronic mass media in the twentieth. The disappearance of childhood therefore implies the appearance of a new type of "adult-child." In 1985, Postman appeared to have lost all hope for any alternative to electronically transmitted entertainment. As it seemed to him, both teaching and television had become amusing activities; thus the final chapter of *Amusing Ourselves to Death* significantly closes on the "Huxleyan warning" about a "brave new world" as a genetically and electronically manipulated world. And yet, in some sense recalling the introduction to *Language in America* from 1969, Postman concludes the final paragraph of *Amusing Ourselves to Death* saying:

What I suggest here as a solution is what Aldous Huxley suggested, as well. [...] He believed ... that we are in a race between education and disaster, and he wrote continuously about the necessity of our understanding the politics and epistemology of media.

To a considerable extent then, Postman focuses on one pervasive theme throughout the well-publicized part of his career: the second half of the twentieth century as characterized by a fundamental restructuring of the public realm and its predominant modes of communication. Formerly, the institutions of school (and, to a lesser degree, family and neighborhood) determined people's time budgets, social activities, forms of intelligence, standards of culturally relevant knowledge and proper conduct. They provided criteria for the orientation of the younger members of society and supplied the framework for authority. The school shaped general standards of accountability to the public and to the nation's future. Yet, school, family, and neighborhood steadily lost their authority over the socialization and education of young people as well as over the communication patterns of American society in general. The balance of communicative habits shifted from education to entertainment, from school to television, from performance and achievement to pleasure without intellectual effort, from serious learning to "amusing ourselves to death." Until the end of the eighties, the only therapy derived from this diagnosis appeared to be *Conscientious Objections*[7].

One of Postman's major complaints springs from the observation that more and more people express what in fact they do not believe. This tendency is strongly reinforced by the functional conditions of big electronic media which provide a plurality of opinions on almost any topic with almost no time for analytic reflection.

The misinformation problem takes a variety of forms, such as lies, clichés and rumours, and implicates almost everybody, including the President of the United States. Many of these problems are related to, or at least seriously affected by, the communications revolution, which, having taken us unawares, has ignited the civil-rights problem, unleashed the electronic-bugging problem, and made visible the sex problem, to say nothing of the drug problem[8].

Contrary to current opinion Postman and Weingartner emphasize that their intention is not to attack or defend the media, but rather to understand their new role in the history of American society. The major media changes that occurred since the invention of the printing press in the fifteenth century and of electronic mass media in the nineteenth and twentieth centuries took place during the last five centuries, which is a minimal time span compared to the evolution of humankind.

In long-term perspective, therefore, the major question is not "What's on television?" or "What's in the newspaper?`" but relates to the medium itself, which "is the message, of course"[9]. Since a "new language" would imply new possibilities of reception, "the new education, in addition to being student-centered and question-centered must also be language-centered"[10]. The major "new languages," however, are the media.

In a world of high-speed, complex, simultaneous, total-field change, the conventional pedestrian academic mode of analytic, linear segmentation and explication itself comprises a threat to our survival. [...] We have new languages to learn if we don't want to talk ourselves to death.[11]

This statement implies that Postman and Weingartner have critical reservations about the use of traditional academic discourse in the contemporary environment. Postman's intellectual shifts of position may be due to the development of the discursive mode during the final decades of the twentieth century, which inevitably lags behind the need for reality-adequate diagnosis of highly accelerated changes. Neither verbal communication nor visual presentation nor spectator entertainment can come to adequate terms with a fast-changing environment. The only alternative – according to Postman – would be a new type of education for a new type of reality.[12]

How can such an education be organized, and which strategies can be devised? These were the questions to be answered in 1971.

The soft revolution has as its purpose the renewal and reconstruction of educational institutions without the use of violence. [...] The central purpose of the soft revolution is to help all of us get it altogether in the interests of our mutual survival.[13]

The major strategy of this revolution is seen as quite similar to one of the arts of self-defense, Judo. "You use your adversary's strength against himself, and in spite of himself (in fact, *because* of himself)."[14] This technique might lead to behavioral changes on the part of the educational establishment

through being challenged and overthrown by their own premises and fundamental values as determined by the Declaration of Independence, the Bill of
Rights, and other 'sacred' texts.

Postman and Weingartner offer numerous examples for soft revolutionary
activities from various scholastic environments all over the United States.
They also discuss the hostile relationship between the students and the "hard-
heads." Most original for the early seventies is their "prospectus for a Ph.D.
program in media ecology." This new subject is supposed to focus on communications technology as an environment for human perception, feeling,
understanding, and evaluation. If realized it would encompass media history,
media literacy and creativity, media research, media perspectives and criticism.[15]

These proposals reflect the authors' concern with the new type of media
mixture in American society of the seventies. They do not reject the Western
literary tradition nor do they assume that its (irrecoverable) predominance in
the competition of different media would in itself be conducive to a better
understanding of reality. Their point is not that the loss of a literary tradition
has to be regretted as such. Rather they argue that neither the effects of literary tradition nor the growing impact of electronic media on social consciousness and behavior are able to provide reality-adequate means of perception,
orientation, and communication. Under these circumstances they call for a
new type of study which they introduce as "speculative research," a type of
research which cannot yet be grounded on empirical analyses, but combines
insights from various disciplines with artistic intuition.

On the basis of their speculative diagnosis of the changing semantic environment Postman and Weingartner[16] offer a major thesis concerning the competition of media, namely "that *two media of communication cannot exist at
the same time if they are trying to do the same thing.*" This assumption of a
general tendency towards monopoly in any historical media mix is certainly
challengeable. Yet, it highlights a major problem for media research: in any
given phase of development and for any given culture we have to specify the
degree of distribution and acceptance of the different media in order to understand the prevalent modes of perception, evaluation, and communication.
Therefore, the crucial question is not whether reading books or pamphlets or
watching television news or sitcoms and soap operas is "better or worse," but
rather how and why observable changes in the overall communication structure take place. Only on the basis of a more adequate diagnosis of this development, can "strategies for survival," as Weingartner and Postman designate
them, become possible.

The development of Postman's intellectual career, however, suggests that
strategies have become replaced by lamentos. In 1973, Postman and Wein-

gartner[17] still believed in childhood as a major phase of individual human development throughout "the history of the human race." But, less than ten years later, Postman recalls "the invention of childhood" and diagnoses its disappearance. His new mood is reflected in his introduction to *The Disappearence of Childhood*[18]: "If one cannot say anything about how we may prevent a social disaster, perhaps one may also serve by trying to understand why it is occurring."

Falling back on Barbara Tuchman's studies on medieval behavior, Postman[19] considers the questions why in the Middle Ages childhood ended at age seven: it was because seven was the age at which children had full command of speech. Since speech was the only medium of communication between human beings, people were able at this age to participate in general communication. However, as soon as the printing press, requiring particular reading and writing skills, became widespread, a new conception of childhood and adulthood came into being. Using Harold Innis's typology of three major effects of changes in communication technology, Postman refers to a change in the structure of interests, in the character of symbols, and in the nature of community, all of which result from the invention of the printing press and the propagation of reading and writing skills since the end of the fifteenth century. "With the printed book another tradition began: the isolated reader and his private eye. Orality became muted, and the reader and his response became separated from a social context."[20] On the basis of a more widespread visualization of human language in terms of durable, repeatable and standardized (printed) letters, a new detachment from language and linguistic usage developed. The

foundations of modern science were laid within one hundred years after the invention of the printing press. [...] From print onward, the young would have to *become* adults, and they would have to do it by learning to read, by entering the world of typography. And in order to accomplish that they would require education. Therefore, European civilization reinvented schools. And by so doing, it made childhood a necessity.[21]

Elaborating results from Norbert Elias's and Philippe Ariès's historical studies, Postman[22] offers a synopsis of cultural change and of alterations in the communication skills of different age groups:

Eventually, knowledge of ... cultural secrets became one of the distinguishing characteristics of adulthood, so that, until recent times, one of the important differences between the child and the adult has been that adults were in possession of information that was not considered suitable for children to know. [...] And because children could no longer be expected to know the secrets of adult public behavior, books on manners became commonplace.

The institutional separation of childhood from adulthood by means of compulsory education took several centuries to take effect. Only towards the end of the nineteenth century did it become fully established in industrial societies. However, in the second half of the 20th century, almost parallel to the development of a post-industrial society, a new institution developed which, at least in terms of its share in the time budgets of young and old alike, supplemented and partly replaced traditional ways of integrating individuals into society by standardizing behavioral patterns. Television greatly changed the social situation, especially the contents, and the mode of gaining access to information.[23] The presentation of information underwent a transformation toward "infotainment," and jolts of entertaining information usually are internalized without any instruction in the context of different age groups. Television became a "total disclosure medium," i.e.

an open-admission technology to which there are no physical, economic, cognitive, or imaginative restraints. The six-year-old and the sixty-year-old are equally qualified to experience what television has to offer. Television, in this sense is the consummate egalitarian medium of communication, surpassing oral language itself.[24]

Not until the late sixties and the seventies did a generation grow up in the United States which had experienced television continually from their early childhood days through their first years as adults.

According to Postman[25], total television disclosure of formerly hidden realms of life implies a

gradual decline of shame ... a corresponding diminution in the significance of manners. [...] In the face of all this, both the authority of adulthood and the curiosity of childhood lose ground. For like shame and manners they are rooted in the idea of secrets. Children are curious because they do not yet know what they suspect there is to know; adults have authority in great measure because they are the principal source of knowledge.

If Postman's argument is correct, the invasion of television as a total disclosure medium inevitably leads towards the disappearance of childhood. This would in effect mean a severe challenge to a cultural system that has derived its major features from the authority of printed material. However, in his writings on media ecology from the eighties, Postman appears to ignore his former analysis of the interplay of different media of communication. As far as social statistics for the second half of the twentieth century indicate, there is a highly significant increase not only in the amount of television programs and television consumption but also in the amount of high school, college, and university education as well as of vocational training. The time invested in personal discussions at the work place or at home has increased, as compared with the second half of the nineteenth century and the first half of the twentieth when the majority of the working population endured eighty to sixty-hour working weeks.[26] On the other hand, Postman extends his argument by pointing towards the disappearance of adulthood and the emergence of a new type of adult-child as an outgrowth of the changing electronic information environment.[27]

In politics, for example, it does not make any difference for the electorate which of several candidates running for office is able to advance sound arguments. Even the widely received evening service of "world news" (which mainly focuses on national news anyway) only confirms

that there are no important differences between one day and another, that the same emotions that were called for yesterday are called for today ... that all events, having no precedent causes or subsequent consequences, are without value and therefore meaningless[28].

What then,

is the effect of a medium that is entirely centered on the present, that has no capability of revealing the continuity of time ... that always asks for an immediate, emotional response? If the medium is as pervasive as television is, then we may answer in this way: Just as phonetic literacy altered the predispositions of the mind in Athens in the fifth century B.C. ... so does television make it unnecessary for us to distinguish between the child and the adult. For it is in its nature to homogenize mentalities. The often missed irony in the remark that television programs are designed for a twelve-year-old mentality is that there can be no other mentality for which they may be designed.[29]

In historical terms, the printing age introduced childhood and education, whereas the television age reinvents an intermingling of age categories and levels of maturity in perception, knowledge and judgment.

In 1985, Postman tried to develop a general social theory on the basis of his speculative analysis of the changing communicative structures. "For on television, discourse is conducted largely through visual imagery, which is to say that television gives us a conversation in images, not words"[30]. It is his intention "to show that a great media-metaphor shift has taken place in America, with the result that the content of much of our public discourse has become dangerous nonsense"[31]. The perception and criteria of truth have changed. Certain faculties of human intelligence and wisdom lose while others gain in social importance, "the epistemology created by television not only is inferior to a print-based epistemology but is dangerous and absurd"[32].

Postman's media ecology from the eighties contradicts some of his statements on education from the late sixties and early seventies. His confidence in the importance of letter-based intelligence appears to have grown measurably, while his formerly expressed expectation that the new media might provide new and enjoyable as well as informative realms of discourse has decreased. He may have changed perspective – if we regard his later writings as more mature and reliable.

At the same time we have to take into account that the media environment, especially television, changed considerably during the one and a half decades under observation here.[33] The use of remote control units and of VCRs also modified the formerly pre-structured viewing patterns. At least some technical control of the electronic visuals, an individual manipulation of its storage and vision, became available for a significant segment of the population. Maybe this distribution of remote control units, VCRs, in conjunction with the distribution of PCs, restructure the audio-visual semantic environment so that Postman's major works of media culture criticism from the eighties may survive only as remarkable examples of fearful apprehensions rather than valid prognostications.

The print age of written exposition is replaced by the visual age of show-business.[34] "[T]he huge amount of time that audiences devote to broadcasting may have far less psychological significance than the sheer number of hours suggests"[35]. More significantly, all television programs seem to favor specific types of conflicts and strategies for their solutions. From the wide array of potential conflicts between man and nature, man and God, man against himself, man and man only the latter (social conflicts) have so far been given preference for the continuous production of television programs. Moreover, individuals are characterized in terms of their physical appearance, environment, and behavior in consonance with highly conventionalized patterns, which reinforces stereotypes. In contrast to former problem-solving models as taught at school, problem solutions in television programs usually favor dramatic outcomes, preferably violent acts.[36]

Prior to the age of telegraphy, the information-action ratio was sufficiently close so that most people had a sense of being able to control some of the contingencies in their lives. What people knew about had action-value. In the information world created by telegraphy, this sense of potency was lost, precisely because the whole world became the context for news. Everything became everyone's business. For the first time, we were sent information which answered no question we had asked, and which, in any case, did not permit the right of reply.[37]

Even the invention of the printing press and the wide distribution of books had changed communication processes towards a more encompassing and modified reception circle, where readers could not directly respond to the author of any book they were reading. Besides, it was impossible even then to select and reselect every bit of information which books, journals, or pamphlets distributed, in accord with one's personal preferences. Postman describes a change in the structure of this 'balance of power' between authors and readers or viewers, yet the widespread tendency towards functional democratization[38] again changes the overall importance of this aspect of the development of communication situations. In a simplified way, with reference to the present phase of the production and reception of visual material, Postman may be right in stating that the

photograph itself makes no arguable propositions, makes no extended and unambiguous commentary. It offers no assertions to repute, so it is not refutable. The way in which the photograph records experience is also different from the way of language. Language makes sense only when it is presented as a sequence of propositions. [...] But there's no such thing as a photograph taken out of context, for a photograph does not require one.[39]

What the communication revolution ushered in by electronic media involves, may be summarized as follows:

– a disconnection of the visual representation of events and the creation of pseudo-events;

– the experience of the world as one to be watched rather than one to be acted in;

– a reaction towards pre-programmed stimuli rather than attempts at self-control (although remote control – it may be added – can provide at least some means of a reconstruction of pre-programmed clips);

– extension of television programs due to the fact that people tend to take for granted the special angle of visualization as the only possible one;

– the representation of socially important discourses subjected to the general rule of entertainment, namely that "the show must go on;"

– disconnection of arguments as they are transformed into entertaining performances put into stimulating sequences, cueing the audience to the 'true' messages of commercials;

– disinformation misleading the public, as events become more and more misplaced, irrelevant, fragmented or superficial, creating in people the illusion of knowledge;

– elimination of reality-testing due to the overwhelming discontinuity of television's visual "discourse";

– projection of discontinuity onto the world it "represents" (what a "present"?), or "re-creates" (what a "creation"?) especially through infotainment that supports and shapes the secular trend towards a politics of televised symbolism;

– imitation of television techniques by other media, as in the case of *USA Today*.

This restructuring of communication even affects formally protected messages, such as sacred sermons, as soon as they enter the world of television.

Even here former standards of conduct based on religious belief are replaced by the pseudo-therapies of commercials. Commercials seemingly offer an easy way out for any human deficiency, not by self-chosen effort but by the easy consumption of a commodity which is constructed and reconstructed for a vicarious experience of the most enjoyable and desirable lifestyle. Among the various lessons taught by any commercial are those

that short and simple messages are preferable to long and complex ones: that drama is to be preferred over exposition: that being sold solutions is better than being confronted with questions about problems [...]. Or that complex language is not to be trusted, and that all problems lend themselves to theatrical expressions. Or that argument is in bad taste and leads only to an intolerable uncertainty.[40]

To put it simply, a new type of behavior pattern emerges, the *immediate* gratification pattern of a zapping and grazing television viewership. What Christopher Lasch in 1979 generally diagnosed as "the culture of Narcissism" coincides with Postman's more particular analysis of media culture and its conspicuous emphasis on immediate gratification.[41]

In 1988, Postman advanced seven theses concerning media technology, corroborating the interpretation that Marshall McLuhan had imposed on media culture – "the medium is the message" – as the major factor of social change. Postman, like McLuhan a quarter century previous, puts media technology into the center of cultural development: (1) culture always pays a price for technological advance: (2) the advantages and disadvantages of a specific technology are never distributed equally:[42] (3) every technology favors a specific and particular world view: (4) technologies compete for domination; (5) technological change takes place in ecological leaps rather than accumulatively; (6) technologies tend to become mythical, i.e. they appear to be components of a natural order: (7) differentiation between technology and media allows for control of social change.[43]

Similar to Marshall McLuhan's limited impact on the academic world[44], Neil Postman's theories were at first little discussed or echoed in major publications such as the *Communication Yearbook*, published by the International Communication Association, the *European Journal of Communication* or the West German journal *Rundfunk und Fernsehen*. Only recent publications by internationally known communication scientists tend to support some of Neil Postman's theses but mostly without placing their own limited and empirically grounded observations in the context of Postman's more encompassing models of media developments as major constitutive factors in cultural and social processes.

Thus, Jerome L. Singer and his wife Dorothy, psychologists at Yale University, summarize the state of research concerning the deterioration of the imagination under the impact of television.[45] Their findings confirm that reading supports the understanding of causal relations and requires a broader cognitive decoding process than the reception of visual presentations on television. The habitualization effected by viewing entertaining television programs increasingly entails a reception of and adaptation to superficial structures.[46] However, this change in the perception skills of the audience does not affect everybody in the same way. Members of social groups who continue reading books, journals and newspapers, also tend to pick up more information from television programs, thus increasing the so-called "knowledge gap" between a better informed minority and the vast majority.[47]

Elisabeth Noelle-Neumann's summary of opinion research in the Federal Republic of Germany supports Postman's thesis that increasing exposure to television programs, including information programs, does not improve people's knowledge about and understanding of actual political developments: Noelle-Neumann also confirms Postman's thesis that this is due to an increase of superficial involvement without a corresponding increase of cognition, which entails the danger of viewers becoming more easily manipulated than readers.[48] Moreover, Noelle-Neumann shares Postman's view that the negative impact of television on the human mind will increase for those generations who from early childhood had adapted themselves to visual stereotypes and are no longer capable of relating them to information picked up and reflected in the context of literal and oral communication.[49] She also shares Postman's focus on a reduction of the mental skills for sustaining arguments, for establishing causal relations, for elaborating and retaining information, for verbal expression, and for developing the imagination – all of which are skills acquired in a culture predicated on literacy, now reduced by a shift to electronic visual media.[50]

Wolfgang R. Langenbucher and Angela Fritz, from the University of Vienna, arrive at similar conclusions: The increasing impact of audio-visual communications has produced negative consequences, such as a partial replacement of personal face-to-face communication.[51] In contrast to Postman, however, they work out different propositions: first, specific requirements for communication research; second, media education; third, media planning. Postman for his own part focuses on media education and is not too optimistic about the chances for a media planning conducted in defense of specific communication skills as developed during the era of literature and the Enlightenment.

The sociologist Elihu Katz questions the Postmanean emphasis on the importance of oral communication in the nineteenth and twentieth centuries.

He argues that only during the industrialization of modern societies and the concomitant trend of the reduction of working time did more opportunities for talk evolve and greater interests in events outside of one's immediate environment develop. Moreover, only the secularization of power structures allowed for unfettered discourse contributing to the pluralism of world views and opinions characteristic of modern societies.[52]

In contrast to the thrust of his arguments in *The Disappearance of Childhood* and *Amusing Ourselves to Death*, Postman in 1988 concluded his interpretation of the development of media technology in a more optimistic vein. We have to take into account his progressive statements on media ecology during the eighties in order to avoid one-sided judgment. I nonetheless deem it necessary to put his arguments into the context of empirically demonstrable changes in both the television audience and television programs as well as other cultural fields.

What Postman largely disregards – and this is the first target of criticism – is the changing television audience[53]: their demographic structure, their level of education, their access to different types of entertainment, their changing ratio of working and leisure time, the growing habitualization processes, the observable development of television towards a mere background medium and the loss of its function as the only home supplier of visual images since its supplementation by VCRs and PCs. There is a conspicuous lack of empirical data substantiating theoretical and critical reflections.

A second major change underestimated by Postman is the *differentiation of television programs* as such. The shift in the United States from a market almost entirely dominated by three commercial networks to competitive forms of audio-visual media distribution through the traditional networks, cable services, and public services in combination with video programs and computer games reestablishes some borderlines between audience groups definable by age categories and educational levels.

The rise of mass media, especially television, to what is practically a fourth power in parliamentary democracies – on a par with the legislative, executive and judiciary branch – evoked specific responses from other quarters such as politics, science, social movements. This rise occurred even under the conditions of so-called deregulation in the United States and an increasing commercialization of the competitive television market in Western Europe during the eighties: This period witnessed "great communicators" whose selection and election was prepared by stereotypes propagated, reproduced, supported, and stylized by mass-distributed television programs. Simultaneously, there was an increasing professionalization in the staging of events by the communication experts of leading politicians. Moreover, the disregard of the role of electronic mass media by academic disciplines came to an end. Theoreticians like Paul Lazarsfeld, Marshall McLuhan, Herbert Schiller, Neil Postman, and Joshua Meyrowitz, as well as numerous empirical researchers like George Gerbner shaped college courses in various schools of journalism or communication. New centers of criticism of television established themselves. During the eighties and nineties even high school courses on the functions and harmful effects of television programs gained ground. Contrary to Postman's propagation of an all-encompassing power of public discourse determined by television, these responses from scientific or public institutions demonstrate its interdependency with other developments. These even include the policies of pressure groups who develop motives and standards of judgment other than "amusement to death."

Along with the changing patterns of both audience and programs, as well as their exposure to other institutional influences, a more differentiated acquisition of visual knowledge easily available for the majority of the audience has evolved. A new generation is thereby enabled to gain some detachment from visual stimuli which initially may have held the power of infinite fascination and exerted the effect of 'brainless' entertainment for some viewers. Thus new expectations and desires for entertainment emerge and previously unknown information patterns converge.

New mediate worlds of news as non-fiction as well as fiction, of news as entertaiment, or news as public and private concerns, of sacred and profane experiences etc. combine in conditioning new personality structures and social relationships. Due to television's indisputable role as a shaper of world views across functionally differentiated realms of activities, a strict borderline between a televised reality in clear contrast to an empirical reality in politics or education or the workaday world cannot be drawn. This does not mean that each and every realm of social life, each and every aspect of human personality is equally subject to the overpowering rule of entertainment. It rather means that different television stations and programs, videos and computer software reflect the functional differentiation and social stratification of modern societies. There is clearly a reciprocal and very dynamic relationship between televised information and public needs, between media content and social change – a relationship that transcends the shaping influence of television, however significant.

Pinning down my assessment of Postman's contribution to contemporary cultural ciriticism to a few major points, I perceive the following inconsistencies and shortcomings in his writings: In consonance with the fundamental critique of major social institutions during the sixties, Postman, collaborating with Weingartner, called for a revolutionary change of the American school system in the late sixties and early seventies and advanced several strategies for survival in what he took to be a polluted semantic environment. Less than ten years later, Postman modified his diagnosis and called for a defense of major values of the established school system which had to be preserved in order to safeguard indispensable moral values and cognitive skills. In the early eighties, all these efforts appeared futile since childhood itself was in the process of disappearing, a new socialization type of "adult-child" taking its place, a human being intent on amusing him- or herself to death. In the jeremiads directed against the role of electronic mass media the media are said to endanger the moral values and cognitive skills which developed during the short era since the Enlightenment, especially the rise and predominance of the printing press and general reading and writing skills.

Against this line of arguments a number of objections may be raised.

(1) Postman's focus on one historical trend comes down to a generalization of partial symptoms into a general social syndrome. Postman does not clarify the historical context of social developments among which media development is only one major trend whose interdependencies with other strands of development require specification.

(2) It is highly improbable that the various trends of development all point in the same direction, viz. a global change of consciousness with pervasively detrimental effects on perception, ideation, conflict solution, etc.

(3) Even if we focus on *cultural* development alone, it is important to keep in mind that the media constitute only one part of the overall cultural system. Habitualization in the reception of television programs redefines its use in everyday life: the increase of education and leisure time contributes to reception patterns different from those in the sixties and seventies.

(4) At the same time, large-scale confrontations with such problems as air and water pollution, war and peace through mass mediated electronic images effect rearrangements in the interdependencies of means of production, destruction, orientation, and communication. Postman's lament about the lowering of educational standards and the loss of excellence is based on the unquestioned assumption of a priority of education in relation to other ways of dealing with social issues. The chief objective of Postman's cultural criticism is what he calls media ecology and the development of more adequate curricula. He ignores the educational effects or side-effects of the media outside the range of education proper.

Finally, going beyond a critique of Postman as one critic of contemporary culture, we must not ignore the fact that interpretive theories of culture and cultural criticism in terms of individual contributions owe themselves to personalized concepts of authorship from the times of the print media. Collective authorship, already predominantly practiced in audio-visual productions, often operates as a hidden force behind individual authorship. Future collections of contributions to criticisms of contemporary culture therefore will increasingly take into account the roles of institutions of teaching and research, of specific journals and television programs, of video productions, and computer software. These collections, however, will no longer be distributed in the physical form of books but transmitted electronically. As such they will combine auditive, visual, textual, and musical modes of presentation. It is probable that Postman's approach to culture is the approach of a dying species.

Notes

1 I am deeply indebted to the editors of this volume for their critical readings of two earlier drafts of this essay and for their pertinent suggestions.

2 Cf. Postman, Weingartner, and Moran 1969.

3 Postman, Weingartner, and Moran (1969, IV) quote Aldous Huxley's "education on the non-verbal level" from *Daedalus* (Spring 1962).

4 *Soft Revolution* is the title of another book by Postman and Weingartner, from 1971.

5 His first major media bestseller from 1982.

6 Cf. Hertha Sturm, "Die grandiosen Irrtümer des Neil Postman – Fernsehen wirkt anders." *Fernsehen, Aspekte eines Mediums.* Ed. M. Kunczik and U. Weber (Cologne and Vienna: Böhlau, 1990) 240-262.

7 This is the title of a collection of Postman's essays from the eighties as published in 1988.

8 Postman and Weingartner 1969, 11-12.

9 As Postman and Weingartner headline Chapter 2 of their book from 1969, placing themselves deliberately in the tradition of Marshall McLuhan who specified in his "Probes," as edited by G. Sanderson and F. Mcdonald. *Marshall McLuhan. The Man and his Message* (Golden: Fulcrum, 1989) 218: "To say that any technology or extension of man creates a new environment is a much better way of saying that the medium is the message." This "probe" points to *media ecology*.

10 Postman and Weingartner 1969, 104.

11 Ibid., 162.

12 "The new education, in sum, is new because it consists of having students use the concepts most appropriate to the world in which we all must live. [...] The purpose is to help all students develop built-in shockproof crap detectors as basic equipment in their survival kits." These are the final words in *Teaching as a Subversive Activity* (1969, 1972[3], 204).

13 Postman and Weingartner 1971, 3-4.

14 Ibid., 5.

15 Concerning later criticism of Postman's own theories of media ecology, the following questions from the section on media research deserve to be quoted: "What will be our new literary forms? Of what use will 'tradition' be? To what extent is technology remaking our language? Have the big media 'polluted' our language environment? To what extent is our language impeding our understanding of technology?" (Ibid., 142).

16 1973, 113, emphasis added.

17 Ibid., 139 and 150.

18 1982, XIII.

19 Ibid., 13.

20 Ibid., 27.

21 Ibid., 35 and 36.

22 Ibid., 49-51.

23 "It is well to remember that the average length of a shot on a network television program is somewhere between three and four seconds, the average length of a shot on a commercial, between two and three seconds. This means that watching television requires instantaneous pattern-recognition, not delayed analytic decoding. It requires perception, not conception" (Ibid., 78).

24 Ibid., 84.

25 Ibid., 88-89.

26 Cf. Peter Ludes, "Visualisierung als Teilprozeß der Modernisierung der Moderne." *Geschichte und Ästhetik des bundesdeutschen Fernsehens, Vol. 1, Das Programm und seine Voraussetzungen.* Ed. Knut Hickethier (Munich: Fink, 1992) (in preparation).

27 "Television ... does not call one's attention to ideas, which are abstract, distant, complex, and sequential, but to personalities, which are concrete, vivid, and holistic. What this means is that the symbolic form of political information has been radically changed. In the television age, political judgment is transformed from an intellectual assessment of propositions to an intuitive and emotional response to the "totality of an image" (Postman 1982, 101).

28 Ibid., 103 and 106.

29 Ibid., 117-118.

30 Postman 1985, 7.

31 Ibid., 16.

32 Ibid., 27.

33 Cf. for example the "Survey of Electronic Media" by Sydney W. Head and Christopher H. Sterling, *Broadcasting in America.* (Boston: Houghton Mifflin Company, 1987). Using as an indicator for the determination of a lead medium the number of full-time employees, even in 1984, commercial television was only number three with 63,170 employees behind commercial radio with 72,639 and cable sytsems with 63,228 employees. Broadcasting headquarters, non-commercial television, cable headquarters, and non-commercial radio came next in a differentiated employment structure in the electronic media business. (Ibid., 217) Also in terms of the advertising volume of major media, television was only a distant second with 19,300,000,000 total dollars in 1985 as compared to the 23,744,000,000 total in the newspaper business. Direct mail, radio, magazines, and cable complemented this advertising market (Ibid., 227).

34 A quote from the results of empirical media research in Head and Sterling, op. cit., 424, may support the validity of Postman's observation: "Entertainment, as well as news and public-affairs programming, tends to play an agenda-setting role. It is safe to predict that any big news story that holds the headlines for any length of time will soon turn up as the subject of a special program or mini series and will influence future episodes of established entertainment series. [...] Fiction influences audience perceptions by reinforcing stereotypes, which are versions of reality deliberately oversimplified to fit in with preconceived images. [...] Even authors capable of more individualized and rea-

listic character portrayals resort to stereotypes when writing for television, in order to save time [...] Stories must be told with the utmost efficiency to fit them into the confines of half-hour and hour-long formates (minus time-outs for commercials, of course.)"

35 Head and Sterling, op. cit., 426.

36 Cf. ibid., 424-431.

37 Postman 1985, 69.

38 Cf. Norbert Elias, "Knowledge and Power: An Interview by Peter Ludes," *Society and Knowledge. Contemporary Perspectives in the Sociology of Knowledge*. Ed. N. Stehr and V. Meja (New Brunswick and London: Transaction Books, 1984) 251-291.

39 Postman 1985, 73.

40 Postman 1985, 131.

41 The Culture of Narcissism: American Life in an Age of Diminishing Expectations (New York: Norton, 1979). Cf. Rosita Becke's contribution on Lasch on pp. 291 of this volume.

42 Here Postman takes into account the results of research on the "knowledge gap," referred to previously.

43 Neil Postman, "Sieben Thesen zur Medientechnologie," Fröhlich et al., op. cit., 9-22.

44 Cf. Peter Ludes, "Marshall McLuhan," *Classics in Cultural Criticism II: United States*, edited by Hartmut Heuermann (Frankfurt/M., Bern, New York, and Paris: Peter Lang, 1991), 421-447.

45 Jerome L. Singer and Dorothy G. Singer, "Wider die Verkümmerung der Phantasie: Fernsehen, Lesen und die Entwicklung der Vorstellungskraft." 98-114, especially 108.

46 Ulrich Saxer, "Wissensklassen durch Massenmedien? Entwicklung, Ergebnisse und Tragweite der Wissenskluftforschung," ibid., 141-189, here 169.

47 Cf. ibid., 169 and 179.

48 Elisabeth Noelle-Neumann, "Das Fernsehen und die Zukunft der Lesekultur," ibid., 222-254, especially 226-235. Noelle-Neumann (ibid., 232) emphasizes that the terminology of a "knowledge gap" neglects different dimensions of "knowledge" like recollection and imagination.

49 Ibid., 242.

50 Ibid., 243-247; Noelle-Neumann explicitly refers to Neil Postman, "The Contradictions of Freedom of Information," paper given at the meeting "Creating Meaning: The Literacies of Our Time" of the Annenberg School of Communications, University of Southern California, February 16-18, 1984.

51 Wolfgang R. Langenbucher and Angela Fritz, "Medienökologie – Schlagwort oder kommunikationspolitische Aufgabe?," ibid., 255-270, here 266.

52 Elihu Katz, "Wird das Fernsehen überschätzt? Konzepte der Medienwirkungsforschung," ibid., 190-221, here 191-192. Katz refers to Gabriel Tarde's classic study "La Conversation," in *L'Opinion et la foule* from 1901.

53 Cf. Robert Bower, *The Changing Television Audience in America* (New York: Columbia University Press, 1985).

The Major Works of Neil Postman

The Languages of Discovery. New York: Holt, Rinehart and Winston, 1965 (with Howard C. Damon).

Exploring Your Language. New York: Holt, Rinehart and Winston, 1965.

Linguistics: A Revolution in Teaching. New York: Delta, 1966 (with Charles Weingartner).

Teaching as a Subversive Activity. New York: Delacorte Press, 1969; Penguin Books, 1971, 1972 (with C. Weingartner).

Language in America: A Report on our Deteriorating Semantic Environment. Indianapolis and New York: Western Publishing Company, 1969 (ed. with C. Weingartner and Terence P. Moran).

The Soft Revolution: A Student Handbook for Turning Schools Around. New York: Delacorte Press, 1971 (with C. Weingartner).

How to Recognize a Good School. Fastback Ser.: No. 30. Phi Delta Kappa, 1973 (with C. Weingartner).

The School Book: For People Who Want to Know What All the Hollering Is About. New York: Delacorte Press, 1973 (with C. Weingartner).

Crazy Talk, Stupid Talk: How We Defeat Ourselves by the Way We Talk – and What to Do About It. New York: Delta, 1976.

Teaching as a Conservative Activity. New York: Delta, 1979.

The Disappearance of Childhood. New York: Delacorte Press, 1982.

College Reading and Study Skills. New York: Macmillan, 1984 (with Barbara Keckler).

Amusing Ourselves to Death: Public Discourse in the Age of Show Business. New York: Viking Press, 1985; London: Heineman, 1986.

Conscientious Objections: Stirring up Trouble about Language, Technology and Education. New York: Alfred A. Knopf, 1988.

Ingrid Rosenberg

Stuart Hall

(1932-)

With characteristic modesty Stuart Hall writes in the introduction to one of his latest books *The Hard Road to Renewal* – the first of, incidentally, which he is the single author –: "The essays have the dubious distinction of having helped to launch the word which has dominated the period – 'Thatcherism' – into our political vocabulary."[1] In fact, Stuart Hall developed into one of the, if not *the* most prominent critic of that curiously mixed socio-economic-political phenomenon which befell Britain in the 1970s and is now commonly known by the term 'Thatcherism'. Perhaps it is a not unfortunate historical coincidence that Margaret Thatcher should have been voted out of power by her own party just at the time when I was working on this essay. It seems a good moment for a retrospective evaluation of Stuart Hall's running commentaries on the characteristic of her politics, which he began delivering almost from the very moment when Mrs Thatcher took office.

Even Hall's critics grudgingly admit his outstanding rank among her opponents. Ralph Miliband, for instance, who vigorously contests one of Hall's central insights, namely that Thatcher had a profound appeal in the working class, grants him that he "has been the most articulate and eloquent of the many proponents of this view".[2] What is characteristic of Hall's criticism is that he, though well read in Marxist economic theory, did not occupy himself so much with a detailed analysis of Thatcher's economic concepts and their precarious consequences (though he did repeatedly point to their importance). Instead he has been fascinated by the secret of Thatcher's popularity among even those parts of the electorate who have been suffering the greatest disadvantages from her government: the jobless, the old, the handicapped, the poor, the working class in general. Stuart Hall here has detected and tried to uncover the workings of ideology – a cultural phenomenon in the modern sense of the word, and one of the greatest consequence.

Before Stuart Hall developed into the chief analyst of Thatcher's skilful handling of ideology and at the same time a sharp critic of the corresponding weakness of the Left, he had come a long way. Born in Jamaica of coloured parents in 1932, he began his studies at Jamaica College. The exceptionally gifted student that he was, Hall won a scholarship that brought him to Britain in the 1950s and opened the doors of Oxford University to him: he studied and obtained his M.A. at Merton College. Both his background and inclination made Hall a partisan of the Left in Britain from the start. When in 1956, as a reaction to the political repercussions and revelations of the year, the British Communist Party went into decline and disappointed members together with other left wing intellectuals formed the New Left, Stuart Hall, though so young, was among the activists of the first hour along with such eminent figures as Raymond Williams, Richard Hoggart and E. P. Thompson. Hall helped to found and in 1957 became the first editor of the *Universities and Left Review*, which, beside the *New Reasoner* edited by Thompson, developed into one of the two most prominent journals of the new movement. When the two papers merged into the *New Left Review* in 1960, the new editor's name was, once again, Stuart Hall. Hall's work for these journals consisted mostly of editorial work while the number of his own contributions remained fairly small (all in all ten, including two reviews and two jointly written articles). In addition, thanks to an unusual rhetorical talent, Hall was a very popular speaker at many political meetings. In 1961 he obtained his first academic position as lecturer for film and mass media studies at Chelsea College, part of London University. The nature of his work there qualified him for a fellowship at the newly founded Centre for Contemporary Cultural Studies at Birmingham University, then run by its founder and first director, Richard Hoggart. Hall joined the Centre in 1964, also the year of his marriage; later a son and a daughter were born to the couple. After four years at the Centre Hall had the honour of following Hoggart as director, who left to work for UNESCO in Paris. Under Hall's leadership the scope of work conducted at the Centre was considerably extended, as will be shown later. Hall left the Centre in 1979 – the year Thatcher came to power – to become Professor of sociology at the Open University, a position he still currently holds. His publishing activities have, if anything, even intensified since his change, be it for teaching purposes, for broadcasting or in cooperation with journals like *The New Statesman*, various media magazines and, most important, *Marxism Today*, for which Hall has written prolifically. It was during his professorship that Hall also became more and more involved in the analysis of current politics; perhaps the nature of his work, which demanded of him the occupation with such basic political concepts as the role of the state, had stimulated his interest.

Hall had begun his writing career in the late 1950s with a book in the field of what one now usually calls "culture proper" though the application of the term in the sense implied here was then still much disputed. With the exception of an occasional article on D. H. Lawrence and a few literary reviews Hall, unlike one of his most important intellectual "teachers", Raymond Williams, never really focused on literature or other forms of "high culture".[3]

Instead he was fascinated by those new, typically twentieth century mass art forms, such as film and rock music, which make use of modern technology. Williams, himself all his life interested in defining the role of "high literature" in society – not perhaps just because he was still closer to the Leavis tradition, but also as a novelist himself – had nevertheless paved the way in his influential second book *The Long Revolution* (1961). In this study Williams had fused the traditional concept of culture as the body of intellectual and imaginative work in a given society with the anthropological conception of culture as the sum of social practices, the "way of life" of a particular society or a group within it. Thus he had arrived at a broad definition in which art figured as only one of many human activities, all forming a meaningful pattern. And, perhaps even more important for Hall at the time, art in Williams's view did not necessarily have to be "the best that has been thought and said" as Arnold's restrictive definition had run. All forms of creative interpretation and forming of social experience were of equal importance in Williams's model. This justified looking with an unprejudiced eye at all forms of contemporary cultural activities, the mass media included. Further stimulation was provided for Hall by the work of Richard Hoggart, who in his famous book *The Uses of Literacy* (1957) had already applied Leavis's reading of "high literature" to various aspects of working-class culture as it had developed between the 1890s and the 1930s.

Stuart Hall wrote his first book *The Popular Arts* (1964) in collaboration with Paddy Whannel while he was teaching at Chelsea College. Their starting point was the difficulty secondary schools were having with the pupils' enthusiasm for film, TV and pop music while they could be less and less motivated to take an interest in literature and other forms of "high art". One of Stuart Hall's characteristic intellectual features showed here for the first time: the alertness, unprejudiced openness and down-to-earth realism with which he registers and accepts new social developments. Hall is the exact opposite of an orthodox thinker. Though profoundly committed to some unvarying basic values of equality and social justice, he has never clung to a fixed theory and consequently never stepped into the trap of normative judgements based on such a theoretical construction.

What is remarkable about the book is its optimistic tone. Hall and Whannel rejected the widespread lamentations in the Leavis tradition about the general cultural and moral decline due to the mass media's influence, lamentations that no longer came mainly from individual conservative intellectuals such as T. S. Eliot but also from such influential national institutions as the National Union of Teachers and the Educational Institute. Hall and Whannel criticised this reaction as inadequate and of little use. Instead they recommended the integration of mass art into the school curriculum, pointing the way by suggesting a number of teaching projects in a long appendix; for – so they argued – mass art has come to stay, not all of it is bad, and it is the teachers' task to train the pupils' aesthetic judgement to enable them to make a selective use. Distinguishing "popular art" from "mass art", they defended the former as an equally genuine art form beside "minority art" (or "high art"). "Popular art" has to be considered as the modern form of pre-industrial "folk art" and is more or less practised in and spread by the mass media. Whereas "high art" "explores new experiences", the true popular artist "shares the experiences and attitudes" of his/her audience while adding the unique quality of his/her individual style: Charlie Chaplin is pointed out as the epitome of such a true popular artist.[4]

The weakness of the book is apparent when it comes to naming the standards for distinction. The argument deteriorates into woolliness when the authors, apparently drawing on but without critically discussing the tradition of humanist idealism, demand that good popular art should "confirm our common humanity" and "remind us, in an affirmative way, of the continuities of life and nature." (PA 78) The bulk of the book then consists of a critical survey of the contents and forms of numerous works of "popular art", "good" ones and "bad" ones, mostly films, Western, thrillers and films about love and romance, but also TV programmes, music and dance forms such as rock-n'-roll, twist and skiffle. It may be worth mentioning that Hall, the Jamaican, in this context carefully (and proudly?) traces the roots of white British teenagers' favourite music all the way back to black American folk culture. One chapter is dedicated to a brief analysis of the audience, i.e. the post-war teenage generation creating its own youth culture, a subject Hall was to take up later and to explore in more detail and on a theoretically advanced level. On the whole the book rings with a humane commitment and a cultural optimism reminiscent of Williams's *Long Revolution*. It is permeated with the belief in cultural progress, not only even if, but also precisely because, the forms have changed. In striking contrast to media critics like the American Neil Postman writing in the eighties, Hall and Whannel in the sixties saw the new technical media, particularly television, as a chance for more democracy in the cultural field. For on the one hand, they hopefully argued, television can carry culture into everybody's living-room or kitchen, and on the other hand, the active participation of the audience in the programmes should and can be extended (though in other places they also deplore the prevalent one-sidedness of communication in the media: usually a few perform for the multitude, not to speak of the handful of owners of the media). Hall has never lost his interest in the media. But with the years he has come to look at them far more sharply and more critically, while the focus of his interest has shifted from cultural to political programmes. We will have to return to this subject at a later stage.

The topic of Hall's and Whannel's book may well have served as Hall's credential for being appointed Fellow at the Centre for Contemporary Cultural studies (CCCS), for it fitted precisely the aims of this institution as outlined by Hoggart in his inaugural speech: studying "neglected materials drawn from popular culture and the mass media".[5] Hall himself has repeatedly told the story of the Centre in interviews and articles, the most detailed being the long essay "Cultural Studies and the Centre: Some Problematics and Problems" of 1980.[6] In this article he names three "intellectual fathers" of the new foundation: Hoggart, Williams and E. P. Thompson. While Williams had assumed a harmonious totality of group cultures, all contributing to a common whole, Thompson, particularly in his classic *The Making of the English Working Class* (1963), had insisted on the element of struggle between different class cultures at all times. As Hall reports, the Centre in its infancy was watched suspiciously from all sides for breaking new ground: the traditional English departments shook their heads over the serious attention given to texts other than those of the Great Tradition while sociologists were warning the new institution not to poach on their territory. Yet that was exactly what the Centre did. The first founded project, a study of social change through an examination of the popular press 1930-1964, later published under the title *Paper Voices*, was carried out by a combination of textual analysis with a thorough historical study of the social context. This interdisciplinary approach gradually led away from the occupation with texts and to an emphasis on "lived culture". The Centre's work diverged into the varied investigation of such areas as youth culture, deviant behaviour, the effect of schooling on social positioning, media studies, language studies, etc. Stuart Hall took an active part in many of these activities, specialising over the years in the fields of youth culture and – more continuously – media studies and racism.[7] The results of his work were published as *Stencilled Occasional Papers* of the Centre, in the Centre's *Working Papers in Cultural Studies* and in a number of journals dealing with cultural and media criticism such as *Signs; Screen; Screen Education; Media, Culture and Society*. Moreover, Hall continually contributed to anthologies and himself figured as editor of many of the books published by the Centre. As H. Gustav Klaus first pointed out in his introduction to a recent selection of some of Hall's most important essays in German translation, it seems worth mentioning that with the exception of *The Hard Road to Renewal* Hall has never published a book all by himself.[8] This is indicative of his attitude to intellectual work: Hall has always preferred cooperation with others not shying away from the notorious difficulties of team work.

However essential the analysis of concrete social phenomena may have appeared to Hall, he became even more involved in questions of theory as the

indispensable foundation for such practical investigations. Partly institutionalized sociology represented a constant challenge for the Centre to justify its
activities, partly the period of the post-war consensus among the political
forces in Britain, resting on relative affluence, was coming to an end and the
clear definition of one's own political stance was becoming more urgent; at
all events the Fellows of Centre set up a General Theory Seminar to study
jointly the works of the international sociological tradition, with the aim of
assimilating what was useful for the definition of their own position. Starting
with the work of the Germans Dilthey, Max Weber, Simmel, Dürkheim, wo
had already dealt with social actions and institutions as structures of meaning,
they then turned to American Interactionism in the work of Mead and the
Chicago School and, more recently, of Howard Becker and the subcultural
theorists. The study of the "history from below"-movement as practised in
Britain by History Workshop, the East London Centreprise group and some
feminist historians like Sheila Rowbotham, also proved fruitful. Yet the
greatest momentum was gained from the discussion of continental Marxist
theory, especially of German and French provenance, i.e. Walter Benjamin,
Georg Lukács and the Frankfurt School on the one hand; Lucien Goldman,
Sartre, later Louis Althusser and the (non-Marxist) Structuralists Lévi-Strauss
and Roland Barthes on the other. This reading of continental sources was for
most of the seminar participants by no means a voyage of rediscovery: the
translation of the texts by New Left Books and Merlin Press from the late sixties on, had first made the study of them possible for many of those who had
little French and no German. Possibly it was mainly due to such language difficulties that the cultural debate among British Marxists – with a few laudable
exceptions like Caudwell in the thirties or Raymond Williams in the sixties –
had so far been conducted on a theoretically rather modest level, more or less
determined by Moscow's crude official guidelines. Be that as it may, the Fellows plunged with eagerness and enthusiasm into the newly discovered intri-
cacies of theoretical debate and became, as Hall reports, "for a time over-pre-
occupied with these difficult theoretical issues."[9]

Despite this self-critical note it was and remained Hall himself who
became the Centre's most prolific writer on theory. Thus it was often he who,
alone or in collaboration with others, wrote the lengthy introductory essays,
setting the theoretical frame, to joint publications such as *Resistance through
Rituals* (1976), *Policing the Crisis: Mugging, the State, and Law and Order
(1978)* and *Culture, Media, Language* (1980). He did so with remarkable
logical lucidity and a special talent for didactic clarity of presentation. Again
and again in these introductions and articles Hall unfolded the theoretical
concepts at which he and the other Fellows had finally arrived and in which
ideas of Marx and Engels were merged with those of twentieth century struc-

turalists like Roland Barthes and Lévi-Strauss, the structuralist Marxist Althusser, the psychoanalyst Jacques Lacan and – perhaps most important of all – the Italian Marxist, Antonio Gramsci. A prominent place was always given to the discussion of the role and function of ideology – for good reasons, as will become clear later. In all these studies Stuart Hall appears less of an original thinker than, for example, Raymond Williams, who developed his very own notion of culture and society by blending ideas of diverse origins with a very personal view. In Hall's approach to theory the different strands of thought always remain neatly kept apart, their creators being scrupulously and repeatedly named. For all his extensive occupation with questions of theory, Hall does not seem interested in them as such, but only in so far as they provided him with a set of tools to explain plausibly cultural phenomena in contemporary British society. As, however, this theoretical base gained such a determining influence, colouring all of Hall's statements about the state of British society, it seems necessary to trace the genesis of his position in some detail.

Of crucial interest to all materialist cultural critics is, of course, the relationship between what is metaphorically called "base" and "superstructure", i.e. between the historically specific organisation of the productive forces on the one hand and the forms of the social structure on the other. No Marxist denies the ultimately determining influence of the "base", but to pinpoint the exact relation between both levels seems difficult. Marx himself, polemicizing against idealist philosophy, had given only rather crude outlines of this complex network of relations in *The German Ideology*. Of the individuals he had written that how they live and what they are depends on what they produce and *how* they produce it, i.e. under which material conditions.[10] What was true of the individuals' lives equally applied to the life of society as the organisation of society and the state grows out of the lives of the individuals. Thus, he argued, the production of ideas, concepts and consciousness is from the start entwined with the material activities and relations of men.[11] Such statements by Marx were subsequently taken at their face value by quite a large number of cultural critics of little subtlety, in the first line the official representatives of cultural politics in the later socialist countries. More sophisticated minds tended, polemically, to call them "vulgar Marxists" or "reductionists" as they deduced from Marx's words a mechanical causal relationship between base and superstructure, assuming that a particular historical stage of production automatically produces definite superstructural forms. It did not help much that Engels had rejected this simplification as early as 1890 as he had done so in a private letter to Joseph Bloch: "Nach materialistischer Geschichtsauffassung ist das *in letzter Instanz* bestimmende Moment der Geschichte die Produktion und Reproduktion des wirklichen Lebens.

Mehr hat weder Marx noch ich je behauptet. Wenn nun jemand das dahin verdreht, das ökonomische Moment sei das *einzig* bestimmende, so verwandelt er jenen Satz in eine nichtssagende, abstrakte, absurde Phrase."[12] So the "reductionist" view lingered on over the decades, despite repeated sharp attacks from influential opponents like Georg Lukács and Walter Benjamin (however much these two differed on many other points). In the sixties the issue was taken up again, first by French Marxists and later by the British New Left; probably the first of the latter was Raymond Williams with his article on "Base and Superstructure" in the December issue 1973 of *New Left Review.*

One of Marx's theorems in the context of the base-superstructure discussion which was to gain particular importance for the debate of the sixties and early seventies was his definition of ideology, which Marx had come to consider as a special superstructural phenomenon. Having discovered that the thinking of the various social classes differs, Marx arrived at the famous conclusion that it is the "philosophy" of the ruling class that determines the thoughts of an epoch. For in order to achieve its goal, he argued, every new class aspiring to domination is forced to disguise its own interests as those of all members of society, i.e. to give its own thoughts the appearance of general validity.[13]

The whole complex of the base-superstructure relation, but particularly the role of ideology became the focus of discussion in the General Theory Seminar of the Centre for Contemporary Cultural Studies under Hall's directorship.[14] It was Louis Althusser's work which first opened a promising route out of the theoretical calamities: it offered instruments which seemed suited for an adequate interpretation of the complexities of post-modern capitalist society from a materialist point of view. Though his position was not accepted in toto, some of his notions were hailed as extremely fruitful, in particular his ideas concerning the reproduction of the social system via the "ideological state apparatuses" and his concept of "overdetermination".[15] Althusser in his work had updated materialist theory by combining Marxist concepts with a Structuralist approach and the insights of modern psychoanalysis, particularly the discoveries of Jacques Lacan concerning the constitution of the "I".

Althusser was an outstanding figure among the Marxist thinkers in the sixties who rejected the still widesprad "reductionist" position – which he himself preferred to call "economism" – as opposed to a true Marxist reading. He did not dispute the ultimately determining influence of the economic base but pleaded for a description of its influence which took more accurate account of the complex realities of actual life. Production, he insisted, is the determining factor, but only in the final instance. Where "economism" saw a simple hierarchy, Althusser recognised a "structured complex whole with a dominant", in which the single components mutually determine each other (for example the productive forces and the conditions of production, the elements of the superstructure and the material existence) while they are all, in the last resort, determined by economy. To this complex fact Althusser applied the term "overdetermination", borrowed from linguistics and psychoanalysis. From the idea of a complex structured whole of all social formations follows a conviction which was to become of great importance to Hall: the conviction that the single parts of the superstructure, in other words the different social practices, all have a certain relative autonomy. They are diverse, may develop differently and at a different pace and exert influence on each other.

Also central in Althusser's work and in turn for Hall's adaptation of it, was Althusser's development of the Marxian concept of ideology. Stuart Hall had already vehemently and repeatedly fought the notion popular among many Marxists that ideology is nothing but "false consciousness". This notion, he felt, does not suffice to explain ideology's power and, besides, declares a large number of people imbecile intimating that they allow themselves to be deceived about reality. Althusser's revision started from Marx himself. Marx, Althusser argued, had already distinguished basically between two different levels within the superstructure: the legal-political level of the institutions of state and law on the one side and the ideological level on the other (the area of political and legal ideas, of religion, philosophy, etc.). But Marx had not yet made an attempt to study the mechanism of this complex network thoroughly, which is what Althusser tried to do. Every social system, according to Althusser, has the innate urge to stabilize and possibly perpetuate its existence, and it does so by making use of both levels of the superstructure. The institutions of the state (army, police, law courts, prisons) contribute to the stabilisation by directly repressive measures while the so-called "ideological state apparatuses" (schools, the family, religion, cultural institutions, etc.) do so in a subtler way: spreading the ruling class ideology, they peacefully win over even the subjects of determination. When Marx had written that each new ruling class is forced to represent its interests as the common interest of all, he had not yet explored by what psychological mechanisms a class could actually achieve this. Althusser now found plausible explanations in Lacan's psychoanalytical theory.

Althusser came to see an analogy between the workings of ideology in the grown-up individual's mind and the early childhood process Lacan had described in his influential essay on the "mirror stage" of 1949.[16] The child, according to Lacan, catching sight of his own image in the mirror for the first time, forms a satisfyingly unified image of selfhood by identifying with the object in the mirror. This seemingly unified self is, however, not real, but merely an image, an idealisation. Similarly, Althusser argues in "Freud and Lacan", the grown-up individual forms an image of himself as a person with a significant relation to society by the impact of ideology on his mind. Ideology is not a system of ideas, but rather a framework for interpreting the material conditions in which a human being lives: it is the set of beliefs and practices which gives the self a centre enabling it to function in society in a particular way. This set, just as imaginary as the child's vision of himself in the mirror, is provided by the social surroundings (family, class) into which a person is first placed and begins to exert its influence even before birth, for example, by class-specific rituals. What is important to realize is that this process is a subconscious one: the individual is not aware of his/her preconditioning and takes the views and habits he or she is brought up to as "natural". In both cases language, the medium of relation to others, is necessary to complete the process of constituting the "I". With the help of language, which replaces reality by the metaphorical, the infant, Lacan taught, enters the realm of the "symbolic order", i.e. of the Father and the (culturally specific) law(s): through language the child learns the norms of its family and society. Althusser went a step further reminding us of the fact, stressed by Saussure, that language is not a system of fixed signs meaning the same to everybody. Rather it is a many-faceted system, arranged by different codes and through various discourses which in their turn depend upon the social (and economic) position of the speakers. (For instance the word "black" will have an utterly different significance for a member of the Ku-Klux-Klan and for a Black Panther.) Thus language becomes the most efficient instrument of ideology. Though we are partly conditioned from our birth on and even before, the decisive part of "interpellation" takes place in the "ideological state apparatuses" through the medium of language. In former times, mainly through the activities of the churches, today above all in educational institutions like kindergarten, school or university, the ruling class "interpellates" the concrete individuals. Along with a few indispensable skills like reading and writing children learn in school how to function in the place society allots them: working-class boys in shabby comprehensives learn how to function as factory hands and in other low-paid jobs while upper-middle-class boys in expensive public schools acquire the attitudes and skills requisite to the craft of leading people in later life.

Though Althusser had briefly hinted at the possibility of resistance forming inside the "ideological state apparatuses" as a logical consequence of their relative autonomy, he had not gone further into this. Focusing on the mechanisms by which a social system reproduces itself, he did not dwell on the subject of its possible overthrow. One of the gravest objections to Althusser's work raised by the Fellows of the Birmingham Centre was precisely the marginalising of this aspect. Althusser's view of society, they felt, was too static and thus too depressingly gloomy: change seemed hardly feasible.

Here it was the work of Antonio Gramsci, the Italian Marxist who had died in 1937 after serving a long sentence in fascist Italy's prisons, that offered a more optimistic perspective. It was in fact Gramsci who eventually became the most important guiding figure for Hall. In an article from 1987 Stuart Hall explains why it was that Gramsci's work, particularly the *Prison Notebooks* written in the nineteen-thirties, had such an immediate and strong appeal for him when he was reading them in the nineteen-seventies. Gramsci, he writes, was in a situation in the nineteen-twenties and -thirties very similar to the one Britain has been experiencing since the nineteen-seventies. Although after the First World War a world revolution might well have been expected, history did not go that way. Gramsci, deeply disappointed by the actual development, was searching for an explanation why and how the Right had managed to take advantage of the historical conjuncture or, to use a key Gramscian expression, to "hegemonise" the moment. Though Britain has, of course, not been in exactly the same position in recent years, Hall has discovered "strikingly similar features": he sees Britain in just such a "crisis of authority" as Europe was undergoing in the nineteen-twenties, and, again, the Right has managed to win the field for the time being.[17] So Gramsci's analysis seemed relevant. As Gramsci had not resigned, but, on the contrary, had stressed the possibility of a continued struggle, his work was well suited to stimulate Hall into an interpretation of his own time that combines an acute analysis of present conditions with optimism for the future.

Though the *Prison Notebooks*, due to the bleak conditions in which they were written, do not present a coherent theory nor use a consistent terminology and even contain occasional contradictions, Hall managed to filter from them the elements of an argumentation useful for his purposes.[18] What apparently impressed him most of all was the great store Gramsci set by the field of culture as a battlefield for political dominance. Gramsci – like many other more profoundly thinking materialists, as we have seen – was convinced that the state of the productive forces does not mechanically determine the formation of a society, but merely sets the frame in which the historical forces can move. Gramsci here – in contrast to others – considered the cultural forces as of equal importance to the economic and the political ones. A fight for power or "hegemony" between the different social groups, he taught, is always possible, and victory is not only decided on the level of economy and with the help of the state's coercive institutions but equally in the institutions of what he called "civil society" (the family, school, the churches, the press, political parties, etc.)[19] A group or class striving for power will be successful only if it has won "hegemony" in these institutions too.

Another of Gramsci's notions to come in handy to Hall, especially for his treatment of questions of class consciousness and racism, was Gramsci's definition of the dominant social group. Though Gramsci sometimes did speak of the "ruling class", for the most part he preferred the expression "the power bloc". This meant an alliance of certain dominant groups within the ruling class (for example politicians and businessmen, in contrast to artists) with the state on the one hand and groups in the subordinate classes on the other, who are granted certain concessions. The notion rested on the realisation – contrary to orthodox Marxism – that classes are not really homogenous groups automatically developing the same outlook on society, but are in fact divided by differing interests. The supportive members of the subordinate classes cannot, of course, be forced to play the dominant group's game; rather they have to be peacefully and silently won over to a "consensus", preferably without their noticing it; and this is what is attempted in the various institutions of "civil society". But these institutions are never entirely in the hands of the ruling bloc; because of their relative independence from the direct influence of the state there is always the chance for opposition voices to make themselves heard. The champions fighting this ideological battle are the "intellectuals" among whom Gramsci distinguished two types: the "traditional intellectuals" defend the old social order at any given time while the "organic intellectuals" are the advocates of the new oppositional forces trying to rise to power. The outcome of their struggle is never certain; even victory is never final as there always remain resistant elements, and hegemony can be lost again.

When pursuing the question how the ruling class might actually win consensus, Gramsci made a distinction between two types of ideology that also proved useful for Hall's interpretation of the British present. There may be ideologies that are coherent philosophies, Gramsci had written; but they are of little political impact as only a minority understands them. "Common sense", however, is the kind of ideology that helps to decide the power question in a society. It is, as Gramsci explains at length in the first part of his long article "The Study of Philosophy", the popular version of philosophical and moral ideas, old and new, filtered down into ordinary people's understanding and mixed in a motley fashion, incoherent, fragmented, often contradictory: it is the "folklore of philosophy", the set of values with which ordinary people make sense of the world. (PN 321-377, esp. 323-343) Any group willing to win hegemony has to play on this set of ideas as on the keyboard of some musical instrument, picking out and stressing the notes that serve its purposes best. The ascent of a new dominant ideology is never the sudden rise of an entirely new philosophy; rather it is a process of deconstruction and reconstruction, of newly accentuating older elements, of "renovating and making critical an already existing activity."[20]

Gramsci's insights into the phenomenon of "common sense" finally led him to a view of the individual that comes astonishingly close to the findings of modern psychoanalysis and therefore must have appeared particularly convincing to Hall. For it is in the individual's mind that Gramsci located the seat of "common sense". When he stressed the fragmentedness and even contradictoriness of the human mind, in which he discovered "Stone Age elements and principles of a more advanced science, prejudices from all past phases of history ... and intuitions of a future philosophy", Gramsci, just like Lacan and Foucault much later, practically denied the existence of a unified subject. (PN 324) The fragmented and often contradictory individual mind then is in Gramsci's theory the object of the ideological battle fought in the institutions of "civil society".

The intense study of theoretical concepts from Marx to Gramsci and Althusser – and, needless to say, a number of related ones: of the contemporaries Nicos Poulantzas' and Ernest Laclau's work deserves special mentioning – outlined here and undertaken in the General Theory Seminar, enabled Stuart Hall to return to current cultural and social phenomena with sharpened perception and a profounder political understanding. In particular he adopted and blended Althusserian and Gramscian concepts concerning the political impact of ideology applying them to the interpretation of present day British realities. One area he had worked in before and which he now approached on the theoretically more advanced level was mass media studies. Stuart Hall discovered the media as perhaps the most important institutions of today's "civil society" and indeed as the decisive battlefield for ideologies.

In a paper "Television as a Medium and Its Relation to Culture" of 1971 the optimistic view of the new media, which had motivated his book of 1964, still prevails. The stress is on the chances television offers to popular art. Praising such series of the time as *Coronation Street, Steptoe and Son, Family at War* and *Monty Python's Flying Circus*, specially tailored to the medium, as superior to adaptations from older art forms (theatre, concert, opera, even film), Hall voices his hope that where at present only a minority produces the programmes for the masses, more people may be involved in active creation in the future. Thus television may be turned into a medium of a "specially democratic kind": "Everything about the medium ... is aimed at a use of the medium for disseminating information and experiences from an elite source to an uninformed audience. Yet what is potential in the very language and form of the medium is a different, and alternative set of relationships: in which, through the mutual exploration of reality, new, transformed realities begin to be jointly created."[21] When talking about documentary programmes on the other hand, Hall already hints at the problem of an only apparent closeness to reality, but does not yet go into the ideological implications of this circumstance.

Only a year later, in another paper on the "External Influences on Broadcasting", Hall first applied the ideological criticism approach that he was to unfold more and more over the following years.[22] The central points of his argumentation concerning the political influence of the mass media may be summarised as follows.

Born in the form of the press in the eighteenth century, the mass media have reached maturity in our own century as the "dominant means of social signification".[23] It is they that provide the images through which we perceive the world and as such have become the most important site of the ideological battle between the "power bloc" and oppositional forces, essentially helping to mediate power in our society. It seems worth emphasising that Hall, however, rejects both simplistic theories, the "conspiracy thesis" and the "displacement thesis", current among some less sophisticated left wing critics, according to which the media are either direct organs of the state or themselves manipulate the state. The cooperation between power, the state, and the media is much more complex, Hall insists. On the one hand the state guarantees the media their relative freedom, which they need to play their role properly, on the other hand state and media function in an analogous way: they both seemingly keep aloof from party struggles, giving themselves the air of a neutral and impartial referee. By this role they both help to maintain the existing social order. Thus the BBC – Hall concentrates on the BBC, not dealing with any additional questions arising from the nature of commercial television – outrightly supports neither the Tories nor Labour. Instead, by allotting roughly the same speaking time to the respective party members in discussion or by an equal news coverage, the BBC supports the two-party parliamentary system as such. Yet the virtues of balance, impartiality and objectivity, to which the corporation has pledged itself, on closer examination, often prove to be merely a masked cooperation with the "power bloc". The simple necessity to select the news and a perspective of presentation implies the possibility of veiled partiality: thus, during major strikes in the recent past television has tended to flood the screen with acts of violence committed by strikers while police brutality was played down, verbal appeals to the "overriding principle" of the good of the whole economy (as opposed to group interests) helping to underline the point. Opposition groups and minorities are certainly occasionally given a chance to appear on television too and defend their positions (though some groups like the IRA are never interviewed – at least since Thatcher, by a rare direct government intervention in the freedom of the press, prohibited it). But Hall reveals the subtle ways by which their views are marginalised so that they do not assume undue weight. He claims that in discussions representatives of the two big parties are always asked first, thus being given the chance to determine the direction of the debate. In various TV-debates on immigration in the seventies, for example, racism was thus from the start reduced to a problem of the "too large number" of blacks and Asians in England. So the real function of including the odd opposition speaker in a programme turns out to be no more than an attempt to improve the media's democratic image without actually endangering the status quo.

Hall's media criticism may appear extreme to some regular viewers of British TV. Yet this impression is partly due to the fact that Hall concentrates on political debates on BBC, leaving other programmes like, for example, critical documentaries, and also other, sometimes more critical broadcasters like Channel Four or Granada out of consideration. As far as Hall's analysis goes, however, it seems convincing enough. A particularly thoroughly worked example is an article of 1974, analysing a "Panorama"-debate, broadcasted a couple of days before the October election of that year. The subject was the "Unity of the Nation", the context the situation after the big miners' strike of 1973/74. The power of the unions, but also small nationalist parties in Ireland and elsewhere seemed to pose a threat to the status quo. Analysing the debate step by step, Hall shows how the representatives of the three big parties, though quarrelling over differing suggestions how to preserve "national unity", agree on its basic necessity, i.e. the necessity to retain the existing parliamentary system. The challengers, on the other hand, are not included in the circle and thus not allowed to explain their position.[24]

To support his insights further Hall applied semiotic theory.[25] It is impossible for the programme makers, he wrote, to pass on a correct reflection of reality; they can only "encode" a message in order to give meaning to events, and they do so on the basis of their ideological conditioning, which is usually unconscious to them and, as a rule, the hegemonic one. Also the codes that are shared by the majority of viewers seem to provide the most "natural" explanations. The connotation of word signs (for instance of "black") and of the iconic signs on the screen (for example the British flag) are of the greatest importance here. The receiver then basically has three options to read the message: if he shares the dominant hegemonic position of most TV professionals, he will decode the message on the same level and fully agree. In another instance the receiver may decode from a "negotiated position", i.e. he agrees fundamentally, but has objections in a particular instance (for example a worker on strike may deplore the frequency of strikes but have good reasons for his own). Finally, a receiver may apply an "oppositional code" and discover that certain messages about the "national good" are in reality in the interest of the "power bloc" (take, for example, the Falkland War). But such viewers will certainly be in the minority.

In the book *Policing the Crisis. Mugging, the State and Law and Order* published in 1978, written by Hall in collaboration with Chas Critcher, Tony Jefferson, John Clarke and Brian Roberts, the study group showed persuasively in one concrete instance how the media can exert political influence more weighty than merely helping to stabilise the status quo, namely in determining the direction of political developments. Between August 1972 and 1973, the media, through an overproportionate and heavily biased newscoverage of muggings, then a new crime in Britain, contributed strongly to the development of the law-and-order state with an extended and tougher police force and disproportionately severe sentences. By an exaggeration of the violence committed by black youths, people's fears were fanned into a kind of hysteria which in turn led to ever louder calls for more police power, which the government was only too willing to obey. As a particularly grave side effect, racism in Britain intensified considerably.

A brief graphical presentation of these results had already been included in a book published in 1975, which was dedicated to another social phenomenon Hall had shown interest in before: post-war youth culture.[26] This was again a collective work, this time for the most part with distinguishable single contributions dealing with subjects such as the cultural profile of different groups (Mods, Skinheads, Teds, Rastas), the cultural meaning of drug use, the role of girls in the groups etc. Again it was Stuart Hall, who together with John Clarke, Tony Jefferson and Brian Roberts, did the theoretical framework in a seventy page introduction. Drawing on Raymond Williams's definition of culture "to refer to that level at which social groups develop distinct patterns of life" and Gramsci's concept of hegemony, the authors interpret the emergence of distinct youth sub-cultures in the nineteen-sixties and -seventies as signifying a crisis in the hegemonic position of the ruling powers. (RR 10) The nineteen-fifties were a period of unquestioned hegemonic domination and of an unspoken, quiet consensus between the different social forces. This consensus began to be shaken in the sixties and seventies under the impact of the national and global economic crises of the time. The formation of youth groups protesting against the lifestyles of their parents and social norms in general by their marked styles of behaviour and dress at exactly that time was read as a symbol of the tremors sent through society from the economic base. Whereas Hall and Whannel in *The Popular Arts* had spoken of "*the* teenage culture", merely dropping a casual hint that about eighty per cent of this culture were working-class, Hall and his co-authors now made a clear distinction between "working-class sub-cultures" on the one hand (Teds, Mods, Skinheads) and "middle-class counter-cultures", on the other

(Hippies, protesting students). The earlier book had breathed a sympathetic, but not very well-founded partiality and optimism towards all youth groups in general: "... the younger generation have acted as a creative minority, pioneering ahead of the puritan restraints so deeply built into English bourgeois mentality, towards a code of behaviour in our view more humane and civilized". (PA 273) This emotional attitude was now replaced by a thorough and scholarly sociological study of the respective groups' behaviour in relation to their parent-cultures and to the dominant culture (which for middle-class youth are, of course, identical). The detailed survey, in parts very illuminating indeed, is unfortunately marred to my mind by a class-biasedness that Hall was to strip off later: the different working-class sub-cultures seem on the whole too positively accentuated, their oppositional character over-estimated while the negative element of social disorientation, caused by the darkening economic situation, leading to aggression and violence is played down. The middle-class counter-cultures, in contrast, though correctly defined as more politically motivated, are undervalued in their protest potential and long-term effectiveness (generally changed attitudes to education and an increased environmental awareness are good examples of this) simply because they stem from the middle class: "... middle-class sub-cultures continue to reveal their transitional class character and displaced position ...". (RR 69) They are even suspected of unwittingly playing into the hands of the dominant groups: "The counter-cultures performed an important task on behalf of the system by pioneering and experimenting with new social forms which ultimately gave it greater flexibility." (RR 66)

A third social phenomenon always at the centre of Hall's interest has been – very understandably – racism. He pursues this topic with special warmth and a particularly sensitive perception. Beside a number of articles and lectures approaching the problem on a more theoretical level, Hall also helped to produce two anti-racist films in 1979 and 1980, *It Ain't Half Racist, Mum* and *The Whites of Their Eyes*.[27] The films were shown on school TV and on Channel Four and triggered a lively discussion among the Left on how to combat racism more effectively.

Hall as a black and a Marxist had been puzzled by the disturbing fact – usually played down by orthodox "reductionists" as a "secondary contradiction" – that racism is by no means limited to the ruling class, but is, on the contrary, deeply rooted in the English working class, perhaps especially there, and is even tending to grow under the present pressure of deteriorating economic conditions for the class. The violence of Skinheads against "Pakis" and blacks in British streets is an all too obvious proof. Again it was Gramsci who provided the theoretical means to accept the uncomfortable truth, his concept of the individual's mind made up of bits and pieces of the "common sense" allowing for contradictory elements existing side by side in a person's mind. Drawing on Gramsci's theory, Hall analysed racism as an ideological tool cleverly handled by the white ruling class of Britain, anxious to defend their hegemonic position, with the purpose of dividing and thus weakening the working class as a whole. Underprivileged white groups, in their desire to upvalue their self-image, are all too ready to listen to a racist discourse: looking down on others makes one feel important and strong. Hall shows how the "common sense" of the lower classes is permeated by racist concepts, which to a large extent rest on a confusion of history and nature: the blacks' low social position in history (slavery), which in turn is the reason for their poor opportunities today, is not explained by the cruel treatment they suffered but by the assumption of their generally lower intelligence. The media, Hall claims, have played a crucial role in perpetuating this image. While in the imperialist period mass literature spread the "white eye's view" of the inferior "aboriginals", later films did the same. Until the nineteen-fifties the same old stock types of the warm-hearted, but stupid black nanny, the grinning black entertainer or the vicious black gangster made their appearance on the screen over and over again. *Gone with the Wind* is a good example. Though today, after the Civil Rights Movement, only few film makers would continue in this line, the old films, being shown again and again, may still exert their influence. Hall also proved, as we have already seen, that even serious political programmes indirectly and probably unconsciously, but perhaps all the more effectively, help to spread racist attitudes. To explain what then happens on the level of social practice, Hall refers to Foucault's concept of discourse, which denies the traditional distinction between the mental and the physical level. According to Foucault, all practices are determined by ideas, while it is equally true that ideas exist only in the form of practices. Thus, Hall says, in present British society racism is exercised in excluding practices, which in turn lead to an intensification of racist feelings: for the past two or three decades blacks have more or less systematically been denied access to good schooling, good jobs, good housing and, as a consequence, have lost even more respect in the eyes of their white fellow citizens.

Hall is, however, far from denying the existence of differences between the various culture groups in Britain. In a remarkable passage referring to Lacan he compared the realisation of racial differences to the infant's realisation of sexual differences necessary for the constitution of the self.[28] Thus Hall came to define as one of the most urgent tasks for the Left the necessity to counter the racist ideology of the hegemonic culture by an effective anti-racist campaign, to be launched in the media, which does not deny differences but underlines the necessity "to live together" – in the interest of all parts of the British community, blacks and Asians as well as whites.

Yet in the bulk of Stuart Hall's work from the late nineteen-seventies onwards, preoccupation with single cultural phenomena, even with racism, gave place to his growing involvement in the debate on current political changes at large, in the process of which Hall changed from a scrupulously observant scholar into an often witty and sharp-tongued polemicist. His final goal was to stimulate the British Left into a counter-hegemonic campaign. As hinted before, Hall's new position as a professor at the Open University may have helped to bring about this widening of his outlook. Overlooking the profusion of his articles on the subject beginning with "The Great Moving Right Show" of 1978, many of them first published in *Marxism Today* and later reprinted in anthologies, one cannot help noticing though that Hall's strength lies rather in analysis than in the creation of an alternative vision for the future. He – like so many left-wing theoreticians, including Marx himself – seems to lack the imaginative power for that. Yet his interpretation of Thatcherism is all the more brilliant, thanks to his intensive study of political theory in general and Gramsci in particular.

Naturally Hall was deeply upset by the swing to the right that happened towards the end of the seventies not only in Britain, but also in the US and Germany. Hall realised that the Thatcherite state represented much more than just another Conservative government. From the fifties to the seventies subsequent Labour as well as Conservative governments had followed certain common political signposts – capitalism, the welfare state, the western alliance, Keynesian economics: Thatcherism now broke with this consensus and thus with a line of politics followed by its own party for so long (with the exception of the Heath government 1970-74, which Hall sees as a forerunner of Thatcherism). Traditional patriarchal Conservatives were now ousted by a new generation of political thinkers believing in a combination of traditional radical liberal and individualist attitudes with monetarist theory as taught by Milton Friedman. What puzzled Hall above all was, as intimated at the beginning of this article, that Margaret Thatcher, though she never promised a bed of roses to all but far more a rough time for many, found her voters not only in the middle class and petty bourgeoisie – her own background –, but also in the ranks of the working class. Despite all disputes over the exact composition of her electorate, there simply cannot be any doubt that a large number of traditional Labour supporters must have voted for her in three consecutive elections. The answer Hall found is deeply indepted to Gramsci.

The miracle was worked – thus runs Hall's central hypothesis – via ideology. Thatcherism has won hegemony not by economic successes (which anyway are now more and more turning out to have been of an only temporary nature: British productivity is again lagging dangerously behind that of other European countries; inflation is back and up to more than ten per cent), but by a broad campaign on all levels from the economic to the cultural, the educational, the moral. In an article of 1988 Hall tries to describe what happened in Lacanian and Althuserian terms: Thatcherism succeeded in "repositioning" "already positioned subjects" by a "new set of discourse".[29] Thatcherite ideology took up, Hall explains, and bent to its own use certain justified complaints of ordinary people, including members of the working class, against social democratic solutions applied by Labour in the past. As the greatest sources of discontent Hall detects the falling standard in public education and, even more important, a weariness of too much state, of a swollen and increasingly ineffective state bureaucracy regardless of the fact that it had also provided social welfare. Such complaints, according to Hall, were then skillfully mixed with ideological elements from political philosophies of the past, from traditional "organic" Toryism as well as from liberalism, to be melted into the strange blend of a new "reactionary kind of common sense".[30] Collectivist thinking was replaced by competitive individualism, self-interest and anti-statism; a new nationalism substituted class consciousness; the idea of "Englishness" supplanted the vision of England as a multi-racial society; the aim of equal educational chances for all was replaced by the parents' right to choose their children's school: finally the old Tory ideals of family, respectability and patriarchism were conjured up to fight the dangers of feminism and to secure the authoritarian structure of the law-and-order society gradually established in the seventies. As Hall emphasizes, the single elements of this new "populist common sense", as a consequence of their disparate origins, are often contradictory, the most blatant contradiction being the juxtaposition of the free market ideal with the call for a strong state able to subdue unruly protests. To indicate this particular inconsistency of the ideological mix by which Thatcherism won and held power, Hall finally coined a term that was to be attacked by other critics of Thatcher: "authoritarian populism".[31] By this paradoxical formulation he wished to stress the very strangeness of insisting on a strong state while at the same time pretending to be the champion of "the little man" and his concerns. As a subtly worked and perfidious side-effect Hall points out that Labour as the party responsible for the growth of the state in the post-war period was made to appear as part of the "power bloc".

This ideological cocktail had carefully been prepared from as far back as the fifties in such institutions as the *Institute for Economic Affairs* and the *Centre for Policy Studies*, founded somewhat later by Sir Keith Joseph. As they were already operating before Thatcher's victory and outside the state organisations then still dominated by social democratic ideology, Hall prefers to call them by the Gramscian name "civil institutions" rather than by Althusser's "ideological state apparatuses". Another branch of "civil society" then popularised the concepts worked out there: the tabloid press, particularly *The Sun, The Daily Mail, The Star* and *The Express*, which by "vivid identification and glorification" spread Thatcherism as the new gospel among the masses.[32] Thus it happened that many working-class people were transformed into what Hall calls "populist political subjects" who no longer adhered to the traditional proletarian view of society as divided into "them" and "us", but were made to believe in Thatcher's slogan "everyone together", forming an alliance across class borders with the "power bloc".[33] For, as Hall had realised and found confirmed by Gramsci, interests are not inborn or given with the class position; they are "made" in the ideological smithy.

Though Stuart Hall's analysis of Thatcher's success has by no means gone uncontested, not even his critics, as already mentioned, deny the logic and consistency of his argumentation. His corresponding criticism of the British Left, however, is much less convincing. It is theoretically less well-founded, less coherent and sometimes even seems unfair. Ever since his article "The Great Moving Right Show" of 1978 Hall has repeatedly scolded the Labour Party for mistakes in the past as well as for its present performance. In the past, he claims, successive Labour governments involuntarily prepared the ground for Margaret Thatcher's victory by neglecting their popular democratic connections and generating a "gigantic state bureaucracy" that disciplined people more than it helped them and protected capital interests in order to keep the party in power. (PTh 14) This sounds strangely similar to Thatcherite criticism of Labour. As to Labour's present role, Hall accuses the party of not having been alert and creative enough under Thatcher's rule to develop a true alternative. Inflexibly, he complains, the party clings to the doctrines of the past still dreaming of reintroducing Keynesianism, which in Stuart Hall's judgment has been made obsolete by developments in the modern world.

In May 1988 Hall took part in a seminar organised by *Marxism Today* with the aim of analysing what exactly this "modern world" or these "new times" are made of and how the Left should react to it. The papers were later published as a book by Hall and Martin Jacques under the title *New Times*. When reading Hall's own contributions one is again impressed by the clear-sightedness of the analytical parts, for instance by the disillusioned clarity with which he registers capitalism's victory not just in Thatcher's Britain, but worldwide: "New Times, after all, is still new times for capitalism, which remains in place, untranscended in all its fundamental rhythms and tendencies. Capital is still deeply entrenched – in fact, more so, globally, than ever before."[34] When saying "globally" he meant the East as well, and that was more than half a year before the socialist governments in Eastern Europe began to collapse in domino fashion. Hall, with almost brutal bluntness, wrote sentences about Eastern society that might come from a book of the New Right: "The Leninist model of society ... is historically exhausted ... The old autarchic model of socialism has disintegrated. It cannot be rescued in its old form." (NT 19) He attacked these régimes even more severely than the British Labour Party. They have become guilty, he writes, of developing "their own species of Fordism – an obsession with quantity, the centralised plan, the masses, the suppression of variety and the suffocating grip of centralism and authoritarianism. In which direction you turn, the Left faces a massive cultural crisis." (NT 16)

Though it may sound like it, this was by no means a farewell speech to Hall's socialist position. Having faced the present imbalance of socialism and capitalism in the world, Hall then proceeds to search for possible new parameters for a new politics of the Left. For, he claims, Conservative rule is not an integral part of New Times: the Left has to make its own sense of the structural changes in the world. First everybody has to realise and accept that our time is a transitional age in which equally important and interrelated changes on the economic and cultural level are taking place. On the economic level Hall sees New Times (which he sometimes also calls "Post-Fordism") as characterised by a number of distinct features: the decline of the old manufacturing base and the rise of computer-based, high-tech industries; a shift to more flexible and decentralised forms of work organisation; the decline in the male work-force and a corresponding rise in the female; growth of part-time work; increasing importance of multi-nationals and, as a result, an international division of labour; the globalisation of financial markets; the leading role of consumption and its growing influence on lifestyles; the emergence of new social divisions (two-thirds/one-third society). (NT 118) For the cultural analysis Hall draws on Lacan and the more recent work of Lyotard, Baudrillard, Alain Touraine and Habermas. To the same extent, he argues, that the traditional collective social subjects have become more segmented and pluralised through the changes in the sphere of work, the individual has won a new importance; not the "whole, centred, stable and completed Ego" of past world views, of course, but the modern "fragmented and incomplete" Ego, "composed of multiple selves'", "positioned by different discourses and practices." (NT 120) The Labour Party, Hall criticises, has overlooked the significance of these fundamental changes and especially undervalued the subjective factor. Still clinging to the collective dreams of the nineteenth century, they have failed to grasp the innovative democratic potential in the diverse smaller movements resting on personal initiative such as the women's movement, the ecological and the peace-movements and various other citizens' initiatives. For Hall they are models for a future orientation of the Left: from them the Left should learn how to make use of individual commitment, which he sees as the only promising route for the future. The Left, Hall maintains, just like Thatcherism has to take seriously and build on the new individualism, if, of course, for another purpose: not for more materialism and selfishness, but for more individual social responsibility. In his readiness to accept realities, Hall even goes as far as maintaining that the market itself could be a school for individual responsibility. Chiding Labour for having occasionally adopted a puritanical attitude to working-class consumerism, Hall stresses that the market has to be accepted as an "expansive popular system" in which people can train their abilities to choose and select.

This reads very much like wishful thining. It is hard to see what selecting the fifth pair of fashionable jeans or a new micro-wave, even a computer has to do with training in social responsibility (except perhaps for such rare occasions when people have to decide for or against a car with a catalytic converter – but even then most will decide according to costs). Yet even if one disregards this unfortunate example, which should perhaps not be taken too seriously, the great hopes Hall places in a new role for the individual, however one may sympathise with his wishes, seem exaggerated. The very fates of the movements he points out as models prove rather their fragility as the sole basis for political hope: the peace-movement had almost dissolved, the feminists are still very much on the defensive in all socially influential areas. But in particular the defeat of the West German Green Party in the 1990 elections has brought home a few unpleasant truths with brutal clarity, of which two in particular seem of interest in this context. For one thing, too much individualism is a mixed blessing, easily tipping over into a force destructive of any group formation, and for another, the clear commitment to only one single political issue and an unclear stance to many others is not enough to gain and hold real political influence for any length of time. It seems worth remembering that in the nineteen-seventies many joined the Greens out of frustration with more comprehensive socialist programmes, turning to the concrete and the limited where the great revolution seemed out of reach. Environmental commitment was for many not a promising first step into a newly discovered responsibility, but, on the contrary, a form of resignation, political withdrawal and self-restriction. It seems that political power cannot be won, especially by those who have no capital and are not part of the power bloc, without a programme that covers all aspects of social life from the economic to the cultural, the moral and international relations – something that may indeed be learnt from the very strategy of Thatcherism, which Hall himself has so admirably analysed. (The intellectual poverty and contradictoriness of Thatcherism as a political philosophy, which Hall has equally precisely analysed, is, of course, another story.)

However much one may agree with Hall's relentless criticism of the communist parties' rule in Eastern Europe, his harsh scolding of the British Labour Party and his allround condemnation of all social democratic policies seem to overshoot the mark. Labour has certainly made mistakes while in power as well as in opposition, and it is true that the party is at a loss for an all-embracing "alternative vision for the future" which would take into account all developments of the "New Times". Yet this is, no doubt, a very complex task and one that cannot possibly be solved by a stroke of genius or an act of will. It seems that such a programme would have to grow and be developed, with contributions coming from many sides, just as the socialist programmes and, indeed, the liberal and the conservative ones of the past were gradually developed. For the time being Conservatism certainly has the upper hand in the ideological duel, and the Left needs patience to work a comeback. Keynesianism, by the way, which Hall had so rigorously declared dead, may well still be fit to form part of a new socialist programme: the FRG, though also under Conservative rule for roughly as long as Britain, has more cautiously preserved some Keynesian elements in its politics, above all a comparatively generous and effective social safety net, with the effect that all parties involved, employees as well as business and the state, have fared better for it than their British counterparts.

Stuart Hall's deeply probing analysis of Thatcherism has made him a well-known figure in public political discourse in Britain over the past decade, whose assumptions have been "quite widely adopted on the Left", as one of his critics has put it.[35] *Marxism Today*, for example, the journal where he first published most of his more recent work, has developed from a minority journal into one widely read and respected by a broad left-liberal spectrum. In all likelihood it was due to his refreshing unorthodoxy and readiness to accept and face social and political developments, even if unpleasant to the Left, that Stuart Hall has found so many open ears for the explanations he derived from Gramsci and a number of the most avantgarde modern theoreticians. In Germany he remains unfortunately known only to a smaller and more strictly Marxist audience, readers of *Das Argument*, in which a number of his articles have appeared in translation. The new selection in book-form, also published by *Das Argument*, and occasional reprints in school text books may help to spread his name a little more widely.

Despite his popularity in Britain, and perhaps not surprisingly, Hall has also been criticised from within the Left. As may be guessed, one of their main objections was his extremely rigorous criticism of all left politics, past and present. To some this did not only seem to go too far, but even come strangely close to Conservative positions. In particular it was held against Hall that he had reproached Labour for "statism", of having exerted a "state-administered socialism" while in office. Ralph Miliband, who in contrast to Hall underlines the essential importance of the state for social democracy, therefore includes him in his list of the "new revisionists" who "have retreated from all essential socialist positions", all formerly illustrious figures of the Left like Eric Hobsbawm, Ernest Laclau, Barry Hindess, etc. (Mil. 6) More objections have been raised against the application of Gramscian concepts and the great importance Hall attaches to the role of ideology, allegedly underestimating the impact of the economic base. Ruth Levitas in her book *The Ideology of the New Right*, for example, confesses to be confused by the fact that both the Left, stimulated by Hall, and the New Right have adopted Gramsci's concept of hegemony to explain what is going on in contemporary Britain: borderlines seem to become blurred (though one might see this general acceptance of Hall's concepts with equal right as a sign complimentary to his intellectual influence).[36] Further she questions whether Thatcherite ideology has indeed been as successful as Hall will have it. It is not true, she polemically claims, "that we are all Thatcherites now". (Lev. 16) Miliband makes the point more precise in rejecting Hall's claim that Thatcher "has won the hearts of the working class". (Mil. 17) Referring to statistics concerning the 1983 General Election he points out that most defections from the Labour Party were to the SDP/Liberal alliance and not to the Conservatives. On the other hand he confirms "a very marked alienation of workers from the Labour Party" (Mil. 18) while Levitas finally admits that, even if Hall exaggerates the trend, "the hegemonic project of the New Right must be deemed to have had some success" (Lev. 17), thereby herself falling back on Hall's categories.

The more detailed criticism of Bob Jessop, Kevin Bonnett, Simon Bromley and Tom Ling published in the *New Left Review* runs on a theoretically more sophisticated level, but basically raises the same points. On this level of "'pure', theoretically-analytical operation" their main goal is to reject the term which Hall, stimulated by Poulantzas, had coined to characterise the special nature of Thatcherite ideological strategy, namely "authoritarian populism", which they declare to be "unclear", "incoherent, mystifying, celebratory, homogenizing, and so forth" – only to then adopt the concept themselves, filling it with what they deem to be a more proper, more precise meaning.[37] Further they criticise Hall for having undervalued the importance of the economic sector in the explanation of Thatcher's success and, moreover, of seeing Thatcherism as a "monolithic bloc", overlooking the fact that in reality it is "an alliance of disparate forces". (Jes. 38)

Stuart Hall rightly replied in a vehement repartee that he had never denied the mixed provenance of the various elements in Thatcherite ideology, but had, on the contrary, all along stressed the "contradictory strands in its discourse – 'the resonant themes of organic Toryism – nation, family, duty, authority, standards, traditionalism, patriarchism – with the aggressive themes of revived neo-liberalism – self-interest, competitive individualism, anti-statism.'"[38] The reproach of having neglected economic realities Hall counters with the modest as well as true statement: "I work on the political/ideological dimension (a) because I happen to have some competence in that area, and (b) because it is often either neglected or reductively treated by the left generally and by some Marxists. But the idea that because one works at that level, one therefore assumes economic questions to be residual or unimportant is absurd."[39]

The general rank of Stuart Hall's contribution to the thinking of the Left over the recent years will become very clear if we finally listen to what his sharpest critics have to say of him towards the end of their article: "Notwithstanding our suggested criticism of Stuart Hall in preceding pages, it is important to pay tribute to his recent interventions. These have been a powerful force in rethinking traditional conceptions of the relations between economy and polity, class and party, structures and strategies. He has also been a central figure in bringing the importance of the political and ideological struggle for hegemony to the attention of the Left in Britain." (Jes. 60) Yet perhaps the surest sign of Hall's intellectual influence is the fact that even the Right has adopted his concepts.

Notes

1 Stuart Hall, *The Hard Road to Renewal. Thatcherism and the Crisis of the Left* (London, New York, 1988) p. 1.

2 Ralph Miliband, "The New Revisionism in Britain", *NLR* 150, 1985, 5-26, p. 17. Quoted as Mil.

3 Stuart Hall, "*Lady Chatterley's Lover*. The Novel and Its Relation to Lawrence's Work", *NLR* 6, 32-35.

4 Stuart Hall and Paddy Whannel, *The Popular Arts* (Hutchinson: London, 1964), p. 59. Quoted as PA.

5 Quoted in Stuart Hall, "Cultural Studies and the Centre: some problematics and problems" in Stuart Hall (ed.), *Culture, Media, Language* (London, Melbourne, Sydney, Auckland, Johannesburg, 1980) 15-47, p. 21.

6 cf. footnote 5.

7 His publications in these field will be discussed later. See p. ###.

8 H. Gustav Klaus, "Vorwort" in Stuart Hall, *Ausgewählte Schriften*, trans. and ed. Nora Räthzel (Argument: Berlin 1989), 5-8, S. 5.

9 Hall, "Cultural Studies", p. 25.

10 Karl Marx, *Die Deutsche Ideologie* (1845-46), *MEW* Bd. 3 (Berlin 1969), S. 21.

11 Marx, *Deutsche Ideologie*, S. 25-26.

12 Friedrich Engels, letter of 21st September 1890 to Joseph Bloch in Königsberg. Quoted in *MEW* Bd. 37, S. 463.

13 Marx, *Deutsche Ideologie*, S. 25-26.

14 The most important of the articles in which Hall has traced his and the fellows' theoretical development are listed in the bibliography.

15 The decisive texts in this discussion were above all: Louis Althusser, *For Marx* (Allen Lane: London, 1969); Louis Althusser, "Ideology and ideological state apparatuses" in *Lenin and Philosophy and Other Essays* (New Left Books: London, 1971); Louis Althusser, "Freud and Lacan", NLR 55 (1968), 49-65.

16 English translation of this report for the 16th International Congress of Psychoanalysis in Zurich of 1949 under the title "The Mirror-phase as formative of the Function of the I" in *NLR* 51, 71-76.

17 Stuart Hall, "Gramsci and Us" in *The Hard Road to Renewal*, 161-173, quotation p. 162.

18 Probably Hall's knowledge of Gramsci rested mainly on his reading of the *Selections of the Prison Notebooks*, ed. and trans. Quintin Hoare and Geoffrey Nowell Smith (Lawrence & Wishart: London, 1971). Quoted as PN.

19 Hall preferred this Gramscian expression to Althusser's "ideological state apparatuses" because it underlined the basically different, more private character of these institutions in contrast to actual institutions of the state.

20 Quoted by Hall in Stuart Hall, "Gramsci's Relevance for the Study of Race and Ethnicity" *Journal of Communication Inquiry* 10,2 (summer 1986), 5-27, p. 23.

21 Stuart Hall, "Television as a Medium and Its Relations to Culture", (1971), *Stencilled Occasional Papers* of the CCCS, Media Series, SP No. 34, July 1975, p. 27.

22 Stuart Hall, "External Influences on Broadcasting: The External-Internal Dialectic in Broadcasting: Television's Double-Bind", *Stencilled Occasional Paper* of the CCCS, Feb. 1972.

23 Stuart Hall "The Rediscovery of 'Ideology': Return of the Repressed in Media Studies" in *Culture, Society and the Media*, ed. Michael Gurevitch et. al. (New York, London, 1982), 36-90, p. 83.

24 Stuart Hall, "The 'Unity' of Current Affairs Television" in *Popular Television and Film*, ed. Tony Bennett et al. (London, 1981), 88-117.

25 A particularly stringent and informative article in this line is Stuart Hall, "Encoding/Decoding" in Hall et al., *Culture, Media, Language*, 128-138.

26 Stuart Hall and Tony Jefferson (ed.), *Resistance through Rituals. Youth Subcultures in Post-war Britain* (1st ed. 1975) (London, 1976). Quoted as RR.

27 Some of Hall's most important articles on racism are listed in the bibliography.

28 Stuart Hall, "Rassismus als ideologischer Diskurs", *Das Argument* 178 (Nov./Dez. 1989), 913-921, S. 920. The article is based on a lecture given in Hamburg.

29 Stuart Hall, "The Toad in the Garden: Thatcherism among the Theorists" in *Marxism and the Interpretation of Culture*, ed. Cary Nelson and Lawrence Grossberg (Basingstoke and London, 1988), 35-57, p. 50.

30 Stuart Hall and Martin Jacques, *The Politics of Thatcherism* (London, 1983), p. 11. Quoted as PTh.

31 For the genesis of the term see Stuart Hall, "popular Democratic vs Authoritarian Populism: Two Ways of Taking Democracy Seriously" (1980) in Hall, *The Hard Road to Renewal*, 123-149.

32 Hall, "The Toad in the Garden", p. 47.

33 Stuart Hall, "The Great Moving Right Show", *Marxism Today* Dec. 1978, reprinted in *The Politics of Thatcherism*, 19-39, quotation p. 31.

34 Stuart Hall and Martin Jacques, "Introduction" to Stuart Hall and Martin Jacques (ed.), *New Times, The Changing Face of Politics in the 1990s* (London, 1989), 11-20, p. 17. Quoted as NT.

35 Bob Jessop et al., "Authoritarian Populism, Two Nations and Thatcherism", *NLR* 147, 1984, 32-60, p. 33. Quoted as Jes.

36 Ruth Levitas, *The Ideology of the New Right* (Cambridge and Oxford, 1986), p. 11. Quoted as Levy.

37 First quotation from Hall's reply: Stuart Hall, "Authoritarian Populism: A Reply to Jessop et al." (1985) in *The Hard Road to Renewal*, 150-160, p. 153. The second quotation from Jessop et al., p. 55.

38 Hall, "A Reply to Jessop", p. 157. The quotation contains a self-quotation from "The Great Moving Right Show" of 1979.

39 Hall, "A Reply to Jessop et al.", p. 56.

The Works of Stuart Hall

Stuart Hall and Paddy Whannel, *The Popular Arts* (London, 1964).

Stuart Hall, "External Influences on Broadcasting. The External-Internal Dialectic in Broadcasting: Television's Double-Bind", *Stencilled Occasional Papers of the CCCS* (Feb. 1972).

Stuart Hall, "Deviance, Politics, and the Media" in *Deviance and Social Control*, ed. Paul Rock and Mary McIntosh (London, 1974) 261-305.

Stuart Hall and Tony Jefferson (ed.), *Resistance through Rituals. Youth Subcultures in Post-War Britain* (first published as *Working Papers in Cultural Studies* no. 7/8, 1975) (London, Melbourne, Sydney, Auckland, Johannesburg, 1976) (several reprints).

Stuart Hall, "Culture, the Media and the Ideological Effect" in *Mass Communication and Society*, ed. James Curran et al. (London, 19771), 315-348.

Stuart Hall et al., *Policing the Crisis. Mugging, the State, and Law and Order* (Basingstoke, 1978) (last reprint 1987).

Stuart Hall et al. (ed.), *Culture, Media, Language (Working Papers in Cultural Studies 1972-1979)* (London, Melbourne, Sydney, Auckland, Johannesburg, 1980) (several reprints).

Stuart Hall, "Cultural Studies: Two Paradigms", *Media, Culture and Society* 1980, vol. 2, 57-72.

Stuart Hall, "Rasse, Klasse, Ideologie", trans. Manfred Behrens and Thomas Laugstien, *Das Argument* 122 (Juli/Aug. 1980), 507-510.

Stuart Hall, "The 'Unity' of Current Affairs Television" in *Popular Television and Film*, ed. Tony Bennett et al. (London, 1981) 88-117.

Stuart Hall, "The Structured Communication of Events" in *Society and the Social Sciences*, ed. David Potter et al. (London, 1981), 269-289.

Stuart Hall, "The Whites of Their Eyes. Racist Ideologies and the Media" in *Silver Linings. Some Strategies for the Eighties*, ed. G. Bridges and R. Brunt. Contributions to the Communist University of London (London, 1981). (Abbreviated German version "Die Konstruktion von Rasse in den Medien", *Das Argument* 134 (Juli/Aug. 1982), 524-533.

Stuart Hall, "The Rediscovery of 'ideology': Return of the Repressed in Media Studies" in *Culture, Society and the Media*, ed. Michael Gurevitch et al. (New York, London, 1982), 36-90.

Stuart Hall and Martin Jacques (ed.), *Politics of Thatcherism* (London, 1983) (last reprint 1987).

Stuart Hall, "Gramsci's Relevance for the Study of Race and Ethnicity", *Journal of Communication Inquiry* 10, 2 (summer 1986), 5-27.

Stuart Hall, *The Hard Road to Renewal. Thatcherism and the Crisis of the Left* (London, New York, 1988).

Stuart Hall, "The Toad in the Garden: Thatcherism among the Theorists" in *Marxism and the Interpretation of Culture*, ed. Cary Nelson and Lawrence Grossberg (Basingstoke and London, 1988), 35-57.

Stuart Hall, "Rassismus als ideologischer Diskurs", lecture given in Hamburg and trans. Nora Räthzel, *Das Argument* 178 (Nov./Dez. 1989), 913-921.

Stuart Hall and Martin Jacques (ed.), *New Times. The Changing Face of Politics in the 1990s* (London, 1989).

Stuart Hall, *Ausgewählte Schriften*, translated by Nora Räthzel (Hamburg, Berlin, 1989).

Rosita Becke

Christopher Lasch

(1932-)

If someone were to wonder why Christopher Lasch is included in the present collection of cultural critics, one could do worse than quote the opening remarks from Reynolds and Norman's *Community in America* which assembled responses to *Habits of the Heart*. They referred to this much noted study by Robert Bellah and his team as:

> the kind of scholarship that periodically kindles broad public interest because it catches and focuses something out there ready to be kindled, a widely shared but not yet fully articulated sense that something urgent and important requires attention. *The Lonely Crowd, The Feminine Mystique, The Culture of Narcissism*, and *Roots* immediately come to mind as books that similarly have captured the public imagination (1).

The reception of Christopher Lasch's *The Culture of Narcissism* (1978) transcended academic circles, it graced the *New York Times* best-seller list for seven weeks – long enough for its title to become a household item when talking about 'the seventies,' long enough for Lasch to be interviewed by *People* magazine, and long enough to make former President Jimmy Carter's reading list (cf. Seaton 184). But whereas "*Habits* is a venture of shared hope" (Reynolds and Norman 1), *The Culture of Narcissism* sketched a darker picture of the American condition.

Christopher Lasch was born in Omaha, Nebraska, right in the American heartland, in 1932. In light of his later career, it is perhaps not irrelevant that his mother was a social worker and later a professor of philosophy and his father an award-winning journalist, thus combining social commitment with a concern for ethics and politics under one roof. Furthermore, Lasch married into the family of a noted American historian: his wife Nell is the daughter of Henry Steele Commager.

Educated as an historian at Harvard and Columbia University, Lasch earned his PhD in 1961 and moved to the University of Iowa. There he resolutely climbed the rungs of the academic ladder from assistant via associate to full professor of history within the next five years. After a brief interlude at Northwestern University, he made Rochester his permanent academic home turf in 1970 (see *Current Biography Yearbook*). As a writer and critic, Lasch has published relentlessly. So far, he is on the record with seven books and a myriad of articles, forewords, epilogues, and reviews. He has a standing column titled "Politics and Culture" in *Salmagundi*, he was on the editorial board of the interesting, albeit short-lived, leftist journal *Democracy*, in 1980-81 he held the Freud Lectures at London's University College – to name only a few of Lasch's lively scholarly activities.

Lasch has talked about himself as someone "who came intellectually of age in the fifties" (*The Agony of the American Left*, viii). That decade has become known for its conformity, intellectual blandness, and a preoccupation with material concerns. Historians like Charles C. Alexander and Eric F. Goldman have detected the wish for an equilibrium on the political stage (cf. *Holding the Line* chs. 4-6; *The Crucial Decade* ch. 12). After the economic and ideological turmoil of the thirties, the strain of World War II, followed close at heel by the Korean War, and the onset of the Cold War with its McCarthyite repercussions on the domestic scene, the U.S. was ready for a period of rest. Cold War anxieties, conjured up by the perceived communist threat and potential atomic destruction, found expression in the official containment policy which was nurtured by the assumption that international peace and liberty hinged on American moral and intellectual supremacy. This internationalist containment policy manifested itself domestically in an ideological closing of ranks.

That the leadership of the so-called 'free world' was lodged in the U.S. seemed to be corroborated by superior economic power. The Korea boom along with large-scale government and consumer spending fired the American economy. Indeed, consumption reached hitherto unprecedented highs: 75% of all families owned a car and a washing machine, even more, namely 87%, had a tv-set (Chafe 112). Economic theorist John Kenneth Galbraith apostrophized America as "the affluent society." And historian David Potter identified economic abundance as the wellspring of democratic institutions in the U.S. But the economy was not only booming, automation and labor-saving devices were transforming it at the same time. The service industry was on the rise and with it the number of bureaucratic, managerial positions. A type of worker emerged that William Whyte called "the organization man": he operated in teams and consequently had to sell his personality alongside his professional skills. This corporate practice fit into a larger social pattern explored by sociologist David Riesman. In *The Lonely Crowd* Riesman described the cultural homogenization as a product of "other-direction": Americans, he claimed, no longer shaped their life according to a more or less consistently applied set of personal values, instead their views and behavior echoed the opinions currently voiced in their respective peer group and the media (21).

As interrelated social phenomena, the Cold War consensus, affluence, and conformity, did not spare the intellectual community, where deep cutting criticism was relegated to the sidelines. The most striking example in this context was furnished by the *Partisan Review*. After establishing itself as the most important radical quarterly in the preceding two decades, in 1952 three issues were devoted to a symposium on "Our Country and Our Culture." The shift signaled by the conspicuous use of the possessive pronoun led maverick sociologist C. Wright Mills to deride the intellectuals' "soft and anxious compliance" (446) with the status quo. Lasch's judgment was even harsher. In *The Agony of the American Left* (1969) he talks of "capitulation" and "the wholesale defection of intellectuals from social criticism" (58) that, as he points out in the preface, contributed to the crisis of radicalism in the sixties (vii-viii). In his penetrating dissection of the Congress for Cultural Freedom Lasch explores the reasons for the intellectuals' reconciliation with American culture:

... intellectuals were unusually sensitive to their interests as a group ... and they defined those interests in such a way as to make them fully compatible with the interests of the state. As a group, intellectuals had achieved a semiofficial status which assigned them professional responsibility for the machinery of education and for cultural affairs in general. Within this sphere – within the schools, the universities, the theater, the concert hall, and the politico-literary magazines – they had achieved both autonomy and affluence, as the social value of their services became apparent to the government, to corporations, and to the foundations ..., partly because of the increasing importance of education – especially the need for trained experts – and partly because the cold war seemed to demand that the United States compete with communism in the cultural sphere as well as in every other (94).

In emphasizing the role played by status concerns and consumption's cornucopia in the social integration of intellectuals, Lasch's view significantly diverges from liberal interpretations which simply diagnosed a process of maturation on the intellectuals' part. Daniel Bell, for instance, welcomed the advent of pragmatic realism supposedly heralding "the end of ideology," to quote the catching title of one of his books. Lasch, however, in unfolding the financial and personal link between the Congress for Cultural Freedom and the CIA, showed not only the intellectuals' corruptibility, but affirmed the power structure's ability to use intellectuals for its own ends without their being aware of it – a sinister view, indeed.

The conformist cultural climate described above was reflected in the historical profession into which Lasch was initiated in the fifties. The paradigm directing the discipline at the time posited a broad liberal consensus as the prime constituent in American history. Thus, historians like Hartz, Hofstadter, or Potter discarded the conflict hypothesis advanced by preceding progressive scholars like the Beards, Parrington, and Turner. In doing away with the assumption that the struggle of classes, interests, or sections determined the unfolding of American history, the consensus historians, as John Higham pointed out, rediscovered "the continuity of American history, the stability of basic institutions, the toughness of the social fabric" (95). And whenever divisive elements had to be acknowledged, they opted for a psychological explanation: "[P]resent-day scholars tend to subjectivize the stresses in American life" (95). This approach is illustrated, for example, by Richard Hofstadter's status anxiety thesis set forth in *The Age of Reform*.

It is certainly a reaction to "the conservative historiography of the fifties" (*The World of Nations* xii) that Lasch would lavish so much of his professional attention on radicalism and would dissect American liberalism from that point of view. Accordingly, his first booklength study *The American Liberals and the Russian Revolution* (1962) was an historical inquiry into the liberals' failure to adequately assess and respond to the Russian Revolution during and after World War I, a failure which, according to Lasch, led to a breach in American liberalism still to be felt forty years later. His next work *The New Radicalism in America 1889-1963: The Intellectual as a Social Type* (1965) traced the development and the limitations of radical thought from populism to the New Left – a theme that he picked up and broadened in the following two essay collections *The Agony of the American Left* (1969) and *The World of Nations* (1973). In *The New Radicalism* Lasch declared that he was "somewhat skeptical of 'pragmatic liberalism'" and admired "whatever was negative and critical in the new radicalism" (xvi), since there he found "the effort to see society from the bottom up, or at least from the outside in" (xv). The radical point of view predicated for Lasch a detachment genuinely appropriate and indispensable for intellectual work which had, however, been sacrificed by "the cold war intellectuals [who] revealed themselves as the servants of bureaucratic power" (*Agony* 94).

Even though Lasch tried to distinguish his approach and the topics of his work from the consensus historians, he remained deeply indebted to at least two of them, namely Louis Hartz and Richard Hofstadter. His conceptualization of liberalism is derived from Hartz, a fact which he leaves unacknowledged. In his influential study *The Liberal Tradition in American History* (1955) Hartz resurrected Tocquevillean ideas as he talked about a "*natural* liberalism as a *psychological* whole, embracing the nation and inspiring unanimous decisions" (14, emphasis mine). Hartz thus not only differentiated American from European liberalism with the latter becoming a consciously chosen political creed and the former being an endemic American socio-psychological fact. He also offered the lack of a feudal past as the single causative factor for this "natural liberalism" and argued for the absence of a clearly defined class consciousness. The corollary, of course, is the limited applicability of a political theory derived from the European context marked by class conflict and ideological strife. If Lasch did not accept Hartz' corollary, he nevertheless adopted the description of liberalism in *The American Liberals* (cf. vii ff), as well as in *The New Radicalism*:

... it is true that in the United States the agencies of social cohesion (church, state, family, class) were never very strong in the first place. Nevertheless, there existed during the first two and a half centuries of American history a sort of cultural consensus at the heart of which was a common stake in capitalism and a common tradition of patriarchal authority. There were social classes but compared to Europe or even to American society during the colonial period, remarkably little class-consciousness; [...] "The whole society," wrote Tocqueville in 1831, "seems to have melted into a middle class ..." Divisive influences tended to be local and regional rather than social; and the very intensity of local and regional rivalries enhanced the social solidarity of each particular part of the country (xi).

The greater influence on Lasch, however, is Hofstadter, his teacher at Columbia University, whose academic accomplishments he genuinely respected (see Lasch's introduction to Hofstadter's *The American Political Tradition and the Men Who Made It*). It is noteworthy in this context that Lasch considers Hofstadter's work propelled by "the attempt of left-wing intellectuals to discover a tradition of their own" (xxi) which happens to agree with his own interests. When Lasch presents his argument in *The New Radicalism* "chiefly by means of a series of biographical essays" (xvii) (not really a standard method for writing social history) he patterns this structure on Hofstadter's *The American Political Tradition*. Besides, there are other indications pointing to a discursive lineage going back to Hofstadter. For instance, the final chapter titled "The Anti-Intellectualism of the Intellectuals" relates back to Hofstadter's *Anti-Intellectualism in American Life* (1963); another example is Lasch's treatment of "The Decline of Populism" in *Agony* recalling *The Age of Reform*, or his 1974 article "Paranoid Presidency" recalling Hofstadter's *The Paranoid Style in American Politics* (1965) in more than just the title's epithet. In fact, it can be argued that Hofstadter's attention to socio-psychological phenomena in U.S. history prepared the ground for Lasch's own look at American society in terms of narcissism.

The foregoing description highlights the fact that while Christopher Lasch was influenced by historiographical developments in the fifties, he still traveled different avenues in his own work which were, however, also removed from the New Left approach in the sixties and early seventies. To paraphrase the main thesis of William O'Neill's book *Coming Apart*, the social fabric in that period was disintegrating. The idealism and expectancies raised by the Kennedy presidency tapered off during the Johnson administration which was torn between funding the ambitious programs for the "Great Society" and financing the war in Indochina. In the resulting polarization of the political spectrum various protest movements – blacks, students, women, anti-war protesters – came to the fore which were modeled on the civil rights movement, the main agent of political reform in the fifties. Demanding the full realization of social equality and an end to the Vietnam war, activists encountered an entrenched leadership elite unwilling to address their issues. The year 1968 with the assassinations of Martin Luther King and Robert Kennedy, urban unrest, and the disastrous Chicago Democratic Convention marked a breaking point. The consequences were described by William Chafe:

As the civil rights movement pursued its inexorable journey toward Black Power, and as the activists in the student movement, the women's movement, and the antiwar movement became disenchanted with the possibilities of incremental reform, the nation witnessed a growing extremism on the left, together with a burgeoning reaction on the right (379).

After Vietnam and Watergate, the U.S. political scene witnessed a disintegration and partly a retreat from politics on the left coupled with a gradual resurgence of conservatism.

As a history professsor approximately ten to fifteen years the senior of student protesters, Christopher Lasch accompanied the rise and demise of the New Left with a critical eye. Whereas in the final essay of *Agony* titled "The Revival of Political Controversy in the Sixties" he had still given credit to the New Left for their insistence on "decentralization, local control, and a generally antibureaucratic outlook" (211), this positive contribution was subsequently submerged as his judgment became increasingly disapproving. In *World* he argued that the New Left profited and, indeed, depended on the liberal climate pervading society at large and never established a radical agenda of their own in cultural discourse. This fatal flaw was linked to an equally fatal lack of historical memory: "the New Left either refused or was unable to learn much from its predecessors, even from their mistakes, and in the end paid heavily for its indifference to the past" (125). Furthermore, it sealed the New Left's fate that when looking for a theoretical framework it fell back on "Marxism in its most rigid and sterile forms, or third world revolutionary doctrines quite inapplicable to the United States, and began to engage in sectarian polemics" (125f). Devastating as this opinion on the New Left may sound – the polemics' very acidity may perhaps be an indicator of frustrated hopes originally entertained in connection with the New Left, it was surpassed in *The Culture of Narcissism* where Lasch pilloried the New Left for its "theatrical conception of politics" (154) geared toward self-dramatization.

Thereby, political issues were drained of their substance; the radical pose, for it cannot be called a position any more, deteriorated into a life style subject to fashion's tides. Moreover, the student movement brought "a militant anti-intellectualism" (257) to the American campus in that established disciplines were revised and new fields inserted along the lines of yet untested, merely asserted, subjective categories of relevance. This caused, Lasch claims, a lowering of intellectual standards across the board.

His own position in those turbulent years was stated in a condensed and, as he himself willingly conceeded, somewhat polemical fashion, in an article on "The Counter-Culture" (*World* 183-202). In the final section he elaborates on "The Cultural Crisis: A Manifesto" (198). This part was initially meant to be the prospectus – and therefore can claim a certain programmatic value – for a journal of historical and cultural studies (envisioned together with Eugene Genovese, Norman Birnbaum, Gerald Graff, Warren Susman, Herbert Gutman, and David Kettler; cf. 336) a venture which was, incidentally, never realized. Lasch starts with a general definition of culture's function: "the expression of standards and principles that transcend the social order and are therefore inherently critical of it" (198). This function he sees neglected in current cultural discourse which is usurped by skirmishes either in defense of the status quo, or in attacks of revolutionary intent. The deflection of a true cultural discourse dealing with "ethical and political questions ... questions of how society can best be organized so as to promote justice, peace, and the fullest realization of human creativity" (199) is aggravated by the split between natural and social sciences on the one hand and the humanities on the other. The dichotomy, engendering a sterile scientism in the former and a degradation to ornamental status for the latter, is replicated in the political left and hinders what Lasch thinks is the foremost work of intellectuals, namely "to produce a critical analysis of all phases of advanced industrial society and to communicate this body of knowledge to non-specialists – that is to train an educated public" (200). He goes on to demand an intellectual community, not yet existant, that would furthermore inquire into "the place of knowledge in a social order to which knowledge seems at once indispensable and superfluous" (202). For this project he proposes a socialist perspective grounded in a critical theory of society as well as in Marxian theory, yet going well beyond it in order to elucidate the relationship between culture and ideology.

Interesting in this manifesto is Lasch's view on culture, since it is informed by the wish to safeguard liberal culture from the onslaught of the New Left (*World* 333), without buying into liberal politics or ideology as the proposed theoretical perspective shows. This idea contains a conceptual flaw revealed in the underlying assumption that the realms of liberal politics and culture can be neatly separated and that there is agreement on where the dividing line is to be located. Similar problems in definition, for instance in connection with authority and the bourgeois family in *Haven in a Heartless World* (1977) and *The Culture of Narcissism*, will have to be addressed later on. Suffice it to say now that such terminological confusions are part of the explanation why many people on the left were appalled by his criticism, while some on the right applauded, and Lasch felt his intentions and meanings misread (cf. *Salmagundi* 46: 194-202). So far, at least three conclusions can be drawn: first, his view of the intellectuals in the fifties on the one hand and the New Left on the other exemplifies that his writing thrives on negation with a polemic element being quite prominent. Second, apart from his critical attitude toward liberalism, the specific tenants of his radicalism remain curiously opaque in that the particulars of a radical agenda which can be positively made out in his work do not materialize. Third, with respect to the emerging attitude toward culture, he seems to fall into a familiar pattern characteristic of a certain segment of intellectuals in that a leftist political outlook is wedded to cultural conservatism.

In the public debate of the seventies "narcissism" was a term resounding through all levels of cultural discourse. Historians and political scientists, for example, applied it in studies on political movements and leadership styles; literary critics advanced the term to explain artistic creativity; journalists used it, for instance, in connection with the awareness movement (cf. Battan 119). Thus, well before Lasch focused his attention on this concept, it had been discussed in a variety of contexts ranging from Richard Sennett's brilliant socio-psychological study *The Fall of Public Man* to New Journalism satires such as Tom Wolfe's "The Me Decade and the Third Great Awakening." Lasch was aware of the widespread and increasingly indiscriminate usage of the term "narcissism" in interpretations of cultural phenomena, which threatened to distort the term's original meaning beyond recognition. Nevertheless, he insisted that this concept harbored yet unrealized analytic potential and might yield penetrating insights into the workings of post-industrial America, if used with proper care. Lasch defined the rules for handling psychoanalytic terminology as follows:

[P]sychoanalysis cannot be regarded as a tool-kit, which historians can delve into selectively as the need arises. It is a theory, and it has to be understood first of all in its own wholeness, secondly in relation to other theories offering contradictory or complementary interpretations of the world, and only thirdly (if at all) as a means of interpreting historical facts ("Introduction" to *Social Amnesia* viii).

This was clearly a sideswipe at the psycho-history of Eriksonian provenance that he deemed "a misconceived enterprise" (*Salmagundi* 70-71: 215).

Starting with *Haven in a Heartless World* Lasch began to integrate psychoanalysis and cultural criticism according to the rules he had set down. A closer look at *Haven* is warranted not only because its argument is entirely absorbed into *Culture*, but also because psychoanalysis is approached in general terms and not yet with the particular emphasis on narcissism, in fact, that concept appears only on the fringes, as when the narcissist is pronounced to be the presently prevalent personality type (e.g. xiii; 156).

The central argument in *Haven* is that the bourgeois family has been in a state of utter decay ever since the 1920's. Lasch starts with a Marxian outline of the changes of the work process – the sphere of production, which he then extends into the family, the sphere of reproduction. In Lasch's sketch the capitalist process of production transformed the workplace and consequently the meaning of work for the laborer throughout the nineteenth century. The industrial system turned artisans and skilled laborers into just another machine stripping them of control over the work process and robbing them of their pride in the finished product. Therefore work was no longer experienced as a meaningful activity beyond its cash value. However, up to the 1920's, so the argument goes, at least the private sphere, the family, still provided a refuge in a "heartless" capitalist world. As husband or wife, the individual found acceptance and love; as father or mother, the individual found meaning in providing for and educating the young. The child in turn experiences stable relationships and a union of discipline and love personified by the parents whose task it was to inculcate lasting values. This allowed the child "to become an autonomous adult" (124). The arrangement was torn apart by an advancing "socialization of reproduction" (cf. 12-21). What Lasch means here is that a conglomerate of outside agents intrude into, and ultimately dissolve, the private sphere, turning it into a replica of the workplace. The relationship between parents and children is eroded by social workers, the school, the juvenile courts, pediatricians, child psychologists, sociologists, and finally the peer group. Their combined influence destabilizes parental authority, and, operating with distorted models of individual growth, rechannels the children's character formation away from the restraints imposed by the protestant ethic and in the direction of self-gratification. Youths are thereby fitted neatly into the consumer society's framework. While parents feel increasingly insecure and inadequate in managing household and child-care without relying on "the helping professions" and outside experts, the marriage bond and, by extension, the female-male relationship become brittle. Again a myriad of influences were conflated in this move: marriage counselors, the advertizing industry, neo-Freudian psychotherapists, sociologists, and proponents of an "alternate life-style" all engaged to create and propagate a picture of the relationship of the sexes as an easy-going partnership, a "non-binding commitment" (cf. 134-41) to be conveniently cleared away should the quest for personal fulfilment require it.

Lasch claims that the intervention from outside agencies that result in the unraveling of family ties were, however, initially motivated by the wish to stabilize a faltering institution through modification. In this context, the theoretical discourse in anthropology, psychoanalysis, and sociology provided the intellectual justification and the guidelines for the helping professions' intrusions. Therefore he devotes a substantial part of *Haven* to reconstructing and criticizing the discursive patterns in these disciplines. The argument he proposes in this context is clearly inspired by the one Russell Jacoby advanced in *Social Amnesia* (1975).

Writing about the development of psychoanalytic thought in the U.S., Jacoby had traced the loss and/or domestication of critical terminology by Freud's disciples from Adler and the neo-Freudians such as Horney and Fromm to psychologists on the left like Laing and Cooper. Following in the footsteps of the Frankfurt School (cf. ch. 4), Jacoby deplored this regression, since it generated what he calls a "conformist psychology" which instituted a "shift from a psychology of the unconscious to one of the conscious, from id to ego, sexuality to morality, repression to personality development, and most generally from libido and depth psychology to surface and cultural psychology" (46). While this made psychoanalysis palatable to a larger audience, it also resulted in a restricted vision concerned solely with the individual's psychological adaptation to "social reality," discounting the social roots of "sickness." The subversive element in Freudian terminology was smoothed over and "forgotten" by subsequent generations.

In *Haven*, Lasch not only adopts the revisionism charge with respect to psychoanalysis (e.g. 76-84), but he extends it to anthropological and sociological discourse. Using the example of Malinowski, he maintains that cultural anthropologists were interested in Freud's ideas because they provided a comprehensive, dynamic approach (sharply contrasted by a static behaviorism) in studying personality and family. Yet Malinowski insisted that Freud's findings were conditioned by a family structure far from universal and hence needed revision. Consequently, when studying so-called primitive cultures, the description of family dynamics rather than the psyche took center stage: "For the study of unconscious mental processes, as revealed in dreams, fantasies, and neuroses, he substituted the study of family structure, child rearing, and the formation of 'sentiments'"(68). The next generation of anthropologists represented by Ruth Benedict and especially Margaret Mead reapplied Malinowski's revision of Freudian ideas for different cultural settings to the American family. Although Lasch concedes that Mead's analyses offer important insights (73), he nevertheless classifies her denunciation of "jealousy and passion" and her attack on Momism as smoothing the path for "cool sex" and, respectively, supporting the case against parental authority (75).

In dealing with sociology as exemplified by Talcott Parsons and his circle, Lasch makes out the same pattern: first, a bowdlerized Freud (120ff); then, a theoretical approach subsuming the family in a larger service network for the socialization of the young and, given the rapidity of the modernization process, questioning the parents' ability to contribute much beyond a purely material basis (125-33); finally, Lasch's indictment that all of this not only proves detrimental to salvaging the family, but, in addition, scientifically sanctions its decay. In fine, he constructs in *Haven* a picture of the American family – disseminated through academia, picked up and elaborated on by the helping professions, consumer economy, and government agencies – as determined by a therapeutic outlook. In this context a disturbing effect emerges in that what formerly was considered a power relationship is now masked as a doctor-patient relationship. In other words, the political and economic power structure is careful not to come across to the individual as an antagonistic other, but to couch its policies and actions in therapeutic terms (184-86), and, consequently, stifle all questions about its legitimacy. Here Lasch spells out the negative potential lurking in Philip Rieff's "psychological man" who "is likely to be indifferent to the ancient question of legitimate authority, of sharing in government, so long as the powers that be preserve social order and manage an economy of abundance" (*The Triumph of the Therapeutic* 26). Yet, Lasch goes beyond Rieff in *The Culture of Narcissism* to feature his own version of a modal psychological type emerging forcefully in the seventies.

Apart from Rieff's "psychological man," Lasch's narcissist was inspired by David Riesman's "other-directed man," and a host of related studies that genealogically all hark back to that old question of Crèvecoeur's about the national character. Lasch sets out to explain the

connections between the narcissistic personality type and certain characteristic patterns of contemporary culture, such as the intense fear of old age and death, altered sense of time, fascination with celebrity, fear of competition, decline of play spirit, deteriorating relations between men and women (75).

After an exposition of his main thesis, he moves beyond what he considers a purely metaphoric use of the term narcissism as connoting self-absorption. He extracts his ideas about the etiology and the manifestations of that phenomenon from authoritative sources, primarily Otto Kernberg. Together with Heinz Kohut, on whom Lasch relies for describing the kind of parenting that fosters narcissism (293-301), Kernberg is the major theoretical innovator in the field ever since Freud's suggestive, but by no means exhaustive 1914 essay "On Narcissism: an Introduction" (reprinted, for instance, in the highly useful collection edited by Andrew P. Morrison *Essential Papers on Narcissism*).

Following Freud's differentiation between small children's primary narcissism and a pathological secondary narcissism caused by regression, it is the latter that is of foremost interest. Quoting Kernberg, Lasch summarizes that a grandiose self, a fiction which enables the individual to compensate the frustration of rebuffed object-love, is he main distinguishing feature. In withdrawing the object libido, narcissism shores up the self, repressing anxiety, rage, and guilt. Thereby, the narcissist severs the ties to the outside, thus losing the means of a realistic assessment of him- or herself and others. In brief, narcissism is characterized by an "inner void"; the emotional life is impoverished, since it holds little more than a vision of a grandiose self that tends to be manipulative toward others, "ravenous for admiration," ridden by fears of physical decay, cultivating a "protective shallowness," and prone to depression should the grandiose self-image be questioned (81-2). The narcissistic condition is linked to an impaired, archaic superego covering up punitive impulses and rage. It relates back to what child psychologists label "less than sufficient" parents (on whom the infant is nevertheless totally dependent), especially a narcissistic mother coupled with a father lacking authority. Building on this psychopathological foundation, Lasch ferrets out the workings of narcissism in all realms of cultural expression. He explores such fields as the workplace, advertizing, politics, literature, sports, education, the family, gender relationships, and aging, often changing swiftly from one subject to another in a matter of a few pages, often restating observations previously made with a polemical edge added.

The racy subtitle of chapter three "From Horatio Alger to the Happy Hooker" with which Lasch strives to glaringly underline the transformations in the protestant ethic illustrates this polemic edge. He dramatizes the switch from inner- to what Riesman called other-direction, arguing that modern bureaucracies force people to prostitute themselves, to peddle an inflated image for the easy consumption of peers and superiors. They have to maintain a likable facade, quite divorced from their actual skills on the job, in order to survive the competitive bureaucratic rat race. This narcissistic preoccupation with self-promotion has spilled into politics. Pointing to Vietnam and Watergate as examples (145-51), Lasch states that the Nixon Administration's obsession with 'credibility' took precedence over all reasonable policymaking and confounded the electorate. The narcissistic lessons the American learns in politics and the economy are reiterated in sports and culture. While the latter used to be offset from ordinary experience by playful ritualistic conventions, these boundaries are breaking down due to "the organization of leisure as an extension of commodity production" (217). Now the spectator finds in the arena the same mechanisms of rivalry and competition that govern the workplace. The spirit of play that formerly provided psychological relief is destroyed. The same holds true for the fine arts, the theater of the absurd and experimental writers like Barthelme and Barth who are cited as proponents of pseudo-self-awareness and an ironic detachment that relentlessly thrusts both bleak reality and the fiction making act into their audience's face. As a consequence the "representational power" is undercut, leading to "a remarkable indifference to reality." Moreover, the audience is denied a recuperative escape to fantasy by the artist's pathological self-consciousness which mirrors that of the narcissist (171).

With respect to the family, education, and the relationship between the sexes Lasch continues the argument advanced in *Haven*. Reflecting on the American home as narcissism's breeding ground, he deems permissive parents unable to assist their offspring in developing an adequate superego (301ff). Furthermore, "the mechanical quality of parental care, so notably lacking in affect, gives rise in the child to ravenous oral cravings and to a boundless rage against those who fail to gratify them" (306f). The misery is compounded in the schools that institute a "steady dilution of intellectual standards" (246) which deprive students of the means to test and develop their abilities. This ultimately leads to the students' "inability to take an interest in anything beyond immediate experience" (258). Men and women socialized in this manner experience shallowness, at best, in each other's company. Relationships exhibit a fundamental incongruity in the give-and-take: while the individual tends to make exorbitant demands on others, s/he is made uneasy by their reciprocal expectations, and proves unwilling to attend to the wishes of others in return. This is reinforced by the fact that instant gratification, while at the same time maintaining independence and control, is glorified in the culture at large, particularly by the advertizing industry which spearheads the consumer economy. As worst case scenario Lasch projects intermittent warfare into interpersonal relationships. It is fueled on the women's side by a "flight from feeling" (338) into self-assertion at times exacerbated by feminism. It is fed on the men's side by fears of inadequacy breeding resentment and rage that are then vented on a perceived female threat.

Lasch caps his interpretation of the pitfalls of a narcissistic culture with a reflection on aging. It is another factor unbalancing the narcissist's mental economy since s/he has no interest in the future (357). No longer valid is the pattern which held that kinship ties transcend generations viz. that parents live vicariously through their offspring. And no longer are the old esteemed for their experience in a society in flux. Cut off from social prestige and other forms of recompense and sublimation, the narcissist, imprisoned in the "now," tries allaying the dread of old age in adopting the outward attributes of youth prescribed by fashion and/or banks on medical progress to stretch the human lifespan ever more.

In *The Culture of Narcissism* Lasch set out to describe how the remnants of American individualism slide into narcissism in twentieth century society. He selected an approach to cultural criticism that subordinates all observed phenomena to a single interpretive key. This procedure, one should again be reminded, bears a structural resemblance to the consensus school's treatment of liberalism. The daring and the dangers in this synthetic approach are underlined by the fact that Lasch himself felt compelled in *The Minimal Self* (1984) "to make clear what *The Culture of Narcissism* seems to have left obscure or ambiguous" (16). It is sensible to avoid repetition in presenting the gist of his argument there and to concentrate solely on the changes and additions to his thesis as stated so far.

One major shift within the larger concept of narcissism is the stress on survivalism:

> Narcissism signifies a loss of selfhood, ... It refers to a self threatened with disintegration and by a sense of inner emptiness. To avoid confusion, what I have called the culture of narcissism might better be characterized, at least for the moment, as a culture of survivalism. Everyday life has begun to pattern itself on the survival strategies forced on those exposed to extreme adversity. Selective apathy, emotional disengagement from others, renunciation of the past and the future, a determination to live one day at a time – these techniques of emotional self-management, necessarily carried to extremes under extreme conditions, in more moderate form have come to shape the lives of ordinary people under the ordinary conditions of a bureaucratic society widely perceived as a far-flung system of total control (57f).

Concomitantly, the support drawn from psychoanalytic literature stems no longer primarily from Otto Kernberg and Heinz Kohut. In fact it is quite conspicuous that Kernberg is quoted only once, Kohut not at all, while both were cited freely throughout *The Culture of Narcissism*. Perhaps their notion of the grandiose self stands in too obvious a semantic contrast with the minimal self advertised in the title. Anyway, apart from Freud, Lasch's interest in psychoanalytic thinking has increasingly been transferred to Kleinian object relations theory, especially that of her student Winnicott. Yet, it was through Kernberg and Kohut that the work of Melanie Klein was finally spread in American Freudian circles in the early seventies (Kurzweil 143, 280f). Historically, the reception had been stifled by the Americans' siding with Anna Freud and her disciples in the controversy that broke out with Klein and her following in London after Freud's death in 1939 (Kurzweil, 132-34, 261-66). Kleinians were disregarded while American psychoanalysts welcomed Anna Freud's work on child psychology alongside with Heinz Hartmann's ego psychology. This background is important not because it shows that Lasch was carried by a wave of renewed interest in Klein, but rather because it points out his allegiances. It explains to some extent his critique of mainstream American Freudians (cf. *Minimal* 208-11) as well as his attack on Hartmann (218-223) whom he sees in a slightly nineteen-eighty-fourish manner as striving for "a rationalization of mental life as a counterpart to the rationalization of the natural environment" leading to "the demand for a new form of behavior control far more rigorous than psychoanalysis" (222).

But let us return to Lasch's reworking of the psychoanalytic framework he uses. Central is the infant's coming to terms with the challenges of union and separation, the premise being that a successful coping with the separation from the mother opens the road to maturity. One way to manage the negative feelings caused by separation is through what Winnicott termed "transitional objects," viz. the teddy bear, the doll, or the cuddly blanket, which for the child symbolically represent aspects of the mother. Furthering the formation of object libido, these transitional objects function as a link between the inner and the outer world; they are the vanguard of culture. Together with the Oedipus complex later on, they provide an important check regarding infantile visions of omnipotent control (194f). In the Oedipus complex the child's vision – regardless of gender – that it could serve as sufficient partner to the mother is once again focused on the craving for a lost union. In overcoming the complex "the infantile illusion of omnipotence" (178) is put into place and set onto a realistic track.

Arguing from this basis, it is Lasch's contention that American culture impedes the development of a self that is able to manage the difficult dialectics of union and separation. One reason for this is that the commodity world principally offers objects devoid of "transitional" value. The dream world it creates thus seems separate and beyond human control, yet paradoxically it also encourages regressive fantasies: "it simultaneously takes on the appearance of a mirror of the self, a dazzling array of images in which we can see anything we wish to see. Instead of bridging the gap between the self and its surroundings, it obliterates the difference between them" (195). Furthermore, the American narcissist "rejects the Oedipal solution to the problem of separation" (184). With Janine Chasseguet-Smirgel, Lasch points out that this leads to a denial of the differences between generations and gender guided by the wish "to restore the sense of wholeness" (185). The outcome, as Lasch sees it, is an emotionally impoverished self barely able to keep its head above the waters of existence, yet yearning for the womb's all-encompassing unity.

He finds reminiscences of this yearning in the holistic, even atavistic, approach to the environment espoused by some ecologists.

A look at the meta-level discourse shows Lasch defending his view that the nexus of consumption and narcissism is related to mass culture's degradation. He directs his critique at the proponents of cultural pluralism (39ff), such as Peter Clecak and Herbert Gans (see also his exchange with Gans on popular culture in *Democracy* 1 and 2). But he also finds the minimal self enshrined in high culture regions. Here he goes to more detail than before to show that it is present in the survivalist novels of Doris Lessing, as much as on the canvasses of Mark Rothko, in the music of John Cage and the reductive characters populating Thomas Pynchon's novels. The most important discursive turn, however, is Lasch's attempt to classify and describe contemporary cultural politics in "psychoanalytic terminology" since it "now provides a more reliable guide to the political landscape than outmoded distinctions between left and right" (198). He arrives at a typology that is based on the Freudian model of the human psyche: a "party of the superego", a "party of the ego" (198), and, although the logical continuation would be a party of the id, he prefers to earmark that position as "the party of Narcissus" (253).

The advocates of the superego stand for a libertarian view of culture and the economy, they treasure minority rights and civil liberties, and want to guard what they consider an American tradition of self-reliant individualism. In their view the commonwealth is endangered by a denigration of morality. They would like to strengthen the superego, therefore they put a stress on "conscience" (201) in order to reinvigorate social stability and a moral consensus rooted in liberalism. It is Lasch's criticism that in holding tight to these inherited core values proponents of this position – he mentions Philip Rieff, Daniel Bell, and the late Lionel Trilling (200) – tend to overestimate the superego. Lasch points out how the superego operates with a consensus determined by restraints. But once the consensus is eroded, the primitive, violent, and punitive impulses hidden in the superego come to the fore, undercutting the very values the party of the superego wants to energize.

The second position features "the rational, the reality-testing faculty, the ego, against both impulse and inherited morality" (205). According to Lasch, it has its roots in progressive conceptions of an autonomous personality, and beyond that goes back to an attack on Calvinist ideas of retribution which are unfavorably compared to "a system of rational 'correction'" (206). Thus, the party of the ego has behavior control and regulation written on its banners misreading Freud's famous dictum "where id was, there shall be ego" as the irreversible outcome in cultural modernization (cf. 220f). It aims at speeding the modernization process through social engineering based on scientific analysis. This, in Lasch's opinion, is the umbrella that shelters such diverse scientific systems as the educational concepts derived from Dewey, Parsonian sociology, Skinner's behaviorism, and neo-Freudian ego psychology. Their main underlying premise is that social organization has reached a level of complexity only manageable by experts. Consequently, a scientific and technological elite strives to devalue and bypass the established democratic political process, the participatory element in democracy, which ideally pervades all levels in society, is blacked out – so Lasch charges.

The third party was galvanized as a response to the shortcomings of the other two positions. For Lasch it "corresponds, more or less, to the thinking of the new left or at least to those who advocate a 'cultural revolution' not merely against capitalism but against industrialism in general" (199). Here he updates his critique of the New Left developed earlier, and it has to be noted that his previous blanket condemnations have been refined considerably. He argues that this socio-cultural position hinges on the observation that the dialects of the enlightenment, first brought home by Nazi death camps and the atom bomb, reiterated by the arms race and environmental destruction, prompted the feeling that physical as well as "emotional survival" is predicated on a cultural revolution (225). He goes on to discuss Herbert Marcuse and Norman O. Brown whose ideas have shaped the New Left. Marcuse's effort to find a way around the cultural pessimism expressed in the writings of Freud and the Frankfurt School centers on the Marxian surplus concept which he projected into the psychological realm in *Eros and Civilization* (1955). More precisely, Marcuse claims that Western culture generates "surplus repression" directed against the body beyond what is necessary to ensure physical reproduction. This leads to a distorted reality principle. In this context Narcissus and Orpheus are interpreted as the mythical harbingers of a different reality principle, one that does more justice to the body than the Promethean one presently in charge (*Minimal* 227-34). In *Life against Death* (1959) Brown shared Marcuse's concern for the neglected rights of the body. In a culture that denies those rights, the psyche, torn between eros and thanatos, turns its destructive instincts outward against Nature and other human beings. In short, Brown saw the root evil of society in a culturally induced incapacity to accept death. The antidote would be a Dionysian indulgence of the body which then facilitates an acceptance of death-in-life (*Minimal* 237-40). Lasch's main critique of the two authors is that for Marcuse the body's liberation is still contingent on "the liberating potential of industrial technology" (234), thus on the very same instrumental reason that implemented its subjection; while Brown tries to abolish the tensions between culture and the instincts. This, in Lasch's view, is a futile undertaking that forgets the intellectual gratifications (in terms of human achievement through work) springing from this differential (240).

The cultural revolution envisioned by Marcuse and Brown took a new turn in Freudian feminism. Authors such as Nancy Chodorov, Dorothy Dinnerstein, and Stephanie Engel held that psychoanalysis, in tune with the rest of Western civilization, favored a concept of the self that was male-centered. They argued against the remnants of patriarchal structures dispersed throughout culture and identified the destructiveness wreaked by instrumental reason solely with the male. Drawing a gender line, they elevated feminine mutuality and condemned the masculine drive for mastery. This feminine mutuality is linked back to narcissism positively understood, i.e. the yearning for unity generates a holistic relation to the human and natural environment different from the male urge for domination. Lasch thinks this feminist analysis has spread from the women's movement to the environmentalists and the peace movement, all of which hail "a narcissistic symbiosis with nature as the cure for technological solipsism" (248) without recognizing that technological solipsism itself is rooted in narcissism. Lasch defines his own standpoint as sympathetic to, yet critical of the third position. In an earlier article on the Freudian left he had pointed to patriarchy as a pseudo-problem deflecting criticism "from the corporation and the state to the family" (*New Left Review* 129:33). Similarly he defends the need for "a firm conception of selfhood" (*Minimal* 253) grounded in the morals of a guilty conscience necessary to gain a tenable, intermediary relation with respect to nature and culture. The sketchy invocation of "communities of competence" at the end of *The Culture of Narcissism* (396) as agents of change reappears when he introduces the Aristotelian "*phronesis* or practical reason" as a corrective to instrumental reason (*Minimal* 253).

Ever since the publication of *The Minimal Self*, Lasch has continued his efforts to grasp and classify American cultural discourse. For instance, the tripartite structure derived from the Freudian concept of the psyche reappears in a modified version in "A Typology of Intellectuals," his contribution to a 1986 *Salmagundi* symposium. There he cites three public roles the intellectual may fulfil: "the voice of conscience; the voice of reason; [and] the voice of the imagination" (27). Then he assigns feminists to the imagination category, Melanie Klein is brought in connection with the voice of reason, and C. Wright Mills serves as the example of the conscience category. However, the difficulties in keeping up his classificatory system are highlighted by his reactions to a position that was voiced emphatically in *Habits of the Heart* (1985), namely the communitarian view. One might assume with the communities of competence and the resort to practical reason in mind that he would relate to communitarians as kindred spirits. Yet, in a 1987 lecture he bluntly caricatured them as

romanticiz[ing] a tightly knit little world in which everyone agrees on a common definition of the good life. [...] The guardians of political morality are thus authorized to stamp out all forms of heresy and to indulge on a grand scale their fanatical determination to mind their neighbor's business ("Fraternalist Manifesto" 17).

This opinion was somewhat moderated in a more balanced article for *Community in America* (1988), an essay collection featuring responses to Robert Bellah and his collaborators' thesis. There he positively reflects on the insistence on community over bureaucracy, on the definition of tradition as past achievements, and the emphasis on practices; while he cautions his readers about "authoritarian implications" (182) in the communitarian social ideal. Furthermore, their criticism of liberalism cannot hide the fact for Lasch that they are ultimately quite close to what they criticize. The article demonstrates that in spite of his attempt to transcend the old markers such as left and right, liberal and conservative in his typology informed by psychoanalysis, he still has a hard time doing without them in contemporary discourse (cf. also "'Traditional Values': Left, Right, and Wrong"). But before embarking on any further reflections on the significance this holds for evaluating Lasch's own stance, let us focus on the reception his ideas have met with in the intellectual community.

Considering Lasch's negative view of American society and the criticism that he voiced about various participants in cultural discourse in his last three books, it was to be expected that he would evoke a strong echo. In 1979 *Salmagundi* devoted an entire symposium to *The Culture of Narcissism*. *Telos* followed in 1980 with a symposium on narcissism in general which was, however, clearly inspired by the widespread reception of Lasch's book. Particularly virulent criticism came from feminists. In their contribution to the *Salmagundi* symposium Doane and Hodges concluded that Lasch was in a "profoundly conservative" manner hankering for the paternalistic family and hierarchical structures (187). Barrett and McIntosh intensified and consolidated that criticism. They detected a "romantic view of the psychological strengths derived from Oedipal conflict underly [sic] his general support for authoritarian styles of socialization" (42). This, in turn, is given as the reason for his distorted account of historical change that purports to be "iconoclastic *within* a socialist tradition," whereas it actually masks a "reactionary" stance (43). They discover a similar discrepancy between the seeming and the real in his view of feminism where "he appears to be treating gender relations in an objective way [but] his standpoint is utterly and exclusively masculine" (44). In this context, Barrett and McIntosh rely on an article by Stephanie

Engel. She had argued that what Lasch was actually attacking in his conceptualization of narcissism was a much needed feminization of society ("Feminity as Tragedy" 97f). Reviewing the controversy between feminist critics and Christopher Lasch, Miriam Dixson pointed out that on both sides misunderstandings were at work which were caused by a male outlook ingrained in the very foundations of psychoanalysis.

Feminists were not alone in raising objections with respect to psychoanalysis in the writings of Lasch. In his study *Psychology of the Self and the Treatment of Narcissism* Richard D. Chessick declared that Lasch confused "Kohut's theory of the 'psychology of the self in a broader sense,' which is meant to be applicable to everybody, with Kohut's discussions of pathological narcissism" (21). Furthermore he pointed to theoretical incompatibilities in the concepts of Kernberg and Kohut that are glossed over in *The Culture of Narcissism*. This point had been raised earlier by Colleen D. Clements in *The Psychoanalytic Review*. She saw Lasch misusing psychiatric models in attempting an easy equation of cultural history and the psychiatric clinical situation. She maintained that this is not only "a significant reductionist error" (284) which breeds "a judgmental, apocalyptic use of narcissism" (288), but also that it may encourage "inappropriate guilt, masochistic notions of sin, self-destructive behavior in many forms" (293). In a response to Clements' article, Roberta Satow wonders why psychoanalysts have been so reluctant to forcefully criticize the glaring misappropriations of their terminology, and, instead, have "made Christopher Lasch the plenary speaker at the American Psychoanalytic Association's 1980 annual meeting" (301). One of her answers suggests that no clear-cut definition of narcissism has yet emerged in psychoanalytic theory itself, making it hard to chastize outsiders like Lasch. Jesse F. Battan rounded off this criticism with a flat denial that narcissism is on the rise in contemporary society. Instead, he believes that transformations within psychoanalysis itself are responsible for the increasing number of patients who are classified as narcissists (206). In order to further demolish Lasch's claim that narcissism is spreading, Battan emphasized that since only a small, rich segment of American society can afford psychoanalytic treatment, any professionally observed increase in pathological narcissism would be negligible, indeed (208). In sum, he thinks that Lasch's perspective on contemporary culture is "little more than a moralistic diatribe cloaked in the clinical terminology of psychoanalysis" (209).

Sociologist Richard Flacks pronounced similar misgivings about the narcissism thesis (*Center Magazine* 28). He implies that Lasch is constructing a trend to fit his ideological persuasion. This remark turns the spotlight away from methodology and terminology, and refocuses attention on the discrepancies in Lasch's writing between a conservative analysis and a socialist credo.

This issue had been brought up not only by feminists, it was also featured by others (Wrong 313; Shapiro 70; Nachman 176; Gronseth 246). Depending on the critic's own stance, Lasch was either condemned for betraying leftist positions, or admonished for carrying useless ideological baggage, Marxist jargon, in his interpretations. A more perceptive observation came from Lenz who deplored the fact that Lasch seemed to have lost sight of his project to contribute to a radical political agenda over publicizing his negative view of things (207).

Very few critics, indeed, were in outright agreement with Lasch (cf. the article by Michael Fischer or Kent M. Brudney, the latter reviewed *Haven, Culture,* and *Minimal* as late as 1987, yet gives little indication of being aware of the criticisms made previously). James Seaton is unique in that he offers a sympathetic attitude toward Lasch, whom he considers "one of the major social critics of our time" (183), but his appreciation is felicitously coupled with a judicious assessment of Lasch's weaknesses. He is intrigued by the paradoxical circumstances that allow for Lasch's criticism to be absorbed and celebrated by its own subject, American society, and assumes that *The Culture of Narcissism* invites such misconstruction on the part of those criticized. He believes that these misreadings are founded on Lasch's "failure to situate his own text within a cultural tradition" (171) – for instance, Jacoby's work or Marcuse's *One-dimensional Man*, also texts by Fromm and Horkheimer's *Eclipse of Reason*. This failure is aggravated, because Lasch never truly elaborates his implicit commitment to socialism. These omissions, Seaton is convinced, were "demanded by the concept of culture which informs *The Culture of Narcissism*" (173): the synthetic narcissism thesis is built on an organic, non-conflict view of culture. This monistic outlook is linked to a "glorification of the 'clinical'" (175) which is the flipside of Lasch's condemnation of theories alien to his own, also criticized by Robert Ehrlich (*Telos* 40: 193). Thus, Seaton astutely lays his finger on a soft spot, since both Freud and Marx, on whom Lasch relies as theoretical authorities, work with a concept of culture based on conflict.

Seaton's able criticism may be supplemented and carried on in various ways. For instance, one could argue that the monistic approach to culture is an off-shoot from the liberal consensus paradigm which Lasch had encountered early in his career as a historian. More interesting, however, is another issue: Seaton had pointed out that the reception of *The Culture of Narcissism* which made it a best-seller was pre-structured by a discussion about self-centeredness and egotism in American society. But it needs to be emphasized as well that what the book reflects are largely mainstream views. For instance, the distrust of a professional elite, which Lasch highlighted from *Haven* onward, is seen as quite typical of the times by Peter N. Carroll in his history of the seventies:

Public distrust of the political leadership represented only the tip of a massive iceberg of discontent. A national opinion survey of 1975 showed that 69 percent of the respondents felt that "over the last ten years, this country's leaders have lied consistently to the people." These suspicions implicated all the major institutions of American society. A Harris poll revealed that between 1966 and 1976, public confidence in the medical establishment dropped from 73 to 42 percent; for the major companies from 55 to 16 percent (advertising agencies fell to 7 percent); the credibility of lawyers slid to 12 percent (235).

Yet Lasch is not simply a mouthpiece for a general mood – for this the idiosyncrasies of his views are too prominent. For example, his reaction to sociological and anthropological theories, outlined in *Haven* and reiterated in *Culture*, is somewhat extreme, as when he links Margaret Mead's ideas to those of advocates of cool sex. In addition, his crusade against Malinowski and Parsons on charges of polluting Freudian terminology is overwrought. After all, the two were applying Freud to their fields which operate with different parameters, i.e. adaptations caused by recontextualizations were not only inevitable but are legitimate scientific practice. Lasch's insistence on orthodoxy reminds one of the sectarian infighting some Freudians have engaged in. One rationale why he is so insistent on orthodoxy might be that he hopes to bolster his own arguments with the prestige of established authorities (this recalls, of course, Seaton's argument about "the glorification of the clinical"). In this context, it should be recognized that some of his ideas are in desperate need of validation. For instance, in *The Minimal Self* he ponders the social consequences of the narcissist's failure to master the Oedipus complex. Chasseguet-Smirgel, his psychoanalytic authority, had hypothesized about a denial of differences between generations and gender as a consequence of an unmastered Oedipus complex. Projecting this from the individual psyche onto the macro-level of society, Lasch finds not only child neglect on the part of narcissistic parents, but he darkly ruminates: "There is some evidence that incest is on the rise" (190). Yet none, statistical or other, is put forth, except the remark that Vance Packard is also speculating about an increasing number of incests. Instances like the preceding one discredit his entire argument. The shadows they throw cloud Lasch's usage of psychoanalysis even where it is more convincing. Furthermore, this example reveals a more basic problem, a problem involving value systems.

In "Forms and Transformations of Narcissism" Heinz Kohut had reflected on the negative evaluation of that pathology which leads to a disregard of the therapeutic possibilities it hides. He deplored the analyst's urge to replace narcissism with object-love in their patients. According to Kohut, this urge

Roszak labels "avuncular carping" the scolding comments of older liberals about the young radicals.[3] But if Roszak's comments are not carping, they are sternly avuncular. They have to be, since his explanation of what formed the flower children is at the same time a description of their vulnerability.

The rearing of the white, educated counter cultural youth, in Roszak's perception, had been caring and protective. Encouraged by their enlightened parents and their permissive society to explore freedom and pleasure, and sheltered from the want that had forced their parents to sell themselves for the pleasures that a modern economy offers, they were able to "build a new, uncompromised personality, flawed perhaps by irresponsible ease, but also touched with some outspoken spirit." But this upbringing, coupled with the newness of the cultural enterprise on which the young of the sixties were embarked, meant that they had available no firm standards by which to make something permanent of the project. The manner of the free universities of the sixties Roszak describes as "a fondling of ideas that resembles nothing so much as an infant's play with bright, unfamiliar objects." The task of "building a sophisticated network of thought" on the healthy but untutored instincts of the young "is rather like trying to graft an oak tree upon a wildflower."[4] And so *The Making of a Counter Culture* proceeds in its purpose of constructing an architecture of ideas on the foundation of the youth rebellion, meanwhile admonishing the young here and there for some triviality or carelessness: it is especially hard on the ersatz and essentially programmed liberation promised by drugs. The book seems a bit apart from its subject. This is entirely appropriate. It was a property of the counter culture not to be overly articulate. But that fact needed someone to articulate and explore if the cultural rebellion was to be understood or to understand itself; and this, of course, means that the counter culture could be spoken about only from some point outside of itself.

It is, then, precisely the rejection of intellect as the seat of understanding that according to Roszak distinguishes the counter culture from the larger society. More particularly, the rejection is of the intellect of science and technology, the mind of what here and in later writing Roszak joins other cultural commentators in labeling the technocracy. For an explanation of that mind, which Roszak calls the objective consciousness, he uses a terminology that will later reappear in his work. The objective consciousness, a psychological state that may exist even if objectivity itself is impossible, makes the clearest possible distinction between an observer In Here and an Out There that is the object of observation. Everything that may clutter the consciousness as it attempts its cold accuracy of observation, every troublesome emotion or need must be banished, to become part of the Out There: it is the intention of In Here to contract into as small and tight a knot of concentration as possible, and to put under observation as much of existence as it can. "The very word 'concentration' yields the interesting image of an identity contracted into a small, hard ball; hence a dense, diminished identity ..." But In Here continues to be inconveniently possessed of wayward emotions that interfere with exact observations. The modern world admires the machine for its clean dispensation from all that messiness, its ability to "achieve perfect concentration, perfect self-control."[5]

But what did the West lose when it drew into its clot of concentration? The answer Roszak gives is not so clear as it might at first seem. A response to the question will indicate something of the difficulty of distinguishing Roszak the practical critic of modern capitalist and collectivist technology from Roszak the mystical transcendentalist.

The Making of a Counter Culture, like Roszak's later work, talks at length about visionary powers, higher faculties, and the like. When he is speaking in this way, it is to be understood that these are what the objective consciousness alienates from itself or denies to the world it puts under observation. The point, he remarks, is not that objective truth is possible (perhaps it is not) but that the personality committed to objectivity is.[6] Would he be willing to propose that neither is transcendental truth available in a stone or a trance, except insofar as philosophy or theology might interpret these: that what is available are experiencings more powerful or more exquisite than the technocracy offers? Whatever is to be made of his language, it postulates states of mind that transport beyond the boundaries of the ordinary experiences of his readers.

There is much in *The Making of a Counter Culture*, though, that would recommend a more modest set of experiences alternative to those offered by the collectivist or free-market present. Speaking, for example, of the makers of music, dance, drama, the plastic arts, and "rhapsodic utterance," Roszak comments that "in the making of these glorious things, these images, these utterances, these gestures, there was a supreme joy"; the "achievement of that joy was the purpose of their work." The individual who has refused to compromise the fullness of personality and its desires knows that the object of living "is to take this raw material of his total experience – its need for knowledge, for passion, for imaginative exuberance, for moral purity, for fellowship – and to shape it *all*, as laboriously and as cunningly as a sculptor shapes his stone, into a comprehensive style of life."[7] The words suggest commonly recognizable forms of creativity and of self-making. And arguing that the modern organization of technology and economics impoverishes them makes for viable cultural criticism.

Here Roszak might have been kinder to present-day technics in themselves, and to whatever may actually exist of the objective consciousness as a foundation of them. As forms of making, they have awakened a sufficient relish to deserve inclusion in the activities he endorses. And if the pursuit of objectivity is as rigorous as Roszak claims it to be, it deserves some place, however subordinate, in the act of self-making that he champions.

The Making of a Counter Culture finds the era to be similar to the time when the lowly and unruly Christians broke in upon the Mediterranean civilization of their time, proclaiming a truth that defied the Apollonian reason and order of the Greco-Roman world.[8] Now that the counter culture has subsided, at first sight the historical comparisons seems dated. But in a more important way the analogy holds, and deserves to have received a more extensive examination than Roszak's suggestive reference accords it. The antinomianism of the counter culture, which in order to be antinomianism must reject history along with any other source of authority outside of immediate experiencing, actually stands in a long history informed by Christianity as well as such strains of western religion as Hasidic Judaism. Western culture has managed to accommodate a trust in rationality and an attentiveness to visionaries; it has alternatively located right conduct in the self-controls of conscience and in the spontaneity of love; it has even sought, in a few works of theology, to compound such opposites. To that extent there was little new – and much of honorable tradition – in the counter culture, and in its quarrel both with conventional society and with the rebels who spoke a political or moral language in place of a language of ecstasy. Roszak's book contains hints, but only hints, of such a perception.

One of the most insightful and analytically close sections of *The Making of a Counter Culture* examines Marxists and later critics who have attempted to revise Marx or replace his ideology with something more promising in the way of a humane radicalism. Briefly noting how little of the humanist implications of *The Economic and Philosophical Manuscripts* got worked out in Marx's later work, Roszak quite convincingly demonstrates that the concept of alienation, which imaginative Marxists have attempted to put to sensitive cultural criticism, had only a narrow meaning in Marx's texts. Through a critical explication of Herbert Marcuse and Norman O. Brown, Roszak pursues the question of why the human race has come to its state of alienation, which can be understood loosely as its apparently perverse and willful determination to sever from itself its warmest desires and needs. In the limited terms of Marxism, for example, alienation amounts to the willingness of the work force to project its collective labors into capitalism (a twentieth-century critic would add state Marxism) and thereby to enchain the act and debase the meaning of labor.

Elsewere in *The Making of a Counter Culture*, Roszak presents alienation as the expulsion from In Here of sensuosity and imagination, and he makes it essentially an event of the recent centuries. *Where the Wasteland Ends* will begin the process at the point when human beings stood upright, therein making the chilly, distancing senses of sight and hearing the center of human awareness and placing the body actually and metaphorically below them. In his discussion of Marxism and its critics, Roszak gives a favorable presentation to Norman O. Brown's conviction that alienation originated in humankind's awareness of mortality and its consequent will to commit its efforts to works that will vindicate its existence.

What is significant in all this for an understanding of Roszak is his conviction that alienation, of an extent and kind that conventional Marxism cannot measure, constitutes the essence of the troubles of the human race. *The Making of a Counter Culture* looks to the communards and flower children of the 1960s for a cure. Later writings pursue other ways of defining alienation. But can those acts and states of mind that belong to the objective consciousness, as Roszak defines it, be recognized as amounting to something more than a condition of sickness?

Where the Wasteland Ends speaks only incidentally of the counter culture. But it may be taken to be Roszak's reflections on the larger cultural meaning of the rebellion he had earlier defined and chronicled as a revolt against the hegemony of modern technology and science. What he now set out to consider, as in *The Making of a Counter Culture* but more extensively, was nothing less than the human psyche itself and why modern civilization is sickening it. *Where the Wasteland Ends* is a big, rich, sprawling, and often quite frustrating book. For the sake of convenience its argument may be split into two. It is a practical commentary on the physical dominance of modern industry and science and what might be done to rewin a livable human life. And it is a book of psychology: not psychology as therapy, though that is among the work's aims, but psychology as an examination of human mind and experience.

That broader objective is founded in an assumption, which will also inform *Unfinished Animal*, that there is a continuity between the most somatic of physical processes and the most rational of the mind's faculties: that thinking of sorts, copious and varied, goes on in every throb of organic sensation and growth. To live fully, Roszak concludes, is to experience this organic thinking freely. A civilization that severs itself from the bountiful experiencing that goes on beneath rational thought has to that extent chosen death. And this is what modern civilization has done.

The harm began in the course of evolution (which *Unfinished Animal* will present as taking the human race out of its present imprisonment). When the human race stood upright and the head came to be a "watchtower" scanning the surroundings, eyes and ears became the dominant sensory organs, the seat of awareness, distancing awareness from the body below.[9] Thereupon humanity was liable to a detachment of the chilly cerebral activities from their hot vital grounding. Modern culture, compounded of science and technology, has completed the detachment. What are children trained to view with disgust? Science fiction and horror literature evoke things that are alive and gooey, things that are sloppy, slimy, clingy. "We cringe from anything as oozy as the inside of our body and look for security to what is clinically tidy, hard-edged, dry, rigidly solid, odorless, aseptic, durable. In another word, anything *lifeless*," like the glass and steel and plastic of industrial interiors. It is not sex that suffers the most repression. Sex still announces its presence. Repression, so deep that modern people no longer feel it, stifles not sexuality but organism itself in its processes of growth and instinct and aliveness.[10]

Demanding sharp analytical perception and methodical verification, modern civilization rejects the dream state. "Last night, as on all the nights of your life, you dreamed much and magnificently," inventing a reality that in wakefulness you forget though it may have had the greatness of Homer or Shakespeare. Tribal peoples trust to what dreaming tells them. But not we. Dreams are unreal according to the modern understanding of reality, which is that it resides in the observable, measurable world that does not alter from moment to moment or does so only in accordance with continuing laws. The dark things of sleep are vague, changing, elusive of measurement. "The alarm rings, and instantaneously an axe falls across the continuum of consciousness, sharply dividing awake from asleep ... . Rapidly, efficiently, the dreams are dispersed from memory and our sharply outlined, compacted, daytime identity is precipitated out of the shape-shifting self we were in our sleep ... ." Alarm clocks, caffeine, the mental requisites of modern technics and science: their object and result are to force the "edge of wakefulness mercilessly against the mind ... ."[11]

The passage catches Roszak at his freshest, with images as clean and brief as the cut of a laser. It fulfills its intention, which is to make the reader recoil from that violence against sleep and the opulent organic and imaginative existence that sleep enfolds. But in imputing to the twentieth-century mentality exactly the clarity and spareness that its aestheticians have attempted to catch in architecture and in the most advanced of machine designs, Roszak's phrases unintentionally reveal that what he calls the technocracy has a case to make for itself beyond its more vulgar claims. Essentially, it is this: to be able to represent an idea of an order of morality.

Any system of morality, or ethics, or honor has to set itself against some sort of spontaneity or appetite, doing so if only because human dignity requires it. A code of courage resists fear, a code of charity resists selfishness, and so on. That slash of wakefulness against sleep and dreams and organic sensibility in general, as Roszak sees the matter, suits fairly well as an act of resistance: to read Roszak's passage is to feel the body's shudder at the morning wake-up call. In moral and spiritual content, to be sure, the whole of modern technics and modern science shrivels beside the beatitudes: to find any adequate content whatever they have to do service to something outside themselves, whether that be democracy or the physical sustenance of a growing population. Nor do they have much to offer in the way of an ascetic regime: their favored western attendants know next to nothing of danger, labor, or pain. But if they do no more than to demand or even merely to symbolize an icy clearness of consciousness that is at contraries to organic sensibility – and that, Roszak eloquently insists, they do – science and technology may make a very modest contribution to a civilization that can be respected. The British art critic T. E. Hulme proposed something not far different early in the century when he detected in the flat geometries of modern art, so resistant to the fleshly three-dimensional fullness that earlier modern painting captures, the representation of a spiritual realm such as Egyptian and Byzantine art imagines. Roszak's presentation of the western twentieth-century consciousness could have led him to reflect on the possibility of a dialogue, however argumentative, between it and the kind of experiencing he locates in organism.

Roszak actually does attribute to science a value distantly related to that which I have in mind. Science, he says, invites people to engage in civilized conversation. Francis Bacon, whom Roszak presents as a catalyst to the technocratic future, came from a time of religious violence; and what he did is to change the groundwork of discussion, advocating a reasoned empirical address to questions. Believing that truth is objective and discoverable by observations and logic, science recommends virtues of patience, openness, "above all, unstinting self-control." Such virtues in Roszak's judgment of them are at least courteous. A defender of the modern ethos may even describe them, rightly or not, as a means to a democratic citizenship.[12]

Thus described, the scientific habits of discourse are both honorable in themselves and of some practical use, if not for preventing a war or two at least for calming some otherwise very nasty disputes. The thrust of Roszak's book, though, is to give them scant credit for either good. The courtesy and the other decencies they embody he finds to be chill and distant. And as for their usefulness: Roszak is convinced that the intellectual servants of technology are for the most part conditioned not to independence but to an impersonal performance of whatever tasks are assigned them, and these can include very lethal tasks. Any small contribution the scientific mind might make to the dispassionate settling of a potentially murderous disagreement it more than makes up for in its servitude to modern war and genocide.

The maiming that twentieth-century science and technics effect on the person is at the same time a maiming of the outer world, or at least a disrespect for it. The habit of examination and technical manipulation of the world makes for a radical distinction between In Here and Out There, in the terminology that Roszak has used in *The Making of a Counter Culture*. In Here, again, is the hard observational consciousness, contracted into as small a knot as possible so that even the function of the self can be an object of cool scrutiny. Out There is everything under observation, kept at cool distance from the observer In Here and looked at without love or sympathy. Even the body gets pushed Out There, remarks Roszak, who has already commented on the detachment of the head from the organic experiencing that lies literally and figuratively below it as its foundation.

Again Roszak has an elegant concept, and again he is able to make his reader experience the cultural event: here, the space between the outside world, which includes the body, and the small isolated observer inside the skull. He assumes that the observational distance implies disrespect and loss of encounter. The assumption is more questionable than the descriptive analysis that precedes it. That the world is outside, along with the body, that we shall never know either in itself, never know even a cell inside the skin or the bone unless it sends, from a distance, a message of pain or pleasure: that is an occasion for the awareness of mystery. A twentieth-century urbanite does not, like a tribesman, believe that he is at once himself and a parrot. He knows parrots as parrots, having their own physical and somatic integrity, living creatures that can awaken speculation as to how or whether they are conscious; creatures of vivid color, and also creatures of mysterious processes of which the biological and chemical sciences can take note, though they know that the notations are only arbitrary ways of selecting among a possible infinity of processes. Parrots are Out There, and the more beautiful for being so. But the warning that Roszak legitimately gives is that the observer In Here must never think itself master of a creature so distant, ultimately incomprehensible.

Whatever specific quarrels a reader may have with *Where the Wasteland Ends*, Roszak succeeds in presenting modern technology and science as a system that intends to have total hegemony over the human consciousness. The more practical discussion is of how the system maintains its hegemony and what is to be done about it.

Maintenance would have to be in part a simple matter of stamping on the minds of each generation the conviction that there is no rationality beyond that of the technocracy, no reality beyond what science defines. Institutionally, the system survives by a dynamic that the early portion of *Where the Wasteland Ends* describes engagingly. Whenever the increasingly complex industrial world goes wrong at some point, as it will, its own experts are called in to fix it, on the proposition that they alone have the knowlege to do so. Their solution will then become a part of the world. Meanwhile, in the West, the technocracy finds remarkably smooth means to incorporate its rebels into itself. Western technocracy, as Roszak presents it, achieves a certain degree of humaneness, which becomes a part of its character of dominator. Here Roszak pays advanced western technocracy its dues, which less discriminating radicals neglect. Technocracy under what at the time of the book's publication seemed like an immovable Communist bloc he describes as grim and heavy in a nineteenth-century way, accompanied by thick social controls and a thick ideology. Then there is technocracy with the aid of the torture police. A valid distinction, Roszak says, is to be made between that kind of society "and a society where dissent fills the Broadway theater and the best-seller lists"[13]: a courteous acknowledgement on Roszak's part that has no traffic with the neo-Marxist dialecticians who would claim that western tolerance is no more than a strategy of intolerance.

For a response to the technocracy, Roszak similarly turns from psychology to thinking about concrete physical and social arrangements. Toward the end of *Where the Wasteland Ends*, he lists some features of the society that he imagines to exist at the end of the wasteland. It would manage a "proper mix of handicraft labor, intermediate technologies, and necessarily heavy industry," recover autonomous, unexploited work, establish an economics in kinship, workers' cooperatives, and barter, make the neighborhood and the commune agencies of welfare services, set up credit unions and mutual insurance as alternatives to big financial institutions, and otherwise replant society in intimate groupings.[14] The most notable thing about Roszak's prescriptions is that however difficult of attainment they may be, they neither require nor promise any radical transformation of consciousness from a technocratic to a tribal or mystical form. They are entirely attractive to anyone who is on the whole favorably disposed to modern technics, modern science, and a modern western rationality, wishing only to make humane rearrangements of its institutions and its clots of population. Roszak's imagined future, in fact, appears to have in it a clear vein of machine technology, of a scale that puts technics firmly in the hands of the users.

Where the Wasteland Ends, like its predecessor, speaks for and beyond the cultural rebellion of the sixties, in a voice of greater calm, larger speculation, and more careful inquisitiveness than the clamors it both respects and wishes to turn to articulateness. Roszak manages again to make of that impulsive insurgency something that the insurgents seldom had an interest in defining for themselves: he places it all in a history. His familiarity with scientific method and intent is sufficient, and his curiosity is broad enough, to make his protest a knowledgeable conversation with an opponent, and he treats that opponent with the kind of civility that scientists themselves, in his description of them, claim to be a part of their discipline to objectivity. Roszak would be uncomfortable at seeing his impassioned cultural criticism equated with bloodless disputations that score themselves by reference to test-tube findings and mathematical logic: but civility is civility. It should be added, for this as for the rest of Roszak's work, that while he can be lengthy to a fault, he can also be brief. "Sense data" in the empiricist use of the term, he says, are "conceived of abstractly as a uniform species of evidence that politely registers its arrival and then waits about to be accounted for in clever epistemological schemes." The phrase suits exactly. So does Roszak's remark that "the darkness, sobriety, and oppressive weightiness of the puritan style betoken a perceived *thickening* of the world's substance, as if the very gravity of matter were on the increase," while in the painting of the period "the light rapidly fails; it is poured over with the 'brown sauce' of heavy oils," all representing a world too dense to allow the spiritual to shine through.[15] A reader need not agree with either Roszak's appraisal of empiricism or his view of Puritanism to take pleasure in formulations so swift and deft.

Unfinished Animal proceeds on a tradition of which Roszak is an engaging expositor, the idea that biological evolution is purposeful, straining toward the creation of higher life. Roszak discusses, with due severity when he detects showmanship or sloppiness, the gurus of the past century who have constructed philosophies or cults upon that foundation. The concept has enjoyed some more solid and conventional support, to which Roszak does not give extensive notice. At the turn of the century it associated itself in American religious thought with the Social Gospel: matter itself works biologically toward a higher life; the human conscience, meanwhile, is to participate in cosmic progress, participating in social action toward the moralization of society and the coming of the Kingdom.

Much of the thinking about evolution as teleological, or at any rate as being evolution upwards, was entirely conformable with the Darwinist explanation of the evolutionary process in itself. The previous explanation offered by Lamarck, that a characteristic acquired during the lifetime of an individual can be passed on genetically, had failed to give any satisfactory explanation of how, say, the giraffe's stretching of her neck to reach the leaves of a tree could get encoded in her reproductive process and so pass the lengthened neck to immediate and remote descendants. Darwin and his successors went around the problem, denying that acquired characteristics can go to progeny, consigning inheritance to traits bestowed by chance. Some giraffes, a Darwinist might observe, happen by genetic roulette to have longer necks and an ability to generate long-necked offspring; these will be more likely to survive an environment stingy in vegetation; over time short necks will be filtered out; and what will emerge is the graceful if peculiar animal that now inhabits the African plains. Since this is more convincing, or at least bypasses the trouble Lamarckianism had presented, it became standard. Those who wished to see evolution as intentional could understand the whole process as being ultimately purposeful, the rules of chance and the rules of survival so shaped as to bring about the lush variety of species now extant and to produce the splendors of the human mind.

So Darwinism contains nothing that would ultimately disprove the existence of purpose, in evolution or elsewhere in the universe. But Lamarckianism, which Roszak favors, describes a more benignly direct and economical procedure. An individual does something advantageous like stretching up to the leaves of a tree, the result imprints itself on offspring and their offspring, and so the whole life process goes about efficiently preserving and bettering itself. The simplest rendering of this does not place intention directly within organisms and their reproductive components. It lets whatever happens to the individual get passed on, the good and the bad, whatever is desired along with whatever has been unsuccessfully avoided, the only encouraging qualification being that a reasonably hungry and pleasure-seeking and sexually appetitive individual will probably do more advantageous than disadvantageous things to itself in the course of a lifetime. But Lamarckianism as Roszak presents it conceives a *"sentiment interieur"* within the organism that works toward evolutionary improvement, an intention of sorts.[16] Roszak gives some arguments for the believability of that perception of evolution.

Roszak uses the term evolution to apply also to cultural change. By way of analogy that usage is common enough, and it is consonant with an idea of purposeful biological evolution, more especially of a Lamarckian sort. Seeing a logical unfolding within human culture, driven both by biology and by the nonbiological imperatives of culture, Roszak makes it the proper work of his contemporaries to go with the true direction of evolution. As the amphibians were to their aquatic kin, as the first human beings who struggled with speech were to their slower companions, so the seers presently among us stand to the majority of people today.

If the human race is object and author of an intentional evolutionary process, in which the end has been embedded in the beginning, then "our task is *to become what we are,*" so Roszak announces: the task that future psychotherapy will aid its subjects in accomplishing.[17] The phrase suggests that intuition will tell the individual, and the whole of humankind, what is the potentiality to be achieved; it suggests also that repression is the enemy. It is not easy to get from Roszak exactly what evolution is reaching toward. An essentially clean and inviting style is frequently invaded by a transcendentalist language, and the human race that Roszak wishes to rediscover the heft of tools and the feel of wood and shell threatens to dematerialize. It is actually in his more concrete and material imagery that Roszak better represents the future he has in mind. What he projects when he is being specific about it is a time when the human species will have discovered the full unity of body and mind, of self and nature: when the touch of the fingers on a smooth pebble, so he may be taken to mean, will be a fully and complexly thought touch, when the thought of a pebble will awaken the sense of touch.

Looking to that unity, the author of *Unfinished Animal* joins other critics in contending that western civilization has torn itself apart with dualities, which he perceives somewhat as the cleft he has presented between In Here and Out There. The discussion, though not the judgment, is suggestive of Harvey Cox's *The Secular City*. There Cox argues that Judaism, Christianity, and Islam have drained magic from nature, setting the human race to a strenuous project of submitting nature to moral objectives. Cox in the writing of *The Secular City* had spoken approvingly of this secularization of nature as assigning due ascendancy to conscience and intellect and respecting the integrity of the secular realm; he would later take a different view of the matter. The time of the counter culture was rife with commentators who claimed that modern industrialization is an ascetic morality gone mad, wrenching the human consciousness from its location in the body and the material world, subjecting the mind to technical abstractions and the body to work in which the rhythms of nature have no part, crushing nature into the metallic shapes of cities and machines. The Vietnam war and the technology that fought it, that argument goes by extension, brought to a logical conclusion the war on life that industrialism had already been waging. *Unfinished Animal* presents clusters of duality that Roszak insists have rent the self: sacred and profane, soul and body, mind and matter, intellect and emotion.[18] (The edited collection *Masculine/Feminine* adds the duality given in the title, and a persuasive essay there by coeditor Betty Roszak argues that the split constrains men as well as women from the fullness of personality.)

What Roszak says of dualism sounds like describing Manicheanism, a particular dualism that haunted the West for centuries with its proclamation that the cosmos is divided into light matter, which is good, and dark matter, which is wholly evil, dark matter being approximately the same as the natural world of flesh and human desire. Though Manicheanism had some resonances with the Christian faith, Christianity fought it as a heresy. The dualities that Roszak assaults can be more affirmatively understood as merely recognizing that in a practical way the mind *is* different from the body, as conscience differs from sensuous desire, or intellect is distinct from passion, or human order distinguishes itself from organic nature, and that their difficult and complex encounters determine the richness of a civilization. The modern ecological understanding of nature, for example, owes itself not only to advanced scientific formulations but to the distancing from nature that modern existence has brought, which makes for a discovery of nature as a separate realm to be respected, examined, and preserved.

This manner of conceiving duality is not, in fact, so far from what Roszak imagines as a proper recomposing of the severed elements of human experience. His denunciations of the worldly asceticism of the West mingle with sharp observations about the self-indulgence that attends much of what passes for Aquarian spiritualism, and the ascetic mystics of the East are his redemptive models. Reflecting upon the violent revelatory experience that his cultural rebels pursue, he admonishes that "there are *structures and disciplines of experience* as well as of intellect, and that these can absorb a lifetime's learning"[19]; and much of the chapter "Ethics and Ecstasy" is taken up with the exquisite rigor of genuine yoga discipline, of which the first step in the order of ascent is the mastery of moral purity in just and loving relationships with the world. Such "structures and disciplines of experience" at once bring comeliness to experience and take it to perfect pitch, so that even the normally automatic act of breathing becomes a practice of mindfulness.

Roszak, of course, is not prepared to admit anything of duality to all this, and conceives instead a oneness of the flesh with the yoga way that brings the flesh to fulfillment; but what he favorably and persuasively describes is in a rough practical way dualistic. It is no more than good psychological bookkeeping to perceive, for instance, that an act of mastery is distinct from the experience mastered, their encounter being something of a cooperative combat. At the instant that it wishes to make some order of the human organism and mind it presides over, whether the project is to get out of bed in the morning or to learn a language or to be faithful to a marriage, the will is going to find that mass of craving waywardness to be a rebel. And it in turn, in its biological desire to sleep or its human desire to break faith or its entirely reasonable desire not to study the German plural endings, is going to find the will to be a tyrant. That is an observable fact of experience, and manners, literature, and religion have spent much time in defining it. Doing so can be a means of paying proper honor to each, the moral will in its austerity and the natural desiring self in its vivid hungering diversity, and perhaps in bringing the two antagonists to fruitfully cooperative terms, however precarious. But some Manichean-like form of moral hostility to nature is an attendant danger; and when Roszak raises his own eloquent voice in concert with orthodox western spirituality to repudiate that mistake, he is doing service to cultural criticism.

Roszak, in any event, concludes that dualism is western, and an assault on sensuality, sex, nature, and life. To this extent he might seem to be reversing the course of evolution, since presumably the western ethos – certainly in its industrialist expression – has come after a time of greater harmony between humankind and nature. There is reason to believe that he is also reversing the order of individual growth. As the student of child development Piaget describes it, the child between two and seven years of age is in an intermediate stage, emergent from a sensory motor mode and working toward a mode of critical thinking: a stage in which causality is perceived as magical and there is little if any distinction between the symbolic and the literal. But nothing that might look like an inversion on his part of the actual succession of events, in history or in individual growth, would mar the evolutionary scheme that Roszak envisions. He does put a time of magic, and of myth and mystery, before a time of more critical and technical thought, which it appears will then give way to an integration of the two ways of thinking. Myth, explains the chapter "Sacred and Profane," preceded and provided the ground for a historical consciousness that can only produce information about an infinity of facts, without the structure that myth provides. Magic was at the origins of technology, which now turns madly against a nature in which it cannot see the intelligence that magic detected in all things. The mysteries carefully guarded in early cults have as their degraded descendants the dry professional methods of modern reason. Describing the secularization of culture as a daring and in its own way magnificent achievement of the modern era, Roszak anticipates a moment when history will reroot itself in myth, technology in magic, and reason in mystery: a return of prodigal children, so he appears to be saying, coming back to their origins not empty-handed but bearing the rich though thorny fruits of their outlaw forays.

Much of *Unfinished Animal* is valuable apart from the idea of evolution it presents. Celebrating the various phenomena he labels Aquarian, Roszak here as in his earlier work refuses to patronize or surrender to the accompanying hedonism, and maintains his position of thoughtful, critically sympathetic observer. His sense that technology or any kind of practical work should be at once production and play, along with his seeking for the element of ritual in common activities, puts him in a tradition of critics who begin, like the Russian anarchist Petr Kropotkin, like Ruskin and Morris and the craft socialists, with questions of how daily work is done and daily relations are conducted. His belief that there is magic to be experienced in materials and in the worker's dance of mind and tools over them is empirically true to the extent that the fashioner chooses to perceive these as magical. Modern culture has not elected to encourage that perception, which ought to extend also to the materials and work and products of modern technics. A reader may fail to be persuaded that such heightened experience occurs within a patterned, inner-driven biological and cultural evolution. But evolution, taken as a metaphor for the working up of human experience into exact and rigorous awareness, moments of delight in making, flashes of ecstasy, states of beatific compassion, does not serve him badly.

In its most general theme and tone, *Person/Planet* sounds at first much like the books that precede it. Roszak speaks of the brutal severing of the human being from nature, the decline of craftsmanship, the injury to the wholeness and the psychic health of the person. But read with *The Cult of Information*, which was published a decade later, it indicates a turn in its author's interest from the cosmos to the human microcosmos, and toward defining fairly small and workable ways of winning back the health that Roszak is convinced the modern world imperils.

A founding thesis of the work is very much in the manner of Roszak's earlier books. The human race has evolved from rock and sea. "The rhythm of the moon is echoed in the cycles of the female body. The remembered shapes of our evolutionary ancestry are recapitulated in every human embryo ... . Even our queer, alienating consciousness rises out of some uncanny potentiality of her elemental stuff." The seeming break between matter and mind looks like a radical denial of this continuity. But suppose that mentality and not matter, crudely understood, is "the basic, irreducible continuum of the universe," as patterns are more basic than their parts: then the continuity holds.[20] The argument is that any artificial rupture in the continuum will damage the human race. A response to that claim taken literally is that if the human race and will and mind are in continuity with nature, so is every apparent rupture, every smokestack factory, every high-tech weapon of commercialism or genocide, and nothing can possibly be wrong. But Roszak's argument should not be taken literally. As metaphor it serves the same purpose as do the uses of metaphor in *Unfinished Animal*: to call a very caring attention to a nature with which the human race does have organic and somatic connections, and to instigate a search into what those connections at their most health-giving might be.

So it is true of *Person/Planet* as it is of the rest of Roszak's most creative social criticism – progressively true of his later writing – that his commentary can be received as an entirely practical investigation into why at the moment things are not working as well for our twentieth-century selves as they might work, even on our own terms. Much of the book, in fact, does not directly address any question of a continuum between nature and humanity. Roszak's central concern is for the defense of the person as having a right to a free career of self-discovery and self-articulation, a process that he along with many other commentators believes to be victim to the century's ills, more particularly to the many ways in which politics, commerce, and the present-day organization of daily work impose false fronts on the person.

The vocabulary of personhood as social critics use the concept always threatens to turn edgeless. How, for example, is it possible to distinguish between an imposed and a true part of the person? How about language – surely imposed, word by word, construction by grammatical construction, and yet entirely interior and expressive of the self? But Roszak in *Person/Planet* is sharp and thorough in dismissing the self-indulgence that in recent years has appropriated the counter culture to pass itself off as a serious defense of personality. Among his specific observations and suggestions are to be found some of the best writing and most appealing commentary in his body of criticism.

Paul Goodman, a rebel occupying a point not far from Roszak on the anarchist left, published in 1971 a book with the subtitle *Notes of a Neolithic Conservative*. An approximate rendering of the phrase, in a volume that calls among other things for freeing from capitalism the more austere virtues of modern science and technology, is that it refers to Goodman's wish to restore a world of neighborhoods, craft guilds, and other groupings of intimate scale: the world, real or romanticized, of premodern times. *Person/Planet* has passages as eloquently reactionary. Fully respectful of the rational, civic libertarian and democratic institutions that are the heritage of modern revolutions, Roszak proposes a rebirth of the idea that prerevolutionary aristocracy assigned only to its proud self, the idea of the person as possessing an inviolable sanctity and dignity. Roszak here looks to be a twentieth-century Jeffersonian, leveling the population upward into the nobility rather than downward into mass democracy.[21] More notable, for a time when cultural libertarians have proudly acclaimed their freedom from the nuclear family and the tiresome tasks of childbearing and child-rearing, is Roszak's insistence that the old biological family, nuclear and extended, deserves to be affirmed. The family, behind the roles that tend to become artificial, has evoked among its members the invaluable virtue of unconditional loyalty, thereby promising the security and assigning the responsibilities that at their best are the condition of mature personhood.[22] Roszak, consciously or not, here resolves for a moment the paradox that what is interior to the self must also be in some sense imposed.

Person/Planet deals at length with modern work. Roszak is severe with both capitalist and collectivist economics, claiming that modern economic practice in general fixes individual work to huge impersonal institutions, whether of money-making or of social production, and therein robs the worker of an honorable responsibility within the act of work. He quite neatly dismisses the American work ethic, or rather the American conviction that the nation has a work ethic, with an observation as brief as it is trenchant: that since Americans understand real work to be no more or less than something that you get paid for, the American creed credits as the most prestigious work the kinds that bring the most money for doing the least. The modern concept of work began in a complex of Protestant ideas meant to give special honor to the working bourgeoisie as conveyers of "human dignity," an "ethic of diligence, frugality, and honest toil." The problem is that these ideas regarded labor not "as a redeeming joy," but for its ascetic function: "to discipline the appetites and humble the will. It was an experience of self-denial, not of self-discovery."[23] If work is not to be an occasion for expressiveness, if its only character is a character of toil and difficulty in the pursuit of a produced object exterior to its own experience, then the worker will have either of two contradictory ways of regarding it: as worthy precisely because it is joyless drudgery and an occasion for sullen hostility, or as a means of getting money or pleasure.

Roszak gives insufficient attention to the nineteenth-century origins of socialism in the determination to make work a fully self-actualizing activity on the part of the individual and the community. He also fails to consider the relationship between work as ascetic and work as self-expressive: self-expressive precisely in being a pressing of will and responsibility against the resistant forces of indolence and hedonism, an inward working of which the outer articulation presses form against the resistant forces within wood or stone, words or numbers. But these are quibbles. A strength of Roszak's commentary on work in the modern world is that he places his emphasis not on some play of the senses and the fancy upon a material to be worked – though his earlier work is eloquent on the subject – but on more mental and moral faculties of responsible freedom. He is not, for example, prepared to denounce modern machine technology, which in his estimation would be an admirable addition to craftsmanship if it were a supplement to the work itself, an extension of the inventiveness of the craft worker.[24] It is centralization, capitalist or collectivist, that is the enemy, centralization that prevents not so much the hand's grip of gnarled wood as the grip of intelligence and conscience upon a process of useful making.

That hunger for a livable scale of community and production makes concrete Roszak's wish to see much of society return to the land and to agriculture. Cities, as he describes them, fall victim to their own virtue, which is the virtue of restless imagination and intellect, the appetite for change and variety. Cities fix an imperial domain over the countryside; they concentrate power, production, and energy. The return of the human race to its origins in rock and water means in practice the return of the worker to the materials immediately available for shaping into sustenance, pleasure, and poetry.

The Cult of Information reads like a continuation of the project of giving some practical applications to Roszak's more general criticism: it is among the most circumspect of his writings, its commentary close to the measure of its specific and limited subject. Modern technology, here in the form of the computer, remains the culprit. But Roszak, insisting that he is no technophobe, justifies the disclaimer. He gives the computer due credit for particular kinds of usefulness and writes of it with a fluency in computer vocabularly that indicates an almost friendly familiarity.

Once conceived as nothing more than small and distinct data, useful or not, and granted little intellectual stature, information according to Roszak has now won enormous prestige, or rather has shared in the prestige that the computer possesses as the processor of information. The ideologues and the promoters of computer technology have convinced the public, Roszak concludes, that the flow of information will give society not only the raw materials of knowledge but knowledge itself in unimaginable abundance, even duplicating and demonstrating the act of thinking. The author of *Where the Wasteland Ends* might have viewed that presumption as a final stage of alienation. But Roszak now confines himself to separating the computer from the preposterous and dangerous claims that have been made of it.

Roszak addresses clearly and authoritatively the confusion between information and thought. It is with ideas and not information, he observes, that the mind thinks. "*Ideas create information* ... . Every fact grows from an idea; it is the answer to a question we could not ask in the first place if an idea had not been invented which isolated some portion of the world, made it important, focused our attention, and stimulated inquiry." Take information about the time of day or the year: simple, self-subsistent clusters of data. Behind this apparently neutral information lies a magnificent idea; "the idea of time as a regular and cyclical rhythm of the cosmos. Somewhere in the distant past, a human mind invented this elegant concept, perhaps out of some rhapsodic or poetic contemplation of the bewilderingly congested universe."[25]

There are, above all, master ideas that determine lives and cultures. These rest on no information whatsoever. That justice demands equality, that the Tao that can be named is not the true Tao, that life is a miracle, that life is a mystery: such ideas can appropriate the same linguistic structure as the announcement that George Washington was the first president of the United States. But they do not refer to facts, "any more than a painting by Rembrandt is a fact, or a sonata by Beethoven, or a dance by Martha Graham. For these too are ideas; they are integrating patterns meant to declare the meaning of things" discovered in revelation, insight, or slowly ripening wisdom.

"Where do these patterns come from? The imagination creates them from *experience*. Just as ideas order information, they also order the wild flux of experience as it streams through us in the course of life." Roszak insists on the clearest distinction between true experience and the little discrete packets of awareness that empiricists mean by the word: he refers to experience that is fluent, inclusive of all the contradictory experiencing of each moment.[26]

So an idea is a response to experience and a patterning and clarification of it. Here is the continuity between Roszak the author of *The Cult of Information* and his earlier self; and here is the distinction. Roszak continues to insist on a consciousness and thought wider than what he associates with reductionist science and technology. But now the thought and the experience are of kinds readily accessible, workaday as well as magical, making their appearance in modern as well as in other cultures. The computer itself issues from ideas that are powerful and admirable.[27]

How generous Roszak has become to his own age is revealed in a passage in which he demonstrates the limits of a computer simulation of an experiment in breeding. The simulation, which is designed to reach a predicted conclusion, eliminates "the real scientific work involved: the careful arrangement of apparatus, the manipulation of materials, the false starts and pitfalls, the watchful, often boring waiting, the painstaking discriminations among results." Above all, the simulation eliminates the risk, which is the essence of experimentation.[28] Whatever is Roszak's intention, genuine experimentation as he presents it here is at once grainy and experiential, in a way that elsewhere he associates with preindustrial craftsmanship, and ascetically observational in a fashion that *The Making of a Counter Culture* or *Where the Wasteland Ends* would have identified as an act of alienation from the world and from the passional self. Here, the asceticism and the concreteness of experiencing are of a single compound.

A chapter discusses, skeptically but sympathetically, the "guerrilla hackers" of the counter culture who attempted from the middle 1970s to the mid-eighties to take the information flow out of the hands of monopoly capitalism. Their hope was in the microcomputer, which in the form of home computers seemed capable of making information democratic and creating informal communities of users within networks. Roszak might usefully have continued his discussion and looked into a phenomenon that has been very much a part of the counter culture: its relish for computers, for video cameras, in general for some of the most technically sophisticated devices of the century.

Some of the appeal is clear enough. Light, swift, sent and received by equipment that comes in small packages, communication by computer seems to retake and extend the public conversation that for a time looked to have been monopolized by radio, television, and the wire services. Some champions of computer networking see in it the creation of an invisible community. The more mundane and practical effect of the technology of videos and computers is to establish a kind of craftsmanship: not of hand skills, but of skill nevertheless, some of it quite advanced and recondite, and under the autonomous control of the individual user. There is a less obvious attraction that modern technics may one day have for the green movement. It is common among animal rights activists to claim that animals need not be exploited for human subsistence, since human beings can substitute synthetic materials for whatever has been stolen from the animal world in the way of bone and skin, eggs and milk and wool. Perhaps there are indications here of an implicit sensibility toward nature that leaves her as far as possible Out There, that respectfully refrains from making from living natural substances whatever can be made within the system of human technology. Green partisans would doubtless prefer that the technology be of the handicrafts, which allow for a lighter touch in the removal of substances from the earth. But the productive and communicative processes of modern technology, at least when these are as unostentatious as the invisible magic of computers, have a character of being self-enclosed, a character almost of introspection; and this might readily lend itself to a conviction that in acts of production humankind should best maintain, whenever possible, a polite apartness from living nature.

The Cult of Information, economical and cautious in its definition of what is wrong with the more extravagant claims for computers and their unending stream of information, is convincing in its definition of the more particular evils of the new technology. They turn out to be attributable not to the technology in itself but to its false uses. That is a rugged practical distinction that technophobes would find irrelevant, and its appearance in the book is one more indication of Roszak's accommodation to much that would have repelled his younger self. Roszak is offended by what he sees to be expensive and unneeded devices that promoters are happy to sell and university administrations are humbly happy to receive, convinced that computer processing must be the way of the future and a necessity for a sophisticated institution. He says of computers that would allow students to stay in their dormitories and submit work to their professors – a submission that can quite satisfactorily take place in a simple walk across campus – that these speak to "the sort of pseudo problem (like 'static cling' or 'wax buildup') that exists only because the hucksters invented it in the first place to sell a product."[29] Roszak demands that schools at every level reject whatever of computer gimmickry and the cult of information distracts from the ultimate educational task of teaching the critical reception and making of ideas. He suggests that a good place for computers would be in libraries: these are true seats of information retrieval, and librarians, "the traditional keepers of the books," have "a healthy sense of the hierarchical relationship between data and ideas, facts and knowledge," a knowledge of when to consult a computer and when to look at a book.[30]

In *The Cult of Information* Roszak speaks, and says that he speaks, as a professor and a humanist. If that makes him a dissenter of sorts from the technocracy, it is not as a seeker for the primitive but as an active, twentieth-century intellectual, speaking his mind in the best common language of his century, aware of the exterior usefulness of the computer technology and respectful of the interior discipline of modern science. Yet a reader of Roszak's earlier books will recognize the connections, more particularly insofar as his notion of the making of ideas, even of the most rationalistic and academic sort, looks to experience that is onflowing, prolific, and ecstatic.

Two novels published between the appearance of *Person/Planet* and that of *The Cult of Information*, in fact, sustain the vision of the earlier work. *Bugs*, published in 1981, tells of the defeat of a futuristic giant computer system in the service of nuclear armament. The victors are bugs of a sort, lifeless insects that swarm out of the computers, lethally at first but in the end benignly in their destruction of a technology that had intended to make the human race obsolete. It is a religious circle, out of what Roszak has been terming the Old Gnosis, that discovers the force of evil in the computers, and the meaning of the bugs. In 1985 Roszak published *Dreamwatcher*, a novel that has as its premise the existence in the psyche of layers of experience and reality that dreams embody: dreams that a few people outside the dreamer have the gift of entering or inducing. By the novel's end, the Christian saintliness of a Guatemalan nun combines with the Indian sorcery of her buried childhood to combat, in a dream state, the evil unleashed by a national intelligence agency making use of science to manipulate minds. Both novels present science, misused in the pursuit of power, as expressive of the force of Thanatos in combat with the force of life. Roszak would continue to perceive the waking and rational life of the human species as founded on psychic (and somatic?) potencies.

A simple placing of the counter culture, as Roszak defines it, within western history is to relate it to the recurrent struggle of the Dionysian idea against the Apollonian (Roszak once makes an analogy to the invasion of Olympia by the centaurs, there to clash with Apollo, guardian and embodiment of ordered rationality[31]). It is a fair assessment of Roszak's thought, especially if it be considered that Dionysus represents not violence and nihilism, not a Freudian id or Thanatos, but a joyful and generous nature that invites human participation.

Roszak escapes, if only barely, from a problem that confronts any critic who wishes to make "nature," in one form or another, the grounding to morality and spirituality. There is nothing, from the behavior of a banana slug to the experiments of a chemical warfare specialist or the asceticism of St. Francis, that is not in some sense grounded in biochemical nature. When Roszak refers a moral or cultural question to nature, he is thinking specifically of organic process that is healthy and appetitive but not greedy or aggressive: sexuality when it is loving and playful rather than exploitive and dominating, or the sensual pleasure that texture brings to the hands of a craftsman. His selection, then, is of a Dionysian nature and life appropriately understood.

That has been Roszak's choice from the beginning, and it makes irrelevant the attacks that, not entirely without the help of some of his own more loosely written passages, critics have directed against him for rejecting objective reason. Reason speaks in every page of Roszak's work: temperate, dispassionate reason. His respect for the reasoned place of appropriate technology got a recent demonstration. A fellow champion of the agrarian life had claimed not to need to use a word processor, since he had the unpaid help of his wife. Arguing that there are better claims against computer technology, Roszak responded that privileged groups throughout history have similarly scorned technology when they had cheap labor to do their bidding.[32]

If there is a quarrel to be made with Roszak's world view, it is this: his wish that human consciousness enjoy a fluent, unbroken engagement of nature and of itself obscures a full recognition of what is involved when the encounter is among separate entities. The ecological sensibility, intricately informed by scientific method that at once marks and traverses the distance between nature and the examining intellect, is an example. Roszak's early writing in particular is an attempt to reconcile the dissonance between intelligence, with its capacity for imagination, and the pulse of nature that can awaken that imagination: to fuse the subject who knows and the object that is observed. Could an existence without dissonances produce minds with the critical urbanity of a Theodore Roszak? It is not, at any rate, in his idea of an all-embracing and holistic nature that he is at his most convincing. At moments when he is talking in that way, enthusiasm overwhelms analysis: biology and spirit tumble over each other without edge, discrimination, or compassion for the reader. Much of his best commentary is in his later and less known books, when he looks at specific questions, the place of social and psychological deviance, the public effect of the information revolution, and most especially the condition of work in modern times. Work, after all, belongs to a broken existence and brings opposites precariously together: pleasure, tactile or imaginative, and submission to the demands of the task; the autonomy of the worker and the communal organization of the project. It is when Roszak is being limited and particular that the kind of existence he describes takes on the deepest grain and texture, and consequently comes closest to embodying that rediscovery of the sensual and biological that he had defined as the purpose of the counter culture.

What Roszak's major writings do not do is give any scheme for dismantling centralized industry, for instance, or sending city dwellers back to the country, or channeling to democratic communities the flow of computerized information. About as close as he comes to being programmatic is to recommend models. Toward the end of *Person/Planet* he looks to the monastic model, which founded community in moments of personal seclusion, and in a seeking for purity outside the fallen world founded a life of orderly, worldly production.[33] He is antagonistic to American capitalism for its competitiveness and its disregard of honest workmanship, and to totalitarian collectivism for its mindless brutalization of work and society. He is not obliged to be more specific and programmatic. He is a teacher, a profession whose calling is to nag and pester. He has been faithful to the station that in his remarks in *The Dissenting Academy* he assigned to the intellectual, that of awakening society to critical moral thought. If work has been severed from responsibility, then it is the responsibility of workers to find ways of making it responsible. If citizens have been turned into irresponsible consumers of glittery hedonistic products, then it is their responsibility to cease being consumers. Programs will not do the job, and it is not Roszak's job to recommend the programs. Or so he could convincingly insist.

Notes

1 *Unfinished Animal: The Aquarian Frontier and the Evolution of Consciousness* (New York: Harper and Row, 1975) 256-257.

2 *The Making of a Counter Culture: Reflections on the Technocratic Society and Its Youthful Opposition* (Anchor Books; Garden City, New York: Doubleday and Company, 1969) 121-123.

3 *Making of a Counter Culture* 26.

4 *Making of a Counter Culture* 30-31, 41, 46.

5 *Making of a Counter Culture* 220, 227.

6 *Making of a Counter Culture* 216.

7 *Making of a Counter Culture* 234-235.

8 *Making of a Counter Culture* 43-44.

9 *Where the Wasteland Ends: Politics and Transcendence in Postindustrial Society* (Garden City, New York: Doubleday and Company, 1972) 93-94.

10 *Where the Wasteland Ends* 95-97.

11 *Where the Wasteland Ends* 79-87.

12 *Where the Wasteland Ends* 204-209.

13 *Where the Wasteland Ends* 45-49.
14 *Where the Wasteland Ends* 432.
15 *Where the Wasteland Ends* 90-91, 126.
16 *Unfinished Animal* 98.
17 *Unfinished Animal* 241-242.
18 *Unfinished Animal* 153, 251.
19 *Unfinished Animal* 243.
20 *Person/Planet: The Creative Disintegration of Industrial Society* (Anchor Books; Garden City, New York: Doubleday and Company, 1978) 53-54, 57.
21 *Person/Planet* 113-114.
22 *Person/Planet* 162-169.
23 *Person/Planet* 224-225.
24 *Person/Planet* 232-234.
25 *The Cult of Information: The Folklore of Computers and the True Art of Thinking* (New York: Pantheon Books, 1986) 87-88, 105.
26 *The Cult of Information* 91-95.
27 *The Cult of Information* 220.
28 *The Cult of Information* 69-70.
29 *The Cult of Information* 61-62.
30 *The Cult of Information* 176.
31 *Making of a Counter Culture* 44.
32 *Utne Reader* 40 (July/August 1990) 11-12.
33 *Person/Planet* 290.

Works by Theodore Roszak

Criticism

The Cult of Information: The Folklore of Computers and the True Art of Thinking. New York: Pantheon Books, 1986.
From Satori to Silicon Valley. San Francisco: Don't Call it Frisco Press, 1986.
The Making of a Counter Culture: Reflections on the Technocratic Society and Its Youthful Opposition. Garden City, New York: Doubleday and Company, 1969.
Person/Planet: The Creative Disintegration of Industrial Society. Garden City, New York: Doubleday and Company, 1978.
Unfinished Animal: The Aquarian Frontier and the Evolution of Consciousness. New York: Harper and Row, 1975.
Where the Wasteland Ends: Politics and Transcendence in Postindustrial Society. Garden City, New York: Doubleday and Company, 1972.

Edited Work

The Dissenting Academy. New York: Pantheon Books, 1968.
Masculine/Feminine: Readings in Sexual Mythology and the Liberation of Women. New York: Harper and Row, 1969 (with Betty Roszak).
Sources. New York: Harper and Row, 1972.

Fiction

Bugs. New York: Doubleday and Company, 1981.
Dreamwatcher. Garden City, New York: Doubleday and Company, 1985.
Pontifex: A Revolutionary Entertainment for the Mind's Eye Theater. Garden City, New York: Doubleday and Company, 1974.

Selected Journal Articles

"An Alternative to the Arms Race: Meeting the New Soviet Threat." *The Nation* 193.7 (1961): 131-135.
"British Peace Movement: Looking for the Marchers." *The Nation* 201.13 (1965): 273-277.
"By Love Depressed." *The Nation* 200.2 (1965): 33-34. Review article on Denis de Rougemont.
"The Case for Cults: Skeptics and True Believers." *The Nation* 228.5 (1979): 137-139.
"The Counter Culture." Part I, "Youth and the Great Refusal." *The Nation* 206.13 (1968): 400-407. Part II, "Politics of the Nervous System." *The Nation* 206.14 (1968): 439-443. Part III, "Capsules of Salvation." *The Nation* 206.15 (1968): 466-471. Part IV, "The Future as Community." *The Nation* 206.16 (1968): 497-503.
"The Historian as Psychiatrist." *The Nation* 195.17 (1962): 343-348.
"In Search of the Miraculous." *Harper's* 262.1568 (1981): 54-62.
"Life in the Instant Cities." *The Nation* 204.11 (1967): 336-340, 350. Commentary on affluent New Towns.
"The Monster and the Titan: Science, Knowledge, and Gnosis." *Daedalus* 103.3 (1974): 17-32.
"Muddling Through Chaos." *The Nation* 202.15 (1966): 428-431. Review article on twentieth-century British politics.
"Science: A Technocratic Trap." *The Atlantic* 230.1 (1972): 56-61.
"Scientists for Peace." *The Nation* 193.10 (1961): 205-206.
"Seduction of the Scientist." *The Nation* 192.22 (1961): 477-481. Refutes the claim that the research scientist working on weaponry is engaged in free creative inquiry.
"Technocracy: Despotism of Beneficent Expertise." *The Nation* 209.6 (1969): 181-184, 186, 188.
"Theologians in Distress: Dilemma of the 'Just War.'" *The Nation* 194.15 (1962): 327-330, 332.

Gary Grieve-Carlson

Susan Sontag

(1933-)

Susan Sontag occupies a singular position in the contemporary field of American letters: much of her work deals with European writers such as Canetti, Cioran, Artaud and Barthes, and is aimed at a fairly narrow American audience, yet at the same time she is well known to the general public. A character in the popular baseball film *Bull Durham* asserts, "The novels of Susan Sontag are self-indulgent, overrated crap," to which another responds, "I think Susan Sontag is brilliant!" She has even been mentioned in an episode of the animated TV series, *The Simpsons*.

This amphibious quality of being at home in very different worlds is perhaps in part a result of what Sontag calls "a completely rootless childhood" (Cott 53). Her parents were Polish Jews who immigrated to the United States and then spent much of their time working in the fur business in China, where their daughter Susan was conceived. Sontag's mother returned to New York to give birth, and then re-joined her husband in China, leaving Susan to be raised by several aunts in the New York area. When her husband died in China in 1939, Sontag's mother returned to New York, and in 1945 married a U.S. Army pilot ("Sontag" is her stepfather's name). The new family moved to southern Arizona, and later to the Los Angeles area, where Sontag attended North Hollywood High School.

The most striking aspect of Sontag's childhood is her precocity. "I was a terribly restless child, and I was so irritated with being a child that I was just busy all the time. I was writing up a storm by the time I was eight or nine years old" (Cott 50). She learned to read, she claims, at age three, and reading *Les Misérables* at age nine "made a conscious socialist of me" ("Pilgrimage" 44). As a child, "other people seemed to me astonishingly unseeing as well as uncurious, while I longed to learn everything" ("Pilgrimage" 38). She devoured Mann, Joyce, Kafka, Gide and Eliot, and at age fourteen, she and a high school classmate telephoned Thomas Mann (then aged seventy-two and living in the Los Angeles area) and were invited to tea, an incident charmingly described in "Pilgrimage." At age fifteen, "I discovered a newsstand on the corner of Hollywood and Highland that carried literary magazines. I'd never seen a literary magazine before; certainly I'd never seen anyone read one. I picked up *Partisan Review* and I started to read 'Art and Fortune' by Lionel Trilling; and I just began to tremble with excitement" (Copeland 87).

Sontag graduated high school in January 1948 and immediately entered the University of California at Berkeley. In the fall of 1949 she transferred to the University of Chicago, where she studied with Kenneth Burke and, as she puts it, "had the good fortune to do undergraduate work in the most ambitious and the most successful authoritarian program of education ever devised in this country" (*Reader* 344). When she earned her B.A. in philosophy in 1951 she was eighteen, the age at which most Americans are graduating high school. At Chicago she met Philip Rieff, a professor of sociology, whom she married in 1950. Upon her graduation, she and Rieff went to Harvard, where she began to do graduate work, earning an M.A. in English in 1954 and an M.A. in philosophy in 1955, while raising their son David, who had been born in 1952. Between 1955 and 1957 Sontag was a Ph.D. candidate in philosophy at Harvard, specializing in modern French philosophy. In 1957 she continued her graduate studies in England at St. Anne's College, Oxford, and in 1957-58 she studied at the Sorbonne. By the time she returned to the U.S. her marriage had dissolved, and while Rieff went off to Stanford University, Sontag and her son in 1959 moved into a two-room apartment in Manhattan. She never completed her Ph.D., but lectured for the next six years in philosophy and religion at the City College of New York, Sarah Lawrence College, and Columbia University.

In 1963 she published her first novel, *The Benefactor*, and in 1964 her essay "Notes on Camp" appeared in *Partisan Review*, and was then reprinted by *Time*. The resulting publicity turned her into a celebrity, and she quickly established a reputation as an interpreter/spokeswoman for the avant-garde. From that point on, Sontag's essays and fiction appeared regularly in vehicles as diverse as *Mademoiselle, Partisan Reviews, Ramparts*, and *The New Yorker*. Rockefeller and Guggenheim Fellowships followed, and her writing proved so profitable that after serving as writer-in-residence at Rutgers University in 1964-65, she no longer needed to attach herself to either a university or a specific journal in order to earn her living.

In the late '60s and early '70s she began to write and direct her own films, and served with the Venice and New York Film Festivals. Her interest in politics also grew more pronounced, and she travelled to Cuba, North Vietnam and China. Awards for her writing began to accumulate, culminating in the National Book Critics' Circle Award for Best Work of Criticism in 1977, awarded to *On Photography*, and her 1979 induction into the American Academy and Institute of Arts and Letters. Sontag's life changed drastically in 1975 when she discovered she had breast cancer and "was told it was likely I'd be dead very soon" (Cott 48). After undoing a mastectomy and many months of outpatient chemotherapy, she recovered and used the experience as the impetus for one of her finest books, *Illness as Metaphor*.

In the 1980s her production of essays and stories has slowed, although she is reportedly at work on a novel on Eastern European emigres in Paris and the U.S., and she remains a major intellectual figure. Her activities in this decade include directing Pirandello's "As You Desire Me" for the National Theater in Italy, the production of a video introduction to the work of Pina Bausch and her Tanztheater Wuppertal, the narration of a documentary film on Sarah Bernhardt, and most significantly, since June 1987, her serving as President of the American chapter of PEN, the international writers' organization, which has involved her in issues of censorship and the suppression of writers and publishers in this country and around the world.

Sontag's biography affects her criticism in two fundamental ways. First, her rootlessness is reflected in her extreme independence; "I never was anybody's disciple or protege" (Cott 53), she claims, and she has produced no disciples or school of thought or style. Second, her childhood precocity has been followed by a childlike adulthood: "Then I felt like an adult, forced to live in the body of a child. Since, I feel like a child, privileged to live in the body of an adult" ("Pilgrimage" 54). Elsewhere she describes herself as "one of those people who is precocious as a child and then takes a long time to grow up, has a very extended adolescence. Sometimes I think I'm still going through mine" (D'Antonio 133). Her writing, for all its brilliance, sometimes displays some of the less attractive traits of adolescence: a tendency to provocative assertion, inadequately defended, and a tendency to deny the inconsistencies and contradictions that exist between her early and late work.

At the time that Sontag burst onto the scene of American cultural criticism with such essays as "Notes on Camp" and "Against Interpretation," the established, so-called "New York intellectuals," with their tradition of left-wing or liberal politics and their literary criticism focused on moral questions, still occupied the center of the critical stage. Although their influence with the reading public had been gradually declining since the 1940s, no group or individual had arisen to challenge their dominance in any serious way until the cultural and political dislocations of the 1960s occurred. Writers such as McLuhan, Mailer, Buckminster Fuller, R. D. Laing and Norman O. Brown demolished traditional intellectual boundaries and procedures in their work, and very suddenly, the older intellectuals seemed unable to explain what was happening in the world around them.

Sontag's challenge to the established criticism is summarized by Andrew Ross:

More than any other publication, [*Against Interpretation*] signaled the challenge, in the sixties, to the tradition of Jewish moral seriousness that had governed the cultural crusading of the Old Left and Cold War liberalism. Not that Sontag is willing to jettison entirely the prerogative of moral discrimination; in fact, she is careful to record her ambivalence about camp ... . Nonetheless, the importance of her own critical intervention in the mid-sixties was in the service of pleasure and erotics, and against judgment, truth, seriousness, and interpretation; against, in short, the hermeneutics of depth and discrimination through which the New York Intellectuals had filtered extra-curricular literary taste since the war. As for the academic New Critics, whose "Christian" moral seriousness was the more hegemonic literary force, Sontag's flight from sincerity was almost too far outside of their orbit to register immediate effects and responses: Camp in the U.S., at the moment that Sontag immortalized it, was an important break with the style and legitimacy of the old liberal intelligentsia, whose puritanism had always set it apart from the frivolous excesses of the ruling class (*No Respect* 47).

Ross is correct, yet it would be a mistake to identify Sontag too closely with the counterculture of the '60s, for in many ways she is much closer to the New York intellectuals than to the Berkeley Free Speech Movement.

All throughout the Sixties, I was horrified by the anti-intellectualism of the movement and of the hippies and of the bright-thinking people ... . Some of the activities of the New Left were very far from democratic socialism and were deeply anti-intellectual, which I think of as part of the fascist impulse. They were also anticultural and full of resentment and brutality, reflecting a kind of nihilism (Cott 49).

Sohnya Sayres, more sympathetic to the values of the counterculture than Ross, argues that Sontag, despite her fame as an interpreter of and spokeswoman for the cultural avant-garde, was limited in her understanding of the new because of her grounding in European intellectual thought and the history of its crises. Sontag remained a "complicating, hyper-self-conscious writer, glutted on ideas and empty of certainty" (219), claims Sayres, despite her championing of the erotic, the immediate and the sensory. Sayres's point is as accurate as Ross's. Sontag was much more attentive to, receptive to, and articulate on the latest developments in film, the visual arts, and "style" (in the broadest sense) than were the established New York Intellectuals, and she was much more willing, at the beginning of her career, to abandon the tone of high moral seriousness that rendered the avant-garde almost unintelligible to many of them. Yet she was one of them, an intellectual intent upon defining, analyzing and explaining the culture around her. She says:

One of the chief ideas of modernism was this new relationship betwen high culture and popular culture. That goes back at least to Apollinaire. And it was my reiterating of this older, modernist position in the early sixties which seemed so distinctive because there was nobody else around who had my commitment to the traditional literary and philosophical culture and who also seemed to know about these other things and to enjoy them (Copeland 86).

In the '70s and '80s American intellectual life has shaped itself into a variety of matrices. Where once political debate occurred largely among the factions of the left, neo-conservatism has developed into an increasingly vocal, aggressive position, challenging the assumptions of traditionally liberal academics. The intellectual Left has splintered into interest-groups focused on various minorities who have been excluded from the cultural center (e.g., women, blacks, Hispanics, native Americans, homosexuals) or committed to the post-structuralist deconstruction of the dead-end corpus, i.e., corpse, of Western metaphysics. In short, there is no longer a coherent center in American intellectual life; journals such as *Partisan Review* and *The New Republic* are no longer read by the entire intellectual community, nor do any individual figures hold the authority to shape the culture's tastes in the way that Edmund Wilson, Alfred Kazin, Dwight MacDonald and Philip Rahv once seemed to. Instead America's intellectuals have retreated to specific departments in large universities, and increasingly they write for other intellectuals as opposed to the general reading public.

Intellectuals such as Sontag, who operate outside the academy, tend to ignore the stylistic conventions of academic prose, and sometimes publish in mass-circulation magazines, are often viewed by the academy with suspicion and/or contempt. Hilton Kramer, who edits the neo-conservative *New Criterion*, labels Sontag a "celebrity intellectual," and others have lumped her, along with Buckminster Fuller and McLuhan, into the "pop intellectual" category, a term which uses popularity as a synonym for trendiness and lack of intellectual gravity. Excluded from the academic, the neo-conservative, the feminist, the post-structuralist, and the Marxist encampments on the current American intellectual landscape, Sontag nonetheless maintains a very high profile. When the sociologist Charles Kadushin compiled a list, based on empirical methods, of America's "leading intellectuals" in 1970, Sontag was included along with Daniel Bell, Noam Chomsky, John Kenneth Galbraith, Irving Howe, Dwight Macdonald, Mary McCarthy, Norman Mailer, Robert Silvers, Edmund Wilson and Lionel Trilling. Six years later, when Daniel Bell named the "second generation" of New York Intellectuals (a label which has failed to persist), the only name from Kadushin's list to appear on Bell's was Sontag's (the others were Norman Podhoretz, Steven Marcus, Robert Brustein, Midge Decter, Jason Epstein, Robert Silvers, Philip Roth and Theodore Solotaroff (Jacoby 10-11).

Sontag's first book, *The Benefactor*, prefigures the concerns of most of her subsequent fiction as well as her early criticism, and its critical reception sets the tone for the subsequent criticism of most of her work. The novel is set in Europe, and concerns a young man whose dreams are so intensely vivid that they begin to dominate his waking life. After vainly attempting to interpret his dreams, he decides to live them. Anticipating the argument of "Against Interpretation," the narrator concludes, "To interpret is to impoverish, to deplete the world – in order to set up a shadow world of 'meanings' ... Perhaps I did not need to 'interpret' my dreams at all ... I wanted to enact my dreams, not simply observe them." This self-absorbed, almost solipsistic narrator embodies the dream-like quality of real life and the concrete, real-life quality of dreams, playing along the border of objective and subjective, conscious and unconscious, self and other. Sontag agrees with an interviewer who suggests that the dominant theme in her fiction is "the predatory habits of consciousness, the desire to hold the whole world in one's head," and then elaborates: "Consciousness as a form of acquisition; and the counter-projects of disburdenment and silence – the temptations of silence ... are unifying notions in my fiction" (Copeland 83); *The Benefactor's* narrator, she says, "searches for some clear state of consciousness, for a way in which he could be properly disburdened."

Death Kit, Sontag's second novel, focuses similarly on a hyper-self-conscious protagonist who thinks he may have murdered a man in a train tunnel, although certain evidence suggests the murder never occurred. Again the themes of perception and interpretation, subjectivity and objectivity, dominate the narrative. One wonders, however, whether such "proper disburdenment" is a desirable goal, or whether it would simply mean the "silence" of autism or solipsism.

Reviews appeared in the *New York Times, Partisan Review,* and *The New Republic*, a remarkable achievement for a beginning novelist, yet they were not altogether positive. Daniel Stern called Sontag "an intelligent writer who has ... jettisoned the historical baggage of the novel. However, she has not replaced it with material or insights that carry equal or superior weight. Instead she has chosen the fashionable imports of neo-existentialist philosophy and tricky contemporary techniques" (5). Most critics agreed. Tony Tanner wrote, "The idea behind [*Death Kit*] is more interesting than the book itself" (448), and Gore Vidal opined: "[her] intelligence is still greater than her talent" (46). Yet Vidal praised Sontag because of her novels' obvious borrowings from the French New Novel, particularly the technical devices of Sarraute and Robbe-Grillet. John Wain also noted Sontag's fiction's "completely European character ... . It owes nothing to any American author or to any American way of looking at things" (26, 27).

Because both novels are most interesting only because of their "acquaintance" with – one might say derivation from – a certain continental style and tone, they have not aged well. Today they are seldom read, and they receive almost no scholarly attention; when Jay Parini reviewed the body of Sontag's work in 1983, he pronounced *The Benefactor* "almost unreadable" and *Death Kit* "unspeakably tedious" (416, 418). Sontag's short fiction, while uneven in quality, is generally much better than her novels. Of the stories collected in *I, etcetera*, "Project for a Trip to China," "Debriefing" and "Unguided Tour" are especially fine, careful depictions of a specific sensibility; for example:

We know more than we can use. Look at all this stuff I've got in my head: rockets and Venetian churches, David Bowie and Diderot, nuoc mam and Big Macs, sunglasses and orgasms. How many newspapers and magazines do you read? For me, they're what candy or Quaaludes or scream therapy are for my neighbors. I get my daily ration from the bilious Lincoln Brigade veteran who runs a tobacco shop on 110th Street, not from the blind news agent in the wooden pillbox on Broadway, who's nearer my apartment. And we don't know nearly enough. (38)

When her fiction remains obsessed with technical experiment – as in "Description (of a Description)," which consists of seven sentences, each fragmented and followed by a paragraph of commentary – it is less compelling because her prose tends then to become flat and lifeless, and her experiments are often dull. Recently she has turned to more conventional narrative, a form completely new for her, and she writes in it with grace and vitality. One feels that in such stories as "The Way We Live Now" and "Pilgrimage" she is releasing a voice which her obsession with technical experiment had kept repressed for decades.

Like her fiction, Sontag's films suffer from hyper-self-consciousness and heavy-handed technical experimentation. Her first, *Duet for Cannibals*, depicts an older couple entangling a younger couple in their perverse relationship, and premiered at the 1969 New York Film Festival. Her second, *Brother Carl* – filmed like the first in Stockholm, and first shown at the Cannes Film Festival – centers around the silent title character, who seems both mad and Christlike.

Both films are difficult to follow, and neither was a critical success; one of Sontag's best critics has remarked that *Brother Carl* "threatens to turn into a primer of elementary film technique" (Bruss 217). Her last film, *Promised Lands*, is her best. Filmed in five weeks in Israel, the Golan Heights, and the Sinai, immediately after the conclusion of the 1973 Yom Kippur War, *Promised Lands* is a documentary (with no voice-over narrative) about that war, its causes and its aftermath. Sontag says that she wanted to "represent a condition, rather than an action," to depict "a mental landscape – as well as a physical and political one" ("Movie" 84), and perhaps because she works here within the constraints of an established genre, this film succeeds where the others fail.

In general, Sontag is far better at writing about other people's fiction and films than at creating her own. She is especially good at introducing her audience to writers or filmmakers who seem at first opaque – too bizarre, too enigmatic, too elusive – and she has played a major role in the introduction of Continental figures to American readers, introducing such figures as Sarraute, Barthes, Artaud, Canetti, Benjamin, Cioran, and Pavese. Her early essays on Robert Bresson, Jack Smith and Jean-Luc Godard exemplify her "celebratory" mode, in which she shows her readers how to appreciate an undervalued or misunderstood artist – with Bresson's films, for example, we must not expect the dramatic suspense typical of naturalistic cinema, but must cultivate a consciousness of form detached from content. In such essays Sontag is prone to provocative assertions as well: "[Bresson] has never had the attention of ... Bunuel, Bergman, Fellini – though he is a far greater director than these" (*Against* 179). Her other chief mode is "debunking," best illustrated in her brilliant attack on Leni Riefenstahl in "Fascinating Fascism." Here Sontag's target is not only Riefenstahl's attempt to deny the political motivation behind her work, but also Riefenstahl's ingenuous supporters (especially American feminists) who refuse to consider the historical and ethical dimensions of her work.

Sontag's literary criticism embodies many of the stylistic features evident in all of her writing. Instead of articulating a problem, stating a thesis, anticipating objections, and carefully developing a line of argument, she writes an impressionistic, epigrammatic prose that circles its topic rather than approaching it directly. Elizabeth Bruss compares Sontag's prose to collage and montage (225), and for these reasons she sometimes reminds me of Emerson and Nietzsche. She resembles them also in her propensity for the extreme position, the self-assured extravagant assertion, the broad generalization; several readers have noted a similarity between Sontag's style and that of the polemical manifestos of the Futurists and Surrealists, and Bruss has characterized her rhetorical strategy as intentionally exacerbating and provocative (267).

Particularly when she writes about a specific author, she tends to focus not so much on particular books or themes or strategies of form as on what she calls a "sensibility," i.e., the complex of attitudes, the stance toward the world, that underlies an author's *oeuvre*. She presents Benjamin by means of the archaic category "melancholic"; Barthes's temperament delights in the aesthetic but cannot accommodate the moral, and his books fit into "that tradition inaugurated by Rilke's *The Notebooks of Malte Laurids Brigge*, which crossbreeds fiction, essayistic speculation, and autobiography" (*Saturn* 175). Simone Weil is important to our liberal bourgeois civilization precisely because she is anti-liberal and anti-bourgeois. Because of their absence today, we value those qualities – the morbid, the hysterical, the enormous indulgence in suffering – which we find in her work. Weil appeals to us because of her capacity for extremism, her sense of the unhealthy, her fanatical asceticism, "her noble and ricidulous political gestures," "a level of spirituality which is not, could not, be [our] own," and "a life, absurd in its exaggerations and degree of self-mutilation" (*Against* 51).

Obviously such an approach has its limitations – "I've probably left out ninety percent of what Canetti is about," Sontag admits in an interview – and her approach is the opposite of the trained scholar's: "There's a part of me that identifies with most of the people I write about; it's almost as if I'd invented them, as if they were fantasy projections of part of myself" (Copeland 83, 87). Nonetheless she is at her best in such essays: insightful, provocative, causing readers to want to return to those writers they have already read, or to read right away those whom they have not yet read.

Sontag is less compelling when she takes on a broader subject such as modernism. In the 1960's, defending the notion of the avant-garde, she argued "that it is the obligation of each art form … and of any artist who is truly serious … to evolve, to systematically evolve – not simply to be original and novel, but to be committed in a process of systematic evolution or development" ("Avant-Garde" 930). The work of Joyce, Woolf and Beckett in the 1920s and '30s fulfills this obligation, but in the late '30s "the novel returned to precisely what had seemed to be outmoded" (940), and no serious literary tradition evolved from Joyce's work. The contemporary novel is "essentially journalistic in conception" and has regressed to "the aesthetic principles of nineteenth-century realism" (940). Bellow, Mailer, Baldwin, Roth, Malamud and Updike are "essentially unconcerned with the problems of the novel as an art" (940), and "the novel is probably the most rear guard art form today … . There is no art form today in which the avant-garde is less relevant, less developed, and less influential" (938).

Sontag's account is simplistic, reductive and unfair to the authors she names. *Finnegans Wake* and *The Unnamable* are stylistic dead ends, and Sontag's argument boils down to a complaint about aesthetic evolution. Her complaint is aimed also at art's audience:

When I started writing in the early Sixties, I was defending the "modern," particularly in literature, because the prevailing approach was very philistine. And for about ten years, the views I espoused became more and more common. But during the past five years, it's not as if people have gone back to the position they had before; it's worse. Before, they didn't like this stuff because they were ignorant. They didn't even know about it. Now they don't like it because they think they know something about it and feel superior to it. So you have to defend Schonberg or Joyce or Merce Cunningham. There's a mean-spiritedness regarding high-modern art now that's so discouraging that I don't even feel like entering the fray in the essay form. (Cott 50)

In 1981 she tells an interviewer, "It seems that people don't want books — or any form of art — to be *hard,* they want art to be decorative." She finds "people more and more finding things hard ... not having the necessary energy," and blames much of this on "the acceptance of television, the mentality and kind of attention that is the given of television. The condition of our attention, the condition of our seriousnees has been progressively altered ... I really think it's the death of western civilization. It's the death of literature, the death of literacy, and the death of politics" (Copeland 86).

This kind of extremism leads Sontag into contradictions. Despite her disparagement of the novel and her prediction of the death of literature, in 1974 she spoke of "a kind of explosion in prose fiction" (Bellamy 114), and told the *New York Times Book Review* (24 October 1982): "I think that the novel is far from being exhausted" (40). The same two interviews reveal one other inconsistency: "I am most interested in ... fiction which moves back and forth between imaginary or fantastic worlds and the so-called real world" (1974); "I want to write fiction which is not solipsistic, in which there is a real world" (1982). Again, in 1966 Sontag refers to film as the "second most conservative art form" ("Avant-Garde" 939); in 1973 she calls cinema "the century's likeliest candidate for the title of master art" (Saturn 32). Inconsistency in itself is no great crime, since it often leads, if examined carefully, to intellectual discovery. Sontag, however, is not a great examiner of her own inconsistencies, and this has limited the development of her thought.

Another limitation to her thinking about literature is her pronounced bias in favor of the continental European. She tells the New York *Times* (10 October 1980) that there are simply "not many American writers in the international class" (34), and whenever she is asked to name writers she admires, the list might include Beckett, Kafka, Kundera, Brodsky, Naipaul, or Calvino, but rarely does she mention an American. More recently she has expressed some admiration for Doctorow, Vidal, Gass, Barthelme and Ishmael Reed, but she does not write about these authors. In a brief essay on Paul Goodman, written shortly after his death, she calls him "quite simply the most important American writer. He was our Sartre, our Cocteau" (*Saturn* 8-9), but this startling claim goes undeveloped and undefended. When the New York *Times* asks her in 1979 to name the books written since World War II that will enter the canon of Western literature, she lists works by Beckett,

Yourcenar, Mandelstam, Calvino, Genet, and Borges. The only quasi-American title on her list is Nabokov's *Pale Fire*. In one sense she does Americans a service by insisting that the best of contemporary literature is being written in foreign languages, and that we need to expose ourselves to this work, much of which is undeniably powerful. But when she so predictably praises the foreign and ignores or demeans the domestic, her claims can seem less than compelling.

Of Sontag's three collections of essays, *Against Interpretation* (1966) is the most well known and provocative. The title essay begins with the distinction between the experience of art and the theory of art; Sontag argues that in the West, theory has smothered experience to such an extent that an audience immediately demands that art be interpreted, or translated, so that they can know what it "really" says. Marx and Freud are guilty of contributing to "the effusion of interpretations of art today [which] poisons our sensibilities. In a culture whose already classical dilemma is the hypertrophy of the intellect at the expense of energy and sensual capability, interpretation is the revenge of intellect upon art" (7). Sontag bemoans the "thick encrustations of interpretation" that have built up around the work of Kafka, Beckett and Proust, most of which first reduce a work that would otherwise be too anxiety-provoking. Sontag's remedy is "more attention to form in art," and she cites Frye, Barthes, Auerbach and Benjamin as critics whose work "dissolves considerations of content into those of form" (12). The weakest part of her essay is her claim that a work of art can "elude the interpreters" if its "surface is so unified and clean, [its] momentum is so rapid, [its] address is so direct that the work can be ... just what it is" (11). This naive notion of aesthetics is celebrated as "transparence ... the highest, most liberating value in art ... [which] means experiencing the luminousness of the thing in itself, of things being what they are" (13). As Westerners, the "steady loss of sharpness in our sensory experience" has so dulled our capacity to experience art that drastic action is called for: "In place of a hermeneutics we need an erotics of art" (14).

The obvious weakness in Sontag's argument is that the concrete, sensory experience of a work of art is inarticulate, and as soon as the subject begins to articulate his experience, even if he merely describes it, he has begun to interpret it. Sontag's more generous readers have claimed she is arguing against externally imposed meanings, or simply refusing the idea of determinate meaning, of constricting single readings. Elizabeth Bruss characterizes the essay as a playful, inflammatory manifesto in the style of Artaud and Breton. But most readers took the essay as a serious challenge, and responded in kind. Alicia Ostriker reduces the essay to "her major premise ...[is] that brains are bankrupt," and claims that Sontag "shares ... in a popular and antirationalist superstition according to which intelligence has not only failed to solve the problems of mankind, but is also directly responsible for getting us into our contemporary fix" (83). Kavolis traces her "flight from systematic conceptual interpretations to momentary sensuous experiences ... back to the beginning of the self-consciously avant-garde culture in French bohemianism of the second half of the nineteenth century" (23). Similarly, Hilton Kramer finds her basic idea "a refurbished and scrupulously up-to-date version of the radical aestheticism that had long been associated with the 'decadent' movement of the 1890's," or more simply, "replacing the Matthew Arnold idea of culture with the Oscar Wilde idea of culture" (90). Among others, Paul Velde notes the irony of a writer "who is against hermeneutics and for form, yet seems to interpret more readily than most; who is for the senses, yet whose criticism is unflinchingly cerebral" (391). Finally, Charles Samuels addresses Sontag's claim that interpretation ignores form and deals only with content: "Where has she been since the advent of I. A. Richards ...?" Samuels notes that the "new criticism" effectively demolished the overvaluing of content decades ago, and labels Sontag's a criticism in which "discernment is abandoned in behalf of sensation, evidence yields to incantatory assertions, and critical elucidation disappears ... . She has lobotomized [art]" (221).

I suspect that Sontag intended to provoke such a response, but it is regrettable that her extreme manner of phrasing left her so very open to rebuttals that could ignore the valid heart of her argument: that aesthetic experience today is needlessly dominated by intellectualization. She makes the point in a review of the painter Francis Bacon: "The principal modern way of looking at a painting is to situate it inside the history of *thinking* about painting" ("Bacon" 136). In interviews, Sontag has explained that she is not "against" analysis, and that she views the intellectual experience as an important part of the aesthetic experience. But people "have been programmed to look for certain things in works of art – and to lie to themselves about what they were actually experiencing. They have been taught to reduce their experience to certain forms of talking about it, the most notable of these being 'what it means'" (Bellamy 121). In another interview, she states, "One of my oldest crusades is against the distinction between thought and feeling" (Cott 50), but in her polemic she seemed to be maintaining the distinction and simply reversing the hierarchy.

"Notes on Camp" is a brilliant series of tentative definitions of the "camp" sensibility, an articulation of a taste and attitude that everyone was somehow aware of, but no one was yet talking about. Sontag classifies camp as a mode of aestheticism, as "*one* way of seeing the world as an aesthetic phenomenon ... not in terms of beauty, but in terms of the degree of artifice, of stylization" (277). Camp delights in the unnatural, in artifice and exaggerations, in surface and style, in passion and glamor and the glorification of "character" – "Martha Graham is always being Martha Graham" (285). Camp is "dandyism in the age of mass culture," one strand in the history of snob taste. As a central element in homosexual aestheticism and irony, camp forms one of the two pioneering forces of the modern sensibility – the other being the tradition of Jewish moral seriousness. The essay is playful, profound and provocative, and in retrospect most interesting in many critics' assumptions that Sontag was defending or celebrating "camp," when in fact she states, "I am strongly drawn to Camp, and almost as strongly offended by it" (276). Again, the fault is partly with Sontag's rhetoric, which in this essay is too often didactic, too often in the tone of the privileged initiate speaking to the uninformed or unaware. Instead of developing that interesting ambivalence in her attitude toward camp, she ignores it and the reader forgets it.

"One Culture and the New Sensibility" is Sontag at her weakest, playing the roles of expositor of the contemporary and inspired prophet of the new order. Here she argues that the "two cultures" – the literary-aesthetic and the scientific – are being fused in a new sensibility, rooted in the condition of contemporary civilization: mobility, crowdedness, the availability of new sensations, and a pan-cultural perspective on the arts. Contemporary art (excluding fiction, which is burdened by excessive "content," reportage and moral judgment) is "an instrument for modifying consciousness and organizing new modes of sensibility" (296). The boundaries between the scientific and the literary, art and non-art, high and low culture, are being erased, and a new non-literary culture (which depends, oddly enough, on "basis texts" by Nietzsche, Wittgenstein, Artaud, Barthes, McLuhan, Levi-Strauss, et al.) is emerging, centered around music, film, dance, architecture, painting and sculpture, which "understands art as the extension of life" and takes as its "basic unit" not the idea, but sensations (300). Sontag invites the charge that again she is simply reversing the hierarchy, valorizing the senses at the expense of the intellect and the visual arts at the expense of the literary.

"On Style" amplifies the argument of "Against Interpretation." It begins quite plausibly: "Though the issue of the adequacy of artistic representation to life has pretty much been abandoned in, for example, painting, such adequacy continues to constitute a powerful standard of judgment in most appraisals of serious novels, plays, and films." Thus most criticism "treats the work of art as a statement being made in the form of a work of art." However, "a work of art encountered as a work of art is an experience, not a statement or an answer to a question" (21). If Sontag had halted here, most readers would agree. But she goes on to reduce art to "nothing more or less than various modes of stylized, dehumanized representation" (30) and to assert that "the world is, ultimately, an aesthetic phenomenon" (28). This extreme position supports the entirely spurious claim that "a work of art, so far as it is a work of art ... cannot advocate anything at all. The greatest artists attain a sublime neutrality. Think of Homer and Shakespeare, from whom generations of scholars and critics have vainly labored to extract particular 'views' about human nature, morality, and society" (26). Sontag has painted herself into a corner from which she must claim that "the knowledge we gain through art is an experience of the form or style of knowing something, rather than a knowledge of something (like a fact or a moral judgment) in itself" (22). The phrase "rather than" illustrates Sontag's propensity to preserve the very boundaries she derides, and her unfortunate habit of deflecting attention from her more interesting points by making stupid assertions – if Homer and Shakespeare were not writing about the truths of human nature, morality and society, then they weren't writing about anything at all. At the end of her essay, Sontag demonstrates that a criticism focusing "on style" in Robbe-Grillet would detect a mode of attention implying "that persons are also things," and in Gertrude Stein, "the dilution of immediate awareness by memory and anticipation" (35). But isn't style then functioning "as an auxiliary to truth" (28), which Sontag asserts is not art's purpose? Sontag's weakness here is that when she is right, she shows "not the slightest awareness of the fact that many of the best modern critics of the arts ... had written, and written at length, on matters of 'form', 'style,' and 'the sensuous experience of the work of art' with an attention to detail and a sense of complexity" (Kramer 91), and when she is wrong, she opens herself to obvious objections.

"Happenings: An Art of Radical Juxtaposition" is an excellent essay in which Sontag introduces her reader to an unfamiliar contemporary art form by carefully describing her experience as a member of an audience at one of these "series of actions and events" without stage, actors or plot. She explains her immediate responses quietly and perceptively, and describes the happening itself very effectively. Her suggestions that happenings are a logical development of the 1950s "New York School" of painting, or of the surrealist sensibility, are interesting and persuasive, quite different from the extreme polemicism of the more theoretical essays.

Styles of Radical Will (1969), Sontag's second collection of essays, is most notable for "The Aesthetics of Silence," a tour de force which, according to Christine Brooke-Rose, is "a landmark essay" and "in many ways a proleptic summary of much that has been said since" (9,14). Sontag begins by considering modern art as a metaphor for the spiritual project, an "antidote to consciousness" akin to the paradoxes involved in attaining the absolute state of being described by religious mystics: beyond knowledge, beyond speech, beyond subject and object. Yet "silence remains, inescapably, a form of speech (in many instances, of complaint or indictment) and an element in a dialogue" (11), as art remains a form of human consciousness, of attention and perception. Why has the most valuable modern art "been experienced by audiences as a move into silence (or unintelligibility or invisibility or inaudibility)" (7)? Why are silence, emptiness, reduction, absence, minimalism such potent elements in our art? Sontag suggests that silence "is a metaphor for a cleansed, non-interfering vision" (16), and that it plays to our desire "for a perceptual and cultural clean slate" (17), ahistorical and unalienated. Because "language is the most impure, the most contaminated, the most exhausted of all the materials out of which art is made" (14), the pursuit of silence answers "a perennial discontent with language that has been formulated in each of the major civilizations of the Orient and Occident, whenever thought reaches a certain high, excruciating order of complexity and spiritual seriousness" (21). The tone of this essay is less antagonistic, less loud, than that of her earlier theoretical essays; her topic is more focused, and her argument far more compelling.

"The Pornographic Imagination" develops the themes of a 1964 essay on the film *Flaming Creatures* (reprinted in *Against Interpretation*). In the earlier essay Sontag defends a film that most critics regard as pornographic trash. Sontag admires the film because of its utter lack of "commentary on or critique of anything" (375); it takes no position on its subject matter, neither approving nor disapproving, and is thus "a triumphant example of an aesthetic vision of the world" (376), "a treat for the senses" (375), rich in the directness, power and lavish quantity of its images. In the space of moral ideas, the film fails, but in the space of aesthetic pleasure, it succeeds.

"The Pornographic Imagination" is more hesitant in its defense of the genre. Focusing on pornographic literature, in particular *The Story of O* and the work of Pierre Louys and George Bataille, Sontag first argues that some pornography does deserve to be considered literature, that no aesthetic principle can categorically exclude pornography from art. Pornographic art makes forays into the frontiers of consciousness, into extreme forms of consciousness, and if its report is original, thorough, authentically powerful, then it deserves to be called art. Sontag's insistent separation of aesthetic values from moral values repeats her earlier arguments, but Andrew Ross misreads the essay when he claims Sontag sees pornography as "a realm of radical chic pleasure" (184). On the contrary, Sontag admits that pornography can be a crutch to the psychologically deformed and brutal to the morally innocent; her half-hearted defense is that "all knowledge is dangerous" and that pornography "is only one item among the many dangerous commodities being circulated in this society" (72). The most interesting aspect of the essay is her attitude toward the human sexual appetite, which she claims is *not* the natural, pleasant function that liberal thinking claims it is, but "a highly questionable phenomenon, [belonging] at least potentially among the extreme rather than the ordinary experiences of humanity. Tamed as it may be, sexuality remains one of the demonic forces in human consciousness – pushing us at intervals close to taboo and dangerous desires" (57). This attutide, surprising in a writer labelled the spokesperson for the radical sixties, resurfaces in a 1979 interview:

> We've been instructed that [sexuality] is the central or only natural activity of our lives. That's nonsense. I mean, it's very hard to imagine what natural sexuality could be. I don't think it's available to any of us. Sexuality is a much bigger, more anarchic thing than one imagines, and that's why, throughout human history, it's been the subject of so much regulation. I don't think people understand why there's been this problem of repression. I would turn it around and say that the reason most societies have been repressive about sexuality is that people *have understood* that it can get out of control and be completely destructive (Cott 52).

Sontag's third collection of essays, *Under the Sign of Saturn* (1980), displays a markedly different tone from her earlier work: much less didactic and polemical, much more skeptical; fewer aphoristic fragments, more developed arguments. The finest essay in the collection is "Fascinating Fascism," which deals with the work of Leni Riefenstahl. Sontag attacks Riefenstahl's defenders, who claim she was always concerned with beauty and that her Nazi past no longer matters. She also details Riefenstahl's intimate connection with Hitler, even before 1932, and her close working cooperation with the Nazi regime. All of Riefenstahl's work, argues Sontag, illustrates the themes of "fascist aesthetics": a preoccupation with situations of control, submissive behavior, extravagant effort, the endurance of pain, glorified surrender, exalted mindlessness, and glamorized death. Fascist aesthetics today are evident in the official art of communist countries, with its taste "for the monumental and for mass obeisance to the hero" (91), its public staging of the will, its drama of leader and chorus. In the contemporary West, fascist aesthetics persist in "the ideal of life as art, the cult of beauty, the fetishism of courage, the dissolution of alienation in ecstatic feelings of community, the repudiation of the intellect" (96). Finally, in a backhanded admission that she is contradicting her earlier stance on the absolute autonomy of the aesthetic, she writes: "Art that seemed eminently worth defending ten years ago, as a minority or adversary taste, no longer seems defensible today, because the ethical and cultural issues it raises have become serious, even dangerous, in a way they were not then ... . Taste is context, and the context has changed" (98). Almost ten years earlier, in "On Style," Sontag had written: "In art, 'content' is, as it were, the pretext, the goal, the lure which engages consciousness in essentially *formal* processes of transformation. This is how we can, in good conscience, cherish works of art which, considered in terms of 'content,' are morally objectionable to us" (*Against* 25), and used Riefenstahl's films as an example of such art. In "On Style" she had argued that Riefenstahl's work transcended the category of propaganda; in "Fascinating Fascism" she claims *Triumph of the Will* is devoid of any aesthetic conception independent of propaganda. When asked about this in an interview, Sontag refuses to admit a contradiction exists, insisting "both statements illustrate the richness of the form-content distinction, as long as one is careful always to use it against itself" (*Reader* 329). She continues: "One of the main assertions in 'On Style' is that the formalist and the historicist approaches are not in competition with each other, but are complementary – and equally indispensable" (330).

Unfortunately, nowhere in the polemical "On Style" does Sontag assert anything like this, and this refusal to examine the tensions within her thought is a weakness in Sontag's work. In interviews she has admitted to this shift, but she has yet to deal with it in any depth in writing. In 1975:

Though I continue to be as besotted an aesthete and as obsessed a moralist as I ever was, I've come to appreciate the limitations – and the indiscretion – of generalizing either the aesthete's or the moralist's view of the world without a much denser notion of historical context (*Reader* 331-32).

In 1981:

If there's been a real change in my views over the years, it's that I've had to give the historicist approach a more central role in my reaction to things (Copeland 85).

One of the more interesting aspects of Sontag's cultural criticism has been her relationship with feminism. In 1972 she wrote a long essay, "The Third World of Women," which seemed as radically feminist as anything being written by Greer, Millett or Steinem. "Support for the emancipation of women," wrote Sontag, "stands today approximately where support for the emancipation of slaves stood two hundred years ago" (180). Her thesis was that

All women live in an 'imperialist' situation in which men are colonialists and women are natives. In so-called Third World countries, the situation of women with respect to men is tyranically, brutally colonialist. In economically advanced countries (both capitalist and communist) the situation of women is neocolonialist ... But the same basic relations of inferiority and superiority, of powerlessness and power, of cultural underdevelopment and cultural privilege, prevail between women and men in all countries (184).

The essay ends with a call for women to violate the "morally defective and historically obsolete" (182) conception of femininity by taking karate lessons, whistling at men in the streets, supporting themselves literally (economically) and metaphorically (psychologically and culturally), converting in sizeable numbers to militant lesbianism, and destroying sexuality as an instrument of repression by challenging the primacy of genital heterosexuality.

In a series of essays for *Vogue*, a women's magazine devoted to fashion and beauty, Sontag argued that "beauty" is a demeaning value that encourages narcissisim, dependence and immaturity. "The conventions of beauty reinforce the image of women as indolent, smooth-skinned, odorless, empty-headed, affable playthings" ("Beauty" 174), and if a woman is beautiful, her capacity to be objective, authoritative and professional is immediately suspect ("Woman's" 119). In the same magazine in 1976, Sontag published an eloquent plea for passage of the Equal Rights Amendment in "a time of exhausted radical hopes and aggressive, well-financed reaction" ("Rights" 100). Yet despite this point of view, Sontag has been a consistent critic of feminism. In an exchange of letters with Adrienne Rich, who had criticized Sontag's "Fascinating Fascism" for its attack on the feminist defense of Riefenstahl, Sontag refers to feminism as a "simple-minded" moral truth, and complains about its demagogic "demand for an unremitting rhetoric, with every argument arriving triumphantly at a militant conclusion." Feminist rhetoric, Sontag writes, is too often anti-intellectual, and its anti-hierarchical egalitarianism is "part of a childish, sentimental fantasy about the human condition" predicated on a shallow psychology and a thinned-out sense of history ("Feminism and Fascism" 31-32).

This attitude reappears in a 1975 interview: "It's not the appropriateness of feminist criticism which needs to be rethought, but its level – its demands for intellectual simplicity, advanced in the name of ethical solidarity" (*Reader* 33). Asked about Helene Cixous' claim that writing reveals gender difference, Sontag replies, "Her statement doesn't make any sense," and continues:

I think it's very oppressive to be asked to conform to a stereotype, exactly as a black writer might be asked to express only black consciousness. I don't want to be "ghettoized" ... I would be sorry to see writing start to be sexually segregated. The attempt to set up a separate culture is a way of not seeking power (Cott 50).

Sontag's politics are as provocative, as extreme and as inconsistent as her aesthetics. In 1966 she wrote:

The role of the writer as critic or dissenter provides the key to everything serious that has happened in our culture in the last one hundred years. The writer is the model of the awake consciousness. ... It seems to me impossible that the writer not be involved in politics. Right now, it seems to me one task of the American writer is to be yelling at the top of his voice at the folly and ugly self-righteousness, at the immorality of and terrible danger entailed by our government's policy and behaviour in Vietnam ... . Writers should be in the vanguard of the dissenting minority ("Role of the Writer" 36).

Twenty years later she tells the *New York Times Book Review* (January 5, 1986):

I subscribe entirely – the correct word might be devoutly – to this modern, secular idea of literature as a calling, which assumes an artistic hierarchy, which assumes literature as privacy – as a social contribution, if you will, but only because the writer knows how to distance herself or himself from the collective din, above all, the din of the state. In my view, literature entails the right to be apolitical (what some would read as irresponsible).[22]

Sontag would be a far more compelling critic if she would directly confront these reversals in attitude instead of pretending they don't exist.

Like Muriel Rukeyser, Mary McCarthy, Denise Levertov, and more notoriously Jane Fonda, Sontag travelled to Hanoi in the summer of 1968 as the guest of the North Vietnamese government, an experience which led to "Trip to Hanoi" (reprinted in *Styles of Radical Will*). Sontag claims to be "passionately opposed to the American aggression in Vietnam" and "neither a journalist nor a political activist ... nor an Asian specialist, but rather a stubbornly unspecialized writer who has so far been largely unable to incorporate into either novels or essays my evolving radical political convictions and sense of moral dilemma at being a citizen of the American empire" (205). The essay is interesting because its focus is on Sontag's own shifting response to what she encounters there. At first she feels confused, often exasperated, and somewhat disappointed. The Vietnamese seem utterly alien: their responses to her questions seem predictable, rote and intellectually simplistic; their aesthetic lacks variety; psychologically they seem simple and uncurious, without skepticism or irony. But as she begins to see the Vietnamese for what they are, and discards her assumptions about what they ought to be, she comes to admire the moral beauty of their unsophisticated, simple world-view. Sontag decides that unlike Americans, who are psychologically "split," the Vietnamese are "whole" human beings (263) unburdened by the complicating, alienating weight of Western consciousness.

The most valuable aspect of the essay is Sontag's insistence on the "otherness" of the Vietnamese, on their radical difference, and on the impossibility of "knowing" the truth about them, an idea which dovetails to some extent with her suspicion of interpretation in the world of aesthetics. She is weakest in the naive, wishful-thinking manner in which she accepts much of what her North Vietnamese hosts tell her about their aims and values – she is far more willing to suspend her skepticism in Vietnam than she is in America. She states that North Vietnam is not "a model of a just state," but then claims it is "a place which, in many respects, deserves to be idealized" (259). Just as she simply reverses hierarchies in much of her early work on aesthetics, so here she simply reverses the official American account of the war, putting the white hat on the North Vietnamese and the black hat on the Americans. The Vietnam War, Sontag writes, illustrates "what's most ugly in America: the principle of 'will,' the self-righteous taste for violence, the insensate prestige of technological solutions to human problems" (234). Her claim is true, but it is a reductive, simplistic way of thinking about a very complicated and horrible episode in our history. Leo Marx, who has written the finest response to "Trip to Hanoi," notes that this essay represents a sharp break from the "resolutely apolitical" assumptions and "frigid aestheticism" of *Against Interpretation*, and correctly identifies its "strongest appeal" as "its lucid expression of the dilemma confronting countless Americans ... who are morally alienated from a society which so abundantly favors them" (570, 571). Sontag concludes that Americans on the left must "reclaim the tarnished idea of patriotism" (266) from its constricted, right-wing usage – an interesting idea that she never develops.

Sontag's political naivete is at its most extreme in her idealization of Cuba. In 1969 Sontag attacks the American New Left, in "Some Thoughts on the Right Way (for us) to Love the Cuban Revolution, " for being concerned only with cultural and psychic revolutions. "Its goal is freedom, not justice," Sontag laments, and such freedom invites the individual's non-participation, disaffiliation and selfishness (10). In Cuba, on the other hand, the revolution is focused on the community and "the moralization of work," and is "astonishingly free of repression and bureaucratization" (14). The Cuban revolution "has meant the discovery of new public values" and cultivated a "peculiarly intense form of fraternal international feeling." In Havana today "one feels more in the world, more in touch with events ... than one ever does in such genuinely provincial cities as Rome or Stockholm," which suffer "the debilitating effects of [the New Left's] habit of over-aestheticizing revolution" (19).

This tone persists in Sontag's introductory essay to *The Art of Revolution: Castro's Cuba, 1959-1970*, in which Sontag claims that Cuba "has by revolutionary aspiration ... repudiated mercantile values more radically than any communist country outside of Asia. ... Leaving out China, Cuba is perhaps the only current example of a communist revolution pursuing that ethical aim [i.e., the raising and complicating of consciousness] as an explicit political goal" (xiii). Reluctantly admitting that poets, such as the imprisoned Huberto Padilla, are "vulnerable" in revolutionary Cuba, Sontag nonetheless praises "the Cuban government's achievement in resisting an ethically and aesthetically philistine treatment of its artists" (xvi), and concludes her essay "Viva Fidel."

This naive, sentimental depiction of Cuba is even more striking when compared with Sontag's "A Letter from Sweden" (1969). Sontag wrote and directed two films in Sweden, with generous support from the Swedish Film Institute, and she has due praise for that Institute's generosity, and for certain traits of the Swedish people, who have a "genuine gift for self-criticism" and are "among the most polite and amiable people I have ever met" (28). Swedish society is "more egalitarian than any other operating within the framework of capitalism" (32), and "the ruling class of this country is genuinely benevolent and filled with good intentions" (35). Yet the thrust of the essay concerns "the profound quarrel [Sontag has] with much of the quality of Swedish life" (23). The Swedes' "reasonableness," claims Sontag, is rooted in their "inhibition and anxiety and emotional dissociation" (26). Their "institutionalized" social life is meager and relatively comfortless (28), and their society "uncompetitive without being genuinely cooperative" (33). Sweden's defects are easily explained: "at no time was the SDP ever committed to revolutionary socialism; Marxist influence in the trade union movement has always been marginal ... . Certainly Sweden is not a socialist country" (34). Thus the reforms of Sweden's welfare state "don't strike at the root of the situation of Swedes as human beings. They have not awakened the Swedes from their centuries' old chronic state of depression, they have not liberated new energy, they have not – and cannot – create a New Man. To do that Sweden needs a revolution" (38). This predictable, knee-jerk political thinking has done Sontag's reputation no good, and to her credit, she has largely refrained from it since then.

Sontag's criticism of the United States is as extreme as her praise of Cuba, and takes its most direct form in "What's Happening to America (1966)" (reprinted in *Styles of Radical Will*), written in response to a questionnaire from *Partisan Review* on the direction of American life. She begins: "Everything that one feels about this country is, or ought to be, conditioned by the awareness of American *power*: of America as the arch-imperium of the planet, holding man's biological as well as his historical future in its King Kong paws. ... American power is indecent in its scale: American policy is still powered by the fantasy of Manifest Destiny" (194, 196). Given the Vietnam War and the Cold War, this sounds plausible, but Sontag isn't finished: "The white race *is* the cancer of human history; it is the white race and it alone – its ideologies and inventions – which eradicates autonomous civilizations wherever it spreads, which has upset the ecological balance of the planet, which now threatens the very existence of life itself" (203). This is a curious metaphor (and one which Sontag later repudiates), since cancer is a disease we "fight" and try to "wipe out."

America is "pretty much the same Yahooland that Mencken was describing," except today our barbarism and innocence are "outsized" and "lethal" (194). Like Mencken, Sontag sees the average American as "boobus americanus": "If the Bill of Rights were put to a national referendum as a new piece of legislation, it would [fail]. Most of the people in this country believe what Goldwater believes, and always have. But most of them don't know it. Let's hope they don't find out" (198). Apparently this ignorance on the part of the electorate explains Goldwater's massive defeat in the 1964 presidential election. This tone of snide elitism – "Let's hope they don't find out," i.e., let's you and I, who write for or read *Partisan Review* and appreciate the moral superiority of North Vietnam and Cuba, share a smile at the ignorance of these boobs – is one of Sontag's less attractive traits.

Another unattractive trait is her penchant for psychoanalyzing entire nationalities: the North Vietnamese are "whole," the Cubans are spontaneously communal, the Swedes are chronically depressed and alienated from their emotions. Americans are psychological wrecks, for "the quality of American life is an insult to the possibilities of human growth; and the pollution of American space, with gadgetry and cars and TV and box architecture, brutalizes the senses, making gray neurotics of most of us" (194). Our energy "is the energy of violence, of free-floating resentment and anxiety unleashed by chronic cultural dislocations which must be, for the most part, ferociously sublimated ... into crude materialism and acquisitiveness ... [or] benighted moral crusades" (195). But neurosis and sublimated violence are insufficiently extreme: psychosis, Sontag decides, is the proper diagnosis:

> The unquenchable American moralism and the American faith in violence are not just twin symptoms of some character neurosis taking the form of a protracted adolescence, which presages an eventual maturity. They constitute a full-grown, firmly installed national psychosis, founded ... on the efficacious denial of reality (196).

Violent psychotics are routinely hospitalized and administered psychoactive drugs, but Sontag does not develop the implications of her metaphor. Her definition of psychosis as "denial of reality" is also interesting coming from a writer who has repeatedly proclaimed her own "agnosticism" about reality. If this essay were a one-time outburst it might be dismissed, but in a 1968 interview she says, "I'm really beginning to lose hope for America. It's not Western civilization that's crazy, it's *this country*," and then claims to see no difference at all between American foreign policy and Nazi Germany's in the 1930s (Toback 114). In 1979 she is less strident, but the theme remains:

"Everything in this society – in the way we live – conspires to eliminate all but the most banal level of feelings, there's no sense of the sacred or of transcendence. Today we don't have much" (Cott 48). In that same interview, however, she pays one compliment to America – "Americans tend to think that everything is possible, and that's something I like a lot about them" (49) – but interestingly speaks of Americans in the third person, as if she herself were a citizen of another nation.

Sontag's most notorious piece of political "cultural criticism" occurred on February 6, 1982, at a rally at Town Hall in New York aimed at showing support for Solidarity after Jaruzelski's imposition of martial law. The speakers included Gore Vidal, Kurt Vonnegut, and E. L. Doctorow, but Sontag's speech caused a greater disturbance than anything she had done since *Against Interpretation*. She was booed and heckled during the speech, and when the *Soho News* published a transcript of it, she filed a copyright lawsuit. *The Nation* agreed to print her speech, but Sontag altered several sections of the original, and the resulting controversy recapitulated Sontag's penchant for obscuring her valid points with polemical nonsense, as well as her critics' tendency to oversimplify her arguments.

Sontag aimed her speech at the American Left (including herself); although she began with an attack on "Reagan the union-buster, Reagan the puppet master of the butchers in El Salvador," she quickly shifted to a consideration of "how long it has taken us" to learn "the lesson of the failure of Communism, the utter villainy of the Communist system" ("Left" 230). She argued that the American Left had to distinguish itself "from others in the chorus of virtuous indignation, to stake out a different kind of support for Poland than that tendered by, say, Reagan and Haig and Thatcher" (230). For too long the Left, "governed by the wish not to give comfort to 'reactionary' forces," had so restricted the scope of its rhetoric on communism that it has "wittingly or unwittingly told a lot of lies … . We were unwilling to identify ourselves as anti-Communists because that was the slogan of the right, the ideology of the Cold War and, in particular, the justification of America's support of fascist dictatorships in Latin America and of the American war on Vietnam" (230). The American Left "believed in, or at least applied a double standard to, the angelic language of communism" (230), and "many of us, and I include myself, did not understand the nature of the Communist tyranny" because "we did not love the truth enough" (231). In conclusion, Sontag urges her audience to use the Polish crisis as a "stimulus to rethink our position, and to abandon old and corrupt rhetoric" (231).

Thus far Sontag's point is valid: in the Manichean atmosphere of the Cold War, the American Left saw its principal enemy as the "professional anti-Communist" of the American Right, and it was often unwilling to join the

Right in condemning the horrors of communism – although not everyone on the Left was as sanguine about Cuba and North Vietnam as was Sontag. But Sontag went further and asserted that the Polish crisis illustrates "a truth we should have understood a very long time ago: that Communism is fascism – successful fascism, if you will" (231). And in a passage she excised from the version of her speech she authorized in *The Nation*, but which the magazine's editors reprinted in their introductory remarks, she said:

> Imagine, if you will, someone who read only the *Reader's Digest* between 1950 and 1970, and someone in the same period who read only *The Nation* or the *New Statesman*. Which reader would have been better informed about the realities of communism? The answer, I think, should give us pause. Can it be that our enemies were right? ("Left" 229)

This kind of provocation unfortunately deflected attention from Sontag's important central point and led to an intense, if short-lived, controversy in leading journals of American opinion.

In the same issue in which it printed Sontag's approved version of the speech, *The Nation* published a series of short "Comments" on it. Diana Trilling labeled the speech "an important defection from the ranks of intellectual sympathizers with Communism" (232), while Aryeh Neier applauded "Sontag's effort to recapture anti-Communism from Reagan" (234), but most of the comments were critical. Philip Green noted that the left *did* speak out against the invasions of Hungary and Czechoslovakia, and that *Reader's Digest* is notorious for its support of the "monolithic conspiracy directed from Moscow" myth (232). Daniel Singer criticized Sontag for oversimplifying the case with her "tactics of collective guilt" (234), while Philip Pochoda attacked Sontag's equation of communism with fascism as a banal and "barbarous assault on valid historical discrimination," and accused her of eviscerating historical context: "At this late date we should not need Sontag to further enlighten us on the horrors of Stalinism" (237). David Hollinger attacked Sontag's reputation for trendiness: "Somehow, I had the impression that a critical attitude toward Communism had been 'in' for some time, and that it was no longer necessary to affect a heroic posture while criticizing Communism" (235). This point is echoed in Bruce Cumings' letter to the March 27 issue of *The Nation*, in which he identifies Sontag's as "one more voice among the many since the mid-1970s ... bespeaking the move from radical chic to conservative chic among so many American intellectuals" (368).

But the conservatives didn't like the speech either. Keith Mano, in the *National Review*, wondered why Sontag didn't admit that America was right to fight against the "utter villainy" of communism in Vietnam, and accused her of rejecting the word "communism" while maintaining her leftist sentiments (440). Peter Shaw claimed that "Sontag emerges as having been consistent over the years chiefly in being wrong" (39), and responding to her reference in *The Nation* to "the democratic movement in El Salvador, whose struggle to overthrow the tyranny backed by the American government I passionately support" ("Left" 238) , he wrote: "To commit oneself to [the El Salvador rebels, funded by the Marxist Sandinistas and Cuba,] 'passionately' on the same day as one had finally come utterly to reject Communism was no easy task" (40).

The most comprehensive attack was Richard Grenier's in *The New Republic*, in which he characterizes Sontag's speech as "another one of her dazzling modernist leaps into incoherence" (15). Grenier reminds us that in her essay on Cuba she had claimed that *Reader's Digest* was "originally connected with the Special Forces' napalming villages in Guatemala." He points out the self-serving naivete of Sontag's claim, in a 1980 interview, that "When I was in Cuba and North Vietnam ... it was not clear to me then [1968] that they would become Soviet satellites" (16), and notes that in the version of her speech printed in *The Nation*, Sontag replaces her statement that she "was utterly unconvinced" by Milosz's 1953 *The Captive Mind* with the phrase that it "troubled" her (19). In 1982 Sontag tells the *Washington Post* that most of her favorable comments on Cuba and North Vietnam were made during the Khrushchev era, but Grenier notes that her major essays on those countries appeared in 1968, the same year the Soviets invaded Czechoslovakia and four years after Khrushchev's removal. Grenier concludes with a reference to Sontag's avowed support for the Salvadoran rebels: "Somehow she'll always passionately support the other guys, and passionately oppose us. We'll always be bad and they'll always be good" (19).

Most of Sontag's defenders were Eastern European. Joseph Brodsky defended Sontag's equation of communism with fascism in *The Nation* (March 27, 1982) "since her main purpose was to bail the American left out of the hopeless swamp of its intellectual provincialism" (354) and in *The New Republic* (May 26, 1982), because "it is still news for both the American left and the American right that to be antifascist means to be anticommunist" (6). In that same issue of *The Nation* Josef Skvorecky defended Sontag's equation of communism with fascism by suggesting that "she was obviously not concerned with terminological accuracy but with an emotionally charged description of recent events in Poland" (369). The Argentine Jacobo Timerman also defended Sontag's "cry of anguish" as morally honest in *The Nation* (March 6, 1982).

The best scholarly defense of Sontag is Robert Branham's, who in a 1989 essay, after tempers had cooled, explored the oddity of the widespread interpretation of the speech as a defection from the left and a source of support for the left's political enemies. Branham claims Sontag's critics read her speech as an ideological recantation like the "public confessions" of former communists during the McCarthy era, and that this prevented them from seeing that she was maintaining her leftist sympathies (and since she was never a communist, she couldn't "defect"). Branham is correct; *The New York Times Magazine* (August 25, 1985), for example, claimed that "Susan Sontag, that most radical of radicals, made a significant rightward shift in her famous Town Hall recantation of 1982" (25) in an article on intellectual conservatism.

In this case, as with her early polemics on aesthetics, many of Sontag's critics and defenders oversimplify or distort her arguments, but the fault lies not only with her readers. Instead of contenting herself with the legitimate points that the American Left's tendency to separate "good" communism from "bad" communism is facile, that the Left tends to limit communist crimes to "Stalinism," that the Russian emigrés who appeared in *Reader's Digest* could not find a forum in *The Nation*, she goes out of her way to provoke and antagonize her readers with sophomoric polemic. Moreover, she is defensively disingenuous when she tells the *New York Times Book Review* (October 24, 1982):

> The problem at Town Hall was simply that I was breaking ranks. ... I think that a very large portion of the left has underestimated the wickedness of the Communists. It's a mistake I shared from the early 60's when I went to Cuba and was terrifically impressed with the Cuban revolution (which was not then even Communist), through the invasion of Czechoslovakia in '68. One forgets that the period between '63 and '68 was one of impressive liberalization in the Soviet Union. Solzhenitsyn won the Lenin Prize. Well, all that was ended by the decision to invade Czechoslovakia. So my political views began changing fourteen years ago (11).

Curiously, Sontag shows us "the right way to love the Cuban Revolution" in 1969, after the invasion of Czechoslovakia. If the Cuban Missile Crisis of 1962, Brezhnev's ouster of Khrushchev in 1964, and Castro's changing the name of his "Party of the Socialist Revolution" to "Communist Party of Cuba" in 1965 did not alert Sontag to the truth before 1968, she is less perceptive than she appears. It is disappointing that a writer of Sontag's gifts does not address directly the decades-long tension between her leftist sensibilities and her discomfort with "real existing socialism." As far back as 1975 she was thinking about the similarities between the "styles" of fascism and communism: "when official art in the Soviet Union and China isn't resolutely old-fashioned, it is, objectively, fascist" (*Reader* 331), a point she develops in "Fascinating Fascism." Unfortunately she prefers the role of self-righteous iconoclast, championing Cuba and North Vietnam in the '60s, and then turning on the left in the '80s and asserting that everyone on the left had been as ingenuous about communism in the '60s as she had been.

Politics is not Sontag's forte. As a cultural critic she is at her best when examining a sensibility, a habit of thinking. In 1977 she published a collection of six essays which had originally appeared in *The New York Review of Books* between 1973 and 1977. Entitled *On Photography*, it stands among her strongest work, and is an unfolding, meandering series of meditations on the meaning of photographs. The book is most interesting in its concern with both the aesthetic and ethical dimensions of photography: "photographs alter and enlarge our notions of what is worth looking at and what we have a right to observe. They are a grammar and, even more importantly, an ethics of seeing" (3). Sontag stresses the aggressive, acquisitive, appropriative quality of photography, a quality which at once establishes the photographer in a position of power and reduces him to the status of voyeur. Because anything can make an "interesting" photograph, photography levels the kinds of discrimination aesthetics and ethics normally involve: "No moment is more important than any other moment; no person is more interesting than any other person" (28).

Photography promises to disclose objective reality in a way denied to the other visual arts, yet the reality it discloses is always colored by the subjectivity of the photographer's vision and by the context in which a photograph generates its meaning: in a police record, as a news item, in an art gallery, in a family album, in a newspaper. Moreover, the proliferation and mass replication of photographs contributes to the erosion of meaning. We see so many, so much, so often – the violent and the cute, the brutal and the tender, the bizarre and the familiar – that our reactions to the "real" are more easily distanced, detached. "Cameras miniaturize experience, transform history into spectacle. As much as they create sympathy, photographs cut sympathy, distance the emotions" (110). In its "easy irony that democratizes all evidence" (75), in its "partly jubilant, partly condescending relation to reality" (80), photography embodies a surrealist sensibility: "... the best of American photography (and much else in American culture) has given itself over to the consolations of Surrealism, and America has been discovered as the quintessential Surrealist country" (48). This capacity to reduce the real to the surreal, and to function as both sensory stimulant and moral analgesic, is one way in which photography demonstrates that "art changes morals" (40) – a surprising assertion from the author of *Against Interpretation*.

In her foreword to *Italy: One Hundred Years of Photographs*, a book based on the exhibit inaugurating the Fratelli Alinari Museum of Photography in Florence, Sontag reflects on the status of photographs as documents of the past:

Photographs are not windows which supply a transparent view of the world as it is, or more exactly, as it was. Photographs give evidence – often spurious, *always* incomplete – in support of dominant ideologies and existing social arrangements. They fabricate and confirm these myths and arrangements. [They] make statements about what is in the world, what we should look at. The way most old photographs look [i.e., posed] expounds the value of uprightness, explicitness, informativeness, orderly spacing; but from the 1930s on, and this cannot only be due to the evolution of camera technology, the look of photographs confirms the value of movement, animation, asymmetry, enigma, informal social relations. Now, for several decades, Italian photography – photographic endeavors by many hands – has participated mightily in the project of unifying Italy culturally (which also means politically) with Europe, with the Atlantic world. Photographic images play a large role in making Italy (be? or only look?) more and more like ... everywhere else. All of Europe is in mourning for its past. Bookstores are stocked with albums of photographs offering up the vanished past for our delectation and reflex nostalgia ... The depth possessed by these images of an older Italy is not just the depth of the past. It is the depth of a whole culture, a culture of incomparable dignity and flavor and bulk ... that has been thinned out, effaced, confiscated. To be replaced by a culture in which the notion of depth is meaningless. That is not meant to be sauntered through. That becomes an abstraction. To be seen as an image (13).

Although *On Photography* is Sontag's only book to be honored with a National Book Critics' Circle Award, although its defenders include the formidable William Gass, and although its tone is far less polemical and capricious than that of much of her earlier work, it remains controversial. George Elliott attacked it in *The Times Literary Supplement*, claiming the book "intensifies, gives the authority of high fashion to, that despairing, never-resting confusion which is endemic in this age." Moreover, "by authorizing a nihilistic confusion for which a likely relief is totalitarianism ... [Sontag's] writing becomes more than just analytic of what is wrong; it is symptomatic and causative as well" (304). Maren Stange complained that Sontag's "arguments are hard to follow. [They] do not have a clear design or outline. Their structure is not the result of disciplined thinking" (12). I find both criticisms obtuse. Elizabeth Bruss is far more incisive in asserting that the book aims "to make it possible to judge photography rather than just consume it, to see around its seeing" (247), and that Sontag's argument "is hardly a linear movement, however, but one that doubles back and inches forward, a rocking motion that achieves gradual and seemingly unpremeditated advances" (257). William Gass agrees: "... the book is a thoughtful meditation, not a treatise, and its ideas are grouped more nearly like a gang of keys upon a ring than a run of onions on a string" (7).

On Photography is brilliant in its recognition of its subject as an activity which, as Sontag later says, "reflected all the complexities and contradictions and equivocations of this society" (Cott 53). It also marks an important break from her earlier insistence on the autonomy of the surface, style, appearance, form emptied of content. Sontag claims that the book is actually about modernity, about contemporary moral and aesthetic attitudes, contemporary ways of feeling and thinking (e.g., consumerist consciousness). Photography is the child of modern art and its audience:

> [Today's audience] is less willing to be serious in that old-fashioned way that modernist art demands. It's very complicated, because part of modernism is the idea of anti-art. So modernism itself, while being the breeding ground for all these great works of art starting from the end of the last century, contained the seeds of its own destruction. Too much emphasis was placed on outrage, and people got used to taking short cuts. Enough artists said we had to close the gap between art and life. Now people aren't willing to put in the work involved in entering these realms of discourse which distinguish art from life. ... More and more, audiences want quick results, they want punch lines from the beginning. Modernism always assumed that the recalcitrant bourgeois audience that could be shocked was going to hang onto its own standards. But when modernism became the established mode, it also became a contradiction in terms. And that, I think, is the situation in which photography has prospered (Simmons 31).

Of all Sontag's books, *Illness as Metaphor* (1978) has met with the least controversy and the most acclaim; in many ways it is her finest piece of work. The book grew out of her reaction to learning that she had cancer – "I was examining my own ideas because I had a lot of the fantasies about illness, and about cancer in particular. I'd never given the question of illness any serious consideration. So if you don't think about things, you're likely to be the victim of the going clichés" (Cott 48).

Sontag never discusses her personal experience with the disease; she simply argues "that illness is *not* a metaphor, and that the most truthful way of regarding illness ... is one most purified of, most resistant to, metaphoric thinking" (3). She focuses on tuberculosis and cancer, the two diseases most "encumbered by the trappings of metaphor" (5) because their causes and cures were/are not understood, so they became loci of mystery and fear. Quoting heavily from literature and private letters, Sontag demonstrates the ways in which tuberculosis in the nineteenth century was rendered meaningful by Romantic metaphors: it became the disease of "romantic agony," its victims genteel, delicate, sensitive, gripped by a consuming passion, an inward burning which "dissolved the gross body, etherealized the personality, expanded consciousness" (20). However, once doctors learned how to cure the disease, the metaphoric connotations which had grown up around it dissolved. Metaphor, Sontag suggests, fills the space between our knowledge of a disease and our fears of it.

In the twentieth century cancer has been similarly rendered meaningful via metaphor: its victims, however, are thought to suffer from insufficient passion, sexual repression, and emotional resignation. A disease which mystifies medicine becomes in the popular imagination an expression of character, a self-judgment. Doctors often tell patients that their "attitude," their own desire to get well, will determine whether or not they recover, which reinforces the myth that emotions cause (or cure) the disease, and places responsibility for its cause and cure in the lap of the patient. Cancer has also become a metaphor for anything evil or socially wrong. Cancer cells "invade" one organ, then "colonize" another site, while the body marshalls its "defenses" and attempts to "kill" the marauding cancer cells, which unfortunately are "alien" or "mutant," and like science-fiction monsters, can reproduce more quickly than normal cells. Like supernatural forces, cancerous tumors may be "malignant" or "benign." And in a more sophisticated and contemporary metaphor, cancer is said to signify the rebellion of the injured ecosphere against the wicked, polluted, techno-industrial world (69).

In political rhetoric, "cancer" may encourage fatalism or incite severe, violent measures. Sontag notes that European Jews were called a cancer that had to be excised, that Trotsky labeled Stalinism a cancer, that Deng Xiaoping called the Gang of Four a cancer, that John Dean explained Watergate to Nixon as "a cancer within," that the Arab states have named Israel the cancer of the Middle East. And she admits to her own metaphor: "the white race is the cancer of human history." Such metaphors reflect the historical conditions surrounding their creation rather than the nature of the diseases they purport to signify (cancer in the nineteenth century, for example, was metaphor-ized in a fashion strikingly similar to tuberculosis). Yet such metaphorical thinking is dangerous to patients and their families, as well as to political discourse: "only in the most limited sense is any historical event or problem like an illness ... it is invariably an encouragement to simplify what is complex and an invitation to self-righteousness, if not to fanaticism" (85). Michael Ignatieff is representative of the book's critics, hailing it as "the first to point out the accusatory side of the metaphors of empowerment that seek to enlist the patient's will to resist disease" and as "an exemplary demonstration of the power of the intellect in the face of the lethal metaphors of fear" (29).

Sontag's most recent book, *AIDS and Its Metaphors* (1988), applies the theme of *Illness as Metaphor* to AIDS. Like other catastrophic epidemics, AIDS has come to signify moral laxity, political decline and contamination by the foreign. It has also rekindled "the oldest idea of what causes illness": punishment. But unlike mental illness and, formerly, tuberculosis, AIDS has not generated a sentimental "compensatory mythology" which designates its victims as romantic, creative or spiritual, probably because it is too closely associated with death.

The book received generally poor reviews; many critics felt that Sontag was repeating, and not acknowledging, points already made by other writers, while others argued that only figures like Jerry Falwell and Jean LePen were guilty of the kind of crude metaphorization Sontag described. And indeed, on the disease itself Sontag is not particularly illuminating or original. Nonetheless, she is still interesting on our response to AIDS as illustrative of other aspects of our culture. For example, on the martial rhetoric of the "war" against AIDS:

Indeed, the transformation of warmaking into an occasion for mass ideological mobilization has made the notion of war useful as a metaphor for all sorts of ameliorative campaigns whose goals are cast as the defeat of an "enemy." We have had wars against poverty, now replaced by "the war on drugs," as well as wars against specific diseases, such as cancer. Abuse of the military metaphor may be inevitable in a capitalist society, a society that increasingly restricts the scope and credibility of appeals to ethical principle, in which it is thought foolish not to subject one's actions to the calculus of self-interest and profitability (11).

Another example:

AIDS may be extending the propensity for becoming inured to vistas of global annihilation which the stocking and brandishing of nuclear arms has already promoted. With the inflation of apocalyptic rhetoric has come the increasing unreality of the apocalypse. A permanent modern scenario: apocalypse looms ... and it doesn't occur. And it still looms (87).

The apocalypse takes the shape of nuclear war, third world debt, overpopulation, global warming, ozone depletion, acid rain – all of which are projected into the future and statistically quantified, as we are told how awful things will be in five, ten or twenty years. Thus "reality" itself is "bifurcated" (89), claims Sontag, due to its electronic simulation and the faith we place in statistical projections and computer models.

Sontag's critical reception has been marked by an animated ambivalence, often in the same writer. Benjamin DeMott's review of *Against Interpretation*, for example, begins by praising "the alertness and integrity with which Sontag details her own responses to the more startling and symptomatic esthetic inventions of recent days" and calls the book "a vivid bit of living history here and now, and at the end of the sixties it may well rank among the invaluable cultural chronicles of these years" (5), but concludes with a curiously dismissive image of Sontag:

The haunting image is that of a lady of intelligence and apparent beauty hastening along city streets at the violet hour, nervous, knowing, strained, excruciated (as she says) by self-consciousness, bound for the incomprehensible cinema, or for the concert hall where non-music is non-played, or for the loft where cherry bombs explode in her face and flour sacks are flapped close to her, where her ears are filled with mumbling, senseless sound and she is teased, abused, enveloped, deliberately frustrated until – Until we, *her* audience, make out suddenly that this scene is, simply, hell, and that the figure in it (but naturally) is old-shoe American: a pilgrim come again, a flagellant, one more Self-lacerating Puritan. (32)

Carolyn Heilbrun is typical of Sontag's admirers in the 1960s:

She writes, she is uncommonly brainy and darkly beautiful, smart enough to tell America off, and glamorous enough to make America like it. Susan Sontag is definitely "in." Susan Sontag, thank God, is the spokesman for the "other side." The one who understands, can explain and speak for: happenings, boredom, *nouvelle vague* films, drugs, the young. In short, the voice which can provide me with a dialogue: defend what I do not find defensible, show me the order in what I find chaotic, the meaning in what I find meaningless. (2)

To *Esquire* in 1968 she is "the most prominent young woman in the literary world ... the 'Dark Lady of American Letters' ... brilliant, articulate, beautiful and productive" (Toback 59).

Such exuberance inspired reaction. John Updike dismissed her as a "loud worrier" and "our glamorous camp follower of the avant-garde" (353, 577). Louis Rubin was more vehement: Sontag is the "high priestess" of Camp who has "charmed all the editors with her particular brand of fashionable anti-intellectualism." Mocking her as "Mme. Sontag" and "La Sontag," Rubin attacks Sontag's essays of the 1960s as "old-fashioned impressionism decked out in new clothes" and "foolish half-truth" (503, 506). Others attacked her facile use of straw men and her taste for sweeping generalizations of history.

Her two strongest defenders in the '60s were Richard Gilman and William Phillips. Gilman saw her difference from the traditional cultural critic in her esthetic intelligence, and labelled her

one of the most interesting and valuable critics we possess, a writer from whom it's continually possible to learn, even when you're most dissatisfied with what she's saying, or perhaps especially at those times. For the past several years she has been the chief voice in America of one main tradition of French criticism, which is one of the reasons, I'm convinced, why she is disliked, where she's disliked, with such ferocity and xenophobic scorn (23).

Phillips admitted that in 1969 Sontag appeared in the public imagination as

the up-to-date radical, a stand-in for everything advanced, extreme and outrageous, for artistic revolt, political disaffection, perversity and that peculiar combination of moral responsibility and moral irresponsibility associated with revolutionary movements – a fusion of Che and Genet (388).

This glitz obscured her stature as "one of our most intelligent and exciting writers," possessed of "a skeptical mind steeped in the unsolved problems that make up the history of thought and a strong, almost willed, feeling for change and discovery" (390).

In the late 1970s Sontag's critics focused on her political polemicism: "In two areas she is ... totally unironic: America is bad (except for the special few who like herself know both that and how it is bad), and revolutionary (as opposed to Soviet) Marxists are good" (Elliott 304). Maren Stange's charges that Sontag's essays are "good journalism and not serious criticism" and "simply intellectualizations of her own responses" (12) are typical of another vein of Sontag criticism.

Her strongest critics include Walter Kendrick, Richard Grenier, Jay Parin and Hilton Kramer. Kramer reduces her appeal to sensationalism:

Whether she wrote about *Flaming Creatures* or Albert Camus, about "Camp" taste or Claude Lévi-Strauss or the movies of Godard and Bresson, Sontag seemed to have an unfailing faculty for dividing intellectual opinion and inspiring a sense of outrage, consternation, and betrayal among the many readers – especially older readers – who disagreed with her. And it was just this faculty for offending respectable opinion that, from the outset, was an important part of her appeal for those who welcomed her pronouncements. She was admired not only for what she said but for the pain, shock, and disarray she caused in saying it ... . She made criticism a medium of intellectual scandal, and this won her instant celebrity in the world where ideas are absorbed into fashions (88).

Grenier finds in her work a consistent hatred for American society, and argues that

even though Sontag is widely considered a home-grown American intellectual, she in fact represents a survival of our condition as a colonial culture. While her feeling toward the United States has rarely risen above loathing, her consistent attitude toward the tastes and prejudices of the continental avant-garde has been, in a word, servile (16).

Parini, reviewing Sontag's work up to 1982, has almost nothing good to say. "Where Sontag is correct, she is often sophomoric; where she is wrong, she is irritating and, frequently, pretentious." He labels her rhetoric "all fizz, without intellectual rigor or moral force" (416), and attacks her for wanting to sit on both sides of the fence: to be an ethically committed, political "radical" and to be a coolly amoral, Wildean aesthete (418).

Walter Kendrick's critique is the most interesting. In a 1980 review, he praises "the literary portraits" of Artaud, Benjamin and Canetti in *Under the*

Sign of Saturn as occasional essays – "the form in which Sontag ... still does her best work" – and calls Sontag "for two decades the foremost interpreter of the European avant-garde to American readers" (44). He identifies her weaknesses as her fondness for platitudinous aphorisms, her inability to sustain an extended argument, and her sacrifice of sense to euphony of phrase. He then argues that Sontag, despite her reputation as cutting-edge interpreter of the new, "sees modernity, as it were, from behind, judging it always in terms of the nineteenth century," and that despite her reputation as a writer heavily influenced by Continental authors, such influences are "red herrings, excrescences on a body of work that belongs squarely in the mainstram of the Anglo-American tradition of the genteel essay," which I think is exactly right. Kendrick calls her "our greatest living Victorian writer" (46), an observation that is exaggerated only slightly.

Two years later, however, he is much harsher. He sees Sontag's talent "confined to the fashioning of memorable phrases and elegant sentences" and her thought limited to "esthetic impressionism":

Sontag's eminence in American letters is disproportionate to the quality of her thought; she perpetuates a tradition of philosphical naivete that has always kept America subservient to Europe and that surely should have run its course by now ... [Her] constant devotion to the Anglo-American tradition of genteel literary discourse has surely outmoded her. She seems to know nothing of semiotics, deconstruction, the reinterpretation of Freud, Nietzsche, Hegel and Marx – the true leading edge of the European intelligentsia ... [She is] an unexpectedly conservative, philosophically retrograde writer whose primary function has always been domestication. (405-406)

The most recent Sontag criticism echoes the complaints of the earliest. In 1989 Andrew Ross labeled Sontag a "pop intellectual" who has not "retained any lasting theoretical respect of the sort that is still accorded to the older liberal intelligentsia" (114), while Joseph Sobran dismissed her work as "dazzling on a first reading, but slightly silly on a second" (49).

The most recent Sontag praise similarly echoes the plaudits of the '60s. In 1988 *Time* called her "a crucial guide to the intentions of the avant-garde" (Lacayo 86), while *Esquire* in 1990 named her "America's best-known philosopher and literary critic" (D'Antonio 131), despite the fact that she is neither philosopher nor literary critic as those terms are usually understood, and that she has scarcely written about the contemporary avant-garde since the early 1970s. Her strongest recent defenders have been Cary Nelson and Elizabeth Bruss. Nelson admires her interest in the difficult, and accurately notes the irony of "her reputation as an enthusiast for works [camp, pornography] toward which she actually expresses considerable ambivalence" (709). He sees the relative lack of overt quotation or extended explication of specific passages as characteristic of Sontag's antagonism toward "the solemn, patronizing, and finally defensive explication that characterizes much academic criticism" (716), an antagonism Nelson admires because it also enables the writer to utilize and explore her own experience of her subject.

Elizabeth Bruss is probably Sontag's finest critic, and her *Beautiful Theories* the best introduction to Sontag's work. Bruss argues that Sontag's strength – the elegant aphorisms, the keen apercus, easily remembered and repeated by her readers – is also a weakness, since it invites inaccuracy and counterargument. Sontag's is a style whose concomitants are "controversy, dissension, cries of pain and outrage" (222). To an extent, such dissension is justified, as I have tried to indicate, but Bruss is correct when she suggests that some of it emerges from an intellectual climate of "increasingly narrow academic specialization" which judges any generalist as pretentious, "speculating beyond her professional competence" (138) if she impinges upon the specialist's ground. Sontag makes the same point in her essay on Paul Goodman: "There is a terrible, mean American resentment toward a writer who tries to do many things" (*Saturn* 7). Bruss is also unfortunately correct when she claims to detect "a vein of misogyny in Sontag criticism" (227) – this is painfully evident in, for example, Louis Rubin's essay.

How are we to judge Sontag as a cultural critic in 1991? Her fiction and her political writing have not aged well, and she has attempted no systematic critique of the general culture. When she claims that "all of my essays, without exception, are attempts to ask what it means to be modern, to delineate the modern sensiblity from as many different angles as possible" (Copeland 84), we must conclude that her delineation of that "sensibility" is idiosyncratic and grossly incomplete. Nonetheless, she remains one of our more interesting essayists because she works so consistently against the grain of prevailing opinion. She said in 1975 that "the most interesting ideas are heresies," and "the only intelligence worth defending is critical, dialectical, skeptical, desimplifying" (*Reader* 346)) – typically exaggerated, but possessed of a truth which her best work embodies. In 1978 she told the New York *Times* (January 39): "For me, writing is a way of paying as much attention as possible" (16). At her strongest, Sontag pays attention to what the rest of us ignore or take for granted in our increasingly crowded quotidian world: why do we use metaphors to talk about disease? What does photography's popularity tell us about ourselves? She provokes us into rethinking the interaction between the formal, the historical and the ethical dimensions of the aesthetic, and challenges our ignorance of literary/cinematic work outside the Anglo-American world. On the other hand, she fails to develop many of her provocative assertions, and never examines the most interesting inconsistencies in her thinking. Hers is a truly singular voice within contemporary cultural criticism, and she is one of the few important intellectual generalists America has produced, yet her voice has remained at the edges of the intellectual stage – impossible to ignore, but rarely entirely persuasive.

Works Cited

Bellamy, Joe David, *The New Fiction: Interviews with Contemporary American Writers.* Chicago: U of Illinois P, 1974.

Branham, Robert, "Speaking Itself: Susan Sontag's Town Hall Address." *The Quarterly Journal of Speech* 75.3 (August 1989): 259-76.

Brooke-Rose, Christine, "Eximplosions." *Genre* 14.1 (Spring 1981): 9-21.

Bruss, Elizabeth, *Beautiful Theories: The Spectacle of Discourse in Contemporary Criticism.* Baltimore: Johns Hopkins UP, 1982.

Copeland, Roger, "The Habits of Consciousness." *Commonweal* 108.3 (February 13, 1981): 83-87.

Cott, Jonathan, "Interview." *Rolling Stone* (October 4, 1979): 46-53.

D'Antonio, Michael, "Little David, Happy at Last." *Esquire* (March 1990): 131.

DeMott, Benjamin, "Lady on the Scene." *New York Times Book Review* (January 23, 1966): 5, 32.

Elliott, George P., "High Prophetess of High Fashion." *The Times Literary Supplement* (March 17, 1978): 304.

Gass, William, "A Different Kind of Art." *New York Times Book Review* (December 18, 1977): 7, 30-31.

Gilman, Richard, "Susan Sontag and the Question of the New." *The New Republic* 160 (May 3, 1969): 23-26, 28.

Grenier, Richard, "The Conversion of Susan Sontag." *The New Republic* 186 (April 14, 1982): 15-19.

Heilbrun, Carolyn, "Speaking of Susan Sontag." *New York Times Book Reviews* (August 27, 1967): 2, 30.

Ignatieff, Michael, "AIDS and Its Metaphors." *The New Republic* 199.28 (26 December 1988): 29.

Jacoby, Russell, *The Last Intellectuals.* New York: Basic Books, 1987.

Kavolis, Vytautas, "The Social Psychology of Avant-garde Cultures." *Studies in the Twentieth Century* 6 (Fall 1970): 13-34.

Kendrick, Walter, "Eminent Victorian." *The Village Voice* 25.42 (October 15-21, 1980): 44-46.

– "In a Gulf of Her Own." *The Nation* 235.13 (October 23, 1982): 404-406.

Kramer, Hilton, "The Pasionaria of Style." *The Atlantic* 250.3 (September 1982): 90-91.

Lacayo, Richard, "Stand Aside, Sisyphus." *Time* (October 24, 1988): 86.

Mano, D. Keith. "The Strange Agony of Susan Sontag." *National Review* 34.7 (April 16, 1982): 439-40.

Marx, Leo, "Susan Sontag's 'New Left' Pastoral." *Tri-Quarterly* 23-24 (Winter-Spring 1972): 552-75.

Nelson, Cary, "Soliciting Self-Knowledge: The Rhetoric of Susan Sontag's Criticism." *Critical Inquiry* (Summer 1980).

Ostriker, Alicia. "Against Interpretation." *Commentary* 41 (June 1966): 83-84.

Parini, Jay, "Reading the Readers." *The Hudson Review* 36.2 (Summer 1983): 415-18.

Phillips, William, "Radical Styles." *Partisan Review* 36 (1969): 388-400.

Ross, Andrew. *No Respect: Intellectuals and Popular Culture*. New York: Routledge, 1989.

Rubin, Louis, "Susan Sontag and the Camp Followers." *Sewanee Review* 82 (Summer 1974): 503-510.

Samuels, Charles, "Contra Sontag." *The Nation* 202 (February 21, 1966): 219-21.

Sayres, Sohnya, ed. *The Sixties Without Apology*. Minneapolis: U of Minnesota P, 1984.

Shaw, Peter, "The Incident." *Encounter* 58-59 (June-July 1982): 38-40.

Simmons, Charles, "Sontag Talking." *New York Times Book Review* (Dezember 18, 1977): 7, 31, 33.

Sobran, Joseph, "AIDS and Its Metaphors." *National Review* 41.3 (February 24, 1989): 48.

Stange, Maren. "Susan Sontag: Recycling the Self." *New Boston Review* (Spring 1978): 12.

Stern, Daniel, "Life Becomes a Dream." *New York Times Book Review* (September 8, 1963): 5.

Tanner, Tony, "Space Odyssey." *Partisan Review* 35 (Summer 1968): 446-51.

Toback, James, "Whatever You'd Like Susan Sontag to Think, She Doesn't." *Esquire* 70 (July 1968): 114-16.

Updike, John, *Picked-Up Pieces*. New York: Knopf, 1975.

Velde, Paul, "The Sontag Sensibility." *Commonweal* 84 (June 24, 1966): 390-92.

Vidal, Gore. *Reflections upon a Sinking Ship*. Boston: Little, Brown, 1969.

Wain, John, "Song of Myself." *The New Republic* 149 (September 21, 1963): 26-27, 30.

The Works of Susan Sontag

The Benefactor. New York: Farrar, Straus, 1963; London:Eyre & Spottiswoode, 1964.

"The Role of the Writer as Critic." *Publishers Weekly* 189 (March 28, 1966): 36-37.

"The Avant-Garde and Contemporary Literature." *Wilson Library Bulletin* 40 (June 1966): 930-32, 937-40.

Against Interpretation. New York: Farrar, Straus, 1967; London: Secker & Warburg, 1968.

Death Kit. New York: Farrar, Straus, 1967; London: Secker & Warburg, 1968.

"Some Thoughts on the Right Way (for us) to Love the Cuban Revolution." *Ramparts* 7 (April 1969): 6, 10, 14, 16, 18-19.

"Letter from Sweden." *Ramparts* 8 (July 1969): 23-38.

Styles of Radical Will. New York: Farrar, Straus, 1969; London: Secker & Warburg, 1969.

Duet for Cannibals. Sandrew Film & Theater AB (Sweden), 1969. New York: Farrar, Straus, 1970; London: Allen Lane, 1970.

"Posters: advertisement, art, political artifact, commodity." In Dugald Stermer's *The Art of Revolution: Castro's Cuba, 1959-1970*. New York: McGraw-Hill, 1970; Köln: Kiepenheuer & Witsch, 1970.

Brother Carl. Svenska Filminstitutet (Sweden), 1971; New Yorker Films, 1972; New York: Farrar, Straus: 1974.

"The Third World of Women." *Partisan Review* 40 (Summer 1973): 180-206.

Promised Lands. New Yorker Films, 1974.

"How It Feels to Make a Movie." *Vogue* 164 (July 1974): 84, 118-19.

"Francis Bacon: About Being in Pain." *Vogue* 165 (March 1975): 136-37.

"Feminism and Fascism: An Exchange." *The New York Review of Books* (March 20, 1975): 31-32.

"Woman's Beauty: Put-Down or Power Source?" *Vogue* 165 (April 1975): 118-119.

"Beauty: How Will It Change Next?" *Vogue* 165 (May 1975): 116-17, 174.

"Can Rights Be Equal?" *Vogue* 166 (July 1976): 100-101.

On Photography. New York: Farrar, Straus, 1977; republ. as *Susan Sontag on Photography.* London: Allen Lane, 1978.

I, Etcetera. New York: Farrar, Straus, 1978; London: Gollancz, 1979.

Illness as Metaphor. New York: Farrar, Straus, 1978; London: Allen Lane, 1979.

Under the Sign of Saturn. New York: Farrar, Straus, 1980.

A Susan Sontag Reader. New York: Farrar, Straus, 1981.

"Communism and the Left." *The Nation* (February 27, 1982): 229-31.

"Description (of a Description)." *Antaeus* 53 (Autumn 1984): 19-21.

"The Way We Live Now." *The New Yorker* 62 (24 November 1986): 42-51.

"Pilgrimage." *The New Yorker* (Dezember 21, 1987): 38-54.

"Foreword" to *Italy: One Hundred Years of Photography*, ed. Cesare Colombo. Florence, Italy: Fratelli Alinari, 1988.

AIDS and Its Metaphors. New York: Farrar, Straus, 1988.

Ingrid Kerkhoff

Fredric R. Jameson

(1934-)

> ... anyone who believes that the profit motive and the logic of capital accumulation are not the fundamental laws of this world [...] such a person is living in an alternative universe ...
>
> Fredric Jameson[1]

> We must [...] begin to think of cultural politics in terms of a struggle for space. We are no longer thinking in the old categories of critical distance.
>
> Fredric Jameson[2]

Fredric Jameson is without dispute the leading Marxist critic and literary theorist of his generation in North America. He earned this reputation not only because he introduced European ideas into the North American cultural debate – structuralist as well as Marxist –, but because he also sustained a resolutely Marxist perspective in the face of subsequent challenges.

Jameson's work over the last three decades shifted its focal point from analysis of "literature" as defined by dominant academic canons to cultural production in a wider sense, including architecture, painting, film, and other cultural products (or "texts") of consumer capitalism. Today, Jameson is at the center of a debate on postmodernism and cultural politics. In conceptualizing postmodernism as the "logic of late capitalism" Jameson rearticulates Marxism, introducing, defending and developing a body of theory in a situation which (in the 50s and again in the 80s) was ignorant of and/or hostile to that radical tradition of which Marxism, in any version, is a key component.

Jameson's intervention in the postmodernist debate was, at first, surprising. He was a Professor of French and Comparative Literature at the University of California, San Diego (1967-1976) and then moved to the Yale University French Department (1976-1983). In 1981 his book *The Political Unconscious* had established him as one of the foremost Marxist *literary* critics of our era. Why did a critic like Jameson get involved in the debate on postmodernism? The purpose of this essay is to present Fredric Jameson as a theoretically adventurous Marxist critic of late capitalist/postmodernist culture, following his trajectory in particular from the moment he crosses the threshold to our contemporary culture. The term culture, with Jameson, is extended to include wider cultural production not just in the arts, but also in the spheres of science, law, morality.

Debates about Marxism often turn out to be sham disputes where each party involved means something else by the terms at issue. As the new types of Marxism offer no ready-made explanations and programs of action but compel us creatively to think through the current historical situation in the light of classical Marxist theory and practice, it is wise to approach Jameson's edifice of thought by discussing the authorities which put him on the way to developing his theory of an expanded Marxism.

Jameson's line of thought is not easy to follow. There seems to be much jargon. On the other hand, from a Marxist viewpoint, the truth about social relations and about the place of culture in them does not lie on the surface of everyday life; it is structurally concealed by those phenomena generated by the presence of commodities around us. And if commodities are the source of this opacity (or obfuscation) of daily life, it will get worse rather than better as consumer society spreads world-wide. This means that any true account of the mechanisms at work *behind* daily life will look "unnatural" and untrue to "common sense", and that one of the strategies of such an account will have to be the destruction of our habits of reified perception. A Marxist description of our social and cultural life is therefore always reflexive and self-conscious, as well as hermeneutic, because part of the point to be made by such writing is precisely our own conscious or unconscious resistance to it.[3]

Fredric Jameson was born in Cleveland in 1934. When he launched into academic literary criticism, he was challenged by a heavy ideological mortgage. Under the impact of McCarthyism in the 50s, the Marxist tradition of the Thirties was reduced to such eminent figures as Michael Gold and journals like the *New Masses*, strongly influenced by Shdanovite prescriptions for a "socialist realism", which relied heavily on evaluating writers on the basis of their class background or an immediate class-political alliance.[4] This version of Marxism became a target against which later bourgeois literary criticism could score easy victories, conveniently equating Marxism with Stalinist policies. It was therefore not unexpected that Jameson, as a young literary critic, was radicalized by his studies in Europe during the 50s.

Marxist theory and politics were never eradicated as completely from post-war European society as they were in the U.S. Through Jameson's appropriations, American Marxist literary theory was influenced by developments in the French, German, and English traditions. Lukácsian theory had a profound influence on Marxism associated with the Frankfurt School. (Adorno, Horkheimer, Walter Benjamin, Herbert Marcuse) The Frankfurt School's approach emphasized late capitalism's tendency to swallow cultural production within

the general process of commodification, thereby reifying and degrading modernist longings for a more liberated social existence to be expressed through
art. Roland Barthes, Michael Foucault, Jacques Derrida and French "poststructuralism" became progressively insistent on questioning the epistemological presuppositions of the literary text and literary criticism. Within the
British tradition Raymond Williams's move from a radical humanist criticism
to a more rigorous Marxist theory of ideology and Terry Eagleton's challenge
of Althusserian initiatives in literary theory prepared the way for a more politicized understanding of culture.

Jameson's first object of philosophical and literary enthusiasm was Sartre.
Scholars in Yale like Henri Peyre, Jacques Guicharnaud and Kenneth Douglas put him on this trail which is still important for him.[5] Wanting to avoid
the reductionist features of "vulgar Marxism" and rejecting orthodox interpretations of the basis/superstructure metaphor in the context of the conformism
of the 1950s, Jameson's choice of Sartre as his philosophical mentor might be
seen as an attempt to create a position for himself among the conformist currents of his epoch. Sartre was the most influential intellectual of the period:

I came to Marxism through Sartre and not against him; and not even through the later,
Marx-oriented works such as the *Critique*, but very precisely through the 'classical' existential texts of the immediate post-war period [...]. For Americans like myself, Sartre represented *the* model of the political intellectual, one of the few role models we had, but a
sufficient one.[6]

Sartre was thus taken by Jameson as a paradigm of the non-conformist,
critical intellectual. There was, however, a ban of silence that hung over Sartre's work in France during the "structuralist" period. The structuralists' turning away from Sartre was part of a more general repudiation of phenomenology, with its emphasis on lived experience and on individual consciousness
– in Sartre's case the emphasis on a Cartesian *cogito*, and the stubborn and
symptomatic return to an individual biographical framework characteristic of
the existential psychoanalysis, but also in the *Critique*, and most dramatically
in the 3000-page work on Flaubert which was to become Sartre's testament:

The Sartre offered to Americans after the War who – along with Camus – generated
low-level, homegrown forms of existentialism (Mailer, Bellow, an enormous volume of
literary-critical rambling about "alienation," and the "absurd"), was a Sartre thoroughly
laundered of all political reference and consequences: the Sartre of "freedom" and
"choice", of *angoisse*. All the numerous and often excellent manuals offered to the American public on Sartre's "existentialism" did not, for a single minute, allow the reader to
guess that, from the occupation to the Lipp strike, Sartre's every thought and every publication was consistently, profoundly, and even obsessively, political.[7]

In 1956-57 Jameson had a Fulbright grant and he studied a first semester in Munich and a second semester in Berlin. His German made it possible for him to assimilate writers like Hegel, Marx, Benjamin and Adorno. Very important for him was going over to East Berlin in those days and buying up the big blue volumes of Lukács. It was in Germany that he first began to learn the essentials of certain types of Marxism. Lukács's work on realism and on the historical novel strongly influenced Jameson's way of seeing and situating literature and, although he never accepted Lukács's polemics against modernism, he appropriated Lukácsian categories, in particular that of "reification"[8], to describe the fate of culture in contemporary capitalism. What was more, Lukács's discussion of individual works always presupposed a synthesis between analysis and evaluation:

(T)here is never found in these pages [i.e. the *Historical Novel*] the dissociation between a neutral, formal (or semiotic) dissection of the text and a manifesto-like defense of the interest, excitement, or "greatness" of this or that cultural tendency – something too frequent in bourgeois criticism, and, indeed, for most of us, a situation or dilemma within which we find ourselves obliged to work, however much we may deplore the limits and distortions it imposes on us.[9]

Jameson reconstructed Lukács's career as

... an exemplary evolution of an intellectual formed in the great middle-class philosophical traditions of Central Europe, and particularly of Germany (and an upper-class intellectual, a banker's son and a characteristic specimen of the Jewish aristocracy of the Austro-Hungarian Empire in its prewar heyday) toward a political commitment, first determined by revulsion against World War I, and then by an intellectual and emotional commitment to Marxism and the ideas of the Soviet revolution in its early period.[10]

Jameson started discarding misconceptions and stereotypes about the historical figure of Lukács whom he considers *the* central philosopher of twentieth century European socialist and communist movements. For Jameson, Lukács's great work, *History and Class Consciousness* (1923), virtually invents a Marxist philosophy. What must be understood, Jameson argues, especially by those for whom Lukács's polemic against Bertolt Brecht seems to mark the former as a traditionalist and also as a representative of some officiel Soviet cultural policy, is that the aesthetic works written and published during this period are all *coded* works. They are not, as Jameson tells us

the defense of a Shdanovite 'socialist realism' by a philosopher, who, in capitulation, was content to become a party hack: They are rather explicit *critiques* of precisely that official Stalinist aesthetic of socialist realism which for obvious reasons of prudence and survival are in Lukács's work designated by the term of *naturalism*. These books, then, involve a dual public: For the West, they are historical discussions of nineteenth century literature which can stand on their own genuine merits as cultural history and analysis. To the East, they are coded interventions into a very real and urgent, dangerous zone which was that of culture and cultural revolution in a post-revolutionary 'socialist' society.[11]

The third authority on which Jameson based his edifice was "Althusserianism" which had an important historical function. Althusserianism improved the "crisis in Marxist theory" through a reassertion of continuity between orthodox Marxist organisations, especially the PCF and the innocence of pure Marxist theory. Aligned to the determinist model of the economy of material progress, these organizations were unable to deal with the new contradictions of advanced capitalism, espcially with regard to culture. Althusser's attempt to rethink Marxism (*Reading Capital*) incorporated developments in psychoanalysis which were considered to promote explanations in areas where orthodox Marxist theory had hitherto been less articulate.[12] The fact that Althusser's approach to the basis/superstructure metaphor soon became the target of a most vehement criticism[13] should not conceal that within the historical context Althusser served the important function of qualifying – in Jameson's work – aspects of Lukács and the Hegelian-Marxist tradition.[14] Althusser had denounced a version of Marxist humanism that was dominant in contemporary mainstream cultural criticism by showing that the early Marx was still anthropologist.[15] In the West, humanist Marxism had lost attraction and it was rather the middle Marx of the *Grundrisse* which had moved into that space.

Best[16] calls Jean-Paul Sartre, Georg Lukács and Louis Althusser Jameson's "Marxist triumvirate". Inspired by that rather polemical remark of Terry Eagleton's who once called Jameson a "shamelessly unreconstructed Hegelian Marxist"[17], Best discussed which of the three authorities Jameson utilized at which step of his itinerary to relativize the other. A list of influences on Jameson's thought should not, however, exclude Lévi-Strauss. Structuralism allowed us – as Jameson phrased it – to see messages at work in cultural objects that were not visible before and which cut across the problem of hidden meanings in a new way. Lévi-Strauss here was probably more important than anyone else.[18] In *The Prison-House of Language* (1972) Jameson offers a sympathetic Marxist critique of the most influential structuralist and formalist academic theories, including those of the French structuralists (Roland Barthes, Claude Lévi-Strauss, J. A. Greimas[19]) and the Russian formalists (Mikhail Bakhtin). He argues that Marxism provides the essential historical dimension missing in structuralist and formalist analyses. It is with this background of influences and inspirations that Jameson was to present, years later (with James H. Kavanaugh), his concept of ideology to the *Left Academy* anthology:

Ideology, then, is not for Marxism just a set of ideas with some relatively explicit political content; it is a system of representations, perceptions, *and* ideas through which people imagine and experience as well as think about their relations to, and their place within, a given socio-economic mode of production and its set of class relations. Ideology is the transformative reflection of the social whole that registers unconsciously as well as consciously, projecting imaginary resolutions of irreconcilable social contradictions, depicting the political and social effects of specific historical actions as the inevitable results of "human nature" or "natural" economic laws. Ideologies are produced in practises, and in modern societies, artistic and literary practises [...] are privileged mechanisms for adjusting or disrupting social subjects' implicit ideological visions of self and social order.[20]

Jameson started his career as a literary critic highly interested in modernism[21] as a literary movement. From a culturally more comprehensive point of view, modernism can be most adequately understood in terms of an intensified commodity production whose all-informing structural influence on mass culture has only lately emerged. For modernism the omnipresence of the commodity form determined a reactive stance, so that modernism conceived its formal vocation to be the resistance to commodity form.[22] There is, however, an important difference between Jameson's stance and the valorization of modernism by the Frankfurt School (or later, by *Tel Quel*).

The Political Unconscious (1981), a collection of earlier essays with an introduction and a postscript, announces its project by way of its subtitle. It had been long prepared.[23] Following Lévi-Strauss, Jameson sees the narrative as a "socially symbolic act," where social conflicts and contradictions are given a pseudo-resolution in an aesthetic form. This process is broadly defined as ideology, but Jameson redefines ideology so that it refers not simply to the more traditional "false consciousness", but also includes a more positive Blochian perspective that seeks to uncover a transhistorical utopian longing for an unalienated social life.[24] As all literary texts are inscribed with the imprints of their social and historical existence, they can be critically en-(rather than de-)coded in a hermeneutical operation which is likely to uncover their multi-dimensional "political unconscious."[25] For Jameson, Marxism is the only discourse which can reveal the full scope of historical development of discourses in their material reality. Therefore a Marxist critique becomes the "hermeneutical epicenter of all possible historiography, social and cultural theory and literary criticism."[26] His most audacious phrases include such statements as "Marxist critical insights serve as an ultimate semantic precondition for the intelligibility of literary and cultural texts,"[27] or Marxism functions as the "untranscendable horizon" that subsumes even the most disparate critical methods "assigning them an undoubted sectorial validity within itself, and thus at once canceling and preservating them."[28] Jameson takes pains not to devalorize other critical approaches like psychoanalysis, structuralism, myth-criticism, close reading etc.: They are integrated in terms of ancillary instruments implementing "the semantic richness" of Marxist literary criticism. Within this hermeneutical framework "interpretation is construed as an essentially allegorical act, which consists in re-writing a given text in terms of a particular interpretive master code."[29]

In establishing his theoretical and methodological framework Jameson makes use of a both fascinating and frustrating eclecticism of references. His work proceeds more in terms of digressions and detours than in the straightforward way of linear thinking, incorporating such disparate critical codes as Greimas's structural paradigms, Lévi-Strauss's reading of collective myth, Frye's anatomy of criticism, Lukács's theory of the novel, neo-Freudian psychoanalysis (Lacan[30]) etc., only to name a few. However, from the retrospective the contours of his interpretive project have become clear.

PU delineates a procedure, which – step by step – uncovers the ideological information of a given text. First, the internal logic of a text must be exhausted. Then the specific problematic – its determinants – must submit to a historical reading. There are various interrelating levels to be kept in mind. As far as modernist literature is concerned, there is first the basic contradiction between the discourses of the bourgeoisie and those of the proletariat, the narratives of the bourgeoisie representing the dominant cultural practice against which the narratives of the proletariat would be opposed in a "contrary" relationship. On a second level the petty bourgeoisie would oppose the revolutionary vanguard. An ideological analysis would therefore exhaust the bourgeois logic by highlighting the repression of revolution as a prerequisite for bourgeois dominance. Within this basic class structure special emphasis is given to the stances of the petty bourgeoisie in relation to those of the political vanguard.

Best sees one of the central moves of *PU* "to defend the importance of the diacritic narrative against a hasty Althusserian dismissal of the narrative as a reductive device which succumbs to an idealistic logic of humanism, historicities and expressive causality."[31] Jameson argues that history is constituted as a type of allegorical form which can only be interpreted textually through a (Lukácsian) narrative.[32] History (with a capital H) is for him, at this stage, "a single great collective story" and every rejection of a master discourse and/or allegory tends to block a critical reading of the "political unconscious" as buried in literary texts. *Critical* narratives[33] make connections and contextualize literary devices within a comprehensive historical storytelling framework. *PU* thus revalidates the critical "narrative" which was long discredited with literary scholars. Jameson restores its favorite place within cultural tradition. In the *critical* narratives of *PU*, he tries to grasp the ways in which economics and social class affect the form and content of narrative paradigms of literary production. He draws attention to the mediations between stages of capitalist development, forms of bourgeois subjectivity, and literary genres and styles. These mediations should not be understood as mere "homologies", but rather as "transcoding" mechanisms, which – reconstructed – reveal insights into the complex relationship between the causes and effects of cultural work. *PU* includes detailed readings of Balzac, Gissing, and Conrad. He takes the novels of Conrad, e.g., as providing key articulations of the intensifying fragmentation of the individual consciousness in an age of growing commodification. Conrad's novels are read by Jameson as articulations of the fear of *Otherness* in Third World cultures during the Age of Imperialism. The vivid perceptual and acoustic elements of aestheticizing modernism are explained as compensatory responses to the reification and fragmentation of life under capitalism, so that *PU* can thus also be taken as an allegory of the history of bourgeois subjectivity.[34] At times, the political strategies which exist as a sub-text to Jameson's critical narratives are highly ambivalent, as a closer look at the *Fables of Aggression*, his confrontation with the novels of Wyndham Lewis, might demonstrate.

Fables of Aggression, published in 1979, two years before *The Political Unconscious*, had already given a detailed impression of what such an ideological re-writing would be like.[35] By "fables of aggression" Jameson refers to Lewis's fictions (= "fables") which are read as representations of psychic aggressivity in narrative forms[36] revealing a particular facet of the ideology of modernism. The fascist aggression is here read as a result of tendencies within capitalism and bourgeois subjectivity. Jameson gives a surprisingly synthetic critique of Wyndham Lewis's prose as a kind of "machine" that demonstrates, in all its fury, the stark contradiction, libidinal power, and ultimate closure of fascist ideology, arguing that Lewis's integrity of style and his rejection of "high" or individualist modernism make his novels – as cultural documents – valuable even though Lewis is a fascist and a sexist.[37] For Jameson at this stage Lewis's style has the unusual ability to function as "the impersonal registering apparatus for forces which he means to record, beyond any whitewashings and liberal revisionism."[38] Jameson emphasized that Wyndham Lewis both accepted and rejected the generic conventions of modernism, and it was this very violation of conventions which made the novel valuable. Jameson was obviously convinced that only moments of *rupture*, of non-conformity and libidinal utopian vision were likely to reveal glimpses of a future society. Within his analytical framework "protofascism" refers to a complex of historical elements which emerge in Lewis's texts as a petty bourgeois and antifascist critique of capitalism. Lewis's psychic aggressivity is not identified in the man himself but in his texts, by means of the concept of libidinal apparatuses, a term from psychoanalysis which is here given historical and social potential.[39] In *FA* as in the essays on Balzac, Gissing and Conrad in *PU*, literature is understood not only as a way of organizing and controlling experience, but also as a process of narrative form-giving which is destined to fulfill a historical, ideological and even proto-political function. In disclosing these sub- and undertexts, Jameson reminds us, literary studies today can recover their urgency and sense of mission.[40]

In the following years Jameson became involved in highly theoretical contexts, developing his concept of postmodernism as the cultural logic of late capitalism.[41] This sudden shift asks for explanation. Douglas Kellner, however, in his thoughtful introduction to Jameson's discussion of postmodernism[42], demonstrated that this new topic was not alien to Jameson's earlier work, but rather the logical consequence of it. In *Marxism and Form* (1971) Kellner discovered what he called the "Jamesonian Urtext":

> ... for the most part, and particularly in the United States, the development of postindustrial monopoly has brought with it an increasing occultation of the class structure through techniques of mystification practised by the media and particularly by advertising in its enormous expansion since the onset of the Cold War. In existential terms, what this means is that our experience is no longer whole: we are no longer able to make any felt connections between the concerns of private life, as it follows its own course within the walls and confines of the affluent society, and the structural projections of the system in the outside world, in the form of neocolonialism, oppression, and the counterinsurgency warfare.[43]

At the end of *Marxism and Form*, Kellner argues, Jameson already presents a striking anticipation of his later theory:

> Nonetheless it seems to me that something more must be said in the face of such defenses of modernism as Susan Sontag's 'new sensibility' or Ihab Hassan's *Literature of Silence*. These theories reflect a coherent culture with which we are all familiar: John Cage's music, Andy Warhol's movies, novels by Burroughs, plays by Beckett, Godard, camp, Norman O. Brown's psychedelic experiences, and no critique can have any binding force which does not begin by submitting to the fascination of all these things as stylizations of reality.[44]

"Postmodernism; Or The Cultural Logic of Late Capitalism" (1984) presents one of the most illuminating analyses of postmodern culture and is probably the "most quoted, discussed, and debated article of the past decade."[45] Jameson does not make the mistake of condemning postmodern commercial culture wholesale as previous cultural critics on the Left had done. He recognized that the new kind of experience embodied in postmodernism is very powerful precisely because it has a great deal of content that seems to come as a solution to existential problems.[46] Jameson's approach in "PCL" is a totalizing one and corresponds to a process of abstraction which serves to defamiliarize from the immersion in the immediate and get a hold on history. Abstraction is here taken as an intellectual device to escape from the "blooming and buzzing" of immediacy, as a radical intervention in the "here and now".[47] Such a step is highly required, because there is, at present, a growing contradiction between the lived experience and structure, or between a phenomenological description of the life of an individual and the more properly structural model of the contradictions of existence of that experience. These two levels drift apart and begin to constitute themselves into that opposition the classical dialectic had described as *Wesen* and *Erscheinung*, essence and appearance, structure and lived experience.[48] The gap between daily experience and the structure of society inevitably leads to a situation in which, as Jameson suggests, we can say that "if the individual experience is authentic, then it cannot be true; and that if a scientific or cognitive model of the same content is true, then it escapes individual experience."[49] Jameson offers a fascinating description of a street scenario in San Francisco to show in which way personal perceptions intermingle with structural phenomena of life in a modern metropolis.

For Jameson the concept of postmodernism suggests two connected things: that we are at a new and different stage of capital, which gave rise to a number of significant cultural modifications, e.g. the end of the avant-garde, the end of the great *auteur* or genius, the disappearance of the utopian impulse of modernism etc. The concept refers to a social formation which has been alternately called "media society", the "society of the spectacle" (Guy Debord), consumer society, the "bureaucratic society of controlled consumption" (Henri Lefèbvre) or "postindustrial society" (Daniel Bell). In the early 1980s the concept of postmodernism was not widely accepted or even understood, partly because of the unfamiliarity of works it covered: from the poetry of John Ashbery to the pop buildings and decorated sheds celebrated by Robert Venturi in his manifesto *Learning from Las Vegas*, Andy Warhol and pop art, the moment of John Cage in music, but also the later synthesis of classical and popular styles found in composers like Philip Glass and Terry Riley and also punk and new-wave rock with groups like the Clash, the Talking Heads and the Gang of Four; in film, everything that comes out of Godard, including the contemporary vanguard film and video, contemporary novels, the work of William Burroughs, Thomas Pynchon and Ishmael Reed.[50]

Jameson's argument about postmodernism has two levels: on the one hand it is an inventory of constitutive features of postmodern culture, and on the other it is an account of a vaster reality which these features are taken to express. His objective was to create a mediating concept, to construct a model which can be articulated in, and descriptive of, a whole series of cultural phenomena. This unity or sytem is then placed in relation to the infrastructural reality of late capitalism.[51] The intention was a positive description, not in any sense one of value (so that postmodernism would then be "better" or "less good" than modernism) but in order to grasp postmodernism as a new cultural logic in its own right, as something more than a reaction.

Jameson's theoretical framework to articulate the moments of the postmodern provides a synthesis of Hegelian-Marxian notions of totality, Mandel's theory of the stages of capitalism, and concepts of the New French Theory such as the "simulacrum" (Deleuze and Baudrillard), "the schizophrenic" (Lacan and Deleuze/Guattari) and "the sublime" (Lyotard). Postmodern culture is essentially distinguished by the effacement of the older (essentially high-modernist) distinction between high culture and the so-called mass or commercial culture, and the emergence of new kinds of texts infused with the forms, categories and contents of that very culture industry so passionately denounced by the ideologies of the modern, from the American New Criticism all the way to Adorno and the Frankfurt School.[52]

Jameson's concept of postmodernism includes a social and political theory in terms of a world-wide disembodied yet increasingly total system of relationships and networks hidden beneath the appearance of daily life. Its "logic" is sensed in programming our outer and inner worlds, even to the point of colonizing our "unconscious." This existential sense of the total system is in itself unpresentable and is detectable only in its effects like an absent cause. Every theory of postmodernism, Jameson claims, contains an implicit periodization of history, and an "implicitly or explicitly political stance on the nature of multinational capitalism today."[53] Following Ernest Mandel's periodization in his book *Late Capitalism* (1975) Jameson states "that there have been three fundamental moments in capitalism, each one marking a dialectical expansion over the previous stage: These are market capitalism, the monopoly stage (or the stage of imperialism) and our own, wrongly called postindustrial, but what might better be termed multinational capital."[54] Jameson chose Mandel as theoretical model because Mandel, for the first time, theorized a third stage of capitalism from a reliable Marxian perspective. Jameson's own thoughts on postmodernism are therefore to be understood as an attempt to theorize the specific logic of cultural production on that third stage, and not as yet another disembodied culture critique or diagnosis of the spirit of the age.[55]

As far as creative work in the age of postmodernism is concerned, Jameson stresses its tendency toward the pastiche. Pastiche is a concept developed by Adorno to describe the recourse of Stravinsky, Joyce, and Thomas Mann to dead styles and artistic languages of the past as vehicles for new works. The pastiche, in Adorno's sense, must be radically distinguished from parody, which aims at ridiculing and discrediting styles which are still alive and influential. Parody involves a distance from a ready-made artistic instrument and technique. Such distance and safe vantage point to assess phenomena of daily life has disappeared with postmodernism.

The pastiche as mode of expression seems to have two fundamental determinations: The first is its subjectivism, the overemphasis and overevaluation of the uniqueness and individuality of style itself – the private mode of expression, the unique "world" of a given artist, the incomparable bodily and perceptual sensorium of this or that claimant for artistic attention. In our global media world, the price for artistic individuality has become, both for producers and consumers, increasingly onerous. The result, in the area of high culture, was the moment of pastiche in which energetic artists who lack both forms and content "canabalize the museum" and wear the mask of extinct mannerisms."[56] The canabalizing of historical styles is correlated to what Jameson calls a "waning of affect", which can be observed in postmodern artistic creation. Affect in the older sense of anxiety as it found its now traditional vehicle in Munch's *Scream*, in Kafka's nightmares or in classical existentialism has suddenly and unexpectedly disappeared.[57] According to Jameson postmodern painting, to quote an example, lacks not only visual, but also interpretive, historical and emotional depth. Anxiety, a primary constituent of modernist poetics, was, to Jameson, a hermeneutical emotion. It expressed an underlying nightmare state of the world, whereas the highs and lows of today's creative products imply no specific emotions. You can feel them on whatever occasion. They are, Jameson concludes, no longer cognitive.[58] At times Jameson speaks of the "hysterical sublime", or the "exhilaration of the gleaming surface." Artistic productions of the postmodern kind are what he calls "disposable texts." Rauschenberg would be a good example: "You go into a Rauschenberg show and experience the process done in very expert and inventive ways; when you leave, it's over." As a pastiche is defined in terms of a simulacrum for which there is no original pastiche art is a derived art which cannot escape the logic of postmodernism.

Since the 60s there has been a gradual and seemingly natural mediatization of North American society.[59] Cinema has become, as Jameson developed earlier on, "… the hegemonic formal expression of late capitalist society."[60] Therefore a Marxist critic cannot ignore this field of creative work.[61] The colonization of the new mediatic and informational phenomena by the Political Right led, by the end of the 60s, to a concentration of critical potential on Cinema Studies. Cinema Studies came of age as an academic subject when most of its closely allied fields – philosophy, literary studies and art history – fell under the thrall of European theories, Marxist and non-Marxist. Therefore new and potentially radical academic discourses deriving from feminist, psychoanalytic and Marxist theory moved swiftly to the center of the discipline, rather than remaining, as was the case in literary studies, marginal or repressed.[62] The majority of cultural critics within the universities, however, regarded this shift of interest from literature to film studies with its concomitant erosion of the distinction between high culture and mass culture as particularly threatening to intellectuals. These developments were, indeed, distressing for academic intellectuals, as Jameson concedes, because the academy always had a vested interest in preserving the realm of high or elite culture against the surrounding environment of "philistinism, of schlock and kitsch, of TV series and *Reader's Digest* culture, transmitting difficult and complex skills in reading, listening and seeing to its initiates."[63] Jameson seems to connect this resentment of the academy against media culture with the lack of self-reflectiveness regarding the tacit doxa and stereotypes of academy-oriented intellectual endeavor.

In order to illuminate the ideological workings of postmodern film Godard is a good example. The films of Godard seem to incorporate for him the logic inherent in the "cultural dominant" in a very pronounced way.[64] Godard favored montage as artistic device, which, reminiscent of Eisenstein, was originally associated with a subversive cultural practice. It is true that in Godard the dissecting process of visual representation is counterpoised to the homogeneity of the capitalist system. However, the formal device of montage is grafted onto an incompatible genre, that of classical character-centered narrative form. This discordance of structures and the way it is provisionally resolved, brings into relief the manner in which montage here functions as a symbolic resolution at the level of form.[65] Two contrary symbolic structures seem to vie for dominance in Godard's cinema: the rhetorical system of critique, conveyed through the technique of montage, and the narrative system, which consists of a conventional chain of actions channeled through an anthropomorphic center, a character. The erstwhile revolutionary aesthetic of montage (Eisenstein) which Godard appropriates and adapts and which specifically abjures narration of an individual protagonist, opting instead for a collective protagonist, has become part and parcel of the "cultural dominant." To paraphrase Fredric Jameson (with Burgoigne): The montage form continues to broadcast its original ideological signals, although the form has been emptied of its original content and converted to the transmission of an entirely different ideological message. Recentered as the pivot of discourse, the character-sytem once again functions as a form-generating center of the text. The refraction of the discourse through the characters' consciousness functions to naturalize the montage form and to bring it into accordance with the cultural dominant.

The artistic productions of postmodernism cannot be described in terms of a "false consciousness." In ideological analysis, the denunciation of works of art for embodying 'false consciousness' was possible only in a heterogeneous class situation, when the working classes were still a nation within the nation and did not consume bourgeois culture. Today, as these class differences are no longer secured by social isolation, and with a continuing process of massive democratic culturalization, there is no space in which the Left can be outside. Jameson seems to wish to encourage a critique which goes through postmodernism in a "homeopathic way": Poison is given in small doses as a temporary remedy. He seems to wish to undo postmodernism with the methods of postmodernism itself: "to work at dissolving the pastiche by using the instruments of the pastiche itself, to reconquer some genuine historical sense by using the instruments of what I have called the substitutes of history."[66] His essay on Syberberg and cultural revolution seems to indicate a direction in which this "homeopathic criticism" might work.

Had Syberberg not existed, he would have to have been invented, Jameson suggests. Syberberg, undertaking in his films a program of cultural revolution, shares some of the values and aims of his enemies on the Left. His aesthetic is a synthesis of Brecht and Wagner in a high-technology medium. Ever more specialized and self-conscious, he suddenly reinvents the role of the naive or "primitive" artist, organizing his vision of the filmic art of the future not around the virtuoso use of the most advanced techniques (as Coppola or Godard do, though in different ways) but rather around something like a return to the home movies. This improvisation effect is derived from the interview format of cinéma-vérité. In *Our Hitler*, which is at the center of Jameson's comment, there is something obscene about the Syberberg child (his daughter) who wanders through the seven hours of *Our Hitler* carrying dolls of the Nazi leaders and other playthings of the German past. Syberberg here demonstrates his conception of the self-effacing mission of the documentary artist. *Our Hitler* spreads a panoply of mythic images before us. Syberberg's philosophical mentor, Ernst Bloch, had suggested that it would be desirable to substitute a fairytale, populist Wagner for the epic-aristocratic one. Syberberg's method can be described, according to Jameson, as a forcible short-circuiting of all the wires in the political unconscious, as an attempt to purge the sedimented contents of collective fantasy and ideological representation by reconnecting its symbolic counters so outrageously that they de-reify themselves. According to Jameson de-reification is a major principle of counterhegemonical culture. Equally important, however, is the task of restoring a sense of historicity.

"Consumer society," "media society," the "society of the spectacle," "late capitalism" – whatever one wants to call this moment – is striking in its loss of a sense of historical pasts and historical futures. For Jameson this loss seems to be a far more pathological symptom of late capitalism than features like "narcissism"[67] or the loss of subjectivity. The concept of postmodernism suggests that the subject has lost his/her identity, his/her capacity to persist over time and organize his or her past and future. It is hard to imagine, Jameson concludes, how the cultural productions of such a subject could be anything but "heaps of fragments" and a practice of the random and the heterogeneous. If postmodernism precludes a loss of the historical past and the historical future, then attempts to "invent" pasts and futures become highly relevant for postmodern culture. Here Jameson sees a chance for literary authors and film directors to reinvent what has been lost.

The historical novel and/or film is not dead: It is alive and thriving as *American Graffiti*, *Ragtime*, and *The Color Purple* may illustrate. The majority of historical novels and films are based on problematical period concepts which usually correspond to no realities whatsoever. Whether they are formulated in terms of a generational logic, or by names of reigning monarchs or according to some other category or typological or classificatory system, the collective reality of the multitudinous lives encompassed by such terms is nonthinkable (or "non-totalizable," to use a current expression) and can never be described, characterized, labeled or conceptualized. What is particular about these attempts to retell and allegorize the past is, as Jameson warns us, their tendency towards the nostalgic. This does not exclude films with a pronounced Leftish stance. Even *Reds* is, for Jameson, a nostalgia film. What he considers as inauthentic about nostalgia films and nostalgia books is their cult of the glossy image, the wide angle-shots, the lavish indulgence on mostly unconnected details, the breath-taking expanses of sun-lit leaf-tracery, big-screen flower-bowls of an unimaginable intense delicacy of hue. These details in historical films seem, for Jameson, obscene, although he concedes that kitsch has to be taken into account as a proto-political act.[68] Yet the final result is not an art of liberation but an art that enthralls.

Whereas the literary or filmic reconstruction of the past – even with such powerful literary authors as Doctorow (*Ragtime*) – mainly remains nostalgia art, Jameson seems to favor Science Fiction as a way to cope with the historicity of the present. Historicity for him is neither a representation of the past nor a representation of the future (although its various forms use such representations): It can first and foremost be defined as a perception of the present as history, a representation which defamiliarizes us and allows us that distance from immediacy which we call historical.

Science Fiction as a historically new and original form offers for Jameson analogies with the emergence of the historical novel in the nineteenth century. To quote the corresponding paragraph:

(I)t seems interesting to explore the hypothesis that Science Fiction as a genre entertains a dialectical and structural relationship with the historical novel, a relationship of
kinship and inversion, all at once, of opposition and homology. [...] For if the historical
novel "corresponds" to the emergence of historicity, of a sense of history in its strong post-
eighteenth century sense, Science Fiction equally corresponds to the waning or blockage
of that historicity today, and particularly in our own time, in the postmodern era, to its crisis and paralysis, its enfeeblement and repression.[69]

For Jameson, the SF-work of Philip K. Dick is one of the most powerful
expressions of the society of "the spectacle and the pseudo-event", in which
"the image is the final form of commodity reification," as Guy Debord put it
in *The Society of the Spectacle*.[70] Dick, who became a cult figure among
French intellectuals[71], was long neglected by the English Departments in the
U.S., which Jameson relates to the fact that Science Fiction was long discarded as a less prestigious art. In postmodernism, however, art is set loose
from the autonomous sphere which once contained its impulse of play and
revolt and is integrated in every-day life beyond anything a utopian avant-
garde would wish.[72]

For Jameson, a mass-cultural sub-genre like SF has different and stricter
laws than so-called "high culture," so that it can sometimes express realities
and dimensions that escape higher literature. For Jameson, Dick emerged as
particularly sympathetic to transformations that America had undergone
under late capitalism. His interest in Dick's novels lies less in their overt
political statements than in what Jameson would describe as their "politics of
experience." The critical question to be asked in relation to Dick's novels is
that about the role of the subject: the decline of the "autonomous", "bourgeois", "centered" subject, variously characterized in terms of "one-dimensionality," "schizophrenization," and the "ecstasy of communication," a persistent
motif of cultural criticism since the 60s.[73] From a conservative point of view,
the "decentered subject" is one which is shaken by disruptions of desire,
which are compensated by renunciations in the realm of social or political
practice. From a postmodern vantage point this "decentered subject" is characterized by the states through which it passes (Deleuze/Guattari). Dick's
novels give in to schizophrenic processes. Their "founding experience" is the
delirious dissolution and the subsequent attempt at reconstruction on a new
basis. Dick's novels show that this delirium is inseparable from the logic of
late capitalist production itself. When Jameson talks about postmodernism as
a "cultural dominant" this doesn't exclude forms of resistance. He leaves a
space for oppositions or enclaves of resistance, all kinds of things not integrated into the global model but necessarily defined against it. In fact, the
whole point for undertaking this analysis was the idea that one would not be

able to measure the effectiveness of resistance unless one knows what the dominant forces were.[74]

The social movements of the Sixties reinvented the question of utopia. The fact that this interest was buried with the post-war economic boom was due to the fact that the "level of fantasy tolerance" was modified by a change in social relations. Jameson's comment:

In the windless closure of late capitalism it had come to seem increasingly futile and childish for people with a strong and particular repressive reality-and-performance-principle to imagine tinkering with what exists, let alone its thoroughgoing restructuration.[75]

However, with the new social movements of the 60s, the utopian impulse became painfully visible ("Freedom Now"). Consequently, the transition from the 60s to the 70s was a passage from spontaneous practice to renewed theoretical reflection with a new generation of literary utopias, the appearence of Skinner's *Walden Two*, Ursula LeGuin's *The Dispossessed*, Joana Russ's *The Female Man*, Ernest Callenbach's *Ecotopia*, Marge Piercy's *Women on the Edge of Time*, to name a few literary examples, along with the rediscovery and renewed study of the anticipatory "philosophy of the future" by Ernst Bloch. Why was this utopian upsurge of the 60s cooptable by the system? The answers Jameson offers embark on a discussion of a problematic of representation in language, or, to put it differently, linguistic referentiality.

What has become clearer today is, to follow Jameson's line of thought, that the demands for equality and justice, projected by the new social movements of the 60s, were not intrinsically subversive. Rather, the slogans of populism and the ideals of racial justice and sexual equality were already part and parcel of the Enlightenment tradition itself, inherent not only in a socialist denunciation of capitalism, but also and foremost in the bourgeois revolution against the *ancien regime*. For Jameson, the values of the Civil Rights movement and the women's movement were pre-eminently cooptable because they were already – as ideals – inscribed in the very ideology of capitalism itself. He attributes this lack of transparency to a loss of referentiality significant of the state of language under capitalism. As (late) capitalism becomes increasingly abstract and reified, language itself follows that course, throwing off the burden of referentiality and attaining a quasi self-referential status. Jameson restaged these insights in the form of a fairy tale:

Once upon a time – at the dawn of capitalism and middle-class society – there emerged something called the sign which seemed to entertain unproblematic relations with its referent. This initial heyday of the sign – the moment of literal or referential language or of the unproblematic claims of so-called scientific discourse – came into being because of the

corrosive dissolution of older forms of magical language by a force which I will call that
of reification, a force whose logic is one of ruthless separation and disjunction, of specialization and rationalization, of a Taylorising division of labour in all realms. Unfortunately
that force – which brought traditional reference into being – continued unremittingly,
being the very logic of capital itself. Thus this first moment of decoding or of realism cannot endure; by the dialectical reversal it then itself in turn becomes the object of the corrosive form of reification, which enters the realm of language to disjoin the sign from the
referent. Such a disjunction does not completely abolish the referent, or the objective
world, or reality, which still continues to entertain a feeble dwarf. But its great distance
from the sign now allows the latter to enter into a moment of autonomy, of a relatively
free-floating Utopian existence – as over against its former objects. This autonomy of culture, this semi-autonomy of language, is the moment of modernism, and of a realm of aesthetic which redoubles the world without being altogether of it, thereby winning a certain
negative or critical power, but also a certain otherworldly futility. Yet the force of reification, which was responsible for this moment, does not stop there either: in another stage,
heightened, a kind of reversal of quantity into quality, reification penetrates the sign itself,
and disjoins the signifier from the signified. Now reference and reality disappear altogether, and even meaning – the signified – is problematised: instead we are left with that
pure and random play of signifiers which we call postmodernism, and which no longer
produces monumental works of the modernist type, but ceaselessly reshuffles the fragments of preexistent texts, the building of blocks of older cultural and social production, in
some new and heightened bricolage: metabooks which cannibalize other books, metatexts
which collate bits of other texts.[76]

A Marxist position must therefore take into account the possibility that
these ideals are already part of the internal logic of the capitalist system,
which has a fundamental interest in social equality to a degree to which it
needs to transform as many of its subjects or its citizens into identical consumers interchangeable with everybody else. A Marxist position strives to dis-
entangle these ideals from their primary mode of representation which is cultural[77] and argues that the system is structurally unable to realize such ideals
even where it has an economic interest in doing so.[78] There is, for the Marxist critic, the necessity of a "constant reinvention of precautions against this
tendency which tradition calls perceptual reification."[79] In reconstructing the
utopian discourse of the 60s an honest Marxist project must meet the feminist
project. Here Jameson, as I read him, reassuringly calls for an alliance of progressive movements. Very interesting and worth discussing in this context is
therefore his statement on the pleasure principle as a radical weapon.

One of the main tenets of the 60s was to turn down the performance principle in favor of the pleasure principle (Marcuse). Later, Deleuze and Guattari
celebreated the consciousness of the ideal schizophrenic as the 'true hero of
desire.' Roland Barthes evoked the *plaisir du texte* as an inspirational quality.
With the Marxist hindsight of the 80s, however, the pleasure principle
became highly ambivalent, not only because it was exploited by the media, in

particular the commercial video market, but also because it included an unreconstructed anti-feminist bias. As far as its sexist component is concerned, Jameson points to Laura Mulvey's essay "Visual Pleasure and Narrative Cinema"[80] as one of the more influential statements. Her program – the destruction of pleasure as a radical weapon – is based on the theoretical identification of the filmic viewing pleasure with the symbolic expression of the male power in the 'right to look', a right whose ultimate object becomes the woman's body, or rather, the woman *as* body.

Something of the politics of Mulvey's article could still, as Jameson suggests, be argued in the older class terms; the right to look, the defense of sexual liberation, including pornography and the whole culture of the libidinal image as such – those would be slogans attractive to males, but symbolically marked (now in gender, rather than in class ways) for women as the practices of the other, of the oppressor, of the form of domination analogous to that of the enemy.[81] Jameson here objects to the current fashionable Left using this term as an omnibus slogan. If the value of 'pleasure' as a political slogan is not merely unattractive to working-class people but also to women, then its ideological effectiveness is a rather diminished one.[82] The utopian project involves the task of trying to imagine how a society without hierarchy, a society of free people, can possibly cohere. Historically, all forms of hierarchy have always been based ultimately on gender hierarchy and on the building block of the family unit, which makes it clear that this is the juncture between a feminist problematic and a Marxist one – not an antagonistic juncture, but – as Jameson tells us – a moment at which the feminist, the Marxist and the socialist projects meet.

Jameson's transition from a critic of postmodern experience to a theorist of a counterhegemonic postmodern cultural politics is signaled in "Cognitive Mapping" (1988), where he emphasizes the need for a new spatial reorientation.[83] The Left in the US (and elsewhere in Western societies) has – as Jameson reminds us – to begin by sorting out priorities, the overall project being the conquest of the legitimacy for a socialist discourse.[84] Here the faddish post-marxism and an honest expanded marxism divide. Faddish post-marxism includes the proposition that class no longer exists, a proposition that might be clarified by the simple distinction between class as an element in small scale models of society, class – consciousness as a cultural event, and class analysis as a mental operation.

Since the 60s, everybody has known that there is a socialist discourse. In TV serials there is always, as Jameson points out, a "radical." The radical, however, has become a social type, or – more accurately – a social stereotype. So while people know that a socialist discourse exists, it is not a legitimate discourse in Western societies. Thus, no one takes seriously the idea that socialism and the social reorganization it proposes is the answer to some of the vital problems with which postmodern societies are confronted today. Discourses of socialism are, in contemporary western societies, no realistic and serious alternatives for people. It is in the context of this general political project that Jameson's (more limited) aesthetic project finds a place.

"Cognitive mapping" derives from Darko Šuvin's emphasis on the cognitive function of art and aesthetics, Kevin Lynch's attempt to discover how people map urban space, and Althusser's theory of the "imaginary representation of the subject's relationship to his or her real conditions of existence." "Cognitive mapping" involves the task of individuals, artists, and theorists in providing orientation, a sense of time (history) and space (place) through theoretical models of how society in its particular as well as in its systemic moments is structured.

In "Periodizing the Sixties" (1984) Jameson anticipated the main tendencies of the 1980s:

> ... the 1980s will be characterized by an effort, on a world scale, to proletarianize all those unbound social forces which gave the 60s their energy, by an extension of class struggle, in other words, into the farthest reaches of the globe as well as the minute configurations of local institutions (such as the university system).[85]

Much of what Jameson prophesied has become fact. It remains, however, to be seen whether the oppressive realities of contemporary capitalist societies are producing a further proletarianization or whether, as Kellner put it, "the glitzy joys of its culture and consumerism will continue to entrap the majority of the underlying population in its massified and commodified pleasures and its simulated politics."[86] Here Jameson sees a vital chance for the honest Marxist intellectual.

Culture is a janus-headed concept. On the one hand it is the cry of the oppressed, but it is also (with Benjamin) a document of barbarism. Therefore a responsible (and usable) Marxist hermeneutics is necessarily a hermeneutics of suspicion, which seeks to demystify, reduce, explain away an illusion. On the other, it is – equally required – a hermeneutics of affirmation where there is a positive message to be deciphered and applied. The purpose of the Marxist theorist is to build as powerful and as all-embracing, systemic, and self-perpetuating as possible a model of capital and its workings as an "absent cause." Jameson calls for a radical culture which is to assume once again the task of showing people the relationship between the quality of their own daily lives and the "untotalizable totality" of a world-wide capitalist system. The formal difficulties of this task increase in direct proportion to the expansion and complexities of that system and the subsequent reification and opaqueness of individual life.

The second task area for the Marxist cultural critic is, however, of equal importance. Without some notion of a total transformation of society and without the sense that the immediate project is a figure for that total transformation so that everybody has a stake in that particular struggle, the success of any local struggle is doomed, or limited to reform. It will lose its impetus, as any number of issue movements have done. Jameson emphasizes the need for reestablishing a vital socialist discourse by quoting an example from the 60s which might serve as a lesson for the future.

In 1968 there appeared a publication by Marvin Surkin and Dan Georgakis entitled *Detroit: Do I Mind Dying* which retold the rise and fall of the League of the Black Revolutionary Workers in that city in the late 1960s.[87] The politcial formation in question was able to conquer power in the workplace, particularly in the automobile factories, and it drove a substantial wedge into the media and informational monopoly of the city by way of a student newspaper. It elected judges, and finally it came within a hair's breadth of electing a mayor and taking over the city apparatus.[88] But then the jet setting militants became media stars. Having acceded to a larger spatial plane, the base vanished under them. Thus, what Jameson considered the most successful social revolutionary experiment of that rich political decade in the United States that were the 60s, came to a sad and undramatic end. This lesson to be drawn from his experience is: You cannot build a socialism in one city and then suppose you can conquer a whole series of large key urban centers in succession.

The linguistic problem that arose was, for Jameson, a "spatial" one: How to build a national political movement on the basis of a city strategy and politics? The movement failed but the representation "triumphantly survived" in the form of a book and a film. Thus documented, the process became an image and a spectacle and although the referent seemed to have disappeared the "uplifting socialist-realist drama of revolutionary triumph" was inscribed in this narrative of defeat[89], thus lending itself to future appropriations. As a basic requirement for the development of class consciousness[90] Jameson names *figurability*, the need for social reality and every day life to have developed to a point at which its underlying class structure becomes *representable* in tangible form. Culture plays a vital role in this process, not merely as an instrument of class consciousness but also even before that as a symptom and a sign of possible self-consciousness in the first place. The relationship between class consciousness and figurability, in other words, demands something more basic than abstract knowledge, and implies a mode of experience that is more visceral and existential than the abstract certainties of economics and Marxian social science. We have to sense the abstract truth of class through the tangible medium of daily life in vivid and experiential ways, and to say that class structure is becoming representable means that we have now gone beyond abstract understanding.

The development of an alternative discourse is, for Jameson, closely tied up with the experience of non-threatening difference. Within postmodern culture, the concept of difference has come to be eroded. New modes of thinking and perceiving have been cultivated, evidenced e.g. by the new video art:

... Nam June Paik's stacked and scattered television screens, positioned at intervals with lush vegetation, or winking down at us from a ceiling of strange new video stars, recapitulate over and over again prearranged sequences or loops of images with at dissynchronous ... in various screens.[91]

The postmodern viewer is called upon "to do the impossible, namely to see all the screens at once in their radical and random difference. Whereas in the 60s the average camera movement did not go below 1 per 7.5 seconds – this was thought the optimum of what human perception could handle – it is now down to 1 per 3.5 or less. "Each training in an increased tempo is a training in feeling it natural to shift from one thing to another."[92] The very perception of breaks and differences becomes a meaning in itself, not a meaning that has content but one that seems to be a meaningful yet new form of unity. The experience of difference is eroded towards a "continuous flow".

Postmodernist culture hampers the experience of difference. At the same time the (modernist) fear of *otherness* persists unconsciously. In the shrinking world of today with its gradual leveling of class, national, and radical differences, it has become increasingly clear that the category of *otherness* is at one with the concept of evil itself. "Evil" characterizes whatever is radically different from me, whatever by virtue of precisely that difference seems to constitute a very real and urgent threat to my existence. So, from the earliest times, the stranger from another tribe, the "barbarian" who speaks an incomprehensible language and follows outlandish customs, or, "in our own day, the avenger of cumulated resentment from some oppressed class, or else that alien being – Jew or Communist – behind those apparently human features an intelligence of a malignant and preternatural superiority is thought to lurk" – these are some of the figures in which the fundamental identity of evil and the other are visible. This relationship of me/us against the other(s) has to be politically reconstructed. For Jameson the point is not that in such figures, the other is feared because he is evil; rather, he is evil because he is other. Here Jameson endows ethnopoetics with a function to reawaken a sense of difference and to revive that feeble, almost extinct, sense that it is really not necessary to live in this particular way, and that people have been able to live otherwise.[93] Ethnopoetics can by developing a sensitivity for difference, reduce our fear of *otherness*. The concept of "Cognitive Mapping" includes a new approach toward the cities in terms of a rediscovery of spatial experience. The neighborhoods of the big metropolitan areas present a multifaceted wealth of ethnically different subcultures whose contact might become mentally and emotionally invigorating. The principal anxiety we have about the city today can, as Jameson tells us, probably be best expressed in terms of sheer urban concentration: here the stereotypes of Science Fiction usually document the unconscious agoraphobia of contemporary bourgeois consciousness, with its monitory images of overpopulation and its logged dystopias of all kinds. From a diachronic perspective, this fear of urban concentration is clearly a nineteenth century variant, a coded or "sedimented persistence, of that older, ideologically more transparent, nineteenth century terror of the mob itself, the revolutionary crowd, which such anxieties thematize in terms of looting and arson, of damage of property, but whose real credentials for menace are to be sought in the great revolutionary days of 1789-1794."

Jameson has epitomized the possibility of an oppositional or radical critique of contemporary culture and thereby positioned himself at the center of a series of contemporary theoretical and political battles. Since the early 1980s there has been a growing interest in his works and a proliferating critical literature which explicates, defends and attacks his works – especially his texts of the last decade.[94] On the whole, critics register their undaunted respect for Jameson's encyclopaedic knowledge. Many of them, in the United States and abroad, try to relate themselves to Jameson's work, extrapolating individual aspects which they endorse or refute. Marxism, however, carries with it the full freight of nostalgia images dissolving into yellowing period photographs of Lenin and the Soviet Revolution, and postmodernism tends to yield a vista of the gaudiest new hotels.[95] A criticism of Jameson's work is, therefore, only helpful if it counteracts these moments of reification which reduce it to futile academic discussions.

Some critics took exception to Jameson's use of the concept of "modes of production" (which was originally worked out in the Scottish Enlightenment).[96] The problematic of "the modes of production" which made its appearance in the *Grundrisse* and re-emerged in sections of Althusser's *Reading Capital* invites us, as Jameson tells us, to see culture and the economic (or superstructure and base – to put it in more traditional terms) as a structural unity in which neither is determinant in the older sense of economic determinism. At the same time it invites us to envisage a whole range of simultaneously coexisting cultural phenomena deriving from historically different and distinct modes of production.[97] The important question for Jameson is why such a concept at a specific historical conjuncture is of relevance. At present, Jameson argues, it is highly relevant and exceedingly urgent because there have been in the last decades a number of attempts to suggest that the advanced First World society today is no longer capitalist in the classical sense of the term for a number of reasons, one being its shift from industrial production to knowledge and information production and the consequent fading away of social classes in the older economic sense. This "new society" has been alternately called "post-industrial-society," "consumer society", "media society", terms which in their very connotations tend to suppress the new economic framework of late (or multinational) capitalism. The notion of "modes of production" accentuates this link between ethics, aesthetics and economics. This is all the more urgent, given the fact that Marxism's primary ambition to unify isolated working-class struggles into a mass movement is hampered today by its seeming inability to catch up with transformations within labor, the new types of geopolitical struggles of post-colonialism, the reticence to seriously theorize the subalternity of women etc.[98]

The second area of criticism turns around Jameson's concept of totality. The 1980s were a difficult time for the Left with the consolidation of power by conservative regimes in the USA, in Britain, Germany and elsewhere. Many 60s radicals turned to theoretical work which more often than not involved an abandonment of the radical perspectives of the 60s. Against these trends Jameson held on to Marxism and his intervention into the debate on postmodernism can be seen as a defense of Marxism against poststructuralist attacks which characterized his version of Marxism as an anachronistically totalizing and reductionist discourse failing to conceptualize the features of contemporary postmodern society.[99] Those who put it more bluntly excoriated him for "reductive and terroristic totalizations," seeing him, with Habermas, as a "dinosaur of a paleolithic Marxism and modernism trying to foist a repressive Enlightenment scheme upon denizens of the postmodern scene."[100]

That in certain deconstructionist versions of poststructuralism (Paul de Man etc.) the modernist project of human emancipation gave way to a frivolous and depoliticized play of textuality[101] might not be conclusive here. Jameson had claimed that totality is "the most dramatic battleground of the confrontation between Hegelian and structural Marxisms."[102] In these debates and hostile face-offs in the "war against totality", the stakes are high and involve issues concerning what type of society and culture we live in and what modes of theoretical comprehension and political groupings are possible and desirable.[103] Jameson attempts to refuse the equation of totality with totalitarianism. Totalizing models have become fairly unpopular with Western intellectuals. For Jameson the interesting question today is not so much why he adopts this perspective and other critics don't, but why so many people are scandalized (or have learned to be scandalized) by it.[104]

The concept of totality is, in itself, value-free. It can be either of two things. It can signify a dystopian nightmare of coercion and an endorsed identity, but it can also mean the utopian dream of personal and collective advancement, of social and ecological harmony, the dream of a non-threatening society realized in a transformed future. The "war against totality" had its political motivation. That a utopian and revolutionary politics associated with totalization might eventually lead to terror is a familiar idea since Edmund Burke and has been revived in this century during the Stalin period or by the Cambodian atrocities.[105] What these "hoary nightmare images" of *1984* on the one hand and the gulags on the other invite us apart from depoliticizing us, is, for Jameson, not quite clear. Concepts of totality have been necessary and unavoidable at certain historical moments, so that the only logical step would be to analyze those moments of the past when such conceptuality seemed possible or even desirable. To conclude with Jameson: "Such an equation, then, is possible for unreconstructed Hegelians but it is quite incompatible with the basic positions of an honest post-Althusserian post-Marxism."[106]

There are places, however, where Jameson is definitely too "totalizing." Some of his articulations are at times "repressive", in particular where he assumes the role of the authoritative humanist. This does not only apply to his rewritings of canonical works of high modernism but is equally true for cultural objects of everyday life. There are brilliant analyses of everyday environments where Jameson unearths contexts which historical, unself-conscious readers presuppose but fail to grasp, e.g. when he describes the streets of San Francisco. Other presentations are less convincing. I tend to follow Featherstone when he comments:

> ... approaches like those of Jameson tend to regard history as the outcome of a particular relentless developmental logic and play down the role played by classes, social movements and groups in creating the preconditions for such a logic in their various power balances, interdependencies and struggles for hegemony.[107]

For Featherstone it would seem important to distinguish between the commentators' experience of postmodernism and the specific experiences of groups and class fractions who use postmodernist cultural goods in particular practices.[108] We are given by Jameson a fascinating interpretation of the Bonaventura Hotel in Los Angeles[109], but little guidance as to how individuals from different groups incorporate the experience into their own respective practices. Do individuals experience a new kind of shock, or are they unshockable? How do working-class audiences react if they ever have the chance to step inside? The same with television: There is a host of different activities in different groups taking place in front of television – eating, talking, working, sex and so forth.[110] Furthermore the actual perception and reading of programs is also filtered through a particular class habitus. Here Jameson just overgeneralizes and demonstrates a lack of sensitivity to the historical concrete. Even examples of a nostalgic culture can act as catalysts of a redeeming postmodern (counter)politics. Documentaries like *Union Maids* (Julia Reichert and Jim Klein, 1975) or fiction films like *Norma Rae* (Martin Ritt, 1978) might appear, to some viewers, as manifestations of a nostalgic culture. But this does not prevent them from becoming highly appraised organizing tools for various political purposes. The process of dereification must not necessarily (or exclusively) happen on the representational plane.

There are continuities in Jameson's work, but there are also learning processes. A last consideration should be reserved for Jameson's self-critique which is worth quoting at full length, as self-criticism is the credential of a major Marxist critic:

... if one takes the position as I generally take, it will mean that all works of quality, whatever their official ideologies, whether they are art-for-art's sake or reactionary or religious, whatever they be, all artistic works of quality have within them concealed or repressed a political impulse of some kind that one must unmask or show as such. This position is a pedagogical one, which attempts to recuperate the classic of a canon of a more elite tradition and so translate those back into active political terms. If that can be done for all kinds of art, what is the state of the *political work of art* (my italics). And I think my own current problems involve trying to rethink what would be the forms of a political art today, to rethink for example, things which had been allowed to go by the board in the canon, for example didactic works. One of the greatest possible functions of art is to teach and to propagandize in the most genuine way. I think that a whole lot of rethinking has to be done about what political art is and should be. *If one is content to say to the artist "Produce anything you like, and we, the critics, will show you that it is finally political underneath all your ideologies": then in another sense we are not doing or performing our political function which ought to be to encourage a political art, to produce a political art and to create a radical political culture* (my italics).[111]

There are three books by Jameson coming out soon, one on Adorno, one on postmodernism and a third on film. Where will Jameson's Marxism lead? Will this academic type of Marxism and the more spontaneous kinds outside the universities meet? And if so, where will they meet? It is to be hoped that an increased level of struggle by new social movements will make such projects an increasingly important part of the Left's theoretical and political tradition. In particular the developments in the East give Marxist intellectuals an urgent new vocation that they may have thought they didn't have before, i.e. to explain and promote socialism. For the moment, however, Jameson's own immediate research projects bear on a return to modernism to see "whether it can be thought of in a new way."[112]

Notes

1 Jameson, "Cognitive Mapping," in Cary Nelson (ed.), Lawrence Grossberg (ed.), *Marxism and the Interpretation of Culture*, Urbana 1988; pp. 347-360 (p. 354).
2 Anders Stephanson, "Regarding Postmodernism – A Conversation with Fredric Jameson," in Douglas Kellner (ed.), *Postmodernism – Jameson – Critique*, Maisonneuve 1980, pp. 56/57.
3 Jameson, "On Jargon," *Minnesota Review* 9 (1977), pp. 30-31.
4 Jameson (with James H. Kavanagh), "The Weakest Link: Marxism and Literary Studies," in Bertell Ollman (ed.), Edward Vernoff (ed.), *The Left Academy, Marxist Scholarship on American Campuses*, Vol. ii, New York 1984, pp.1-23.
5 Personal Communication (Letter May 15, 1990).
6 Jameson, "On Aronson's *Sartre*," *Minnesota Review* 10 (1982), pp. 116-127 (pp. 122-123).
7 Jameson, "On Aronson's *Sartre*," p. 119.
8 See Georg Lukács, "Reification and the consciousness of the proletariat," in *History and Class Consciousness*, Cambridge, Mass. 1971, and for a theory of the consumer society Guy Debord, *La Société du spectacle*, Genova 1967.
9 Jameson, "Introduction" to Georg Lukács, *The Historical Novel*, Lincoln, Nebr. 1983; pp. 1-8 (p. 2).
10 *ibd.*
11 *ibd.*, p. 8.
12 For a discussion of Jameson's *The Political Unconscious* in the light of Althusserianism see William C. Dowling, *Jameson, Althusser, Marx. An Introduction to The Political Unconscious*, Ithaca, New York 1984.
13 For a detailed discussion of Althusserianism see John Practice, *Enclytic* 7 (Spring 1983), pp. 104-116. For Jameson's own comment on the collapse of Althusserianism see "Cognitive Mapping," p. 354.
14 Stephen Best, "Jameson, Totality, and the Poststructuralist Critique." in Douglas Kellner (ed.), *op. cit.*, p. 347.
15 Ayyappa Paniker, "A Dialogue with Fredric Jameson," *Littcit* 8 (December 1982) 2, p. 17.
16 In Kellner, *op. cit.*, p. 345.
17 See also Terry Eagleton, "Fredric Jameson: The Politics of Style," *Diacritics* 12 (Fall 1982), pp. 14-22.
18 Personal Communication (Letter May 15, 1990).
19 For Jameson and Greimas see Con David, "Theorizing Opposition: Greimas, Jameson, Said," *L'Esprit créateur* 27, Minneapolis 1987, pp. 5-18.

20 Jameson, "The Weakest Link," p. 2.
21 The classic age of modernism spans from the revolutions of 1848 to the aftermath of World War I.
22 Jameson, "Reification and Utopia in Mass Culture," *Social Text* 1, 1979, pp. 130-148 (p. 134).
23 See in particular Jameson's Essay "Metacommentary," *Publication of the Modern Language Association* 86, January 1971, pp. 9-18; abbr. "MTC".
24 Best in Kellner, *op. cit.*, p. 340.
25 For a discussion of decodings, encodings and transcodings in the context of a demand for a non-reductive literary hermeneutics see Haynes Horne, "Jameson's Strategies of Containment," in Kellner, *op. cit.*, pp. 268-300.
26 Best in Kellner, *op. cit.*, p. 341.
27 Jameson, *The Political Unconscious: Narrative as a Socially Symbolic Act*, Ithaca, New York 1981, abbr. "PU"; p. 75.
28 *PU*, p. 10.
29 *ibd.*
30 For Jameson and Lacan see Michael Clark, "Imagining the Real: Jameson's Use of Lacan," *New Orleans Review* 11, 1984, pp. 67-72.
31 Best in Kellner, p. 342.
32 Jameson, *PU*, pp. 34ff.
33 See also Marshall Grossman, "Formalism, Structuralism, Marxism: Fredric Jameson's Critical Narrative," *Dispositio* (Notes) 4, 1979, 11-12, pp. 259-272.
34 For reviews of and comments on *PU* see Geoff Bennington, "Not Yet," *Diacritics* 12, 1982, pp. 23-32; William C. Dowling, *Jameson, Althusser, Marx. An Introduction to The Political Unconsious*, Ithaca, New York 1984; James Iffland, "The Political Unconscious of Jameson's *The Political Unconsious*," *New Orleans Review* 11, New Orleans 1984, pp. 36-45; James H. Kastely, "Towards a Politically Ethical Criticism: Narrative in *The Political Unconscious* and *For Whom The Bell Tolls*," *Style* 22, 1988, pp. 535-558; Dominick LaCapra, "Marxism and the Textual Maelstrom: Fredric Jameson's *The Political Unconscious*." *History and Theory* 21, 1982, pp. 83-106; Jean-François Lyotard, "The Unconscious, History and Phrases: Notes on *The Political Unconscious*," *New Orleans Review* 11, 1984, pp. 73-79; Patrick Parrinder, "Fredric Jameson: *The Political Unconscious*." *Modern Language Notes* 98, 1983, pp. 780-787; James Seaton, "Marxism Without Difficulties: Fredric Jameson's *The Political Unconscious*," *The Centennial Review*, 1985, pp. 122-142; Michael Sprinker, "The Part and the Whole," *Diacritics* 12, 1982, pp. 57-71; Samuel Weber, "Capitalizing History: *The Political Unconscious*," *Diacritics* 13, 1983, pp. 14-28.
35 See also Jameson, "Wyndham Lewis as Futurist," *Hudson Review* 26, 1973, pp. 295-329.
36 Alan Munton, "Fredric Jameson's Fables of Aggression: Wyndham Lewis, the Modernist as Fascist," in Seamus Cooney et al. (eds.), Blast 3 (1984), pp. 345-351.
37 Philip Goldstein, "The Politics of Fredric Jameson's Literary Theory: A Critique," in Kellner, *op. cit.*, p. 352.
38 Jameson, *Fables of Aggression. Wyndham Lewis. The Modernist as Fascist*, Berkeley 1979, abbr. *FA*; p. 21.
39 For a discussion of *FA* see Michael Sprinker, "The Part and the Whole," *Diacritics* 12, 1982, pp. 57-71.

40   For a discussion of Jameson's concept of literary politics see Philip Goldstein (note
     37).
41   Jameson presented his first attempt of defining the features of postmodern culture in
     an essay "Postmodernism and Consumer Society" which was the publication of a
     Whitney lecture from 1982. In Hal Foster (ed.), *The Anti-Aesthetic*, Port Townsend,
     WA 1983, pp. 111-125. He synthesized and elaborated its main concepts to become
     "Postmodernism: Or, The Cultural Logic of Late Capitalism," *New Left Review* 146,
     1984, pp. 53-92.
42   Douglas Kellner, "Jameson, Marxism, Postmodernism," in Kellner, *op. cit.*, p. 35.
43   Jameson, "Preface" to *Marxism and Form: Twentieth Century Dialectical Theories
     of Literature*, Princeton 1971, abbr. *MF*.
44   Jameson, *MF*, p. 413.
45   Kellner, in Kellner, *op. cit.*, p. 2.
46   Anders Stephanson, "Regarding Postmodernism – A Conversation with Fredric Jame-
     son," in Kellner, *op. cit.*, p. 49.
47   Jameson, "Marxism and Postmodernism," p. 33.
48   Jameson, "Cognitive Mapping," p. 349.
49   *ibd.*
50   Jameson, "Postmodernism and Consumer Society," p. 111.
51   Stephanson, in Kellner, *op. cit.*, p. 43.
52   Jameson, "PCL", pp. 54-55.
53   "PCL", p. 55.
54   "PCL", p. 78.
55   Jameson, "Afterword," in Kellner, *op. cit.*, p. 71.
56   Jameson, "The Shining," *Social Text* 4, 1981, pp. 114-125, p. 114.
57   Jameson, "On *Diva*," *Social Text* 6, 1982, pp. 14-119, p. 117-118.
58   Stephanson, in Kellner, *op. cit.*, pp. 44-45.
59   Jameson, "Marxism and Postmodernism," p. 32.
60   Jameson, *PU*, p. 160.
61   For Jameson's film comments see "Reading Hitchcock," *October* 23, 1982, pp. 15-
     42; "Class and Allegory in Contemporary Mass Culture: *Dog Day Afternoon* as a
     Political Film," *College English* 38, 1977, pp. 843-859; "On *Diva*", *op. cit.*, "The
     Shining," *op. cit.*, "Hans-Jürgen Syberberg and Cultural Revolution," *October* 17,
     1981, pp. 99-110.
62   See Robert Sklar, "Oh, Althusser!: Historiography and the Rise of Cinema Studies,"
     Radical History 41, 1988, pp. 10-35.
63   Jameson, "Postmodernism and Consumer Society," p. 112.
64   For a discussion of the application of Jameson's concept to Godard Studies see Robert
     Burgoyne, "The Political Typology of Montage: The Conflict of Genres in the Films
     of Godard," *Enclitic* 7, 1983, 1, pp. 14-23.
65   *ibd.*
66   Stephanson, in Kellner, *op. cit.*, p. 59.
67   See Christopher Lasch, *The Culture of Narcissism*, New York 1978.
68   Jameson, "The Shining," p. 116.
69   Jameson, "Nostalgia for the Present," *South Atlantic Quarterly* 88, 1989, 2, pp. 517-
     537.

70 Jameson, "Futuristic Visions That Tell Us About Right Now (on P. K. Dick)," *In These Times*, 1982, May 5-11, p. 17.

71 *ibd.*

72 P. K. Scott Durham, "From the Death of the Subject to a Theology of Late Capitalism," *Science Fiction Studies* 15, 1988, 2, p. 177.

73 Scott Durham, *op. cit.*, p. 173.

74 Stephanson, *op. cit.*, p. 51.

75 Jameson, "Of Islands and Trenches: Neutralization and the Production of Utopian Discourse," *Diacritics* 7, 1977, 2, pp. 2-21.

76 Quoted from "Reading Without Interpretation," pp. 222-223.

77 Jameson, "RMC," p. 139.

78 Jameson, "*Dog Day Afternoon*", p. 844.

79 Jameson, "Afterword – Marxism and Postmodernism," in Kellner, *op. cit.*, pp. 369-388 (p. 372).

80 Laura Mulvey, "Visual Pleasure and Narrative Cinema," *Screen* 16 (autumn 1976); rpt. in Constance Penley (ed.), *Feminism and Film* (London 1988), pp. 69-79.

81 Jameson, "Pleasure: A Political Issue," in T. Bennett et al. (eds.), *Formations of Pleasure*, London 1983, pp. 1-14 (p. 7).

82 Jameson, "Pleasure," in Bennett, *op. cit.*, p. 8.

83 See also David Gross, "Marxism and Resistance: Fredric Jameson and the Moment of Postmodernism," in Kellner, *op. cit.*, pp. 96-116.

84 Jameson, "Cognitive Mapping," p. 358.

85 Jameson, "PTS," p. 209.

86 Kellner, *op. cit.*, 1989, p. 30.

87 Jameson, "Cognitive Mapping," p. 351.

88 *ibd.*

89 Jameson, "Cognitive Mapping," p. 352.

90 This identification of class content of postmodern culture does not imply for Jameson that "yuppies" have become something like a new ruling class or "subject of history," but merely that their cultural practices and values, their logical ideologies, have articulated a useful dominant ideological and cultural paradigm for this stage of capital. See Jameson, "Afterword," in Kellner, *op. cit.*, p. 376.

91 Jameson, "Postmodernism and Consumer Society," p. 66.

92 Stephanson, *op. cit.*, p. 46.

93 Jameson, "Collective Art in the Age of Cultural Imperialism," *Alcheringa* 2, 1976, 2, pp. 108-11 (p. 108).

94 William C. Dowling, *op.cit.*; *Jameson Issue of Diacritics*, 1982; *Georgia Review* 1984; Kellner, *op. cit.*

95 Jameson, "Marxism and Postmodernism," p. 31.

96 Scotland was in the 18th century a complex and interesting case, as last of the emerging First World countries and the first of the Third World ones. Jameson here used Tom Nairn's provocative idea in *The Break-Up of Britain*. See Jameson, "Afterword," in Kellner, *op. cit.*, p. 376.

97 The standard list is: primitive communism, the ancient mode or the Greek polis, the Asiatic mode, feudalism, capitalism, communism.

98 See Gayatri Spivak, *In Other Worlds: Essays in Cultural Politics*, New York 1987; Gayatri Spivak (ed.), Ranajit Guha (ed.), *Selected Subaltern Studies*, New York 1988.

99 Discussed in Kellner, "Postmodernism as Social Theory".

100 Quoted by Best in Kellner, *op. cit.*, p. 335.

101 Best in Kellner, *op. cit.*, p. 338. See also Michael Ryan, "The Marxism-Deconstruction Debate in Literary Theory," *New Orleans Review* 11, 1984, pp. 29-35.

102 Jameson, *PU*, p. 50.

103 Best in Kellner, *op. cit.*, p. 334.

104 Jameson, "Afterword," in Kellner, *op. cit.*, p. 371.

105 Jameson, "Afterword," p. 374.

106 Jameson, "Cognitive Mapping," p. 354.

107 Mike Featherstone, "Postmodernism, Cultural Change, and Social Practice," in Kellner, *op. cit.*, p. 120.

108 Featherstone, *op. cit.*, pp. 126-127.

109 Jameson, "PCL", pp. 80ff.

110 Featherstone, *op. cit.*, p. 127.

111 Paniker, *op. cit.*, p. 21.

112 Personal Communication (Letter May 15, 1990).

The Works of Fredric R. Jameson

Sartre: The Origins of a Style (New York 1961. New Haven: Yale University Press; Rpt. 1984); abbr. *SS*.

"T. W. Adorno; or, Historical Tropes," *Salmagundi* 5 (1967), pp. 3-43.

"Walter Benjamin; or, Nostalgia," *Salmagundi* 10-11 (1969), pp. 52-68.

"Metacommentary." *Publications of the Modern Language Association* 86 (January 1971), pp. 9-18; abbr. "MTC".

Marxism and Form: Twentieth Century Dialectical Theories of Literature (Princeton: Princeton University Press; 1971); abbr. *MF*.

The Prison-House of Language: A Critical Account of Structuralism and Russian Formalism (Princeton: Princeton University Press; 1972); abbr. *PH*.

"The Great American Hunter; Or, The Ideological Content of the Novel," *College English* 34 (1972), pp. 180-197.

"Benjamin as Historian: or, How to Write a Marxist Literary History." *Minnesota Review* 3 (1974), pp. 116-136.

"The Ideology of the Text," *Salmagundi* 31-32 (Fall-Winter 1976), pp. 204-246; abbr. "ITT"

"Figural Relativism, or, The Poetics of Historiography," (Review Article on Hayden White, *Metahistory: The Historical Imagination in Nineteenth Century Europe*, 1973), *Diacritics* 6 (1976) 1, pp. 2-9; abbr. "FRP"

"Political Painting: New Perspectives on the Realism Controversy," *Praxis* 2 (1976), pp. 225-230.

"Reflections in Conclusion" in Fredric Jameson (ed.), *Aesthetics and Politics. Ernst Bloch, Georg Lukács, Bertolt Brecht, Walter Benjamin, Theodor Adorno* (London: New Left Books; 1977), pp. 196-213; abbr. "RIC".

"Imaginary and Symbolic in Lacan: Marxism, Psychoanalytic Criticism, and the Problem of the Subject," *French Yale Studies* 55-56 (1977), pp. 338-395.

"Marxism and Historicism," *New Literary History* 11 (Autumn 1979), pp. 41-73; abbr. "MAH".

Fables of Aggression. Wyndham Lewis, The Modernist as Fascist (Berkeley: University of California Press; 1979); abbr. *FA.*

"Reification and Utopia in Mass Culture," *Social Text* 1 (1979), pp. 130-148; abbr. "RMC".

The Political Unconscious: Narrative as a Socially Symbolic Act (Ithaca, NY: Cornell University Press; 1981); abbr. *PU.*

"From Criticism to History," *New Literary History* (Winter 1981), pp. 367-389.

"Beyond the Cave: Modernism and Modes of Production," in Hernani, Paul (ed.) *The Horizon of Literature* (Lincoln & London 1982), pp. 157-182.

"Postmodernism and Consumer Society," in Hal Foster (ed.) *The Anti-Aesthetic* (Port Townsend, WA: Bay Press; 1983), pp. 111-125; rpt. *Amerikastudien/American Studies* 29,1 (1984), pp. 55-73.

"Pleasure: A Political Issue," in T. Bennett et al. (eds.) *Formations of Pleasure* (London: Routledge & Kegan Paul; 1983), pp. 1-14; abbr. "PPI".

(with James H. Kavanagh), "The Weakest Link: Marxism and Literary Studies," in Bertell Ollman (ed.), Edward Vernoff (ed.) *The Left Academy. Marxist Scholarship On American Campuses*, vol. ii (New York: Pantheon; 1984), pp. 1-23.

"Foreword" to Jean François Lyotard, *The Postmodern Condition: A Report on Knowledge* (Minneapolis: University of Minnesota Press 1984), pp. vii-xxi; abbr. "FJF".

"The Politics of Theory: Ideological Positions in the Postmodernism Debate," *New German Critique* 12 (Fall 1984), pp. 53-65; abbr. "PTI".

"Postmodernism; or, The Cultural Logic of Late Capitalism," *New Left Review* 146 (July-August 1984), pp. 53-92.

"Periodizing the Sixties," in Sohnya Sayres (ed.), Anders Stephanson (ed.), Stanley Aronowitz (ed.), Fredric Jameson (ed.) *The 60s Without Apology* (Minneapolis: University of Minnesota Press; 1984. 2nd ed. 1985), pp. 178-209; abbr. "PTS".

"Architecture and the Critique of Ideology," *Architecture Criticism*. Revisions: Papers in Architectural Theory and Criticism (Princeton: Princeton Architectural Press; 1985), pp. 51-87; abbr. "ACI".

"Third World Literature in the Era of Multinational Capitalism," *Social Text* 15 (Fall 1986), pp. 65-88; abbr. "TWL".

"The State of the Subject (III)," *Critical Quarterly* 29 (Winter 1987), 4, pp. 16-26.

"Cognitive Mapping," in Cary Nelson (ed.), Lawrence Grossberg (ed.) *Marxism and the Interpretation of Culture* (Urbana: University of Illinois Press; 1988), pp. 347-360; abbr. "CMP".

"Reading Without Interpretation: Postmodernism and the Video-Text," in Nigel Fabb (ed.), Derek Attridge (ed.), Alan Durant (ed.) and Colin MacCabe (ed.), *The Linguistic of Writing. Arguments Between Language and Literature* (Manchester 1987), pp. 199-223.

"*History and Class Consciousness* as an Unfinished Project,'" *Rethinking Marxism* 1 (Spring 1988), pp. 49-72: abbr. "HCC".

"Postmodernism and Utopia," Boston: Institute of Contemporary Art 1988 March, pp. 11-32; abbr. "PAU".

"Postmodernism and Consumer Society," in E. Ann Kaplan (ed.), *Postmodernism and Its Discontents* (London: Verso Press; 1988), p. 13-29; abbr. "PCS".

The Ideologies of Theory, Essays 1971-1886: Vol. 1 *Situations of Theory.* Vol. 2 *The Syntax of History* (Minneapolis: University of Minnesota Press; 1988); abbr. *IT.*

"Marxism and Postmodernism," *New Left Review* 176 (1989), pp. 31-45.

Messages of the Visible: Film/Theory/Periodization (New York: Routledge & Chapman, Hall [forthcoming]).

Postmodernism, or, The Cultural Logic of Late Capitalism (Durham: Duke University Press; 1991)

Dialectical Aesthetics (London: Verso Press [forthcoming]).

Blanche Linden-Ward

Kate Millett

(1934-)

Kate Millet's writings, beginning with *Sexual Politics* (1970), epitomize the tenet of late-sixties American "radical feminism" that the "personal is political" – or, in her words, "sexual distinctions are political definitions." *Sexual Politics* has been acclaimed as catalyst for modern feminist literary criticism and as the first shot fired in the attack against the American literary canon. Millett herself won a reputation as one of the "big four" mothers of the "new feminism" along with Betty Friedan, Gloria Steinem, and Germaine Greer. Millett's subsequent books, dominated by her personal, autobiographical voice, sometimes seem superficially narcissistic yet reveal deep levels of cultural criticism related to her own experiences as a public figure in the bourgeoning feminist movement and as a private person plagued by an unhappy family life and allegations of insanity.[1]

Katherine (Kate) Millett, born on September 14, 1934 in St. Paul, Minnesota, was the second of three daughters born at five-year intervals to Helen Feely and James Albert Millett. Her father, a contractor and engineer for the state highway department, raised the family standard of living above that of their Depression era neighbors; and Kate had a comfortable early childhood imbued with Midwestern and Irish Catholic values reinforced in a parochial school education; but she later complained, "We were constantly reminded that we weren't sons ... that we were mistakes" (Cohen 237). Friends affectionately dubbed her "Tomboy Kate" because of her propensity for sports, her love of riding her bicycle along the banks of the Mississippi River (Cohen 73). Her mother, a graduate in English literature from the University of Minnesota, instilled a respect for education in the family as well as a hatred for bigotry.

Such rationalism led to skepticism. Kate began early to question Church doctrines like the Immaculate Conception and the Assumption, shocking her pious mother with heresy. As Marcia Cohen observes, "a profound rebellion had taken root, a rebellion that was both thrilling and terrifying." To challenge the authority of the Church that surrounded her youth "was to dare all." Kate engaged in youthful feminist analysis: "Men were the popes. Priests had all power over the nuns. Boys get to serve Mass. They get to wear little red skirts and sing the Tenebrae in Latin" (Cohen 75). She felt the injustice of being marginalized by a patriarchal church.

That nascent feminist awareness was given a cuttingly personal edge in 1948 when her father abandoned the family for another woman precisely at the time when American media were celebrating marriage, family, togetherness. Her mother sold insurance to support the children, and the fourteen-year-old Kate also worked. In *Flying*, Kate remembers the pangs and recriminations of her mother: "We have no money. We will starve. Everyone in St. Paul knows about his drinking. You can be darn sure they talk about how he's left us. And the two of you are Jim Millett for sure. Took up right where he left off." Such venom accentuated Kate's adolescent resentment and rebellion. It also instilled self-doubt: "If I'm like my father, am I still a girl?" She fantasied having been adopted as a way she, too, could leave. Yet superficially, she remained the solicitous, dutiful daughter. She remembered, "I did the being-a-good-girl-in-school act because they had convinced me I was so ugly I couldn't make it any other way. I did my shuffling that way" (Cohen 77-78, 237).

Kate had a very close female friend for a time in high school until her sister Sally's fiancé warned her mother that she was a lesbian. After a stressful confrontation, Kate promised good behavior which she maintained until enrolling in 1952 at the University of Minnesota. Although just across the river in Minneapolis, she felt completely independent from home. Running counter to the cultural currents of a time in which two-thirds of "co-eds," women students, dropped out of college for marriage, Millett proclaimed an iconoclastic feminism, vociferously questioning the domestic ideal for women. Reflecting the standard psychological theories about "healthy" women, her classmates told her she was "sick" and should see a therapist (Cohen 80). She scandalized her family by living in a love relationship with a woman. Still, she continued her academic excellence, graduating Phi Beta Kappa and magna cum laude in 1956.

Millett then studied literature at St. Hilda's College, Oxford, and earned first honors and a second B.A. in two years. Her wealthy aunt Christina Millett, who later disowned her, payed her way to correct her "increasingly apparent tendency to flout convention" but really to get her away from her lesbian lover (Cohen 143). In Europe, Kate underwent a "conversion experience." Travelling from one gallery and museum to another in Italy, she decided that although she had been "brought up to be an English major" by her mother, a college graduate, her real calling was in art (Raven and Rennie 36). Although she hoped one day to have her own gallery, she returned to a position teaching literature at the Women's College of the University of North Carolina. There, her female lover had urged her to paint; and Millett produced about forty abstract expressionist works before resigning from her job to move to New York to pursue an art career. She took classes with Seymour Lipton, got her own studio, and for two years experimented in clay, then plaster sculpture.

Millett went to Japan in 1961 to sculpt, supporting herself by teaching English, having her first one-woman exhibition in Tokyo, and rooming with Fumio Yoshimura, a young sculptor of delicate hanging mobiles of bamboo and rice paper. Back in New York in 1963, she exhibited "Pop Art" furniture – chairs with human legs and pianos with fists poised over the keyboards. In 1965, the bi-sexual Millett married Fumio and settled into the Bowery in a loft featured by papers as "an archetype of loft living" (Millett 1990, 80).

Millett joined the National Organization for Women (NOW) in 1966, the year of its founding by Betty Friedan and other moderate, "egalitarian" feminists; and she was active in the founding in February 1967 of the New York chapter, the most radical in the 45 national chapters and the largest with almost a third of the national membership. There, Millett worked with chapter President Ti-Grace Atkinson, attorney Florynce Kennedy, and playwright Anselma dell'Olio. As Chair the Education Committee of New York's NOW, Millett's authored a pamphlet, *Token Learning* (1967), her first work, challenging the validity of curricula in women's colleges and the tracking of young women into nursing, teaching, and home economics. Millett decried socialization that squelched ambitions of young women to enter traditionally male professions: "By the time a girl is ready for medical school, she doesn't want to go any more. She never really had a choice. She's been conditioned to her role ever since she got the doll to play with, and her brother got the gun" (Lear). Jean Faust, first New York-NOW President, sent her a memo in March 1969 criticizing the stance as "intellectually arrogant" and "sarcastic," tinged with a "down-with-the-government-and-capitalistic-society" tone incompatible with the moderate philosophies of NOW leaders (Cohen 154, 165).

Millett's reputation spread beyond NOW. She was invited to join several professional women from law, architecture, and federal employment as a featured speaker at the April 11, 1970 conference which marked the founding of the Professional Women's Caucus (PWC), "perhaps the first nationally organized women's right group to have been influenced by the organizational ideology of radical feminist groups", lacking a traditionally hierarchical slate of officers run by a 30-member steering committee. A 17-hour PWC meeting was attended by over 300 academics and professionals "interested in upgrading the status of women" and airing "their ideas on how to do it" (Hole and Levine 102). Millett presented the paper criticizing the opportunities for women both as students and as professors in academe.

Millett did not quit NOW in disgust as did Atkinson and Kennedy, although she joined their "October 17 Movement," later renamed The Feminists. Still, she was not content to conform to a moderate agenda dictated through the organizational structure of NOW and divided her attentions among all facets of new women's movement (Cohen 154, 165-66). New York from 1968 on was a focal point of the development of radical feminism, characterized by a number of small and sometimes eccentric organizations – Women's International Terrorist Conspiracy from Hell (WITCH), Society for Cutting Up Men (SCUM), the Redstockings, and especially New York Radical Women (NYRW). Millett joined NYRW and became a regular along with feminist theorists Shulamith Firestone, Anne Koedt, Robin Morgan, Kathie Sarachild, and Ellen Willis. Hence, for a time, Millett tried to span the ideological division between the radicals and the egalitarians in the new but increasingly factionalized feminist movement.

Barnard College hired Millett to teach part-time in the fall of 1968; and in order to keep her job, she was simultaneously "forced into" working on her doctorate in English and comparative literature at Columbia. Meanwhile, she helped found the Columbia Women's Liberation Movement and marched for abortion law repeal with her own sign reading "Nobody should legislate *my* right to *my* body." Her outspoken activism at faculty meetings against the Vietnam war and on behalf of civil rights, women's liberation, and especially the student movement as an active observer of the 1968 Columbia Strike cost her the position after one semester. She was fired (Cohen 165)

In a speech she delivered to a women's group at Cornell in 1968, Millett articulated the premise that "sexual politics" were involved in all male power relationships with women. The so-called "sexual revolution" that had taken place over the course of the sixties had not necessarily been liberating for women. While "sexual freedom has been partially attained," Millett contended, "it is now being subverted beyond freedom into exploitative license for patriarchal and reactionary ends." She argued that feminism would further women's freedom of sexual expression and bring "an end to sexual repression." It would either "bisex" and bring about "the end of enforced perverse heterosexuality" or "unisex, or the end of separatist character structure, temperament and behavior, so that each individual may develop an entire – rather than a partial, limited, and conformity personality." Although the Cornell talk was a feminist political tract, widely circulated among feminists, especially when reprinted in *Notes from the Second Year: Women's Liberation*, edited by Shulamith Firestone and Anne Koedt, it contained some ideas Millett developed through literary analysis in the thesis for her doctorate.[2]

Although completed quickly through 18-hour days of writing by March 1970 because of the added incentive that Doubleday would publish it immediately, Columbia awarded Millett's dissertation *Sexual Politics* "distinction." It was a complex example of sophisticated cultural and literary analysis. The book skyrocketed Millett from relative anonymity to become overnight a literary and media celebrity with a position of prominence in the bourgeoning feminist movement. She won acclaim as a pioneer, one of the first to formulate serious feminist literary and cultural criticism. Its impact on the general public, on feminists and scholars was immediate, selling 80,000 copies in its first six months.

Sexual Politics is an exhaustively documented, devastating attack on male, patriarchal literature. Millett focuses on the writings of D. H. Lawrence, Henry Miller, Norman Mailer, and Jean Genet but also considers George Meredith, Charlotte Brontë, George Eliot, Thomas Hardy, and others. She indicts Lawrence, Miller, and Mailer as representative of modern male voices expressive of a personal, counterrevolutionary fight, using sex as a weapon, in the name of patriarchy. She castigates Lawrence for his glorification of masculinity, Miller for his violent denigration of women, and Mailer for chauvinistic celebration of a virility cult. Millett draws connections between literature, literary criticism, and other cultural agents and reactionary politics of which "chivalry" or sexism was one manifestation. Millett decries "power-structured relationships" as "the most pervasive ideology of our culture" used by one group, essentially male, to govern others, to create "vast gray stockades of sexual reaction." *Sexual Politics* argues that artistic violence presages violence in real life, that images condition as well as reflect reality.

Millett insists on the long unused capability of criticism "of seizing upon the larger insights which literature affords into the life it describes, or interprets, or even distorts." Going against critical trends dominant from the 1930s through the 1960s and transcending the limitations of New Criticism and literary history, she takes into account the larger cultural context in which literature is conceived and produced (Millett 1970, xii, 178).

Sexual Politics was the first major work of cultural criticism of the new feminism and of great "ovular" importance on development of feminist literary and cultural criticism in the 1970s and 1980s. It was a major literary event which helped launch the "women's renaissance" of the seventies; but feminist literary analysis was not unprecedented. Millett drew inspiration and a model from Simone de Beauvoir's *The Second Sex* (1949), translated into English in 1953. In a section on "The Myth of Woman in Five Authors," de Beauvoir analyzes Montherlant, Claudel, Breton, Stendhal, and D. H. Lawrence, the latter indicted for "Phallic Pride." De Beauvoir used literary references throughout the book which inspired much of the new feminist thought in America in the sixties. Mary McCarthy also included a collection of critical essays on literature and the arts written between 1946 and 1961 in *On the Contrary: Articles of Belief* (1962).[3]

Mary Ellman's *Thinking About Women* (1968) also criticizes sexism pervading all levels of literary culture, particularly in the work of Norman Mailer. It focuses on women's voices in literature and the negative male response to it – "phallic criticism." Intellectual historian Dale Spender summarizes Ellman's conclusions that men "produced and legitimated society's reservoir of knowledge, and in it, men were central, positive, various, active, admirable, while women were sex-objects, seen only in relation to men; women were 'other,' where they were deemed to exist at all." Chapters include "Feminine Stereotypes," "Differences in Tone" between male and female writers, "Phallic Criticism," "Sexual Analogy," and "Responses" of women writers to personal experience. Ellman blames the academic establishment, especially graduate literature departments, for systematically excluding women from admission and hence making the professional teaching, creation, and criticism of literature a male domaine. Ellman charges, "Books by women are treated as though they themselves were women, and criticism embarks, at its happiest, upon an intellectual measuring of busts and hips" (Ellman 29).

Shulamith Firestone's *Dialectic of Sex*, also published in 1970, similarly argues that the masculinization and formalism of twentieth-century literature "is a direct response, indeed a male cultural backlash, to the growing threat to male supremacy"; but Firestone blends Marxism with feminism, calling for elimination of sexual class by revolutionary seizure of control of reproduction analogous to the need for proletarian revolt and seizure of the means of production.

Like Firestone, Millett's *Sexual Politics* links literature to larger trends in society, politics, and culture. Both attack psychological constructs based in Freudianism; but Millett extends her criticism to others like Eric Erikson who replaced the theory of penis envy with "uterine glorification ... a gentler form of persuasion." She decried the pattern in which science had systematically rationalized male power in biological-physiologial terms, thus giving "patriarchy logical as well as historical origin" (Millett 1970, 213); and she had no patience for "liberals" like Erikson who urged a place for women in the public realm only because of inherent virtues – "realism of householding, responsibility of upbringing, resourcefulness of peacekeeping, and devotion to healing" traditionally exercised in their private sphere (27). She reacted: "One cannot but note ... that the force of this recommendation is to urge that women participate in political power not because such is their human right, but because an extension of their proper feminine sphere into the public domain would be a social good." Millett called this an argument "from expediency rather than justice" (210). But such an argument echoed the beliefs of earlier social feminists – Jane Addams, Florence Kelley, Frances Perkins, and Eleanor Roosevelt. Rejection of them represented a radical rejection of a main current in earlier American feminism and of basic concepts of the nature of women deeply embedded in American culture.

Ernest Van Den Haag complained about Millett's "biased" choice of writers who were "sitting ducks for feminists … . Some writers have not gone beyond the phallic stage of development and rationalize their failure in their writing. Why do their wishful fantasies show that society oppresses females?" (Van Den Haag 1004-05). Another reviewer in *The New Yorker* correctly complained that "the authors she has chosen are in such psychological trouble themselves that it is hard to agree that they express typical attitudes toward women … . Most of Miss Millett's masculine theorists writing about women are the sexual equivalent of Hitler writing on government: striking, unsound, and out of the main line of cultural evolution" ("Sexual Politics" 137). More recently, Helen Vendler summarizes, "The feminist literary criticism that appeared in the Sixties and Seventies was frequently naive," focusing on how women were represented in literary works by male writers. Those like Millett "wrote about literary characters as if they were real people (though sophisticated ideas about narrative since Aristotle would have suggested otherwise) and they predictably found women characters treated less sympathetically by men than they would like. They also wrote as though authors had a public duty to be ideologically correct on sex, race, and class (correctness being defined in contemporary terms), and could be criticized and patronized when they were not." Vendler rhetorically questions why no one thought "to deplore the stiff, idealized, antagonistic, or calumniatory portraits of men by female novelists from Jane Austen to, say, Fay Weldon" (Vendler 19).

Yet *Sexual Politics* is far more complex than the literary criticism with which Millett begins and ends the book. Her analysis is interdisciplinary, challenging as reactionary the dominant twentieth-century Freudian psychological, functionalist sociological, and social anthropological theories with more vigor than her critique of literature. Here, again, she found sources upon which to build. In *Adam's Rib* (1948), Ruth Herschberger discusses the idea of rape as part of the masculine power mystique, a male symbol, myth, and ritual of aggressiveness, violence, superiority, and supremacy. *Sexual Politics* also probes historic context in cross-cultural perspective. She considers the likes of Ruskin and Freud for their "counterrevolutionary" response to the "first phase" from 1830 to 1930 of the "sexual revolution," by which she means not the opening of female sexuality of the 1920s (and 1960s) but dramatic shifts in the political relationships between the sexes" in politics, law, economics, education, employment, and activism brought about by social and technological changes. All amount to a move away from feudal "chivalry" used to keep women as a separate caste (61). Internationally, the 1930-1960 period witnessed a reactionary or counter-revolutionary undermining of feminism through ideology. *Sexual Politics* presented a sweeping worldview tapping recent scholarship in a diversity of disciplines. It intended to formulate a new theoretical approach for assessment of various aspects of culture, not simply literature. Yet it is known almost entirely as literary criticism.

Following de Beauvoir's example, Millett blamed psychological theory as a form of anti-feminist ideology. She attacked Freud, his followers and popularizers as trying "to rationalize the invidious relationship between the sexes, to ratify traditonal roles, and to validate temperamental differences" (Millett 1970, 178). She equally criticized Erik Erikson for substituting the idea of women's joy of "inner space" for Freudian "penis envy," thus creating "uterine glorification" as "a gentler form of persuasion" which still leaves women separate but not equal (213). Social scientific language, especially in psychology and psychiatry, Millett suggests, thus become an agency for social control. Critic Claire Tomalin correctly judged, "if she had stuck to her discussion of these topics, she would have produced a small, sharp additional weapon for the feminist armoury. Unfortunately she feels impelled to pad out her book with huge sections devoted to literary criticism ... not central to her argument" (Tomalin 429).

Millett argues that male supremacy is grounded in cultural and historical, not inherent and natural factors, perpetuated in many subtle ways through "interior colonization" that is "sturdier than any form of segregation and more rigorous than class stratification, more uniform, certainly more enduring" (25). She excoriated chivalry as the basis for modern etiquette, a token substitute for true respect and equal right for women. Although she admitted that chivalry was better than "machismo" or "oriental behavior," she realized "how much of a concession traditional chivalrous behaviour represents – a sporting kind of reparation to allow the subordinate female certain means of saving face. While a palliative to the injustice of woman's social position, chivalry is also a technique for disguising it" (Millett 1970, 37). Such was the kindness of master for servant, a calculated behavior intended to please in the short run and in the long run to keep women in their place. Millett also questioned courtly or romantic love as a ploy concealing intentions to control women's submissive behavior in conformity to a traditional norm. This attitude reverberated through a generation of feminists, no longer pleased when men gestured to open doors or help them be seated; and it gradually revolutionized social formalities.

Millett confirmed feminists' realization that sexism was deeply ingrained in culture and especially in language. Linguist Ethel Strainchamps wrote that the word "man" originally meant human being before males appropriated it. English usage of the word in compounds descriptive of occupations of skill or power – such as chairman, foreman, handyman – traditionally monopolized by males or defined as "men's work" embedded discrimination into society. Feminists wanted to reform language in a sex-neutral way; and they extended their criticism to media in general, to the stereotypical images of women presented in mass culture.

Sexual Politics ends on a optimistic, if naive and somewhat polemical, note, like that on which she began in her Cornell talk. Millett finds "evidence in the last few years that the reactionary sexual ethic … has nearly spent itself." Although she touches only briefly on class, omitting consideration of racism or imperialism, she anticipates with the second "sexual revolution" that "women might come to play a leadership part in social revolution quite unknown in history," forging bonds based on "fundamental values" shared by "a coalition of expropriated groups" including blacks, youth, and the poor (Millett 1970, 363). She calls for no less than abolition of patriarchy as part of a larger feminist agenda of social reform premised upon the cultural.

A remarkably large number of reviews and articles appeared almost immediately after the release of *Sexual Politics*, particularly in the popular press and mass circulation magazines. Betty Prashker, her editor at Doubleday, had circulated advance copies that spring. Many of the reviews were positive. Christopher Lehmann-Haupt reviewed the book for the *New York Times*, agreeing that "all vestiges of male chauvinism ought by rights to melt and drip away like so much fat in the flame of a blowtorch" and he personally owned to "the particular brand of guilt that, as Millett herself points out, all oppressors feel toward the people they oppress." But he complained that the unforgettable "book itself is too masculine, itself a denial of femininity" (Cohen 235). Other reviews were far less objective, sympathetic, or positive. *Time* magazine ran two articles on Millett in one month. On August 2, 1970, a reviewer predicted, "There will always be a few … who may want to invite Millett outside to settle the question of Women's Liberation in a manly manner." A second reviewer correctly observed, "Until this year with publication of a remarkable book called *Sexual Politics*, the movement had no coherent theory to buttress its intuitive passions, no ideologue to provide chapter and verse for its assault on patriarchy … . In a way, the book has made Millett the Mao Tse-tung of Women's Liberation. This is the sort of description she and her sisters despise, for the movement rejects the notion of leaders and heroines as creations of the media" (*Time* Aug. 31, 1970, 20). *Time* contributed, rejecting her suggestion that a group photograph of movement activists would be appropriate for its cover, instead featuring an unflattering portrait of Millett by a primitive painter depicting her as a wild animal crouched and ready to spring. Millett became a celebrity overnight, interviewed on television, controversial and even notorious, a "household name" for millions who would never read her writings. The negative tone of the publicity even alienated some of her feminists friends.

Millett had rightly feared the immediate and visceral reaction her work would inspire. George Stade, one of Millett's thesis advisors at Columbia, told *Time*, "Reading the book is like sitting with your testicles in a nutcracker"; but rather than writing a more detailed critique on the book, he devoted much of his writing through the seventies to challenging and reacting against Millett's thesis. In the *Partisan Review*, in 1977, he defends and commends Mailer and Miller with a blend of militant nostalgia and Freudianism. In his novel *Confessions of a Lady-Killer* (1979), he uses Millett as a model for his "ugly" and "aggressive" feminist villain, Judith (Jude) Karnofsky, "prize-winning authoress of *The Precedence of Women*, itinerant lecturess, talkshow personality, and cryptolesbian" (Stade 14). The novel is murderous and misogynist, written as if deliberately to outdo the combination of violence and sex in Lawrence, Miller, or Mailer. Ironically, Millett served as catalyst not only for the development of feminist literary theory but for a flowering of a reactionary literary response – texts nostalgic for the old paternalism as rhetorical and cultural force.[4]

Sexual Politics had struck painful nerves, particularly among many male critics who expressed their outrage in words rarely seen in published reviews. Irving Howe wrote a lengthy diatribe against "The Middle Class Mind of Kate Millett" in the December 1970 issue of *Harper's* magazine. Howe's tantrum involved calling Millett names – a "feckless," "morally shameful," "squalid," "female impersonator." He accused her of "historical reductionism. ... crude simplification ... middle-class parochialism ... sexual monism ... methodological sloppiness ... arrogant ultimatism ... cosmic ignorance." Condescending only to call her "brilliant in an unserious way," Howe found "that such a farrago of blunders, distortions, vulgarities, and plain nonsense could be passed by the English Department of Columbia University for the doctoral degree is an interesting fact" (Howe, 124, 129). A grotesque, sexist cartoon accompanied the review.

Mailer got even more personal, turning his review, "The Prisoner of Sex," in *Harper's* in March 1971, into a combination of obscene confessional, self-exhibitionism, and tantrum. In a book-length diatribe, Mailer complains that "his ghost-phallus," his reputation, "was apparently being chewed half to death by a squadron of enraged Amazons, an honor guard of revolutionary (if we would only see them) vaginas" (Mailer 15). Mailer counter-attacks Millett as "a pug-nosed wit" and "an honor student in some occult school of thuggee" whose "pure Left totalitarian" arguments are clouded by distortion and "the smudge pots of her indignation." He described her work as a landscape where "the food served at every inn was ... ideological lard, a grit and granite of thesis-factories turned out aggregates of concept-jargon. ... Bite and bubbles of intellectual flatulence coursed in the river, and the bloody ground steamed with the limbs of every amputated quote. Everywhere were signs that men were guilty and women must win" (72, 124). Mailer vascillates between being enraged, patronizing, sarcastic, and blatantly gross. Somewhere amid the purple prose, Mailer correctly points out some of Millett's omissions of historical periods and literary misinterpretations; but the voice of reason whispers briefly between lengthly passages of emotional, bellowing invective that only serves to justify Millett's thesis and her judgment of Mailer.

Gore Vidal was slightly gentler in his *New York Review of Books* critique that July. He recognized that Millett had opened up more than an Pandora's box of feminist rage; her intellectual arguments would lead to the opening up of academe and related intellectual and cultural professions in the decades ahead (Vidal, 11).

Social anthropologist Lionel Tiger, author of *Men in Groups*, simply denounced Millett as wrong, explaining away the popularity of the book: "Women's Liberation is very much a minority movement. It's evangelical. It's a movement that makes people feel good, and there will be a lot of people reading these books who won't do a thing to change the conditions of their lives; still, they like reading about revolution. In one sense it constitutes a kind of pornography; it's a fantasy about the different ordering of things without individuals really doing anything about the ordering" (Tiger, 21). Tiger simply pontificated without commenting on the substance of Millett's thesis, leading the reader of his review to suspect that, at best, he had barely glanced at the book.

Sexual Politics and the author's starring role in the new movement drew attention to Millett's private life. She had raised sexual preference as an issue for discussion and some radical feminists used this opportunity to push their own agendas to the fore in the movement. Teresa Juarez, a member of Radicalesbians, forced Millett to restate publically at a forum sponsored by Gay People at Columbia University that, despite being happily married, she was indeed a lesbian. This was not news for those in the movement since Millett had participated in a "zap action," the takeover by lesbians of the second annual Congress to United Women that May. This time, however, *Time* magazine sent a reporter with a tape recorder and seized upon the revelation.

In its cover story, "Women's Lib: A Second Look," in the "Behavior" section, *Time* belittled the 35-year-old author as "a sometimes sculptor and long-

time brilliant misfit in a man's world." It used her for "lesbian-baiting," media
exploitation of diversity of choice as a means of discrediting all feminists.
Time predicted, "Kate Millett herself contributed to the growing skepticism
about the movement by acknowledging at a recent meeting that she is bisexual. The disclosure is bound to discredit her as a spokeswoman for her cause,
cast further doubt on her theories, and reinforces the views of those skeptics
who routinely dismiss all liberationists as lesbians" (*Time*, Dec. 14, 1970,
50). Kate's sister Sally had warned her, "middle America simply can't take
this sort of thing" (Cohen 245), but that was precisely why *Time* exploited
the issue.

Millett felt *Time* used her "as a club to beat the movement." Her sudden
fame was "fun for ten days, then awful." The media, she recalls, "almost
made an iron-clad safe out of [*Sexual Politics*] and locked me in. And I'm
claustrophobic" (Raven and Rennie 37). Yet Millett explained the media
response with dispassionate analysis: "The women's movement began for
them as entertainment, but then it became serious. It began to make economic
demands. Maybe you'll have to pay women equal pay, the whole clerical
level of Bell Telephone, for instance. Here was a minority group, a pressure
group, and they were getting someplace. So it became necessary to down-
play, to do a number on me that week" (Cohen 247).

The negative publicity, however, shook the women's movement, forcing
even conservative feminists to come to terms with lesbians' social and cultural dilemma. It precipitated an emergency strategy meeting in Dolores Alexander's New York apartment. Although Friedan lived in the same building,
she absented herself from the meeting. Friedan thought *Sexual Politics* was
"genuinely dangerous to the movement" since the media was ready to use it
to discredit even moderate feminists; but even without the negative publicity,
Friedan would have remained personally opposed to expanding her feminist
agenda to include sexual preference, declaring that "no serious, meaningful
action emerges from a sexual emphasis. There is simply talk, anger, and wal-
lowing. It is also based on a highly distorted oversimplified view of our society, men and women, family relations, relations to children" (Friedan 157,
163, 189-90, 210-13). Friedan was determined not to associate herself with
Millett or issues of lesbianism; but Ivy Bottini, President of New York NOW,
declared that the "real test of sisterhood" had begun because "lesbianism as
an issue had never before surfaced [publically] in any earlier phase of feminism" (Cohen 247-50).

By 1970, according to Faderman, "many feminist writers began to declare
lesbianism to be a logical extension of feminism." "The women who joined
the feminist movement first and then chose to become lesbians were not hampered by the weight of all the old images. The New Women found strength

and solidarity in their examination during consciousness-raising of their choice to be lesbians." Many had not read the Freudians and had not internalized the feeling of being "sick" – not that such knowledge would have mattered much because these women were coming out in "a society that had far less respect for authority" than did the women who came out in the 1950s, "an era when respect for 'experts' was at a height" (Faderman, 382-84). New feminist journals and publishing houses provided an antidote against derogatory, demeaning images of lesbians from "cheap paperbacks that promised tales of lurid passion." Finally, new lesbians did not have to come out in isolation because either they had a support group of women "who would help them validate their choice, or – if they had no physical support – lesbian-feminist literature, which by 1970 was being published all over the United States in the form of newspapers, newsletters, magazines, pamphlets, and books" (Faderman, 476); but not only was *Time*'s exposé on Millett unprecedented in journalism, it was the first time in a century and a half of American feminism that lesbianism became a public issue in terms of the movement.

In response, radical feminists led by Ti-Grace Atkinson, Susan Brownmiller, and Florynce Kennedy won support from NOW, Columbia Women's Liberation, Radicalesbians, and the long-established Daughters of Bilitis to stage the "Kate Is Great" press conference on December 18, 1970 at New York's Square Methodist Church, decorated with banners reading "We Stand Together as Women, Regardless of Sexual Preference," "Sisterhood is Powerful," and "Is the Statue of Liberty a Lesbian, Too?" Millett read a statement declaring that women's liberation and homosexual liberation are both struggling toward a common goal: A society free from defining and categorizing people by virtue of gender and/or sexual preference. 'Lesbian' is a label used as a psychic weapon to keep women locked into their male-defined 'feminine role' ... defined in terms of her relationship to men. A woman is called a lesbian when she functions autonomously. Women's autonomy is what women's liberation is all about" ("The Lesbian Issue"; Abbott and Love 119-34; Hole and Levine 241-42). Millett was not disavowing lesbianism; she was trying to end use of the term as an epithet by anti-feminists.[5]

The meeting temporarily ended lesbian-baiting by the press, but homophobia within NOW persisted. Friedan threatened NOW colleagues with a suit because, writes Marcia Cohen, "this coalition – her coalition – had never asked her permission to make the pro-lesbian statement" (Cohen 247-51). But Friedan could not stop the momentum of feminist indignation. At its mid-1971 convention, NOW passed a resolution supporting lesbianism "legally and morally," heeding Millett's plea that the organization acknowledge "the oppression of lesbians as a legitimate concern for feminism." Many radical feminists considered lesbianism as a political statement – epitome of "the personal is political." Millett called coitus "a charged microcosm" of "sexual politics" (28); but her ideas were not the cause but merely an articulation of a trend in progress.

Through all the publicity and controversy surrounding "SexPol," Millett remained active in the women's movement. Speaking at a march of about 10,000 on New York's Fifth Avenue, part of the general strike staged nationally on Women's Rights Day, August 26, 1970, fiftieth anniversary of ratification of the women's suffrage amendment, she declared the official start of a revolution: "Today is the beginning of a new movement. Today is the end of millenniums of oppression." In a Duffy Square rally, Mary Orvan began the ceremony honoring Susan B. Anthony with a prayer and the sign of the cross, "In the name of the Mother, the Daughter and the Holy Granddaughter, Ah-Women. Ah-Women." That day, thousands of women went out "on strike" in other cities as well in protest of inequalities and to demand legal abortions, day care, and equal educational and employment opportunities. Miami feminists staged a "liberation garden party," smashing dishware. Karate instructors gave self-defense lessons to women in Philadelphia's Rittenhouse Square. Housewives in Los Angeles marched with their pots and pans. Two thousand marched in San Francisco where a small girl bore a sign, "I Am Not a Barbie Doll." Placards, banners, and posters revealed rage, determination, and even humor: "Don't Iron While the Strike is Hot," "Don't Cook Dinner Tonight — Starve a Rat," "Up Against the Wall Male Chauvinist Pig Doctors," "Repent, Male Chauvinists, Your World is Coming to an End," "Pray to God/She Will Help." In several cities, small groups of women "liberated" male-only restaurants, bars, and clubs. Others invaded corporate offices protesting advertisements portraying women as "servants and sex objects" (Hewlett 141-42). Feminism had become a national movement.

Millett consistently attempted to be a peacemaker at times of factionalism. In 1975, she signed a feminist petition in support of Jane Alpert, a member of the Weather Undergrond who had recently emerged from hiding as a legal fugitive and was accused of informing on former colleagues. Two other petitions by leftists and feminists were highly critical of Alpert. The issue further fragmented the women's movement; but Millett preferred to sympathize with Alpert as a "sister" and "underdog" (Judith Coburn, "The Issue That's Splitting Feminists," quoted in Wandersee 14).

Through her close association with New York radical feminists, Millett's analysis of patriarchy and sexual politics undoubtedly influenced other theorists and activists even before publication of her book and her sudden rise to fame. For instance, the manifesto, "Politics of the Ego," drafted in December 1969 by Shulamith Firestone and Anne Koedt for their new group, New York Radical Feminists (NYRF, not to be confused with NYRW), stated: "We believe that the purpose of male supremacy is primarily to obtain psychological ego satisfaction, and that only secondarily does this manifest itself in economic relationships." Koedt believed that "male ego identity" was sustained only through destruction of women's egos, that men dominate women "out of a need for a sense of power," that the system of domination was perpetuated through socialization and deeply ingrained in the culture (Echols 187-89).

Millett began *The Prostitution Papers* (1973) as a chapter for *Women in a Sexist Society* (1971), edited by Barbara Moran and Vivian Gornick, a *Village Voice* journalist and activist in NYRF which co-sponsored with The Feminists a conference on prostitution in December 1971. Ti-Grace Atkinson called the prostitute "the only honest woman left in America because they charge for their services, rather than submitting to a marriage contract which forces them to work for life without pay" (Cohen 167). Millett attended the program at which prostitutes complained "that the organizers assumed a judgmental stance toward them" (Echols 194). She perceived "the accusation, so long buried in liberal good-will and radical rhetoric − 'You're selling it; I could too, but I won't' − was finally heard. Said out loud at last." Kathie Sarachild castigated conference organizers for "assuming that they could theorize about prostitution without consulting the women with first-hand experience" (Millett 1973, 38). Millett personally set out to break that pattern and to document through the voices of the prostitutes themselves the nature of their oppression. She edited oral testimony elicited from two prostitutes and a feminist attorney, adding a sympathetic introductory essay arguing that prostitution was only one of the most visible of the many ways in which women were turned into commodities. In a chapter entitled "Quartet for Four Voices," she stipulated that the narratives be printed side by side in columns; but her publisher abandoned the plan which would have been an innovation in style as well as format anticipatory of Deconstructionists of the eighties.

Millett argued that second to marriage, women's prime occupation was prostitution. She focused on an occupation that traditionally concerned feminists and frequently produced controversy. Since the writings of Mary Wollstonecraft, a number of feminists in the nineteenth and twentieth centuries had considered women's economic role in marriage as equivalent to prostitution. While nineteenth-century feminists tried to convert prostitutes to the "cult of true womanhood," Millett and some of her generation of radical feminists went so far as to sympathize and empathize with prostitutes, to identify elements of a common female condition in that shunned occupation. They even helped organize groups like the Prostitutes Union of Massachusetts (PUMA), providing legal aid and other services to members of the "oldest profession."

One of Millett's subjects, "J.," testified, "I'd like so much to have the illusion that I had some freedom of choice. Maybe it's just an illusion, but I need to think I had some freedom. Yet then I realize how much was determined in the way I got into prostitution, how determined my life had been, how fucked over I was. ... So I believed I'd chosen it. What's most terrifying is to look back, to realize what I went through and that I endured it" (Millett 1973, 78-79). Certainly, such a linking of prostitution with marriage and the fundamental cultural role of women was not new; it appeared in the writings of Mary Wollstonecraft, Victoria Woodhull, and Charlotte Perkins Gilman, among other feminist writers since the late eighteenth century. Millett updated the argument with a sympathetic interest in the professional prostitute and augmented her argument in the 1976 revised edition of the book with a personal account of the 1975 French prostitutes' revolt. She placed the choice to sell sex in contemporary economic perspective, noting "With a Ph.D. and after ten years' experience, I was permitted to make only $60 a week," while one of her subjects made $800 a week (Millett 1973, 95).

Millett turned to her own first-person narrative. Instead of writing *about* literature, she spent four years to create her own – "the whole discovery of writing. ... a first book, really, one book of your own" (Millett 1990, 77). Her fourth book was the autobiographical *Flying* (1974), the plea of a deeply personal voice trying to counteract the negative, sensationalized, and misunderstood image of her as a strident "women's libber," to impart a sense of her passion for politics, art, and feminist friendship in the context of the first wave of the contemporary lesbian-feminist movement. *Flying* attempts to provide a wholistic self-portrait in a postmodern way, integrating her public and her private selves through a series of cinematic scenes – flashbacks, flashforwards, vignettes, brief character sketches, memory fragments seemingly excerpted from a journal, and free association, all containing thematic motifs and narrative threads, "almost tiny film clips of association and reference," writes Annette Kolodny. Its structure reflects Millett's philosophy that "inch by inch growing older we become what we came from and left" and her "wondering ... always if I am going forward or backward" (Kolodny 544, 548). It is a personal story rather than the scholarly treatise on homosexuality Millett initially planned. Through this rambling, autobiographical defense, she aimed to make the public understand her as a person rather than as a two-dimensional stereotype. Catharine Stimpson judges that "like other autobiographies by contemporary women, hers deliberately pushed back the boundaries of permissible 'women's speech'" (Stimpson 1073).

Favorable reviewers called Millett's intensely personal style "an essential breakthrough in a developing genre of women's writings"; many remarked that she was creating a new mode of discourse since traditional patriarchal language was inadequate for expressing women's experience (Rule 22-27; Juhasz 62-75). Susan Wolfe commented on the syntactical experimentation, the innovative circularity of form (Wolfe 134-43). Julia Stanley asserted that Millett's work shattered the myth of women's lack of objectivity; and Millett explained that she was breaking women's literary silence, especially about her sexuality (Stanley 52-62).

But many critics, even women, were extremely negative about *Flying*. René Kuhn Bryant berated the book as "an endless outpouring of shallow, witless comment" about a year, documented "minute by remorseless minute" (Bryant 990). Muriel Haynes called it an "assemblage of raw materials" that "refuses and eludes any literary category" and "a leviathan ... that demands of the reader an analyst's endurance" (Haynes 28). Elinor Langer complained that "free association has supplanted thought" in a confessional work that "is not disciplined autobiography" (Langer 74). Millett replied that it was no longer possible to constrain or restrict the kind of information in or about women's lives (Millett 1975, 26-29).

Annette Kolodny defended Millett's style, arguing that *Flying* could not be judged by traditional male "norms of importance, personal and/or cultural" or by structuralists' "formulaic dictum." Women, Kolodny wrote, internalized a picture of themselves that itself precluded the kind of self-attention which might generate autobiography" – not the same reality experienced by men; and Millett had "produced a text which in no way resembles that disengaged, self-critical, self-distanced, and self-scrutinizing brand of [male] autobiography we have been taught to read and critics have come to expect" (Kolodny 543-44). Kolodny insisted that "the feminist critic/reviewer must ask her colleagues to accept the various ways in which the moment-to-moment content of a life may shape the form of its narrative, and, further, she must insist upon a serious examination of the resulting text – however odd its form may at first appear, and in spite of any personal misgivings one might have about the details of the life depicted" (Kolodny 559). One precedent for Millett's approach to breaking previous codes of silence through personal narrative was Doris Lessing's *Golden Notebook* (1962).

Flying and Millett's later writings proved models for the writing of autobiography as political history. *Sita* (1977) was like *Flying* in experimental style, but on a narrower personal and lesbian subject – her painfully dissolving romance with an older woman, the breakdown of her marriage, and reluctant incarceration in a mental hospital. She sculpts confessional narrative, repeatedly restating her theme but from different perspectives, building up a mantle of emotions around a set of personal events. She remembers that while writing *Sita*, "I prayed every night to Proust and Colette. I wanted to get all of the *nostalgie* and all of the bitter-sweetness" and to "capture the sorrow of romance. Love is essentially tragic, and to lose a love is like losing a life" (Raven and Rennie 37).

Millett seemed repeatedly drawn to analysis of tragedy. Critics have called *The Basement: Meditations on a Human Sacrifice* (1979) a cage of words, similar to the sculptural constructions she made in the sixties; and all were inspired by the torture and murder in a basement of eleven-year-old Sylvia Likens by her female guardian, Gertrude Baniszewski, and a group of teens. For over a decade, Millett's obsession became the news story and grisly police photograph of the girl's nude body, lip bitten through from pain and stomach carved with the words "I am a prostitute and proud of it" (Cohen 383). It inspired her to sculpt open cages and eventually to write a nonfiction narrative which she intended to combine "scholarship and philosophy" to explore "the nature of evil." Millett explained, "It explores the terrible antagonism around sexuality. But I'm also writing it as writing too. I have to be in Sylvia Likens' mind as she dies: the last time she sees the vague bit of grey light coming into the basement windows when she dies." Millett admitted, "I was Sylvia Likens … . She was what happens to girls." Millett also attempted to penetrate the torturer's mind, to "try to know something that may be beyond understanding … wickedness beyond meanness" (Raven and Rennie 37). Millett imbues the book with tension created by a dialectic between her own voice and those of her protagonists with their language revealing a brutalized, selfless version of the human experience; but none of the voices can explain, rationalize, or ultimately understand the crime. Frieda Werden writes that Millett "verbalizes the bars of the cage – her subject's poverty, their isolation from societal restraints, their rationalizations and guilts and enjoyment of petty drama – and fills the cage with monologues representing the interior voices of torturer and victim" (Werden 54).

Despite her prolific writings, through the seventies, Millett insisted that she considered herself first a sculptor and only secondly a writer, although she produced art only when commissioned to do a show. For instance, after not sculpting for four years, she was asked by the Women's Interart Center in New York to show her work; and a promotional poster was being printed before she began work with her team of assistants she dubbed "my angels." Her "Terminal Piece" – a stage-light arrangement of a human mannequin and chairs in a cage – was influenced by Ionesco's "The Chairs" and Samuel Beckett's *Waiting for Godot* (1952). It was similar to her "sculpture environment" titled "The Basement," described by Millett as theatre. Two other works produced for a special show in 1977 at the new Los Angeles Women's Building were mammoth environmental sculptures titled "The Naked Ladies" – huge female figures fashioned of papier-maché over chicken wire, one looming over a real shopping cart. Millett preferred showing her work in these "women's environments" newly established in New York and Los Angeles rather than in the "male art world system in which the artist is sort of a semi-nitwit in funny clothes who they try to keep sober." She wished she could be like Louise Nevelson, who persisted in her art despite the difficulties: "She kept right on doing it – she didn't run around and write books or make speeches. ... I felt rebuked." Yoko Ono also encouraged Millett to persist with her sculpture (Raven and Rennie 37-39).

Millett experimented in other visual arts. In collaboration with Louva Elizabeth Irvine, Susan Kleckner, and Robin Mide, she made the 70-millimeter film *Three Lives* (1971), acclaimed as the first feature-length women's liberation documentary. It presented portraits of a young lesbian, a divorcée, and a middle-aged woman in a *cinéma verité* style associated with new trends in "direct cinema" of the 1960s. Using interviewing techniques borrowed from oral history, the film features the voices of the subjects. Millett was director of an all-woman crew, producer, and co-editor of the cinematic documentary; but it was Irvine and Kleckner who had the cinematic experience. The film was shown at the First International Festival of Women's Films in New York in June 1972. Millett also experimented with photography – largely Lesbian Erotica with "little short stories" written on the pictures – but they were not well received when she exhibited them in New York (Millett 1990, 253). She also occasionally exhibited her drawings and prints such as "Nudes," inspired by Japanese calligraphy.

Going to Iran (1981) was based on her own brief odyssey to Iran with her lover, Canadian photojournalist Sophie Keir, on invitation from the Committee to Defend Women's Rights and the Committee to Artistic and Intellectual Freedom in Iran (CAIFI), humanitarian groups of dissenters. The Shah had just been deposed and women, in particular, wanted Millett's insight on the direction of Iranian revolution, being threatened by Moslem fanatics led by the Ayatollah Khomeini. Marching with Iranian women led to Millett's deportation, more fortunate than the fate that she risked in a country that executed homosexuals. The book highlighted news accounts of the intense, endemic discrimination against women as part of fundamentalist Moslem culture.

At the end of *Going to Iran*, Millett summarizes in a very personal way, emphasizing how she learned to treasure personal freedom and mobility. Released after her arrest, she quickly made the transition "from a cell and submachine guns to a brasserie" in Paris, thankful for airplanes, "Because the madness in one place is not the madness of another. If there is an airplane, as long as there is an airplane, as long as you can get on it, and they'll let you – the government, the limiters of freedom, the appropriators of imagination and possibility, the unquestioned thieves of human life, liberty, and pursuit of happiness. If they permit, and as long as they do – so guard what is left of that liberty – you may not only go home, you may go to Paris … . To the city of light streaming in the sun-filled sky, Paris" (Millett 1982, 331).

Such a personal response to Iranian oppressiveness and the dangers she faced there can only be fully understood in light of Millett's own history of incarceration told in *The Loony-Bin Trip* (1990) – a series of tales of her humiliation, degradation, depravation of freedom and even reason through forced medication engineered by her sisters, mother, husband, and female lovers utilizing the international legal and psychiatric system. In her case, the personal truly resonated with the political. She was a case study of the plight of so many women from the 1950s through the 1970s. Robin Morgan wrote in "Goodbye to All That," one of the founding documents of the new radical feminism, "There is something every woman wears around her neck on a thin chain of fear – an amulet of madness" (Cohen 215). Medical researchers found in statistical studies that physicians prescribed almost twice as many psychotherapeutic drugs for women because of stereotypes they held about the female personality (Cooperstock; Linn and Davis); and they identified "an underlying sexual basis for this prejudice" that also led to inordinate institutionalization of women (Lennane and Lennane).

Millett's story began late in 1973 in Oakland when she was teaching as a full professor at Sacramento and leading an international campaign to save the life of Michael X (Mallik), a Trinidadian political activist condemned to death. She and others including John Lennon, Yoko Ono, and attorney William Kunstler believed him falsely accused of murder. Appalled by the money she was pouring into the crusade for commutation of his sentence, her family and friends determined to quell her fanaticism. Aided by Kate's husband Fumio and her lover Sita, her elder sister Sally, then a Nebraska law student, tricked Kate, under the guise of visiting a psychiatrist to relieve the stress, into a hospital – "a mental jail" – and slammed the door behind her. The claustrophobic Millett spent a night in solitary. Against her wishes, doctors forceably administered mind-altering Thorazine – "the business of poisoning consciousness with drugs … such an invasion of soul." The "white police" beat her "to the floor of the parking lot … big guys … and then I was trussed upside down on a stretcher." They had put her in "a locked box," her own cage; the hospital was "like the circles of Dante's Hell, floor after floor, each door locked behind."

After retreating home to New York via St. Paul two weeks later, her mother again committed her on the advice of another doctor – perhaps because Kate questioned him about whether he had read the psychological theories of R. D. Laing or Phyllis Chesler. Feminists summoned legal aid for her, and she was released after three days. Millett exaggerates that the trial she arranged "established a precedent, so no one can be committed to a mental institution without a trial." She observed, "The treatment is not to cure me but to take away my freedom." She concludes, "It's like being a felon without ever having committed a felony." (45)

The bouts with asylums coincided, not surprisingly, with a period in which her husband left her, vacating the loft where they'd lived for fifteen years, which itself was condemned and torn down. The divorce became final in 1984. Acutely depressed, Millett made six suicide attempts, remembering: "Janis and Plath and Sexton beckoned; it seemed time to bow out as a writer too; the residual effects of suicide on artistic reputation might cover over the fact that I had nothing else to write – *Flying* had done it all, said it all" (Millett 1990, 75). But there was another book to tell of how she took the mind-dulling lithium for a total of 13 years to regulate what was diagnosed as manic depression. Twice, she tried to free herself from it. She retained skepticism and even hatred of those who prescribed the drugs with their side effects – sluggish thought, hand tremor, diarrhea, and fears about damaged kidneys.

She remained active in patients' rights groups, helping form the Network Against Psychiatric Assault (NAPA) out of the Madness Network in San Francisco. Her experiences left her justly distrustful of those close to her. In 1980, her lover, Sophie Keir, and other friends, pretended to support her voluntary withdrawal from the drug, which Millett considered "a form of social control" (55); but they tried with Millett's younger sister Malory (originally Mary), an actress, to commit her again. Millett successfully resisted, going on a speaking tour of Ireland, her father's homeland, where she spoke to pro-IRA radicals of her pacifism. She discovers an "amazing international system of mental policing" (195) as American authorities persuaded the Irish to arrest her for withdrawing from lithium. She was drugged and confined in another mental hospital there for several days. Through coincidence and adventure, her Irish friends rescued her. But depression on her return to America led her voluntarily to return to lithium for another six years.

Millett learned that "Institutional treatment of women often involves conditioning in and enforcing sexual stereotypes" (Millett 1990, 39-40). Such conditioning could be mild such as including use of cosmetics and clothing as part of therapy or requiring female inmates to do domestic chores in the institution or even in doctors' homes. A patient who forgot how to cook "remembered like magic" after a few electroshock treatments. Women were "singled out and punished for mildly aggressive behavior which would be tolerated in men, simply because they depart from the clinician's expectations for 'normal' women" (Roth and Lerner, 801-03). Phyllis Chesler points out that "'depression' rather than 'aggression' is the female response to disappointment or loss ... Women are in a continual state of mourning – for what they never had –

or had too briefly, and for what they can't have in the present, be it Prince Charming or direct worldly power. ... It is important to note that 'depressed' women are (like women in general) only verbally hostile" (Chesler 44-45). Chesler suggests that women with normal responses to stress in a sexist society were often diagnosed as mentally ill.

Not until 1989, under confidence with two patients' rights advocates from the National Association for Rights, Protection, and Advocacy, did Millett finally quit lithium. She has even reconciled with family: "I had lost my family over being gay, over being an artist, and now I was going to lose them over being crazy. ... it seemed too stupid. I'm an inveterate peacemaker and an habitual teacher. I insisted that if I could somehow make them see my side of it and question it, we would side against the shrinks" (Millett 1990, 55).

Millett spent four years from 1982 to 1985 writing *The Loony-Bin Trip* (1990), another very personal vindication and defense of "the integrity of the human mind and its sacredness," another chapter in her yet unfinished autobiography that documents her travels through diverse cultures of the late twentieth century. At first the book was just therapeutic: "The only way out [of a bout of severe depression] is to write: the manuscript I called the Deathbook with all the notes and passages, the fragments from the first bust and lockup, and the attempts at suicide ... . A fight back, a writer's solution to the panic ... . So this time confront, don't run. Heal yourself. Stand your ground. ... This time spill the beans and speak." She determined to turn "what happened in those joints" into "not just a catastrophe but a source" (Millett 1990, 254-55).

The book obviously has other functions. It ends her conspiracy of silence with so-called "loved ones" who exercised such arbitrary power over her "for her own good," thus eliminating some of the possibility it could happen again. She takes the reader into confidence, as if there remains only the reader who she can trust, to whom she can present evidence of self and sanity. In the end – although she does not explicitly say so – it is no longer the monolithic force of patriarchy that Millett must confront but the newer myth of sisterhood. Even this she anticipated in *Sexual Politics*, commenting that "everyone knows that having internalized the disesteem in which they are held, women despise both themselves and each other." She presaged her own fate in that first book: "Generally an accused woman acquires a notoriety out of proportion to her acts and due to sensational publicity she may be tried largely for her 'sex life'" (Millett 1970, 55-56).

Millett now lives in relative quiet on her eighty-acre farm outside Poughkeepsie, New York, and participates in a women's community in the region. She had struggled for years, at times at great emotional cost, to turn it into a self-supporting artists' colony for women financed by the sale of Christmas trees. Two pines flanking the entrance commemorate Simone de Beauvoir, whose funeral Kate attended in Paris in 1986 (Cohen 384).

Throughout her career, Millett has been consistent in resisting dogmatism as an outspoken proponent of principles of justice, freedom, pacifism, and equal rights, even when it alienated family, friends, and associates in the women's movement. She remembers, "I grew up in an orthodoxy; I really know about think-crime. In Catholicism, all kinds of thoughts are crimes." She equally resists orthodoxy even in the interest of causes she might otherwise support. At times, her principles have made her a victim of "horizontal warfare" – "trashing" or "zapping" by other women in organizations and audiences who felt that even her radical views did not conform with what they considered "correct." In a 1975 debate with Herbert Marcuse, she reacted immediately to his suggestion that after "the" revolution which social radicals anticipated there would have to be repressive measures against the former elite. "No revolution that requires force and repression of human rights is a revolution," she countered. Millett defends the Bill of Rights as "one of the greatest advances in human behavior and theory of government. ... Very few tribes, classes, industries, religions, parties, states have ever permitted such a thing as free speech. Now if that could be extended to freedom of life, you've got a revolution" (Raven and Rennie 41; "Dialog" 20).

Notes

1   Sara Davidson ranks her with radical feminists Ti-Grace Atkinson, Susan Brownmiller, Marilyn Webb, and Anselma Dell'Olio in her article "Foremothers," in the special issue on "The American Woman" of *Esquire* 80:1 (July 1973), 71-87.

2   The essay Millett wrote in 1968 was published as "Sexual Politics: A Manifesto for Revolution," in Shulamith Firestone and Anne Koedt, eds., *Notes from the Second Year: Women's Liberation* (New York: New York Radical Feminists, April 1970).

3   Feminists attempting to rid the language of sexist elements preferred the term "ovular" to "seminal." Ravon and Rennie, 36.

4   George Stade quoted in "Who's Come a Long Way, Baby?" *Time* (Aug. 31, 1970), 20. See also Stade, "Romantic Anxiety," *Partisan Review* 40 (1973), 494-500; "Mailer and Miller," *Partisan Review* 44 (1977), 616-24. (Doane and Hodges 140).

5   Other prominent participants included Sally Kempton, Myra Lamb, and NOW Board Chair Wilma Scott Heide. Bella Abzug, Caroline Bird, and new NOW President Aileen Hernandez sent formal messages of support for Millett.

The Works of Kate Millett

Token Learning. New York: National Organization for Women, 1967. Pamphlet.
"Sexual Politics: A Manifesto for Revolution," in Shulamith Firestone and Anne Koedt,
    eds. *Notes from the Second Year: Women's Liberation*. New York: New York Radical
    Feminists, April 1970. Essay written in 1968.
"The Debate over Women: Ruskin versus Mill," *Victorian Studies* 14 (Sept. 1970), 63-81.
Sexual Politics. 1970.
Three Lives, 70-mm documentary film, 1971.
in Vivian Gornick and Barbara Moran, eds. *Women in a Sexist Society* (New York: New
    American Library, 1971).
The Prostitution Papers. New York: Avon, 1973.
Flying. New York: 1974.
"The Shame is Over," *Ms* 3:7 (Jan. 1975), 26-29.
Sita. New York: 1977.
"Introduction" to Cynthia MacAdams, *Emergence*. New York: Chelsea House, 1977. The
    book contains MacAdams' portrait photographs of women, many active in the feminist
    movement.
"Introduction" to *Caterpillars: Journal Entries by Eleven Women*. New York: Epona
    Press, 1977.
"Introduction" to Maryse Holder, *Give Sorrow Words: Maryse Holder's Letters from
    Mexico*, New York, 1979.
The Basement: Meditations on a Human Sacrifice. New York: Simon and Schuster, 1979.
Going to Iran. New York: Coward, McCann & Geoghegan, 1982. With photographs by
    Sophie Keir.
The Loony-Bin Trip. New York: Simon and Schuster, 1990.

Other works cited:

Sidney Abbott and Barbara Love, *Sappho Was a Right-On Woman: A Liberated View of
    Lesbianism*. New York: Stein & Day, 1972.
The Alyson Almanac: A Treasury of Information for the Gay and Lesbian Community.
    Boston: Alyson Publications, 1989.
René Kuhn Bryant, "Drowning in Claustrophobia," *National Review* 30 (Aug. 1974), 990.
Phyllis Chesler, *Women and Madness*. New York: Doubleday, 1972.
Marcia Cohen. *The Sisterhood: The Inside Story of the Women's Movement and the Lead-
    ers Who Made It Happen*. New York: Fawcett Columbine, 1988.
Ruth Cooperstock, "Sex Differences in the Use of Mood-Modifying Drugs: An Explana-
    tory Model." *Journal of Health and Social Behavior* 12 (Sept. 1971): 239-43.
"Dialog: Millett and Marcuse." *Off Our Backs* 5 (Aug. 1, 1975): 20.
Janice Doane and Devon Hodges. *Nostalgia and Sexual Difference: The Resistance to
    Contemporary Feminism*. New York: Methuen, 1987.
Alice Echols, *Daring to be Bad: Radical Feminism in America. 1967-1975*. Minneapolis:
    Minnesota UP, 1989.
Mary Ellmann, *Thinking About Women*, New York, Harcourt, Brace, Jovanovich, 1968.
Lillian Faderman, *Surpassing the Love of Men: Romantic Friendship and Love Between
    Women from the Renaissance to the Present*. New York: William Morrow, 1981.

Muriel Haynes. "Sexual Energy." *New Republic* 6 (July 1974), 28.

Sylvia Ann Hewlett. *A Lesser Life: The Myth of Women's Liberation in America.* New York: Warner Books, 1986.

Judith Hole and Ellen Levine, *Rebirth of Feminism.* New York: Quadrangle, 1971.

Irving Howe, "The Middle Class Mind of Kate Millett," *Harper's* 241 (Dec. 1970): 124, 129.

Suzanne Juhasz, "Toward a Theory of Form in Feminist Autobiography: Kate Millett's *Flying* and *Sita*; Maxine Hong Kingston's *The Woman Warrior.*"*International Journal of Women's Studies* 2:1 (1979): 62-75.

Annette Kolodny, "The Lady's Not for Spurning: Kate Millett and the Critics." *Contemporary Literature* 17:4 (autumn 1976): 541-62.

Elinor Langer, "Confessing." *Ms* (Dec. 1974): 74.

Martha Weinman Lear. "The Second Feminist Wave." *New York Times Magazine* (March 10, 1968).

K. Jean Lennane and R. John Lennane. "Alleged Psychogenic Disorders in Women: A Possible Manifestation of Sexual Prejudice." *The New England Journal of Medicine* 288 (Feb. 3, 1973): 288-92.

"The Lesbian Issue and Women's Lib." *New York Times* (Dec. 18, 1970).

Laurence S. Linn and Milton S. Davis. "The Use of Psychotherapeutic Drugs by Middle-Aged Women." *Journal of Health and Social Behavior* 12 (Dec. 1971): 331.

Norman Mailer, "The Prisoner of Sex." *Harper's* (March 1971), reprinted as a book. New York: Little, Brown, and Company, 1971.

Arlene Raven and Susan Rennie, "Interview with Kate Millett." *Chrysalis* 3 (Oct. 1977): 35-41.

Robert T. Roth and Judith Lerner, "Sex-based Discrimination in the Mental Institutionalization of Women." *California Law Review* 63 (1973): 796-801.

R. Z. S. "Up Against the Men's Room Wall." *Time* (Aug. 3, 1970).

"Sexual Politics by Kate Millett." *The New Yorker* 46 (Sept. 19, 1970): 137.

George Stade, *Confessions of a Lady-Killer.* New York: Norton, 1979.

George Stade, "Mailer and Miller." *Partisan Review* 44 (1977): 616-24.

George Stade, "Romantic Anxiety." *Partisan Review* 40 (1973): 494-500.

Julia P. Stanley, "Fear of *Flying*?" *Sinister Wisdom* 1:2 (1976): 52-62.

Catharine R. Stimpson, "Literature as Radical Statement." in Emory Elliott, ed. *Columbia Literary History of the United States.* New York: Columbia Univ. Press, 1988, 1060-76.

Lionel Tiger, "An Unchauvinist Male Replies." *Time* (Aug. 31, 1970): 21.

Claire Tomalin, "Liberty, Equality, Sorority." *New Statesman* (March 26, 1971): 429-30.

Helen Vendler, "Feminism and Literature." *The New York Review of Books* (May 31, 1990): 19-25.

Gore Vidal. "In Another Country." *New York Review of Books* (July 22, 1971): 11.

Winifred D. Wandersee, *On the Move: American Women in the 1970s*, Boston: Twayne/G. K. Hall, 1988.

Frieda Werden, "Kate Millett." in Langdon Lynne Faust, ed. *American Women Writers*, vol. II. New York: Frederick Ungar, 1979: 54.

"Who's Come a Long Way, Baby?" *Time* (Aug. 31, 1970), 18-21.

Susan J. Wolfe (Robbins), "Stylistic Experimentation in Millett, Johnston, and Wittig." *Fireweed* 5/6 (1979/80): 134-42.

Günter H. Lenz

Edward W. Said

(1935-)

In the Preface to his important book, *Intellectuals in Power: A Genealogy of Critical Humanism* (1986), Paul A. Bové writes: "Edward Said has produced the most powerful model of oppositional critical practice within the American literary academy. In large part, Said's project results form his organic relationship to an oppressed and homeless people ... . Said, therefore, appears frequently in this book because his position reveals what a critical humanism is capable of when it sets out to fulfill its progressive secular potential" (Bové xiii). Bové's assessment of his colleague's achievement gives some indication of what I consider the most consequential objectives of Said's critical project and the crucial questions his work as a "radical intellectual" has raised: How can "oppositional critical practice" in the United States reconstitute itself after the poststructuralist deconstruction of the Western humanist tradition and the crisis of radical literary and cultural criticism at home? In how far does the common institutional context of the American intellectual, the university, enable, accommodate, depoliticize the radical scholar's work? If it is one of the major problems for the "critical intellectual" today to "situate" his or her work and relate it to a clearly defined "constituency," Edward W. Said, as a Palestinian in Western exile, seems to be in a particularly difficult, but also productive and challenging position. But what does Bové's "organic relationship" actually mean? Can it – or should it – overcome the experience and the intercultural construction of "otherness" and "difference"? How can Said succeed in combining, or negotiating, his (Western) avantgarde work as a radical literary and cultural critic with his political commitment to, and his active interventions in, the Palestinians' fight for national recognition, regional independence, and cultural "enunciation"? In which sense can a "critical" and "secular" humanism reaffirm the "moral" dimension of critical cultural work after Foucault's "discourse analysis," which had suspended the category of the "subject," without reestablishing the radical critic as a new (or old) culture hero? And how can the radical Western intellectual and the postcolonial intellectual define the formal strategies of their critical discourse?

Since his first book, *Joseph Conrad and the Fiction of Autobiography* (1966), Edward W. Said has most unrelentingly and most creatively explored these questions in his work. Born in 1935 in Jerusalem in what was then Palestine, a mandatory territory of Great Britain since 1920, he left with his family for Cairo, Egypt, in 1947, when the United Nations decided to divide Palestine into a Jewish and an Arab state and to place Jerusalem under international control. A year later the state of Israel was founded, incorporating additional territory from the part of Palestine assigned by the UN to the Arab population. More than 700,000 Arab Palestinians were dispossessed and displaced and became refugees. In Cairo Said attended the American School and Victoria College, in the early Fifties began his studies in the United States, got an A.B. from Princeton in 1957, and his M.A. and Ph.D. from Harvard in 1960 and in 1964 respectively. Since 1963 he has been teaching at Columbia University in New York City where he became a full professor in 1970 and was later promoted to distinguished Chairs in 1977 and in 1989. Since 1977 he has been a member of the Palestinian National Council, the Palestinian parliament-in-exile.

Since his dissertation on Joseph Conrad Edward W. Said has published six books. *Beginnings: Intention and Method* (1975) is his highly original and difficult contribution to avantgarde literary (and cultural) theory, to a radically historical theory of authorship and author-ity. *Orientalism* (1978) develops his critique of the ideological and imperialistic implications and consequences of Orientalism as a totalizing, ethnocentric Western discourse inherently based on the inferiority of "the Orient." *The Question of Palestine* (1979) offers an account of the historical experience of the – of his own – Palestinian people and their "traumatic national encounter with Zionism" and a passionate plea for the (re-)construction of a political identity of the (of his) Palestinian people. In *Covering Islam: How the Media and the Experts Determine How We See the Rest of the World* (1981), Said exposes the biased and distorted depictions of "Islam" in American mass media, in the academic community, and among experts in "area studies" and government policymakers, using the Iranian revolution and the Teheran hostage crisis of 1979 as a case study. *The World, the Text, and the Critic* (1983) is a collection of essays in literary and cultural theory and criticism that pursue in detail Said's notion of a radical "secular criticism" between the normative discourse of "Culture" and totalizing theoretical "systems." Finally, *After the Last Sky: Palestinian Lives* (1986), a multivocal text with photographs by Jean Mohr, tries to complement his earlier, often polemic attacks on the victimization of Palestinians by Western and Israeli discourse and neocolonialist politics with fragmentary reflections, direct expressions of Palestinian everyday life, and self-conscious assertions of cultural and political identity.

If Said has widely been recognized among American literary and cultural critics as one of the most pronounced and powerful models of oppositional critical practice today, the reactions to his work have been very divergent. He has been attacked, and denounced, by mainstream critics and "Orientalist" scholars for transgressing the boundaries of literary and cultural criticism, for his idiosyncratic critical vocabulary, and for his double commitment to radical scholarship and to political activism in the name of the Palestinian people (see Bové, "Closing Up the Ranks"). Critics from the Left have criticized his theoretical work for lacking clarity and consequence in terms of Marxist theory and have found his engagement with French poststructuralist thought less than satisfactory. Some American critics such as Paul Bové or Jim Merod who have acknowledged the profound impact of Said's work on their own redefinitions of oppositional criticism and the role of the humanist intellectual have expressed reservations concerning the political thrust of Said's critical practice. Bové who emphasizes Said's specific "organic relationship" to an oppressed people – which seems to make him a "natural" model of the Gramscian ideal of an "organic intellectual" with the kind of a real "constituency" radical Western intellectuals have been looking for – charges Said with reintroducing in his revisionary reading of Foucault's discourse analysis and theory of power the ideal of the intellectual as hero who continues to work with "those enabling figures basic to the origins and perpetuation of the dynastic discourses against which the oppositional critic always struggles" (Bové, *Intellectuals in Power* 31f., cf. 218). In his wide-ranging study, *The Political Responsibility of the Critic* (1987), Merod takes exception to Bové's rather single-minded defense of Foucault against Said, but in his exposition of the problematic he critically reads, reexamines, and complements Said's theoretical reflections and projects of the oppositional intellectual by the crucial insights and strategies of Foucault's "transgressive intellectual" (see esp. 180-95). As we will see, Said's work raises a number of questions, and critics such as Bové and Merod have carefully investigated important issues. What is amazing, however, in all these critical, but sympathetic responses to Said's critical practice is that almost all of them exclusively focus on his explicit contributions to literary theory or redefinitions of Western humanities and ignore, or only mention in passing, his work on Orientalism and the politics, culture, and discursive formations of the world of Islam. If they refer to *Orientalism*, they discuss the book mainly as the prime example of an American (revisionary) Foucauldian analysis of discourse and power, but they fail to take up the challenge of cultural (and intercultural) otherness and difference indicated in the book and further developed in Said's later work on the world of Islam and postcolonial discourse and to explore the repercussions of these reflections on Said's project of oppositional, interventionary criticism "at home."

The essays in *The World, the Text, and the Critic* most explicitly and most concretely, but also most self-critically define and elaborate Said's project of oppositional cultural practice and its specific critical (counter-)discursive strategies. His notion of a secular, "interventionary" criticism that resists the dominant culture and remains rigorously skeptical grew out of his commitment to a fundamental reconstitution of American literary criticism vis-à-vis French poststructuralism, an increasingly radical questioning of the ethnocentrism of Western discourses, and a reformulation of the moral responsibilities of a politically active intellectual.

Said situates his critique in a powerful reassessment of contemporary European literary and cultural "theory" and a reconstruction of American "Left" literary criticism, past and present. He responds to the "radical" philosophical propositions of French "post-structuralism" (Derrida, Foucault) and criticizes its "depoliticization" in American literary deconstructive criticism which in his view has displaced – in spite of its radical rhetoric – poststructuralism's critical potential and philosophical thrust by isolating "textuality" and the "self-deconstruction" of the language of literature. Ironically, American avantgarde literary criticism has canonized deconstruction as a new theoretical system or master-discourse. Said also points out the failure of American "leftist" criticism to draw on "the American radical movement that ended with the McCarthy period" (*World* 166) and to work out an oppositional, revisionist, historical critique of the hegemonic power of contemporary culture. In his wide-ranging essay "Reflections on American 'Left' Literary Criticism," first published in 1979, he writes:

> No one would have any trouble finding a Left in American culture between the twenties and the fifties ... To [F.O.] Matthiessen ... literature and criticism are nourished by the very same experiences out of which economics, material history, and social conflict are generated ... The problem is to see how he spoke so passionately and politically of the critic's responsibilities and why, twenty-odd years later, critics like de Man (whose current influence is very estimable) direct their attention to the impossibilities of political and social responsibility (162).

Said does not answer this question, even though he does complain about a "relative absence of the historical dimension" in literary studies since the 1960s, "even in their Marxist variety" (165f.). He knows that "the transition from the notion of the Left in politics to the Left in literary criticism [is] a difficult one to make" (160) and that history has destroyed some of the foundations of Matthiessen's radical criticism and subverted the meaning of the very terms "Left" and "Right":

> So far as I have been able to tell, the kind of Marxism practised or announced in university literary departments owes very little to the American radical movement that ended

with the McCarthy period. The new Marxism came to this country partly as a result of the interest in French criticism and later the Frankfurt School, partly because of the general wave of anti-war agitation on the campuses. It did so in the form of sudden discovery and just as sudden application to literary problems. Its main weaknesses were the comparative absence of a continuous native Marxist theoretical tradition or culture to back it up and its relative isolation from any concrete political struggle (166).

In Said's view, this unmediated adoption of European "theory," this relative "absence of the historical dimension," and this "isolation from any concrete political struggle" have led to a form of academic literary studies on the Left that, "far from producing work to challenge or revise prevailing values, institutions, and definitions, have in fact gone too long a way in confirming them" (168). Or, they have, in restricting their domain to "something called literature," as Gerald Graff and Christopher Lasch have also argued, "effectively confirm[ed] the culture and the society enforcing those restrictions" (175; see Lenz, *Tradition*). In his essay, Said briefly discusses the internal and external challenges to the dominance of modernist (New Critical) literary criticism during the late 1960s and the often unmeditated search for "relevance" and new interdisciplinary programs. But he does not reconstruct in more detail the specific historical processes that led to the "comparative absence of a continuous native Marxist theoretical tradition of culture" in the United States or alternative forms of radical literary criticism. Obviously, there cannot be a "body" of works or movements that constitute something like a "radical tradition" the cultural critic could simply hold on to or recover. If there is an indigenous radical tradition in the United States, it is, in Theodor W. Adorno's words, a "tradition of the anti-traditional," of discontinuity, of the critique and questioning of the form of tradition that has been institutionalized as ideology, "affirmative culture" (Herbert Marcuse), or the "politics of Culture" (Alan Trachtenberg). It is a tradition of social critique as well as of counter-cultures, sustaining alternative ways of life that have to be discovered, "wrested away from conformism" (Walter Benjamin), and redefined and reconstituted ever again.

If Said does not provide a genealogy of (the failure of) American Left Literary criticism, he pursues instead the question how — under these circumstances — effective strategies of an oppositional literary and cultural criticism in advanced capitalist societies in the West can be developed, how problems of power, authority, and cultural formations can critically be addressed and worked out at all. What most American literary and cultural critics have failed to realize and consciously to explore is the fact that all intellectual and cultural work is enmeshed in relations of power in history and society and "occurs somewhere, at some time, on some very precisely mapped-out and permissible terrain, which is ultimately contained by the State" (169). Drawing on Antonio Gramsci's analysis of hegemony and of the complex functioning of "culture" and cultural pluralism in sustaining the power and authority of the "modern Western State" as well as on Raymond Williams' notion of "cultural materialism," Said poses the question of the role of the radical intellectual today, of "modern critical consciousness, of oppositional criticism" (174). He briefly characterizes his explicitly "secular" concept of "affiliation" as providing the focus for a genuinely historical and politically oppositional understanding of cultural formations, defining "affiliation" as "that implicit network of peculiarly cultural associations between forms, statements, and other aesthetic elaborations on the one hand and, on the other, institutions, agencies, classes, and amorphous social forces" (174f.).

In other programmatic essays in *The World, the Text, and the Critic*, Said offers a more detailed analysis of these affiliations in an oppositional discourse on literature and culture. The critic's responsibility is, as he writes in his "Introduction: Secular Criticism," to face not only the "text," but also the "world," to "affirm the connection between texts and the existential actualities of human life, politics, societies, and events" (5). For Said this does not mean to relate the literary text to some kind of environment or background, but to rediscover that the text itself is a dynamic field, that texts always "are in the world, and hence worldly," that texts "to some degree ... are nevertheless part of a social world, human life, and of course the historical moments in which they are located and interpreted" (4). Texts have to be studied in a "worldly" and "historical" way. Critics have to determine "the social and external constraints upon production, as well as the discursive and cultural (that is, internal) systems that provoke and assimilate literary production." In being in the world, being worldly, "texts are fundamentally facts of power, not of democratic exchange," as the discursive situation, "far from being a type of conversation between equals, ... is more usually like the unequal relation between colonizer and colonized, oppressor and oppressed" (48).

If texts are worldly and facts of power and if the discursive situation is inherently political, then criticism as well, or literary theory, is always embedded and reconstituted in institutional contexts, is "always situated: it is skeptical, secular, reflectively open to its own failings" (26). It cannot simply be transferred from one period, place, or discursive formation to another without undergoing crucial transformations. In his essay "Traveling Theory," Said sketches a general framework for analyzing the patterns of influence or interaction between theories of different countries or times that transcends the common debate, or polemic, of the accommodation and appropriation of "radical" European social and cultural thought by American critics in terms of misunderstanding and misinterpretation that could easily be corrected if the critics had more adequate knowledge and a more articulated political consciousness. Said discovers a "discernible and recurrent pattern to the movement of the [transplantation, transference, circulation, and commerce of theories and ideas]," namely "three or four stages common to the way any theory or idea travels" (226). Said does not talk of theories or ideas in the sense of a combination of concepts and items that can be (re-)assembled in different ways and "used" with different political intentions and results. What he has in mind is the complex constellation and agonistic process of critical thought in particular historical and social contexts. The key concepts in his understanding of the pattern of "traveling theory" are "place" and "time" as specific situations and the "distance" between them. His approach is radically historical, particularly as there does not exist any consensus among critics of different times and places on the enclosing limits of "literature" and "literary criticism" and as the critic should not renounce his or her historical responsibility by resorting to "the theory of limitless intertextuality as an Archimedean point outside the two situations" (237). In studying "the extent to which theory is a response to a specific social and historical situation of which an intellectual occasion is a part," the critic of traveling theory will "judge misreadings (as they occur) as part of a historical transfer of ideas and theories from one setting to another" (236f.). The historical transfer of ideas and theories, therefore, *necessarily entails transformation* of their forms and functions, a transformation the critic of traveling theory has to reconstruct and analyze. As significant examples Said discusses the "influence" Georg Lukács' *History and Class Consciousness* had on Lucien Goldmann in France and on Raymond Williams in England, and the response to Foucault's work in the United States. As any theory tends toward "closure, like social conventions or cultural dogma," or "overextension" to a "bad infinity" (in Lukács' case), the critic has to develop the "faculty for locating or situating theory" (239, 241). Yet it is important to realize that Said's emphasis on "place," on "situating" theory does *not contextualize or root* criticism in reality, but that he has in mind a "critical consciousness" that is aware of the *difference* between "situations" and the "resistances to theory" and that opens up theory "towards historical reality, society, human needs and interests" (242f.). "Theory, in short, can never be complete, just as one's interest in everyday life is never exhausted by simulacra, models, or theoretical abstracts of it" (241). "Critical consciousness" has to beware of the "closure" of theory, but it also has to keep from "overtotalizing ... social reality" and "degrading theory," as Said accuses Foucault of tending to do (242f.).

Nevertheless, Said in his essay focuses exclusively on examples of an "appropriation" of "revolutionary" theories that have robbed them of their "insurrectionary quality" and have led to "impoverishment" or "rarefaction," without pursuing the question in which sense these European "theories" may have in their transformation, in the crucially *different* academic, cultural, and political situation in the United States, effectively contributed to repoliticizing and rehistoricizing American literary criticism. This hesitation may find its explanation in his rigorously tentative, skeptical, and self-reflexive notion of a "secular criticism" he sets out to locate "between culture and system" (the title of one of the key essays in his book). Said defines "culture" as closure, as "a system of discrimination and evaluation," as "a system of exclusions legislated from above but enacted throughout its polity, by which such things as anarchy, disorder, irrationality, inferiority, bad taste, and immorality are identified, then deposited outside the culture and kept there by the power of the State and its institutions" (11). In his analysis, the institution(s) of "culture" perform their hegemonic function through a process of constant re-definitons and re-articulations of difference: "The dialectic of self-fortification and self-confirmation by which culture achieves its hegemony over society and the State is based on a constantly practised differentiation of itself from what it believes to be not itself" (12). On the other side, the critic has to beware of "system," of the "impersonal system of disciplines and methods," of the domestication of oppositional, "interventionary movements" – such as French poststructuralism – into a theoretical system abstracted from "the events, the physical senses that made it possible and render it intelligible as the result of human work" (4). It has to prevent critical thought from being absorbed by "the ethic of professionalism" (4).

If criticism wants to overcome "the overall compliance of the intellectual class to which critics belong" and to subvert "the regulated, not to say calculated, irrelevance of criticism" (25), not excluding "Left" criticism, it must keep distance and situate itself between the dominant culture and the totalizing forms of critical systems, place itself "skeptically between culture as a massive body of self-congratulating ideas and system or method, anything resembling a sovereign technique that claims to be free of history, subjectivity, or circumstance" (202). Only by working at this critical "nodal point" can it be true to the dialectic at work in "affirmative culture" (Marcuse) or "hegemony" (Gramsci) which in turning "culture" into ideology, power, and system of exclusion and oppression, *at the same time* have produced their very opposites, namely a powerful resistance to domination and domestication and enabling forms of cultural critique. Said writes: "If culture exerts the kinds of pressure I have mentioned, and if it creates the environment and the community that allows people to feel they belong, then it must be true that resistance to the culture has always been present" (14). Intellectuals have often contributed to the working of hegemony, but they have also "stood for values, ideas, and activities that transcend and deliberately interfere with the collective weight imposed by the nation-state and the national culture" (14).

Said's "oppositional criticism," then, (re-)constitutes itself through the awareness and unrelenting discursive dramatization of *distance* and *difference*: "If criticism is reducible neither to a doctrine nor to a political position on a particular question, and if it is to be in the world and self-aware simultaneously, then its identity is its difference from other cultural activities and from systems of thought or of method" (29). It is only through this identity in difference that for Said oppositional criticism can pursue its *positive* goal, "noncoercive knowledge produced in the interests of human freedom" (29).

This description of the oppositional quality and dynamic of criticism has far-reaching implications. How does Said's commitment to the "project of modernity," the ideas and ideals of the enlightenment, and the responsibility of the intellectual relate to his critical reception of the attack on the humanist tradition in French poststructuralism, especially in Derrida and Foucault? How does he "situate" his oppositional criticism in the intellectual and social world? Said, first of all, emphasizes the *individual moral* commitment of the intellectual, the "individual consciousness placed at a sensitive nodal point" (15). But he knows that contemporary literary criticism has achieved its methodological independence only "by forfeiting an active situation in the world," by celebrating modernist alienation and "homelessness," that it has replaced a concern with the "relations of power at work in history and society" by a "rhetorical enthusiasm for buzz words like scandal, rupture, transgression, and discontinuity" (173). Said, therefore, argues that the individual critical mind must be very much aware of "the *collective* whole, context, or situation in which it finds itself" (15, my emphasis) and must combine this "worldly self-situating," this "sensitive response to the dominant culture" with the knowledge that the individual consciousness is a historical and social actor in the world. That is, the critical intellectual must – and here Said quotes Raymond Williams – "act on behalf of those alternative acts and alternative intentions whose advancement is a fundamental human and intellectual obligation" (30).

This commitment to enlightenment, to noncoercive knowledge in the interest of human freedom, and to solidarity with the oppressed and alternative acts and intentions returns Said to the question what the "between" in his project of oppositional "criticism between culture and system" actually means, how key terms such as "text," "discourse," and "world" can mediate between the individual critical consciousness and the collective context and social responsibility without collapsing the difference.

Said pursues these problems in his lengthy discussion of the works of Jacques Derrida and Michael Foucault in his essay "Criticism Between Culture and System." In his comparison of Derrida and Foucault he finds that both – in spite of their divergent views on criticism – "consciously attempt to take revisionist positions toward a reigning cultural hegemony" and that they are "aware of the danger that what they do might turn itself into a critical orthodoxy, an unthinking system of thought impervious to change and insensitive to its own problems" (208). Both produce criticism in Said's sense, but in contrasting their critical strategies Said finds Foucault more challenging to contemporary "insular and scholastic" American criticism than Derrida, as he not only "moves us into the text," but "in and out" (183), reading the inscriptions of power in the text as its claim on actuality. Derrida's definition of a text concentrates on its "deconstruction," on its self-difference, on the imperceptibility of the text that always "hides" from the first glance "the law of its composition and the rules of its game" (184). In his more recent work, Derrida has radicalized his deconstructive work on often hybrid texts at the boundaries of disciplinary discourses by experimenting with alternative forms of writing, by exploring, as Said puts it, quoting Derrida, an "*écriture double*, one half of which provokes an inversion of the cultural domination Derrida everywhere identifies with metaphysics and its hierarchies, the other half of which 'allows the detonation of writing in the very interior of the word, thus disrupting the entire given order and taking over the field'" (185). But Said accuses Derrida's "reading method" as being "unable to get hold of the local material density and power of ideas as historical actuality" (212), of collapsing the difference between the text and the world: "the search *within* a text for the conditions of textuality will falter at the very point where the text's historical presentation to the reader is put into question and made an issue for the critic" (212). Derrida explicitly distinguishes his notion of deconstruction from dialectical thinking – Said quotes from *Disseminations* where Derrida says of his "anticoncepts, antinames, counterideas" that reveal textuality: "these points of indefinite pivoting ... mark the spots of what can never be mediated, mastered, sublated, or dialecticized through any *Erinnerung* or *Aufhebung*" (206). Yet Derrida's balancing act in his (intertextual) deconstructive readings between a philosophical critique of the complicitous use of language and his tentative projection of alternative terms is characterized by a strong ascesis that directs its "dedefinitional energies" on the undecidability and indeterminacy in a text and not on its effective historical power. Derrida's "programmatic hesitation toward his historical situation, toward his work's affiliation with certain types of work and not with others" (210) has kept him from a pronounced historically specific deconstructive critique of social formations, institutions, and manifestations of power.

Foucault also stressed the difference of his notion of "discourse" from dialectial thinking, as Said pointed out in his review essay on *The Archeology of Knowledge* in *Diacritics* (1974) and in his book *Beginnings* (1974). "Archeology" is the "retrieval of the archive" as the "place of discourse," discourse being "an historically and particularly apprehensible order where a statement occurs" (*An Ethics* 29f.). Discursive practices take place within an *épistémè*, a "system of distances," a set of moving constraints that establish an outer limit of knowledge" (*An Ethics* 34) at a given moment in history. "The filled, activated space of a given epoch," Said writes in his book *Beginnings*, "Foucault calls an *épistémè*; the filling is *discourse*, a body that has temporal duration and is comprised of *énoncés* (statements)" (295). For Foucault, "discourse is not dialectical" (*An Ethics* 34), but characterized by "difference," by "reversibility," "discontinuity," "specificity," and "exteriority," as Said emphasizes in his exposition of *L'ordre du discours* (1971) in *Beginnings* (297-313). The method is "postnarrative" (*Beginnings* 282), as Foucault understands "history" no longer as linear, as a narrative sequence, but as *genealogy*, as "decentered," as a break of the present and the past, as shaped by "dispersion," "displacement," "transformation," "discontinuity," "coincidence." As Foucault defines the concept in an interview in 1977: "[Genealogy] is a form of history which can account for the constitution of knowledges, discourse, domains of objects etc., without having to make reference to a subject which is either transcendental in relation to the field of events or runs in its empty sameness throughout the course of history" (Foucault, *Power/Knowledge* 117). In *Beginnings*, Said mentions Foucault's argument that Hegel's dialectic "so compelled thought into continuities that any radical philosopher since Hegel has to think against Hegel" (296). Foucault set himself the task of reincluding elements of "chance, discontinuity, and materiality" into thought and of elaborating a "theory of discontinuous systematizations" (Foucault, *L'ordre du discours*, quoted in *Beginnings* 296). His understanding of discourse tries critically to uncover the power of texts by reading them as integral to the "social processes of differentiation, exclusion, incorporation, and rule" (*World* 212). As Said concludes in his essay "Criticism between Culture and System":

Foucault's greatest intellectual contribution is to an understanding of how the will to exercise dominant control in society and history has also discovered a way to clothe, disguise, rarefy, and wrap itself systematically in the language of truth, discipline, rationality, utilitarian value, and knowledge. And this language, in its naturalness, authority, professionalism, assertiveness, and antitheoretical directness, is what Foucault has called *discourse*. The difference between discourse and such coarser yet no less significant fields of social combat as the class struggle is that discourse works its productions, discriminations, censorship, interdictions, and invalidations on the intellectual, at the level of base not of superstructure. The power of discourse is that it is at once object of struggle and the tool by which the struggle is conducted (*World* 216).

For Foucault, the master discourse of society became "invisible" some time near the end of the 18th century when it began to hide the "systematic rules of its formations and its concrete affiliations with power" (217). Language was dispersed into special disciplinary discourses, in the plural, that in their institutionalization in the culture obscured their interrelationships as well as their uses as means of social control. This process in the history of culture, of knowledge, defines the intellectual's political task: He has to read the text and the network of intertextuality as social practice and make the discourses visible again. Said writes:

Foucault's interest in textuality is to present the text stripped of its esoteric or hermetic elements, and to do this by making the text assume its affiliations with institutions, offices, agencies, classes, academies, corporations, groups, guilds, ideologically defined parties and professions. Foucault's descriptions of a text or discourse attempts by the detail and subtlety of the description to *resemanticize* and forcibly to redefine and reidentify the particular interests that all texts serve (212).

If the master discourse of society works as "power," as systematic "exclusion" and "incorporation," the critic's own discourse serves as a "countermemory for the text" (184) and has to function as a counterdiscourse. It is at this point that Said considers Foucault's work as lacking in consequence. He acknowledges that Foucault "has written his books in solidarity with society's silent victims, to make visible the actuality of discourses and to make audible the repressed voices of its subjects" (216). And he emphasizes a major shift in Foucault's work after 1968, when he began to analyze the function of discourses, no longer Discourse with a capital "D," and the genealogy of knowledge less "in terms of types of consciousness, modes of perception and forms of ideology, but in terms of tactics and strategies of power," as Foucault put it in an interview in 1976 (quoted in *World* 219, cf. *Beginnings* 303). Yet Said criticizes Foucault for being "unable to deal with, or provide an account of, historical change" (*World* 152), as he does not seem to be interested in investigating the *causes* of the development of "discourses," as he "takes a curiously passive and sterile view not so much of the uses of power, but of how and why power is gained, used, and held onto" (221). Said does not accept the theoretical and political consequences of Foucault's critique of the concept (and critique) of ideology as being delimited by being in opposition to "something like truth," by presupposing "something of the order of a subject," and by depending on "the infrastructure or economic or material determinant for it" (Foucault, *Power/Knowledge* 118). Said sees the reason for Foucault's "passive and sterile view" of the omnipresence of power in his "disagreement with Marxism," that is, in Foucault's truncated understanding and use of the dimension of historical change, of "the central dialectic of opposed forces that still underlies modern society" (*World* 221f.). In his essay "Traveling Theory" he writes: "In human history there is always something beyond the reach of dominating systems, no matter how deeply they saturate society, and this is obviously what makes change possible" (246f.). The lack of self-reflexivity in Foucault's theory of power that is a consequence of the suspension of the notion of a subject as a historical agent has a price Said is not willing to pay: "In short, power can be made analogous neither to a spider's web without the spider nor to a smoothly functioning flow diagram; a great deal of power remains in such coarse items as the relationships and tensions between rulers and ruled, wealth and privilege, monopolies of coercion, and the central state apparatus" (212).

In Said's view, the limitations of Foucault's theory of power become even more glaringly evident if we situate it in the wider context of the postcolonial world. Neither Derrida nor Foucault have been particularly committed to dissolving, in the presuppositions and the procedures of their own work, the Western, or French, *ethnocentrism* they have criticized in general political terms. Foucault does not seem interested in the fact, Said writes in *The World, the Text, and the Critic,* that

history is not a homogeneous French-speaking territory but a complex interaction between uneven economies, societies, and ideologies. Much of what he has studied in his work makes greatest sense not as an ethnocentric model of how power is exercised in modern society, but as part of a much larger picture involving, for example, the relationship between Europe and the rest of the world. He seems unaware of the extent to which the ideas of discourse and discipline are assertively European and how, along with the use of discipline to employ masses of detail (and human beings), discipline was used also to administer, study, and reconstruct – then subsequently to occupy, rule, and exploit – almost the whole of the non-European world (222).

It is at this point near the end of his key essay "Criticism Between Culture and System" that Said's re-construction of American, or Western, literary and cultural theory confronts the consequences of his scholarly historical and critical work on Orientalism, of his political engagement in Near Eastern politics, and of the Islamic world's representation in the West. He argues that the very notion of the West, the superiority of Western society and culture was constituted, and has always been reconstituted, by processes of exclusion, by essentializing the "Orient" as the West's inferior "Other." What we are used to consider the meaning of "our" culture has always been constructed in a process of *intercultural* production. Said refers to his book *Orientalism* (1978) in which he offers a genealogy of the Western discourse of (mainly British and French) "Orientalism" (of the Islamic Near East) and its transformations from the early efforts of "knowing the Orient" during the 18th century to its secularization, professionalization, and institutionalization in the universities and public discourse in the century after Napoleon's occupation of Egypt (Chapters One and Two). The final part of the book analyzes the system of ideological fictions and political institutions in the wake of British and French late 19th century and early 20th century imperialism and colonialism and, finally, its crisis and reformulation in the service of the American bid for control of the whole area and as a reaction to some resurgence of political and cultural strength among the peoples in the Near East. What had been a "fundamentally philological discipline and a vaguely general apprehension of the Orient" has been turned during the last decades into "a social science speciality" of "area studies" policy experts supporting American economic and political interests (290). What has *not* changed, however, is the powerful totalizing construction of "the Orient" by the West as its inferior Other, a construction that has *never* been challenged or tested by the "reality" of the Near East, as "the Orient" in the Western mind is arrested ontologically, outside history, at a more primitive stage of mankind and can never change and never "represent itself" (cf. 12, 21, 70f., 96, 203, 222, 239, 246, 283, 293, 307, 322).

For Said, then, Orientalism is not a system of ideas or of simple lies and distortions of the truth that could easily be corrected, but an "integral part of European *material* civilization and culture" which Orientalism expresses and represents "culturally and even ideologically as a mode of discourse with supporting institutions, vocabulary, scholarship, imagery, doctrines, even colonial bureaucracies and colonial styles" (2). He explicitly conceived his book on Orientalism as a case study in Foucauldian "discourse analysis," as a study of a total network of interests, of "power," of "domination," complemented by a Gramscian emphasis on "hegemony" and on the constraining as well as enabling, productive effects of "culture" (6f., 14). Said does not accept in his analysis of the "anonymous collective body of texts constituting a discursive formation like Orientalism" (23) Foucault's elimination of the notion of the historical subject. He emphasizes instead the *dialectic*, the "dialectic between individual text or writer and the complex collective formation to which his work is a contribution" (24). The questions he raises are:

What is the meaning of originality, of continuity, of individuality, in this context? How does Orientalism transmit or reproduce itself from one epoch to another? In fine, how can we treat the cultural, historical phenomenon of Orientalism as a kind of *willed human work* -- not of mere unconditioned ratiocination – in all its historical complexity, detail, and worth without at the same time losing sight of the alliance between cultural work, political tendencies, the state, and the specific realities of domination? (15)

These questions concerning the interrelations of politics and culture can only be answered in the specific historical circumstances of the individual study. In the case of *Orientalism* two consequences are crucial for Said's book. First, *Orientalism* methodologically is characterized by a "hybrid perspective" (23) broadly historical and anthropological which permits to combine a genealogical analysis in terms of Foucault's "discursive formation" with a hermeneutic interpretation of individuals' intentions and their moral responsibility as expressed in texts. The "antihuman" oppressive and devastating effects of the discourse of Orientalism in all its political and institutional repercussions on the people of the Near East – to whom Said as a Palestinian in exile belongs himself – ask for an approach that can also clearly assign causes and responsibility where they belong – and that can specify the role and task for the critical intellectual who wants to see things changed. Even though Said points out in a Foucauldian move that he does not want to talk about the "truth" of Orientalism vis-à-vis Near Eastern "reality," but about the powerful effects of the internal consistency of Orientalism and its ideas about the Orient, he feels bound to ask how we can "undertake studies in contemporary alternatives to Orientalism."

This also indicates the second aspect, the fact that Orientalism is an expression of Western ethnocentrism, that a study of Orientalism necessarily brings up the question of how "we" can "represent" *other cultures*, or, particularly, how they can *represent themselves*, a problematic that will be more extensively discussed later. Said does *not* opt for a pure "insider" perspective, as if only a Palestinian could write about Palestinians or a black American about black Americans (322), but for something like an *intercultural dialogue* that might help to transcend the constraints and limitations of power in "our" understanding of non-Western cultures and societies without constructing their "difference" as a way of controlling them. Yet in *Orientalism* Said tends to recover and define the "alternatives to Orientalism" too much within the boundaries of the Western discourse he sets out to dismantle. As John Carlos Rowe writes in his brilliant critique of *Orientalism*: "Said must conceive of this tradition to be a sort of 'anti-tradition,' or 'counter-culture,' which marginalizes itself with respect to the dominant culture. And yet this process of marginalization is mythologized by Said himself until it clusters into a single, albeit complex, image of a margin inhabited by: the avant-garde artist, the Orient, Woman, the 'third world,' and the genealogical critic himself" (*The Authority* 62).

Said pursues these questions in his next two books. *The Question of Palestine* (1979) sets before the American reader a picture of the specific Palestinian experience in history, its "traumatic national encounter with Zionism" (ix), which has systematically been excluded from public knowledge by "the hypocrisy of Western (and certainly liberal Zionist) journalism and intellectual discourse" (x). Said considers it his own moral duty to penetrate this ideological smokescreen and to show things as "*they actually are* for Palestinians and for Arabs" (214f.), to expose the historical reality (whatever the epistemological status of "reality" might be). As Bruce Robbins put it: "The reality of the Palestinians is not what they have lost, but the state of loss itself" (Robbins 70). What is most important in this undertaking is not to be held captive by a thinking in terms of simple oppositions of good and bad. Several times in his book Said points to the unique historical experience of the holocaust for the Jews which to a large extent explains Israel's fear and uncompromising attitude toward the Palestinians (*Question* 60, 231). He writes:

We Palestinians are clearly struggling for our self-determination but for the fact that we have no place, no agreed-upon and available physical terrain on which to conduct our struggle. We are clearly anticolonialist and antiracist in our struggle but for the fact that our opponents are the greatest victims of racism in history, and perhaps our struggle is waged at an akward, postcolonial period in the modern world's history (122).

This also means that the main objective of his book is not primarily to elaborate the victimization of Palestinians by Zionism, but to show, and to contribute to, the Palestinian people's collective fight for constructing and "representing" a national cultural identity and political consciousness of their own. "It must not be forgotten that the Palestinian was not simply a function of Zionism. His life, culture, and politics have their own dynamic and ultimately their own authenticity ..." (114, cf. 141,155). In his historical experience of always "*being represented*, never able to speak for [himself or herself]" (25), the Palestinian turns out to be "at once a representative and an outcast" (154). In fact, as an "outcast, as transnational exterritorial being, [or] as oppressed nonentity inside Israel," the Palestinian is "central to, or at the core of, the Middle East problem" (169). And we could add, the Palestinians in their homelessness seem to be the collective incorporation of, as well as a radical challenge to, the (modern) Western intellectual's constitutive "homelessness."

Said's project demands a specific historical method and a vision of historical change. He quite clearly points out that "Zionism" in its effects can only be studied *genealogically* "in the framework provided by imperialism," but, at the same time, also as a practical system "for *accumulation* (of power, land, ideological legitimacy) and *displacement* (of people, other ideas, prior legitimacy)" (57, 73). Only through this methodological move could Said transcend the study of ideas of individual authors as well as of anonymous political and ideological traditions. Only this dual approach could provide a perspective that would make it possible to see Palestinians and Jews within a common historical perspective, a common "self-conscious rational struggle conducted in the interests of human community" (235), a struggle based on fundamental human rights such as self-determination, being allowed to "live free from fear, insecurity, terror and oppression, free also from the possibilities of exercising unequal or unjust domination over others" (53), and also of having a home you can call your own. Said's openly utopian vision is not a reaffirmation or reestablishment of the traditional ethnically more or less homogeneous national state (or one dominated by the largest national group). It is not a return to "origins," to an original "place," but is "utopian" – Said uses the term "nonplace" (124) – in the sense that it explicitly acknowledges the "unstable identity," the "dispersion and exile," and the "cubistic form of Palestinian existence" (162) in his (tentative) idea of a "secular democratic state in Palestine for Arabs and Jews" (220), an idea he has actively supported as a member of the Palestinian National Council.

Said's next book, *Covering Islam* (1981), takes up the problems of understanding and (mis-)representing other culture(s) for the *American* context in a study of how the media and the experts controlled the way Americans were to perceive and interpret the world of "Islam," particularly the Iranian revolution and the Teheran Embassy hostage crisis. The "consensus on 'Islam' as a kind of scapegoat for everything [the Americans] do not like about the world's new political, social, and economic patterns" (xv) led to a widely distorted and reductive picture of the Islamic world which in the age of U.S.-dominated mass media even may be said "to be learning *about itself* by means of images, histories, and information manufactured in the West" (52, cf. 67). Ironically, the strong Western commitment to the idea of a monolithic, unchanging, backward state of "Islam" prevented Americans from realizing the political and social processes at work in contemporary Muslim societies that were directed against the autocratic, "medieval" traditions the West continued to identify the world of "Islam" with (cf. 64, 94). Yet this powerful and devastating "ideology of difference" also has bred its own "counteralternative practices," as Said elaborates in his essay "An Ideology of Difference" (1985). Therefore, what Said focuses on in *Covering Islam* is the question of how we can get beyond these pervasive longstanding misrepresentation of "the Orient" or "Islam," how we as Americans or Europeans can really understand the Muslims' *own interpretations* of the complex societies of Islam and their internal developments, how we can understand a non-Western culture – which means, at the same time, how we can understand our own Western culture in a less homogeneous and exclusionary way. This seems to be a particularly formidable task in a country like the United States which has been characterized by a totalizing, transhistorical nationalist consensus and myth of "America" (Sacvan Bercovitch) (cf. 49).

Near the end of his earlier book *Orientalism*, Said had pointedly raised the general theoretical questions: "How does one *represent* other cultures? What is *another* culture? Is the notion of a distinct culture (or race, or religion, or civilization) a useful one, or does it always get involved either in self-congratulation (when one discusses one's own) or hostility and aggression (when one discusses the 'other')?" (325) If "culture" is a "hegemonic system," if a culture always is trying to appropriate other cultures, how can we "study other cultures and people from a libertarian, or nonrepressive and nonmanipulative, perspective" (24)? How can we understand and accept the genuine differences among human cultures, if there can be no "true representation," if all representations, "because they *are* representations, are imbedded first in the language and then in the culture, institutions, and political ambience of the representer" (272)? In *Orientalism* these questions mean, "what of some alternative to Orientalism? Is the book an argument only *against* something, and not *for* something?" (325) How could an *oppositional critical consciousness* work out alternatives to Orientalism? At the time of writing *Orientalism*, Said's as yet undeveloped "theory of culture as a differentiating and expressive ensemble rather than as simply hegemonic and disciplinary," as James Clifford put it in his important review essay on *Orientalism*, does not permit him, however, to take into account any (national) oppositional movements (Clifford 212, 214), but allows him only to indicate how *individual* (Western) scholars such as Louis Massignon (267-74) or, even more impressively, *individual* writers such as Gérard de Nerval or Gustave Flaubert (181-90) somehow succeeded in transcending or subverting the "power" of "Orientalism." In theoretical terms, Said could only briefly suggest ways out of the totalizing system of "Orientalism" through reflexive "methodological self-consciousness," a "continual self-examination of … methodology and practice," and a "direct sensitivity to the material before them" (326f.), qualities he found in the works of some *individual* scholars working on the margins of institutions or on the boundaries of disciplines. Yet these remarks remain more or less moral appeals and do not provide convincing arguments for alternative ways of knowledge and practice.

A few years later, in *Covering Islam*, Said discusses the possibility of understanding another culture more extensively, referring to the debate in anthropology over the "complicity between imperialism and ethnology" (131). He defines two conditions that must be fulfilled if we want to achieve a knowledge, however tentative that may be, of another culture: first, "uncoercive contact with an alien culture through real exchange," and, second, "self-consciousness about the interpretative project itself" (142) or the awareness that this knowledge is a "social activity and inextricably tied to the situation out of which it arose" (156). Said also takes a first step in overcoming the failure he accuses Western scholarship on Islam of that it never has systematically dealt with *Islamic* writing on Islam, Islamic writing that may be *different* in its strategies from what the West regards as "scholarship." Still, when he comes to characterizing the "*antithetical knowledge*" (149) of Islam that we have, he mentions three groups of scholars and intellectuals who have worked as outsiders and radicals *in the West*, giving Islamic scholars only a minor voice in this endeavor. Instead of exploring in more detail the problems and prospects of *intercultural knowledge* in general or of the double status of being a Palestinian by birth and an intellectual educated in the West, an experience he shares with quite a number of other Palestinians, Said again emphasizes the critical stance and position the *Western oppositional intellectual* has to achieve. It remains, finally, a *moral decision of individuals*, even though the individual is now seen as supported by an intellectual *community*. As he writes in the final paragraph of *Covering Islam*: "Underlying every interpretation of other cultures – especially of Islam – is the choice facing the individual scholar or intellectual: whether to put intellect at the service of power or at the service of criticism, community, and moral sense" (164).

It is this tension between a radical systematic critique of Western discourses on "other" cultures and the enabling articulations of other cultures representing themselves, between intercultural dialogues and Western antithetical or oppositional knowledge, and between the community of intellectuals and the people on the one hand and the precarious positioning of a homeless scholar who is always in exile on the other that Said pursues in his most recent work. In his essay "Opponents, Audiences, Constituencies, and Community" (1982), Said addresses directly the role of a "politics of interpretation and the politics of culture" in "the Age of Reagan," in the contemporary United States (*Opponents* 1). Oppositional criticism has to uncover and expose the "actual *affiliations* that exist between the world of ideas and scholarship, on the one hand, and the world of brute politics, corporate and state power, and military force, on the other" (2). Said traces again the "depoliticization" of American literary criticism and the "sustained self-purification of humanists" and interprets them as an "integral part of the historical moment presided over by Reaganism" (19f.). He proposes to counter the non-interference demanded by the academy, the government, and the corporate elites with a "program of interference" that crosses "borders and obstacles," reopens "the blocked social processes ceding objective representation (hence power) of the world to a small coterie of experts and their clients," and acknowledges that "the audience for literacy is not a closed circle of three thousand professional critics but the community of human beings in society" (24f.).

Clearly, this "program of interference" – which Said, again, defines as a "dialectical response" (24) – expresses his hope of finally overcoming, or at least mastering, the tensions between his "two separate lives," as he had put it in an interview in 1976 (*Interview* 35), between his own work as an avant-garde literary critic and intellectual in the West (his books *Beginning* and *The World, the Text, and the Critic*) and as a political intellectual and activist involved in Near East political affairs, multi-culturalism, and post-colonialism in the so-called Third World (his books *The Question of Palestine and Covering Islam*). It is, finally, to comprise *both* "Western cultural radicalism" *and* the "radical nationalism of the non-Western world," as he had written at the end of his early review essay on Foucault (*An Ethics* 37).

But his agenda for an oppositional "politics of culture" and "politics of interpretation," as he applies it to the politics, society, and culture in the United States, is in danger of emptying cultural criticism and the "world of ideas and scholarship" too radically of a political potential of their own, when he confronts the critic too directly with the "world of brute politics" in "the Age of Reagan." He situates his critical, rigorously secular exposure of the politics of culture and of literature in Reagan's America in an analysis of the peculiar "configuration of constituencies and interpretive communities" (17) in order to find a perspective for change: "How can interpretation be interpreted as having a secular, political force in an age determined to deny interpretation anything but a role as mystification?" (19) Yet the crucial difference of cultural criticism from the world of political organizations and structures, the limitations of criticism, but also the political implications of the literary and cultural critic's work he had elaborated in his critical reading of Derrida's and Foucault's work and in his studies of Orientalism and the world of Islam are impatiently put aside by the type of question Said quotes from Terry Eagleton's critique of Fredric Jameson's *The Political Unconscious*: "How is a Marxist-structuralist analysis of a minor novel of Balzac to help shake the foundations of capitalism?" Said concedes that obviously "the answer to this question is that such readings won't" (15), and he also attacks Eagleton for failing to provide an alternative of his own. But I think his own polemical conclusions, permeated by his strong longing for community or constituency and for politically meaningful, effective cultural work, are somewhat premature, or rather mistaken, when he argues, with Eagleton, that Jameson's and Frank Lentricchia's work is characterized by "their political 'unclarity,' their lingering pragmatism, eclecticism," and even by "the relationship of their hermeneutic criticism to Reagan's ascendancy" (15). It is too easy to charge Jameson and Lentricchia with "marginality and vestigial idealism" and an

"apolitical content and methodology" that simply accepts the "cloistral seclusion" of "literature" and "Marxism" (15f.), if Said, in other contexts, emphasizes the crucial importance of a radical dismantling of Western discourses,
the "distance" and "difference" of oppositional criticism, and the working out
of counter-discourses.

Radical cultural criticism, therefore, must assume a complex and wide-
ranging important political significance in the social and cultural process.
"Interpretation always makes a difference," as Lentricchia put it in his
response to Eagleton and Said in his book *Criticism and Social Change*
(1983) (11). But we also have to accept the limited political role and impact
of cultural criticism, of cultural productions, and have to acknowledge the
different, discontinuous forms of expression and communication it has
worked out, if we want to grasp the political potential it may have. If the
"paradoxical" identity of "oppositional criticism," as he puts it in *The World,
the Text, and the Critic*, is defined by the "social goals ... [of] noncoercive
knowledge produced in the interest of human freedom," this is not just an
empty hope or abstract utopia, but can find some "potential space inside civil
[capitalist] society" (29f.). Twice in his book Said quotes Raymond Williams'
statement that "however dominant a social system may be, the very meaning
of its domination involves a limitation or selection of the activities it covers,
so that by definition it cannot exhaust all social experience, which therefore
always potentially contains space for alternative acts and alternative intentions which are not yet articulated as a social institution or even project" (29,
240). Yet in the essays collected in, or written for, *The World, the Text, and
the Critic*, Said has not yet fully brought this insight to bear on American
literature and culture which he tends to portray in too generalized and homogeneous a manner, a portrait that necessarily focuses on isolated oppositional
intellectuals and writers at the expense of the potential of ethnic, minority, or
other oppositional sub- or countercultures. If we understand, with Said's reading of Foucault (and with Bakhtin), discourse as a form of social action, as a
form of power and desire, the radical cultural critic has to uncover and
expose the power game of master discourses and institutions, of Discourse, of
Culture, of History, and of Tradition, all with capital letters. But he or she has
also to articulate and project the alternative discursive practices, the alternative histories, traditions, and counterdiscourses, in the plural, within Western
capitalist societies *and* to face and respond to the "discourses" and "histories" of "others," of the societies and cultures of the so-called Third World. It
is in this sense that American cultural criticism as "discourse theory" must
transcend and redefine its traditional boundaries, acknowledge the heterogeneous and multicultural character of culture(s) in the United States, and
become radical *cultural studies*.

In his essay "Orientalism Reconsidered" (1985), Said briefly discusses quite a number of "interventionary" analyses and theoretical projects in American (and English) cultural and literary studies. He succeeds in providing a much more complex and convincing account of the *common endeavor* of these oppositional intellectuals which explicitly accepts *plurality, difference, and unstability* in their work without renouncing the claim to attaining the social and political goal of "noncoercive knowledge in the interest of human freedom." He strongly reaffirms the "consciously secular, marginal, and oppositional" (*Orientalism Reconsidered* 106) character of these practices with reference to the dominant culture and authoritative systems they want to dismantle and to replace. His emphasis, however, is now less on systematic comprehensiveness than on "local" knowledge and political practice in a common project of alternative critical work: "We note a plurality of audiences ..., a plurality of terrains, multiple experiences, and different constituencies, each with its admitted (as opposed to denied) interest, political desiderata, disciplinary goals. All these efforts work out of what might be called a decentered consciousness, not less reflective and critical for being decentered, for the most part non- and in some cases anti-totalizing and anti-systematic" (105-106). Said briefly mentions the importance of the intellectual and political work done in the U.S. by "subaltern groups, women, blacks, and so on" (certainly not a particularly happy phrase), but warns against any form of "possessive exclusionism" some representatives of these groups have been favoring, claims, that if we take them seriously, would make any inter- (and intra-) cultural understanding impossible (106). Said finds equally dangerous the quest for a new "grand synthesis" which could too easily "wipe out both the gains and the oppositional consciousness provided hitherto by these counterknowledges" (107). He does not elaborate, however, how these counterknowledges could help to rearticulate his own understanding of the oppositional potential for change within American culture and society at large.

Said discovers most of the kind of oppositional work he proposes in recent American anthropology. In his critical essay "Representing the Colonized: Anthropology's Interlocutors" (1989) he discusses books by Marxist anthropologists, feminist anthropologists, anthropologists of praxis, and other politically committed schools and individuals. He also mentions the programs of postmodern anthropologists who have been heavily influenced in their critique of the traditional ethnocentric ethnographic work of their discipline and in their own discursive strategies by poststructuralist literary and cultural theory, anthropologists such as James Clifford, George Marcus, and Michael M. J. Fischer. Nevertheless, Said finds "a genuine malaise about the sociopolitical status of anthropology as a whole" (*Representing* 208), namely its complicity as a discipline with imperialism and colonialism, a complicity the new oppositional schools in his mind do not seem to have overcome:

In fact, there is no way that I know of apprehending the world from within our culture (a culture by the way with a whole history of extermination and incorporation behind it) without also apprehending the imperial contest itself. And this I would say is a cultural fact of extraordinary political as well as interpretive importance, because it is the true defining horizon, and to some extent, the enabling condition, of such otherwise abstract and groundless concepts like 'otherness' and 'difference.' The real problem remains to haunt us: the relationship between anthropology as an ongoing enterprise and, on the other hand, empire as an ongoing concern (217).

Said attacks in a polemical manner the pervasive "fetishization" of "difference" and "otherness" in Western ethnographic and critical discourse in general and the "textualization" of other cultures and societies in postmodern anthropology (213), as they tend to ignore, or obfuscate, the problem of how "the colonized represent themselves," or, in Gayatri Spivak's words, "how the subaltern can speak" (Spivak 271-315). Said's objections raise crucial questions concerning the practice and theory of anthropology today, but he much too quickly dismisses the work "postmodern" anthropologists such as George Marcus, Michael M. J. Fischer, or Paul Rabinow (whom he mentions in passing) have been committed to.

Again, *how* can the "other" cultures "represent themselves," *how* can they speak? How can they become "interlocutors" in an intercultural dialogue and not remain "native informants" "constructed" by Western anthropology and (neo-)colonialism? How can the key concept of "culture" be redefined in a way that it does not fall victim to the totalizations of the institution(s) of Culture in the West or the "anthropologizing" of "other" cultures nor dissolve into a set of arbitrary signs and expressions of collective human behavior? How can *they* develop indigenous cultural textual strategies in a situation of a neo-colonial encounter? How can the *anthropologist*, or a *Palestinian-Western critic* "between cultures" such as Said, negotiate and tentatively project critical textual strategies that could communicate and testify to the critical, reflective, decentered consciousness traversing a plurality of terrains, multiple experiences, and different constituencies Said had envisioned in his essay "Orientalism Reconsidered"?

In *The World, the Text, and the Critic*, Said had claimed the *form of the essay* as a "radically skeptical form" (26) for his secular criticism. More than anything the "essential formal incompleteness" of the essay and its specifically literary strategies enable the oppositional critic to escape "closure" and to decode the text's "dialectic of engagement in time and the senses," without relinquishing "the essay's consciousness of its marginality" to the (apparant) formal completeness of the text it analyzes (50f.). "The central problematic of the essay as a form is its *place*, by which I mean a series of ... ways the essay has of being the form critics take, and locate themselves in, to do their work" (50). Said stresses the reflective, exploratory, as well as committed character of the essay, its "ironic" mode that makes it an expression of "willed homelessness," as Said puts it in another context (7).

In *Orientalism*, Said had pointed out that "history" and "narrative" could be used as powerful counter-strategies against the totalizing, essentializing "permanence of vision" of Orientalism, provided they are conceived and "written" in a radically secular, demystified way that opens up human institutions and actualities to change: "Narrative, in short, introduces an opposing point of view, perspective, consciousness to the unitary web of vision: it violates the supreme Appolonian fictions asserted by visions" (240). In his later essay "Representing the Colonized," he takes up the recent wide-ranging theoretical discussion of "narrativity" and reclaims the political power of *narrative*, namely the disruptive and culturally enabling emerging counternarratives of non-Western peoples' fight for national liberation and cultural articulation, against Jean François Lyotard's postmodernist dismissal of the two great narratives of emancipation and enlightenment in favor of smaller local narratives of performativity. Here the self-reflective, experimental, open textual strategies of postmodern anthropologists – and writers, of course – *can* be very helpful to the oppositional cultural critic who faces his or her own dilemma as an intellectual as well as the challenges of the "unrepresentability" of "subaltern" experiences and consciousness. Postmodernism in this sense, however, is not the reductive version as an "aesthetic of quotation, nostalgia, and indifferentiation" (222) Said offers, but "situates itself" in a post- (or neo-) colonial world that demands, and makes possible, an intercultural dialogue, or polylogue, of the de-(and re-)constructive forms of more recent Western writing and the various cultural representations of the so-called Third World in their distinctive "otherness." After we have become aware of the intimate interconnections of modernism and colonialism, of their historical dialectic, different political readings of many of the great modern writers as well as new forms of articulations of postcolonial cultures beyond the fixed and essentializing notions of nativism and cultural nationalism have become possible (see Said's essay "Yeats and Decolonization," 1989). As Said writes in his essay "Intellectuals in the Post-Colonial World" (1985): "Many of the post-colonial writers bear their past within them – as scars of humiliating wounds, as instigation for different practices, as potentially revised visions of the past tending towards a future, as urgently re-interpretable and re-deployable experiences in which the formerly silent native speaks and acts on territory taken back from the colonialist" (54f.). Both for the Western oppositional intellectual and the post-colonial intellectual, though in different ways, the dream of finding a *stable identity* by situating theory politically or of *overcoming* the "difference," the tensions between Western and non-Western cultures, within "our (or their) own" culture(s) as well as between cultural criticism and political activism, must be relinquished. Yet these tensions, these differences, these interactions *can* be illuminated, explored, and negotiated in a secular perspective and represented in "experimental" forms of cultural practice and "counternarrative" forms of writing that tell a different story and tell the story differently.

At the end of "Representing the Colonized," Said writes: "Exile, immigration, and the crossing of boundaries are experiences that can therefore provide us with new narrative forms or, in John Berger's phrase, with *other* ways of telling" (225). One important and productive alternative is a form of genuine *intercultural dialogue*, such as the study by "postmodernist" anthropologist Michael M. J. Fischer and "native" anthropologist Mehdi Abedi called *Debating Muslims: Cultural Dialogues in Postmodernity and Tradition* (1990), which in its ambiguous title plays upon the dialogues, multiple discursive positionings, contestations, and polyphony among Muslims, between Muslims and non-Muslims, and between the two authors, one a Muslim insider and one a non-Muslim outsider, each drawing not merely upon their individual opinions but upon the several cultural traditions which have constructed each of them.

Said has not ventured into this area as yet, but his own latest book, *After the Last Sky: Palestinian Lives* (1986), a text with photographs by Swiss photographer Jean Mohr, can be taken as another powerful model that dramatizes and exploits Said's positioning "between" Western and non-Western cultures. Said's text succeeds in responding to the photographs of Palestinian "everyday" life (and suffering) and in capturing a complex, highly charged political and cultural reality and the confusing experiences of his fellow Palestinians in various places of exile in "essentially unconventional, hybrid, and fragmentary forms of expression" and in "alternative modes of expression" (6). It is a "personal rendering of the Palestinians as a dispersed national community," a "multi-faceted" portrayal informed by a "double vision" (6). It is a book that sets out to find the scattered traces of Palestinian lives in their discontinuity, in autobiographical memories, in cultural traditions, in oral narratives, and in Palestinian literature. It is at the same time a story of the quest for origins and homes lost in the ordeal of history *and* a utopian construction, or creation, of peoplehood in a fight for national representation and liberation.

Since our history is forbidden, narratives are rare; the story of origins, of home, of nation is underground. When it appears it is broken, often wayward and meandering in the extreme, always coded, usually in outrageous forms – mock-epics, satires, sardonic parables, absurd rituals – that make little sense to an outsider. Thus Palestinian life is scattered, discontinuous, marked by the artificial and imposed arrangements of interrupted or confined space, by the dislocations and unsynchronized rhythms of disturbed time (20).

After the Last Sky is a very tentative, meditative, and fragmentary book, free of Said's often sharp polemical attacks in his political statements and writings. It is characterized by "formal instability," a "broken narrative, fragmentary composition, and self-consciously staged testimonials" (38), and it is permeated by Said's experience of being an insider and an outsider at the same time, a distinction, however, that the Palestinian experience has confused:

For Palestinian culture, the odd thing is that its own identity is more frequently than not perceived as "other." "Palestine" is so charged with significance for others that Palestinians cannot perceive it as intimately theirs without a simultaneous sense of its urgent importance for others as well. "Ours" but not yet fully "ours." [...] Thus the insider becomes the outsider. Not only have the interpositions between us and Palestine grown more formidable over time, but, to make matters worse, most of us pass our lives separated from each other. Yet we live in comradely communications despite the barriers. Today the Palestinian genius expresses itself in crossings-over, in clearing hurdles, activities that do not lessen the alienation, discontinuity, and dispossession, but that dramatize and clarify them instead (40f.).

After the Last Sky is a testimony to Said's own dispersed identity that finds, or posits, its "center," however, in his strong moral commitment no noncoercive forms of knowledge and of living together.

The Works of Edward W. Said

Joseph Conrad and the Fiction of Autobiography. Cambridge, MA: Harvard University Press, 1966.
"Eclecticism and Orthodoxy." *Diacritics* 2, Spring 1972. 2-8.
"An Ethics of Language." *Diacritics* 4, Summer 1974. 28-35 (quoted as *An Ethics*).
"Contemporary Fiction and Criticism." *TriQuarterly* 33, Spring 1975. 231-56.
Beginnings: Intention and Method. New York: Basic Books, 1975, new edition with new preface, New York: Columbia University Press, 1985 (quoted as *Beginnings*).
"Interview." *Diacritics* 6, Fall 1976. 30-47 (quoted as *Interview*).
Orientalism. New York: Random House, 1978, Vintage Books, 1979 (quoted as *Orientalism*).

The Question of Palestine. New York: Random House, 1979, Vintage Books, 1980 (quoted as *Question*).

"Preface." *Literature and Society*. Ed. Edward W. Said. Baltimore: Johns Hopkins University Press, 1980. vii-xi.

Covering Islam: How the Media and the Experts Determine How We See the World. New York: Pantheon, 1981 (quoted as *Covering*).

"Opponents, Audiences, Constituencies, and Community." *Critical Inquiry*, 9, September 1982, 1-26 (quoted as *Opponents*).

The World, the Text, and the Critic. Cambridge, MA: Harvard University Press, 1983 (quoted as *World*).

"French Philosopher Michel Foucault: Death at an Early Age." *In These Times*, September 5-11, 1984. 18-19, 22.

"An Ideology of Difference." *Critical Inquiry* 12, Autumn 1985. 38-58.

After the Last Sky: Palestinian Lives. With Photographs by Jean Mohr. New York: Pantheon Books, 1986 (quoted as *After the Last Sky*.)

"Intellectuals in the Post-Colonial World." *Salmagundi*, nos. 70-71, Spring-Summer 1986, 44-64.

"The Horizon of R. P. Blackmur." *Raritan* 6, Fall, 1986, 29-50.

"Orientalism Reconsidered." *Cultural Critique*, no. 1, Fall 1985, 89-197 (quoted as *Orientalism Reconsidered*).

"Introduction." *Blaming the Victim: Spurious Scholarship and the Palestinian Question*. Ed. Edward W. Said and Christopher Hitchins. London and New York: Verso, 1988. 1-19. Reprints the following essays by Said: "Conspiracy of Praise," "The Essential Terrorist," and "Michael Walzer's *Exodus and Revolution*: A Canaanite Reading."

"Yeats and Colonialism." *Remaking History*. Ed. Barbara Kruger and Phil Mariani. Seattle: Bay Press, 1989. 3-29.

"Representing the Colonized: Anthropology's Interlocutors." *Critical Inquiry* 14, Winter 1989. 205-25 (quoted as *Representing*).

"*Intifada* and Independence." *Social Text*, no. 22, Spring 1989. 23-39.

Other Works Quoted

Bové, Paul A., "Closing Up the Ranks: Xerxes' Hordes Are At the Pass." *Contemporary Literature* 26, 1985. 91-106.

Bové, Paul A., *Intellectuals in Power: A Genealogy of Critical Humanism*. New York, Columbia University Press, 1986.

Clifford, James, "Review of *Orientalism*." *History and Theory* 19, 1980. 204-23.

Current Biography Yearbook 1989. New York: Wilson and Co. 493-97.

Foucault, Michael, *Power/Knowledge: Selected Interviews and Other Writings, 1972-1977*. Ed. Colin Gordon. New York: Pantheon, 1980.

Lenz, Günter, H., "Tradition, Discontinuity, and Counterdiscourse: Some Problems in American Radical Cultural Criticism Since the 1960s." *The Crisis of Modernity: Recent Critical Theories of Culture and Society in the United States and West Germany*. Ed. Günter H. Lenz and Kurt L. Shell. Frankfurt/M.: Campus, and Boulder, Col.: Westview Press, 1986. 191-249.

Merod, Jim, *The Political Responsibility of the Critic*. Ithaca, NY: Cornell University Press, 1987.

Miller, J. Hillis, "'Beginning With A Text'" (review of *Beginnings*). *Diacritics* 6, Fall 1976. 2-7.

O'Hara, Daniel, "Criticism Worldly and Otherworldly: Edward W. Said and The Cult of Theory." *Boundary 2* 12, no. 3, and 13, no. 1, Spring-Fall 1984. 379-403.

Riddel, Joseph N., "Scriptive Fate/Scriptive Hope." *Diacritics* 6, Fall 1976, 14-23.

Robbins, Bruce, "Homelessness and Worldliness." *Diacritics* 13, Fall 1983. 69-77.

Rowe, John Carlos, "'To Live Outside the Law, You Must Be Honest': The Authority of the Margin in Contemporary Theory." *Cultural Critique*, no. 2, 1985. 35-68.

Spivak, Gayatri Chakravorty, "Can the Subaltern Speak?" *Marxism and the Interpretation of Culture*. Ed. Cary Nelson and Lawrence Grossberg. Urbana, IL: University of Illinois Press, 1988. 271-315.

White, Hayden, "Criticism as Cultural Politics" (review of *Beginnings*). *Diacritics* 6, Fall 1976. 8-13.